Crossroads:
A History of St. Charles County, Missouri
Steve Ehlmann

ISBN: Hard Cover: 0-9747864-2-X
    Soft Cover: 0-9747864-3-8

Publisher: Lindenwood University Press
209 S. Kingshighway
St. Charles, MO 63301

Credits: *Daniel Boone, pioneer and trailblazer, Lindenwood University*
Rose Philippine Duchesne, educator Missouri State Archives
Rufus Easton, Congressman, Missouri State Archives
David Barton, U.S. Senator, Missouri State Archives
Edward Bates, State Senator, Missouri State Archives
Unidentified Sioux Indian that Visited St. Charles in 1880s
John J. Buse Collection, 1860-1931, Western Historical Manuscript
    Collection - Columbia, MO
Mary Sibley, co-founder of Lindenwood College, Missouri State Archives
John Stumberg, soldier and local leader, St. Charles County Historical
    Society
Herman Esselmann, German immigrant whose citizenship oath appears on
    the cover.
Arnold Krekel, Civil War colonel and federal judge, Missouri State Archives
Ellis Keen, African-American plaintiff in civil rights litigation. Frenchtown
    Museum Corp.
Courthouse pictures: (clockwise from top)
1. First courthouse built 1848,
    John J. Buse Collection, 1860-1931, Western Manuscript Collection,
    Columbia, MO
2. Courthouse built in 1903, St. Charles County Government web. page
4. New Courthouse, St. Charles County Government web. page

Editor: Charles W. Stewart

Printed by:
Walsworth Publishing Company
Commercial Book Division
306 North Kansas Avenue
Marceline, MO 64658-2105

All profits and royalties from the sale of this book will be used to fund the H.K. "Kriete" Stumberge, Memorial Scholarship at Lindenwood University

1

Crossroads: A History of St. Charles County, Missouri

By Steve Ehlmann

Table of Contents. . .2

Dedication and Acknowledgements . . .4

CHAPTERS

I. French and Indian Accommodation 1769-1804... 5

    A. Geology, Ecology and Geography... 6

    B. French Colonization and Spanish Administration... 13

    C. Life of the *Voyageur...* 21

II. American Predominance 1804-1850... 32

    A. Territorial Status and Statehood... 33

    B. Frontier Life... 45

    C. "The Progress of Agriculture"... 61

III. Immigration, Emancipation and Transportation 1850-1890... 79

    A. The Civil War... 80

    B. Post Civil War Politics... 96

    C. Successful Economic Revolution of
the Radical Republicans... 112

    D. Failed Social Revolution of the Radical Republicans... 129

IV. Germanization, Republicanization
and Industrialization 1890-1929... 148

    A. German Predominance... 149

    B. Republican Ascendancy... 172

    C. Industrialization and Urbanization... 190

V.   Depression and War 1929-1945... 208

    A. Depression Memories and the Home Front... 209

    B. Revolution and Restoration... 225

    C. New Deal and War Production... 239

VI.   Postwar Period 1945-1964... 257

    A. Growth and Prosperity... 258

    B. Homecoming and Baby Boom... 274

    C. Politics of Prosperity... 291

VII. Challenges of Growth 1964-1980... 305

    A. New Cultural Conflicts... 306

    B. Political Parity... 316

    C. Building the American Dream... 326

VIII. Recent Developments... 345

End Notes... 416

Bibliography... 425

Index... 436

DEDICATION

This book is dedicated to the memories of Professor William Leverette, who first suggested to me the study of history as the key to understanding the human condition; Professor Gray Dorsey, who taught me the effect of history on the law; and H.K. Stumberg, Esquire, who helped me appreciate the rich history of the community in which we both grew up.

ACKNOWLEDGEMENTS

I am indebted to all those who have chronicled the history of St. Charles County over the years. Where possible, I have attempted to add to the story. I have not attempted to be exhaustive. At all times I have attempted to provide an interpretive framework for what was occurring in the county and show how it related to broader developments in Missouri and the country. To the extent I have succeeded, I am indebted to Douglas Boschert, Hon. Joseph Briscoe, Ervin Davis, Fred Dyer, Erich Ehlmann, Karen Ehlmann, Henry Elmendorf, James Fitz, Carol Geerling, Keith Hazelwood, Wayne Hoffman, Gene Katz, Ron Kjar, Ray Machens, Andrew McColloch, Gary McKiddy, Joseph Ortwerth, Melvin Plackemeier, Carolyn Roth, Robert Sandfort, Cordelia Stumberg, Melvin Washington, Roland Wetzel and Robert Wohler, who read portions of the manuscript at different stages and offered helpful suggestions on how to improve it. Ida Kaplan, Ozzie Maher, Allan Schade, Eugene Steinhoff, Richard Tillman and Oscar Waltermann also provided helpful information. The staffs at the St. Charles County Historical Society and the Kathryn Linnemann Library were helpful at all times. The support and encouragement of Dr. Dennis Spellmann and C.W. Stewart of Lindenwood University were greatly appreciated as well. I am especially indebted to Anita Mallinckrodt and Walter Kamphoefner for their translations of numerous German primary sources, and to Vicki White for her sketches. Any historical errors are unintentional and the sole responsibility of the author.

CHAPTER I
French and Indian Accommodation
1769-1804

In the mid-eighteenth century, the fate of the colony of Louisiana was in the hands of European generals and diplomats, not the people who lived there. This part of the world was a small pawn in an international chess game between France, who had been the greatest military power in the world and Great Britain, the premier naval power. The chess game included the French and Indian War, which historian Hiram Chittendon has suggested, "was, in its far reaching consequences, the most important war ever waged upon the soil of America, excepting possibly the late Civil War in the United States."[1] As the diplomats sat to sign the Treaty of Paris in 1763, they were deciding the future of what became St. Charles County. France lost its empire in North America. The area east of the Mississippi came under the control of Great Britain and many of the French-Canadian settlers moved across the Mississippi River to new settlements, including what became St. Charles. The French gave the colony of Louisiana to Catholic Spain, making the Mississippi River an international as well as an ecclesiastical boundary. The same treaty, by ending English settlement west of the Appalachians, also sowed the first seeds of discontent between Great Britain and her American colonists who gained their independence 20 years later. As the French settlers from the Illinois country arrived, the District of St. Charles became a crossroads where French and Indian culture met. Those two peoples coexisted in a land blessed by nature and strategically located.

A. Geology, Ecology and Geography

The history of St. Charles County has often been a response to events in Paris, France; Washington D.C.; Hanover, Germany or St. Louis, Missouri. However, the one constant throughout the county's history has been its geological qualities and geographical position. Speaking in 1852 before the Mercantile Library Association in St. Louis, Ralph Waldo Emerson suggested that the confluence of the Missouri River with the Mississippi made the area "the greatest cross-roads the world ever saw."[2] Geologically, northern and southern Missouri meet in the county with topography conducive to building the roads, railroads and highways that became the transportation crossroads of the nation. Ecologically, it is between the wide prairies where agriculture could flourish, and the abundant forests that insured the availability of wildlife to feed the early inhabitants and provide the furs for trade. The natural landscape, with the rivers that crossed it, not only made St. Charles County a crossroads for westward expansion in the nineteenth century and interstate transportation in the twentieth, but made it the crossroads between St. Louis and "outstate" Missouri.

In St. Charles County, there are two major geological areas, the uplifted Ozark Dome, characterized by steep hills and rugged terrain, and a second area characterized by gently rolling hills and prairies. The Ozark Dome covers most of southern Missouri and Arkansas and its northern-most point extends into the southwestern part of the county.[3] Trails, roads, railroads and highways could easily be built across the second area of gently rolling hills. Long before the Interstate Highway system the *History of St. Charles County* recognized this geological advantage, stating in 1885:

> St. Charles lies right in the line of our national highway of travel, and the topographical conformation of our county places it there. The south side of the Missouri River is a broken, jagged, mountainous region, unfitted for cheap, direct lines of communication; while north of the river roads may be run through the country at will, without encountering any permanent impeding obstacle. For example St. Louis, Jefferson City and Kansas City all lie on the south side of the Missouri, and yet, in stage coach times, the great route between these points was through St. Charles and on the north side of the river. Again, in this day of railroads, if we wish to make the quickest time, for passengers or freight, to Kansas City Atchison, Leavenworth, St. Joseph or Omaha, the route lies through St. Charles, and at St. Louis we take the St. Louis, Kansas City and Northern Railroad. In earlier times, 50 or 60 years ago, the United States engineers, in locating the great National Turnpike, understood this matter fully. From Maryland the route through the states pointed directly to the shores of the Missouri River, via St. Charles, to Jefferson City, its termination, as the cheapest and most direct route.[4]

When highways came to the state, they followed the same routes. U.S. Highway 40 and later Interstate 70 roughly paralleled the route of the old North Missouri Railroad through St. Charles County. The projected Page Avenue extension roughly follows the old Booneslick trail. All have avoided the rough and hilly areas to the south and north.

St. Charles County is located at the point where the Missouri and Mississippi floodplains meet.[5] Here, before man changed the natural vegetation, two smooth grassy mounds projected out into the prairie some distance from the main bluffs. An early history records, "They were named by the early French pioneers *La Mamelles*, from their fancied resemblance to the human female breasts. These mounds have an elevation of about 510 feet, and afford an extensive view of a most beautiful country, lying east, west and north."[6]

With a vegetative cover, the loess soil that covers the county is resistant to wind and water erosion. When cut into by running water and plowing, it erodes rapidly producing deep ravines and gullies.[7] This phenomenon can be seen in the blufflands adjacent to the floodplains along the Katy Trail and the I-370 corridor. In the last 50 years its soil has made St. Charles County more attractive to residential developers than counties in the Ozark Dome. The soil is very easy to grade and move with modern earth-moving equipment, making it cheaper to develop subdivisions in St. Charles County than in Jefferson or Franklin counties.

Where the loess contained more clay, it was used for brick making. According to the *History of St. Charles County*, "An abundance of the best red clay, is found in and around St. Charles, and in many other parts of the county. Brick made of this material are of a bright red color, and for beauty, solidity and durability are not excelled in any part of the country."[8] The first brick masons arrived in 1790 and built the first brick house for Colonel Timothy Kibby on what is now the corner of Pike and Main Streets. Throughout its history, most of the structures built in St. Charles were built of brick.

Loess soil is fertile, but not as productive as the alluvial soils of river bottoms. These alluvial soils attracted pre-Columbian Native Americans to the area that today is Cahokia, Illinois.[9] This "Mississippian" culture flourished during a period of global warming between 900 and 1350 that allowed improved varieties of squash and maize and the introduction of beans. One historian notes, "As the agricultural revolution gradually spread, for the first time these 'Three Sisters,' rather than hunting and gathering, became the principal food source for Native people throughout the east, with the exception of the far northern regions where the growing season was too short."[10]

Between the tenth and thirteenth centuries, the indigenous population built a city of about 20,000 people not too far from the confluence of the Mississippi and Missouri rivers at Cahokia. The surrounding 125 square mile area encompassed 10 large towns and more than 50 farming villages. There are several sites in St. Charles County that could have been outposts of the Cahokian civilization. Several Cahokia-type mounds have been located within Portage des Sioux, while several more have been identified near the *Mamelles* north of St. Charles. By the fourteenth century the Cahokian culture had peaked and begun to decline, probably because of the onset of a "Little Ice Age" that continued into the 1800s.[11] The same soils that attracted pre-Columbian Native Americans later attracted settlers from Virginia, Tennessee and Kentucky. After 1824, the settlers began to cultivate tobacco on a small scale in St. Charles County, where the average altitude of 550 feet above sea level was perfect for the crop.[12] Later still, German immigrant farmers further developed the agricultural potential of these soils for corn, wheat and beans, helping make the American Midwest the world's leading agricultural region.

The rivers guaranteed a supply of fur-bearing animals that could be trapped and their pelts sold in the European markets of the eighteenth and early nineteenth centuries. The ecology of the Missouri and Mississippi Rivers varied because of the nature of each river. The Missouri River has an average gradient is one foot per mile that enables it to move more sediment. Because it drains the loess-mantled region, it carries high suspensions of loess materials, giving the river its famous muddy color. In its natural state, the Missouri River channel was broad and shallow with numerous islands and sandbars. Before the twentieth century, it was approximately twice its present width, occupying 30 to 50 percent of the width of its floodplain. The Missouri River bottoms had natural lakes or perennial wetlands in St. Charles County, including *Marais Croche* and *Marais Temps Claire*.

Since the late nineteenth century land hungry farmers have narrowed the river by draining these wetlands and built agricultural levees to protect their fields. The US Army Corps of Engineers, by maintaining a channel of sufficient depth for barge traffic, has also contributed to the narrowing of the river. Channelization led to the destruction of habitat for several species. Environmental groups have attempted to persaude the federal government to release more water from upstream dams in the springtime to restore the original habitat. Farmers, who fear that higher river levels in the spring will increase the chance of floods, have vigorously opposed the proposal. Federal regulation has arrested the disappearance of wetland habitat and the Missouri Department of Conservation has purchased land and restored the *Marais Temps Claire* wetlands.

The Mississippi River above the confluence with Missouri River had a natural gradient half as steep as the Missouri River. Its watershed is more vegetated and carries less silt. Because the gradient is so much less, to carry its load the river cannot meander as much as the Missouri. The Mississippi floodplain is wetter than that of the Missouri and is a much better habitat for wildlife.[13] The *History of St. Charles County* boasts of the "vast quantities of water fowl and game birds of passage," claiming that the county has "every variety of duck known on the North American waters." It goes further to explain:

> These, twice a year, pass up and down their great line of migration, which
> follows the course of the Mississippi leading north and south, on their way

in leaving the lakes, rivers and plains of British America and the North, in the fall for the warm bayous, streams and marshes of the Gulf States, and again in returning north in the spring. We are located directly under the great aerial highway of the wild fowl, and in both spring and autumn they stop in vast numbers on our lakes, rivers and prairies.[14]

In the 1880s the area contained the Dardenne and Richfield Hunting Clubs composed of wealthy gentlemen from St. Louis. Even today, the Mississippi floodplain along Highway 79 in St. Charles County has some of the best duck hunting, as well as some of the finest hunting lodges, in the country.

The rivers not only affected the wildlife but also human habitation, and often made the county an unhealthy place for humans in the days before modern medicine. The lakes and natural wetlands of St. Charles County were a source of diseases, and as late as the 1930s St. Charles County residents contracted malaria. In his landmark book on climatology published in 1857, Lorin Blodget asserts, "India itself has not been more certain to break the health of the emigrant than the Mississippi valley," though he softened the embarrassing comparison by stating, "the American forms of the disease were always attended by smaller ratios of mortality."[15] As a result, the primary goal in the river bottoms until the last quarter of the twentieth century was to drain them of their standing waters.[16] For over a century, farmers drained these wetlands and farmed them until restricted by federal policy. That policy, designed to protect remaining wetlands from conversion, conflicts with long-held ideas of property rights. As part of the reconstruction of the Melvin Price lock and dam, the federal government created over 1,700 acres of wetlands adjacent to the dam in extreme eastern St. Charles County in the 1980s.

The extensive lowlands and numerous wetlands also affect the weather in the area. One historian relates how one experienced traveler likened summer in St. Louis to the "Black Hole of Calcutta." Charles Dickens, however, tried to be restrained in his description of the city. St. Louis, he noted in 1842, was as healthy as any territory with "vast tracts of undrained swampy land around it."[17] In the 1980s and 1990s, that weather had greatly increased the amount of pollution in the air and contributed to the St. Louis area being designated a "modified non-attainment" area by the Federal Environmental Protection Agency. To avoid further penalties from the federal government, the state has imposed measures like reformulated gasoline and emissions testing to reduce pollution.

The rivers have also contributed greatly to the scenic beauty of the area. The wide expanse of the rivers has been an inspiration to painter and photographer. Referring to these aesthetic qualities, historian Paul Nagel points out:

However it took a migrant New England clergyman and Harvard College alumnus to picture best the rich legacy Missouri had from nature's hand. The Rev. Timothy Flint's famed *Recollections of the Last Ten Years* became a widely read classic. Published in 1826, it emphasized years Flint and his family spent in the Missouri River village of St. Charles. Flint believed that no one could be unmoved who saw this "river which rises in vast and nameless mountains, and runs at one time through deep forests, and then through grassy plains, between three and four thousand miles before it arrives here." It was a river "more fierce and unsparing in its wrath" than the Mississippi, which Flint also watched awestruck. As for the Missouri countryside, Flint said it was unnecessary "to be very young or very romantic, in order to have dreams steal over the mind, of spending an Arcadian life in these remote plains, which just begin to be vexed with the plow, far removed from the haunts of wealth and fashion, in the midst of rustic plenty, and of this beautiful nature."[18]

The rivers also contributed to the beautiful scenery indirectly. The scouring action of the channel against the bluffs, removing rock and debris at the base, and thus keeping them sharply vertical, created scenic bluffs in St. Charles County along the Katy Trail. An even better example of this phenomenon is the Mississippi River bluffs in Illinois across the river from Portage des Sioux.[19]

Finally, the rivers served as the primary mode of transportation in St. Charles County until the 1850s. Long before Europeans arrived, the Indian tribes had used the rivers as their main source of transportation. Algonquian language tribes including the Sac and Fox, whose lands stretched to the north and east, traveled by canoe on the Mississippi, Illinois, Ohio, Wabash and Great Lakes. These transportation habits gave one of the towns in St. Charles County its name. The Osage tribe came to the state between 1400 and 1500, and was concentrated in the area to the west of St. Charles County. The Sioux, with whom the Osage shared their Siouan language, were located to the north, on the west bank of the Mississippi River north of the Des Moines River. When members of an Osage hunting party killed members of a Sioux hunting party, a fleet of canoes traveled down the Mississippi River and up the Missouri River to attack the Osage village. The Sioux massacred a large number of Osage and fled the scene. The Osage followed the Sioux canoes down the Missouri in hot pursuit. When the enemy was in sight, the Sioux made a turn in the river and, now shielded from the Osage' view, pulled their canoes from the water and hid along the river bank until the Osage had passed. They then carried their canoes across the two-mile strip of land and put into the Mississippi River at a point that became known as Portage des Sioux. This gained them 20 miles on their pursuers and guaranteed their escape.[20] The system of rivers was the conduit for French, Spanish, and later American settlers as they made their way to new areas of settlement.[21]

The rivers were the exclusive highways of commerce until the mid-nineteenth century. Most of the pre-railroad westward expansion through St. Louis, including the nation's access to the commercial Santa Fe Trail and other western trails, moved up the rivers.[22] Many of the railroads were built along rivers. Even after the steam-

High bluffs line the banks of the Mississippi River across from Hideaway Harbor County Park, near Portage des Sioux.

boats were gone the river commerce continued to grow. In the 1930s the federal government built a series of locks and dams on the Mississippi River to aid barge navigation, and one of them was built at Alton, Illinois. When it was replaced, the new Melvin Price locks and dam were the largest public works project in the history of St. Charles County. Paul Nagel has noted that Senator Daniel Webster in 1837, called Missouri an "infant Hercules," referring to its economic potential.[23] Its location at the confluence of the Illinois and Mississippi Rivers as well gave St. Charles County tremendous advantages in the period before the coming of the railroad.

Its location at the confluence has not only been a blessing but a curse, as flooding has been a continuing problem for farms in the low-lying areas of St. Charles County. The first recorded flood was in 1844, when both the Missouri and Mississippi were high at the same time. From Hermann to St. Charles, the river was nearly 15 feet above flood stage and at St. Louis, with the addition of the equally bloated Mississippi, the water level rose to 39 feet, nine feet above flood stage.[24] In the twentieth century, the floods were even more devastating with the worst flooding in history occurring in 1993.

Because of its location between two great biomes, grasslands and forests, the resources of both have been available in St. Charles County. The grasslands were first used as open range by bison and later by cattle. Manuel Gayosa De Lemos, visiting *San Carlos del Misuri* in 1795 stated, "To the rear of San Carlos immense savannahs begin which extend as far as the hunters have penetrated in all directions," on which all livestock would prosper."[25] In their natural state, the woodlands were

11

home to wild game such as turkey and deer. After the "Mississippians", but before Europeans, Woodland Indians lived in St. Charles County and hunted its forests. They lived in villages and practiced limited agriculture. The Woodland Indians departed about 400 years ago and may have been driven out by the Osage and Missouri, Siouan tribes that occupied the area to the west and south of St. Charles County. They also lived in villages and practiced horticulture and hunting in woodlands. The Osage men shaved their heads except for a strip called a scalp lock while both men and women tattooed their bodies.[26] To the east and north were the Algonquian tribes, including the Fox and Sac. In his autobiography, Sac Chief Blackhawk stated:

> We always had plenty – our children never cried with hunger, nor our people were never in want. Here our village had stood for more than a 100 years, during all which time we were the undisputed possessors of the valley of the Mississippi from Ouisconsin (Wisconsin) to the Portage des Sioux, being about seven hundred miles in length.[27]

As late as 1885, the *History of St. Charles County* concluded, "Wild animals of almost every species known in the wilds of the west were found in great abundance. The prairies and woods and streams and various bodies of water were all thickly inhabited before the white man came, and for some time afterward."[28]

The European settlers in the late eighteenth and early nineteenth century also needed a certain percentage of their homesteads to be woodlands, on which they could hunt and procure food for their families. The wooded lands of St. Charles County included an abundant supply of lumber that was initially used to construct homes, fences and barns. Later, skilled craftsmen made barrels at a cooperage in St. Charles, a town also known for the quality of the wagons, carriages and buggies that were manufactured there.[29] Hardwoods such as cherry, walnut and oak were available to make fine furniture.[30] Before the Civil War, St. Charles had seven furniture factories and its craftsmen had a reputation for making fine furniture.[31]

In the middle of the nineteenth century, bottomland timber was cut to provide fuel steamboats, leading to rapid deforestation of the floodplain. The steamboats required 12 to 75 cords of wood per day and carried only a day's supply. Boat owners or local entrepreneurs operated wood yards along the riverbanks.[32] By 1850, a large number of individuals in St. Charles County listed "woodchopper" as their occupation.[33] Three-fourths of St. Charles County was originally timbered. While large quantities had been cut for lumber, firewood, fencing, and cultivation, in 1885 the *History of St. Charles County* stated that timber "remains sufficient for generations to come."[34] In the twentieth-century, managed forests like Busch Wildlife Area became major recreational areas.

Not only is St. Charles County located between two great biomes, but it is also located between the two chief cultural and political divides in Missouri history – St. Louis and "outstate" Missouri. When St. Charles was 23 years old in 1792, Zenon

Trudeau, lieutenant governor of Upper-Louisiana described it as "an isolated settlement more than five leagues up the misuri (sic), too far from St. Louis for easy communication."[35] Nevertheless, St. Charles became tied to St. Louis because of their common French culture and economic ties through the fur trade. However, as St. Charles County received an influx of American settlers in the nineteenth century, the county came to have more in common with the Booneslick Region that became known as "Little Dixie" inhabited by settlers from Kentucky, Tennessee and Virginia. Then, the arrival of German immigrants after the 1830s again created cultural ties with St. Louis, where large numbers of Germans also immigrated. Nevertheless, the economy of the county continued to be tied to "Little Dixie" until the Civil War. While St Charles County remained primarily agricultural for the remainder of the nineteenth century, the North Missouri Railroad provided a link to the St. Louis market for its agricultural products. While still a typical small Missouri town in the first half of the twentieth century, St. Charles was developing industries like St. Louis, and a streetcar across a new bridge linked the two. Post-World War II prosperity and interstate highways permanently linked the future of St. Charles County to the future of the St. Louis Metropolitan Region.

Geographically, St. Charles County was situated between urban and rural Missouri; geologically, it contained topography characteristic of northern and southern Missouri; and ecologically it was where the prairie and forest met. The county also marked the crossroads at which different cultures met as French, Americans, Germans and suburbanites moved into the area. The natural resources of St. Charles County easily sustained the sparse Native American population. As successive groups of Europeans arrived, each exploited these natural resources in different ways and with varying degrees of success. The first to arrive were the French.

B. French Discovery and Spanish Administration

The first European settlers in St. Charles County came from European colonies whose political systems were quite different from the governments that were developing in the English colonies along the Atlantic coast. In the French and Spanish colonial systems decisions were made in the capitals of Europe by monarchs confident in the Divine Right of Kings. After 1763, under direction from Madrid, Havana, New Orleans and St. Louis, local officials regulated the fur trade, protected settlers from Indian attacks, kept the peace and promoted Catholicism. However, the distances involved made it difficult for governments in those far-away European and territorial capitals to impact the day-to-day activities of the settlers in the colony of Louisiana. As a result, the inhabitants of the District of St. Charles had considerable control over their local affairs under Spanish rule. As Spanish administration began, Louisiana was seen primarily as a buffer between the thousands of Protestant Americans across the

13

Mississippi hungry for land and the Spanish possessions to the southwest. By the end of the century Louisiana had become a magnet rather than a buffer.

The first recorded presence of Europeans in St. Charles County occurred in June 1673, when Father Jacques Marquette and his companion Louis Joliet discovered the muddy waters of the Missouri River flowing into the Mississippi River. Marquette wrote, " I have seen nothing more dreadful. An accumulation of large and entire trees, branches, and floating islands was issuing from the mouth of the river, with such impetuosity that we could not, without great danger, risk passing through it."[36] While the French explorers did not venture up the Missouri River at that time, they did claim the territory that it drained for France. By 1700 French fur traders, who had come down from Canada, were trading with the Osage Indians, who lived over 100 miles up the Missouri River from its confluence with the Mississippi River. By that time, France had claimed the lands along both banks of the upper Mississippi River

French speaking *Voyageurs. Sketch by Vicki White.*

and named the area "Illinois Country," a part of France's empire in North America, called "Louisiana."[37] After 1720 Fort Chartres, about 15 miles north of Kaskaskia, served as the French seat of government during the French presence in the Illinois Country. In 1723 Etiene Veniard de Bourgmont, commandant of the Missouri River, constructed Fort Orleans in what is now Carroll County, Missouri and successfully negotiated treaties with the Indian tribes, whose chiefs accompanied him on a visit to the French court. While the chiefs returned to Missouri, de Bourgmont did not and his fort was abandoned in 1729 having proven to be economically unsuccessful.[38]

While the first French penetration into the Missouri River country was not successful, this period marked the heyday of trade between the French and Indians in the Illinois Country. That trade led to a series of wars between France and Great Britain, whose own colonies were located to the east of the Illinois Country. In 1760, during the last of these conflicts, the British captured Quebec City, thus sealing France's fate in North America. In 1762 Spain had joined France in the unsuccessful endeavor against the British that had now assumed global proportions.[39] The peace treaty ending the French and Indian War, as it was called by the English colonists, gave Protestant Britain title to Canada, including the Illinois Country. France had earlier transferred its territory west of the Mississippi River to Spain, compensating its ally for its losses and assuring that the area west of the Mississippi River remained Catholic, thus making the Mississippi River an ecclesiastical as well as an international political boundary. Spain's interest in Louisiana was as a buffer against British advances.[40]

In 1767, the Spanish asserted their rights to Upper Louisiana by building at the confluence of the Missouri and Mississippi Rivers, in what is now St. Louis County, a fort named for their King Charles VI. A blockhouse was also built across the river in what is now St. Charles County. The first Europeans to take up residence in St. Charles County were the 15 Spanish soldiers stationed at the blockhouse to ensure boats going up the Missouri River had a trading license from the Spanish government. While the British were no problem, flooding eventually forced the Spanish to abandon the blockhouse north of the river. Local French and Indian resentment of Spanish attempts to regulate commerce eventually forced Spanish authorities to retreat to New Orleans.[41] In 1769, Spain reasserted control over all of its Mississippi valley holdings by sending Alejandro O'Reilly to govern Louisiana. He partitioned Louisiana into northern and southern administrative units and appointed Pedro Piernas as lieutenant governor of Upper Louisiana.[42]

In the same year a French-Canadian named Louis Blanchette, and called *chasseur*, ("hunter"), established a settlement at what is now the South Main Historic District in St. Charles. Blanchette named the village *Les Petite Cotes* ("Village of the Little Hills"), because it was located on the first high ground on the north bank of the Missouri River.[43] The first evidence that the Spanish were even aware of Blanchette and his village was in 1771, when Piernas was designated lieutenant governor of St. Louis, St. Genevieve, and "all the districts of the Missouri River."[44] Louis Blanchette was commissioned as the first civil and military commandant of St. Charles by the Spanish lieutenant governor of Upper Louisiana and served in that post until his death. His main duties were to enforce Spanish trade policies, protect the settlement from Indian tribes and maintain order. By 1776 a fort was erected on the site of the present county jail, a point commanding a view of the Missouri River and the prairies surrounding the fort. After 1801, duties were paid and travel passes obtained at a customs house in St. Charles.[45]

The Spanish continued the fur trading policies of the French by issuing a limited number of licenses to the highest bidders among their subjects. However, with the coming of the Spanish administration there was a complete reorientation of the economic interest of Upper-Louisiana toward the south and the Gulf of Mexico, and away from Canada, from which many of the French inhabitants had come.[46] British traders operating out of Canada worked to divert much of this trade from New Orleans to Montreal. During the winter of 1772, a British trading party, led by the Canadian-born Jean Marie Ducharme, managed to slip past Fort Don Carlos with two boats of trading supplies. They traveled up the Missouri and traded with the

Osage for four months, until Lieutenant Governor Piernas dispatched Pierre Laclede with a party of 40 men who captured Ducharme's party although Ducharme escaped to Canada.[47] To strengthen their control and to dissuade further incursions by British trading parties, the Spanish began recruiting additional settlers from among the French Canadians living in the Illinois Country, promising land, grain, livestock and essential farming implements. Some of these transplants from the Illinois Country settled in the St. Charles District.[48]

During the American Revolution, the British made alliances with many of the native tribes along the upper Mississippi River and made further inroads into the Spanish control of the fur trade in that area. When Spain declared war on Britain in 1780, towards the end of the American Revolutionary War, the Spanish had to defend St. Louis against British attacks. Even when the war ended, the British did not leave the area of the upper Mississippi, making Upper Louisiana's fur trade increasingly dependent on the tribes along the Missouri River.[49] Spanish companies made two unsuccessful expeditions to the Mandan villages on the upper Missouri; the last in 1795 was led by James Mackay, a Canadian trader who had recently become a Spanish subject in the St. Louis District.[50]

This Sioux Indian visited St. Charles County in the 1880s. *John J. Buse Collection, 1860-1931, Western Historical Manuscript Collection-Columbia, MO.*

Like the French before them, the Spanish provided liquor to the Indian tribes while prohibiting traders and tavern owners from selling any alcoholic beverages to them. By the 1790s Indians were able to get liquor from the Americans across the Mississippi and Governor Carondelet relented and allowed the sale of alcohol to the Indians "for medicinal purposes."[51] In 1794 Carondelet granted Auguste Chouteau a monopoly on the fur trade with the Osage and he started a trading post on the Osage River. With the reorientation of the trade towards the Missouri River, St. Charles took on added importance. A Spanish visitor to *San Carlos* in 1795 reported, "A large part of the residents are employed in voyages to the upper regions of Missouri."[52] Trapper James Mackay succeeded Charles Taillon, who had succeeded Louis Blanchette, as commandant of St. Charles and remained in that post until the purchase of Louisiana by the United States.

In addition to enforcing Spanish trade policies, a second responsibility of the commandant at St. Charles was to protect the village from Indian attack. Lieutenant

Governor Trudeau named Charles Taillon, an experienced militia officer who had fought to defend St. Louis against British attack in 1780, as commandant of St. Charles District, upon the death of Louis Blanchette. In a report to Carondelet in 1793, Trudeau wrote:

> At this time, I am uneasy about a band of 20 Indians which have appeared at the village of San Carlos del Misury and of which I was warned by other savages who came to give me advise of it. However zealous Monsieur Tayon (Taillon) Commandant of the place, might be, it would be truly difficult to prevent them from taking some scalps with his having to leave the village.[53]

Local historian Jean Fields concludes that Taillon's reputation as a tough Indian fighter discouraged the Osage and other tribes from attacking the settlement at St. Charles.[54] Manuel Gayoso De Lemos observed in 1795, "Don Carlos Taillon (Tayon), Captain of the militia and commandant of this establishment is a subject of much merit and very suited to the post, since in addition to being zealous in the discharge of his duty, he is valiant and determined which causes him to be respected by the Indians."[55] North of the Missouri River were the Sac and Fox tribes, supplied by French Canadians working for the British at Prairie du Chien. The Sac and the Fox began to establish villages on the northern edge of Osage country, and the land between the Des Moines, Chariton and Grand Rivers became a battle zone for the warring tribes.[56]

Finally, the third duty of the commandant at St. Charles was to maintain order. Spanish officials restricted the sale of alcoholic beverages by granting tavern licenses at public auction to people of good character. Licensees who failed to report disturbances, the presence of criminals, vagabonds and prostitutes, or swearing and blasphemy, were fined or lost their license.[57] Local historian Edna McElhiney Olson writes, "No one, not even an older resident, was permitted to travel in the country more than 20 miles without a passport from the post commandant, in which was stated specifically the road to be traveled going and returning."[58] However, the Spanish never had the type of control over the population that they would have liked. For purposes of administering their widely scattered possessions, the Spanish established five districts, St. Charles, St. Louis, Ste. Genevieve, Cape Girardeau and New Madrid.[59] St. Charles was described by one lieutenant governor as the "residence of the savages, mongrels, and worst scoundrels in Illinois."[60] Criminal prosecution there was difficult since the criminal could escape to the other side of the Mississippi River and be in another country.[61]

The jurisdiction of the commandant of the District of St. Charles expanded to the north and west and so did the influence of the local Catholic parish, St. Charles Borromeo. Dardenne, near present-day old-town in St. Peters, was settled around 1796 when John Baptiste Blondeau began cultivating land along Dardenne Creek. The Dardenne settlement grew and became a dependency of the St. Charles Borromeo Parish until 1815.[62] Nicholas de Finiels, writing a report in 1803 entitled, "An Account of Upper Louisianna," wrote, "Despite the lethargic state in which St. Charles has remained for nearly 20 years of its existence, a small colony has sprung up on the banks of the Dardenne."[63] He added that, "The settlement at the Dardenne Creek had, however, still another objective, which was to establish a presence close to the mouth of the Illinois River. In that way the portage between the river and St. Charles, which is almost three leagues in length, could be avoided."[64] The settlement, which was midway between the rivers (Mid-rivers), was located at old town St. Peters.[65]

Borromeo records also occasionally mention a colony of Catholics at *Maraise Croche*, north of St. Charles, later called Boschertown. [66] However, after St. Charles, the largest French settlement in St. Charles County was Portage des Sioux. Francis Lesseur, a resident of St. Charles, decided in 1799 that the site would make a good village as it was at a higher elevation than the surrounding countryside. Lieutenant Governor Zenon Trudeau encouraged Francis Saucier to establish a settlement on the site and made grants of land to a number of families from St. Charles and St. Louis. Many French from the Illinois Country came to live in Portage des Sioux. Antoine Soulard, surveyor of the colony, was ordered to make a survey of the village and Saucier was appointed commandant. The distance at Portage des Sioux between the Missouri and Mississippi is scarcely two miles, making it a convenient place for Indians to carry their canoes from one river to the other.[67]

Above the local commandant was a hierarchy of governmental officials each responsible to the official above them. The lieutenant governor's responsibilities were to command the citizen militia; try non-violent crimes; regulate surveys and conveyances of lands; collect taxes and fees; and propagate the Catholic faith. While the governor presided over the trial of serious and violent crimes, in Upper Louisiana, because of the distance, the lieutenant governor heard the cases, made a record of the evidence and sent it to the governor in New Orleans who actually decided the case.[68]

To perfect a land grant after 1798, the request first had to be approved by the lieutenant governor. The land had to be surveyed, and then, under the "Rules of Morales," the document required validation by the *Intendant* at New Orleans. Grants of land by the lieutenant governor were common and, in 1797 the official surveyor for Upper Louisiana, Antoine Soulard, surveyed the St. Charles area with the assistance of St. Charlesan Gabrielle Lattrel.[69] However, the last step, requiring a trip to New Orleans, was cost prohibitive for most residents of Upper Louisiana.[70]

The first tax in St. Charles County was a levy of 1\26 of each parishioner's harvest, payable in bushels of wheat or corn, deerskins, or very rarely in cash. The Spanish also imposed an alcohol tax and a tavern license fee to support the local St. Charles Borromeo Parish.[71] Fees charged for baptizing, marrying or burying parishioners also supported the local parish priest, who worked hand in hand with the civil authorities to promote Catholicism.

Based on these facts, the stereotype later developed among Americans that the Spanish regime was undemocratic, authoritarian, centralized, dominated by clerics and incompetent. Americans thought the democratically elected constitutional government of the United States, with its strong emphasis on local government, constitutional protections and toleration of all religions, should replace it. Professor Stuart Banner suggests that since the lieutenant governors of Upper Louisiana appeared to have unchecked power and the inhabitants possessed none of the constitutional guarantees of their liberty, Americans equated Spanish rule with the British tyranny they had recently overthrown.[72] Americans had an equally poor opinion of the Spanish military. In 1831 Judge Wilson Primm contended that Captain Fernando de Leyba was an "imbecile governor" and a "Spanish Benedict Arnold" for his handling of the defense of St. Louis against British forces in 1780. John Francis McDermott has examined the historical record and concludes, "Documents known today show that Captain de Leyba was effective in his defense of St. Louis. None have been discovered which corroborate the allegations made against him."[73]

In fact, conditions in Upper Louisiana were never as authoritarian, centralized or clerical as they appeared. Not only could criminals flee the country by crossing the Mississippi River, local officials were delegated the authority to try all but the most serious cases. The Spanish also continued to allow the French settlers to refer civil disputes to arbitrators of their own choosing.[74] The decisions in these cases were not based on written law, handed down from the monarch in Madrid, but on unwritten local custom.[75] The system of land grants, while centralized in theory, was quite chaotic in application. It was difficult to find surveyors in a society where most of the inhabitants were illiterate, and most landowners did not have their grants approved in New Orleans.[76] Although Spanish law required grantees to inhabit the land, often grantees did not take possession and were simply land speculators. Noting the graft and corruption practiced by these usually wealthy grantees, Local historian William C. Lloyd writes, "Through their connections these people were given grants they did not settle, but held to sell later. Reviews of the early concessions reveal interesting connections. It seems that many were either related or in business together, in many instances both."[77] While the governor had the power to tax, smuggling, especially of alcohol, was a constant problem that the Spanish government sought to eliminate, usually without success.[78]

In spite of the Spanish government's support for the Catholic Church, Blanchette's settlement had a hard time even keeping a resident pastor. Lieutenant Governor Trudeau explained the ongoing need for a priest in 1795, stating, "St. Charles is too distant from St. Louis for Don Didier to offer to go there; the customs are so depraved there, due to its being in a most out of the way location.... A cure' would be for them a God who would restrain them in their vices."[79] In 1798 the much-awaited pastor, Father Charles Leander Luzon, finally arrived. As a result of the transfer of Louisiana from France to Spain in 1762, ecclesiastic authority had passed from the Archbishop of Quebec, Canada to the Archbishop of Havana, Cuba making the ecclesiastic authority even further away that the civil authority in New Orleans. When the desire for religious conformity clashed with the need to assure public safety, the Spanish often proved to be very pragmatic. Initially Spain tried to restrict settlement to Catholics, but this policy kept villages like St Charles small and vulnerable to Indian raids. In

1787 Spain decided to allow Protestant settlers, provided that they promise to have their children baptized in the Catholic Church.[80]

The Catholic register of marriages at St. Charles Borromeo Parish was a "Who's Who" of English-speaking people in the St. Charles area. Among those whose marriages were recorded are Morgan Boone, son of the famous pioneer, and St. Charles District Commandant James Mackay. The records also contain familiar family names such as Musick, Spencer, Howell and Zumwalt.[81] Still, in 1798 the lieutenant governor noted that many were leaving the St. Louis area for their eastern homes, "because they are obliged to celebrate their marriages and baptism by means of our Catholic priest."[82]

Finally, because of the long distances that separated king and governors from the people, local government was important in Upper Louisiana. The earliest deliberative body in St. Charles met on a Sunday in 1801, upon notice given by Commandant Taillon, for the purpose of deciding whether to fence the commons below the village. The record reflected, "all the inhabitants being present, they agreed that the commons should be fenced." [83]

The weakness of Spanish control of Louisiana can be seen in Spain's relations with the new American republic now across the Mississippi River. In 1784, the Spanish closed the Mississippi River to American commerce, hoping to use navigation of the river as leverage to negotiate a settlement of their differences. The move only antagonized American frontiersmen who threatened to use force to reopen the river. Realizing their tenuous hold on Louisiana, the Spanish settled all outstanding differences with the United States in 1795, guaranteeing free navigation on the Mississippi. Having reached the conclusion that further attempts to develop Louisiana into a buffer against American penetration were a waste of money and effort, in 1796 the Spanish circulated handbills to attract American settlers by offering liberal land grants.[84]

The Treaty of Paris in 1763 brought French settlers and Spanish rule to the St. Charles District. The Spanish administration in the St. Charles District, contrary to the stereotypes propounded by later American settlers, was necessarily decentralized, reluctantly democratic and much more tolerant than the Spanish crown preferred. In 1800 Louisiana again became the possession of France. A few years later, for the second time in 40 years, diplomats in Paris determined the future of the St. Charles District. This time one group of diplomats was receiving instructions from Thomas Jefferson, President of the United States.

C. Life of the *voyageur*

While under Spanish administration at the time of its founding, it was French customs and habits that took root in the St. Charles District after the settlement of *Les Petite Cotes*. The French culture that took root was not the culture of France, or New Orleans, or even St. Louis; it was the culture and traditions of the inhabitants of the Illinois Country, whose families had come from French Canada. These *voyageurs* had established customs and traditions that allowed them to co-exist and trade with the Indians since the beginning of the eighteenth century, and they brought those customs to the District of St. Charles. They also brought their religion, a system of slavery, and a semi-communal village-based agriculture, all uniquely different from the institutions developing across the river in the new American republic.

In St. Charles, conditions were primitive and life was brutally hard. On the other hand, just as in New Orleans and St. Louis, Catholicism, slavery and a common field system of agriculture could be found in the District of St. Charles. Viewed from the racially segregated, competitive world of mid-nineteenth century America, with its Victorian social mores, the life of the *voyageur* seemed scandalous and uncivilized. From the viewpoint of the twenty-first century, it seems remarkably congruent with the integrated, cooperative, multicultural and sexually permissive American society of the last third of the twentieth century. The social stereotypes of the French popularized by the American writers after the Louisiana Purchase were just as misleading as the political stereotypes. Janet Lecompte points out the condescending attitude of the Americans to the Pidgin English, folk-customs, songs, dances and costumes of the French, and identifies many of the comparisons between *voyageurs* and English-speaking trappers in the literature of the fur trade.

> Voyageurs were "very deficient in physical courage," says Chittendon, "and their fears when upon dangerous ground were often ludicrous in the extreme." Washington Irving links their cowardice to an addiction to comfort and safety, and contrasts it with the noble recklessness of the Anglo-Saxon. Their "volatile gaiety" and frivolity was compared to British gravity and dignity. Some of their habits were judged to be disgusting: Townsend saw voyageurs eating like "half-famished wolves." Others described their "frolicking" or inebriation which led to shocking scenes of public sexual promiscuity with Indian women, and subsequent venereal disease.[85]

Many of the earliest settlers of the District of St. Charles came from nearby St. Louis, Cahokia, Kaskaskia or Prairie du Rocher. They also came from more distant locales such as Vincennes, Prairie du Chien, New Orleans and Quebec.[86] The new arrivals' cultural values were a synthesis, the result of the previous 100 years of contact between French settlers and Indian tribes. To understand the ways of the *voyageur* in the District of St. Charles in the late eighteenth century, it is necessary to understand the 265 years of interaction between Algonquian tribes and the French in the area from which most of the residents of the district emigrated. In his book, *The Middle Ground*, historian Richard White suggests that these two alien cultures interacted between 1650 and 1815, and constructed a multicultural world in the region north of the Ohio River, east of the Mississippi and south of the Great Lakes.[87]

After a series of wars between tribes and greater contact with the French and other Europeans, the Native Americans were devastated. There are no reliable estimates, but anywhere from 25 to 90 percent of them died of European diseases in the late seventeenth and early eighteenth centuries as the European population increased. With their numerical superiority shrinking, the Indians reached an accommodation with the French that Richard White has called the "middle ground." The "middle ground" assumed the inability of either side to gain its desired ends through force of arms, and thus the need for the parties to find a non-violent means to gain the cooperation or consent of each other. To succeed, each side had to accept some of the reasoning of the other side and use it to their own purposes.[88]

This accommodation can be seen in the fields of sexual relations, criminal punishment and the fur trade. Interracial marriage between French and Indians was not uncommon. Bernard Guillet crossed the Missouri River into what is now St. Charles County around 1740, built a hut and began trapping the rivers and streams. After killing a Dakota Sioux who was stealing from his traps, he was captured by Dakota warriors and taken to their village. He was tortured and about to be burned at the stake when a Dakota woman, having recently been widowed, intervened and claimed Guillet as her husband. Having been spared, he lived with the tribe and eventually married the chief's daughter. Upon his father-in-law's death, Guillet became chief of the Dakotas.[89]

Less dramatic and less formal unions between French males and Indian females were more common. The absence of French women meant that French males actively sought out native women as sexual partners. For the French the supreme authority on all such matters was with the celibate clergy. In France, and the rest of Catholic Europe, there were strong societal pressures against pre-marital sexual relations. The main concerns of the Catholic Church were prostitution and adultery. But most sexual contact in North America took place between Frenchmen and single Indian women, who enjoyed considerable sexual freedom but were not prostitutes.[9]

Not only did these women have sexual relationships with their male partners, but they also cooked, cleaned and sewed for them. They were free to leave any time they desired. White explains, "These relationships were not contracts between families. They were, instead, a bridge to the 'middle ground,' an adjustment of interracial sex in the fur trade where the initial conceptions of sexual conduct held by each side were reconciled in a new customary relationship."[91] Of 21 baptisms recorded in the French village of Kaskaskia between 1704 and 1713, the mother was Indian and the father was French in 18 cases.[92] Likewise, in the District of St. Charles later, cohabitation without the benefit of clergy was common due to the scarcity of priests. Spanish law did not recognize common law marriages and the Borromeo parish archives do not even mention divorce. The high percentage of illegitimate children, including Blanchette's own, made discrimination toward them unlikely, although the priests continued to inquire whether brides and grooms were "legitimate" or "natural" children of their parents. Between 1792 and 1795, nearly half of the weddings celebrated at the Borromeo church joined white men with women of at least some native blood. Although by then the couple had three adult children, in 1790 Father Le Dru married Louis Blanchette and Tuhomehenga, a woman of either Osage or Pawnee origin. Such biracial weddings dropped off after 1795, probably because that there were then more white women available for marriage.[93]

A second example of accommodation on the "middle ground" was in the area of criminal punishment. Algonquian society provided that the families of those people killed by members of allied tribes could be compensated with gifts, slaves or by the killing of another member of the offending group. The decision about how to proceed was made by the dead person's family, with social pressure exerted to accept compensation short of blood revenge. In French jurisprudence the state took responsibility for punishing murder, in most cases by requiring the death of the murderer.[94] An accommodation acceptable to both cultures had to be found.

In 1792, the people of *San Carlos* were already dealing with crop failures when a band of Iowa Indians stole virtually every horse in town from their lightly guarded pasture near what is now Lindenwood University. The citizens called upon Lieutenant Governor Trudeau for assistance in getting the horses back. At about the same time a band of Iowa had attacked a camp of Kansas Indians, killing 18 and taking 23 women and children prisoner. When the chief of the Iowa learned of the attack, he feared war with the powerful Kansas and asked Trudeau to intercede and mediate a peace. He agreed to mediate on the condition that the horses were returned to the people of St. Charles. The wrongs inflicted on the *San Carlos* settlers and the Kansas tribe were not punished through a criminal justice system, but instead were handled through negotiations.[95]

The assault of Madame Laurin by Angelique, the Indian wife of a French trader, also shows the influence of the "middle ground' in *San Carlos*. For real or imagined insults, the record is not clear, Angelique took the law into her own hands and physically assaulted Laurin. The husband of the offended party complained to the commandant of the St. Charles District, Charles Taillon, that the woman was a menace and that violence was *"ordinaries de la nature"* to her race. Ten of the most prominent citizens of the town came to her defense explaining the Indian custom of these matters being settled between the families. They explained, "Such was the Indian way, but not, she now realized, the way of the French."[96] The record shows no formal disposition of the case and writer Judith Gilbert concludes that Taillon simply let the matter drop, rather than indict Angelique. Gilbert concludes, "This particular episode has meaning, however, beyond her life alone. It is a glimpse into the multi-cultural world of the American frontier, a world in which people of different cultures rubbed shoulders with one another and worked out ways of getting along."[97]

Conflicts in jurisprudence are also obvious in the case of "Little Crow," a Sac warrior who, while under the influence of alcohol, killed Antoine LePage in Portage des Sioux in 1807. The following year Joseph Thibault and Joseph Marechal were killed by two Iowa Indians claiming self-defense. The Sac chief offered a number of horses to Antoine LePage's family in return for Little Crow's freedom. Since the U.S. government was offering $200 as payment for each Indian death at the hands of an American citizen, the offer of the horses seemed fair to the Sac.[98] Nevertheless, the offer was rejected and the three men were brought to trial in St. Louis, where feelings against them ran strong. The court convicted the two Iowa braves, granted them a new trial, and eventually dismissed the cases against them because the crimes were committed outside the jurisdiction of the court. While waiting for the appeal of that decision they escaped and returned to their people. Meanwhile, Little Crow remained in custody until President Madison eventually pardoned him. That action was taken upon the advice of Indian agent William Clark who was acting in the best tradition of the "middle ground."[99]

A third area of cultural conflict for which "middle ground" was sought was the fur trade that provided a livelihood for many in the District of St. Charles. The fur trade was organized around a head trader, or *bourgeois*, who held a license from the government to trade. Under him was a *commis*, or clerk, who made side expeditions to native villages or operated subsidiary trading posts. In 1805 a *bourgeois* hired Joseph Marie, from St. Charles, as his *commis*.[100] Jacques D'Englise, who became famous for his exploration of the Dakotas, came to *San Carlos* in 1792, prospered and built two cabins. Other famous fur traders also had ties to St. Charles County including Baptiste Chalifoux, who was probably related to Joseph Chalifoux, who lived near Portage des Sioux between 1802 and 1807.[101] It is also possible that Joseph Gervais, born in 1777 in Quebec, was the same person of that name who lived on "little prairie" in the St. Charles District in 1800 and signed a petition to the president of the United States in 1805.[102] James Bordeaux, whose parents purchased property in the St. Charles District in 1798, was born in 1814 and, like his father before him, entered the fur trade in 1826.[103]

Those who performed the manual work in the fur trade were known as *engages*, and if they spent one or more winters on expeditions they were known as *hivernants*, or winterers.[104] An early commentator on the French-speaking people of St. Charles stated, "Their young men were engaged during the summer in hunting, boating and trading, whilst the old men and boys were left with their families to cultivate the little farms. In the winter the young men returned to the village, and the winter season was gaily spent in balls, dancing and merriment."[105]

The customs and institutions of the fur trade had been established long before the founding of *Les Petite Cotes*. Indians and trappers had become part of a worldwide market that stretched across the Atlantic to Europe. Since both sides had their own ideas about what constituted equitable exchange, an accommodation on the "middle ground" was required. The French recipe for successful trade called for a company of

French merchants to receive a monopoly on fur exports who, with the advice of the government, set the price for furs, based on the demand in Europe. Mercantilist economic policies of the time did not allow trade with colonies of another European power or with another European country. Under this system the market in France, subject to supply and demand in that country, was the ultimate determinant of the price of furs.[106]

The first goal of the Algonquians in an economic transaction was not to secure the maximum material advantage but to satisfy the needs of each party. The relationship of buyer and seller was critical to the transaction and the need of the buyer was a critical factor. For the Algonquians that need operated contrary to the way it operates in a free market system, where the greater the need the more one is willing to pay. Among the Algonquians, the greater the need of a person with the proper relationship, the greater the demand that person had on the commodity.[107] They buried European-made goods with their dead and generally used goods as gifts to cement social relationships. White adds, "The flow of goods in these relationships seemed backward to the French: leaders did not amass wealth, but, rather, gave it away; the dead did not leave property to the living; instead, the living bestowed scarce goods on the dead. Algonquians had put European goods to the service of an existing social reality."[108]

The accommodation that was eventually worked out for the fur trade was based on a paternalistic system where the French father was expected to show his generosity to his Indian children. The tribes reciprocated with gifts of furs, the value of which remained the same regardless of the market for those furs in France. Thus, the French government often found itself subsidizing the fur trade in the interest of its alliance with the tribes, which guaranteed the safety of the Illinois Country from the British.[109] After the French government handed over Louisiana, the Spanish adopted the French system, providing gifts to the tribes, spending on the average of $13,500 per year. Thus, the French passed on to the Spanish, whose experience had been with the imperial Indians of Mexico and Peru, the practices which the French had developed in dealing with the semi-nomadic tribes of North America.[110]

Later American commentators recognized, but did not appreciate, the tradition of the "common ground." Janet Lecompte relates how:

> The French were thought to be "better with the Indians" than the English. John Wyeth, who accompanied his older brother Nathaniel on his first expedition to the Oregon country, cleverly turned French advantage with Indians into a joke against the French: "[The French] please and flatter the Indians, give him powder, and balls, and flints, and guns, and make a Catholic of him, and make out to live in friendship with the red man and woman." [111]

The French traditions lived on in Spaniards like Manuel Lisa, who often traded in St. Charles.[112] He helped initiate the American fur trade on the Missouri River after 1807. Over a period of 13 years Lisa traveled the Missouri River as far as the Mandan villages at least 12 times and worked hard to develop good relations with the

Indians by giving them gifts in the tradition of the "common ground." Lisa tried unsuccessfully to persuade others that the initially expensive investments in Indian friendship paid dividends in the long run. In the short run, however, the gifts threatened the profits of struggling St. Louis fur businesses.[113]

Along with the customs of the "middle ground," the French brought to the District of St. Charles their Catholic religion, slavery, river transportation, village life and agricultural practices. When Protestant Great Britain gained control of the French settlements east of the Mississippi River, French Catholics became alarmed. After the founding of St. Louis in 1764, many of the inhabitants of the Illinois Country, believing their eternal salvation was at stake, crossed the river into the territory of Catholic Spain.[114] *Les Petit Cotes* was served by traveling missionary priests until 1791. The year before Lieutenant Governor Manuel Perez had written to his superiors, "the inhabitants of the small hills on the other side of the Missouri have also agreed to build a church of their own, and have already begun to work on it. The people have decided to choose as patron, St. Charles, in the name of our august sovereign."[115] A log church, the first of many churches, was built and dedicated on November 7, 1791.[116] On that same day Perez officially changed the name of the settlement to *San Carlos* in honor of St. Charles Borromeo, patron saint of Charles VI, the King of Spain. When Meriwether Lewis passed through St. Charles with William Clark on their famous trip in 1804, he wrote that its inhabitants, "Live in a perfect state of harmony among each other; and place an implicit confidence in the doctrines of their spiritual pastor, the Roman Catholic priest, as they yield passive obedience to their temporal master the commandant."[117]

The Catholic Church brought a thin veneer of civilization to a rugged frontier outpost. When it came to the quality of life in *San Carlos*, even some French commentators of the time agreed with the later American stereotypes. A visiting Frenchman recorded his impressions of the residents of St. Charles late in 1779. He described them as, "poor and indolent," and blamed their lack of civilization partly on the Missouri River, that impeded communications between St. Charles and St. Louis, and partly on the *voyageur* way of life, "which drew most men up the river to hunt, trap and trade during warm weather months."[118] French spy George Victor Collot offered an opinion of *San Carlos* after he visited the village that same year stating, "it would be difficult to find a collection of individuals more ignorant, stupid, ugly and miserable. Such are the side effects of extreme poverty."[119]

With Catholic priests available to read and interpret the Bible, few parishioners had much reason to read or write. Marriage registers show that many of the parish leaders, including Louis Blanchette, never mastered the art of signing their own names. Every witness to a marriage in 1779 marked with a cross rather than a signature. Baron Carondelet appointed the first school teacher of the district who taught all the grades and was granted land by the Spanish government in payment for her services.[120]

As farming gradually replaced hunting and hired hands proved ineffective, the French turned to slaves to work on their farms. Slave traders sent Africans northward from

New Orleans and many American slaveholders moved west into Upper Louisiana with their slaves following the passage of the Northwest Ordinance of 1787, outlawing slavery in the Northwest Territory. Spanish officials passed Black Codes making it illegal for slaves to leave their owner's property without a pass, to carry arms, to assemble, to engage in trade or to own property. However, the codes were not strictly enforced and, in 1781, Lieutenant Governor Cruzat expressed concern about the unruly conduct of the slaves in St. Louis.[121] The Creoles treated slaves as more than mere property, and the institution lacked the severe racism of slavery in the American South. St. Charles Borromeo records show that by the end of Spanish rule there were quite a few enslaved blacks and mulattos living in *San Carlos* and even a few enslaved natives.[122]

Under the Spanish, racial intermarriages were rare, but less formal unions were not. Borromeo baptismal registers note several instances when black mothers presented mulatto babies for baptism. As in most cases of illegitimacy, the record did not name the fathers. Distinctions were made between children whose parents were both of African ancestry, and mulattos, with the latter holding a higher place in society. John Baptiste Point du Sable was a Haitian born fur trader of French and African descent. He was the first non-Indian settler of the Chicago area, where he lived with his wife and children before moving to *San Carlos* around 1800. He resided at Second and Decatur Streets in St. Charles until his death in 1818. A monument in the Borromeo parish cemetery commemorates his place in history as the founder of Chicago and a public park in St. Charles bears his name.[123]

The entire province of Upper Louisiana had an estimated population of only 10,350 in 1804, most of whom were clustered along the banks of the Mississippi River and its tributaries. Roads were almost nonexistent and the French residents traveled by water whenever possible. The *pirogue*, made from a hollowed out log and resembling a canoe, was used for short trips. Larger cargoes were transported in the flat-bottomed *bateau,* or later a keelboat. When the cargo was bulky and headed to New Orleans, it was often loaded on simple flatboats that were dismantled and the lumber sold when they reached their destination.[124] With this reliance on waterways, it is not surprising that many of the major creeks and streams in St. Charles County received French names like Cuivre, Peruque, Dardenne, Blanchette and Femme Osage.

The French preferred to live in villages, where the area along the river was laid out in town lots that were owned by individual inhabitants in fee simple. On these lots the French constructed their residences that often doubled as places of business. The dwellings were scattered and interspersed with gardens, orchards, barns and stables. Most of the structures were built of logs, set in the ground vertically with the cracks plastered over with mortar. The nicer houses had a steep hip roof with an abundance of porches, but most of the inhabitants lived in one-room cabins with dirt floors.[125] In 1791, when the settlement's name was changed to *San Carlos*, there were still only about a dozen houses and these were inferior temporary huts for the commandant and other hunters.[126] An observer in 1797 noted that the houses in *San Carlos*, "can be distinguished from one another only on the basis of which is most dilapidated."[127]

Conditions improved as other business and professional men followed the *chasseurs* and *voyageurs* to the community. Born in 1774 in Quebec, Francis Duquette was one of the most successful businessmen in *San Carlos* by 1796. He engaged in land speculation, the fur trade, retail trade and money lending. He was godfather to many children and advisor to many men.[128] In 1795 he purchased the four-block tract of land now occupied by the Academy of the Sacred Heart and resided there with his wife, who was one of the few literate women in *San Carlos*. By 1787 the village had its first physician, Dr. Antoine Reynal, who became one of the leading citizens of the community and by 1800 had the finest home in *St. Charles*. In 1804 he built a two-story building near the foot of what is now First Capitol Drive that became in 1808 the St. Charles Fur Trading Post. Records indicate that du Sable, Manuel Lisa and Chouteau traded there along with many Sioux tribes.[129]

While they resided in villages, from a very early date individuals recognized the agricultural potential of the St. Charles District. When Francois Marie Perr du Lac toured the area, he pointed out the vast prairies and wide variety of grains. In his view *San Carlos* possessed meadows, "superior to those in St. Louis," with lands that were "better cultivated," and "produce corn, barley, maize, potatoes, in a word, everything necessary for man and beast." [130] In 1796 more than one-fourth of the wheat and one-fifth of the tobacco in upper Louisiana was grown in the St. Charles District.[131] Still, as the villages grew and prospered, all the French settlers continued their "charming, unhurried quality about life,"[132] as they raised just enough vegetable and grain to keep them alive. Spanish Louisiana never achieved agricultural self-sufficiency and regulations had to be passed to assure an adequate food supply.[133]

How could an area that three generations later became part of the richest agricultural area in the world struggle to feed itself? At least part of the explanation is to be found in the system of land tenure. In *San Carlos* and Portage des Sioux, as in all of Upper Louisiana, French colonizers held much of their productive land in common. The practice of establishing common fields and commons had been brought from France to Canada and then to Louisiana.[134] The land tenure systems of the French and the Spanish were similar and the use of *comunales* (community owned lands) was practiced by the settlers of French Louisiana before the coming of the Spaniards.[135] Beyond the village were the common fields; long narrow strips of land, that were granted to individual residents. Each strip was customarily 40 arpents, or nearly a mile and half, long, by one arpent, or 192.5 feet, wide. Between spring planting and fall harvests, each holder of a common field lot was obligated to maintain his fence. Each grantee was entitled only to what he could produce in his common field until after the harvest, when the common fields became a true commons on which all the inhabitants of the village were allowed to graze animals until the following spring. The Spanish government granted individual strips in the common field, without charge, to anyone who could show a need.[136]

Once granted, the common field strip could then be bought and sold like privately owned land and became part of a deceased owner's estate.[137] The common field grantee had property rights somewhere between the rights of an owner of a privately owned village lot and the interest everyone held in the publicly owned commons. The only limitation was that they could not exclude others from their land for roughly half the year and could not use the land for a purpose other than farming, though nothing suggests anyone ever tried. Ambitious farmers could consolidate numerous strips, but farming was never lucrative since, given the expense of transportation, the excess product had to be sold in the local market.[138] Both France and Spain condemned land speculation and neither colonial government ever sold any public lands in Upper Louisiana.[139] Agriculture was not the focus of entrepreneurial effort that was more likely directed at trading and mining.[140]

The commons, usually located beyond the common field, was a large tract in which all inhabitants of the town had a right to graze animals and to gather timber for firewood. Having a mixture of grassland and forest, these commons could be used by anyone, although, in practice, only those living nearby used them. As in any collective endeavor, each inhabitant was allowed to take as much as he wanted, while the upkeep of the commons fell on all the inhabitants collectively.[141] One Spanish official, Charles de Lassos noted the inefficiencies in the common field system in his report to the governor in New Orleans in 1793 and again in 1797 calling them, "a great inconvenience prejudicial to the progress of agriculture."[142] He also pointed out that farmers were unable to grow profitable crops during the winter because the common fields were open to livestock after the autumn harvest. His proposed solution, reflecting the absolutist mercantilist policies of the Spanish crown, was not privatization of the property, but better regulation of the animals.[143] Even de Lassos understood that the inhabitants were over-consuming and under-maintaining the resources of the commons. It was reported that, "[A] prodigious quantity of wood has been lost because the residents [of St. Charles], cutting down trees for their heat, were content to take only the branches, and left the trunks to rot on the ground."[144] Again, the solution proposed by the villagers and ratified by the government, was not to divide up the commons, but rather to "prohibit all persons from felling any tree, or any part, on the Commons, unless they take away the entire tree."[145] The common field system, like the fur trade, was driven by consideration other than market forces. Social concerns, including the need to farm close together so as to defeat or deter Indian attacks, justified the inefficiencies of the system.[146] Social considerations did not trump economic realities on this scale again in St. Charles County until the New Deal of the 1930s.

The commons occupied a category of land ownership unknown in the United States at that time. Stuart Banner explains that Americans are accustomed to view land in two categories, private and public. While individuals or fictional entities such as corporations own private land, public land is owned by the government, as a representative of all people within the jurisdiction. Commons fell into neither category. They were not owned by any individual, organization or government body, but by the public directly without the intermediation of any government. One description of the St. Charles common field described it as being bound by "public land."[147]

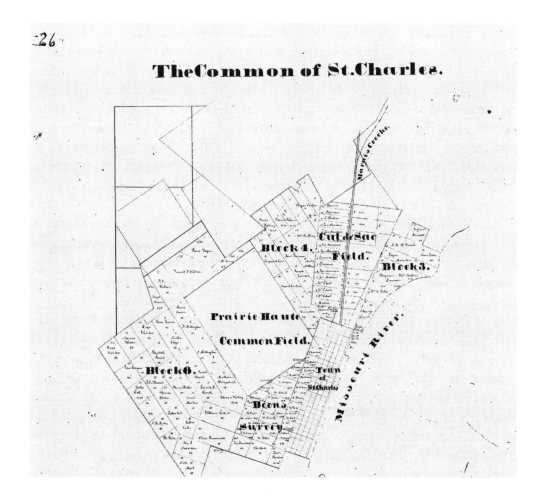

A map of "The Common of St. Charles," *St. Charles County.*

The distinction between the two types of public land became obvious when a government official attempted to grant land within the commons. In early 1804, only a few days before American officials took control, the commandant in *San Carlos*, James Mackay, seemed on the verge of granting a parcel to himself, after surveying the land in the *San Carlos* commons. Villagers immediately protested vehemently and Mackey admitted defeat, agreeing that the commons were for the general use of anyone who was a resident of the village. Public pressure had forced the government official to recognize the existence of a category of public land owned by the inhabitants collectively and not within the government's power to sell.[148] Under the Spanish system, what the inhabitants owned in common did not belong to the crown.

French residents, not the representatives of the Spanish crown, regulated the commons. In *San Carlos* farmers assembled, adopted rules, and appointed a syndic each year to, "make his inspection around the fences of the common field, and if he finds them open or broken, he will warn the farmer who owns the fence in question to repair it immediately."[149] The syndic was to make his inspection every Sunday, and on Thursday during harvest time. If a farmer did not fix his section of fence the syndic was authorized to "seize the first objects he finds belonging to the farmer, to be sold for cash, in order to pay for this repair; furthermore this delinquent farmer will suffer 24 hours in prison for the first offence."[150] In *San Carlos* meetings took place when the commandant summoned all residents to, among other things, "decide if the bottom end of the common should be enlarged."[151] Control of the commons presented an opportunity for local self-government in an absolute monarchy.

As the year 1804 approached, the French settlers in *San Carlos* and throughout Upper Louisiana were easy-going, accommodating to the Indians, civil to their slaves, inefficient in their agriculture and devoted to their Catholicism. All these traits would distinguish them from their new neighbors.

CHAPTER II
American Predominance
1804-1850

In 1821, representatives from throughout the new state of Missouri traveled the rivers, streams, trails and primitive roads to come to St. Charles, state capital of Missouri. Ruluff and Charles Peck had built two buildings on Main Street for their residence and store. When the legislature was deciding where to locate the state capitol, St. Charles offered them the buildings rent-free. The second floor of the Peck building was used as the assembly hall for the General Assembly and the building next door was used as the governor's office and committee rooms.[152] On June 4, 1821, the first session of the General Assembly convened on Main Street in St. Charles in response to the call of Governor McNair. Men in not very fancy clothes met in these not very fancy quarters to launch representative government in Missouri. The members of the General Assembly could look out the back windows of the capitol buildings and see the Missouri River, a highway of local commerce for the French and Indians, now, with the introduction of steam, soon to become a highway of national commerce. The common fields and commons of St. Charles County were being replaced by larger homesteads occupied by yeomen farmers, who, as the years progressed, sold more of their product in regional and national markets. The General Assembly adjourned for the last time in St. Charles on January 21, 1826. The French resisted many of the social values of the Americans, but the American governmental and economic systems were triumphant and were not seriously questioned in St. Charles County for the next 100 years.

A. Territorial Status and Statehood

The trickle of American settlers who came to the St. Charles District at the invitation of the Spanish authorities, became a steady stream after the Louisiana Purchase and a river after the pacification of the hostile Indian tribes. American political institutions completely replaced the Spanish system as the area grew and Missouri achieved statehood in 1821. Formerly a frontier outpost, St. Charles became the first state capital, as residents of St. Charles County played key roles in the history of the new state. With Missouri as one of the United States, democratic practices replaced elitism as the political factions that had developed during the territorial and early statehood periods developed into full-blown political parties by the 1830s. Both the Whig and Democratic Parties grew and prospered in St. Charles County in the period before 1850 as St. Charles County politicians continued to play important roles in state, and even national politics.

In the last years of the eighteenth century, Spanish authorities in St. Louis looked across the Mississippi River to the new republic of the United States and saw people who they hoped to use to settle, and therefore strengthen, their hold on Louisiana. In fact,

Keelboats provided transport on area rivers. *Sketch by Vicki White.*

as one historian asserts, "Basically, the Spanish years did little more than prolong the Latin and Catholic character of the nearer Trans-Mississippi for another four decades after the British victory of 1763, which was really only the first stage of the ultimate Anglo takeover in the first half of the nineteenth century."[153] That takeover began when Spanish authorities promised free land to anyone who took a loyalty oath to Spain.[154] Among the first to take up the Spanish offer and settle in the District of St. Charles was the family of Daniel Boone, the famous pioneer from Kentucky.[155] Morgan Boone scouted the area of Femme Osage Creek in 1797 and his father Daniel Boone, having lost his lands in Kentucky by reason of defective title, followed his son to St. Charles County in 1799. In 1800, Lieutenant-Governor Carlos Delassus appointed the elder Boone commandant of Femme Osage District and granted him 1,000 arpents of land in the Femme Osage District, promising an additional grant of 10,000 arpents when he brought 100 families from Virginia and Kentucky.[156] Until the followers of Boone settled in Darst Bottom in Femme Osage, few white men dared venture far from the Spanish military post at St. Charles. Samuel Griffith, who had planned to come to St. Charles County with Daniel Boone, arrived earlier and settled on land around Portage des Sioux in 1795. He was the first farmer in that vicinity to establish a farm outside the village in the tradition of the Americans.[157]

Warren and Ira Cottle had come to the area in 1798 to scout out a possible settlement. They returned in the winter of 1801-1802 with a group of settlers from Vermont including Zadock Woods. Some of them settled at the mouth of the Cuivre River at what became Old Monroe. Others proceeded further up the river to a spot that became the settlement of Troy. As the northernmost European settlement in Upper Louisiana, these settlers were on the front lines against Indian attacks and Zadock Woods' house was used as a fortification against such attacks.[158] Warren Cottle settled on a Spanish land grant he had received in 1798 located in the area that became known as Cottleville. The names of other early American pioneers are familiar today as they have also become associated with the areas they settled: John (fort) Zumwalt, Francis Howell (school district), Robert Spencer (creek), James Green, ('s Bottom), David Darst ('s Bottom) and Joseph and John Weldon (spring).[159]

People in the District of St. Charles first heard that the United States had purchased Louisiana in the late summer of 1803, and Upper Louisiana was turned over to Amos Stoddard, the representative of the United States, on March 9, 1804. Meriwether Lewis and William Clark took time out from their trip preparation to attend a lavish celebration in St. Louis marking the transfer. Since December 1803 the pair had been assembling men and supplies at Wood River, Illinois for their expedition up the Missouri River. The Corps of Discovery broke camp May 13, 1804 and under Clark's guidance, proceeded to St. Charles, where they stopped to await the arrival of Lewis. On May 20 he arrived from St. Louis with Stoddard, Auguste Chouteau and other prominent citizens of the territory. After a night of partying in the village Lewis and Clark began their historic voyage on the next day. St. Charles resident Jean Baptiste Deschamps became the lead boatman on one of the two pirogues, while James Mackay provided the expedition with some maps. Dr. Seth Millington, a local physician, sold castor oil to the crew. Crewmembers Pierre Cruzatte and Francois Labiche joined the Corps of Discovery in St. Charles.[160]

President Jefferson was not only concerned about the exploration of unsettled western land, but also the transition of the already settled lands to American control. He put William Henry Harrison, governor of Indiana Territory, in charge of Upper Louisiana, which was not made part of Indiana Territory since the Northwest Ordinance had outlawed slavery there. The president recommended to Harrison that the existing governmental divisions be retained and the governor responded with proclamations recognizing the districts of St. Charles, St. Louis, St. Genevieve, Cape

Girardeau, and New Madrid. Each of the five districts had a Court of Common Pleas, a Court of General Quarter Sessions, a Probate Court, and individual justices of the peace.[161] Jefferson commissioned Return J. Meigs, Jr., as commandant of St. Charles.[162] Francis Saucier, Aaron Rutgers, Daniel Morgan Boone, Francis Duquette and Robert Spencer, "or any three of them," were commissioned to hold a Court of Common Pleas for the District of St. Charles.[163] Francis Duquette leased the old Spanish fort in St Charles to the Court of Quarter Sessions and it was used as a jail for several years.[164]

The government of the territory began functioning on July 4, 1805 with a governor; a secretary to record and preserve papers and proceedings; and three judges, serving four-year terms, who could establish inferior courts. A Land Commission was also established to validate land titles.[165] James Wilkinson was appointed governor of the territory, while Return J. Meigs Jr., commandant of St. Charles, was appointed by the president judge of the Superior Court, making him an ex officio member of the territorial legislature along with John B. Lucas and Rufus Easton.[166] Rufus Easton was also appointed the first postmaster of St. Louis and served in that capacity from 1805 until 1814.[167]

Congress nullified all land grants in Louisiana made after October 1, 1800, sanctioned the use of force to remove unauthorized persons from settling on the public land and failed to mention anything with regard to slavery in Upper Louisiana. These measures were a real threat to the French ruling elite and they immediately petitioned Congress for changes. Rufus Easton, who had come to the territory only a short time earlier, explained in a letter to President Thomas Jefferson that the petition to Congress did not represent the wishes of the people of the District of Louisiana, but only those of a small group of men seeking confirmation of questionable land claims.[168]

By October 1805, two factions began to emerge concerning the land title question. One faction supported Governor James Wilkinson and included the territory's French inhabitants and the Americans with the largest Spanish land claims. Edward Hempstead of St. Charles was one of the leaders of this group that became known as the "Junto." The opposing group was composed almost entirely of Americans who had arrived since the purchase, including a group of young and energetic American lawyers who sought advancement through land speculation as well as politics. Among those with ties to St. Charles were Rufus Easton and David Barton.[169] Upon the return of the Corps of Discovery, Jefferson rewarded Meriwether Lewis by appointing him governor of the territory, while William Clark was appointed Indian agent for the territory. It took Lewis over a year to arrive at his post and, when he committed suicide in 1809, President Madison replaced him with Benjamin Howard.[170]

That same year the push began for second-class territorial status. A bill passed Congress in 1811 making the Territory of Louisiana the Territory of Missouri, thus avoiding confusion with the State of Louisiana that was admitted to the Union in the same year. As a result, there was a popularly elected territorial legislature and representation for the territory in Congress.[171] In the first territorial legislature there were

Jacob Zumwalt erected this "fortified" log house in 1798 for protection against Indian attack. In 1936 the site became Ft. Zumwalt State Park. *John J. Buse Collection, 1860-1931, Western Historical Manuscript Collection-Columbia, MO.*

four members from the District of St. Charles. Benjamin Emmons and James Flauherty represented the county in Council and John Pittman and Robert Spencer served in the House of Representatives.[172]

The District of St. Charles was organized as a county on October 1, 1812 by a proclamation issued by Governor William Clark in accordance with legislation passed by Congress. The County of St. Charles had no definite boundaries and extended from the Missouri River on the south to British possessions on the north and from the Mississippi River on the east to the Pacific Ocean on the west. It retained these dimensions until 1816, when Howard County was cut off from the western part of St. Charles and organized into a separate county. The eastern boundary of Boone County was established as the line between St. Charles and Howard. In 1818 Montgomery, Lincoln and Warren Counties were organized and St. Charles County was reduced to its present boundaries. The first territorial delegate to Congress was Edward Hempstead, a lawyer from St. Charles. Tragically, in 1817 he collapsed in a courtroom and died at the age of 38. Rufus Easton, another distinguished lawyer and jurist with St. Charles ties, was twice elected to Congress. St. Charles County men were very influential in territorial politics and had a lot to do with the fact that, following admission of Missouri to the Union, St. Charles became the first state capital.[173]

The primary concern of the territorial government was to provide for the safety of the people. The first time Governor Harrison came to Louisiana Territory the Native American threat was critical as residents of scattered settlements in St. Charles

County were in constant fear of Indian raids. When Sac and Fox warriors killed some settlers in northern St. Charles County, tribal leaders turned over one of the guilty warriors and asked Governor Harrison to pardon the other three and release a fourth on a technicality. This type of negotiation, deeply rooted in the custom and tradition of the "middle ground," was opposed by the military commander of the regular troops in the district, who demanded that the crimes be prosecuted. Harrison, in the spirit of the "middle ground," obtained a presidential pardon for the Indians.[174]

Governor Harrison's main concern was not justice, but the cession of Indian lands and he convinced the Indian delegation sent to negotiate to make a vast cession. It included a sizable portion of their hunting grounds on the west bank of the Mississippi River, on which they were permitted to live and hunt until the United States disposed of it by sale. These lands included all of the present Missouri counties of Ralls, Pike, Lincoln, Warren and St. Charles, along with parts of Marion, Shelby, Monroe, Audrain, and Montgomery counties. Many tribes contended that the delegation did not have the authority to cede the land and the transaction became the cause of resentment by the Indians against the Americans for the next 30 years.[175]

At this early stage, the inhabitants of St. Charles County and vicinity were not at war with the tribes, but the tribes were at war with each other and American settlers sometime got caught in the middle. Between 1805 and 1808 one Frenchman and nine Americans were killed in the District of St. Charles by Indians.[176] Aware of lingering hostility between the Osage and a confederation of Algonquian tribes led by the Sac and Fox, the governor of the territory asked all concerned to send a delegation to St. Louis in 1805. Even though the tribes signed a treaty, hostility between them continued to the detriment of isolated white settlers. The governor threatened to cut off all trade and supplies for the Osage, but the situation did not improve.[177] In fact, the worsening relations between the United States and Great Britain in 1807 increased the threat of Indian attacks from the north so the federal government worked to ensure the loyalty of the Osage to the west.[178] In 1808 Governor Lewis sent an expedition to set up a new trading post at the mouth of the Osage River. The leader of the expedition, George Sibley, was under orders from Washington to, "Be conciliatory in all your intercourse with the Indians and so demean yourself toward them generally, and toward their chiefs in particular, as to obtain and preserve their friendship and secure their attachment to the United States."[179]

A short time later, William Clark and a company of dragoons from the District of St. Charles began an overland march to join the expedition at the proposed trading post. Nathan Boone led the party to their intended destination and the *Missouri Gazette* reported, "It is with heartfelt pleasure that we announce the patriotism displayed by the St. Charles troop of horse, a few days ago; they offered their services to accompany General Clark up the Missouri, in order to protect and assist in the building of the intended Fort."[180] A treaty was negotiated with the Osage marking their return to the American fold. When war came against the British and Indian tribes to the north, the treaty guaranteed the security of the left flank of the Missouri settlements.[181]

His policy was not as successful on the Mississippi where Governor Lewis had to dispatch volunteer companies of militia to relieve the garrison at Fort Madison. He also ordered the construction of a series of blockhouses in the District of St. Charles and placed the militia in St. Charles and St. Louis on a war footing, ordering St. Charles to enroll 41 riflemen.[182] As early as 1805 the Sioux had suggested a confederation of ten Indian nations that would unite with the British to defeat the "white devils."[183] The British declined to join the proposed alliance until war broke out between Great Britain and the United States in 1812.[184]

The prophet Tenskatawa and his brother, Tecumseh, had for several years been carrying on a desperate war against the American settlers in the Wabash region in what is now Indiana. By March 1809, Indian attacks on the frontier were becoming widespread and soon after that the people of the St. Charles District learned that Tenskatawa, was inflaming the tribes against the American settlers.[185] Raids continued to keep settlers on edge and, in 1811, Governor Howard traveled to St. Charles as part of an inspection tour to select sites for further fortifications in the event of war.[186] When the war came, local residents received the news of the war with mixed feelings. Meetings in St. Louis and St. Charles adopted a series of unanimous resolutions supporting the war, and calling upon the national government to supplement local military resources.[187] The Sac, Fox and other tribes in the Mississippi River country made common cause with the British, under the leadership of Blackhawk, with their base of operations on the upper Mississippi River near the mouth of the Rock River in Illinois.[188] Companies of rangers were formed in St. Charles County, including one under the command of Nathan Boone, who received his commission from President Monroe, and proceeded to the northern frontier of the state. The biographer of Nathan Boone points out that the rangers provided an important mobile defense, and notes:

> In July of 1812, the editor of the *Louisiana Gazette* hailed Boone's Rangers as 'Spartan Warriors,' who deserved well of their country. However, had an Indian army moved into Missouri, Boone's Rangers would have needed to be Spartans to stop them, because as late as June 6, only 241 regular soldiers were stationed on the Mississippi.[189]

A town meeting in St. Charles on December 3, 1812 resolved that "we consider our lives, our property all neglected, and miserably forgotten by the general government."[190] Missouri's newly elected delegate to Congress, Edward Hempstead of St. Charles, tried to assure constituents of his labors to secure a vigorous prosecution of the war and worked closely with territorial delegates from the Illinois and Indiana territories to improve frontier defense.[191] In 1813 William Clark became governor, blockhouse fortifications were constructed at Portage des Sioux, and the Missouri Territory was given permission to recruit three new companies of rangers, including Callaway's Company, composed principally of volunteers from St. Charles County.[192] The inhabitants of St. Charles County never felt that the federal government was doing enough to protect them.[193] Settler William Van Burkleo explained how, during the War of 1812:

The Indians attacked my house one night. They fired into the bed where my wife and myself were asleep. They broke my wife's leg and hit me with seven buckshot in my thigh, which awoke me. I knew what was up and sprang to my gun, which was hanging on the rack over my head. But as I got the gun from the rack, one of them came into the house. My wife said he pointed his gun at me, fired and ran out of the house. The powder burned and blinded me, so that I never got to see the rest of them dodging around.[194]

A sadder outcome befell the Ramsay family who were killed by Indians at their home near Femme Osage during the war. According to one account:

Mr. and Mrs. Ramsay both died from their wounds. When Nathan Boone and other settlers who had heard of this raid came to the place, one of the children, a boy about five years old, who had been scalped, still breathed, and as he opened his eyes and saw his father, he attempted to get up, and said, "Daddy, the Indians did scalp me," and died.[195]

In March of 1813, a farmer near Portage des Sioux was killed, and the following August six settlers were attacked and one killed near the Cuivre River. Boone's troops followed the Indians across the Mississippi but were ambushed and had to withdraw. By the time General Howard returned with a larger force the Indians had fled north. His diplomacy was more successful as he was able to persuade 1,500 friendly Sac and Fox to cross the river and rendezvous at Portage des Sioux, from which they were relocated to what is now Moniteau County, Missouri.

Trading on the Missouri River had to be abandoned and small groups of tribal warriors continued to terrorize settlers throughout 1814, but a major attack on the St. Louis region never came.[196] When, in 1814, Lieutenant Zachary Taylor brought a company of soldiers to Woods' Fort in Troy, then a part of St. Charles County, he was not there to protect the frontier from Native American attacks but to recruit troops to join General Andrew Jackson against the British forces expected to arrive in New Orleans.[197]

On December 24, 1814, the representative of the United States signed the Treaty of Ghent ending the War of 1812. The Indian tribes had not been defeated and in March of 1815 Captain James Callaway and several of his rangers from St. Charles County were ambushed and killed by Indians in what is now Montgomery County. Nevertheless, the treaty required the Americans to restore to the Indians, "all possessions, rights and privileges they had enjoyed in 1811."[198] It was July 1815 before the leaders of the hostile tribes agreed to assemble in council at Portage des Sioux to treat for peace. The commissioners on the part of the United States were Governor Clark of Missouri, Governor Ninian Edwards of Illinois, August Chouteau of St. Louis, and Robert Walsh of Baltimore, secretary of the commission. Manuel Lisa and Pointe du

Sable served as translators at the negotiations.[199] The federal government gave the assembled tribes $20,000 worth of presents to facilitate the negotiations under which Chief Keokuk confirmed the former cession of an immense territory on both sides of the Mississippi north of the Missouri and Illinois rivers. [200]

Richard White concludes, "After the end of the War of 1812 the imperial contest over (this region) came to an end and politically, the consequence of Indians faded. They could no longer pose a major threat or be a major threat to an empire or a republic, and even their economic consequence declined with the fur trade."[201] Of course this was not clear at the time to either settlers or Indians and most settlers in the Missouri Territory resented both the Treaty of Ghent and the treaties signed with the Indians at Portage des Sioux. On the other side, Chief Blackhawk knew the cession of land was a fraud and he became a rival of Chief Keokuk. In 1832 Blackhawk's followers refused to leave the ceded land, occasioning the "Blackhawk War."[202] Captain Nathan Boone again organized a company of rangers in St. Charles County. Before they could engage, Blackhawk was defeated, mainly by Illinois troops.[203]

In fact, the fate of Blackhawk's followers had been sealed long before when a steady stream of pioneers began pouring into the Missouri Territory after the War of 1812. While settlement had practically ceased during the war, the territorial population increased from an estimated 25,000 in 1814 to more than 65,000 in 1820. Another company from St. Charles County was later sent to the Indian Territory to protect the Southwest Missouri settlements. Some volunteers from St. Charles County even went to fight the Seminoles in Florida with Andrew Jackson. But the Indian threat in St. Charles County was over.[204] Among the Illinois troops who fought in the Blackhawk War was a young Abraham Lincoln. When it was over, he returned home to Springfield as Boone's rangers returned home to St. Charles. With the Indians pacified, political disagreements now took center stage.

Nationally, the period following the War of 1812 became know as the "Era of Good Feeling." In Missouri, during the same period, party divisions failed to develop but local groups vied for control, and land claims were the dominant local issue.[205] In St. Charles County candidates were chosen for their personal popularity.[206] Referring to partisan elections, a journalist for the *Missourian*, wrote in 1820, "It has, however, been the great fortune of the old county of St. Charles, always to escape those violent commotions which have so justly been described as 'the madness of many for the gain of the few'."[207]

There were highly contested elections during this period such as John Scott's challenge of Rufus Easton, territorial delegate to Congress, in 1816. Governor Clark, a Scott supporter, declared Scott the winner, based on a set of late returns brought to St. Louis by Scott himself from the township of Cotes Sans Dessein in what was then St. Charles County, now Callaway County. The results were disputed and the matter went to the House of Representatives where the Committee on Elections recommended that Easton be seated. However, the entire House voted to declare the seat vacant and ordered a new election. In the second election Scott won easily.[208]

These buildings were the site of Missouri's state capitol from 1821 until October, 1826, when the capital was moved to Jefferson City. *Sketch by Vicki White.*

Statehood had been discussed since the War of 1812 and Samuel Hammond, representative from St. Charles County in the territorial legislature, drafted an application in 1816. In the debate over Missouri's admission to the Union, the Kentuckian John Scott worked hard for slavery, which the majority of his constituents clearly favored. His predecessor, Rufus Easton from New York, had actually co-sponsored a bill in Congress in 1816 to abolish slavery west of the Mississippi River. Since the admission of Missouri alone as a slave state would have given the slave states a majority in the U.S. Senate, a compromise was worked out to admit Missouri to the Union as a slave state and Maine as a free state. An additional term of the "Missouri Compromise" prohibited slavery in the Louisiana Purchase territory north of Missouri's southern boundary, except for Missouri.[209]

There were 15 counties in the state, and St. Charles County was entitled to send three delegates to the first Constitutional Convention - Benjamin Emmons, Nathan Boone and Hiram H. Baber. When the elderly Daniel Boone died while the Convention was deliberating, Benjamin Emmons offered, and the Convention passed, a resolution that the members wear "the usual badge of mourning" for 30 days.[210] While the state was entering a new era, the Convention was composed generally of conservative wealthy men, including the "Junto" from St. Louis, who had dominated territorial affairs. The document they approved was very similar to the constitution of Kentucky,

41

especially in its provisions dealing with slavery.[211] The new constitution required the General Assembly to pass a statute banning free African-Americans from entering the state. This threatened to upset the delicate compromise, as northern congressmen began to insist that Missouri agree to gradual elimination of slavery. The Missouri legislature, meeting in St. Charles, promised that they would never enforce the clause of the Missouri constitution banning new freed slaves from the state. Henry Clay got Congress to accept the promise and, on August 10, 1821 President James Monroe proclaimed the admission of Missouri into the Union as the 24th state. Governor McNair officially informed the legislature during the November 6, 1821 session that Missouri had been admitted to the Union. Sometime later, the General Assembly, still meeting in St. Charles, in what Nagel calls, "one of Missouri's most disgraceful moments," went back on its word and passed a statute keeping freed slaves out of the state.[212]

St. Charles County had several newspapers, including the *Missourian*, a newspaper that had been established by Robert McCloud before Missouri became a state and continued publication while St. Charles was the state capital. When it ceased publishing there was a series of unsuccessful attempts to publish a local newspaper until the *Clarion* appeared, edited after 1837 by William Campbell, a prominent Whig politician in St. Charles County. In 1839 purchasers change the name to the *Free Press*. From 1842 to 1853 local papers were called the *Advertiser, The Western Star*, the *Chronotype* and the *Reveille*.[213]

When it became the state capital, St. Charles had fewer than a thousand people and the western limit of the town was Fifth Street between Jefferson and Chauncey Streets. Actually, not many houses were built beyond Third Street. One publication suggested:

> The 43 members of the General Assembly presented quite a contrast. Many were well educated and well mannered; however, some were rough characters. Most dressed in homespun clothes, buckskin leggings and hunting shirts, and homemade shoes or moccasins. Most wore hats of skins of wild cats or raccoons. Governor McNair must have stood out among them. He wore a coat in "pigeon-tail" style and a beaver hat – the only fine cloth in the assembly.[214]

Many prominent politicians moved to St. Charles including Rufus Easton, the state's first attorney general, and William Pettus, the first secretary of state.

In October 1826, the capital was moved to Jefferson City and St. Charles lost its position of preeminence in the politics of Missouri. While a farewell party was given in his home for the departing state officials, William Pettus remained, was appointed probate judge of St. Charles County, and was later elected a state senator. He was a leading citizen of the county until he moved to St. Louis in 1855 to pursue business opportunities. Rufus Easton remained in St. Charles until his death in 1834 and is buried in a cemetery on the Lindenwood University campus. Writing in 1841, one commentator stated, "While the town enjoyed the perogatives [sic] of a state capital, it flourished and promised to be a place of very great importance, but it since declined considerably, until recently a new impetus has been given to it, and it has renewed its promise of future consequences."[215]

The constitution that allowed the state to join the Union was also the source of the first political debate within the new state. The people, who had not been allowed to vote on ratification of the state's constitution, worried that the new constitution's provision for an independent judiciary might be used to curb the popularly chosen legislature.[216] In the first gubernatorial race, Missouri voters elected Alexander McNair, who had opposed the power of the judiciary, over William Clark, the candidate of the conservative St. Louis "Junto." The legislature appointed David Barton and Thomas Hart Benton as U.S. senators. Although political parties did not emerge until 1832, the divisions created by the adoption of the constitution continued and the two factions coalesced around the two United States senators, both of whom had connections to St. Charles. David Barton had been a resident of St. Charles for several years and served as the county's first circuit judge in 1815. He became the owner of the city block containing the old Spanish Fort, that he later donated to St. Charles College after helping to establish it in 1833. Thomas Hart Benton had arrived in St. Louis in 1815 and joined Edward Hempstead, who built a law practice around the defense of technically defective Spanish land titles. In 1817 he filed a suit on the behalf of St. Charles Borromeo Parish seeking to establish good title to certain lands also claimed by Andrew Wilson and Uriah Devore, recent American arrivals.[217]

Although enjoying the support of the French elite when first elected, Senator Benton became popular with the common man because of his sponsorship of two bills in Congress. The first proposed a gradual reduction in the price of public land until it was purchased, thus allowing even those of limited means to buy the land that the better off did not want. Each year that an acre of land remained unpurchased, its value would have been reduced by 25 ¢. The second bill introduced by Benton would have abolished the Electoral College. This proposal became even more popular after the House of Representatives decided the presidential election of 1824, Andrew Jackson having received a plurality of the vote, but no Electoral College majority. His sponsorship especially ingratiated him with all the Jackson supporters after the House of Representatives chose John Quincy Adams as president.[218]

Congressman John Scott, who had voted for Adams in the House, and Senator Barton became the leaders of the Adams forces in the state. By 1830, Adams was no longer president, Barton was no longer senator and Scott was no longer congressman. Led by Benton, the Jacksonians had been triumphant in Jackson's election to the presidency in 1828, garnering 70 percent of Missouri's eligible vote, and an even larger percentage in St. Charles County. In 1835, they adopted the label "Democrat" and were the clear majority party in Missouri until the Civil War.[219] They were also the majority party in St. Charles County as German immigration to the county after 1830 increased the Democratic strength. Although the *History of St. Charles County* called his family, "somewhat aristocratic in their tastes and manner of life," one of the leading Democrats in the county was Judge Carty Wells. James R. McDearmon, also a local Democratic leader, served as state auditor. Pines H. Shelton served in the State House and Senate, as did Dr William McElhiney, who was a member of the committee that notified Franklin Pierce of his election to the presidency.[220] Democratic power in the rural areas of the state increased in 1841 when 17 new counties were created. There were already 98 members of the House of Representatives and the constitution provided for a maximum of 100. Since the constitution also required that each county have at least one representative, the resulting reapportionment created added power for the thinly populated rural counties and St. Charles County dropped from two to one representatives between 1846 and 1850.[221]

In the 1832 presidential election Henry Clay out-polled President Jackson in St. Charles County. There was also a strong Whig vote in the elections of 1836 and 1840. But, beginning with the election of 1844, the county consistently went Democratic. Nevertheless, Whig candidates were occasionally elected due to their personal popularity.[222] In 1826, Felix Scott, after serving for several terms in the House of Representatives, was elected to the Missouri Senate and was eventually elected president pro tem of that body. Between 1815 and 1835 William Christy Jr. was an active leader in St. Charles County Whig politics, serving as clerk of the county, circuit and Missouri Supreme Courts. Other influential Whigs included Major George Sibley, founder of Lindenwood College, William Campbell, politician and editor, Ludwell E. Powell, a skilled political organizer and state senator, and John D. Coalter, a member of the House of Representatives. Senator William Allen was known for his ability to play the pro- and anti-Benton factions of the State Democratic Party against each other.[223] Senator Allen could also exploit those issues where local self-interest trumped the Jacksonian philosophy. The *History of St. Charles County* explained:

> The Democrats were unanimously opposed to internal improvements by the general government. But Congress had passed an act making an appropriation for, and authorizing the building of a national turnpike from the Atlantic seaboard westward through the different state capitals along the general route of the road. As this would have come to Jefferson City, it could not fail to pass through St. Charles County, and of course the great advantages that would accrue to the county could be dwelt upon with great fervor and effect. Democrats though the majority of the people were, the advocacy of this particular road was a winning card, and Maj. Allen had the tact to see this and the address to use it for all it was worth.[224]

Actually, the Jacksonian Democrats in Missouri were not unanimously opposed to internal improvements and in 1830 a General Assembly dominated by Democrats, asked Congress to expedite the completion of the National Road. Historian James

Neal Prim contends "Jackson's supporters in Missouri were more loyal to the man than to his measures. Jackson meetings might applaud general statements of hostility to the American System but when Missouri interests were involved Jacksonians could make exceptions."[225]

The leader of the Whigs in St. Charles County was Edward Bates, younger brother of Frederick Bates. He served as prosecuting attorney for St. Charles, St. Louis and Washington Counties before his election as state representative from St. Louis County. The principle author of the constitution of 1820, in 1823 he married Julia D. Coalter, sister of John D. Coalter, quit the legislature and began practicing law with Joshua Barton. He was elected to Congress in 1826 but lost his re-election bid in 1828. He then moved to a farm in St. Charles County where he lived from 1828-1842. While elected to represent St. Charles County in the State Senate in 1830, when Edward Bates wished to run for the Missouri House of Representatives in 1834, the Jackson forces had become so strong that he filed as a resident of St. Louis County, where a Whig candidate had a better chance of victory.[226] He won the election and eventually replaced Scott and Barton as leader of the anti-Jackson opposition, turning down a position in President Fillmore's cabinet and serving as president of the Whig Convention in Baltimore in 1856.[227]

In the period from 1804 until 1850, Americans settled large sections of the state, including most of St. Charles County, drove out the Native Americans, and brought representative government and democratic institutions to Missouri. The influence of the French and Indians all but disappeared as the American political system wiped out all vestiges of the Spanish administration. The U.S. Constitution and its legal system became the greatest contribution of the American settlers. Some were already insisting that its protection should be extended to African-Americans as well.

B. Frontier Life

Americans who moved into the Louisiana Territory brought with them not only their political system, but also social customs and habits that created conflict with French, Indian and black populations. Americans replaced the village agriculture of the common field with pioneer homesteads and the religious monopoly of the Catholic Church with numerous struggling Protestant congregations. Just as the French settlers had brought the traditions of the "middle ground" from the Illinois Country and applied it to their relations with the Indians, the Americans brought the Indian fighting traditions of Kentucky and Tennessee with them to Missouri, to the great detriment of the Native Americans. The new settlers also had different attitudes about lawyers, slavery, honor and schools. By 1850 the French were a small minority in St. Charles County; Indians were removed to the west; black slaves were firmly in bondage; and the Americans were firmly in control. A new society of American roughneck pioneers, slave-holding farmers and ambitious lawyers replaced the society of the French *voyageur*.

The first American pioneers to settle in St. Charles County were boisterous, ambitious and pugnacious. They upset the quiet peaceful life of St. Charles, which now became a wild frontier town where whiskey and gambling were unchecked. The settlers, having been raised in the Kentucky and Tennessee wilderness, came to the Missouri country to get rich, by land speculation if possible, by farming if necessary.[228] On the scattered homesteads there was little social interaction as months often passed before settlers saw anyone outside their own immediate families. The loneliness and the solitude of living on isolated farmsteads dominated the life of these American pioneers in their simple homes.[229] A window in a log cabin was a sign of prosperity, even though they were often made with greased paper and delivered little light. The stone fireplace for heating and cooking made the room very smoky.[230] As no one had much, the social interaction that occurred was between equals. As a result, a sense of community and cooperation developed among the earliest American pioneers that prompted the *History of St. Charles County* to remark, "they were practically Communists."[231] Within a few decades these "communists" became very good capitalists as cheap land, slavery and transportation improvements led to an expansion of agriculture and the emergence of a land-owning aristocracy.

But in 1820 St. Charles County was still in the "frontier stage" with a population of only 3,970 according to the census of that year, and lacking some important social and legal institutions.[232] With civil authority feeble and often unable to afford protection, the early pioneer settlers had to rely on neighbors for protection. The *History of St. Charles County* stated, "Each man's protection was the good will and friendship of those about him and the one thing that any man might well dread was the ill will of the community."[233] Law enforcement developed slowly as St. Charles County elected its first sheriff, Uriah J. Devore, in 1816. When the authorities could not apprehend a criminal, the people often took the law into their own hands. In 1844 St. Charles Countians formed vigilante groups known as "slickers" who, when they caught their culprit, "slicked" or whipped them with a hickory switch and told them to get out of the county and not return. A group of slickers had organized in Lincoln County due to some counterfeiters in the area. They handled the problem but overstepped their bounds and attacked some innocent people in St. Charles County, whereupon a company of anti-slickers was organized in the vicinity of Flint Hill for the purpose of dispersing the Lincoln County slickers.[234] In 1849 St. Charles, governed by a Board of Trustees since its incorporation as a town in 1809, received a charter from the General Assembly to operate as a city and was able to provide added police protection and take another step away from the "frontier stage."[235]

As early as 1805, Governor Harrison had appointed a Court of Common Pleas for the St. Charles District. Like the first grand jurors, the judges were all Americans, and for many years they met in "crowded rooms in homes, taverns and churches," including the home of Antoine Reynal. Local historian Anita Mallinckrodt suggests that many people today would be shocked by, "the informal dress of the lawyers, the democratic and off-handed manner of administering justice, the loquaciousness and youth of the bar" and the "roughly dressed farmers and villagers" who served as jurors. Despite this informality, she concludes that the courts were "generally respected."[236] Frontier traditions did not disappear as everyone, including the judge and lawyers brought weapons, often concealed, to court, causing one historian to conclude, "The constitutional right to bear arms, both concealed and open, became a hallowed tradition in the courtrooms of the Missouri frontier."[237] Legal institutions continued to develop and in 1848 the County Court built a courthouse that had a "whipping post" where criminals were punished, and a "slave block" where slaves were bought and sold.

Also characteristic of the frontier stage was the lack of organized religion. While a few of the English speaking settlers were Irish Catholics who became members of

Daniel Boone died in this house belonging to his son Nathan Boone, located on Femme Osage Creek. Today the Boone Home is owned by Lindenwood University, *John J. Buse 1860-1931, Western Historical Manuscript Collection-Columbia, MO.*

St. Charles Borromeo Parish, most of them were from Protestant families and had no church home when they first arrived. [238] According to one Presbyterian minister, Timothy Flint, who came to St. Charles in 1816, the town was filled with "hoodlums from Kentucky." There was not a single Presbyterians in the town prior to his arrival and Flint complained, "there's no Sabbath and the profanity, I believe, is unparalleled." According to the *History of St. Charles County*, Daniel Boone, "never made any profession of religion, or united with any church," and "died the death of a philosopher rather than that of a Christian."[239] Mary Easton Sibley's family had shown little interest in formal religion and Mary had described George Sibley as a critic of the churches. By the 1830s, the Sibleys had begun to take a greater interest in the Presbyterian Church.[240] For, as the French had brought Catholicism, the Americans brought the Presbyterian, Methodist, Baptist, Episcopalian and other Protestant denominations to St. Charles County.

The "Old Blue Church" was erected in 1883. *Sketch by Vicki White.*

Presbyterian preachers had come to St. Charles County even before the Louisiana Purchase. Timothy Flint preached in the town for two years but no congregation was formed until 1818, when Reverend Salmon Giddings, actually a Congregational minister, established the First Presbyterian Church of St. Charles with only nine members. Soon, it was the strongest Protestant body in St. Charles County and the only one with a resident pastor. Services were held in the homes of members and in a building on Main Street owned by Catherine Collier until the "Old Blue Church" was erected on the Southwest corner of Third and Madison. The Dardenne Presbyterian Church was established in 1819 and the Olivet Presbyterian Church was established in Flint Hill in 1835.[241]

Methodist bishops of the west licensed young preachers to, "travel around circuits of up to two hundred miles, preaching in houses, barns, or churches, wherever people were willing to hear them."[242] These Methodist "circuit riders" came to St. Charles County. The *O'Fallon Centennial Program* states,

> The Methodists were the first organized religious group in the vicinity of the present City of O'Fallon. They can trace their founding back to the historical walls of the house of Jacob Zumwalt. In 1798, "the hard riding, shooting, long-praying sons" of John Wesley came to St. Charles County as well as other parts of Missouri. In these pioneer days of traveling preachers, they were not the least in leaving their imprint on the character of the towns. The early fire-and-brimstone religious services were conducted in private homes.[243]

While the first church was erected near Fort Zumwalt in 1807, the congregation grew and it became necessary to build a new and larger church in 1853.[244] Bethlehem Church was built between Wentzville and Flint Hill in 1836, while other Methodist churches were built at Flint Hill in 1846, Cottleville in 1854 and Darst Bottom (Pleasant Hill) in 1856. Catherine Collier, founder of St. Charles College, paid for the erection of a Methodist church building in St. Charles in 1831 that was also available for other Protestant denominations to use.[245]

In 1817, the Baptist Triennial Missionary Convention sent John Mason Peck and James Welch to the frontier. After arriving in St. Louis Peck visited St. Charles and established a mission and a school in 1818.[246] At about the same time another Baptist Church, with 14 members, was organized at Femme Osage.[247] The Trinity Episcopalian Church was organized in 1836 and met for many years at the church building that still stands at the corner of Benton and Clark Streets in St. Charles. The Hickory Grove Christian Church was organized in 1857 just north of Foristell.[248]

The Protestants also brought with them fraternal organizations that excluded the French Catholics. In 1819 Benjamin Emmons IV brought back from Nashville, Tennessee the first Masonic charter for St. Charles County.[249] The local lodge prospered until the capital was moved to Jefferson City, after which it dwindled to nine members and became inactive in 1826.[250] The Masonic lodge was revived in 1837 and included among its members Reverend John Fielding of St. Charles College and Mayor Ludwell Powell of St. Charles.[251]

Protestant condemnation of alcoholic beverages put them at odds with the "Kentucky hoodlums" and the French Catholics. Whiskey was one of the chief cash crops derived from the excess grain produced by the local farmers, and thus its supply was plentiful. The success of the whiskey industry was guaranteed in St. Charles County and elsewhere by the presence of many Scots, Irish, and Scots-Irish, for whom whiskey had been the drink of choice in the old country. Distillers had plentiful water, abundant grain, and ample wood to fuel their stills. Additionally, the federal whiskey tax, that had prompted the Whiskey Rebellion in western Pennsylvania, had been repealed in 1802.[252] As a result, the national rate of consumption of alcohol in 1830 reached a peak of four gallons per capita, nearly double its rate today.[253] The rate of consumption was probably higher in St. Charles where there were six taverns in 1832.[254]

Most Protestant denominations condemned public drunkenness, but it was the revivalist Methodists who most vigorously opposed alcohol.[255] In 1841, the Protestants in St. Charles cooperated in hosting a revival led by a Methodist preacher named Maffett, which according to George Sibley, "produced a great deal of apparent religious feeling," and 60 conversions. It also created the usual mixed emotions from the established churches.[256] The increase in the amount of alcohol consumed had created a nationwide movement that established temperance societies in every town.[257] The Dardenne Temperance Society was organized in 1831, "to secure and extend the Pure and Holy, the Rich and inestimable Blessings of Temperance."[258] By 1842 local Protestants became so disturbed by drinking that the Washington Temperance Group collected over 400 pledges in January of that year.[259] Describing Pines H. Shelton, the *History of St. Charles County* said he was, "honestly and justly opposed to intemperance," and added, "he would carry temperance to the extreme of putting it beyond the power of anyone to obtain a stimulant, under any circumstances, which could possibly be made to intoxicate."[260] There was enough support for the temperance movement that Pines H. Shelton was elected to represent St. Charles County in the Missouri House of Representatives and Senate.

Vices other than drinking existed in St. Charles. Protestants discouraged dancing, especially on the Sabbath. In 1845, the elders of the Presbyterian church considered reprimanding George Sibley and W. C. Thompson for dancing, but refrained when a delegation determined that the men had repented and resolved to not dance again.[261] Timothy Flint wrote:

> The town is crowded with the refuse of Kentucky. Fighting, maiming, the most horrid blaspheming, thieving and every species of riot and outrage are the order of the day and night. Balls on the Sabbath are common…The billiard room crowded every Sabbath and there is but one, or two heads of families, who are not occasionally there….[262]

Flint also complained about the horseracing on Sunday and the gambling that surely accompanied it.[263] The first anti-gambling law in Missouri was enacted by the territorial legislature in 1814. Enforcement was another matter. By 1835 the religious element was in the majority in St. Charles and they were able to place a tax on those forms of entertainment where gambling was likely to take place. Any "keeper of billiard tables and pin alleys, the latter generally known by the name of ninepin alley," had to pay a tax of $50 every six months.[264] In 1842 the General Assembly passed an act outlawing lotteries and a prohibition on the same was included in the 1865 Missouri Constitution. Gambling continued on the riverboats where local jurisdiction was questionable and enforcement lax. One historian suggests that, with the introduction of riverboat gambling, "The rivers served as major routes inland for rascality."[265]

Communities in Missouri evolved much like the communities had in Virginia and Kentucky from which the Americans had come. Communities emerging from the frontier stage not only built churches and regulated vices, but deferred to a class of powerful landowners, doctors and lawyers who provided a paternalistic leadership. Ordinary citizens were not expected to play an active part in local political life.[266] This traditional ruling elite had to deal with at least four other groups: the French, the Indians, their own black slaves and the lower classes of the American community.

Americans had to deal with the French settlers, most of whom were alarmed at the changes to their communities after the Louisiana Purchase. The American pattern of frontier settlement was very different than previously seen in the District of St. Charles, giving the countryside a quite different appearance. The Americans brought with them the Land Law of 1800, also known as the Harrison Frontier Land Act, which divided public lands into 320 acre blocks to be sold at $2.00 per acre.[267] Consequently, unlike the French common field system where the farmers lived in a village, there were now isolated homesteads across the county. While the French settlers had built log cabins with logs placed vertically, the American pioneers brought to St. Charles County the traditional log cabin in which presidential candidates bragged about being born.

The American legal system was also much different than the *Coutumes de Paris*, which had been adapted by the French to Canada and the Illinois Country. Under this customary law civil suits were decided quickly, either by the lieutenant governor or a panel of leading citizens. While there had been a total of one lawyer in St. Louis in the 1770s, in the 1790s French businessmen observed the American legal system in Kaskaskia and Cahokia, where there was a right to jury trial on civil cases involving more than $100. They thought the Americans overly litigious and believed that lawyers were the chief beneficiaries of the legal system.[268] The *History of St. Charles County* relates the following case heard by Justice of the Peace Daniel Colgin.

> Two citizens of St. Charles had a quarrel about a piece of ice which one had sold to the other, and which fell short half a pound. While they were quarrelling the ice all melted away, and the dealer went to Colgin and sued the other man for the price of the ice, which was 6 1/4 cents. Colgin gave judgement in his favor but made him pay half the costs (75 cents), because he thought it was right that the costs should be divided between them for being "such blamed fools as to quarrel about a little piece of ice that he could eat in five minutes any warm day."[269]

An examination of the circuit court files of St. Charles County for 1822 reflects a large number of cases, given the population of the county. Interestingly, many of the community's leading citizens are parties to the cases filed. In that single year, John Mullanphy sued Benjamin Emmons who later served in the State House of Representatives and Senate. George Collier, who later became the founder of St. Charles College, foreclosed on a mortgage to collect a $850.00 debt from James and Delinda

Craig. Ninian Edwards, former Governor of Illinois, sued C.B. and J.H. Penrose over a $393.98 debt. Finally, M. Gilbert sued Rufus Easton, who two years prior had been the territorial delegate to Congress, for $1,500 on a promissory note.[270]

Likewise, the first American officials in Spanish Louisiana were not impressed with its legal system and initiated some very negative stereotypes. Frederick Bates thought the shortcomings of the native inhabitants were attributable to having lived under such an oppressive legal system. He stated, "If their commandants spurned them from his presence; deprived them of half their estate or ordered them to the black hole, they received the doom as the dispensation of heaven, and met their fate with all that resignation with which they are accustomed to submit indifferently to sickness and health, to rain and sunshine."[271] Other Americans believed that the defects in Upper Louisiana's legal system were in large part traceable to the character of the inhabitants, whom they did not hold in very high esteem. These Americans concluded that the poverty of the people encouraged the arbitrary exercise of power.[272] Banner explains that the negative stereotypes served an important purpose for the Americans. The French were a problem for the Americans since they could not be ignored on the grounds of racial inferiority as the Indians were. Many were farmers, using the land exactly as the Americans planned to use it. Furthermore, many had formal written land grants from a duly recognized government. The negative stereotypes of stupid, lazy, depraved French, incapable of understanding a more sophisticated American jurisprudence, were necessary to justify American expansion into the area.[273]

In fact, by modern standards, the French legal system was superior in some regards. In the area of family law the French recognized wife and husband as contractual partners, limited disinheritance and provided for the legitimization of children born out of wedlock. American jurisprudence at the time, in contrast, merged the couple under the husband's authority, allowed complete disinheritance of family members and had no provision for legitimizing children. In Spanish Louisiana all free persons had full rights of citizenship, whereas American common law denied full civil rights to any person having even a fraction of "colored" blood.[274]

Despite conflicts with the American newcomers, French families and French custom did not disappear. The French influence in Portage des Sioux continued much longer than in St. Charles. Election records show that, in the election for trustees of Portage des Sioux in 1822, 19 out of 20 men who voted had French surnames.[275] The state legislature passed a law allowing municipalities to dispose of their commons and most of them did so by selling the land in fee simple. In St. Charles, however, purchasers were given a 999-year lease. In the Portage des Sioux commons the individual lots were leased "in perpetuity," and "for agricultural purposes." The leasehold was conditioned on the payment of a yearly rent of six percent of the assessed valuation, which is established on each twentieth anniversary of 1835, the year the lease was granted.

Certain French social customs appear to have survived until 1830. In that year, a student in St. Charles described his social life thusly:

Since Christmas we have here French balls and American each week alternately…. The French ladies are the most beautiful and graceful dancing I have ever seen, dancing nothing here but cotillions and Waltses [sic]. I engage ever [sic] pretty French lady I dance with to learn me to Waltse and talk French. For beauty and fashion here I could oftentimes imagine myself at Paris.[276]

Paul Nagel writes concerning the French, "There was a charming unhurried quality about life inherited from the French which often struck the compulsive Americans as indolence. The fact that nearly everyone claimed to be a Roman Catholic added to the strangeness felt by most newcomers from the United States."[277] Catholicism struggled in the post-purchase era since it no longer enjoyed the financial support of the state as it had under

Rose Philippine Duchesne - founder of the Academy of the Sacred Heart and Saint of the Catholic Church, came to St. Charles in 1818.
Missouri State Archives

Spanish administration. When the U.S. Constitution and its first amendment came to the St. Charles District in 1804, Father Luzon, pastor of St. Charles Borromeo, and 26 priests of the Mississippi valley received a circular from the Bishop of Havana advising them of their options. They could stay with their parishes and try to survive on contributions and occasional fees or be reassigned to other churches still under the control and support of Spain. Father Luzon and 21 other priests left the colony of Louisiana.[278] St. Charles Borromeo Parish was served by missionary priests for the next two decades, and, by the early 1820s, the parish was barely functioning. However, in 1828 Bishop DuBourg persuaded the Jesuit Order to come to St Charles and the parish became a Jesuit missionary church.[279] By the 1830s, the parish records reflect an increase of the use of English as French surnames began appearing less and Irish and German names began appearing more.[280]

The most lasting French contribution to St. Charles took place in August 1818, when Bishop DuBourg sent Mother Rose Philippine Duchesne to the town with four other French-speaking nuns to start a school for girls. On September 14, 1818, these religious of the Sacred Heart opened the first free school west of the Mississippi River. The school was soon closed when the nuns moved to a convent in Florissant, but was reopened when they returned to stay in 1828.[281] The school enrolled as many as 70 day students and 50 boarders. In 1835 construction was begun on the school buildings that remain to this day.[282] According to St. Charles Borromeo Parish historian Jo

Ann Brown, Bishop DuBourg intended, in sending Mother Duchesne to St. Charles, to benefit the entire community through the secular and religious education of the upper classes.[283]

Although there were several private schools available in St. Charles, many wealthy Americans sent their daughters to be educated by the French women of the Sacred Heart Order in St. Charles.[284] Nevertheless, the Americans continued to feel culturally superior to their French neighbors and French influence diminished as time passed. By the time the legislators arrived in 1821, St. Charles had lost much of its French character and one commentator has suggested, "A typical American arriving in the town on the eve of Missouri statehood would have been able to worship his God, drink his liquor and buy and sell his slaves, just as easily as he had been able to do in Virginia, Kentucky or any of the other southern states from which he would most likely have come."[285]

Americans also had to contend with the Native Americans. The new settlers had not come to the area just to trade for furs and co-exist with the Indians, but to transform the land by turning hunting ground into farms. While the French had come from the Illinois Country with a long tradition of cooperation with the Indians in the fur trade, many of the Americans had grown up fighting Indians in Kentucky and Tennessee, coming to Missouri with bitterness that made them "Indian haters."[286] They chopped down trees, built cabins and started small farms on the Indians' hunting ground.[287] Richard Wright explains that Indian hating was not confined to those Indians that waged war against whites. Indian haters killed friendly Indians who warned them of raids or scouted for their military expeditions. Man or woman, adult or child, warlike or pacified, pagan or Christian, it made no difference.[288] Such an "Indian hater" was John Johnson, who settled on "the point" in St. Charles County in 1805, having come from Tennessee. According to the *History of St. Charles County*:

> The Indians killed his father when he was a small boy, and he grew up with a natural antipathy to the race. He became a noted Indian fighter, and never let an opportunity pass to slay a red man. On one occasion, while the people collected in the forts, during the War of 1812, he saw an Indian hiding behind a log not far from the fort, disguised as a buffalo, with the hide, to which the horns were attached, thrown over his body. The disguise was so transparent that Johnson had no difficulty in penetrating it, and he at once decided to give the Indian a dose of lead for the benefit of his health. So he cautiously left the fort, and making a wide circuit, came in behind the savage, who was intently watching for an opportunity to pick off some one of the inmates who might come within range of his gun. But a ball from Johnson's rifle put an end to his adventures here, and sent him speeding on his way to the happy hunting grounds of the spirit land.[289]

Of course, not everyone was an Indian hater and some Americans attempted, as the French had done, to cross the boundaries between societies and cultures. The boundaries were often undermined during Indian captivity and many captives could not resisted adoption of Indian ways. During his captivity, Daniel Boone became temporarily and partially Algonquian, the adopted son of a Shawnee chief. White concludes, "Adoption tainted him; the great Boone eventually found himself on trial as a traitor when he returned from his captivity."[290] Likewise, anyone who tried to reach a peaceful solution with the Indians, was suspect. Those who signed the peace treaties at Portage des Sioux in 1815 were called the "Indian treaty men," and their critics believed that peace could be assured only after the tribes had been soundly defeated.[291] It was suggested that William Clark lost the race to be the first governor of Missouri in 1821 because he had interceded with President Madison to obtain the pardon for Little Crow.[292]

George Sibley, who later founded Lindenwood College with his wife, reported that Indians, like all people in a state of ignorance, "are bigoted, and obstinately adhere to their old customs and habits."[293] The attitude of other American settlers was less emotional. They believed that they had God and history on their side. Whether one appealed to history, theology, logic or common sense, there was a consensus among Americans that the continent could not be left to uncivilized nomadic tribes. The famous frontiersman John Sevier was explaining the sentiment when he stated, "by law of nations it is agreed that no people shall be entitled to more land than they can cultivate."[294] President Monroe expressed it best when he said in 1817, "No tribe or people have a right to withhold from the wants of others more than is necessary for their support and comfort."[295]

But even the "Indian haters" did not place the Native Americans at the bottom of the social ladder. That position was held by the third minority group with which the Americans had to deal the African-Americans in bondage. Slavery had existed in the District of St. Charles since the days of Spanish rule. The Jesuits had brought slaves with them when they came to St. Charles and even Philippine Duchesne, for a time, owned a slave that had been presented to her in payment of tuition.[296] The incidence and nature of slavery changed with the coming of the Americans. As the number of slaves in Louisiana increased, the relationship between slave and master deteriorated. For Missouri as a whole, the percentage of black slaves remained constant at about 15 percent through the territorial period, while the total number of slaves increased from around 3,000 to 10,000.[297] The first tax assessment of St. Charles County, made in 1805 by the sheriff of the district, showed the population to be 765 people. There were 275 heads of families, 95 taxable single men, and 55 slaves. By 1819, the census showed that the white population had increased by about 30 percent, while the slave population had more than doubled, with five free Negroes residing in St. Charles.[298]

A foreign visitor to St. Charles County in the 1820s commented, "The usual price of a male slave from 19 to 30 years of age is four to 500 dollars. The price of a female slave is a third less. Sometime there is a guarantee against running away, often not. It is always advisable to take this into consideration."[299] The concern about runaways and the constant fear of slave revolt caused officials to enact codes tougher than those of the Spanish, regulating all African-Americans, slave and free. From the beginning of the territorial period, the codes prohibited any slave from traveling without a pass from their master. Pursuant to such codes, the St. Charles County Court appointed Samuel Slater captain of a St. Charles Township patrol in 1823. Any African-American, free or slave, that they caught without a pass could be given 10 to 39 lashes on their bare back. In 1830 St. Charles established a similar patrol, that was apparently more lenient as it gave only five to 25 lashes. In the aftermath of Nat Turner's Rebellion in Virginia in 1831, the Missouri legislature passed an act in 1833 to, "prevent mischief and dishonesty among slaves and Negroes." Slaves were prohibited from assembling on the premises of stores and taverns, and public whippings of up to 20 lashes were authorized to punish those who did. Pursuant to such legislation, the constable of St. Charles was authorized in 1837 to break up "all unlawful gatherings of Negroes."[300] African-Americans were prohibited from testifying against whites in court and from administering medicine. Prohibitions against slave abuse that had been in the Spanish codes were deleted.[301] By 1850, only 20 counties in Missouri had a higher percentage of the population in slavery than St. Charles County.[302]

As the nature of servitude deteriorated, two sisters went to great lengths to prove their Indian ancestry and thus avoid the chains of slavery. Catiche and Marguerite, sisters who claimed to have had three black grandparents and one Indian grandparent, were involved in litigation between 1825 and 1833 to determine whether they were slaves or free persons. Their Indian grandmother had been a member of the Natchez tribe that was defeated and enslaved by the French. The Chouteau family had held their grandmother, along with her children and grandchildren, as slaves. In their litigation they first argued that their grandmother had been a prisoner of war and could not have been enslaved under international law. They also argued that, when Louisiana was ceded to Spain, a resolution by Governor O'Reilly had freed the children of all Indian slaves. The broader question was whether the Louisiana Purchase Treaty language, protecting the inhabitant's "liberty, property, and religion," referred to Catiche and Marguerite's "liberty," or their owner Pierre Chouteau's "property." Although the sisters lost in the first trial, the Missouri Supreme Court reversed the decision and sent the case to St. Charles County to be tried again. After another transfer of venue to Jefferson County, Marguerite eventually prevailed at the trial level. The Missouri Supreme Court upheld her victory, and Justice John Marshall dismissed the appeal to the U.S. Supreme Court on jurisdictional grounds.[303]

By the 1840s, the Missouri courts were solidly in support of the institution of slavery. Because of the close proximity to the free state of Illinois, the slave codes prohibited masters of boats from transporting slaves who did not have written permission from their master. This provision was tightened further in 1841 when the Missouri legislature made it a crime for any one to aid the escape of a slave by riverboat, even if the aid was unintended. When a steamboat captain was convicted under this statute after he allowed passage of an African-American who showed him forged papers granting his freedom, he appealed his case to the Missouri Supreme Court. The court upheld the conviction stating:

The greater portion of our eastern frontier, being only separated by a navigable stream, from a non-slaveholding state, inhabited by many who are anxious, and leaving no stone unturned to deprive us of our slaves: our interior being drained by large water courses, by means of which its commerce in steamboats is maintained with the city on our frontier, render it necessary that the strictest diligence should be exacted from all those navigable steamboats on our waters, in order to prevent the escape of our slaves.[304]

As in the courts, pro-slavery sentiment was strong among the people of St. Charles County. The county Grand Jury handed up a bill of indictment against Congress' criminal activity in denying Missouri admission to the Union as a slave state.[305] A toast delivered at a 4th of July celebration in 1819 typified local disdain for Congressman James Talmadge of New York, who had offered an amendment to exclude slavery from the territory. "Messrs. Talmadge and Taylor – Politically insane. – May the next Congress appoint them a dark room, a straight waistcoat and a thin water gruel diet."[306] As abolitionists became more active, pro-slavery attitudes became even stronger. In 1837 the legislature passed an act, "to prohibit the publication, circulation, and promulgation of the abolition doctrines." Elijah Lovejoy fled St. Louis for Alton, Illinois in 1835 because of views he expressed in his paper, *The Observer*, critical of a St. Louis Grand Jury that had refused to indict the leaders of a mob that had lynched a black man. On October 1, 1837, five weeks before he was killed by an angry mob in Alton, Lovejoy attempted to preach in St. Charles but had to flee a pro-slavery mob and barely escaped on horseback.[307]

Pro-slavery sentiment in St. Charles County and the ongoing battle in the courts over slavery met in the person of Colonel Alexander Sanford. He was one of 12 members of a committee of the St. Louis Anti-Abolitionist Society, chaired by John O'Fallon, organized to fight the, "evil designs of abolitionists and others" who threatened slavery.[308] Dred Scott was the slave of Dr. John Emerson, a commissioned officer in the U. S. Army serving at Jefferson Barracks. When Emerson was transferred to Fort Snelling, in the Wisconsin Territory (now Minnesota), where the Northwest Ordinance had prohibited slavery, Dred Scott accompanied him there. In 1840 Dred Scott and his wife Harriet moved back to St. Louis and, when Dr. Emerson died in 1843, Irene Sanford Emerson became the owner of the Scott family. Her father, Colonel Alexander Sanford, was the owner of four slaves on a farm in St. Charles County. He now became his daughter's financial advisor and she reflected his proslavery attitudes when she rebuked Dred Scott's attempts to purchase his freedom.[309]

Dred Scott won his case at the circuit court level but lost in the Missouri Supreme Court. Colonel Sanford died in 1848 but the Sanford family continued to resist the Scotts' freedom suit. Irene Emerson now looked for advice to her brother John Sanford, who had inherited his father's small St. Charles estate; but he sold it, together with the four slaves, and moved to New York, creating diversity jurisdiction, thus allowing Dred Scott's lawyers to file a case in the federal court. Their case against Sanford alleged, "Dred Scott, of St. Louis, in the State of Missouri, and a citizen of the United States, complains of John F.A. Sanford, of the City of New York, and a citizen of New York, in a plea of trespass."[310]

Many in St. Charles County supported slavery; some did not. In 1835 the Presbyterians divided into an anti-slavery "New School" and a pro-slavery "Old School." The majority of Presbyterians in St. Charles followed the "Old School" that preached, "it is the peculiar mission of the Southern Church to conserve the institution of slavery and to make it a blessing both to master and slave."[311] Likewise the Methodists broke apart into northern and southern branches in 1844, with all Methodist congregations in St. Charles sticking with the southern branch.[312] By 1852 the percentage of slaves in St. Charles County had increased to 14 percent, nearly the same percentage as the state as a whole.[313] The future of slavery in the nation and the county hung in the balance as the U.S. Supreme Court considered the appeal of the Dred Scott case.

The American elite, whose wealth and power were based on land and slavery, also had to deal with the lower classes of American society. Historian Dick Stewart writes that wealth and power within the American elite gravitated to men who had first gained the respect of their group or class. He concludes, "Status was in turn determined by how well one lived up to the predominant values of the community. Those values idealized courage and a vigorous defense of honor."[314] The honor of the new aristocratic class often had to be defended in a duel, and the practice was common in the state of Missouri and not unknown in St. Charles County. In 1820, native Virginian Felix Scott was challenged by his son-in-law to a duel after a heated political debate. The duel took place on Scott's St. Charles County farm, where Scott allowed his son-in-law to fire first. When the shot missed, Stewart tells us, "Scott then proceeded to give the upstart a beating with fisticuffs that the son-in-law never forgot." Scott's reputation was a political attribute that helped him to be elected justice of the peace, state representative and state senator.[315] In the late 1820s Joshua Barton, brother of Senator David Barton, was killed in a duel on "Bloody Island" in the Mississippi River and brought back to St. Charles to be buried on his brother's property.[316] In 1842, James Shields challenged Abraham Lincoln to meet him on an island in the Mississippi River adjacent to St. Charles County for a duel. When the tall Lincoln chose broadswords as the dueling weapon, his much shorter opponent reconsidered and the two opponents reconciled.[317]

The land-owning slave-holding class used dueling as a means to set themselves apart from the lower classes of American society. During an 1822 debate in the legislature meeting at St. Charles on a bill requiring elected officials and lawyers to take an oath forswearing duels, one member complained that such a measure deprived the state of much of its leadership and, "the effect would be to place the citizens of the community upon equal footing."[318] The bill, which passed, also held seconds, abettors and counselors, as well as principals, accountable for murder when a duelist was killed or died within three months of a wound suffered in a duel. Fines of $500 were authorized for anyone conspiring to duel. The law was arguably unconstitutional and sporadically enforced. Frederick Bates, Missouri's second governor, refused to take the oath when he was elected. When it was enforced and a conviction obtained against a Howard County attorney who was fined $150 and disbarred, a bill was quickly introduced and passed by the General Assembly to reinstate the attorney.[319] The vote on this bill suggests that there was support for dueling in St. Charles County as the senator from the county voted "aye," as did one-half the representatives from St. Charles and St. Louis Counties. A bill was passed later that required anyone involved in a duel to be publicly flogged. Governor Bates promptly vetoed the bill and his veto was sustained with those members of the House of Representatives representing the counties between St. Charles and Cape Girardeau voting thirteen to six to sustain the veto of what became known as the "whipping bill." While dueling was made a felony, and challenging someone to duel was made a misdemeanor in 1835, gentlemen continued to travel to the field of honor to settle their differences and to set themselves apart from the lower elements of society. [320]

Another guarantor of continued control by the elite was the deplorable condition of the public schools. The congressional action making Missouri a separate territory in 1812 reserved certain lands for the support of schools. But Congress also confirmed title to lands where the individual was in possession prior to December 20, 1803, leaving little land available to fund the schools in St. Charles County. When Missouri was admitted to the Union in 1821, Congress set aside every sixteenth section for the support of the schools, but Edna McElhiney Olson suggests, because of all the speculation and land grabbing, there was never enough income from the sale of these federal lands to support decent public schools.[321] In 1825, the Missouri legislature authorized each County Court to appoint three commissioners in each township to manage the lands set aside for the support of the public schools. A school district could be formed upon the petition of two-thirds of the households in any township, the territorial unit for school government until 1874 in Missouri. Portage des Sioux Township did not petition to organize "for school purposes" until 1846.[322]

Even though the general assembly provided funds from revenue derived from its salt springs, tuition for public education during the 1830s could be as high as $4 per quarter for basic courses in reading, writing, English and mathematics.[323] Anita Mallinckrodt reports that her German ancestors thought that the "Missouri educational system was making slow progress."[324] It was slow indeed. By 1839 only 114 public schools districts had been organized, serving in substandard schoolhouses only about 5,000 of Missouri's 100,000 eligible children. As in the southern states from which the St. Charles County settlers had come, there were no public high schools, only private academies.[325] While Jeffersonian ideals stressed the importance of education to an enlightened electorate, the Jeffersonian distrust of centralized government and dislike of taxes meant that schools were underfunded and inadequate. The "aristocratic element" among the Kentucky and Tennessee settlers did not believe in education for the masses.[326] Most education continued to be provided in private schools

This courthouse was built by the St. Charles County Court in 1848. Attorneys such as Edward Bates, Barton Bates, Arnold Krekel, and Theodore Bruere argued cases there. *John J. Buse Collection, 1860-1931, Western Historical Manuscript Collection-Columbia, MO.*

or by private tutors until 1822. Nancy Callaway Castlio explained at the time, "It was their practice an' belief that education was the responsibility of fam'ly, or church, not government – most feel the same today."[327] When the first free public school in St. Charles was established on the southeast corner of Second and Jefferson Streets, private school children teased the children who attended the "poor school."[328] Even the "poor school" was not supported by a general property tax but rather by a user fee assessed against the property of "all those in said precinct having scholars to send to such school, agreeably to the number each shall send."[329]

Meanwhile, to meet the higher education needs of the "aristocratic element," two institutions were founded in St. Charles. Catherine Collier and her son George Collier founded St. Charles College in 1834 at a cost of $10,000, for the purpose of training men for the Methodist ministry. The school was chartered by the state in 1837 and, to meet the military interest of the "aristocratic element," eventually became a military academy. By 1837, one publication wrote, "St. Charles College is a valuable literary institution, devoted to the cause of useful practical education. Its buildings are handsome and substantial. There are in the college four talented and experienced professors, and near 100 students. Few literary institutions deserve to rank higher for usefulness."[330]

More of the "aristocratic element" also began to seek higher education for their daughters. While most women had been illiterate before education for women became more common in the nineteenth century, by 1850 most white women were literate.[331] In 1827 Mary Easton Sibley, daughter of Rufus Easton, started teaching young ladies in her father's home on Main Street in St. Charles. Two years later, she and her husband Major George S. Sibley obtained 120 acres just outside the city where a log cabin was erected in 1830 amongst a grove of trees which the Sibleys called "Linden Wood." Here a school, originally composed of 20 students and faculty, grew and became widely recognized by the 1850s when, according to an alumni directory, "many of the area's most prominent families were patrons of what is now known as Lindenwood College, and soon stagecoaches from all points of the new frontier were bringing young women to the gates of the college."[332]

While these institutions existed for higher education, the best elementary and secondary education in St. Charles County was still provided by the French Mothers of the Sacred Heart. The free public school system as we know it did not arrive until after the Civil War. But little else that was French survived as *voyageur* gave way to pioneer and pioneer gave way to slave-holding planter, as the egalitarian chaos of the frontier gave way to a hierarchical society of order, where, according to historian James Neal Primm:

> A rough democracy prevailed on the streets, in the taverns, or at the polling places; and equalitarian doctrines poured from the rostrums and the presses; but gentlemen only fought duels with other gentlemen; they caned their "inferiors" or had them arrested. Senator Benton may have been the voice of the people, as he said: but he did not claim to be one of them, nor was he expected to be.[333]

C. "The Progress of Agriculture"

The economic system introduced by the Americans, like their political system, proved totally triumphant. Generally, the mercantilist policies of the Spanish-controlled fur trade gave way to the free market policies established by the Congress of the United States. In St. Charles County the socially motivated French common field system gave way to a system of privately owned farms that, theoretically, were to function with very little governmental interference. But just as under the Spanish administration, reality did not always match theory. While the legislature and courts set up a system of laws to encourage entrepreneurial liberty and promote capitalist development, the government continued to intervene in economic affairs when instructed to do so by the majority of Missourians. With improvements in transportation, Missouri farmers provided products for regional, and then national, agricultural markets. By 1850, capitalism had largely replaced the mercantilist commercial notions and the collectivist agricultural practices of the French and Spanish. While it was not the free market capitalism of Adam Smith's theory, men were generally free to sell their crops, their property and their labor to the highest bidder – or at least white men were.

When the transfer of Louisiana took place, Europeans had been trading for furs with the Indians along the Missouri for over 100 years. The fur trade, however, did not become a major business until after the explorations of Lewis and Clark, when the trappers moved into the mountains of the west. Its heyday was from 1807 until 1843 and St. Louis was the business center of that trade. There were three ways for the companies to procure furs; by barter with the Indians, by hiring trappers and paying them wages, or by purchasing the furs of independent trappers who had ventured into the wilderness alone.[334] Many of the inhabitants of St. Charles County were in the fur trade. Historian Frederick E. Voelker points out the key role played by men of French birth or ancestry and states:

> Some of them were sons and grandsons of the men who had come up the Mississippi River from New Orleans with Laclede and Auguste Chouteau, and of this group some were native St. Louisians and many more came from the Mississippi River settlements established prior to the founding of St. Louis, such as Fort Chartres, Kaskaskia, Cahokia, and Ste. Genevieve. Later they came from St. Charles and other settlements along the lower Missouri, and from Florissant and Portage des Sioux, the latter two having since their founding furnished numerically respectable contingents to the ranks of the mountain men.[335]

Historian R. Douglas Hurt mentions that when Nathan Boone first saw the town, St. Charles, "had become a well-known site for hunters and trappers to sell their skins, buy supplies, and drink whiskey. Certainly St. Charles had rough social edges, but no more than any other frontier town that had been involved with the fur trade in Kentucky."[336] A few years later Meriwether Lewis found those involved in the fur trade "miserably poor, illiterate and when at home excessively lazy." But much of the time they were away from home and author Stephen Ambrose notes, "To support their families, the men either undertook hunting trips to collect furs, or hired themselves out as voyagers to paddle traders up the Missouri, the Osage, and other rivers. They were gone from six to 18 months at a time."[337] One American fur trader from St. Charles was William Sublette, who came with his family at age 18 from Kentucky in 1817. After serving as constable of St. Charles, and with nothing but his rifle and a buckskin suit given to him by the people of the town, he joined the expedition of General William H. Ashley that blazed what became the Oregon Trail through the Rocky Mountains. He returned five years later and became a successful merchant in St. Louis.[338]

In 1796, Congress had appropriated money for the government to establish factories, or trading posts, where Indians could exchange their furs and receive supplies at costs. It was similar to the previous policies of the French, British and Spanish governments over the previous 150 years, except that private fur trading concerns were allowed to compete against the factories. During the same period, the British had granted a monopoly to the Hudson Bay Company. After Louisiana came under the jurisdiction of the United States, and as the private traders grew in importance, there was political pressure on the U.S. government, with Missouri's Senator Benton leading the effort, to get out of the fur business. It did so in 1822.[339] A business that had always been intertwined with government policies designed to insure good relations with the Indians was now exposed to the rigors of unbridled competition in an area where the normal police powers of the state were virtually nonexistent.[340]

In fact, Congress did impose one regulation on the trade, a complete prohibition on the sale of alcohol to Indians. This was a regulation that the American companies' chief competitor, the Hudson Bay Company, did not have. But since the traders were allowed to take a ration of liquor for their own men it was nearly impossible to enforce the prohibition on selling to the Indian tribes.[341] For better or for worse, free-market capitalism had triumphed with regard to the fur trade.

The French inhabitants of St. Charles County preferred the fur trade over farming which, according to Meriwether Lewis, they regarded as a "degrading occupation."[342] The American settlers from Kentucky and other states of the "Upland South" were much more interested in agriculture. One commentator described St. Charles in 1819 as follows:

> When Lewis and Clark ascended the Missouri, the town of St. Charles was said to be one hundred houses, the inhabitants deriving their support principally from the Indian trade. This source having in great measure failed… the town remained in a somewhat declining condition for several years; but as the surrounding country was soon occupied by an agricultural population, a more permanent though less lucrative exchange is taking the place of the Indian trade.[343]

With the increased importance of agriculture, there was an even greater interest in the former Spanish land grants. From the very beginning, judges had to decide whether to recognize Spanish land grants. Congress had promised to recognize grants made after 1800, the year Spain ceded Louisiana back to France in the secret Treaty of San Il Defonso, a treaty not known in Upper Louisiana, only when the recipient had actually settled on the land. Therefore, in order to confirm a land grant it was necessary that the grantee be in possession. The wealthy often used their influence to obtain grants that they did not intend to settle, but held to sell later.[344] As the grantees were quick to point out, the law in existence at the time such grants were made had not required them to settle on their land. They argued that transfer of sovereignty could not alter individual private property rights.

Another problem for the grantees was that the American government, unlike the Spanish, also required precise surveys in order to recognize land grants and claims.[345] Under Spanish law, in order to confirm a land grant after 1798, it had also been necessary to obtain the signature of the *Intendant* in New Orleans. If one neglected to comply with this regulation his title was declared invalid. Daniel Boone had been granted 1,000 arpents of land by the Spanish lieutenant governor when he settled in St. Charles County. He was granted an additional 10,000 arpents after fulfilling his promise to bring 100 families from Kentucky. Both these titles were declared invalid because he had failed to obtain the necessary signature of the *Intendant* in New Orleans, although the first title was afterwards confirmed by a special act of Congress in 1810.[346] If Missouri courts had required strict compliance with the Spanish law there would have been very few valid claims. If they had allowed every grant there would have been little government land left to sell to the new settlers.[347]

As the courts struggled with the issue, ambitious lawyers came to the Missouri Territory looking for the opportunity to profit from land litigation and speculation.[348] Congress set up a Board of Land Commissioners, but the question of confirming land titles remained contentious between the land hungry pioneers and the French settlers.[349] Disputes arising from Spanish land grants in Missouri were litigated for the rest of the century. From the St. Louis area alone, the Supreme Court decided at least 25 cases involving Spanish land grants, the last of which was not decided until 1888.[350]

The land grant issue was made worse by the fact that as of 1816 not a single acre of public land in Missouri had been offered for sale. This was due to problems other than the inability to settle the Spanish titles. While the federal government was preoccupied with the War of 1812 and extinguishing Indian titles, the Federal Land Law of 1800 required all public lands be surveyed and divided into 640-acre sections before sale. When Nathan Boone was not fighting Indians, he was a surveyor. In 1806 he contracted to survey the counties of St. Charles, Lincoln, Warren and Montgomery. He did extensive survey work on the two common fields in St. Charles, afterwards known as "Boone's Survey." By 1823 Boone was the deputy surveyor of St. Charles County and in 1826 he surveyed in the area of Dardenne Creek.[351]

But the surveyors could not keep up with the stream of new settlers who, in frustration, began to settle illegally upon the land and to make improvements to the land. Congress attempted to keep settlers from settling on public land before it was offered for sale and authorized force to remove these "squatters." This policy was controversial and when Colonel Alexander McNair refused to use his militia troops against the squatters, the federal government had to relent.[352] The governmental interests in order, respecting Indian rights and controlling speculation were countered, according to geographer D.W. Meining, by the argument that:

> This vanguard of settlers was creating homes for their families and by their improvement bringing great benefit to the entire country and increasing the value of adjacent land; they had transformed the derisive term "squatter" into an honorable one, they represented the strength and future of the Republic; and blame should rest on the government for not putting sufficient land on the market to meet an obvious demand. Such sturdy pioneers, it was fervently argued, had earned the right to "preemption" – that is, to

purchase the lands they had actually occupied, at the minimum price, once such tracts were officially surveyed and readied for sale.[353]

Squatting became the "custom or common law of the settlers," although officially still illegal until Congress passed the Preemption Act of 1841. The long awaited notice of public land sales in Missouri appeared on June 5, 1818, when President Monroe ordered the sales to begin in St. Louis and Howard County. Federal policy required the public lands be offered for sale at public auction to the highest bidder, with a fixed minimum price of $2 per acre, and a minimum purchase of 160 acres.[354]

Another problem was land speculation, made worse by the liberal credit terms extended by the federal government. On the day of sale the buyer needed to pay only for the survey, the application and five percent of the selling price. Within 40 days the next 20 percent of the selling price would be due, but the next 25 percent was not due until two years after the date of sale. Many people purchased lands, not with the intent to develop, but with the intent to sell at a profit before the payments were due to the federal government. Commenting on the land speculation, a resident of St. Charles commented that, in the period between 1816 and 1819, "the rage for speculation was at the highest," and "the zeal to purchase amounted to a fever."[355]

In 1820, Congress reduced the price to $1.25 per acre and it remained at that price for several decades. Minimum purchases of 80 acres were allowed in 1820 and 40 acres in 1832.[356] After statehood land policy continued to be an important political issue and Senator Benton's proposal, to gradually reduce the price of unwanted land, continued to be very popular. In 1829 the Missouri General Assembly passed a resolution praising the proposal. The other Missouri senator, David Barton, was concerned the proposal would increase land speculation and was the only western senator to vote against Benton's bill. Even he relented in 1830, while Congressman Edward Bates did not and was defeated in his bid for re-election.[357] The land hunger of the people needed to be fed.

Another troubling legal question concerned the status of the commons and the common fields. The United States assumed sovereignty over the area with a promise to recognize all land grants, "made agreeably to law, usage and customs of the Spanish government."[358] The common fields had never been the subject of any formal Spanish grants as grantees had received their fields from local Spanish officials, yet few had gone to the expense of obtaining formal confirmation from the Spanish government in New Orleans. As a result they had the same problem as the fee simple owners. The American officials had no experience with the concept of the commons. When the inhabitants of St. Charles claimed further grazing rights in the commons in 1806, it took the Board of Land Commissioner six years to decide, and reject, the claim.[359]

After a petition from a group of leading citizens from St. Louis, Congress clarified the status of title to the common fields with an 1806 statute recognizing the land claims of those who could prove they had cultivated their common field in 1800. They were made fee simple owners despite absence of formal approval from the Spanish government. In 1812, Congress also resolved any controversy over title to the commons, providing:

> The right, titles and claims, to towns or village lots, common field lots and commons, adjoining and belonging to the several towns or villages of Portage des Sioux, St. Charles, St. Louis, St. Ferdinand, the Village of Robert, Carondelet, St. Genevieve, New Madrid, New Bourbonnais, Little Prairie and Arkansas, in the Territory of Missouri, which lots have been inhabited, cultivated, or possessed, prior to the 20th of December, 1803, shall be and the same are hereby confirm to the inhabitants of the respective towns or villages aforesaid.[360]

The Americans had little experience with common ownership and favored private ownership of property. When the now predominantly American residents of St. Charles petitioned Congress in 1819 to preserve their commons, they did not even mention the importance of pasturing, wood gathering, or any of the traditional uses of the commons. They asked Congress instead to confirm their claim to the commons so that they could "lease, sell, divide or dispose of the same for the benefit of the inhabitants of said town."[361] By the 1830s, it was generally believed that the best use of the commons was to sell them and use the proceeds for other local government expenses. The inhabitants of St. Charles were already planning to raise a fund of at least $20,000 to be used for public improvements.[362]

The Missouri legislature authorized St. Charles, "to sell in fee simple for ever, all, or any part, of the town lots, outlots, common field lots, or commons."[363] Banner suggests that the transformation in the popular understanding of the commons was now complete. The General Assembly did not make the distinction between the "government" and the "inhabitants" as the Spanish law had. Instead the legislature categorized the commons as public land owned by the government, which the government had the authority to convey in fee simple.[364] The issue of commons ownership was settled by the Missouri Supreme Court when St. Louis brought suit against the lessee of a lot in the commons. In the case of *Morgan v. City of St. Louis*, the court rejected the defendant's argument that the land was held by the "inhabitants" of the city, not the city itself. In American jurisprudence the people are the government, so there was no reason to make a distinction between land held by the "crown" and land held by the "inhabitants."[365]

At the time of the Louisiana Purchase, there were hardly any lawyers among the 10,000 inhabitants of Missouri. Within a year after the purchase they were everywhere and not all had come to litigate Spanish land claims. The initial demand for lawyers came not from prospective clients, but from the United States government that intended to establish an American court system and needed people with legal training to fill judicial and prosecutorial positions. After 1805 Congress severed Louisiana from the Indiana Territory and the government had to appoint local officials.[366] Later the demand for lawyers came from American settlers, mostly from Kentucky,

Tennessee, Virginia and the older states at the same latitude, who brought with them the habits of Americans, including the habit of hiring lawyers to resolve disputes. Like the legislature, the first Supreme Court of the new State of Missouri met in St. Charles and the first case decided by that court was a St. Charles County case, *Collier v. Wheldon and Wife.*[367]

The interaction of these lawyers with public officials often led to their entry into politics.[368] On the national level, while less than one-third of the members of the original Congress were lawyers, by 1813 they constituted a majority of the members. The author of the *History of St. Charles County* wrote, "the profession of law, in itself a profession of the highest character and usefulness, has ever been the great school in which the wisest and best legislators and judges have received their training."[369] As members of legislatures, lawyers pushed legislation that aided the commercial interests that were often their clients' interests. More importantly, by becoming judges they, "fashioned a legal revolution."[370]

After the Louisiana Purchase, old informal norms, which for decades had served as rules for resolving litigated disputes especially in commercial cases, continued to play a role until legislation occupied the gaps formerly filled by custom. Historian Charles Sellers states, "Lawyers were the shock troops of capitalism. The number of lawyers mushroomed, as there was a proliferation of contractual relationships in the new market economy. During the commercial boom merchants abandoned informal arbitration and relied increasingly on lawyers and the courts to settle disputes."[371] He contends they were able to do this through their interpretation of the common law of England, which the territorial legislature declared to be in effect in Missouri Territory in 1816.[372] Sellers writes:

> But the law being taught to the young republic and enforced in its courts was not the old English law. Once the common law empowered lawyer/judges to exploit the law-making potential of the courts, they stood Blackstone on his head. Continued adherence to ancient common law principles, said one judge, would "prevent improvement in our commercial code." With growing confidence judges modified Blackstonian precedents to facilitate commercial ends.[373]

Lawyers also went to the General Assembly seeking corporate charters, under which their clients conducted business while limiting their personal liability. Anti-corporation sentiment, which viewed incorporation as a privilege for the special interests, was strong in Missouri. There was a significant decline in the number of corporate charters granted by the legislature between 1840 and 1845, and the Constitutional Convention of that year proposed a constitution that would have restricted the power of corporations and made stockholders individually responsible for the debts of the corporation.[374] The voters rejected that new constitution and the majority of Missourians obviously agreed with the editor of the *St. Charles Clarion* who denounced demagogues for their portrayal of corporations as "monsters without souls," and contended that, with proper restrictions, corporations were useful and no more dangerous than partnerships.[375] The following year the number of corporations chartered increased and an amendment to hold stockholders individually liable failed by a vote of 55-38 in the Missouri House of Representatives.[376]

While these decisions were being made by the legislature, state and federal courts issued decisions making land more marketable and property owners less liable.[377] More importantly, the United States Supreme Court, in *Marbury vs. Madison* established the principle that federal courts could overturn laws that they believed to be unconstitutional. These two trends converged in legislation passed by the Missouri General Assembly in the summer of 1821. Responding to the economic depression that had been caused by the Panic of 1819, the legislation delayed foreclosures unless creditors agreed to take less money in satisfaction of the debt. The act also attempted to put more money into circulation. The provision requiring creditors to take property worth two-thirds of the value of the original debt or wait two years to foreclose on the property was challenged in state court. The Missouri Supreme Court, led by Chief Justice John McGurk, ruled that the provision was an ex post facto law and that it impaired obligation of contract in violation of the U.S. Constitution. The enactment also set up state loan offices that issued loan certificates backed by the credit of the state and secured by its salt springs. The St. Charles Third Loan Office District gave notice on August 29, 1821 that it was receiving applications for loans and began dispersing money on October 17, 1921. After being upheld by the state courts, the matter made it to the U.S. Supreme Court in 1830 where, by a four to three decision, the court held that the provision violated the constitutional prohibition on states issuing "bills of credit."[378] The decisions greatly expanded the power of courts, creditors and the federal government, at the expense of the legislature, debtors and the state government.

While title to land was being litigated in the courts, the land in St. Charles County was being domesticated in a distinctly American pattern. There was a sequential development of agriculture on the American frontier and specifically in St. Charles County. Historian Lewis Atherton writes:

> E.P. Fordham pictured western society in 1817 as composed of four classes: the hunter who lived by the rifle; the first settlers, who did some hunting but devoted most of their time to farming; the true farmers and the enterprising men from Kentucky and the Atlantic states who founded towns and trade, speculated in land, and began the fabric of society; and a fourth class of old settlers, who really constitute the maturation of the third stage.[379]

Nathan Boone is a wonderful example of the first stage settler. His biographer, R. Douglas Hurt, tells us that he left St. Charles County in the autumn of 1800 to go hunting south of the Missouri River and did not return until January with meat for his family and skins to sell in St. Louis. Like his father, Nathan was an indifferent farmer but a good hunter. While profits from the land were meager and required backbreaking work, the woods provided a bounty of skins, furs and meats. Nathan Boone loved the life of the hunter, in spite of its hardship and privation.[380]

The period of the hunter-farmer produced the enduring symbol of the log cabin and a mythology surrounding its occupant, the yeoman farmer, who, according to one historian, was, "celebrated as the backbone of the Republic," and was "the prototypical American of his day and indeed long after."[381] Unlike the French farmers of the common fields who continued to live in a village and trade with other villagers, the agricultural household of the yeoman farmer was an isolated flexible productive unit sustained on its own raw materials and labor. Charles Sellers points out, "Paradoxically, European technology made white farmers more independent of the market. Fabricating tools from iron, spinning and weaving cloth, and distilling whiskey, they produced for themselves important use values that Indians had to buy."[382]

Each of these subsistence farmsteads had pasture for small herds, some tilled land to furnish grains and garden vegetables, and forested land to supply fuel and timber. Work began each year after the spring thaw when fields were cleared, spread with manure and furrowed by a team of oxen pulling a wooden plow. The winter wheat was harvested in midsummer. After a brief respite in August the frantic harvest and rush to store grain and put up fruit from the orchard began. Local farmers growing tobacco had only slightly different work rhythms. Livestock and poultry needed tending all season. In the wintertime, the farmer cut cordwood, repaired implements, and erected houses, barns, and buildings. Planting and harvesting required the efforts of the entire family; especially when frost or floods caused late planting or rainy weather threatened the harvest. Otherwise, there was a strict sexual division of labor.[383] The men worked the fields, made their own equipment, slaughtered the animals, fished the streams and hunted the forest for deer, turkey, squirrels and various other kinds of plentiful game. Fur animals were abundant, including otter, beaver, muskrat, panther, fox, wildcat and bear, and could be trapped to provide extra income.[384] The women made cloth, sewed clothes, preserved fruits and vegetables, took care of the garden, milked the cows, kept the homestead clean and fed the family.[385]

However, the subsistence farmer was not totally independent. When a new barn was needed, rather than hire a carpenter to build it, the surrounding community was summoned to a barn raising that usually turned into a social event as well. Likewise, within the neighborhood, certain farmers might possess special skill like blacksmithing, shoemaking or even preaching. These services were traded within the neighborhood or exchanged for foodstuffs.[386] This "pioneer society," with its emphasis on self-sufficiency, did not disappear at once and lingered on in some parts of the state until the 1830s.[387]

The next sequential stage in the evolution of the frontier involved the development of a local market between the farmers and towns and villages. This happened early in St. Charles County, with its French villages already in existence when the yeoman farmers arrived.[388] Since the farm families could not produce everything they needed, some commodities were obtained from traveling merchants or at the general store. Ray Donald Cook points out, "Since money was not always available on the frontier, Duff, Green and Co. (in St. Charles) was willing to accept furs, beeswax or tallow in exchange for their merchandise from Philadelphia and Baltimore."[389] In addition to the towns of St. Charles, St. Peters and Portage des Sioux, other small towns sprang up in St. Charles County to which farmers could bring their crops for processing and in which they could trade their surplus products for manufactured goods. Joseph and John Weldon settled at Weldon Spring in 1798 and built a log mill and a flourmill that became the focal points of the community. The spring had a constant temperature of 54 degrees and was located on the edge of an area known as Howell Prairie, named after the Howell family, early pioneers who had come from North Carolina. The largest employer in St. Charles before the Civil War was a steam flourmill that employed 175 men. The town also had a woolen mill located on the northeast corner of South Main Street at Booneslick Road.[390]

Each small town or village had a general store. As the farmers had more surplus crops, they were able to purchase more and the stores came to carry merchandise not previously seen on the frontier. One author comments:

> The drygoods and clothing stock was so varied that one can do no better than list the goods offered for sale in the newspaper advertisements. John Collier and Company of St. Charles, Missouri, advertised the following items in 1820. "Superfine and common Cloths, superfine and common Casimers, Callicoes, Ginghams, Irish Linens, Brown Holland, India, Book, Mull, Jaconet, Cambrick, Leno and Figurd Muslin, Nankeens, Senshaws, and Sasanets, Shawls, and Handkerchiefs, Plain and Figures Cotton Crapes, Hosiery and Gloves- Straw Bonnets, Seersuccer and Cotton Cassimers, Bombazetta & Diapers - Vesting, Ribbons, Steam Loom Shirtings, Russia Sheeting, Plaid and Stripes, Sheeting, Shirting & Bed Ticking, Shoes and Boots, Morrocco Hats and Skins…" The list is impressively long and varied.[391]

If markets were accessible, farmers could begin to concentrate on cash crops. Grain was sent to Europe via New Orleans during the Napoleonic Wars, but this market disappeared with peace in 1815. At that time, it was estimated that grain could be sent profitably no more than 20 miles by land, leaving the river as the primary form of transportation. Grain that reached New Orleans was in a buyer's market and sometimes rotted on the docks. The corn could be fed to hogs, but the market was not much better for hogs.[392] So the western farmers turned to distilling and in 1812 New Orleans received 11,000 gallons of whiskey, in 1816, 320,000 gallons, and by 1824, 570,000 gallons.[393] W.J. Rorabaugh, in his book *The Alcoholic Republic*, states, "before 1825, it was estimated that a farmer who sent 1,000 bushels of corn to New Orleans would be lucky to recover his shipping costs. If he could convert his corn into hogs, oxen, or horses, he might make $120. But if he shipped his corn as spirits, he could make $470."[394] The Griffith family in St. Charles County operated a sizable whiskey still as an important source of revenue on their farm.[395]

No doubt, some of the whiskey made from St. Charles County corn made its way in the opposite direction; up the Missouri River where it was sold to mountain men at a rendezvous. After months of solitary existence in the mountains, these trappers and traders exchanged their pelts for cash, supplies and liquor, and then went on a drinking binge that might last several days. W. J. Rorabaugh has stated, with regard to the whiskey presented to the Indians in exchange for their furs, "this concoction cost 5¢ a gallon to make and sold for 50¢ a bottle."[396]

As markets developed, farmers looked to put more land into production and the size of farms increased. By 1850 the median amount of improved farmland for American farmers in St. Charles County was 40 acres. They were likely to have twice as much unimproved land, mostly woodland that was later cleared. Almost every farmer had a team of horses and a milk cow or two, while 75 percent of them raised cattle, 90 percent raised swine and 50 percent raised sheep. While 75 percent grew wheat, 92 percent grew corn, the yield of which was twice that of all other crops combined. Corn was popular because it could be planted between tree stumps on newly cleared land; could be used to feed man and beast; and could be harvested at a leisurely pace without damage from the weather.[397] Not only did the size of the farms increase, but the quality of farm life also improved. Lewis Atherton suggests, "Where the hunter-farmer still lived in an age of buckskin, the pioneer farmer lived in an age of homespun, and both ages existed simultaneously in Missouri in 1821."[398] Farmers coming from Kentucky, Virginia, North Carolina and Tennessee, desired amenities like glass windows, iron stoves, schools for their children, and necessary farm tools. In 1829 an investor from St. Louis stocked a store in St. Peters with $17,000 worth of merchandise.[399] Farmers now also sought more slaves to work their larger farms. By 1850 non-slaveholding American farmers owned an average of 10 fewer improved acres, harvested 37 percent less wheat and 20 percent less corn than the overall averages of American farmers.[400]

Some amassed considerable holdings in land and slaves. Daniel Griffith, the eldest son of Samuel Griffith, began acquiring land in the Portage des Sioux area at the age of 13 and continued to expand his holdings there until 1836. In 1830 he began purchasing land in the Cave Springs area as well and by 1840 Daniel Griffith's land holdings in St. Charles County totaled 2,412 acres, 1,230 of which were part of the Griffith Plantation at Cave Springs. With his 15 slaves, Daniel Griffith was far from being a yeoman farmer. A nine-room Georgian-style plantation house replaced the log cabin.[401] Likewise, Dr. William J. McElhiney and his wife came to St. Charles County from Maryland and established Bel Aire Plantation about three miles south of St. Charles. It eventually comprised about 1,700 acres between the Booneslick Trail and

Originally a tobacco factory, this building in Wentzville was constructed in the 1850s. It was in this building that Ligget & Meyers Company had its beginning in the tobacco industry. *St. Charles County Historical Society*

the Missouri River where slaves grew tobacco, burnt lime and harvested salt from a nearby creek. Their home had four fireplaces on each floor, with large high-ceiling rooms trimmed in walnut.[402] In 1841, Charles Ferney came from Virginia, bringing many slaves with him and established a tobacco farm near Defiance. Tobacco required barns in which to dry the leaf over a three-year period and Ferney built a 35 x 90-foot barn, the largest in St. Charles County, and another example how far the county had moved from subsistence farming. Market-driven agriculture in St. Charles County also got a boost when settlers from Virginia, led by Captain Taliaferro Grantham, formerly of Flint Hill, Virginia, settled in northwestern St. Charles County in 1836 and began growing tobacco.

Twenty percent of American farmers in St. Charles County were growing tobacco by 1850.[403] Much of it was sold to tobacco factories in St. Charles County. Wentzville alone had seven factories and was well know for its "twist" chewing tobacco and its cigars. There was a tobacco factory in Flint Hill. The northwestern part of the county was at the extreme southeastern edge of a large tobacco-producing area known as "Little Dixie," that stretched westward across the State of Missouri. Tobacco from "Little Dixie" was sold in New Orleans and the members of the first General Assembly, meeting in St. Charles, passed an act requiring the inspection of tobacco. When growers objected, the regulations were lifted during the next session

As late as the 1890s steamboats like the *General Meade* stopped at *Marais Croche* to take on cargoes of wheat. *John J. Buse Collection, 1860-1931, Western Historical Manuscript Collection-Columbia, MO.*

of the General Assembly. The result was to lower the value of Missouri tobacco in the markets, compared to the tobacco of Virginia and Maryland, where the product was inspected and regulated. Objections by the growers to regulation did not equate to objection to government subsidies as the legislature appropriated money in 1843 for a state-owned tobacco warehouse in St. Louis that competed with private entities.[404]

Cash crop farmers also prospered as transportation systems improved. Before 1850 rivers were still the primary means of transportation within the state and the primary means of getting crops to regional or national markets. The earliest steamboat to land in St. Charles was the *Independence*, on its way from St. Louis to Franklin in 1819. By 1825, there was a great increase in the number of settlers coming to the area by steamboat, while even larger numbers used the boats to journey west during the California and Colorado gold rushes. Mail was arriving on the steamers by 1833; in 1836, 76 steamboats landed in St. Charles.[405] But most of the commerce was moving in the opposite direction. While the steamboat improved passenger travel, D.W. Meining writes, "The remarkable reduction in marketing costs of western farmers rather than the speed of passenger travel was the more fundamental change."[406] In 1841, one commentator stated, "the introduction of steam boats broke up the keel boat trade and threw a large portion of the French villagers out of employment, and in a great measure revolutionized their business and habits. The keel-boat and the *cordelle* having gone into disuse, many of them are now engaged in the Rocky Mountains, in the Santa Fe trade, and as pilots, engineers or firemen on steamboats."[407] The steamboats greatly lowered shipping rates for agricultural goods. Courts eventually invalidated franchises, such as the one Robert Fulton had received to operate his steamboat on the Hudson River. As a result, entrepreneurs were free to compete and St. Charles County was especially well situated to take advantage of the competition. By the 1820s rates to transport agricultural goods to the east fell as a fleet of over 75 riverboats had linked the cities of New Orleans, St. Louis, Louisville, Cincinnati, Pittsburgh and Nashville. While the rates on the Missouri River from St. Louis to St. Charles at mid-century had fallen to 25 ¢ per pound, the steamboats also had their problems as the Missouri and upper Mississippi Rivers were more difficult to navigate than eastern rivers. St. Louis became an important riverboat port because larger boats, built to operate in four to six feet of water could come as far north as St. Louis. Their cargoes then had to be transferred to other vessels designed to navigate in water 30 inches deep on the Missouri and upper Mississippi rivers.[408]

Although steamboat travel on the Missouri River was cheap, it was also treacherous because of spring floods and winter ice jams. Between the mouth of the Missouri River and Kansas City, 273 steamboat wrecks were known to have occurred.[409] In 1832, the steamboat *Car of Commerce* sank while attempting a shortcut around Pelican Island, just below Musick Ferry landing. The area where it sank is still labeled "Car of Commerce Chute" on the map. Further downstream, the side-wheel packet steamboat *Cora* ran aground in 1869, causing Cora Island to form in the river just below the present Highway 367 bridge.[410] In addition to navigational difficulties, in the three decades prior to the Civil War, there were 100 boiler explosions on the Missouri River.[411] One of the worst disasters occurred in 1842 when the boiler of the *Edna* exploded near the mouth of the Missouri River, killing 55 German immigrants.[412] Explosions like this prompted state and federal governments to pass legislation regulating steamboats in 1838. Many riverboat captains lived in St. Charles County after their retirement, including Edward L. Fulkerson, who is said to have taught Samuel Clemens riverboat lore and operations.[413]

To take advantage of cheap transportation on the rivers, the farmer had to get his crops to the river. To trade in the local market, the farmer also needed to get his crops to the population centers. In the beginning, according to the *History of St. Charles County*, "there were no roads, no bridges, no ferry boats, and scarcely any conveniences for traveling," and, "so many rivers and treacherous streams were to be crossed and such a trip was often attended by great danger to the traveler when these streams were swollen beyond their banks."[414] When the Europeans arrived, native tribes had already established trails in St. Charles County. Ken Kamper has discovered the "Trail to the Village of the Missouris," from a 1684 map of the French explorer Franquelin. The trail ran from present-day West Alton to St. Charles along the Burlington and old MKT right-of-ways. Past St. Charles, the trail followed today's

Highway 94 and Highway N.[415] When a large contingent of Kentuckians led by the Boone family marched west from Cincinnati to the Mississippi River, they crossed that river into St. Charles County. In bypassing St. Louis, they avoided the necessity of crossing the Missouri River. Kamper points out:

> According to a reliable early account…the Kentuckians and other eastern families who migrated to the Missouri territory with their family, stock, and other belongings, used this trail above the mouth of the Missouri River, while the trail to the village of St. Louis was used mainly by the "well-mounted gentlemen cavaliers" who traveled to the town of St. Louis "to see the famous city."[416]

While during Spanish administration there had been no public mail delivery, a post office was established in St. Charles soon after the purchase. Mail was carried by horseback from Chambersville, Pennsylvania, the furthest point west of any stage line. In 1810 post roads were announced from St. Louis to St. Charles and mail that reached St. Louis was delivered every Tuesday. By 1819 there were also post roads from St. Charles to Clarksville and Louisiana, and from St. Charles to Pinckney (in Montgomery County) and Franklin. By then the mail came down the Ohio River to Shawneetown and then across southern Illinois to St. Louis.[417]

The Missouri territorial legislature on July 9, 1806 passed a law providing that 12 freeholders of the county could petition the Court of Quarter Sessions to establish a public road through the county. By 1815 a network of primitive roads in St. Charles County led from the farms to the nearby village, that is, to the mill, the cotton gin, or the country store. Typically the village was located on water navigable for at least small boats during part of the year. The village could not be far away from navigable water since the prices paid for the produce of the farm, could not absorb the cost of extended transportation by land routes.[418] By 1832 St. Charles had a market house where farmers could bring their produce to be sold.[419]

By 1824, it was possible for a St. Louis legislator to make the four–hour commute to St. Charles for the legislative session. Another stage ran between St. Charles and Franklin County.[420] John Batiste Belland established the first licensed ferry across the Missouri River in 1805 and by 1821 there were several competitors. Thomas Howell operated a ferry from the end of Old Bon Homme Road (now Olive Street Road) in St. Louis County to Howell's Ferry on the St. Charles County side.[421] Even though the County Court set the ferry rates after 1821, one disgruntled traveler wrote in his diary in 1826, "when I came to St. Charles I found the ferrymen to be a deceitful, cunning, shuffling band of men disposed to use all manner of chicanery."[422] Territorial, and later state, laws licensed and regulated the ferryboats. The operators had to pay five dollars per year for their licenses, post a $500 bond and pay fines for safety violations or imposing "delays in crossing" for other than safety reasons.[423]

The roads of St. Charles County not only had local and regional importance, but also were important to westward expansion. The National Road, authorized in 1802, was to have connected Baltimore to the east bank of the Mississippi River at a point somewhere between St. Louis and the mouth of the Illinois River. The editors of the *Missourian*, the local newspaper published in St. Charles, applauded when Congress approved the money to survey the National Road in 1820.[424] The National Road, a victim of sectional rivalries in the period before the Civil War, fell 70 miles short of the Mississippi River and ended at Vandalia, Illinois. From Vandalia travelers on the National Road could make their way to Alton, where Rufus Easton had initiated a ferry service to St. Charles County in 1818, or they could proceed to St. Louis, from which they proceeded to St. Charles. Others used the river system, rather than the National Road, to get as far as St. Charles.[425]

The road west from St. Charles followed the route of the present Highway 94 and Highway K to the Warren County Line. As early as 1795 a Spanish official, referring to the same route, suggested:

> I consider it the most direct route to the kingdom of Mexico, and if we fail to attend to this very interesting object, it will not be very many years before the English merchants may establish themselves there, and after them the forces will follow. It would be advisable to form a chain of small Posts from the Missouri, San Carlos and Carondelet, and continuing until they join with those of the Internal Provinces.[426]

The same trail was used by the Boone family to reach the salt licks of central Missouri and it became a road for settlers headed for the Booneslick country. What became known as the Booneslick Trail connected to the Santa Fe Trail. Benjamin Reeves, George Sibley, and Thomas Mathers, commissioners appointed by President John Quincy Adams in 1825, met in St. Charles to write their report concerning the survey marking the trail to Santa Fe.[427] By 1830 St. Charles County had a population of 4,320 and stagecoaches left St. Charles weekly for points west, as did hundreds of individual wagons and carriages.[428] Timothy Flint observed, "An 100 persons have been numbered in a day passing through St. Charles, either to Boone's Lick, or Salt River."[429]

Towns like Harvester and Dardenne sprang up along the Booneslick Trail. Cottleville was located where the Booneslick Trail crossed Dardenne Creek. After John Pitman and his family arrived from Kentucky in 1810, the town began to prosper, primarily because of it location. When the Dardenne Creek was at flood stage or the flood plain was too muddy, travelers on the trail had to remain in Cottleville until conditions improved. By 1846, with several hotels, blacksmith shops and stores, Cottleville had grown sufficiently that a petition was presented to the County Court to make the town the county seat.[430] The town was incorporated in 1853 but declined in importance after the railroad, rather than the Booneslick Trail, became the primary mode of transportation for settlers moving west.

Although the Booneslick Road eventually became a state road in 1851, private corporations shaped much of the national infrastructure. In many cases competition, rather than rational planning, established the geographic pattern and progress of roads.[431] But the profit motive guaranteed that the immediate transportation needs were met.[432] After 1834, when the first one was built in Canada, plank roads were built by private corporations that collected a toll. The planks were usually three inches thick and eight feet long and were laid horizontally across the roadbed. They were built where there was a supply of lumber including St. Charles County, where the St. Charles and Western Plank Road Corporation was organized in 1851 for the purpose of building a plank road along the Booneslick Trail. Some $34,000 in stock was subscribed for and the plank road was built from St. Charles to Cottleville and was used for many years.[433] In 1853 the Plank Road Company built a plank road across the Portage commons connecting the ferry crossing the Mississippi at Elsah, Illinois with the Musick Ferry crossing the Missouri River to St. Louis County.[434]

The federal census of 1810 gave St. Charles County a population of 3,505, while the census by the territorial legislature in 1814 gave St. Louis County only 3,149 people.[435] Forty years later St. Charles County's population numbered 11,454 while St. Louis had become the eighth largest city in the country. St. Charles fell on hard times after the state capital was moved to Jefferson City. St. Louis had emerged as the major city of the west by 1850 and was the jumping-off point for settlers headed for the frontier. In his work *Yankee Merchants and the Making of the Urban West*, historian Jeffrey Adler explains that the phenomenal growth of St. Louis in the 1840s was due to the influx of Yankee newcomers to the city, bringing their entrepreneurial ethic, capital and eastern business connections to St. Louis. He states, "As long as St. Louis served as the principal Yankee outpost of the region, cities such as Quincy, St. Charles, and Chicago remained starved for economic sustenance and underdeveloped."[436]

There had always been Yankees in St. Charles County as well. Warren Cottle was one of a group of settlers, including relatives, in-laws and friends, who came from Vermont before the Louisiana Purchase.[437] Rufus Easton, territorial delegate to Congress in 1814, was born in Connecticut, as was his predecessor in Congress, Edward Hempstead. Benjamin Emmons, member of the first Council of the territory, had come to St. Charles County from New England. Yet the number of Yankees, while perhaps large for rural Missouri, was small compared to St. Louis. By 1850, the fur trade was at an end, many settlers were now taking trains to the west and there was little commercial expansion in St. Charles County, whose population had now reached 11,454. The economic wellbeing of St. Charles County now rested entirely with its agriculture. Nevertheless, one commentator, writing in 1841, observed,

> Though some of the older inhabitants consider the balmy days of St. Charles
> departed with the removal of the seat of government, (for some years after
> the event the town declined,) yet of late many emigrants have settled in the

town itself and its vicinity, both of which are daily becoming more populous and wealthy, and evince a steady advance in improvement, which justifies the prophesy that St. Charles may yet rank among the proudest of her sister towns anywhere west of the Mississippi.[438]

In the period from 1804 to 1850 significant economic changes took place that had a lasting effect on St. Charles County. While Congress passed unenforceable regulations, in general the fur trade saw monopoly replaced by open competition. In the area of land ownership, government grants to the favored few were replaced by auction of government land. Communal ownership of fields and pasture was replaced with fee simple private ownership. A combination of efforts by government and the private sector yielded improved roads, as advances in technology led to better transportation on the rivers. These changes accelerated the demise of the yeoman farmer and made possible the beginnings of a market economy in agriculture. Looking back from 1843, the year that Charles Dickens wrote *A Christmas Carol*, a 60-year-old *voyageur*, remembering Spanish subsidization of the fur trade and free land to anyone who could show a need, might have thought the government of the United States a "Scrooge." While the new free-market economy was subject to the pragmatic intervention of non-ideological politicians, government had become an umpire, not a benefactor. While the market economy created wealth, the fluctuations of the business cycle exposed the county, like the rest of the country, to economic recessions and depressions. However, the benefits of free market capitalism would not be seriously questioned in St. Charles County until the Great Depression of the 1930s, and up until that time economic expansion would continue.

CHAPTER III
Immigration, Emancipation and the Transportation Revolution 1850 –1890

On November 9, 1870, newspapers in St. Charles County reported the end of Radical Republican rule in the State of Missouri. The Civil War had allowed Republicans to exclude enough Democratic voters, because of their sympathy for the Confederacy, to guarantee their own election during and after the war. In 1870, the Republican Party in Missouri split over whether these former rebels should be re-enfranchised. After they were again allowed to vote the Democratic Party was able to control state government for the next 35 years. Four days after the election, the newspapers in St. Charles County reported the collapse of a portion of the North Missouri Railroad Bridge across the Missouri River at St. Charles. That railroad had brought significant economic changes as farmers could now get their crops to national and international markets. The inability to finish the bridge earlier was symptomatic of the economic decline experienced by St. Louis as more railroads were going to Chicago. Finally, in the preceding months the same papers had been full of stories of Prussian military victories over the armies of the Second French Empire. Within several weeks, Bismarck announced the unification of Germany under the leadership of Prussia. The influx of thousands of German immigrants had significantly changed social and cultural patterns in St. Charles County. Likewise, the Civil War and the support of those German immigrants for the Union had significantly altered the political landscape. The end of slave labor and the coming of the railroad brought economic changes that greatly benefited the Germans. By 1890, St. Charles County had become a radically different place from what it had been 60 years earlier.

A. The Civil War

From the time the sectional crisis began until the end of the Civil War there were three groups active in national, state and local politics. On one extreme were those sympathetic to slavery, dedicated to preserving the society that had grown up around it, and willing to secede from the Union if necessary. In the middle were those dedicated to preserving the Union and the property rights of slaveholders. On the other extreme were those committed to an economic, and even social revolution, where the economic system of slavery would be abolished and the former slaves would, to some extent, be integrated into American society. There were people from each group in St. Charles County. Some of those in the first group, mostly descendants of the settlers who had come from Kentucky, Tennessee and Virginia, left their homes in 1861 to become Confederate soldiers while others stayed behind and dealt with their pro-Union neighbors, federal occupation and martial law. Those in the second group, known as Conservatives in Missouri politics after the war began, were led by men like former St. Charlesan Edward Bates, who took pragmatic steps aimed at keeping Missouri in the Union. The third group, most of them with German names like Krekel, Bruere and Muench, fought to defend the Union when war came and supported Radical leaders in Missouri intent on destroying slavery and the political, economic and social power of the slaveholding class. As the Civil War began, Abraham Lincoln was on the side of the Conservatives in Missouri - before it ended, he was on the side of the Radicals.[439]

In 1845 the United States found itself at war with Mexico. The immediate impact on St. Charles County had been to give the men another excuse to leave their families and go off and fight as they had in the earlier Indian wars. A company of 90 men from St. Charles County under the command of Ludwell Powell and David McCausland set out for Fort Leavenworth, Kansas to join the Army of the West under the command of General Stephen Kearny. Before they arrived, Kearny had set out to capture Santa Fe. Therefore, the St. Charles volunteers spent the balance of their enlistment fighting Indians on the upper Missouri and Platte Rivers.[440]

This war had added vast new territories to the United States, raising questions as to whether slavery should be extended to these new territories. That issue split the Democratic Party in Missouri and the nation. After opposing efforts to bring Texas into the Union, Senator Benton had been forced to work hard to win re-election to the Senate in 1844. Former allies, like David R. Atchison and Claiborne Fox Jackson, opposed Benton and in March 1849 the General Assembly passed the "Jackson Resolutions," instructing Missouri's Senators to oppose any efforts to limit the extension of slavery into the territories. Benton ignored the resolutions and thus split the Democrats in the General Assembly, giving the Whigs the balance of power. On the fortieth ballot Whigs and anti-Benton Democrats elected Henry C. Geyer, a pro-slavery Whig, as United States senator. Senator William Allen, state senator from St. Charles County, was a leader of the Geyer forces, earning him the gratitude of Senator

Barton Bates was the son of Edward Bates and resided with his family (pictured above) in St. Charles County. He served on the Missouri Supreme Court during the Civil War. *St. Charles County Historical Society*

Geyer.[441] The brilliant Senate career of Thomas Hart Benton ended on January 22, 1851.[442]

Not all Whigs in Missouri lined up with the pro-slavery wing of the Democratic Party. Major George Sibley, one of the leading Whigs in St. Charles County, freed his slaves and pledged his loyalty to the Union. Edward Bates had moved from St. Charles County back to St. Louis, where he attended a meeting called by attorney James O. Broadhead to organize the anti-Geyer Whigs. Broadhead, a native of Virginia, had moved to St. Charles County in 1837 and became a protege of Edward Bates. Bates hired him at his home near Dardenne as a tutor, and directed his study of the law.[443] Historian Louis Gerteis asserts that these two men, along with Frank Blair and Gatz Brown, began laying the foundations of the Republican Party in Missouri.[444]

The emerging Republican coalition contained more than anti-slavery Whigs and Benton Democrats. German immigrants constituted an important constituency in the party. Their story in St. Charles County had begun with the arrival of Gottfried Duden in America in 1825. He had lived in Warren County for several years and wrote letters published in German newspapers describing life in America. Upon his return to Germany he had assembled them in a book which encouraged his countrymen to migrate to the Missouri River valley.[445] The book brought wealth to Gottfried Duden and thousands of German immigrants to St. Charles County. By the time of the Civil War approximately one-half of the population of the county was of German ancestry, and more than one-sixth of the Germans in Missouri lived in St. Charles County.[446]

The German immigrants had originally shown an overwhelming preference for the Democratic Party, identifying readily with its Jeffersonian and Jacksonian principles. The Whigs, regarded as aristocratic and unfriendly toward foreigners, were especially unpopular among the Germans because of their flirtations with the "Know-Nothing" Party and with other nativist groups in the period before the Civil War.[447] The nativists were concerned that the immigrants coming to the United States brought with them cultural and religious beliefs that threatened American ways, and the anti-immigrant feelings seemed to be strongest when the immigrants were Catholic. By 1837 Freemasonry, with its anti-Catholic biases, had begun to prosper again, and, in September 1845, the Native American Organization held its first meeting in St. Charles. When the pastor of St. Charles Borromeo parish marched in the July 4th parade in 1845 George Sibley had commented, "How strange that the Jesuits, whose prime object among us is to enslave our country, should place themselves in the front ranks of our people."[448]

By the 1850s, slavery had replaced nativist concerns as the dominant political issue. Dr. Jasper Newton Castlio later recollected how:

> The Southerners who were slaveholders, an' the Dutch who opposed slavery were often at one another's throats. Whenever boys from both sides happened t' cross paths, the 'redshirt' went up an' a bloody nose or broken bones resulted. Many a fight happened after a day in the school-house. Boys would walk a bit away from the schoolmaster's wary eye an' just have at it. Those fights were but warning of worse things to come.[449]

A second wave of German immigrants, the so-called "Forty-Eighters," began to arrive after the failure of the 1848 Liberal revolutions in Germany. Like the "Latin farmers" before them, these new arrivals immediately became politically active and assumed leadership roles in the German community.[450] They joined the German Liberals already here to espouse the political principles that had failed in Germany. These German Liberals generally supported the goals of the French Revolution, minus its more radical abuses. To these German Liberals, it was quite clear that America had betrayed the goals of its own revolution by its toleration of slavery.[451] Speaking at a meeting in Augusta, Friedrich Muench expressed the view of the German Liberals. Identifying two schools of thought about human relations, he stated:

The first is that there must be masters and servants, rulers and subordinates, free persons and slaves, that one is born with spurs to ride and the other with the saddle on his back to be ridden…. The other view is that which first found public expression in the Declaration of Independence: "all men are born with the same rights."[452]

Germans around Augusta aided runaway slaves and John H. Wilke was indicted by the St. Charles County Grand Jury in 1857 for allowing 78 slaves to congregate on his farm in Orchard Farm.[453] Less idealistic Germans had more practical reasons to oppose the extension of slavery. While the southern states defended the institution of slavery and used their power in the Senate to preserve it, they also opposed the Homestead Act that would have created free land in the territories for small farms utilizing free labor, rather than large plantations where slavery could expand and flourish. In an 1860 editorial the *Demokrat*, a German language newspaper, explained that the German voter in St. Charles County had always favored the Democratic Party of Andrew Jackson, who had declared that "the Union must and will" be maintained, not the Democratic Party that had become dominated by the slave-holding interests of the South. It concluded that Democrats were no longer the friends of the German immigrant because they opposed the Homestead Act that would provide free land.[454] Leaders of the German community, like Arnold Krekel, who had been the candidate of the pro-Benton Democrats for the office of Missouri attorney general in 1856, now became Republicans. Krekel had been born on March 12, 1815 in Prussia. In 1832 he immigrated to the United States with his parents, settling near Augusta. He attended St. Charles College for three years and was a surveyor both for St. Charles County and the federal government. He was admitted to the bar in 1844, serving as attorney for both the city and county of St. Charles. In 1852 he became editor of the *Demokrat*, and in the same year was elected to the Missouri House of Representatives. While in the House he favored state aid to railroads and public schools.[455]

In December 1859, an "opposition meeting" was held at the St. Charles County courthouse where a pro-Union resolution was passed, along with a resolution supporting Edward Bates for the Republican presidential nomination.[456] The following March the Missouri Republican Convention also recommended Edward Bates to the Republican National Convention to meet in Chicago.[457] Initially, Arnold Krekel of St. Charles and Gustave Koerner of Belleville, Illinois supported the Bates nomination along with St. Louisan Frank Blair. However, most German delegates followed Carl Schurz and opposed Bates because of his past sympathy for the nativist cause, and initially supported William F. Seward of New York. Eventually, German support enabled Abraham Lincoln to get the nomination and Schurz and Koerner persuaded the Republicans to incorporate several "Dutch Planks" in the Republican Party platform, including equal rights for foreign-born citizens. Friedrich Muench reported in June 1860, "the Germans were the only immigrant group represented at the Chicago convention," and added that Germans would have political influence in the Republican Party, "if we act as American citizens."[458] The "Dutch Planks," along with Abraham Lincoln's freedom from any nativist taint, led to a widespread shift of German voters to the Republican Party in 1860. [459]

Republicans nominated James Gardenhire of Cole County, a former Democrat, as their candidate for governor in the state elections held in August 1860. Meanwhile, Democrats split in August, just as the national party would split in November. Claiborne Jackson was the candidate of the Stephen Douglas Democrats on the national level. Sample Orr was the Constitutional Union Party nominee, as John Bell of Tennessee was nationally. Many Democrats and Jackson were masquerading as Douglas supporters; actually they favored Breckenridge and the extreme pro-slavery and states' rights position. Jackson received 46.9 percent of the vote statewide and 30.9 percent in St. Charles County. Sample Orr, candidate of the Constitutional Unionists, who were for slavery but against secession, received 36.4 percent in the county and 42 percent statewide. The Republican Gardenhire received, 21.8 percent in St. Charles County, while statewide he received only 3.9 percent. The First Senatorial District of Missouri, comprising St. Charles, Warren and Montgomery counties, elected a Douglas Democrat and St. Charles County elected a Constitutional Unionist as its state representative.[460]

As the November presidential election approached, the *Demokrat* exhorted its reader, "Go to it then, German countrymen! It nears, the great battle day, on which it must be decided if freedom or slavery shall be victorious. If then the patrols also come to us, so they shall find us at our post, awake, courageous, and steadfast. And we know the password – it is 'for Lincoln and Hamlin!'"[461] When the votes were counted, Missouri was the only state won by Stephen Douglas with 35.5 percent statewide and 40.6 percent in St. Charles County. The other centrist candidate, John Bell, did well, losing to Douglas by less than 500 votes statewide and 200 votes in St. Charles County. Breckenridge did poorly in the state with 18.9 percent, and did even worse in St. Charles County. It has been suggested that his states' rights ideas may have scared slave owners in Missouri where they were not sure they would always have an electoral majority to insure slavery's continuation.[462] On the Republican ticket, Abraham Lincoln carried only two counties, St. Louis and Gasconade. St. Charles County gave him 530 votes, a number higher than his vote in Gasconade County and second only to St. Louis County. He received no votes at all in 17 counties and fewer than 10 votes in 20 more Missouri counties.[463] Lincoln was no more popular in certain precincts of St. Charles County. When two brothers named Hill, who had come from Illinois, attempted to vote for Lincoln near Darst Bottom, an area inhabited by slave owners, they were turned away. The election clerk exclaimed, "no damn black republican vote will be cast at Hays' Mill."[464]

After the election, John Jay Johns, a slave-owning Virginia native, expressed the view of many of his St. Charles County neighbors,whose roots were in the South. He wrote in his diary on December 13, 1860, "The North has agitated the subject of slavery until the South is maddened to desperation and, unless she retraces her steps, the Union cannot stand."[465] A week later South Carolina seceded, followed by North Carolina, Georgia, Florida, Alabama, Mississippi, Louisiana and Texas. Lincoln named Edward Bates to be his attorney general as the debate over secession raged in Missouri. Governor Jackson, in his inauguration speech on January 3, 1861, suggested that Missouri should, "stand by her sister slaveholding states." The General Assembly called for a Convention to consider secession. There were to be three delegates from each senatorial district and almost 700 people attended a meeting in Cottleville at which Judge W.W. Edwards was nominated to be one of the three candidates. Judge Robert B. Frayser, a slave owner from the Dardenne area and brother-in-law of Edward Bates, was also a nominated. The *Demokrat* endorsed Edwards saying, "maintenance of the union is the major goal for us… We cannot and will not support anyone who is not for unconditional preservation of the Union."[466]

Frayser was elected delegate to the State Convention. Much to Governor Jackson's disappointment, former State Supreme Court Justice Hamilton Gamble, another brother-in-law of Edward Bates, chaired the Committee on Federal Relations and guided the Convention towards a rejection of secession on March 21, 1861. He expressed a pragmatic belief that geography and military necessity dictated, "connection with a Southern confederacy is annihilation for Missouri."[467] But all was not going well for the Republicans either. The General Assembly, concerned about the pro-Union militia activities in St. Louis, had taken control of the St. Louis police force from the mayor and given it to a Police Board appointed by the governor. Then, on April 1st Daniel G. Taylor, running on a "Union Anti-Black Republican" ticket, defeated the Republican candidate John How for mayor of St. Louis. Commentators at the time blamed the defeat on concern surrounding the arming of pro-Union German Home Guards.[468] Such a Home Guard regiment, composed primarily of Germans, began forming in St. Charles County in April under the leadership of Gustave Bruere, editor of the *Demokrat*, John Bruere, Judge Friedrich Gatzweiler, E.F.Gut, Henry Machens, G. Hoover and Arnold Krekel. Other Germans serving as officers included Richard Vogt, Herman Wilke, John D. Hollrah, Conrad Weinrich and Henry Denker. It was eventually armed from the government arsenal in St. Louis by order of Union General Nathaniel Lyon.[469]

A company of Pro-Union Home Guards drill on a vacant lot, later the site of Benton School, in St. Charles. *John J. Buse Collection, 1860-1931, Western Historical Manuscript Collection-Columbia, MO.*

Meanwhile, on April 22, Governor Jackson had ordered the militia to muster throughout the state and a company of militia was raised in St. Charles County as part of what was called the "Missouri State Guard." Captain Richard Overall, First Lieutenant David Schultz and Second Lieutenant Chap. Lucket led the company of 50 men, who drilled at the St. Charles County courthouse. The company was organized for artillery service, but when men were sent to Jefferson City to procure cannon from the state armory, all the ordnance of the state had been distributed.[470] Militiamen reported for the muster in St. Louis, gathering at an area that they named Camp Jackson in honor of their governor. The militiamen were clearly enthusiastic for the Confederacy and railed against the "damned Dutch" and the "black Republicans."[471]

In St. Louis, General Nathaniel Lyon took charge of federal troops and began raising volunteers for the Union, including some men from St. Charles County.[472] General Lyon launched a pre-emptive strike against Camp Jackson, taking most of the militiamen prisoner. The prisoners were quickly paroled but the balance of power had now radically shifted in the St. Louis area in favor of the Union. Former St. Charles Countian James Broadhead, now a leader of Union supporters in St. Louis, recalled, "The night after the Camp Jackson affair was a bad night for mobs."[473] A 13-year-old student at the St. Charles College at the time, remembered the aftermath of Camp Jackson differently and related years later:

> That night a meeting was held at the Courthouse at St. Charles and a company organized to join the army of the South, my father being elected 1st lieutenant. Great excitement prevailed and the streets were crowded with people anxious to enlist, and other companies were projected. The cadets of our school organized a company, and I was appointed sergeant – we got homemade gray uniforms. Our haversacks were stamped, "Dixie Guards" and we drilled, enthusiastically, in Rice's Grove, confident we would soon be on our way to win the war for the South.[474]

Operating under the protection of federal troops, local enlistments for the Union were much more numerous. The St. Charles County "Home Guard" was accepted into service in July 1861 and included over 1,300 men. Composed primarily of Germans and known as "Krekel's Dutch," they drilled at Camp Krekel in Cottleville and spent most of their time attempting to thwart southern enlistments.[475] John F. Dierker, a storeowner from Wentzville, organized a company of men for the Eighth Missouri Infantry. They later became part of the Forty-Ninth Missouri and served under General William Tecumseh Sherman. According to the *History of St. Charles County*, more than 2,000 men from the county fought for the Union.[476]

A second effort to recruit soldiers for the Confederacy in St. Charles County began in December 1861, when 112 men joined the Confederate Army in response to a call by General Sterling Price for 50,000 men. Under the command of Dr. Charles Montgomery Johnson, they rendezvoused with other recruits but were intercepted at

Shiloh Church in Boone County and defeated by Union troops before they could join Price. Of the 112 from St. Charles County, four were killed, 20 wounded and 25 captured.[477]

Life also became difficult for civilian supporters of the Confederacy soon after the fall of Camp Jackson. One such supporter remarked:

A week later, a regiment of Union troops came to St. Charles from St. Louis, took possession of the town, and arrested all the men who had taken part in the Court House meeting, and made them take an oath of allegiance to the United States. All who did not were taken to the military prison in St. Louis.[478]

John C. Fremont took command of the Department of the West in July 1861 and was even more aggressive than General Lyon, declaring martial law in St. Louis on August 14 and extending it to the rest of the state on August 30, 1861.[479] Frances Marten, an immigrant from Prussia and a captain in the Home Guard, was appointed provost marshal for St. Charles.[480]

In St. Louis, a slave pen, confiscated from its disloyal owner, became the Myrtle Street Prison. The McDowell Medical College on Gratiot Street became a prison in the same manner. The Department of the Missouri established a new prison in Alton, Illinois, to which prisoners from Gratiot and Myrtle Street prisons were often sent. These facilities housed not only prisoners of war but also political prisoners, Union army deserters, and federal soldiers awaiting trial for crimes. Citizens arrested for disloyal activity went before military tribunals that either released them on bond or sentenced them to prison or death.[481]

Joseph H. Dougherty, a resident of St. Charles County, after his capture in Monroe County in March of 1862, spent six months in the Alton prison before being exchanged at Vicksburg, Mississippi. Captured again near Jackson, Missouri in April 1863, he was examined at the Myrtle Street prison by Captain George Strong.[482] Dougherty was a farmer with no children and no slaves, who admitted he was a southern sympathizer and claimed to be a prisoner of war. When examined he indicated, "I never took the oath of allegiance to the United States nor do I desire to." Captain Strong recommended that he be exchanged.[483]

Civilians from St. Charles County were held in the prisons as well. On August 17, 1862, Arnold Krekel, provost marshal for St. Charles, Lincoln and Warren Counties, reported the following to the provost marshal in St. Louis:

Sir,

Your note of the 9th requesting me to report on the case of William Chambers whose case I have investigated is before me. Mr. Chambers has been a violent secessionist, has been in the Southern army and refused to go forward to take the oath of allegiance and was finally taken and confined. This confinement has been for some 3 or 4 months and on the whole I think he may be released on oath and bond in the sum of from 3 to 5,000 dollars. I think this will secure his future quiet.

Very respect,

A. Krekel.

William Chambers was released on September 10, 1862 on bond of $5,000 by order of Brigadier General John Schofield.[484] Krekel, who was later clearly aligned with the Radicals, was fairly moderate as provost marshal. In 1862 he conducted the spring elections in a normal manner, tried to be fair to civilians when they had a complaint against the army, and was willing to administer the test oath to almost anyone willing to take it.[485]

Several pro-southern ministers from St. Charles County were imprisoned for refusing to take the test oath, including Reverend Robert P. Farris, minister at the First Presbyterian Church of St. Charles, who was confined in Gratiot Street prison. The history of that church tells us, "He held that his commission to preach the gospel came from the Lord Jesus Christ, not from political power."[486] Reverend Tyson Dines, pastor of Mt. Zion Methodist Church in O'Fallon, was imprisoned in St. Charles where Union troops had taken over the old woolen mill (now Trailhead Restaurant). The St. Charles College (across from the present county executive office building) was also converted to a prison. According to local historian Gary McKiddy, "The conditions of the prison were very cordial; since both guards and prisoners were local residents. Many evenings were spent playing cards in the guards quarters on the first floor of the building before men were taken upstairs to be locked up for the night."[487] At the other extreme was the federal military prison at Alton, Illinois. It had opened in 1833 as an Illinois State Penitentiary, but had been closed in 1860 because the small cells and poor design made sanitation difficult. When hundreds of prisoners died of smallpox at the prison in 1863, a tent hospital was set up on Sunflower Island in the Mississippi River between Alton and St. Charles County, where many of those who died were buried.[488]

Later in the war, Reverend Dines was imprisoned for a second time in St. Louis. Concerned about the prison conditions, his wife Mary S. Dine convinced Major Edward Harding to ask the provost marshal to allow her to visit her husband in prison. A month later Mrs. Dines wrote to Major General Merrill, asking that he "permit my husband to return home." She wrote, "I can vouch for his loyalty. Though southern by birth, we have never been guilty of one disloyal act. I am, Sir, truly a loyal woman, a Union woman and I still cling to the old flag of that government that has protected me from infancy."[489] She added a post script, "remember there is one who daily prays for you."[490]

The imposition of martial law not only affected the civil liberties of southern sympathizers but also pitted neighbor against neighbor. When disagreements over the coming war led to an altercation between pro-Confederate Richard B. Keeble and Unionist James Humphreys, Keeble, believing a St. Charles County jury would be

88

sympathetic, filed a civil lawsuit against Humphreys, who hired attorney Arnold Krekel to represent him. With the imposition of martial law, *Keeble v. Humphreys*, before St. Charles County Circuit Judge Andrew King, now became *United States vs. Richard B. Keeble*, in the court of Provost Marshal Arnold Krekel. His neighbors came forward to present evidence to the provost marshal against Keeble. One witness quoted him saying that he would "give the shoes off his feet to bushwhackers and help them to fight at any time they would ask him to do so." Rudolph Nagel swore in an affidavit that Keeble had called Humphreys a "poor pitiful Union son of a bitch and that he would kill him." Another affiant stated that, "several times he heard R.B. Keeble say that he hoped the United States forces would be cut to pieces and the confederate government established," and that the Confederates "would destroy Peruque Creek Bridge on the North Missouri Railroad and then they would have sway [in St. Charles County]." It was charged that two Confederate soldiers visited Keeble's home in October 1861 before he was taken into Gratiot Street Prison. He was later released on bond and in March 1863 Krekel, no longer provost marshal and now colonel in the militia, wrote to the provost marshal asking permission to return Keeble's shotgun since he had taken the oath of allegiance.[491]

In spite of martial law, southern sympathizers continued to show their support throughout the war. As late as February 1865, the provost marshal ordered a subordinate to "proceed without delay to the vicinity of Millville, St. Charles County and arrest and bring one A.S. Mason, charged with harboring bushwhackers."[492] But as a practical matter, neither Home Guards nor provost marshals were necessary to insure the loyalty of St. Charles County. Although, at one point, General Price's army fled across the Missouri River near Augusta to escape Union forces, St. Charles County was too close to St. Louis and Illinois for any anti-Union groups to operate successfully. The county was important to the Union efforts to eliminate the guerilla forces operating in outstate Missouri. To that end, Union regulars were stationed in St. Charles under the command of General Simeon Bunker. They established a fort on the hill at the top of Reservoir Street, and named the hill and the fort after their commander. The large cannon of the fort faced the river and was used to fire on boats attempting to re-supply Confederate forces in central Missouri.[493]

To control northern Missouri and move its troops and supplies across the state, federal forces also had to control another vital transportation link, the North Missouri Railroad.[494] The St. Charles County Home Guard built a two-story fort to protect the North Missouri Railroad Bridge over Peruque Creek. They also defended against raiders from neighboring counties, at one point occupying Troy in Lincoln County, a hotbed of rebel activity.[495] In July 1861 the Eighth Missouri Infantry skirmished with guerrilla forces just outside Wentzville. Seven men were killed on each side and the 30 wounded were taken to a temporary hospital at the Wentzville Hotel. Robert Darnell was six at the time but remembered:

This fort was built by the Home Guard to protect the bridge that carried the North Missouri Railroad over Peruque Creek near present day Lake St. Louis. *John J. Buse Collection, 1860-1931, Western Historical Manuscript Collection-Columbia, Mo.*

The women did all they could that night to help the men and cried when one fine young man died from a wound. The next day the soldiers were taken away, some as prisoners. The very next day someone set fire to the hotel and it was completely destroyed. Which side set the hotel on fire is your guess.[496]

As the war continued, questions concerning the Home Guard, enlistment of slaves in the Union army, and emancipation dominated political discussions in St. Charles County and throughout Missouri, where politics revolved around Radical and Conservative factions. The German leadership in St. Charles County, although not all Germans, were Radicals and the *Demokrat* was their mouthpiece. The Radicals supported Home Guards under federal control, black enlistments, immediate emancipation and revenge on the rebels. The Conservatives were led by men like Charles F. Woodson, a slaveholder from Dardenne, who served as St. Charles County Court Judge from 1862-63, and lieutenant colonel of the Home Guard. They wanted protection for the slave property of loyal Missourians, a State Militia under the control of the governor and a policy focused more on reunification rather than revenge. The Lincoln administration tried to keep both factions happy and Missouri quiet while waging war in the South.

Until regular elections were held in 1864 the State Convention had established a provisional government headed by Hamilton Gamble, who became the leader of the Conservative faction that included Edward Bates and James Broadhead. In June 1862 the Convention passed an ordinance requiring all voters to take an oath of allegiance to the United States and Missouri constitutions. This had the effect of disenfranchising all Confederate sympathizers and thus changing the political landscape significantly as Radical Germans like Wm. Follenius and Conrod Weinrich were elected to the Missouri House of Representatives and Friedrich Muench was elected to the State Senate.[497] In 1863 Krekel wrote to the provost marshal, "Persons continue coming in and taking the oath and I begin to think a number of them are sincere."[498] But the *Demokrat*, expressing the Radical position, concluded:

> We Germans have become uncomfortable with Mr. Gamble. We completely disagree with his view of punishment for the rebels; we consider everyone who now swears the Loyalty Oath but previously supported the rebellion, openly or secretly, to still be traitors in their hearts, even if the Loyalty Oath is sworn a thousand times.[499]

Governor Gamble also disagreed with the Radicals over the role of the Home Guards, a force under federal control and a tool of the Radicals. With the help of Attorney General Bates, Gamble secured permission from Lincoln in 1861 to replace the Home Guards with a state militia; a plan that, "disgusted Fremont and worried Blair."[500] As General John C. Fremont's reputation declined, Gamble convinced the Convention to create the Missouri State Militia to suppress guerrilla activity. The Lincoln administration agreed to cover the cost of raising the state troops, who served under a federal commanding general. The governor appointed all field officers and the force could not be used outside the state except for its "immediate defense."[501] The four companies of Missouri State Militia recruited in St. Charles County numbered about 400, were commanded by Lieutenant Colonel Arnold Krekel and served until November 1862.[502]

When a Conservative colonel in command of Union troops at Fulton allowed 12 slaves working as teamsters to be seized by their late masters, Surgeon John Brueve, from St. Charles, swore out a complaint in November 1862.[503] Radical militia commanders, on the other hand, began freeing escaped slaves who informed on their masters. On March 10, 1862, Colonel Krekel reported, "A Negro boy gave valuable information in conducting the command, and I would ask for permission to retain him until the war is over, as he cannot safely return."[504] That same year Krekel led his forces into Callaway County, an area he described as "full of bushwhackers" and "certainly the center of the rebellion in northern Missouri."[505] Conrad Weinrich, described in a letter home, dated November 16, 1862, how:

The campaign advanced, through Calloway Co and Fulton, the headquarters of the *Sisesch* in North Missouri, and on October 15 we came back home. The entire time we got nothing from the government but a couple of barrels of *Krakers* and some coffee. All the rest, like horses and all our equipment, except for our clothing, we had to take from the *Sisesch*, because there was no other way to get anything. We had our food and drink provided by the *Sisesch,* when we found some, and when they didn't want to cook for us, we threatened to take everything away from them and cook for ourselves, but then they livened up and cooked what we wanted to have.[506]

Krekel lost men in September when rebels attacked a scouting party. Later that month, a cavalry force engaged about 200 rebels near Fulton, Missouri with each side suffering the loss of 15 men. Gamble reacted against "Krekel's Dutch," who the *Columbia Missourian* reported had been disarmed because of "disorderly behavior," and ordered to return to the people of Callaway County their horses, Negroes and other possessions, "acquired through a Jayhawker procedure."[507] The *Demokrat* reported this as politically motivated, complaining , "Once again the Gamble administration has shown through the sudden and very unusual manner of dissolving the battalion, that it is much more concerned with having secessionists and southern sympathizers as friends as with punishing betrayal."[508]

The enlistment of black slaves in the Union Army was the issue that separated Conservatives and Radicals the most. Lincoln had declared his war aim in July 1861 to be the preservation of the Union, not the abolition of slavery. He had also rescinded the August 30, 1861 order of General Fremont freeing slaves in Missouri, and had excluded slaves in the loyal slaveholding states from his Emancipation Proclamation.[509] After his Proclamation in January 1863, Lincoln stopped opposing the enlistment of black troops, and, by the spring of 1863, he had authorized such enlistments in all the border-states except Missouri. Military service implied citizenship and the arming of African-Americans was controversial almost everywhere, and especially in Missouri. Conservatives seemed to be more concerned with the property rights of slaveholders than winning the war.[510] But Radical leader Charles Drake declared, "No traitor is too good to be killed by a Negro, nor has any traitor a right to insist to be killed by a white man."[511]

In 1863 the Radicals nominated Henry A. Clover, David Wagner, and St. Charles County's Arnold Krekel for Supreme Court judges against the Conservative-backed incumbents, including Barton Bates of St. Charles County, the son of Edward Bates, who had been appointed the year before. The Conservatives narrowly won the election but St. Charles County went for the Radicals. Local historian Bob Schultz warns, lest we overestimate the popularity of the Radicals in St. Charles County, "Krekel's presence on the ticket probably had an enormous effect on the vote in St. Charles county, given his popularity among the Germans, and his war record."[512] Nevertheless, the strong showing of the Radicals in the election for state circuit and Supreme

Court judges convinced Lincoln that recruiting Missouri slaves was politically feasible and he sanctioned such a step. In November 1863 General John Schofield ordered that "all able-bodied colored men, whether free or slave, will be received into the service."[513]

The order was ineffective in some parts of the state because Conservative provost marshals, including James D. Broadhead, did not enforce it.[514] Even though loyal owners were to be compensated at the rate of $300 per slave, in southern Pike County whites patrolled the roads to apprehend slaves trying to enlist. Those caught, and the wives of those who were not, received "barbarous treatment."[515] Once again, proximity to St. Louis made it almost impossible for St. Charles County slaveholders to detain their slaves. One St. Louis newspaper observed, "The patriotic fever is running high among Africa's able sons. Many slaves marched in arms or traveled clandestinely through the night to thwart efforts of their masters to detain them from reaching the recruitment station in St. Louis."[516] When a German immigrant turned in a slave attempting to cross the Missouri River to enlist for military service, outraged people in Augusta removed the immigrant from his position as school board trustee. Then they seized the slave from his owner and sent him on his way.[517] By 1864 it was no longer necessary to cross the river as there was a recruitment station in St. Charles and over 40 slaves were recruited by February to meet the quota assigned to the station.[518] Edna McElhiney Olson, whose grandfather, Dr. William McElhiney, had a farm just south of St. Charles, relates, "Many of the slaves fought in the war and so many men were fighting, so good manpower was hard to find to work on the fields. Gradually the doctor sold most of his land and with his sons in the war, he moved to South Main Street in St. Charles."[519]

In Louisiana, Missouri Unionists protested the "most deplorable conditions," endured by the families of the black enlistees. At the same time, Dr. William McElhiney established an addition to St. Charles between Randolph Street and Gallaher Street, named after the doctor's mother, and, "gave to each of his slaves the same size lot and built them a house. As his slaves joined the army their families were freed and established in this addition."[520] The fate of slaves in a place like Flint Hill, located half way between Louisiana and St. Charles, lay somewhere between these two extremes. In March 1865 Congress gave the families of black recruits their freedom. Unlike Dr. McElhiney, Congress never gave them all a lot and house.[521]

By January 1864, the Radicals convinced Lincoln to replace General John Schofield, who had cooperated at times with Governor Gamble, with General William S. Rosecrans. To ensure Missouri met its draft quota, Rosecrans prohibited the exportation of slaves and stepped up the recruitment of black troops.[522] At the same time, guerrilla activity by Confederate sympathizers continued unabated. On September 27, 1864 an offshoot gang from Quantrill's Raiders, led by Bloody Bill Anderson, rode into Centralia Missouri. On that same day 25 unarmed Union soldiers boarded the North Missouri train at St. Charles. Andersen blocked the tracks at Centralia and forced the Union soldiers off the train. Little Archie Clement, his second-in-command, murdered all but one of the troops. [523] The *Demokrat* reported the details of the "bloody affair at Centralia," as they became available.[524] General Rosecrans called for more troops. While suggesting that one or two companies could certainly be raised in St. Charles County, the *Demokrat* explained:

> But General Rosecrans errs greatly if he thinks that a military organization can be brought about without partisan considerations. No loyal citizen – at least none among those who through their decisive action at the outbreak of the rebellion saved St. Charles and the neighboring counties from secessionists riots – will ever stand in ranks with disloyal, southern traitors or secret rebels. It is not the bushwhackers who endanger us most. Rather, their numerous friends who, behind hypocritical masks of loyalty, provide the knights of the woods with help and support when and wherever it can occure without danger… To really achieve Rosecrans' goal, we see no other way than to proceed with practical implementation of Martial Law. Missouri may not be treated as a loyal state, but must instead feel Martial Law in all its harshness.[525]

The County Convention of the Radical Union Party took place in Cottleville on September 7, 1864 and resolved in favor of preservation of the Union, support of Thomas C. Fletcher for governor and complete abolition of slavery.[526] The *History of St. Charles County*, written 20 years later, states, "the Germans, in 1860, almost in a body, joined the Republicans and have continued to vote and act with that party ever since."[527] This was certainly the case in November 1864, when Lincoln received 78 percent of the vote cast in St. Charles County. However, in that election 52,000 fewer Missourians voted than had done so four years earlier. The decline was due to the test oath requirement, in addition to the fact that many had left the state to fight for the Confederacy.[528] In addition to re-electing Lincoln in November 1864, the Republicans elected Thomas C. Fletcher governor and carried both houses of the new General Assembly by large majorities. In congressional races they swept all but one district and the Radicals were now in control of the state government.[529]

The end of the Civil War brought extremes of revenge and reconciliation. Shortly after the war a group of bushwhackers came through St. Charles County with the intention of killing the family of Herman Wilke, a captain in the Home Guard during the war. After the marauders broke through the doorway, one of them started through a bedroom when a shot from upstairs killed the intruder. The rest quickly picked up the body and immediately departed.[530] On the other extreme, other St. Charles Countians were tired of war and anxious for "normalcy." Willing to forget the deep divisions of the war years, Captain Charles Montgomery Johnson (Confederate) and Surgeon John Bruere (Union) operated a joint medical practice in St. Charles for almost half-a-century after the war.[531]

The war divided institutions along sectional lines. The Presbyterians split into northern and southern branches in 1866. French Strother, president of Lindenwood

President Lincoln appointed Colonel Arnold Krekel as Federal District Judge, *Missouri State Archives.*

College, leased the college and spent much of his own money on improvements. In 1870 a lawsuit determined that the property belonged to the northern branch of the church. Strother gave up his lease, although his daughter later wrote, "By placing his membership in the Northern church he could have held the college, but this he refused to do."[532]

The veterans of both armies who returned to their civilian pursuits kept the memory of the war alive. Both white and black chapters of veterans' organizations like the Grand Army of the Republic were established in St. Charles. Colonel George W. Tainter moved to St. Charles some years after the war. Tainter had enlisted in Boston in 1861. He was wounded and left for dead on the battlefield, but he recovered and enlisted in the Navy. He lived until the age of 102 and helped keep the memory of the Civil War alive for many decades.[533] As late as 1950 the *Banner-News*, in reporting the death of Robert Darnell, related the story he had told throughout his life about a party of marauding Union soldiers. Four years old at the time, he took refuge under a bed when he saw them approaching his house. When he suddenly emerged and confronted them with a shotgun, the Union men laughed. However, when he shouted, "Git, or I will blow out your brains," they decided that there was not much there worth stealing and they left.[534]

With the war over, the Radicals now had to face opposition, not only from the former Confederates, but also from former Conservative Unionists, who were not willing to accept the revolutionary changes desired by the Radical Republicans. Edward Bates, now retired and upset over Arnold Krekel's support for black suffrage, made the following comment in his diary:

> Mr. Krekel is the only prominent man of the party who has secured a safe retreat-U.S. judge of the Western District. He is wholly unfit for the place, and will not fail to display in it, his ignorance and his perverse notions of law and government. He owes his appointment wholly to Senator Henderson who got bitten in supposing that by making Krekel a judge he had "bought the Dutch."[535]

B. Post Civil War Politics

The hatred that developed during the Civil War dominated political expression in Missouri in the post-war period. The victors passed a new constitution while the war was still raging that became the focus of debate. Its radical nature guaranteed Republican electoral success in the short run but Democratic domination in the long run. Without the war to hold them together, the many factions that made up the Republican Party disagreed about how to handle the ex-slaves and the secessionists. Even after the party reunited, the wartime Republican majority in St. Charles County disappeared as social issues like parochial schools, prohibition of alcohol and English language requirements split the German vote in the 1880s, guaranteeing a strong two-party system in St. Charles County through the 1892 election.

At the November election in 1864 the proposal for a State Constitutional Convention carried by 29,000 votes. Statewide, 67.8 percent voted for a Convention, while in St. Charles County the percentage was 80.5 percent.[536] The first issue taken up by the Convention was emancipation of the remaining slaves in Missouri. On January 11, 1865, Arnold Krekel from St. Charles County, president of the Missouri Constitutional Convention, signed the ordinance of emancipation by which slavery was abolished in Missouri.[537]

Another issue before the delegates was disenfranchisement of the "rebel" element. Moderates wished simply to pass an ordinance as they had for emancipation. The Radicals, led by Charles Drake, wanted to include an "ironclad oath" in the constitution. It required voters, office-seekers, teachers, lawyers, pastors and some others to affirm that they were innocent of 86 different acts of disloyalty against Missouri or the Union. The acts included:

> Taking up arms and rebellion; giving help, comfort, sustenance, or support to anyone who did so; contributing money, goods, letters, or information to the enemy; advising anyone to enter confederate service; expressing sympathy for the rebel cause or for any specific foe; and engaging in guerrilla warfare or aiding and abetting those who did. The oath would be a prerequisite for voting and for holding public office, as well as for jurors, lawyers, corporation trustees, teachers, and ministers.[538]

Catholic Germans protested at the oath requirements for their priests. The *Demokrat* contended that this was not an attempt to control what was preached but only who was allowed to preach it. The paper pointed out, "It is even less an intervention in the rights of the Catholic Church, for in other countries the Catholic clergy also take a loyalty oath to the provincial government or the prince."[539]

Charles Drake made at least one appearance in St. Charles. An unknown author, writing in 1891, tells us that local lawyer Boswell Randolph, "annihilated the great Charles Drake in a political contest in the old courthouse in St. Charles."[540]

Drake spent one highly controversial year as a Democrat in the Missouri legislature just before the war, where he antagonized the Germans and others by his advocacy of strict "blue laws," and flirtations with the "Know-Nothing" Party.[541] From the beginning of the convention, the German delegates suspected Drake's motives in opposing suffrage for aliens and other efforts to dilute German voting power in places like St. Charles County. Some German delegates questioned his narrow definition of religious freedom. While it did not become part of the constitution, Drake had advocated taxing church and other charitable properties and restricting churches from holding property not actually used for worship. The Catholics were especially suspicious of these proposals.[542]

Enough delegates shared Drake's views to allow him to pass the constitution and place it on the ballot in early June 1865. President Lincoln's assassination shortly before the election increased support for the Radical movement. Nevertheless, the vote was so close that the result hung in the balance for three weeks awaiting returns from Missourians serving in the Union Army. On July 1, 1865 the official canvass showed a majority of 1,862 in favor of the new constitution out of 85,478 ballots cast. The soldiers had carried the day while the civilian population actually opposed the new constitution by 965 votes.[543] Opposition by German voters was evident in the election returns with only 31.1 percent of the eligible voters in St. Charles County voting for the Drake Constitution.[544] While the highest concentrations of opponents were in areas that had a high percentage of American slaveholders, like Wentzville. Voters in St. Charles and St. Peters, with large numbers of Germans, many of them Catholic, voted no by large margins. Only the heavily German and Protestant areas of Augusta, New Melle, Femme Osage and Schluersburg favored the Drake Constitution.

Polling Place	Constitutional Vote		
	For	Against	Total
St. Charles Courthouse	71	213	284
St. Charles Market House	72	286	358
St. Peters	2	100	102
Cottleville	57	76	133
Wentzville	15	153	168
Wellsburg	7	116	123
Portage des Sioux	8	85	93
Femme Osage	17	31	48
New Melle	132	6	138
Augusta	93	29	122
Schluersburg	38	8	46

To guarantee immediate control of the state by the Radicals, the constitution contained an "Ouster Ordinance" which declared vacant, as of May 1, 1865, the offices of all judges and clerks of the Missouri Supreme Court, the circuit courts, the county courts and the county clerks. One of the officials ousted in St. Charles County was John McDearmon, Democratic county clerk. Twenty years later the *History of St. Charles County* complained:

> The "Ousting Ordinance," presumably adopted to place the official position under the state government and the different counties in the hands of loyal men, but really to secure a general "divide" of all the offices among those who were making a profit, as well as a virtue, of loyalty. Mr. McDearmon was an earnest, consistent, unswerving union man all during the war, but had to give way, nevertheless, to influences that were interested in making it appear that he was disloyal.[545]

The "ironclad oath' guaranteed Radical control by prohibiting former Confederate sympathizers from, among other things, serving as grand jurors. In 1868 Federal District Judge Arnold Krekel was told by a prospective grand juror from Columbia that the only aid he had given the Confederacy was to retrieve his dying brother, who had been wounded serving in General Price's army. He concluded, "That was the only time I ever attempted to help anyone connected with the cause of the South." Judge Krekel replied, "Well Mr. Gentry, if you did that you are not qualified to serve on a United States grand jury. Stand aside."[546] The "ironclad oath" was also used to keep former Confederate sympathizers from voting in the 1866 elections. There were near riots in Wentzville when large numbers of ex-Confederates were not allowed to register to vote. Order was restored but the *Demokrat* warned:

> The Union people in Wentzville and surrounding areas fear very much that this appearance could be repeated in a more serious way. They live with anxiety and fear. The events throw a sharp light on the spirit of these ex-rebels and show what conditions will soon begin in St. Charles Co. if this class of people succeed in gaining the upper hand at the next elections.[547]

The impact of the ironclad oath in St. Charles County can be seen in the number of voters rejected in each precinct during the 1866 general election.

Precinct	eligible voters	rejected voters	percent rejected
Portage de Sioux	148	32	17.8
Augusta	187	9	0.6
Femme Osage	92	10	9.8
New Melle	194	15	7.2
St. Peters	116	8	6.4
Wilke's schoolhouse	51	6	10.5
Wentzville	135	118	46.6

Schluersburg	85	4	4.5
St. Charles	985	26	2.6
Cottleville	84	24	7.8
Wellsburg	165	10	5.7
Total	2442	262	9.7[548]

Conrad Weinrich reported in a letter on November 29, 1866, "I have been elected to the state legislature, and we elected the entire Radical Ticket without exception, and the conservatives are hanging their heads. I heard that two days after the election, the barbers in St. Charles were charging double the price to shave a conservative, because their faces are so long now."[549] After three years under Missouri's new constitution, the entire Radical Republican ticket swept to victory in November 1868, with General Ulysses S. Grant receiving 57 percent of the presidential vote in St. Charles County. The Radicals were at the zenith of their political power in Missouri and began to push through an agenda that included not only the franchise, but also full civil rights for African-Americans. In February 1865, they had passed a measure in the legislature allowing former slaves to come before a justice of the peace and have their previous unions registered as marriages and the children of those unions legitimized.[550] They attempted to give the franchise to the freedmen even before the passage of the 15th Amendment. Public schools were established for the freedmen and taxes were raised to support all public schools in the state. These proposals were revolutionary for the time and could not have commanded a majority if all Missouri men were allowed to vote. The Radical Republicans had resorted to anti-democratic means to achieve their results.

Not all Republicans shared the revolutionary social agenda of the Radicals. Even with large numbers of Missourians disenfranchised, the Radical Republicans were not able to overcome racist arguments used to defeat the amendment calling for black suffrage. The *Demokrat* complained that Negro equality, "is the bogeyman with which the Democrats would like to scare the people," and assured its readers, "Every person who does not wish contact with certain classes of people can easily stay away from them or keep them away."[551] In what Walter Kamphoefner believes was an attempt to discredit Conrad Weinrich, the *Anzeiger des Westens* reported, "Mr. Weinrich from New Melle, the radical candidate for the legislature [...] is said to have recently told some gentlemen that he regards the Negro as quite his equal in political and social terms. He also remarked that if four of his five daughters were to marry white men, and one married a Negro, he would treat his black son-in-law just like the white husbands of his other daughters."[552] While Weinrich was elected, only 39 percent of New Melle voters supported the referendum to grant voting rights to blacks. African-Americans in Missouri did not get the right to vote until the passage of the 15th Amendment to the U.S. Constitution in 1868.

Radical Republicans also lost further ground with Catholic voters. In 1865 many of the clergy had taken the ironclad oath; others could not. Peter Kenrick, the Archbishop of St. Louis, sent a pastoral letter to his priests deploring the oath and hoping that it would not be enforced among the clergy. He had refused to take the required oath to enable him to receive, on behalf of the church, a $20,000 legacy under the will of Mary Lamarque of Washington County. The Circuit Court of that county set the legacy aside as a violation of the Missouri constitution. After the Supreme Court upheld the decision of the Circuit Court, one Catholic prelate sermonized , "Under Radical rule in Missouri a horse thief… was competent to be a legatee, but not Peter Richard Kenrick, Archbishop of St. Louis."[553] John A. Cummings, a priest in Louisiana Missouri, took the archbishop's letter to heart and refused to take the oath. He preached as usual on Sunday morning, was indicted by the Grand Jury, appeared before a circuit judge, refused to post bond and demanded an immediate trial. At the trial he charged that the Radical Republicans were persecuting him because of anti-Catholic bias. After being convicted, his case was appealed all the way to the United States Supreme Court. The court, in a five to four decision, gave the Radical Republicans a serious setback when it declared the test oath provisions, as applied to professional groups, to be unconstitutional.[554].

The Radical Republicans suffered another setback in 1866. Missouri Senator John B. Henderson, along with seven other Republicans, had refused to vote to convict President Andrew Johnson at his impeachment trial. When Henderson was ousted as a result, Carl Schurz was elected to replace him. Schurz was a prominent Republican figure when he moved to St. Louis to become an editor of the *Westliche Post*, the largest German language newspaper in the state. He had come to the United States as a German émigré in the wake of the revolutions of 1848. He had been a key link between Lincoln and the German community and was equally adept at addressing audiences in English or German. He was chairman of the Missouri delegation at the Republican National Convention in Chicago in 1868, where he delivered the keynote address.[555]

When the legislature met in January, despite opposition from Drake, Schurz was elected U.S. senator on the first ballot. On March 1, 1868, having heard that the 15th Amendment assuring the vote for African-Americans had passed both houses of Congress, the Radicals in Jefferson City rushed through resolutions adopting the amendment.[556] Having achieved the Republican goal of universal male suffrage, Liberal Republicans, led by Carl Schurz, now insisted that it was time to end the "ironclad oath" and invite all Missourians back into the political process. With ratification of the 15th Amendment, and the likelihood that most African-Americans would vote Republican, even some Radicals began to listen.[557] The *Demokrat* suggested,

> But agitation for returning the voting rights to ex-rebels and their colleagues will be carried on stronger and harder. One can anticipate that all former political rights will again be valid, if not yet in next autumn's election then next year at the latest. Unfortunately, there are still many former rebels who carry the old anger and hate against the Unionists in their hearts and frequently express it openly. Nevertheless, the number of people who are for lifting the voting ban continually grows, even among the Radicals. And, in fact, if

Negro suffrage is introduced, the major reason for the voting ban disappears – this regulation was passed not as a punishment, not out of revenge, rather as an emergency measure against the defeated, but in no way destroyed, enemies of the union.[558]

William Grosvenor, editor of the *Missouri Democrat*, had managed Schurz' election to the U.S. Senate and was one of the leading Republicans in the state. He and Schurz now also parted company with the national Republicans over the tariff issue. Schurz had been fighting in the Senate against the high tariffs favored by the Grant administration to protect U.S. manufacturers from competition.[559] At an early date Grosvenor decided not to support Governor McClurg in his re-election bid in 1870. A staunch prohibitionist, McClurg had irritated the Germans by refusing to serve liquor at receptions at the Governor's Mansion. The Republican Party was headed for a split.

When the State Republican Convention refused to support re-enfranchisement in principle, wishing only to "recognize the right of any member of the party to vote his honest convictions," the Liberal Republicans left the hall of the House of Representatives and moved to the Senate chamber to establish their own party. They nominated Gratz Brown for governor on a platform dictated by Grosvenor to include re-enfranchisement, lower tariffs, civil service reform, tax reduction, and opposition to government subsidies to railroads. The *Demokrat* announced, "The Liberal Republican Party is the new party of progress which has the courage to break with the reactionaries and German-devourers. Its victory means the victory of progress, and undoubtedly the Germans, one and all, will stand with the party."[560] Seeing that the Liberals had embraced several of their issues, Democratic leaders endorsed Gratz Brown and did not run a candidate of their own.[561]

More than 160,000 Missouri voters went to the polls on Election Day in 1870 as the Liberal Republican ticket swept to a smashing victory. Gratz Brown swamped McClurg by 40,000 votes statewide and by 2,190 votes in St. Charles County. The Democrats contended that they probably contributed two-thirds of his total vote. The Democrats did well in the congressional and state legislative races. They carried 77 of the 138 seats in the Missouri House and, with the Liberal Republicans, could control the State Senate.[562] They elected John McDearmon, a Democrat who had been ousted from the post in 1865, as county clerk of St. Charles County. A.H. Edwards, also a Democrat, was elected state representative.[563] The *St. Charles News* warned, "we now have a Democratic legislature and the governor is pledged to Democratic principles, and the moment he fails to carry out those pledges he is wise enough to know he has signed his political death warrant. Therefore we have, in reality, a Democratic administration."[564]

Constitutional amendments, including one lifting the "iron clad oath," passed by overwhelming majorities; but discussion of the disenfranchisement of so many Missourians continued for a long time. Responding to an article by Friedrich Muench, a highly respected Republican leader, the *St. Charles News* regretted that he had, "within his bosom a simmering hatred of 'rebels,' as though there were still any 'rebels,' to hate."[565] Muench responded:

The constitution excludes none but the direct and indirect aiders and abettors of the late rebellion. In fact it is an unwarranted provocation to place that class of our citizens as " the best and most faithful" in opposition to the others who, with their lives and property, supported the cause. If the Democrats continue to assert that it was a crying injustice on the part of the loyal citizens of Missouri to take the work of reconstructing our state into their own hands, while war was still raging, and to exclude those who even then were in arms against the state government, we must reply that, in the name of common sense, they could not have acted otherwise.[566]

The *St. Charles News* called for the election of Frank Blair, who had returned to the Democratic Party, to replace Charles Drake in the U.S. Senate and he was elected.[567] The future of the Democratic Party in Missouri was now assured.

In St. Charles County, where incumbent Republican Governor McClurg received less than 11 percent of the vote, most Republicans supported the Liberals. Appealing to them, the *St. Charles News* stated:

I believe Senator Schurz represents the sentiments of a majority of the Germans of the West, and it is well known to this large and influential class of our fellow citizens that the Democratic Party has always been a staunch friend and defender. All want to forget the terrible issues of the war, let us unite our forces against the monopolies of the East in order that we may the better work for the good of our people again, General Schurz is with the Democrats on the tariff question, and when we throw the "dead nigger" away, he is with us on every question.[568]

Further trying to exploit the split in Republican ranks, the Democrat-leaning *St. Charles News* reported, "liberty loving Germans of our county would not much longer submit to the narrow and one-sided views of the radical Party, but would demand the real enfranchisement of their old neighbors and friends."[569] The *Demokrat* demanded that the Republican Party remain the party of progress and support civil service reform, introduction of the one-term principle, and abolition of protective tariffs.[570] Fourteen months later the paper had a new owner and announced that, in the future, it would be "unhindered by political cliques."[571]

While the Republican Party was committing political suicide in Missouri, its position nationally was also beginning to erode. While Republicans controlled the U.S. Senate for seven of the ten sessions of Congress between 1875 and 1895, they had a majority in the House of Representatives only twice during that period. Their presidential candidate did not receive a majority in any of the elections between 1876 and 1892. The Republicans controlled Congress and the presidency only during the 51st Congress and by 1892 their share of the national vote had dropped to 43 percent.[572] The Democratic Party controlled the presidency and both houses of Congress simultaneously only in the 1893-1895 session. Historian Paul Kleppner, in his work *The Cross of Culture, A Social Analysis of Midwestern Politics, 1850-1900*, concludes that Republican strength in the Midwest declined perceptibly between 1860 and 1892. He concludes, "This decline did not elevate the Democrats to a majority position. Instead, the two parties attained a relatively even balance in which neither was able to command an electoral majority."[573] This political stalemate existed in St. Charles County as well. The *History of St. Charles County* explained that only since 1882 had parties made regular party nominations and stated, "up to a few years ago, party nominations were rarely made by either party. This is attributed to the fact that the parties were so evenly balanced and the candidates prefer to run unhampered by party nominations, alone on personal merits and popularity."[574]

In 1872 the Liberal Republicans nominated Horace Greeley and Gratz Brown and the Democrats did likewise. In St. Charles County a Greeley and Brown Club was formed. Reporting on one of its meetings at New Melle in October 1872, the *Demokrat* called attention to the fact that, "the old pillars of radicalism in this region, men who formerly would not have missed any radical meeting and always belonged to the prominent voices, stand today on the side of reform, peace and insight."[575] The paper reported prior to the election, "People who voted for Grant in 1868, and still for McClurg in 1870, are now for Greeley and Brown and are decisive opponents of all that smells like Grant."[576]

Although it lost nationally, the ticket did well in Missouri, with most of its support coming from Democrats. Liberal Republicans gathered at Cottleville and Schurz, Friedrich Muench, Wm. Follenius and Emil Pretorius were invited to speak.[577] The presence of Greeley and Brown on the Liberal Republican ticket explains why they received 52 percent in St. Charles County. Many of the original Liberal bolters returned to the Republican Party, especially in counties with large German populations. In the presidential returns the trend was not as noticeable because of the German dislike for both Grant and Greeley.[578] Much of the dislike for Grant had developed when the administration sold arms to France during the Franco-Prussian War. Closer to home, even though Gratz Brown had been elected Governor and Carl Schurz remained Senator from Missouri, Grant allowed the defeated Radical Republicans to continue to control federal patronage in the state. Schurz had broken with the administration on annexation of the island of Santo Domingo and on its Reconstruction policy. The dislike for Greeley was because he was a prohibitionist, anathema to the Germans. [579]

St. Charles County Democrat A.H. Edward was elected in 1874 to the Missouri Senate district that included St. Charles and Warren counties. Callaway and Montgomery counties were later added to the district, insuring that it would continue to be held by Edwards. Although a strong two-party system continued in St. Charles County for the next two decades, as the Radical Republicans had predicted, after 1872 the Democrats dominated statewide elections for the next 35 years. In 1874 Charles Henry Hardin of Audrain County was the Democratic nominee for governor, and

William Gentry, a Pettis County farmer, was nominated by the Republican and People's Parties. Hardin's victory mirrored the next two gubernatorial elections, receiving his strongest support from those Missourians whose families, like Hardin's, had come from Kentucky. While Southwest Missouri voted Republican, the Democrats carried every county in the other three quadrants of the state except Adair, Andrew, Atchison, Caldwell, Dekalb, Grundy, Mercer and Putnam, where large numbers of citizens traced their ancestry to northern states; and Gasconade, Osage, Perry, Warren and St. Charles, where significant German populations resided.[580]

In St. Charles County most of the former Liberal Republicans eventually found their way back to the Republican Party and opposed the "present misgovernment of the Bourbon Democrats (Southern Conservatives)...."[581] The exception was the *Demokrat*, which reverted to advocating Democratic principles and Democrats for president such as Tilden in 1876, Hancock in 1880 and Cleveland in 1884.[582] The *Demokrat* regretted that almost all the Liberal Republicans had returned to the Republican Party by 1876.[583] To a large extent, political alignments in St. Charles County reflected statewide alignments in which Missourians voted for the political arm of the army in which their fathers had fought. Republicans could count on support from black voters. They complained that naming the Democratic state officeholders in 1886 was "like calling the roll of the Confederate army." Among circuit court judges and state legislators elected in 1890, all 27 Confederate veterans were Democrats.[584]

Civil War veterans dominated politics in St. Charles County after the war. A former provost marshal, Captain Francis Marten, served on the St. Charles City Council and school board; Captain John Hackman was elected mayor of St. Charles in 1884; and First Lieutenant J. Philipp Hoehn served as city councilman, marshal, collector and treasurer. Veterans were also among the leaders of the political parties. Democratic leaders included Colonel John K, McDearmon, who held the office of county clerk from 1872 until 1886, and Major James Edwards, the Democratic chairman of the Congressional District Committee. McDearmon had served in the Home Guards, but Edwards had been a Confederate officer.[585] Anglo-Americans dominated the leadership and composed much of the membership of the Democratic Party. The *St. Charles County Portrait and Biographical Record*, published in 1895, lists 74 non-Germans, 68 of which are identified as supporting a political party. Fifty-eight were Democrats. Of the ten who were not, four were from north of the Mason-Dixon Line, and one was born in France. Five of the 68 were from Pennsylvania or Ohio; the rest were from Kentucky, Virginia, Maryland, North Carolina or Tennessee.[586] Typical of the group was John Jay Johns, a native of Virginia who came to St. Charles County in 1846. He moved from his farm near Point Prairie to St. Charles in 1851. A graduate of Miami University of Ohio and an elder in the Presbyterian Church, he was a leader of the Democratic Party in the county.[587]

Veterans also led the Republican Party. Captain John F. Dierker was elected sheriff and collector of St. Charles County. Former members of the Home Guard were elected to several local offices. Captain Charles Daudt was state representative for one term and was, for many years, chairman of the Republican County Committee. Captain Gustave

Aging veterans from St. Charles County are shown here at a GAR meeting. *John J. Buse Collection, 1860-1931, Western Historical Manuscript Collection-Columbia, MO.*

Bruere was elected county clerk in 1866 and served for the next six years. Lieutenant Henry Machens was sheriff of St. Charles County from 1867 until 1871. Captain John Hollrah served as presiding judge of the County Court from 1866 until 1874. Lieutenant Frederick Grabenhorst was a popular state representative from St. Charles County during the 1880's. After serving in the Home Guards, Henry F. Pieper served as county treasurer from 1878-1884. John Henry Stumberg, who had served as a surgeon with the 29th Missouri Infantry during the Civil War, was elected state representative in 1900.[588]

Most of the Lutheran and Evangelical Germans had returned to the Republican Party by 1876. In other states in the Midwest the German Lutherans did not form a cohesive Republican voting block and, even in St. Charles County, Henry Bode, the editor of the now pro-Democratic *Demokrat*, belonged to the Immanuel Lutheran Church. However, an analysis of the *St. Charles County Portrait and Biographical Record* shows that of the 44 individuals who were identified as Lutherans and gave a political preference, 41 were identified as Republicans and only one as a Democrat.[589] Orchard Farm, New Melle and Harvester, all with Lutheran Churches, registered consistently high majorities for Republican candidates. Clearly the Missouri Synod Lutherans in St. Charles County were heavily Republican.

R. Hal Williams believes, "Religious views, especially the tension between liturgicals and pietists, strongly shaped political alignments in the late nineteenth century."[590] He explains that liturgical denominations, like the Catholic Church, stressed the rituals and institutions of the church, assigning responsibility for individual salvation and morality to the church. They consequently restricted the role of the state in prescribing personal morality, a position consistent with Democratic traditions that also limited state authority. Members of pietist denominations were comfortable with the Republican Party's activist outlook. Pietistic Methodists, Presbyterians, Baptists and others downplayed church ritual and believed in individual salvation evidenced by proper behavior. They believed the state was an appropriate instrument to insure that behavior by promoting prohibition, Sunday-closing laws, and other measures.[591] Paul Kleppner suggests that Missouri Synod Lutherans, where pietism had a greater influence, were more likely to be Republican than those of the more liturgical Wisconsin Synod.[592] Kleppner explains that Wisconsin Synod Lutherans considered the Missouri Synod essentially Calvinistic and subversive of "true" Lutheranism.[593]

German Evangelicals were even more influenced by pietism than the Missouri Synod Lutherans.[594] Political commentator Kevin Phillips concludes that this pietism emphasized, "the individualism, pursuit of redemption, and reform so characteristic of pro-Republican U.S. Protestant denominations."[595] He concludes, "German Evangelicals and Methodists – more pietistic and concerned about personal redemption, social reform, and eradication of sin – were the most Republican, resembling the Yankee and Protestant Evangelicals in their commitment to Temperance, Sabbath-keeping, and distaste for slavery."[596] Indeed, of the 26 Evangelicals in the *St Charles County Portrait and Biographical Record* whose political preference was identified, 21 were also identified as Republicans. Likewise, all three German Methodists were Republicans.[597]

According to historian Paul Kleppner, German Lutherans, regardless of synodical affiliation, voted more Republican when they were in the same community with German Catholics. Their religious differences trumped their ethnic similarities, leading the Lutherans to avoid the Democratic Party since the German Catholics were solidly Democratic.[598] Like the Lutherans, the German Evangelicals also took the German Catholics as a negative referent and voted Republican.[599]

In the presidential race of 1876, Republicans "waved the bloody shirt," attempting to link the Democrats with secession. Democrat Samuel Tilden won St. Charles County by 450 votes over Republican Rutherford B Hayes. Tilden also won the popular vote nationally, but fell one vote short of a majority in the Electoral College, with 19 electoral votes from Florida, South Carolina and Louisiana in dispute. In January 1877 Congress set up a 15-member commission, five senators, five representatives and five members of the Supreme Court, to investigate and report its findings. In the end, Hayes became president after a deal was stuck where the Republicans agreed to end Reconstruction in the South. John Jay Johns, a St. Charles County Democrat, wrote, "The Electoral Commission has completed its work and counted in

Hayes as President. A Most Iniquitous business. A President put in by fraud. The members of the Supreme Court degrading themselves to mere partisans. Refusing to inquire into the fraud of the Louisiana Returning Board which threw out 10,000 Tilden votes."[600]

The vote for Tilden showed that not all the Germans in the county had returned to the Republican Party. Of the 36 Catholics identified in the *Portrait and Biographical Record*, only two priest were not identified as the member of a political party and only six Catholics were not identified as Democrats. German Catholic Democrats included Louis Meyer, postmaster of Dardenne, Captain Henry Denker, three-term St. Charles county treasurer, Louis Brecker, mayor of St. Charles, John Steiner, county sheriff; and Henry Kemper, county collector.[601] In spite of the declining percentage of Anglo-Americans after the Civil War, German Catholics kept the Democratic Party competitive in St. Charles County through the 1892 election.

Catholic support for the Democratic Party was rooted in German history, their own American experiences and social issues growing out of theological differences with American Protestants. Many of the German Catholics had arrived after German unification in 1870. Their resentment of the Protestant Prussian State had been further inflamed by the *Kulturkampf* of the 1870s, an unsuccessful attempt by Bismarck and the Liberals to destroy Catholic power in the new German Empire. Bismarck's efforts were thwarted by Ludwig Windthorst, a Catholic leader, who formed the Center Party in Germany to protect Catholic schools, hospitals and other institutions from state control.[602] It was natural for German Catholics to turn to a single political party to protect their institutions in their new homeland against German Liberals in the Republican Party. During the nativist attacks of the 1850s, Catholics of German origin suffered more at the hands of German Liberals than at the hands of old stock Americans.[603] In 1885 the *History of St. Charles County* stated:

> Democrats have always thought a little hard on this, in as much as it was they who saved the Germans from outlawry and stood up for the protection of their rights, including full citizenship; and that the Germans should then turn on them in the South and assist to take their slave property from them without compensation – moreover even to put their slaves to rule over them in many of the states, seemed a little ungrateful.[604]

After the Civil War, German Catholics returned to the Democratic Party. This was true throughout the Midwest, irrespective of residence, wealth or occupation. Of all the precincts studied by Paul Kleppner, no German Catholic precinct abandoned the Democrats between 1875 and 1888.[605] Their allegiance to the Democratic Party was strengthened in Missouri where Republicans Carl Schurz, Friedrich Muench, Julius Mallinckrodt and Arnold Krekel were sworn enemies of the Catholic Church; Radical Republican Charles Drake tried to tax church property; Governor McClurg did not approve of their beer gardens; and State Superintendent of Schools Parker wanted to ensure that no state revenue went to the parochial schools to which they sent their children. Many German Liberals had supported the revolutions of 1830 or 1848 in Europe before coming to Missouri. Since the Catholic Church had supported the monarchists and opposed those revolutions, anti-clericalism was characteristic of the German Liberals. In 1844, 38 members of the Friends of Religious Enlightenment had gathered in Augusta to found the Association of Rational Christians. Friedrich Muench and Julius Mallinckrodt were elected president and secretary respectively, while Arnold Krekel was elected a director. Its program had reflected, "fear not only of synodical encroachments but also of the wave of revivalism sweeping the area after the economic crises of the 1830s and 1840s. The association had warned against 'irrationality,' 'superstition,' and things 'specifically miraculous.'"[606] Muench was a frequent contributor to the *Hermann Licht-Freund,* a rationalist journal and his *Treatise on Religion and Christianity, Orthodoxy and Rationalism*, was translated into English in 1847.[607] More conservative members of the 1865 Constitutional Convention considered Arnold Krekel a, "pure radical who wished to make the new constitution a reflection of German liberal doctrine in politics and religion."[608] The Jesuit pastor of St. Charles Borromeo wrote in 1853:

> But I must say that our congregation would be much more flourishing and pious were it not for a multitude of German radicals and infidels that came to reside in St. Charles, where they established an infidel and radical association called the freemen's society, with a library and reading room for the dissemination of their principles. It is not, however, that they do harm by their learning or talents, because they have no extraordinary man among them; but they have good strong, capacious lungs, they can talk loud and boldly, laugh and ridicule every kind of religion, teach a doctrine apparently easier than ours, and by demoralizing people they are far more injurious than all the sophisms of Rousseau, Kant and many others of the same gang.[609]

Generally, the American Catholic hierarchy during this period followed the Vatican and attacked abolitionists, free-soilers and various Protestant Reform movements as the equivalent of "Red Republicanism" in Europe.[610] Additionally, many American Catholics shared the fear of their Irish co-religionists who were competing with African-Americans at the bottom of the social order and who, before the Civil War, were strongly opposed to the abolition of slavery. Since the Irish tended to dominate the hierarchy of the church, Irish views often became the rule, especially in St. Louis where the Irishman Peter Kenrick served as archbishop.[611] The Jesuit Pastor of St. Charles Borromeo from 1851-1868, Father Peter J. Verhaegen, did not have to rely on the Irish churchmen. The intellectual equal of the freethinkers, he had served on the faculty of St. Louis University and as president of a Jesuit university in Kentucky. He wrote, "The town of St. Charles has a population of 2,000 souls. And for so small a town it has a large share of bigoted infidels and apostates. These people have succeeded in exciting prejudice against the Church. With such enemies we must deal prudently but strenuously."[612] To counteract the impact of the Freemen's Library he started a library at Borromeo that had 1,716 books in 1885.[613]

Historian David Thelen notes, "Missourians mobilized the quest for offices around ethnic and sectional loyalties, not wealth or occupation. Voters subordinated candidates' claims to the all-important mission of aiding the party as the agency to protect their cultures."[614] The German Catholics looked to the Democratic Party to protect them, not only against the German Liberals, but also the Lutherans and Evangelicals of the Republican Party that was now pushing other divisive cultural issues like temperance, Sunday closing laws, public schools and required English instruction in schools.[615] Members of American pietistic denominations favored prohibition of alcohol, especially on Sunday. They agreed with local Presbyterian Elder John Jay Johns, "It is impossible to estimate the evils of whiskey and beer, nothing but a Divine Power can destroy them. The great source of evil is the saloon, shut them up and more than half the evil will cease."[616] Most Germans were opposed to the "Puritan Sunday" and even those who were religious did not see alcohol as a moral issue. They observed the "Continental Sunday" that might include a trip to a wine garden or church picnic where beer was served.[617] When the Fourth of July fell on a Sunday in 1880, Johns further observed, "The governor has appointed tomorrow to be observed as the legal Fourth or holiday. But the German Societies have their celebration today. They hold very loose ideas of the Sabbath, both Catholic and Lutheran."[618]

As before, the Republican Party again identified with the pietistic groups in the 1880s and lost support among Germans, especially Catholics. Attitudes toward alcohol had been a cultural difference between German immigrants and many Americans since the 1830s. State Representative Conrad Weinrich wrote in 1868, "The Sunday laws have been made even worse again, but I hope that the bill won't pass the Senate. The Sunday bigots and temperance supporters are hard at work here, but I hope they won't get far with their absurd bigotry."[619] The *Demokrat* applauded State Senator Theodore Bruere in 1869 for legislation allowing wine farmers to sell their wine in any quantity they wished without a license. At the same time the paper lamented that innkeepers had to get the permission of a certain number of their neighbors to obtain a liquor license. The *Demokrat* regretted, "All licensed inn-keepers, therefore, in coalition with all water-drinkers and hypocrites, will do everything possible to again destroy the generally good law."[620] When temperance forces could not prohibit alcohol, they worked to ban its sale on Sundays. As early as December 1855, the *Demokrat* editorialized concerning the recently passed Sunday closing law:

> There certainly will be much resistance to the law just passed by the Missouri Legislature withdrawing innkeepers' licenses if they sell alcoholic beverages on Sunday. The Sunday law may now have lost general value and effectiveness because it is exploited by ministers in whose interest it was passed.…. But if our legislature goes further and intends to prescribe the morality of the people, one might well ask who gave our representatives such a guardianship over us.[621]

The *Demokrat*, noting temperance victories in Ohio, Indiana and Illinois, reported an 1873 temperance convention in Jefferson City and warned that Missouri would have to fight the movement at the voting booths.[622] To take advantage of German dissatisfaction with the Republican temperance position, the Democratic *St. Charles Journal* published a temperance speech by the Republican governor of Kansas, in which he stated, "We now look to the future, not forgetting that it was here on our soil that the first blow was given that finally resulted in the emancipation of a race from slavery. We have now determined upon a second emancipation, which shall free not only the body but the soul of man."[623] The *Journal* noted that drinking was not a crime and outlawing alcohol could not be justified.[624] On February 8, 1872, the Democratic *St. Charles News*, in reference to temperance laws proposed by Republicans, suggested that the Republican Party:

The beer stand at a church picnic was a popular place for thirsty German-American men. Many of their non-German neighbors favored prohibition of alcohol, at least on Sundays. *John J. Buse Collection, 1860-1931, Western Historical Manuscript Collection-Columbia, MO.*

…would give evidence of having entirely forgotten the unanimous patriotic services rendered by the German element of this state to maintain the position of Missouri in the union, in time of severe trauma, and at time requiring all physical and mental energy of a race, not then, and not now enervated by dissipation, who need no guardians and curators to tell them what to drink or what to eat.[625]

In 1880 the *Demokrat* criticized the Republican presidential victor, James Garfield, because he was connected with the Credit Mobilier scandal and was a tee-totaler. After Garfield's assassination the *Demokrat* was pleased with his successor Chester Arthur who, "long ago attracted the hate of the temperance supporters because in the White House he too follows the custom of a European cosmopolitan."[626] The *Demokrat* observed in 1880:

Now the Germans, and generally all adopted citizens, have always felt themselves more drawn to the Democratic than the Republican Party because the former was the friend of immigration. The latter, because of its nativism, Know-Nothingism, temperance and Sunday laws, always showed a clear rejection of immigrants and made life as bitter for them as possible.[627]

Senator Carl Schurz from Missouri had made civil service reform a national issue. In the 1884 presidential election, Democrat Grover Cleveland promised to carry out such a program if elected and Schurz led a non-partisan movement on Cleveland's behalf. Some historians believe that, without Schurz' support, Cleveland probably would not have been elected.[628] In the closing days of the campaign, a Protestant minister at a public gathering denounced the Democrats as the party of "Rum, Romanism, and Rebellion." These four words implied that immigrants drank too much, the Catholic Church was evil, and the Civil War was the fault of the Democrats. Blaine blundered in failing to condemn the statement immediately. [629] The Democrats took advantage of this fact and, with a large Catholic turnout, Blaine still received a slim majority in St. Charles County, but Cleveland became the first Democratic president in 24 years.

Parochial schools and German language issues also hurt the Republican Party among Germans in the 1880s. Throughout the country political disputes arose over the use of public school funds, Protestant Bible reading in public schools, free textbooks, the use of Catholic nuns as teachers in the public schools, and the language of instruction in parochial schools.[630] In Missouri, the battle over the public school fund had ended when a constitutional amendment banning public funding for parochial schools was overwhelmingly approved in 1870. In the most Catholic county, Osage, 34.6 percent opposed the amendment; in St. Louis County it was 16.9 percent. In St. Charles County the vote against the amendment was 13.7 percent, about the same as the average of the ten most Catholic counties.[631] In the 1876 presidential campaign, the Republican platform favored an amendment to the U.S. Constitution that would have prohibited the use of public funds to support parochial schools. The proposed amendment remained part of the Republican agenda into the 1880's.[632]

Parochial schools like St. Peter's Parish grade school kept the German language alive. *John J. Buse Collection, 1860-1931, Western Historical Manuscript Collection-Columbia, MO.*

Statutes in Wisconsin and Illinois required that English be the principle language in every school. Both Catholic and Lutheran Germans hated these laws, which had a devastating impact on the German vote for the Republican Party in Wisconsin and Illinois. In 1887 the Missouri legislature redrew the St. Louis School Board districts in such a way as to minimize the number of Germans elected. John Jay Johns, who had served as the first public school commissioner in St. Charles County in 1854, made the following entry in his diary: "This is the day of the election in St. Louis for public school Directors to decide whether German should be taught in the public schools any longer. The teaching (of) German or any other foreign language is an outrage. The public system was established to teach our children the common rudimentary branches of an English education."[633] The newly elected board ended German language instruction in the city's schools. Although laws in Missouri required the use of English in certain legal and business documents, efforts requiring the use of English in parochial schools were unsuccessful. Most parochial schools in St. Charles County continued to teach at least part of the day in German.[634]

Nationwide, the temporary exodus of some Germans from the Republican Party certainly contributed to Cleveland's election in 1892. These defections meant that the Republican presidential candidate that year, Benjamin Harrison, won St. Charles County by only 37 votes. Cleveland won the non-German precincts of Mechanicsville, Foristell and Wentzville. He also won the German-Catholic precincts of Josephville, Dardenne, St. Paul, St. Peters and Portage des Sioux.[635] Having freed the slaves and preserved the Union, the Republican Party had been torn apart by internal divisions in Missouri. Even in a county like St. Charles, whose German population had been solidly behind the Union during the Civil War, the Republican Party managed only slim majorities in three of the five presidential elections between 1872 and 1892. It had become bogged down in social issues, taking positions contrary to the beliefs of most German immigrants and their children. As a result, Republican majorities dwindled in St. Charles County and nationally. Summing up the 1892 election, historian Richard Jensen states:

> The basic weakness of the GOP was that it was a shelter for the Pietistic Reformers who harped on divisive cultural issues. The Party weakened all along the line, but especially among the immigrants. Only if the professionals could curb the moralistic crusading of the amateurs, or if new issues would appear, could the GOP recover control of the Midwest and the nation.[636]

C. Successful Economic Revolution of the Radical Republicans

After the Civil War Radical Republicans hoped to replace the traditional slaveholding society of the South with the progressive free labor society of the North. Germans in St. Charles County were entirely behind these revolutionary economic changes. The large inefficient plantations based on slavery gave way to an efficient system of small farms, owned and worked by free men, the overwhelming majority of which were Germans. Meanwhile, the many non-German small farmers who had never owned slaves, continued to look to the frontier and sold their small farms to newly arrived German immigrants. German settlers also supported Radical Republican efforts to finish the railroads that had been started before the Civil War. Finally, the German farmer benefited from technological changes that increased agricultural productivity and allowed for international marketing of farm products.

St. Charles County's close proximity to St. Louis meant that its economic fate was closely linked to the fate of that city. After 1850 the Yankee-dominated business class of St. Louis continued to promote economic development. In addition, businessmen of Southern origin worked to keep Missouri in the Union because they realized it was in their interest to do so.[637] Men from both groups continued to influence the commercial development of St. Charles County, where the population had reached 16,523 according to the 1860 census. While the *St. Charles County Portrait and Biographical Record*, published in 1895, lists only 10 of 74 Anglo-Americans with family roots above the Mason-Dixon line, seven of them were involved in non-agricultural pursuits including brick manufacturing, real estate, insurance, riverboat captain, ferry engineer and railroad engineer. State Senator William Allen, a resident of Wentzville, was instrumental in obtaining a charter for the North Missouri Railroad, the incorporators for which were primarily from St. Charles County.[638] Former Supreme Court Justice Barton Bates, son of Virginia-bred Edward Bates, served on the Board of Directors of the corporation that built the Eads Bridge in St. Louis.[639]

What St. Charles County lacked in American business initiative, it more than made up for with its German population. Of the 118 Germans mentioned in the *History of St. Charles County* in 1885, 53 were listed as "merchants." But the first revolutionary economic changes in St. Charles County did not occur in business, but in agriculture; the Germans were the leaders of that revolution that affected ownership, labor and farming methods.

The Germans who immigrated to St. Charles County before 1850 had come primarily for economic reasons. Three-fourths of them came from the northwestern part of Germany, with Hanover providing the most, while the adjoining German States of Oldenberg and Brunswick provided the next largest concentrations. Many also came from the Prussian province of Mechlenburg, which bordered on Hannover.[640] Before the 1830s this entire area had a thriving cottage linen industry. Families spun and wove linen cloth in the home to supplement the family's income from their small agricultural plots. The Industrial Revolution, with its machines and factory system, put the linen spinners out of business. Historian Walter Kamphoeffner suggests that this made it nearly impossible for families to make a living on the small tracts of land that were common in this part of Germany, thus prompting large numbers of people to leave Germany.[641] The American publishers of the *History of St. Charles County* already recognized by 1885 that the German immigrants "caused barren hillsides to blossom with grapevines and fruit trees, and opened large farms in the midst of dense forests. Swamps and marshes were drained and fertile fields took the place of stagnant ponds...."[642]

Even though two-thirds of adult males in St. Charles County in 1850 were farmers, there was a good deal of specialization in the German occupational structure.[643] Numerous *Heuerleute* had been artisans such as carpenters or blacksmiths to supplement the meager incomes they derived from farming in Germany.[644] They were land hungry when they arrived in St. Charles County and constituted the highest percentage of landowners in every economic category in the 1850 census.[645] Kamphoeffner has analyzed the 1850 census and found German farmers were unique. Their households tended to be smaller and less likely to be headed by females. Custom dictated that a father would turn his estate over to a son and the father would move out of the main house to a special cottage. While other Americans viewed land as an unlimited commodity and took land ownership for granted, German immigrants accustomed to land scarcity in Europe, put a higher value on land ownership. The value of German-owned real estate in St. Charles County in 1850 was less than half that of the Americans and barely exceeded that of the farmers of French descent. However, more than half the men of German descent owned at least a small plot of land.[646]

The 1850 census, for the first time, had a detailed inventory of crops and livestock. Having arrived later, the average German farmer in St. Charles County was not as well off as his American neighbor. The median German holding was only 25 improved acres, with twice as much unimproved land as non-Germans. Germans were more likely to grow potatoes, just as likely to grow corn, and not nearly as likely to grow tobacco as were their American neighbors. Tobacco was grown by one-fifth of the American farmers but by very few Germans. Only five percent of Germans, and 15 percent of their neighbors, did without potatoes. Only three percent of the Germans in St. Charles County grew any rye. Surprisingly, of the dozen winegrowers, half were non-Germans, and German brewers apparently bought their hops from six American growers. While the value of implements per unit of improved land was higher for the Germans, this was probably due to their small holdings and lack of slaves to share in the work, rather than greater intensity in their agriculture.[647]

Kamphoeffner concludes that the distinctive agriculture of the German farmer had not yet proved superior to that of his neighbors as of 1850.[648] Because of their determination to have a piece of land they could call their own, Germans were forced to farm the less productive land. By 1860, Friedrich Muench recorded in the *Demokrat*:

> The hill land which the Germans bought with a lot of money – and had to cultivate with almost overwhelming effort because the Americans called the fat meadows and rich bottom lands theirs – became a good source of income through the industrious, active hands of their cultivators. The Germans were proud of their property.[649]

Many families in the Northwest German states had supplemented their incomes by spinning and weaving linen cloth in their homes. These students at Immanuel Lutheran School in 1916 recall the time their grandmothers spent at the spinning wheel. *John J. Buse Collection, 1860-1931, Western Historical Manuscript Collection-Columbia, MO.*

German farmers eventually gained a reputation for practicing a distinctive type of agriculture. Because of population density European agriculture was more labor-intensive than American. Since most fields had been cultivated for generations and the land that was available was of marginal quality, German farmers put greater emphasis on maintaining fertility. When they arrived in St. Charles County, the immigrants were familiar with such progressive techniques as planting clover to add nitrogen and applying lime to reduce soil acidity. They already practiced a complicated system of crop rotation and they were more aware than other Americans of the value of animal manure.[650] According to Kamphoeffner, a common saying of the day was, "Prayer and manure will not be in vain." The punch line was that "manure will help for sure."[651]

Kamphoeffner suggests that Germans quickly adapted to the geographical conditions and adopted many American crop-farming techniques. Germans, however, "drew the line" when it came to adopting the tobacco culture and slavery.[652] Out of more than 1,000 German heads of families in 1850, only 17 owned slaves. None of their slave holdings were large and involved only one slave in half the cases.[653] Slaveholding among the Americans remained substantial as the Civil War started with the largest slaveholders in the county being Colonel John Pitman of Dardenne Township (23), Captain John Woodson of Callaway Township (25), Francis Howell of Dardenne Township (23), Judge Daniel Griffith of St. Charles Township (23) and Major Nathan Herald of Dardenne Township (20).[654]

The Germans favored the emancipation of slaves in Missouri during and after the Civil War because it was in their economic self-interest to do so. Carl Schurz proclaimed "a free labor society must be established and built on the ruins of the slave-labor society."[655] By 1864 the *Demokrat* reported:

> Those among our fellow citizens who until now owned slaves and cultivated their farms with them, increasingly try to change their residence and activities to adjust to the new order of things. Through this change a good deal of valuable land is put on the market – more than those living here can use. Thus, immigration becomes a very inviting matter.[656]

Robert Sandfort, in his work *Hermann Heinrich Sandfort, Farmer and Furniture-Maker from Hahlen, Germany*, relates the fate of the Griffith plantation and its owner, Judge Daniel Griffith, during the Civil War and after. In the 1860s, one industrious man and his family could farm around 100 acres. The Griffith family, in the traditions of the southern aristocracy, bought slaves to do the actual farming and domestic work on their 1,200-acre plantation. The Griffith family saw its 17 slaves run away, enlist in the Union army or become emancipated in 1865. Harassed by Unionists during the Civil War because of its southern sympathies, the family was forced to continue to sell parcels of land to German immigrants. Before the war they had sold land to Dietrich Thoele, John George Pfaff, Jacob Peters, Hermann Osthoff, Henry Gronefeld, Johann Dietrich Zumbehl and Johann Dietrich Hollrah. After the war, major portions of the plantation were sold to Hermann Dennigmann, Hermann Dietrich Boenker, Hermann Dietrich Ehlmann, Hermann J. Bruns,

Bernard Wilmer, Henry Ermeling, Henry Bruns, George Schierding, Hermann Arnold Hesskamp, Johann Wilhelm Hafferkamp and Hermann Dietrich Sandfort.[657] The same was true of the Bel Aire Plantation. After most of the slaves ran off and joined the Union Army, Dr. William McElhiney, a former Democratic politician, sold his land to German immigrants and moved to South Main Street in St. Charles.[658] Whig turned Republican, George Robards Buckner, moved with his family and 32 slaves to a 900-acre farm in Dardenne Township in 1858. He paid $17,500 for his farm and sold it after emancipation in three parcels for about $34,000.[659] In this manner many of the larger plantations in the hands of Anglo-Americans became small homesteads giving German immigrant farmer a chance to farm some of the best land in the county.

German families replaced the American families who had never sunk very deep roots anyplace and were always ready to sell out and move on to escape closer settlement, or to make a profit.[660] This mobility of the American farmers, originally due to the habit developed in Virginia of farming the land to exhaustion and moving further west to new lands, was now further encouraged by the end of slavery.[661] Emancipation led to the demise of tobacco agriculture since "farmers no longer had slaves to do the tedious work of planting, picking, spreading, drying the natural weed...."[662] The tobacco harvest in Missouri shrank from a high of 25 million pounds in 1860 to 8.5 million pounds in 1890. The Methodist Church in Flint Hill closed its doors and moved to Troy, in Lincoln County. As slavery and the tobacco culture were replaced by a market-driven agriculture, conducted by free men, one contemporary Anglo-American came to believe, "the day of the Southern man was nearly over in St. Charles County."[663]

Unlike the American farmer, the German farmer was in St. Charles County for the long haul. In 1976, of the 37 "Centennial Farms" in St. Charles County, farms that had been in the same family for 100 years, 32 belonged to families of German descent.[664] At an early stage the *Demokrat* boasted of the farming skills of the Germans:

> While the German is accustomed from home (Germany) to rational land use and thereby thinks not only of the moment but rather cares for the future, so one finds a distinctly exhaustive use of the soil by Americans. Among them there is little conservation to be found. The present is everything; the future can take care of itself. As an unavoidable consequence of this false use of agriculture, those counties with a large German population now show the greatest progress; where the American population dominates there is little movement forward. Through his exhaustive agriculture the American exploits the land until it stops being productive. Then he sells it and moves westward and there the entire drama is repeated.[665]

Just as the French had fished, trapped and traveled the streams and given them French names, and as the American pioneer had established towns and laid out trails that bore their names, German farm families named Jungermann, Muegge, Willott, Zumbehl, Kisker, Hackmann and Ehlmann had farm-to-market roads named after them. In 1879 Friedrich Muench wrote:

Where American and German farmers live next door to each other – in former slave states as Missouri – it is almost the rule that the Americans are in debt, above the value of their property, while the Germans improve their financial position from year to year. They use outside capital only to buy land, in the secure expectation of soon being able to take care of their debts.

Opportunities for this arise from the situation that former slave-holding families have to sell their indebted land because their misguided children have not learned to work or save (and there no longer are slaves to do the work!). In this way, from year to year, the Germans acquire more land, and expand their settlement. Only in rare cases is German land property for sale – it stays in the same family from generation to generation.[666]

By 1885 even the American author of the *History of St. Charles County* would praise the Germans for their "superior farming skills."[667]

The revolutionary economic changes that took place with the demise of the tobacco culture received a boost from significant pieces of economic legislation passed during the Civil War by the Republican Congress, including the Homestead Act. This legislation provided free land for settlers in the west, thus reinforcing the practice of American farmers in the Midwest selling their farms to newly arrived German immigrants. These pioneer farmers would then move out to a new "homestead" further west. While the yeoman farmers who settled the American West took on heroic proportions in American legend, the German immigrant saw the frontiersman as, " a product of an environment that often brought out the worst in people." The German also saw them as "free spenders," "rootless" and "lazy."[668]

The Civil War Congress also passed the Morrill Land Grant College Act of 1862, granting federal lands to the states for the building of colleges devoted to education in agriculture and mechanical arts. Congress also created the National Academy of Sciences to boost technical knowledge and development; and the Department of Agriculture to sponsor research on improved farming techniques. Research sponsored by the new Department of Agriculture and information disseminated by the agency to American farmers bolstered agricultural productivity.[669] The University of Missouri was a land grant institution under the Morrill Act, and the governor appointed Dr. George Buckner of St. Charles to the Board of Curators. In 1865 the Missouri legislature also established a Department of Agriculture to promote agriculture, and Dr. Buckner was the first person named to serve on the State Board of Agriculture. The Board of Curators in 1870 established at the University of Missouri a College of Agriculture that became an important resource for the farmers of the state. To encourage competition and promote excellence the Department of Agriculture promoted county fairs. By 1890 there was an annual county fair in St. Charles County held on the site of the present Blanchette Park in St. Charles.[670]

While serving on the State Board of Agriculture for 16 years, George Husmann used his position to promote the burgeoning Missouri wine industry.[671] Germans in St.

The St. Charles County Fair, held at what is now Blanchette Park, attracted crowds that filled the grandstand in the 1890s. *John J. Buse Collection, 1860-1931, Western Historical Manuscript Collection-Columbia, MO.*

Charles County and elsewhere had made wine since their arrival from Europe. By 1833 a German immigrant had built a winery in St. Charles. In 1857 the *Demokrat* stated, "Vineyards and orchards are especially stressed in the Augusta area. Mr. Meyer's grapes, as well as the finished products of his vineyards, enjoy a well-deserved reputation."[672] With the state's encouragement, by the 1880s, about 400 acres in St. Charles County were planted in vineyards, with over half the acreage in Femme Osage and Augusta. The county produced more that 100,000 gallons of wine annually. The two favored grapes for wine making were the Norton's Virginia Seedling and the Concord grape. There was a wine cellar in Wentzville, three in St. Charles, eight in New Melle and 20 in Augusta.[673]

Agriculture got another boost from the federal government when President Grover Cleveland appointed Norman J. Colman of Missouri Commissioner of Agriculture in 1885 and the first Secretary of Agriculture in 1887. In 1889, the Department of Agriculture began issuing weekly agricultural bulletins and by 1900 both elementary and secondary school curricula offered courses in the new scientific management of agriculture.[674] Another significant change from the pre-Civil War era came in 1863, when Republican lawmakers passed the National Currency Act, creating nationally chartered banks, something the Democrats had opposed since the demise of the Second Bank of the United States. The first National Bank of St. Charles received one of the first charters in the state and helped provide capital to farmers for the improvements in agriculture that came after the war.[675]

During the Civil War, Congress approved funds for a transcontinental railroad to spur development of the west. Republican leaders also believed that railroads could help transform the South into a more industrialized society, with a diversified agriculture creating opportunities for black and white alike.[676] Many Democrats in Missouri had come to this conclusion years earlier. In 1837 the Missouri General Assembly had chartered 18 railroad corporations in Missouri, but none of them built railroads because of the Panic of 1837.[677] The laws of the Ninth General Assembly, published in 1841, had included an "Act to Incorporate the St. Charles Railroad Company," proposed to be built in St. Charles County, between Portage des Sioux and St. Charles. Like the rest, it was never built.[678] In 1847, the General Assembly had chartered the Hannibal and St. Joseph Railroad Company, but there was still no public financing. In 1849 the legislature adopted a comprehensive plan to charter seven state-aided railroads including the Hannibal and St. Joseph Railroad and the Pacific Railroad Company line between St. Louis and Jefferson City, (Union Pacific today).[679] In 1852 the Missouri legislature authorized $4.75 million in bonds for three railroads, including the North Missouri Railroad.[680] Missouri had renounced any Jacksonian reluctance to fund internal improvements in favor of a pragmatic approach to funding needed railroads that the private sector simply could not finance on its own.[681]

St. Charles County had no problem with such a pragmatic approach. At the celebration of the opening of the railroad at St. Charles in 1855, the *Demokrat* stated that Mayor Thomas W. Cunningham had noted:

> …the old French village of St. Charles was waking up. The magic influence of the locomotive whistle seems to have broken through the slumber which surrounded us. Similar to Rip Van Winkle of old, as he awakened from his long sleep in the Catskill Mountains, so we shake off the dust of the past and march forward on the firm footing of progress.[682]

Indeed, the "old French village" would see its population increase from 1,498 in 1850 to 3,239 in 1860, and 5,570 after the 1870 federal census. But, as the Civil War began, the North Missouri Railroad was unfinished and railroad cars were transferred across the Missouri River by boat at St. Charles.

As the war ended, Radial Republicans took up railroad building with renewed enthusiasm. While the 1865 Missouri Constitution forbade the lending of state credit to private businesses, including railroads, it also assisted railroad development by allowing county governments to more easily issue railroad bonds.[683] In 1865 the state, under Radical control, exchanged its first lien on the North Missouri for a second mortgage, allowing completion of the North Missouri Railroad. Investors later bought the state's $6.96 million interest for $200,000 and posted a half-million dollar bond to guarantee completion of the railroad, including a branch line from Moberly to the western border of Missouri. In agreeing to this the legislature required, as a condition, that the line to Iowa be completed within nine months; the line to Kansas be completed within 18 months; and the bridge at St. Charles be completed within three years.[684]

The North Missouri Railroad became insolvent in 1871 and was sold off, eventually to become part of the Wabash system. Before it became insolvent it had fulfilled all the conditions of its agreement with the state, including completion of the bridge at St. Charles.[685] But the experience with railroad building was not a pleasant memory for all St. Charles Countians. Edna McElhiney Olson points out, "The farmers who had subscribed to build the railroad did not get back one cent."[686] As a result, the state constitution passed in 1875 contained strong prohibitions on the use of public credit for private purposes.

With bridges needed across the Mississippi at St. Louis and across the Missouri at St. Charles, money was not the only problem for railroad builders. Three separate disasters struck the St. Charles Bridge across the Missouri River. The first occurred even before the completion of the structure when, in November 1870, a hoist machine malfunctioned and dropped four tons of metal killing 19 men and injuring a number of others. Nevertheless, the bridge was completed in 1871 at a cost of $1.75 million. Disaster struck again eight years after the bridge's completion. A span gave way while a train was crossing, throwing 18 cars into the river, killing five men. The same thing happened again in 1881, this time hurling 31 cars into the water and sand below. At this point the bridge was reconstructed with wrought iron replacing the cast iron, and the bridge remained in service until 1936.[687]

The railroad brought new people – many Irish Catholics - to lay the railroad tracks. These immigrants, having fled Ireland during the potato famine, were mostly destitute and ended up either in cities like St. Louis or working on the labor gangs that built America's railroad system in the 1850s and after. Sometime in that decade one of the priests stationed at St. Charles Borromeo wrote:

> A railroad was under construction which was to lead from St. Louis to Hannibal, a town on the Mississippi River, there to connect with a road leading to St. Joseph. Many Irish laborers were employed on this work; and exposed as they were to the hot sun, lodging in miserable huts and destitute of wholesome food, the cholera broke out among them. In consequence the Fathers of this House were called on, day and night, to attend the dying.[688]

The writer goes on to explain that by ministering to these Irish laborers, "many were brought back to their religious duties; and, what was more consoling, some of them were married, settled their home in St. Charles, where they are now leading Christian lives among our parishioners."[689] Although they were certainly not all Catholic, the 1870 census indicated 576 people in St. Charles County were Irish-born.[690]

Two such boats ferried North Missouri Railroad cars from the foot of Morgan Street to the St. Louis County side of the river from 1856 to 1871, the year a bridge was completed. *John J. Buse Collection, 1860-1931, Western Historical Manuscript Collection-Columbia, MO*

Finally, the railroads would also bring another surprising human cargo. Beginning in 1854 the New York Children's Aid Society started a policy of placing children in rural foster homes by sending them on a train to the Midwest. By 1860, midwestern families had adopted over 5,000 such children. In the late nineteenth century, these orphan trains came through West Alton, Machens and other St. Charles County communities, where many orphans were adopted.[691]

Even before the bridge was completed the North Missouri Railroad stimulated economic activity in St. Charles County as towns were established along the line. The Jesuits had established a mission school along the Dardenne Creek in 1819 at the point where the floodplain ended and the hills began. Joseph Trendley, the first permanent settler had arrived in 1823, but had not bothered to plat the settlement. When the North Missouri Railroad came through, Henry Reineke and H. Deppe laid out St. Peters. In 1875 the Hannibal & St. Louis Railroad that ran south from Keokuk, Iowa, through Hannibal, Louisiana, Clarksville and Old Monroe was making slow progress through the floodplain of St. Charles County. Therefore, the K Line was built connecting it to the North Missouri at St. Peters until the main line could be completed.[692] St. Peters became an important railroad town, as it was now the junction of these two railroads.

O'Fallon was laid out in 1857 on land owned by Arnold Krekel, who named the town after John O'Fallon, a well-known capitalist from St. Louis, and a member of the Board of Directors of the North Missouri Railroad. Nicholas Krekel, a brother of Arnold Krekel, surveyed and platted the town, for which he was appointed postmaster in 1857.[693] The city flourished as a shipping point on the railroad for farmers in the area.[694] A pamphlet celebrating the O'Fallon Centennial states:

The completion of the railroad bridge in 1871 considerably shortened the time needed to traverse the 23 miles from this train station in St. Charles to St. Louis. *John J. Buse Collection, 1860-1931, Western Historical Manuscript Collection-Columbia, MO*

These bands of steel became a new artery of trade. Farmers could now produce a surplus, assured that it would reach market without too much delay. People could be sure of scheduled passenger service as well. So with the coming of the railroad, the community began to pass from an advanced pioneer stage to a very early modern one.[695]

In towns like O'Fallon, the railroad stimulated the establishment of retail business as the train could now bring manufactured products to the small towns of St. Charles County.

Other points along the railroad achieved temporary importance, only to disappear over time. The point at which the railroad crossed Peruque Creek was known as Beck's Landing. During the Civil War, the Union army built a fortification nearby known as "Fort Peruque," to protect the railroad-bridge over the creek.[696] After the war, the place lost its importance until a dam was constructed just upstream of the area to create Lake St. Louis in the 1970s. Gilmore, another town on the line, does not survive but was located where the former St. Louis, Hannibal & Northwestern Railroad joined the North Missouri Railroad. The railroad had a repair shop and engine house there.[697]

The station at St. Peters became important after the Hannibal & St. Louis Railroad built the K Line to connect to the North Missouri Railroad in order to use the bridge at St. Charles. *John J. Buse Collection, 1860-1931, Western Historical Manuscript Collection-Columbia, MO*

Wentzville and Foristell sprang up and prospered along the North Missouri route. Wentzville was named after Erasmus Livingston Wentz, an engineer with the North Missouri Railroad. The land, donated by William M. Allen to establish a station, was platted in 1855, patterned on the "symmetric" design, first developed by the Illinois Central Railroad. In the symmetric design, the track became the central throughway for the town, with a wide right of way for lumberyards, grain elevators and other facilities that needed direct rail access. Two streets ran parallel on either side of the track.[698] Wentzville served as a shipping point for local farmers and the railroad allowed the city to prosper. The town became a manufacturing center for tobacco products in the 1870s, when several successful St. Louis businessmen got their start in St. Charles County. The list included George H. Myers, co-founder of the Liggett and Myers Tobacco Co., James T. Drummond of the Drummond Tobacco Company, Paul Brown of the Brown Tobacco Company, and Caleb Dula, president of Liggett and Myers after 1911.[699] The commercial activity justified the building of a sizable hotel in Wentzville in 1867.[700]

Foristell was laid out in 1857 and was known as Millville until 1877 when it was named after Pierre Foristell, a wealthy farmer and cattle dealer in the area. It also was a shipping point on the North Missouri Railroad for local agricultural products.[701] Thomas J. Mason built an early tobacco factory and Frederick Blattner operated a general store there following the Civil War.[702] Grain elevators were located in these towns and others, where farmers could store their grain until the train came through.[703] Hiram Beverly Castlio opined, "But that blest new railroad was a God sent help t' farmers. Once again goods could be sent off t' St. Charles an' t' St. Louis markets. Those necessaries a body couldn't make or grow could be got the same way. All of us, villagers an' farm families alike, all thanked the Lord for the railroad."[704]

The building of the North Missouri Railroad brought prosperity to St. Charles County and the entire state. By 1860 the state had authorized the purchase of $23 million worth of stock of its chartered railroads. Nationwide, government assistance amounted to 30 percent of all investments in railroads before 1860.[705] In Missouri that percentage was 66.[706] In spite of these efforts, Chicago, not St. Louis, became the primary depository for the agricultural products of the West and Midwest. Chicago was located in the middle, not the southern fringe, of the vast glaciated plains of the upper Midwest that could now be cultivated because of the John Deere plow. Its location at the southern tip of Lake Michigan made it the collection point for all the agricultural products of the upper Midwest, from which products would have quick access to the markets of the East. The same type of geological and geographical factors that made St. Charles County, not Franklin County, the route for pioneers going west, made Chicago, not St. Louis, the entrepot for agricultural goods headed east. As a result St. Louis became an important regional center for areas to the southwest and St. Charles County, with a population of 21,304 according to the 1870 census, remained a place of farms and small towns.[707]

The railroads also created some problems for St. Charles County farmers. Regarding the railroads, the author of the *History of St. Charles County* realized by 1885:

The road has proved a great benefit to St. Charles County. It opened up the county to the outside world and gave the people a convenient and rapid means of transportation to all the markets of the country. Of course the county has suffered some from what seemed rate extortions, but the benefits received far outweigh the burdens borne. To be sure, there is some complaint that the road is not assessed and taxed, proportionately, as heavily as the other property and that it even refuses to pay the taxes levied against it.[708]

Farmers quickly realized that the same train that took their crop to market could bring other foodstuffs to St. Charles County.[709] The farmer was now in a very competitive market and had to specialize in the production of agricultural commodities based on demand in distant urban markets. The farmer brought more land into production and purchased more new equipment. As a result, he went further and further into debt.[710] To add to the problem, farm prices generally declined after 1873 as vast new areas in Russia, Australia, Canada and Argentina came under cultivation. The price of corn, for example, went from 67¢ per bushel in 1874 to 24¢ per bushel in 1875, and remained in the 20s and 30s for 13 of the 15 years between 1876 and 1890. Livestock prices behaved in a similar fashion, controlled by supply and demand in an increasingly competitive market. Despite the fact that Missouri agriculture increased its acreage from slightly over nine million acres in 1870 to nearly 17 million in 1880, the value of the products they produced actually declined.[711]

One manifestation of the farmers' discontent was the creation of the Patrons of Husbandry, commonly referred as the Grange. Originally formed to improve social life on isolated farms in the 1870s, the organization strove to alleviate the economic woes of agriculture. In 1875 there were 2,000 chapters in Missouri; the most Granges established in any state. Intended to be nonpolitical, the Grange sought to organize farmers into buyers' cooperatives that would take steps to give the farmer better bargaining power in the market.[712] Granges were organized throughout St. Charles County and the surrounding counties in 1874. Granges in St. Charles County included Ballantine Grange, located four miles below Portage, 17 members; the Dardenne Grange with 21 members; the Hansel Grange near Portage with 22 members; the Walnut Grove Grange in Black Walnut which passed resolutions favoring the exemption of real estate from taxation and abolishing the offices of state and county Superintendents of Public Schools; Black Jack Grange west of St. Charles with 16 members; and the Missouriton Grange with 28 members. There were also Granges in Wentzville and Flint Hill. A membership list of over 100 names did not include any German names. The Grange seems to have been an organization favored by the older American farm families.[713] One explanation was that the Grange actively supported the temperance crusade.[714] Another was that the Germans cherished their economic independence too much to lose any control of their farms by joining a farmer's cooperative.[715]

In addition to low prices, another problem for the farmer was railroad rates. Before passage of the Interstate Commerce Act, a railroads could name its price if it were the only one in the area. This remained a problem as late as 1885 according to the *History of St. Charles County*. The building of the Hannibal and St. Louis Railroad and the St. Louis, Keokuk and Northwestern line alleviated the problem. Further relief came with the building of the Missouri Kansas and Texas Railroad (Katy), that followed the bank of the Missouri River and joined the now completed Hannibal and St. Louis at Machens. Trains from both eventually crossed the Missouri or Mississippi Rivers on new railroad bridges at West Alton. With at least three major railroads in the county, no St. Charles County farmer was at the mercy of any one railroad since he would be close to competing lines.

By 1888 the Central Missouri Railroad had extended tracks along the north bank of the Missouri River from St. Charles to Hamburg. The Missouri, Kansas and Texas Railroad replaced the failed CMR in 1893 and began extending the tracks toward Marthasville. The railroad was built through Matson after Richard Matson deeded the railroad 20 acres of land for a station. One of his principal competitors was James P. Craig, who lived two miles to the north. Craig persisted until the railroad located a station on his property. He did this in defiance of Matson, so he called the place "Defiance."[716] When the MKT was being built through Green's Bottom, T. George Jung made a concession of land on which the railroad built Jung's Station, from which the local farmers could ship their crops and produce.[717] In 1892 the railroad built a depot with ornate detail, a fine example of Victorian railroad architecture, in St. Charles.[718] Other towns sprang up along the route, including Black

Walnut, named for a nearby grove of trees, and the site of a grain elevator. Henry Ernst Machens and his family had arrived from Gross-Algermissen, Germany in 1848. He and his four sons, James, Andrew, William and Joseph, were instrumental in bringing the railroad to the town called Texas Junction. In 1894 the town was renamed Machens in honor of the family.[719]

At the beginning of the 1890s, the Hannibal and St. Louis Railroad, that had connected to the North Missouri at St. Peters in order to use its railroad bridge over the Missouri River, was rerouted. The new route extended through the floodplain to Orchard Farm, Machens, West Alton and then across the new Missouri River Bridge to St. Louis County. Before 1874 West Alton was known as Missouri Point. In that year the residents applied for a post office but found there was already a town of that name. The name was changed to La Mothe, after a rich local landowner, until 1895 when the railroad requested that the name be changed to West Alton. With the coming of the Hannibal and St. Louis Railroad, the entire town moved closer to the tracks.[720]

In St. Charles County, crops were taken to grain elevators along the railroad, from which the grain was shipped to St. Louis and other cities. There were also ten shipping points on the Missouri and 11 on the Mississippi, from which agricultural products were shipped to St. Louis. To get their crops to local markets, river shipping points or the railroads, a system of roads developed in St. Charles County. Mexico Road followed the same route that it does today, while the Marthasville Road branched off the Booneslick Road in Harvester and followed the route of Highway 94 South to the Warren County line. On the north end of the county the St. Charles and Alton Road roughly followed the right-of-way of Highway 94 North. Howell's Ferry Road ran from Flint Hill to Howell's Ferry near Defiance, roughly along the line of Highway 40-61. The lettered highways in the county were county roads by the 1880s.[721]

Not only could the railroads get commodities to market quicker than previous forms of transport, they could also handle the larger quantities farmers were now able to grow due to the mechanization of agriculture. The county produced 1.5 million bushels of corn, 250,000 bushels of oats and 1.1 million bushels of wheat in 1880. While the population of the county had grown to 23,065 according to the 1880 census, it now took far fewer workers to produce the same harvest. Colman's Rural World noted in 1879, "With the improved implements and machines which we now have, a farmer with one hired man can carry on farming on a larger scale than he could a generation ago with half a dozen hired men."[722] Indeed, the most significant changes in agriculture in St. Charles County were not the result of emancipation, education or transportation; but of mechanization. By the 1870s, land in St. Charles County had been cultivated for nearly 80 years without the aid of fertilizers. Successive crops of wheat had been grown for more than 30 years without any rotation. Still, the land produced from 25 to 40 bushels of wheat an acre. In 1871 it was estimated that St. Charles County produced one-eighth of the wheat grown in 114 counties of the state.[723] During the same period the average yield for corn was about 40 bushels an acre. Writing in 1879, Friedrich Muench stated, "Only a few German farmers still help themselves with old, imperfect implements. Instead, most demand the very best field implements for sowing, mowing and threshing, as well as machines for sawing wood and chopping chaff."[724]

In 1885 the State Bureau of Labor statistics noted, "The barshare plow, requiring three to four men per acre a day of plowing, has given place to the sulky plow, asking for but one man per day for three acres of plowing."[725] In St. Charles County, small plows, pulled by one horse, or larger plows, pulled by two horses, were replaced by the three-wheeled sulky plow, complete with the seat for the farmer to ride. These were pulled by three horses side by side or by as many as five horses. Even so, the black stick and gumbo soils on large tracts north of St. Charles were not farmed until steam engine tractors were developed which could pull plows effectively through these heavy soils.[726]

Likewise, the corn planter had replaced ten men.[727] Corn was usually planted after the 10th of May and had to be cultivated several times during the summer. The standing corn was harvested by hand and thrown into a wagon that was fit with an elevated "bump board." A good shucker, or "husker" could keep an ear in the air at all times while the team of horses pulled down the row. He could shuck about 80 bushels per day. About one-half the crop was shucked and left in the fields until used as feed in the winter. The estimated yield of corn in 1871 in St. Charles County was 3,103,000 bushels. The only fertilizers used were the plowing down of legumes and the broadcasting of manure. Near the turn of the century some yields exceeded 100 bushels an acre although the county average was 45 bushels an acre.[728] Cyrus McCormick was the first to mass-produce and market a reaper. First developed in 1834, by 1860 he was turning out 4,000 machines per year. Each could do the work of ten men. As early as 1850 inventors managed to attach a separator to a thresher so that the same machine - the combine - did the whole process of threshing and winnowing.[729] Wheat was grown throughout St. Charles County and speed drills for sowing wheat had first appeared in the 1830s. In the 1870s newspapers advertised the latest farm implements, and the earliest evidence of mechanical wheat harvests in St. Charles County was in the 1880s. The winter wheat was sown in September or early October, and was harvested as early as mid-June. After the wheat was cut, it was put in shocks. By the 1870s, it was threshed by a steam-operated threshing machine hauled from farm to farm by a team of horses. The *Agricultural History of St. Charles County* describes how:

> A group of seven or eight farmers would help each other in a "threshing circle." The owner of the machine had his crew too. On the older machines, which had to be fed by hand, five men were needed. Two men took turns feeding the machine, because this was a difficult and tiring job. One had to watch the machine; one was an engineered to operate the steam engine and one hauled water. On the newer machines that were self-fed, the bundles were simply tossed into the machine by the crews hauling it from the stack. Only three men were needed for this permanent crew.[730]

Once the railroad was completed, depots at Orchard Farm and elsewhere were the collection points for milk cans, which were loaded into boxcars and shipped daily to St. Louis. Dairy farming became important in St. Charles County as more scientific methods of dairy farming were developed. An expert from the College of Agriculture in 1890 explained, "We call a cow a machine

This advertisement appeared in a St. Charles County newspaper for a McCormick Reaper, guaranteed as "the best now in use." *St. Charles Journal, May 18, 1871*

for converting hay grain and grass into milk and butter."[731] The milk producers formed a cooperative association in St. Charles County and the size of the herds and sophistication of the operations continued to increase.[732]

While the arrival of the railroads and advent of mechanization changed the nature of farming throughout the entire state, the changes came to St. Charles County first. David Thelen suggests that these changes did not take place uniformly across the state of Missouri. The rate of change depended on the extent of penetration of the market economy, largely determined by the extent of railroad construction, which depended on geographical location. The cash value of agricultural production in a particular county was an indication of the extent to which the market regulated its activities. In 1880 the average farm yielded products worth more than $1,000 only in St. Charles and Franklin counties. Because of their proximity to St. Louis, farmers there could easily transport to that urban market.[733]

In the second half of the nineteenth century, agriculture in St. Charles County changed from inefficient, subsistence agriculture, to an efficient, market driven, wheat, corn and livestock operation. Family farms, using the most modern equipment, produced more than anyone could have imagined a generation earlier. The United States rail network expanded from less than 40,000 miles when the first transcontinental railroad was completed in 1869, to 240,000 miles in 1890.[734] Freight trains carried crops to market and manufactured goods, processed foods and new immigrants to the countryside. In 1883 railroads abolished "local mean time," a pre-industrial practice whereby each community set its own clocks by the sun, and replaced it with the four standard time zones that exist today.[735] Before railroads it had cost as much to ship wheat the 35 miles from Huntsville, Missouri to Glasgow, Missouri, as it would cost after the railroad to ship the same quantity from Huntsville to Glasgow, Scotland.[736] The German farmers, who now dominated agriculture in St. Charles County, welcomed the changes.

D. Failed Social Revolution of the Radical Republicans

Historian Eric Foner identifies four interrelated areas where the Radical Republicans attempted to reshape southern society: the labor system, economic development, education and race relations.[737] Most Republicans embraced changes in the labor system and the building of railroads, the economic components of the revolution proposed by the Radical Republicans. Race relations and education, the social components of the revolution envisioned by those same Radicals, was a different story. The social program of the Radicals was based on full civil rights for African-Americans, free public education for everyone, and a national culture. This envisioned a society where African-Americans were fully integrated and German-Americans were fully assimilated into a society based on the social values of the Radicals. The people of St. Charles County, like most of the rest of the country, were not ready to accept the Radical Republicans' vision.

Before the Civil War, the attitudes of Germans towards slavery varied depending on the time of their arrival and their religious affiliation. In 1863, shortly after Lincoln's Emancipation Proclamation, the *Demokrat* wrote, "it is precisely the Germans who oppose the institution of slavery not only for economic and political reasons, but fight it more so because it stands in direct contrast to their feelings of justice and morality."[738] This opinion more exactly represented the beliefs of the secular Liberals, many of them refugees from the failed Liberal revolutions in Europe, who, "equated slavery with their former situation."[739] The Catholic Church had taken an anti-slavery position in 1839. Yet a year later Bishop Peter Kenrick stated, "slavery was not demonstrably inconsistent with the natural law."[740] Likewise, German Lutheran churches did not publicly oppose slavery. In fact, Dr. C.F. Walther, leader of the Missouri Synod, stated publicly that scripture supported slavery and considered abolitionism "a child of unbelief and its unfolding, rationalism, deistic philanthropism, Pantheism, materialism, atheism and a brother of modern socialism, Jacobism and communism."[741] Nevertheless, privately most Germans, in spite of their religious leadership, linked slavery with the oppression they had experienced in Germany.[742]

Given these facts, one would have expected to see some German slaveholding among the religiously inclined, though less among the Liberals. In fact, the opposite was true. While the percentage of slaves in St. Charles County was 13.2 percent, higher than the 9.8 percent average found in the state as a whole,[743] only 17 of the more than 1,000 German families in St. Charles County in 1850 owned slaves. Half of them owned only one slave while the largest German slaveholder had seven. Although there were 3,000 slaves in St.

Charles and Warren Counties in 1850, only about 75 were in the hands of Germans. One-fifth of American farmers without real estate owned slaves but no German did. Likewise, among people with less than $1,000 worth of property, 28 percent of non-German farmers, but only one percent of German small farmers owned slaves.[744] Historian Walter Kamphoefner points out that Germans of the "better classes," especially if they had married Americans, were more likely to have slaves. This included many German Liberals, including Friedrich Muench and Arnold Krekel, who would later become Radical Republicans. For these individuals, slaveholding was part of public life and a function of their social class, for all had upper-middle-class origins in Germany and were well educated.[745] While most Germans in St. Charles County refused to hold slaves themselves and opposed the extension of slavery into the territories, few were active abolitionists.[746]

Before the German immigration there had been some efforts to educate slaves. Reverend Timothy Flint had operated a school for slaves in St. Charles from 1816 until 1826.[747] Although warned by Bishop DuBourg that frontier society "stood firmly against acceptance of blacks and even their light skinned children," Philippine Duchesne and the Mothers of the Sacred Heart had admitted mixed race children to the day school.[748] Catherine Collier taught white and black children at the Methodist Church building and had night classes for black adults. Some clandestine educational activity continued even after passage of the 1847 constitutional amendment forbidding the education of African-Americans in Missouri.[749]

The Missouri General Assembly, under the control of the Radical Republicans, rescinded the restrictions on education of African-Americans in the spring of 1865. However, the action came too late to have much effect in that school year. In addition, the legislators made no monetary appropriation so most of the black schools that were in operation that fall were maintained by white benevolent societies, including the American Missionary Association. That organization, in cooperation with the Northwestern Freedman's Aid Commission, conducted schools at Rolla, Warrensburg, St. Charles, St. Joseph, Weston, Sedalia, and Columbia.[750]

Under the 1865 statute, each township or city Board of Education was required to establish and maintain separate schools for black children if the number of black children exceeded 20. The school was to be kept open for a winter-term equivalent to that for white students unless average attendance for any month dropped to less than 12. Superintendent Thomas A. Parker later pointed out that, unfortunately, the legislature had not provided a penalty for noncompliance. In summarizing the progress of black education in 1867, Parker noted, "56 schools had been established in 30 counties. The majority of these institutions were privately run. Public schools for blacks existed only in the larger towns."[751] St. Charles was one of those towns.

The St. Charles school board acknowledged its responsibility to black students in 1866 when it directed that Jacob Weston be issued a warrant for $20.00 as partial payment for teaching the black students.[752] As in Jefferson City, the Radicals, including German Liberals in St. Charles County, were among the biggest supporters of public education for black and white children. The *Demokrat* stated in 1867:

Opposition against schools is like royalty's resistance against the so-called "over education of the under classes" in Europe. "Keep the people ignorant and dumb so we can govern them better and exploit our advantage." That has always been the motto of tyrants and aristocrats in Europe, and that is the slogan of their noble ideological colleagues here.[753]

The 1870 census revealed that while there were 42,000 black students in the state, only 21 percent were getting any kind of education. Locally, 46 percent of eligible black children, 77 out of 160, were enrolled in school in 1867.[754] By 1870 there was a school for black children in the "African Church" at Second and Pike Street, to which the school board paid the sum of five dollars per month as rent until the board purchased the building in 1871. Like many such schools, it was eventually named Lincoln School after the slain president. The black children on the north end of town attended the "African School" or "Blue Ville School" at Gallaher and Olive Streets.[755] Of the 425 public school students in St. Charles in 1885, 75 were African-Americans.

Black schools also came to the rural areas of St. Charles County. By the spring of 1866 black children were attending an integrated school in Augusta. African-Americans organized their own Salem District School near Augusta in 1867. When it was burned down the *Demokrat* complained that it was "a sad sign of the intellectual level of a certain class of people."[756] By 1872 there were 11 black public schools in the county, including one in Cottleville on land donated by David K. Pitman and another near West Alton on ground provided by Eli Keen. By the 1880s Dr. Russell B. Lewis had established a public school for African-Americans at Flint Hill, where L.A. Kern taught for a three-month term. [757] There was a public school in O'Fallon for black students at the foot of Elm Street.[758] These and other black schools in St. Charles County were desperately in need of black teachers. To meet this need throughout the state, Lincoln Institute was founded in Jefferson City with the assistance of Arnold Krekel, who served on the institution's first Board of Trustees.[759] Nevertheless, by 1872 much of the idealism of the German Liberals was beginning to wear thin. The *Demokrat* opined, "as long as enough schools for Negroes are available with teachers equally as good as for whites, we do not see why Negroes should be forced into white schools."[760] There was little opposition when the Missouri Constitution of 1875 required that public schools be racially segregated.

The new system of public schools introduced by the Radical Republicans was controversial, not only because it educated the former slaves, but also because it taxed those who did not use the schools. Before 1866, "public schools" were supported primarily with revenues from the sale of local lands. Since 1825 the legislature had assessed school taxes on the basis of how many children the taxpayer had attending the school. Now, county taxpayers without children were taxed to support the public schools. After the Radical Republican victories of 1868, Superintendent of Schools Thomas A. Parker directed legislation through the General Assembly to allow school boards to approve tax increases for new school buildings without a popular vote.[761] Parker was up against the old "southern attitude" that viewed public school as a "Yankee idea," that robbed working families of their money.[762] As late as 1867 Mary Mowatt arrived from England and opened a private school in St. Charles for children of the "better class," that continued to operate until 1890.[763]

The followers of Daniel Boone still comprised half the population of St. Charles County before the Civil War. Lawyers, landowners and doctors continued to hold positions of authority and controlled the important institutions. Dr. Ludwell E. Powell in 1849 and Dr. Samuel Overall in 1854 were elected mayor of St. Charles. [764] Daniel A. Griffith, whose grandfather, Samuel Griffith had been among the first Americans to come to the county in 1795, was one of the largest landowners and slaveholders in the county. He served 12 years as county court judge of St. Charles County, his last term from 1858-1862.[765] Planters like Dr. William McElhiney represented St. Charles County in the state legislature before the Civil War.[766] Very few Germans were elected to public office before the Civil War. After the war, a large majority of council members, county court judges and legislators were of German descent.[767]

Public schools like the Jefferson School, on Fourth and Jefferson, were central to the Radical Republican vision for the future of the nation. *John J. Buse Collection, 1860-1931, Western Historical Manuscript Collection-Columbia, MO*

Older Americans, and the churches they attended, retained exclusive control over higher education. The state legislature placed St. Charles College under the control of the Methodist Episcopal Church South. Like his mother before him, George Collier established a trust fund to support the school after his death in 1852. Under the leadership of Reverend John H. Fielding, the school prospered until the Civil War, during which the school was used as a federal prison. After closing in 1861, St. Charles College regained control of its buildings only after a lengthy court battle following the Civil War.[768]

Lindenwood College, prospering with the help of Judge and Mrs. Samuel S. Watson, was another institution that reflected the social values of those families that had come before the Germans. In 1853 Lindenwood College obtained a charter from the state legislature and in 1859 began construction of Sibley Hall. George Sibley had bequeathed his 120 acres to Lindenwood, "A school wherein the Bible shall ever have a prominent place and be in daily use. In which the entire system of instruction and discipline shall be based on the religion of Jesus Christ as held and taught in the confession of faith and catechism of the Presbyterian Church…."[769] The General Regulations of 1863 dictated, "On Sunday, the young ladies are required to attend the Sabbath School, also morning and evening services at one of the churches."[770] One student explained:

> Sunday was our most trying day of the week, and we were glad there were but four a month. There were trials all day – a very long walk to church, a very long Presbyterian sermon, a prayer fully as long, when we stood first on one foot, then the other, until our hips must have been several inches difference; the long walk home, and an hour of religious reading in the afternoon.[771]

In 1862 another school was founded in O'Fallon, first called the Fairview Institute, renamed Woodlawn Institute in 1876. Daughters and sons of Methodist ministers were allowed a 50 percent reduction in their tuition and the rules stated, "Students are not allowed to make or receive calls on the Sabbath."[772]

Many of these American social customs and beliefs were totally alien to the German immigrants in St. Charles County. Beginning in the 1830s, emigration societies, composed of intellectuals and people from the higher ranks of German society, had sought to transplant German *Kultur* in America. Organizations like the Solingen Society, that led a party of 120 middle-class Germans to the U.S. who settled mainly in Jefferson County, had no intention of adopting the culture of the Americans. In 1832, Baron Johann Von Bock founded Dutzow, just over the St. Charles County line in Warren County, along with members of the Berlin Immigration Society. Two former members of a liberal student movement in Germany, Friedrich Muench and Paul Follenius, had organized the Giessen Society after the failure of the 1830 revolutions in Germany. They had planned to found a model German Republic in Arkansas but instead ended up in St. Louis before scattering to various locations including St. Charles

County.[773] Muench himself settled with approximately 10 families in Femme Osage Township, where he dreamed of concentrating Germans in a territory that would be admitted to the Union as a state. In 1859 he published a book entitled *The State of Missouri, An Account with Special Reference to German Immigration*, for the benefit of Germans considering immigration. Having spent 24 years in the state, his book was much more accurate than Duden's earlier work, but was just as effective in attracting immigrants to St. Charles County.[774] Other important German intellectuals, referred to as "Latin Farmers," included Julius and Emil Mallinckrodt, who had come to St. Charles County in 1834, determined to preserve their German customs.[775]

Walter Kamphoefner believes that, since these "Latin Farmers" were the ones to leave a written records from this period, their influence in the settlement of St. Charles County is often exaggerated. He points out that they were "more proficient in the

Chartered by the state in 1853, Lindenwood College began construction on this building in 1859. It was dedicated in 1869 and named Sibley Hall in honor of the school's founders, George and Mary Sibley. *John J. Buse Collection, 1860-1931, Western Historical Manuscript Collection-Columbia, MO.*

classics than in agriculture," and did not seriously influence the patterns of settlement in the county.[776] Indeed, upon arriving in Missouri in 1834 Friedrich Muench had noted that there were already, "a considerable number of Westphalian *Heierleute* (sic) in the neighborhood."[777] The German immigrant farmers, usually with strong religious beliefs, continued to arrive and clung to their German customs and beliefs as tenaciously as the Latin Farmers. Many of the German immigrants in the 1870s were Catholics and by the end of the decade they outnumbered the Lutherans and the Evangelicals. The rural area of St. Charles County reached its peak immigration in the 1880s.[778] The *History of St. Charles County* explains that by 1885, "Most of the Germans who came to America with money, lost it by injudicious speculation in lands, but those who came poor generally prospered on their small beginnings, and soon became money-loaners and land-owners."[779] Kamphoeffner suggests that the more adaptable peasantry that followed them came closer to realizing the Latin Farmers' dream of a new Germany in America.[780]

Their method of migration from Germany made it easy for them to retain the habits and customs of the old country after arriving in St. Charles County. At least two-thirds of the German immigrants in the county came from an area in northwest Germany about 60 miles long and 30 miles wide. Eighty percent spoke *Hoch Deutsch*, (Low German).[781] In his study of settlement patterns in the county, Walter Kamphoefner has identified evidence of "chain migration," where the immigrants in an area of St. Charles County had been neighbors in Germany. For instance, the Alsatians in St. Charles County lived in St. Charles Township. Seventy percent of the Germans in New Melle and surrounding Callaway Township were natives of Hanover, where the town of Melle was located. Of a group of more than 100 Oldenburgers in St. Charles County in 1860, most lived along the Missouri River between Augusta and Dutzow and formed the nucleus of a single German-Catholic parish. All but one of ten successive families in the 1850s census was from the same village in Oldenburg, just across the border from the Osnabruck District.[782] Of the 37 founders of the Immanuel Lutheran church in St. Charles, most were from Hanover and many specified Menslage as their birthplace.[783]

Germans took advantage of the revolutionary economic changes that were taking place but, in the area of social relationships, little change took place. By 1870 first and second generation Germans constituted a majority in St. Charles County, but they would remain separate and distinct from non-Germans in their social habits for some time. Recorded statements by German immigrants indicate that they considered themselves to be a people separate, unique, and in some respects superior to other groups. They not only rejected integration of African-Americans into white society, but also opposed their own assimilation. They had low regard for the French inhabitants who kept to themselves and remained culturally distinct. The *Demokrat* observed that the residents of the French village of Portage des Soux, "support themselves less from agriculture and artisanship, than from hunting, fishing and boating on rivers. A log cabin with a few acres of cleared land to plant vegetables and some corn was the most property the easily satisfied Frenchman accumulated. It is unbelievable how little influence the changes of the last 50 years has had on them." [784] Gustave Koerner, a leading German on a tour of Missouri in 1833, had agreed that the French he encountered were, "Indifferent farmers, fond of hunting and particularly fishing … living in villages, where they could have music and dancing and could play at cards. They were a gay and harmless people, and indolent, though their young men would frequently hire themselves out to the fur companies for a year or two as hunters or trappers."[785] After criticizing their cabins, gardens and cornfields, he also stated, "their young men hate all work, and spend the greater part of their lives in the woods or on the rivers as hunters, trappers and fur traders."[786]

Germans did not have a lot of respect for the Americans either. Kamphoeffner points out that the Germans' image of the Americans was more complicated than their image of the French. It involved at least three stereotypes: the aristocratic planter, the shiftless frontiersman and the Yankee trader.[787] Americans of southern origin were represented by two contrasting stereotypes. The "aristocracy" usually meant any farmer that had slaves. The Germans resented the nativist attitudes of this group, about which the *Demokrat* stated, "The families constituted a kind of closed society among themselves, and from here the fate of St. Charles County is determined, or at least so they believe."[788] Most German interaction, however, did not come with aristocrats but with the frontiersmen, who the German saw as a product of a frontier experience that often brought out the worst in people. They were the descendants of Scots-Irish pioneers that had been on the move across the American frontier for the last 100 years, and the Germans considered them, "brutal, ignorant, and ashamed of their ancestry if they were still aware of it."[789] A Femme Osage pastor's wife, Adelheid Garlichs, had written in 1836 that Americans were "sharp traders, such free spenders, not at all frugal, and still so interested in dealing and so egotistic that they hardly consider it a sin to cheat in business or to swear a false oath."[790] It was ironic that she also abhorred their willingness to sell their farm for "petty profit," since German immigrants were making the purchases. Kamphoeffner concludes that Germans admired the "true American spirit, the spirit of free institutions," rather than the Americans themselves, and believed that they understood American ideals better than those who were born here.[791] The so-called aristocrats lost much of their economic power when their slaves were emancipated. Many frontiersmen eventually sold out to German immigrants and moved further west, or stayed and became more respectable.

An article in the *Demokrat* spoke of the dark side that, "grows out of the pursuit of the dollar among the Yankees, such as the deceit and corruption in the present legislature and in trade, the destruction of human life on exploding steamboats for the sake of money and the systematic swindling of immigrants."[792] Of course this was the same stereotype that Americans from the South had of the Yankees, and would disappear as German merchants became more established and German politicians got their own opportunities at "deceit and corruption." Germans also disliked the Yankee's "religious hypocrisy" and "temperance movement."[793] Nevertheless, when German immigrants learned English, the English they spoke was the north midland dialect of most of the Yankees in St. Charles County.[794]

Given the isolation of their existence and prejudices they harbored, it is not surprising that the Germans had low rates of intermarriage with other ethnic groups. By 1850, they constituted a strong minority in St. Charles County, making up 44 percent of the heads of families, as compared to 49 percent who were American and five percent who were descended from the original French inhabitants. While some Germans had been living in St. Charles County for nearly 20 years, the amount of intermarriage that had taken place with Americans was still negligible. Only 11 German women in 100 had American husbands, while only four percent of German men married outside their ethnic group. German men married at a greater rate than the men of any other group, yet only four percent turned to Americans for wives. To encourage marriage within the congregation, St. John German Evangelical church established a *Jugendverein* (Young People's Society) in 1882. The Immanuel German Lutheran Church formed a *Jung Frauenverein* (Young Ladies Society) for the same purpose. [795] Nancy Callaway Castlio observed, "That (intermarriage) was not done much in those times, a weddin' 'tween the de'cendents o' Southern set'lers and the new Dutch. There was some consid'rable diff'rence in outlook 'tween the two groups; questions o' culture, politics, religion, education, slav'ry farmin' an' sech."[796] As late as 1879 the *Demokrat* reported, "Marriages between Germans and Americans occur only rarely."[797]

In the summer of 1867, Carl Schurz gave a speech in St. Charles County where he said the immigrants were preserving the best of German life. By 1870, German immigrants had been coming to St. Charles County for almost 40 years, and having started out in the poor hills of the county, were taking over the fertile river bottoms as well. Another local German leader remarked, "The Germans, from year to year, conquer more ground and extend their settlements. Only in rare cases is German real estate offered for sale - it stays in the same family from generation to generation."[798] The Germans avoided contact with other Americans, even in the economic sphere. In 1860 the Mutual Fire Insurance Company of St. Charles was formed. Arnold Krekel was elected president, Theodore Bruere, secretary and Albin Morgner, treasurer. The fine print in the insurance policies was printed in English and German.[799]

As the followers of Gottfried Duden slowly overwhelmed the followers of Daniel Boone in St. Charles County, a period of social conflict ensued during which the former withstood tremendous pressure by the latter to conform to "American" standards and give up their language, schools and social customs. If little assimilation took place within the German community in the early years, probably even less took place later, after their numbers became sufficient to sustain community life. The immigrants who came first were under the most pressure to assimilate and those that came later could fit into a transplanted community, where ethnic groups lived isolated from each other. Over 40 percent of Germans in St. Charles County lived in ethnic enclaves founded by the German immigrants. Five miles north of St. Charles there was one string of over 100 German families in the 1850 census. This area, known as the Royal Domain, was connected to St. Charles by a road called the *Rue Royal*, later anglicized to Kingshighway. In 1831 the first Boscherts had come to the area from Germany, and the area became known as Boschertown.[800]

There were other areas as solidly German. The first settlers had come to New Melle around 1838, and within a few years there was a thriving community. Settled by immigrants from Melle, Germany, the first settlers were Ernest Bannerman and Henry

Hardach. The homogeneity of the community is suggested by the high percentage of immigrants in the surrounding area who were natives of Hanover.[801] Heinrich Wilhelm Gerdemann, a former resident of Wester-Kappeln in Germany, founded Cappeln by establishing a store there in 1845. The nearby town of Femme Osage had been settled primarily by German immigrants in the late 1830s, as was Schluersburg in the 1840s.[802] Orchard Farm was originally known as Point Prairie and had been settled by Mrs. John Wilke and her two sons, who came from Hanover in 1842 after her husband died. The name was changed when the townspeople wished to recognize the fine fruit crops that were grown in that area.[803] In 1834, six German families had settled Hamburg along the Missouri River, upstream from Weldon Spring.[804]

The crown jewel of German communities in St. Charles County was Augusta. Located on the bluffs overlooking the Missouri River, it was reminiscent of German villages along the Rhine River. Originally called Mount Pleasant, it had been laid out by Leonard Harold, a Pennsylvanian who came to the area shortly after the War of 1812. Many of the Germans who had arrived after 1835 were from Augusta in Germany. When the village applied for a post office and found out there was already a Mount Pleasant in Missouri, the name of Augusta was adopted. Vineyards began to appear in the 1850s and in 1856 the Augusta *Harmonie-Verein* was established when the German residents of Augusta objected to local enforcement of the temperance laws. In January 1856, they went out onto the ice that covered the Mississippi River, erected a tent, and organized the Augusta musical and social society, that in later years used a flat boat on the river as a meeting place.[805] In 1858 a library was opened and Conrad Mallinckrodt prepared a final village plat. The town was a popular stop for riverboats until 1872, when a flood changed the course of the river, moving the river channel several miles away.[806]

Germans settled in other established communities in St. Charles County like Harvester, Weldon Spring, St. Peters, O'Fallon, Dardenne, Josephville and St. Paul, quickly outnumbering their predecessors. The French remained the most highly segregated ethnic group, being restricted to St. Charles and Portage de Sioux townships.[807] *The Demokrat* reported the ethnic make-up of St Charles County in 1873 as follows:

Town	Population	percentGerman
Cottleville	250	87
Weldon Spring	50	100
Hamburg	50	90
Augusta	300	100
Femme Osage	50	100
Schluersburg	30	100
Mechanicsville	50	0
Pauldingsville	?	0
Millville	75	0
New Melle	250	100

Wentzville	350	33
Flint Hill	30	0
Wellsburg	20	100
St Peters	175	100
O'Fallon	75	75
Boschert Town	75	100
Portage des Sioux	100	0 (100 percent French)[808]

The resistance to assimilation became even greater during the Civil War, when Germans actively supported the Union and the majority of non-Germans in St. Charles County, either outwardly or quietly, were in sympathy with the Confederacy.[809] Hiram Beverly Castlio commented, "1865 was the beginning of a long time of pulling away between German and southern families, a time of gathering in town centers, schools an' churches with folks of ones own kind."[810]

The biggest impediment to assimilation was the reluctance of the Germans to give up their language. The *Demokrat* explained in 1861:

Although it is unavoidably necessary in our present situation to have our youth instructed in the English language, so it, nevertheless, also is of great importance to promote the German language as fundamentally as possible, above all in our German Schools. The richness and convenience in conversation, as well as the invaluable literature of our dear mother tongue is never to be replaced by other languages.[811]

Twenty years later the same paper, writing on the same subject, bemoaned the lack of German instruction in the public schools and blamed it on the lack of bilingual teachers.[812] Still it was not the secular German-language newspaper editors who kept the German language alive; it was the Christian churches - Protestant and Catholic. The *Demokrat* wrote in 1887:

Even the most radical German doubter will have to concede that continuation of the German language in this country is dependent for the most part on the German churches…. The great majority of Germans are religious and church oriented. Evidence is found in the increasingly large number of German churches which can be founded and maintained with only the greatest sacrifice of congregation members. Millions of German-Americans and their children will remain loyal to the German language as long as the churches to which they belong are German… (that is) preaching in the German language. One can be rather assured about the German Protestant Churches. Namely, the two biggest German-American denominations, the Evangelical and the Evangelical Lutheran, have done much for training institutions and seminars in which also American-born youths are trained to be good preachers in German….[813]

German immigrants began settling in the area north of St. Charles know as Boschertown as early as 1831. *John J. Buse Collection, 1860-1931, Western Historical Manuscript Collection-Columbia, MO*

In religion, as in marriage, Germans preferred to stay among their own. Because they generally continued to use German in their services, membership of non-German speakers was rare in German congregations and parishes, creating religious continuity from Germany to America. Like the Saxons who had formed the Missouri Synod Lutheran Church, in the 1830s some East Prussians had emigrated in protest of their government's attempts to unify the Lutheran and Reform Churches. In 1836, they established an American counterpart to the Prussian Union Church called the German Evangelical Synod.[814] The denomination was within the German pietistic tradition that, according to Nagel, had changed little since the Reformation. Its characteristics included literal reading of the Bible; an impatience with formal theology or rationalism; a scorn for Roman Catholicism; and a fierce opposition to any state involvement in religion.[815]

At one time, German Evangelicals were the largest Protestant denomination in Franklin, Gasconade, St. Charles and Warren counties, as well as in St. Louis.[816] The first German Evangelical congregation in St. Charles County had been founded at Femme Osage, with Reverend Hermann Garlichs as the pastor. He served five other churches including New Melle and Schluersberg in St. Charles County. He had been

141

a delegate to the meeting where the German Evangelical Synod of North America was founded.[817] As the demand for ministers increased, the Association of Evangelical Churches of the West opened a Theological Seminary in 1850 on a 60-acre tract between Marthasville and Femme Osage.[818] German was spoken exclusively until 1892, when the decision was made to teach English to the students from Germany.[819] Evangelical congregations were established in St. Charles County: (Friedens in 1836), Augusta, (Ebenezer in 1863), Cappeln, (St. John's in 1865), Cottleville, (St. John's in 1866), and Weldon Spring, (Emanuel in 1874). In 1868, the members of the Friedens congregation living in St.

Wilhelm Koch established the Augusta Wine Hall in the 1880s. The wineries of Augusta are an important part of that community's tourist industry today. *St. Charles County Historical Society*

Charles organized the St. John congregation in the city. St. Paul's, a second Evangelical congregation in St. Charles, is no longer in existence.[820]

The second major German Protestant denomination was the German Evangelical Lutheran Church Missouri Synod. The oldest German Evangelical Lutheran congregation in St. Charles County was St. Paul's in New Melle, founded in 1844. The German Evangelical Lutheran congregation in St. Charles had been founded in September 1847, and by 1885 had over 500 members.[821] The Christ Lutheran congregation was formed in Augusta in 1859 when a conservative faction split off from the local Evangelical Church. Another congregation was established in Orchard Farm, where Trinity Lutheran Church was dedicated in 1876. It was originally under the care and supervision of its sponsor, Immanuel Lutheran in St. Charles, but received its own pastor a year later and joined the Missouri Synod in 1888. Zion Lutheran was established in 1884 in Harvester, where the Immanuel congregation had operated a grade school since 1851.[822] The Immanuel Lutheran congregation in Wentzville was established in 1874 and a new church was built in 1899 and a school in 1900.[823] All of these churches conducted services in German, thus keeping the language alive but the German immigrants socially isolated.

The only established Protestant denomination with much appeal for the German immigrants was the Methodists which, in keeping with German pietism, criticized religious ritual and stressed the conversion experience. In 1841 Ludwig Jacoby had come to St. Louis as a Methodist missionary to the Germans and in 1845 had organized a German district for Missouri, Illinois and Iowa. When the Methodists split over slavery in 1844, the Germans went with the northern branch. The German Methodist Church in St. Charles had been founded in 1847 and another congregation was founded in New Melle in 1871.[824] Their reason for existence was to preach Methodism in German.

The German language also flourished in the German-Catholic parishes established throughout the county. Priests in German-Catholic parishes were concerned with, "the preservation of the German language, German customs and German thoroughness in the children of the German immigrant." They felt that, "to hurry on the development of a German into a 100 percent American was tyrannical, imprudent and worse than useless." Furthermore, retention of their German language was "highly conducive to the preservation of the faith of the German immigrants and their children."[825] St. Peter's Parish had been organized in 1848 to serve the German Catholics in St. Charles who did not want to attend St. Charles Borromeo, where the services were in English.[826] Germans had begun to arrive in Dog Prairie in 1838. By the 1860s their numbers were sufficient to attract a German priest, Father Conrad Tintrup, who immediately renamed the community and the church St. Paul. German immigrants had also organized the St. Joseph Catholic Church in Josephville in 1848 and took the village's name from the parish. In 1852 they built a log church and a priest from All Saints Parish in St. Peters came over to say Mass.[827] Father Theodore Krainhardt came to Josephville in 1868 and remained for almost 30 years. He was described as, "a German writer of note gifted with an easy natural style that appealed to the priests and people alike."[828] When Flint Hill began to prosper again with the arrival of German-Catholic immigrants, Father Theodore Krainhardt traveled to Flint Hill to say Mass and, in 1883, the congregation built a church and dedicated it to St. Theodore in honor of Father Krainhardt.[829]

In 1841, fifteen German-Catholic families had settled in Augusta and held church services in the Krekel barn until a small wooden church was erected in 1851.[830] By 1866, 35 German-Catholic families lived near Cottleville. As it became more difficult for the priest from St. Peter's Parish in St. Charles to come out, or for the people to get across Dardenne Creek to attend Mass at All Saints Parish, they decided to build their own church. In 1876, Father Joseph Reisdorff, fluent in German, became the first resident pastor.[831] Immaculate Conception Parish was established on Dardenne Prairie in 1872. In 1880, Father W.A. Schmidt became its pastor and, because of the influx of German-Catholic immigrants, a new church was built in 1896. Likewise, in 1869, Catholics from St. Peters and St. Paul met to discuss building a school in O'Fallon. Instead they decided to start a new parish, composed of 17 German families from St. Peters and seven from St. Paul. By 1871, Assumption Parish had a new brick church and a log cabin school. In 1876, Father Henry Brockhagen became pastor of the parish of 130 families, almost exclusively German in their background.[832] German immigration led to the establishment of a Catholic parish in Wentzville in 1882, with a school building by 1909.

The influx of Germans also revitalized several older parishes in St. Charles County. In Portage des Sioux, St. Francis Parish dated from the French settlement. After an influx of German-Catholics in the 1870s, visiting Jesuits were replaced by diocesan priests in 1875, the first being Joseph Schroeder, followed by Henry Mehring, a native of Luxembourg, whose new church was completed in 1879. In 1883 German-born William J. Rensmann became the pastor of the once primarily French St. Francis Parish.[833] Although French settlers had established the Church of St. Peter along Dardenne Creek by 1819, in 1831 there had been only ten families in the parish. By 1837 there had been 60 families and 400 parishioners, mostly German-Catholic immigrants. By the time a new church was built in 1840, it was too small.[834] The corner stone for the fourth church in St. Peters, now called All Saints, was laid in 1874 and the structure was completed in 1882.[835] Like most of these parishes, All Saints opened a parochial school in 1863. It was run by the Sisters of St. Francis who taught all the lessons at the school in German.[836] The German Catholics in these parishes agreed with the priest who explained "in English you must count your dollars, but in German you speak with your children, your confessor, and your God."[837]

Most Lutherans and Evangelicals would not have disagreed with this sentiment. As a result, Germans who sent their children to parochial schools did not embrace the public schools that would serve the Radicals' social revolution. German Lutherans, Evangelicals and Catholics in St. Charles County were more likely to attend parochial than public schools.[838] In St. Charles alone, St. Peters (Roman Catholic), St. John (German Evangelical), St. Paul's (German Evangelical), Immanuel (Lutheran) and the German Methodists all had parochial schools. Adding St. Charles Borromeo, which would also have more German parishioners by the end of the century, and the Academy of the Sacred Heart, the number of parochial and private school students in St. Charles far exceeded the 425 public school students in the St. Charles school district in 1885.[839] Many of the Catholic parochial schools in St. Charles County were run by the Sisters of the Most Precious Blood, a religious order of German women who had moved to Alsace-Lorraine in 1848 when expelled by the Swiss Government. After 1870 Alsace-Lorraine became part of a unified German Empire, supported by the Liberals and ruled by the Protestant *Hohenzollern* dynasty. These groups, along with Chancellor Otto von Bismarck, suspected the loyalty of the Catholics of the new empire. The German state broke relations with the Vatican and passed the May Laws of 1872, requiring civil marriage, suppressing parochial education and allowing the state to seize the assets of religious and charitable organizations. To escape Bismarck's *Kulturkampf*, the Sisters of the Most Precious Blood moved to the St. Louis area and established a motherhouse in O'Fallon by 1875. In 1878, St. Mary's Institute, run by the order and located in O'Fallon, was chartered as a boarding school for girls.[840]

Catholics who sent their children to parochial schools in America wanted to protect them from the strong religious overtones that permeated early public education. They were concerned about the way Protestant teachers criticized the Catholic faith, and feared that the Protestants sought to use the public schools to "Christianize" the Catholics.[841] At the very least, the public schools promoted the social values of the Protestant Americans. The "Rules for Rural Missouri Teachers – 1872" required that female teachers who married were to be dismissed and male teachers were allowed to "take only one evening per week for courting purposes, or two evenings if they go to church regularly." All teachers were expected to spend their evenings "reading the Bible or other good books." Finally, "Any teacher who smokes, uses liquor in any form, visits pool halls or public halls, or gets shaved at a barber shop, will give good reason for people to suspect his worth, intentions and honesty."[842]

Catholic suspicions about the Radical Republicans and their schools increased after 1870. With new sources of revenue now available for public schools in Missouri, Superintendent Parker wanted to make sure that politicians did not disperse any educational dollars to the state's parochial schools. In his report to the Missouri legislature in 1870, he recommended a constitutional amendment to ensure all school funds remain solely for public education. While the amendment also affected Lutheran and Evangelical parochial schools, the debate over the amendment made it obvious that the main target was the Catholic Church. The tenor of the discussion made it clear to any German-Catholic in St. Charles County that the dominant Protestant culture did not consider them real Americans. The political debate exposed a "cultural war," in some ways reminiscent of the *Kulturkampf*, being waged by the Radical Republicans against the Catholics.

There was tremendous animosity toward Catholic education by Radical Republicans such as William Grosvenor, who wrote in 1870 that the editor of the *Catholic Watchman*, "Quotes chapter and verse from the Syllabus in proof of his position that all those who support the public schools, or even send their children to attend them, are heretics." Issued in 1864 by Pope Pius IX, the Syllabus of Errors condemned European Liberalism, strongly anti-clerical because of the church's support of the old regime. Grosvenor, however, read it as a condemnation of American democracy and an attack on public education. He argued, "the tenants of that church are hostile to that independence of thought and action upon which self-government is based," and called upon his readers to support the constitutional amendment that would prohibit state aid for parochial schools.[843]

The constitutional amendment was adopted by the vote of a large majority and was a victory for the Radical Republicans. Yet the *Demokrat* continued to show its disdain for sectarian schools in 1875 when it related a horror story about a local parochial school and lamented, "Such unconscionable things happen naturally in the name of religion. The state retains the right to examine its teachers before they are hired and to observe how they deliver the instruction. Why does it not retain the right of supervision over all the sect institutions which have been established for stupefying, not ennobling."[844] Reflecting the concerns of the American Catholic clergy, in 1876 the Vatican spoke out against public schools, encouraged parochial schools in every parish and allowed the denial of the sacraments to parents who sent their children to public school without "sufficient cause."[845] The Radicals also lost support among German Protestants who sent their children to parochial schools for religious instruction and to keep the German language alive. In St. Charles County the Radical Republican social agenda remained controversial.

Not only the churches, but also the newspapers, helped keep alive the German language in St. Charles County. Three of the five newspapers published in the county in 1882 were published in German. In addition to the *Demokrat*, now Democratic in its politics, the *Republikaner* was founded in 1880 by Heinrich Conrad Sandfort as a Republican paper. As Rothensteiner has pointed out, the Catholic Germans "were not of the class of the 'Latin Farmers' or the Forty-Eighters, men of university training and revolutionary antecedents. They were, for the most part, people of sufficient intellectual culture to appreciate an honest outspoken press in their own language."[846] The *Katholicher Hausfreund*, a weekly German language paper with countywide circulation, published by Father Brockhagen, fulfilled that need. The *Friedensbote*, the denominational paper of the German Evangelical Synod, was published in St. Charles County.

By keeping their language alive the Germans isolated themselves socially from other Americans. Religious Germans' social life revolved around church activities including church picnics. Many of the congregations in the county had annual parish picnics, a practice that continues to this day. The Catholic picnics were usually on Sundays and an integral part of the picnics was, and still is, the beer stand. Lutheran and Evangelical picnics were not held on Sundays, and whether beer was served often depended on the strength of pietistic influences in those churches, or the whim of the pastor, at any given time.[847] Over their history, both the St. John Evangalical and Immanuel Lutheran congregations have sold or, at times, refused to sell beer at church picnics.[848] For both believers and nonbelievers, there were beer gardens and wine gardens in St. Charles County where friends would drink, socialize and enjoy *Gemuetlichkeit*.

The American Methodist, Presbyterian, Baptist or other pietistic congregations frowned upon these activities. In 1885, the author of the *History of St. Charles County* described the good reputation of a certain German-American saloonkeeper, "notwithstanding the Pecksniffian prejudices of some against his business."[849] In 1887 it was reported that Father Reisdorf, pastor of St. Joseph Parish in Cottleville offended the non-Catholics of the community by "taking part in family gatherings on Sunday afternoons, where it was the custom to play cards and indulge in drinking beer. His non-Catholic neighbors considered such conduct entirely unbecoming a clergyman."[850]

German customs were severely threatened when the Missouri legislature passed Blue Laws prohibiting the sale of alcohol on Sunday. After criticizing the "puritanical

Blue Laws," and pointing out that there was no state religion in this country, the *Demokrat* described Sunday in St. Charles after the passage, in 1878, of a local Sunday closing ordinance:

> Last Sunday St. Charles looked like a Puritanical eastern city, for all life on the street had been ended through strict implementation of the Sunday laws…. If for most of Sunday there was no life to be seen on St. Charles' streets, there was much more in the surrounding area. In the nature park in Boschertown, in Brotherton over there in St. Louis County, almost everywhere in the area there were picnics with wine, beer, cigars, etc. The poor St. Charlesans, forbidden through the Sunday ordinance to give out their money in their own town, went in crowds to these locations to spend their money.[851]

Describing the exact same Sunday, John Jay Johns, an elder in the Presbyterian Church, recorded in his diary, "Yesterday the Sunday law was enforced in our town. All business houses and saloons closed after 9:00 a.m. There was a delightful quiet all day."[852]

In 1883, after the Sheriff had arrested some merchants for violating the Sunday closing law, the *Demokrat* explained, "So we hope, and surely the great majority of all Germans with us…, that the Grand Jury meeting next week will not issue charges against the Sunday law violators. It is in their hands to ignore the old, but warmed up, law."[853] In 1884 the *Demokrat* quoted the Mayor of Milwaukee who contended, "The conflict between German and Puritan view of Sunday observance and temperance will continue for now and bring many a hot struggle. Therefore we should be on guard and prepared at all times to defend our good rights with all our strength."[854]

In the post-war period most people in St. Charles County, German and non-German, rejected the modern integrated, secular and homogeneous society envisioned by the Radical Republicans. Whites lost interest in the segregated black schools. The German immigrant was not interested in becoming an American if it meant giving up his parochial schools, language and *Gemuetlichkeit*. He did not wish to treat African-Americans as equals. At the same time, neither the German immigrants nor the recently freed blacks were fully accepted in American society, though the Germans soon would be.

IV
Germanization, Republicanization and Industrialization
1890-1929

In 1903, St. Charles County officials occupied a new courthouse at the corner of Third and Jefferson Streets. The old courthouse on Main Street had served the county well for many years. Lawyers including Edward Bates, Arnold Krekel and Theodore Bruere had practiced there. The people of St. Charles County remained fiscally conservative and they had expressed their distrust for government by twice defeating, by heavy margins in 1888 and 1894, proposed bond issues for the new courthouse.[855] In 1897, at the request of the St. Charles Retail Merchants Association, the Republican County Court ignored the popular votes and proceeded with the project, paying for it from surplus county funds.[856] The county seat, with a population of 7,982 after the 1900 federal census, had become an industrial center, with the car shops of American Car and Foundry visible from the new courthouse. Within a few years, a highway bridge would be completed across the Missouri River and a new shoe factory would open. St. Charles County had gone solidly for Theodore Roosevelt in the previous presidential election. Between 1896 and 1932, no Democratic candidate for president would get a majority in St. Charles County. Almost all the elected officials of St. Charles County were Republicans. Almost all of them were the sons and grandsons of German immigrants, who were now the political, economic and social leaders of St. Charles County.

A. German Predominance

By 1890, the German immigrants, their children and grandchildren, constituted an overwhelming majority in St. Charles County. They shared fully with the non-Germans in the economic prosperity of the turn of the century, but the German-Americans continued to quarrel over religious issues and refused, along with their Anglo-American neighbors, to accept African-Americans as equals. Describing his grandparents, Nagel writes, "The Nagels and most of their neighbors whose roots were in Warren and St. Charles Counties had grown up with an outlook that their parents and grandparents had brought from Europe. This was racial and religious intolerance, a poison whose source can be traced back in the history of Germany and of all mankind."[857] In addition they continued to feel culturally superior and reject assimilation, traits that would make life difficult when the U.S. went to war with Germany in 1917. Calvin Castlio, from a prominent family of early pioneers, observed, "the Germans had their day of comeuppance coming – just as the Southerners, years earlier, had their own." He continued, "Just as the southern families had to change with the times following the Civil War – give up old ways and old beliefs – so it was for the Germans when America and Germany faced off in that great cataclysm."[858]

Anglo-American John Jay Johns had written in 1880, "The peculiar condition of things in this community are very unfavorable to the growth of our Protestant American churches. The American population diminishes gradually. Our young people go away as they grow up. The Germans have the predominancy."[859] By 1882, the *Cosmos-Monitor* had become enthusiastic about the ability of Germans and other Americans to work together for economic betterment in St. Charles:

> In a community comprising such a diversity of population as was the case in the earlier history of this city, such unanimity of sentiment and concord of action could not have been expected. But the old settlers have most of them gone to the grave or retired from business, while their descendants and successors form frequent business contacts, have learned to know and esteem each other and feel the force of that power which makes the child of every foreign-born citizen as much an American as if his ancestors had come over with Captain John Smith, or landed with the Pilgrims on the then inhospitable shores of New England.[860]

When the *History of St. Charles County* was published in 1885, 118 out of the 221 leaders of St. Charles County identified in the publication had German backgrounds.[861] German influence in St. Charles peaked in 1914 when Robertus Love, a legendary St. Louis newspaperman and humorist, described the city and its Mayor, John Olson.

> Big chief Olson is the epitome of St. Charles, except for his descent, which is Danish. It was a startler to find a Dane at the head of the municipality.

We had understood that with the possible exception of Daniel Boone and the Indians, nobody but Germans inhabited St. Charles. There has been a story afloat to the effect that a man named Smith lived there, but upon investigation, we discovered his name was Schmidt.

It is a notable fact that the German town reads English at sight. A common scene on Main Street is a citizen with a German paper in one hand and an English paper in the other hand, reading German with one eye and English with the other. Meanwhile he talks what they term Dutch-Missoo, and its pretty good German-American.[862]

The German language press continued to flourish in St. Charles County. The *Demokrat* published the following excerpts from a speech by a now very elderly Carl Schurz in 1897:

The German-American family is the most effective school in this country. There the German language is cultivated through entertainment, reading, and letter writing and so kept alive for the children. If the language dies out in the family it will become subordinate in school instruction…. The German press in America is an imperative as long as there are German immigrants. However intelligent, ambitious and thirsty for knowledge these immigrants may be, there will always be a great many of them (who need to read German).[863]

The *Demokrat* was the principal protector of German customs and traditions in St. Charles County. Once, when rowdiness developed, the paper criticized the German Day celebration in St. Charles. The paper's editorial writer explained that he wanted "nothing to do with the celebration of 'German Day' where the only, or primary, amusement is beer-drinking and ends in an obligatory fight…."[864] On the other hand, in 1893 the *Demokrat* reported that the German Day in Augusta consisted of parades, orchestras, speeches and dancing. The article concluded, "We do not exaggerate if we contend that all present left the festival grounds with the feeling that they had celebrated German Day in Augusta in a really German manner."[865]

German theatre groups often performed in small towns throughout Missouri. The Young Men's Dramatic Club of St. Peter's Parish was organized in 1888 and staged plays regularly. German-Americans generally did not object to the participation of women in stage production, and the young ladies of the parish began appearing in productions of the Young Men's Dramatic Association after 1904.[866] Reflecting the German love for music, the *Concordia Verein* had been organized in New Melle in 1874. A German studio singing society, the *Eintracht*, thrived in St. Charles. There were also several bands in the county, including the New Melle Band, established in 1875, and the St. Charles Cornet Band that started playing concerts in 1897. Fred Jacoby organized the O'Fallon Cornet Band in 1890, while Craven's Band was performing in the Wentzville area by 1906. Like Rummel's Military Band in St. Charles, they performed at picnics, concerts and parades.

German organizations like the *Eintracht*, a studio singing society, flourished in St. Charles County. *St. Charles County Historical Society*

In 1927, a municipal band was formed in O'Fallon and, in 1929, St. Charles passed a tax to support its municipal band. In the 1920s St. John Evangelical Church had a 20-piece orchestra. One commentator suggested that these bands helped make St. Charles an "outpost of Gallic and Teutonic culture."[867]

By the 1890s, the first generation of German leaders had passed away, moved away or retired. One historian has established a social hierarchy for American towns during this period. At the top were the bankers, lawyers and doctors. Next came other professionals, including printers, teachers and clergymen. Then came retail storekeepers and their clerks. Finally, at the bottom of the hierarchy were the craftsmen, with millers the highest and wage laborers and the indigent at the very bottom.[868] In St. Charles, German-Americans were well represented in each of these groups.

In 1906, there were four banks in St. Charles and all were led by men with German surnames. Judge Henry F. Pieper was the president of Union Savings Bank; Theodore Bruere was the president of St. Charles Savings Bank; Edward Gut was the president of First National Bank and H. F. Knippenburg was the president of Central Bank of St. Charles. All were political leaders as well. Of the 12 directors, officers or employees highlighted in the 1906 business directory, nine had German surnames.[869]

Among the lawyers listed in the directory were Wm. Achelpohl, Theodore C. Bruere, Charles and Carl Daudt, R.C. Haenssler and Henry Schoenich, along with four non-German names, including B.H. Dyer, an influential Republican leader in the community. Theodore C. Bruere, who served as prosecuting attorney for St. Charles County for over 26 years, also served as a commissioner of the St. Louis Court of Appeals for eight years.[870]

As in previous periods, lawyers provided leadership for the community and German-Americans were now well represented in that profession.

Seven of the 13 physicians listed in the directory had German surnames, including Carl Bitter, John Bruere, Kurt Stumberg and Benedict Wentker. Dr. Bruere had been an important leader in the community since before the Civil War. Dr. B. Kurt Stumberg had served as a medical sergeant with the sixth Missouri Infantry during the Spanish-American War, and was chief of the medical staff at St. Joseph Hospital. Dr. James R. Mudd served as mayor of St. Charles. Dr. John Talley of Wentzville, Dr. Oscar Muhm of New Melle, Dr. Jasper Newton Castlio of Howell and Dr. Russell B. Lewis of Flint Hill were community leaders. Their education and status continued to make doctors important civic leaders in St. Charles County. [871]

German-Americans were the majority among other professionals as well. John Henry Bode was still the editor of the *Demokrat* and R. Goebel was taking photographs that still provide us a look at the community as it existed in the late nineteenth century. Among the clergy, Father F.X. Willmes had been appointed assistant pastor of St. Peter's Church in 1877. With the exception of a three-year stint in Cape Girardeau, he was the pastor there until he retired in 1931.[872] Reverend Jules Friedrich was called to Immanuel Lutheran in 1901 and remained until 1923. The retail storekeepers were almost entirely of German background, including some German Jews. By 1906 every city and county elected official except two, had a German surname. German-Americans were now not only a large majority of the population, but were also a large majority within the professional and commercial elite of St. Charles County.

Decades of German immigration had left its mark on the institutions of St. Charles. The Sisters of St. Mary had begun in 1872 when Sister Mary Odelia Burger and four companions left Germany for St. Louis. They could not speak English but they had experience as battlefield nurses in Europe. Having left Germany to escape Bismarck's *Kulturkampf*, they settled in St. Louis, where their assistance with the smallpox epidemic earned them the name "smallpox sisters." In 1873, when Father Edward Koch, Pastor of St. Peter's Church, called upon the sisters to treat smallpox in St. Charles, Sister Odelia and three other sisters had come and ministered to the sick. Eleven years later the sisters were again called to St. Charles and the following year the Franz Schulte family had given the sisters the house at 305 Chauncey Street, where they opened the first St. Joseph Hospital with 20 beds in 1885.[873] In 1897 the Carmelite Sisters of the Divine Heart of Jesus opened their first novitiate in the Netherlands. The order first came to the United States in 1912, and opened the St. Joseph's Carmelite Nursing Home at Eighth and Clay Streets in St. Charles in 1920. By 1928 the Eighth Street addition allowed the sisters to serve 55 elderly residents.[874]

The Immanuel Lutheran Congregation operated a grade school, as did the German Methodist church. There were two German Evangelical congregations, St. John and St. Paul's. St. John Hall was erected in 1911, and the congregation maintained a parochial school until 1930. The Emmaus Home, an "asylum for epileptics and the feeble minded," was established in 1902 under the sponsorship of the St. John Evangelical Church.[875]

The parochial school at St. Peter's, a German-Catholic parish, was conducted by the School Sisters of Notre Dame. That order, founded in Bavaria in 1833, had come to the United States in 1847 and worked mainly in German parishes.[876] The morning instruction at the school was in German, while English was spoken in the afternoon. A parish hall was built in 1900 and the parish opened St. Peter's High School in 1924, offering a two-year curriculum until 1929, when a full four-year program was instituted.[877]

The brick church of St. Charles Borromeo had been built in 1869 in the Gothic style of most churches in St. Charles County. Like St. John and St. Peter's churches, it was designed by John Henry Stumberg, who also oversaw the construction of Immanuel Lutheran church.[878] As the nineteenth century progressed, St. Charles Borromeo also had welcomed more and more German-American parishioners. When the brick church was dedicated in 1869, one sermon was given in English and one in German.[879] These Protestant and Catholic schools and institutions continued to keep the German language and culture alive in St. Charles.

Other institutions in St. Charles County remained the exclusive preserve of the Anglo-Americans. The large corporations operating in the city tended to be run by professional managers, often brought in from elsewhere, who were usually Anglo-Americans. An early example of this was Benjamin Pratt, a civil engineer who had surveyed and constructed the North Missouri Railroad. He became a successful farmer and served as judge of the County Court. The St. Charles chapter of the Daughters of the American Revolution was organized in 1909, and by 1921 it had dedicated monuments marking the Booneslick Road, the burial site of Rebecca and Daniel Boone (in Warren County) and the headquarters of Commandant Louis Blanchette. Anglo-Americans such as Benjamin L. Emmons, whose family had been in the county for five generations, wrote the local history that has come down to us. The *History of St. Charles County*, written in 1885, has a distinct prejudice in favor of the Democratic Anglo-Americans over the Republican German-Americans. Describing the politics of Benjamin Alderson, it states, "Being a man of sterling, old-fashioned ideas of honesty in public affairs, he is of course a Democrat, strongly opposed to the new regime of extravagance and corruption that prevails in the government."[880] Another important Anglo-American institution that prospered in St. Charles between 1913 and 1924 was the annual Chautauqua, held under a huge tent that was set up at Eighth and Washington Streets. Edna McElhiney Olson explains, "the entertainment was spectacular and truly typical of America. Speakers, singers and entertainers were booked months in advance and the better they were the more season tickets were sold. The first day and the last day were always the best."[881] In September 1915 William Jennings Bryan gave a "neutrality speech," at the St. Charles Chautauqua.[882]

St. Charles College had reopened after a lengthy court battle and was eventually paid $6,600 by the federal government for the interruption. In 1902, it was made a military school and officers from Jefferson Barracks drilled the cadet corps. The Missouri General Assembly made the school a post of the National Guard of Missoui, and required the governor to commission the president as a colonel.[883] In its later years the college offered business courses and admitted women. In 1915 the college closed, the board donated its land to the school district. In 1922 and St. Charles High School was built on the site at Kingshighway and Waverly Streets.[884]

Lindenwood College continued to thrive and received accreditation as a junior college in 1913, was accredited by the North Central Association of Colleges and Universities in 1921, and awarded its first baccalaureate degrees in that same year. In 1914 Dr. John L. Roemer assumed the office of president and began a major building program that, between 1915 and 1929, included three dormitories, a new administration building and a library. By 1922 Lindenwood had a large endowment, and five days of celebration in 1927 marked the centennial of the school's founding.[885] The involvement of German-Americans in St. Charles College or Lindenwood College remained minimal. One notable exception was the Stumberg family. Dr. John Henry Stumberg served as the St. Charles representative on the Lindenwood College Board of Directors from 1877 until 1903. His son, Dr. Bernard Kurt Stumberg, served in the same position from 1903 until 1943. Johann Heinrich Stumberg had been one of the founders of the Immanuel Lutheran Church in 1847. But his son John Henry left the church in a dispute over his purchase of life insurance. He joined the Presbyterian Church and became a supporter of Lindenwood.[886]

Most of the Anglo-Americans sent their children to the public schools and many were strong supporters of public elementary education. Nationally, almost 25 percent of students in 1920 attended a one-room school.[887] The percentage in St. Charles County was much higher, as there were 91 common school districts in the county in 1899 and 77 still remained in the 1920s.[888] Dedicated teachers like Mary Emily Bryan (Mechanicsville), Louis Saeger (Friedens) and Willie Harris (Black Jack) taught in these one-room schools.

Francis Howell Institute, established in 1881 under a provision of the will of Francis Howell Jr., served the southern part of the county. Though not tied to the state common school system, the institute charged no tuition and had no particular religious orientation. In 1901, Hiram Castlio further endowed the institute, where classes were held in a three-story building, with the second and third stories used to board students. The first teacher at the institute had been Cora Bates, granddaughter of Edward Bates and daughter of Barton Bates. The newly formed consolidated district, that purchased ground for a new Francis Howell High School in 1915, absorbed the Institute.[889] In 1896, a two-year high school opened in Wentzville. By 1910 there were two new public schools in the O'Fallon area, where high school classes were offered until 1918 when a Catholic High School opened. After that date, public high school students from O'Fallon attended school in Wentzville or St. Charles. A two-year high school opened in Augusta in 1914, and expanded in 1922 to offer four years of instruction.[890]

In St. Charles, Benton School was opened in 1896, McKinley School in 1905 and a new Lincoln School in 1930. When the old high school, located on the corner of Fourth and Jefferson Streets, burned down on February 14, 1918, it took four bitterly contested elections between November 1921 and June 1922 to approve the bonds to build a new high school at the corner of Kingshighway and Waverly Streets. This was partly due to resistance to taxes among the voters.[891] Indeed, in 1885, while ranking fifth in assessed valuation, St. Charles County had ranked sixteenth in taxes paid. In 1916 St. Charles had the lowest school tax rate of any city half its size.[892] It was also difficult to get the two-thirds majority necessary for the bonds when almost 55 percent of the students in the city attended parochial schools.[893] The *Cosmos-Monitor* complained that 13 counties had smaller populations and paid less in state taxes, but received larger appropriations from the school fund. This was because funding ignored the large number of parochial school pupils in the county. The paper complained, "Still their parents pay state taxes and it hardly looks fair."[894]

Anglo-American churches continued to expand and multiply. In 1872, the St Charles Presbyterians had moved into a new church at the corner of Jefferson and Benton Streets. The following year the Point Prairie and South Dardenne Presbyterian Church had been organized, though the latter continued to share the Union Church of Mechanicsville with the Methodists until 1888. The first Congregational Church in the county had been established at Pauldingville in 1873. The Second Street Baptist Church had been organized in 1888 with 19 members. While the congregation of Trinity Episcopal Church had built a new building at the corner of Benton and Clark Streets in 1871, it did not become well established until 1902 when a rectory was added.[895] In 1906 the Methodist Church at Fifth and Washington Streets was the largest English-speaking congregation in St. Charles.

By 1890, a new source of potential ethnic and religious conflict had emerged in St. Charles. For decades German Jews had been merchants in St. Charles County, including Simon Baer, "one of the energetic, enterprising business men of St. Charles County," who had emigrated from Baden in 1873 and opened stores in St. Peters and Cottleville.[896] The 1891 *St. Charles County Directory* advertised a dry goods business in the Opera House building run by Julius Frank and another business named "Kohn's Big Boot," with Louis Kohn as the proprietor.[897] In 1899 Emil Weil bought out Kohn and another business owned by Ike Constam and opened the Palace men's clothing company on Main Street. Weil was an immigrant from Alsace-Lorraine who became a successful businessman in St. Charles.[898]

By the turn of the century, a second Jewish immigration was bringing Russian Jews to the St. Louis area. The Willner family was the first from this new wave of Jewish immigrant to come to St. Charles County in 1907.[899] By 1910, Russian-Jewish families had established businesses in St. Charles. Harry Caplan (shoe repair), Samuel and Paul Polski and Charles Shapiro (The Famous and Hub Clothing) all had businesses on Main Street. German Jews of St. Louis were leaders in the garment industry and many Russian Jews worked in their factories before entering the tailoring or retail clothing business.[900] By 1929, Herman Braufman (clothing), Samuel Rosenblum (tailor), Joseph Wolfson (The Famous – women's clothing) had also opened busi-

As late as the 1920s there were still 77 common school districts in St. Charles County. Many of them operated one-room schools like the Cul-de-Sac School pictured here. *John J. Buse Collection, 1860-1931, Western Historical Manuscript Collection-Columbia, MO*

nesses on Main Street. Jewish families in St. Louis were active in the lumber business and Benjamin and Jacob Kaplan were operating a lumberyard in St. Charles in 1929. Closely tied to the lumber business was the furniture business and the Willner family operated the Hub Furniture store.[901] Harry Willner, Abraham Kaplan, Julius Kaplan and Samuel Kaplan raised livestock on the outskirts of St. Charles.[902]

While never consisting of more than 20 or so families, Jewish families were a significant part of the St. Charles business community. In the larger community, where Germans and their descendants did not always get along with Americans that had arrived earlier, where Protestant and Catholic German-Americans shunned each other and both abhorred the free thinkers, Christians also had their prejudices toward Jews. Professor Nagel relates how the anti-Semitism of his German grandparents was cultural rather than personal. "It was simple: Jews were not Christians," and Christianity constantly reminded them of the Jewish role in the crucifixion of Jesus Christ.[903]

More surprisingly, animosity sometimes existed between the German Jews and the Russian Jews. Historian Walter Ehrlich explains that German Jews looked condescendingly upon Russian Orthodox Jews as religious fanatics and "schnorrers." At the same time, Russian Jews saw the German Reform Jews as arrogant "goyim." German and Russian Jews existed as almost completely separate Jewish communities in St. Louis.[904] The same was true in St. Charles, where the Weil family belonged to Temple Israel, the leading Reform congregation in St. Louis. The Russian Jews in St. Charles practiced Orthodox Judaism and met in a spare room in the home of Abraham Kaplan on the High Holidays. A Rabbi would come out from St. Louis until the early 1930s when the St. Charles Directory lists Julius Hess as Rabbi of the St. Charles Jewish congregation.

In 1890, African-Americans continued to reside throughout St. Charles County. The attitudes of some Anglo-Americans had not changed much since the Civil War. John Jay Johns, a former slaveholder, made the following diary entry in 1890:

> If the North will keep hands off, the two races will work it out but the white will always be the dominant race. It is the duty of the white to do all they can to help the negro in his dependent and ignorant condition, but his condition must be one of subordination – but if under the influence of the Northern whites he should resort to force he will be inevitably crushed. The best friend of the negro are the whites of the South who have been raised with him and know his good and bad qualities.[905]

Some descendants of slaveholders continued to understate the evils of slavery. They argued: 1) the slaves had been well treated, 2) there had been a kind feeling between the owner and the slave, 3) the slaves had been a "happy carefree group." In contrasts to the industrial wage earner, it was pointed out, "slaves had been free of labor Saturday afternoon and all day Sunday and their masters supplied them with food and fuel…."[906]

Racial attitudes of those German-Americans who had fought against slavery and their descendants were not much better. Leaders like Emil Mallinckrodt feared race mixing, and wrote:

> Viewed entirely without prejudice, an amalgamation would be a misfortune for the white or caucasian, element. There are only two human races on earth whose complete amalgamation disparages neither, rather may have good results through their mixing – that is, the Germanic and Semitic tie. Their intelligence and progressive development has conquered the world – Mongolian, Malayan, Indians and Negroes, even under the most favorable relations, will never lift themselves to such intellectual greatness.[907]

By 1890, the *Demokrat* had adopted many of the Democratic Party's attitudes on racial issues. It perpetuated racial stereotypes, starting in 1893, "St. Charles is becoming a big city, or is one already, if the norm is the number of crimes and disturbances happening daily. For some time now a mood of disrupting the peace prevails, especially among the colored population. It can be controlled only through energetic legal procedures."[908] In fact, rank and file German-Americans were never as idealistic as some of their Liberal leaders. Racism was not a disease that the German-Americans caught from their neighbors.

In this atmosphere, the former slaves and their families struggled with little or no economic assets. Many continued to live in those areas where their masters had held them in bondage before 1865. Dr. Jasper Newton Castlio stated, "Sharecropping and tenant farming then became more common as freed blacks began to seek ways to

The Weils were a successful German-Jewish family in St. Charles who owned this business on Main Street. *John J. Buse Collection, 1860-1931, Western Historical Manuscript Collection-Columbia, MO*

feed their families."[909] Others moved from "Little Dixie" to St. Louis looking for economic opportunities. The black population of St. Louis, which grew from 4,000 in 1860 to 22,000 by 1880, no doubt included many from St. Charles County. Still, as late as 1900, ten percent of the 24,474 population of St. Charles County was African-American; down from 15 percent in 1860, when the population was 16,523. Many freedmen who had been agricultural laborers before the Civil War moved to towns like St. Charles, O'Fallon or Wentzville looking for work. Others stayed in the country, sharecropping or even owning small plots of ground. By 1900, 47 percent of African-Americans in Missouri lived in cities, while in St. Charles County only about a third lived in St. Charles. At one time, there were three black churches in O'Fallon: the African Methodist Church, the Wishwell Baptist Church and the Northern Methodist Episcopal Church. The Hopewell Baptist Church was in Wentzville and another black Baptist church had been built in Cottleville on land donated by David Pitman after the Civil War.[910]

Black economic opportunities were scarce and the percentage of African-Americans in St. Charles County shrank to seven percent in 1910 and 5.5 percent in 1920. The exodus is not well documented. Apparently, according to one story, many had to sell their small farms in the Dardenne Creek floodplain when that creek was straightened in the 1920s. A 30-year tax was imposed on the land, which most black farmers could not afford to pay. From 1910 to 1920 the black population of St. Louis increased from 6.4 percent to nine percent, as the city grew by 11.1 percent while St. Charles County's population fell to 22,822, a decline of 1,867 since the 1910 census.[911] Although prejudice existed in St. Louis as well, there were better economic opportunities in the large cities.[912] James Neal Primm explains that, even though they received only menial jobs, African-Americans justified their situation by explaining "better to be a lamp post on Targee Street than the Mayor of Dixie."[913]

St. Charles fell somewhere between Targee Street and Dixie. The percentage of African-Americans in the city fell from 9 percent in 1900 to 5.3 percent in 1930. Slaves had built their first church in St. Charles at 554 Madison Street in 1849.[914] After the Civil War there were four black churches in St. Charles: St. Johns A.M.E., St. Paul M.E., Mount Zion Missionary Baptist and the Church of God in Christ, the only one of the four not still in existence.[915] African-Americans in St. Charles attended their own churches and lived in their own neighborhoods, including Africa Hill across from Blanchette Park in the McElhiney Addition, Goose Hill at the end of Washington Street, as well as smaller neighborhoods in Frenchtown and on South Main Street. In 1906, a new subdivision, Roosevelt Place, was platted north of Tecumseh Street and West of Third Street. Because the land had been reclaimed from a swamp, the neighborhood became known as "frogtown." The developer was an attorney from Belleville, Illinois named August Barthel; one of the streets in the neighborhood is stilled named for him. The deed to every lot in the subdivision contained the following language: "It is expressly agreed and understood between the parties to this deed that the lot herein described and conveyed shall not at any time be sold, leased to or occupied by any person or persons of the African or negro (sic) race." On the east side of Third Street another subdivision, Riverside View, had the same restrictive racial covenant in its deeds.

The biggest impediment to African-Americans moving elsewhere in the city was not enforced residential segregation but lack of money to buy a home in a nicer neighborhood.[916] The Relief Association of St. Charles, Missouri was organized at St. Johns A.M.E. in 1911 for the relief of poor and needy in the black community. The organization sponsored an annual picnic in Blanchette Park and, in its first 25 years of existence, raised over $30,000. The organization was non-religious and non-political; it rendered assistance to whites as well as blacks when requested to do so.[917]

Racially segregated schools had been required in Missouri since 1875. In 1897, all black students in St. Charles were moved to Lincoln School, at Second and Pike Streets. In 1902, Reverend H.H. Peck appeared before the Board of Education and requested, "the board give the children of Lincoln School a full day's instruction," rather than the one-half day they were receiving. The board granted the request and hired another black teacher. Franklin School, at Franklin and Third Street, was made a second school for black students living north of Clark Street. In 1914, the district expanded the Franklin facility and transferred all the black students to it.[918] While white students were offered two years of high school in 1902 and four years by 1905, only counties with a population over 100,000 were required to have a black high school pursuant to a law passed by the legislature in 1921. In that same year, the state superintendent of schools wrote the St. Charles school board, "I note that you are doing no high school work in the Franklin School. Since Negroes are to have a University in Missouri, I wish to recommend that you plan the work in your school to add two years of high school work."[919] Franklin School provided two years of high school the next year, but would not have a three-year high school until the 1930-31 school year, or a four-year high school until 1932-33. Until that time, ambitious black students had to commute to St. Louis to attend Sumner or Vashon High Schools.[920]

African-Americans still constituted ten percent of the population of St. Charles County in 1900. They remained segregated from the white population and had their own social organizations like the Odd Fellows pictured here in front of the county courthouse . *John J. Buse Collection, 1860-1931, Western Historical Manuscript Collection-Columbia, MO*

In other areas, Missouri law and Missouri courts continued to deny African-Americans their civil rights. In 1851, upon the death of his father, Eli Keen had purchased one of his father's slaves named Phoebe, with whom he began cohabiting. They lived together in the West Alton area until about 1883, with their eight children, six of whom were born prior to emancipation. In 1883 Eli and Phoebe separated and Phoebe eventually moved to St. Charles. Eli went to West Virginia, married and then conveyed a life estate in the family farmhouse to Phoebe, with Phoebe's daughters to inherit upon her death. In his will of 1900, Eli devised his entire estate to his sons except for certain provisions for his West Virginia wife, Sophronia. When Eli died in 1901, Sophronia renounced the will, claiming that she was entitled to one-half the estate as the wife of Eli Keen, and filed a suit to eject the family of Eli Keen from the farm. The attorney for the Keen heirs was D. P. Dyer, who as U.S. Attorney had uncovered the corrupt "whiskey ring" almost 30 years earlier.[921] After hearing the case, St. Charles County Circuit Judge E.M.Hughes held:

> My conclusions of law from the above facts are that no marriage at common law ever existed between Eli Keen and Phoebe Keen, and that Eli Keen died without any child or children or other descendant in being capable of inheriting from him, and that plaintiff is entitled to recover possession of an undivided one-half of the lands described in the petition.

The Missouri Supreme Court upheld the circuit judge, explaining that Phoebe had been incompetent to enter into any contract, including a marriage contract, while a slave. It distinguished another case where the marriage of two slaves had been upheld because their masters had consented. After emancipation the law in Missouri specifically made any marriage between white and black persons "void." Statutes provided, "the children of all persons who were slaves, and were living together in good faith as man and wife at the time of the birth of such children, shall be deemed and taken to be legitimate children of such parents," and further "the issue of all marriages, decreed null in law, or dissolved by divorce shall be legitimate." The Supreme Court held that the children of Eli Keen were not legitimate under the former provision because their father had not been a slave. They were not legitimate under the latter because no "marriage" had taken place.[922]

In addition to this *de jure* discrimination so characteristic of southern states, African-Americans in St. Charles County also had to deal with what E. Terrence Jones describes as a "kind of northern indifference to race," characterized by a "lack of social interaction of any kind."[923] African-Americans were excluded from sports, the public library, the St. Charles Hotel, St. Joseph Hospital, and every restaurant and bar in the community.[924] When American Car and Foundry had a party for its workers, the whites were invited on one night and the blacks on the next.[925] Local historians who have looked at the issue confirm the indifference. Mark Poindexter suggests the treatment of African-Americans in the *Cosmos-Monitor* newspaper, shows that, for the most part, the paper, "ignored the existence of Black people."[926] Lori Breslow believes that the white citizens of St. Charles, "were not particularly affected by the presence of Blacks in their town."[927]

This "northern indifference," sometimes degenerated into outright hostility. Three thousand people had witnessed the execution by hanging of William Barton, an African-American, in 1879 for the murder of a white man. Some of the interest may have been due to his age,15, rather than his race.[928] Between 1900 and 1930, there were 22 lynchings in Missouri, 17 involving black men.[929] The *Demokrat* condemned the practice of lynching, stating that, "Whoever gives lynchers the word must also support a return to the painful question about torturing and drawing and quartering, to whipping posts and branding. He must learn that society should be just as gruesome, merciless and bloodthirsty as the lowest criminals, and that the primary purpose of law is revenge."[930]

In 1916, Lacy Chanley, a black man, shot and killed Sheriff John H. Dierker when the sheriff tried to arrest him for the attempted murder of Ernest Plackemeier. Chanley was tracked down by sheriff's deputies, trapped in a barn and surrounded by an angry mob. According to John Buse, "Chanley attempted to surrender but the angry men were determined to have his life. He appeared at the barn door and 100 shots were fired at him. He then set fire to the barn and again he appeared with his hands in the air when perhaps 1,000 shots were fired at him and he fell in the doorway."[931] Apparently, some time in the 1920s racial tensions in O'Fallon caused most of the black families to move out of town.[932] Other stories persist about whites taking the law into their own hands against blacks in the county. With their civil rights often unprotected and their economic opportunities dwindling, many African-Americans moved out. By 1930 they comprised only 4.2 percent of the population in the county.

Social conflicts persisted between whites in St. Charles County as well. Calvin Castlio commented on the cultural differences when he compared the "Southern village" of Howell to the "German village" of Hamburg, whose "menfolk liked their beer, liked music and a dance now and again. Hamburg was a right lively place. Someone always had a fiddle or a harmonica, or even a piano. Howell was more staid – like I said – churchy."[933] The "churchy" Anglo-Americans especially disapproved of the drinking, music and theatre of the German-Americans when they occurred on Sunday. Though a sizable majority in the county, Americans of German descent were a minority in Missouri and were especially upset when the legislature passed a "Sabbath Law" making it a misdemeanor to engage in certain commercial enterprises on Sunday, a day important to the German cultural tradition of *Gemuetlichkeit*. St. Charles had two breweries; the Schibi Brewery, since torn down, and the Moerschel-Spring Brewing Company, whose facilities still stand at Second and Water Streets. Wepprich's Wine Garden opened in 1901 and there is still a wine garden on the site today. The city had 14 taverns and the "continental Sunday" was commonly observed. Three thousand people attended the St. Francis Parish picnic in Portage des Sioux on the first Sunday in August 1912 and consumed 48 kegs of beer.[934]

The German-Americans resented the efforts of some Protestants to legislate morality. The *Demokrat* reported in 1895:

> At the next session of the Circuit Court, the English Protestant ministers here seem resolved to bring a charge before the grand jury against pub keepers who keep their business open on Sunday…. Sensing the pending filing of a claim against them, two pubs here were closed last Sunday. That is, the front door was closed, while the back door was open for anyone who wanted to add fuel to the fire. The agitators have the law on their side, and it is not improbable that they will succeed in their intent to introduce the Puritanical Sunday. Catholic and Lutheran clergy here are not part of the movement[935]

Never missing a chance to demonstrate its anti-clericalism, the *Demokrat* added, "The (pastors) have Sunday every day and 'work' only on those days when other people may celebrate. They should just permit people to have their way of life, for they cannot improve or reform them with force."[936] The temperance reformers responded by asserting, "With five saloons in town, it does seem everyone could get drunk enough in the six working days of the week, without having to resort to Sunday."[937]

By the 1890s, temperance forces were moving beyond mere enforcement of Blue Laws. Nationally, many pietistic Protestants believed that the new urban industrial society had made intemperance an even greater problem. Later arriving immigrant groups were not nearly as prosperous as the Germans, yet used alcohol just as much. The sober Protestants blamed the poverty and dysfunction of these immigrant families on the "demon rum." Although few in St. Charles supported it, the temperance movement was active and frequently tried to close the saloons. In 1909 the Women's Christian Temperance Union warned the editor of the *Cosmos-Monitor*, "The safety of our young manhood and young womanhood are in danger by the disregard of the enforcement of the city and state laws enacted for our moral protection."[938] One month later a saloon was closed down for violating the dramshop law.[939]

The pressure to conform to pietist ideas about the Sabbath was nothing compared to the scrutiny endured by those of German descent when the United States went to war against Germany in 1917. One German-American in Belleville, Illinois faced the kind of mob violence usually reserved for African-Americans. German language and *Kultur*, long a point of ethnic pride, were now the targets of patriotic fervor. Prior to 1917, appreciation for things German in St. Charles also encompassed pride in what a unified Germany had achieved since 1870. Since the 1860s the German Liberals in America, like their counterparts in Europe, had applauded Otto von Bismarck's leadership in uniting Germany.[940] In St. Charles County, the *Demokrat* had reported in 1869 that Bismarck, unlike his predecessors, realized, "the Germans in the U.S., even if in fact separated from the motherland, still had direct and indirect connections," and he saw how desirable it was, "to secure the friendship of North America."[941] The *Demokrat* had followed with interest the German victories against France in 1870, which led to the announcement of the German Empire the following year. Those of German ancestry in St. Charles County continued to express pride in the accomplishments of a united Germany.

When World War I broke out in August 1914, most German-Americans sided with Imperial Germany, especially the editors of German language newspapers. However, support for Germany's war aims was not uniform throughout the community. After Bismarck broke with the German Liberals in the 1880s and formed a government with the assistance of the Conservatives, many German-American Liberals were no longer as enamored by the regime. Bismarck's *Kulturkampf* against the Catholic Church certainly did not endear the regime to German Catholics. Finally, many of the immigrants in St. Charles County had not come from Prussia, but from other German

163

Kuhlmann's Grove, located at what is now the main entrance to Heritage Subdivision, was a popular place for German-Americans to picnic, drink beer and enjoy *Gemuctlichkeit. St. Charles County Historical Society*

states like Bavaria, Baden and Hanover. Many had immigrated to the United States to avoid universal military training required of all adult males in the German Empire. An old letter from Germany, found by local historian Judy Sigmund, captures the feeling against the *Kulturkampf*. A young German girl writes, "Weddings are now very different. We will not have a celebration at the church, but we will go before the magistrate." While German censorship of letters was mentioned, the greatest complaint was against the military training and service required of all young men.[942]

In Missouri, the German-American Alliance led the fight against prohibition. In October 1914 the *Cosmos-Monitor* announced a mass meeting of the German-American Alliance at the county courthouse where a former assistant prosecuting attorney spoke on the "great danger" of national prohibition. The article made it clear that the speaker would be "speaking in English." After the outbreak of war in 1914, the German-American Alliance sought to ensure the neutrality of the United States. Many local German-Americans opposed war with Germany, not because they approved of the Kaiser's regime, but out of concern for the well being of relatives who would be fighting on the other side. In 1915, responding to anti-German pressure, John Cardinal Glennon, Archbishop of St. Louis, banned sermons and announcements in German at Catholic church services.[943]

While the predominance of German customs was a problem in St. Charles County when the United States declared war on the Central Powers, the German-Americans were anxious to prove their loyalty.[944] An ordinance was introduced in the St. Charles

City Council to ban the publication of newspapers in German. The German-American Bank in O'Fallon changed its name to Commercial Bank. When the Immanuel German Evangelical Lutheran Church dropped the word "German" from its name and made English its official language, the St. John German Evangelical Church did the same. The *Cosmos-Monitor* applauded the change and said, "hereafter nothing but English, the pure United States language, will be taught to children at the school. Three cheers for the Lutherans."[945] St. Peter's Catholic School stopped instruction in the German language, as did the common schools at Hamburg, Weldon Spring and Friedens. Thirty-five men from St. Peter's parish volunteered or were called for the draft, while the rest of the congregation participated in war relief efforts.[946] A War Bond drive was launched with a big parade. Led by Julius F. Rauch, the drive doubled its quota and collected $1.1 million.[947] In fact, St. Charles County's unity behind the war effort earned it an award for buying more war bonds per capita than any county in Missouri.[948] Parishioners from St. Peter's Parish subscribed to more War Bonds than any other congregation in the county.[949] Of the 1,166 St. Charles County men who served in the armed services during the war, 759 (65 percent) had German surnames. Of the 49 St. Charles countians who died in service to their country during the war, 29 had German surnames. An even larger percentage of local German-Americans served in the Home Guard formed in 1918 to provide security in the state while the Missouri National Guard was fighting in France.[950]

Nevertheless, by 1918 the German population in St. Charles County came under serious scrutiny. Early in the year, the State of Missouri required all German-born residents to either produce their naturalization papers or register as citizens of Germany. Sixty St. Charles residents registered with the chief of police by February 20th:

> Many were interested in becoming naturalized citizens and the local papers carried instructions on how that could be done. Ninety-one–year-old William Lentz, a retired farmer, was one person who applied for citizenship. Lentz came to the United States from Uchtdorf, Germany in 1883 and was reported to be the oldest man ever to apply for citizenship. In an article in March of 1926, the *Banner-News* reported that "approximately ninety applicants visited the naturalization bureau. Fifty nine applications were filed by three o'clock and about thirty-five were in the corridor awaiting their turn."[951]

A division of the American Protective League, under the direction of the U.S. Department of Justice, was formed to cover St. Charles and Warren Counties. Dr. Will L. Freeman and Ronald M. Thompson, editor of the *Banner-News*, headed the division. Dr. Freeman alleged:

> The activities of the League included concerted, intelligent effort to overthrow the German spy system in the United States, to defeat the underhanded work of the German propagandists, to prove or disprove the loyalty of prominent citizens, to curb disloyal remarks and enemy activities, to secure evidence against alien enemies and disloyal citizens and bring about internment or conviction.[952]

The Missouri Home Guard of St. Charles County was comprised of 61 men who were exempt or too old for the military draft. They drilled and functioned at all military funerals in the county until disbanded in June of 1919. *John J. Buse Collection, 1860-1931, Western Historical Manuscript Collection-Columbia, MO*

The German-Americans now received some of the same kind of scrutiny that Americans of southern origin had received during the period of martial law during the Civil War. At the end of its seven months of operation, the League had made complete reports on 34 cases and partial reports on 63 suspects with 14 cases still under investigation. Mob violence erupted in Collinsville, Illinois, where Robert Praeger, a 45-year-old unemployed coal miner, had applied for naturalization and tried to join the U.S. Navy. At a gathering of socialists, he apparently offended the community's pro-war sentiments by criticizing President Wilson. Although the police put him in jail for his own safety, an angry mob dragged him out, made him kiss the Stars and Stripes and, after allowing him to write a farewell letter to his parents in Germany, hanged him.[953]

While German-Americans were trying to prove their loyalty, the entire community supported the war effort. Farmers attended mass meetings on food production at the St. Charles County courthouse in May 1917. They elected officers to head the recently established St. Charles County Farm Bureau and resolved to cooperate with the Missouri College of Agriculture to increase crop yields. They also recommended that the government establish minimum prices, provide loans and make all farmers exempt from military service.[954] Over 4,000 individuals from the county signed the following pledge card:

To the Food Administration, Washington, D.C.

I am glad to join the service of food conservation for our nation and I hereby accept membership in the United States Food Administration, pledging myself to carry out the directions and advice of the food administration in my home, in so far as my circumstances permit.[955]

Builders announced no new buildings would be constructed during the war. The county sheriff asked the newspapers to publicize letters he had received from the U.S. marshal, asking for his cooperation to "maintain order and respect for the American flag in St. Charles County." Citizens volunteered for the local chapter of the American Red Cross that provided shelter, medical attention, and nurses to the men disabled by the war. A sewing room was established and the volunteers made over 4,000 items including sweaters and socks for the soldiers. The Red Cross presented a comfort pack to every soldier who left the county containing a knife, handkerchief, soap, toothbrush, toothpaste and post cards.[956] Latona Rodgers, Olive Rauch and Celeste Rauch, all from St. Charles, served with the Red Cross in France.[957] After a large patriotic rally, 25 men from St. Charles County enlisted in the armed services.[958]

Throughout October 1918, the people of the county followed with interest the German retreat. At news of the armistice, businesses shut down and, along with the high school band and the St. Charles Military Band, 8,000 people paraded in the streets.[959] St. Charles recognized the returning soldiers at a 1919 Labor Day picnic. As they had after the Civil War, many veterans joined organizations like the newly formed American Legion. The first meeting of American Legion Post 262 in Augusta was held at the "G.A.R. Hall" in the autumn of 1920.[960] Those who did not return were honored with a statue on the courthouse grounds, unveiled on November 11, 1920. As a further tribute, Memorial Hall in Blanchette Park was dedicated in 1929 to the 49 men from the county who lost their lives in the conflict.

After WWI the world was never the same, and neither was St. Charles County. Parochial schools, the German language and anti-temperance attitudes did not disappear; but they could no longer be defended in the name of German *Kultur*. In 1920, the Missouri Catholic Union, meeting at the St. Peter's Parish hall, voted down a resolution to make English the official language of the organization. In explaining their decision to use both English and German, the organization claimed to "assume the liberal attitude that members of the Union may use either German or English."[961] The German Catholic Benevolent Society of St. Peter's Parish continued to raise money in the name of charity, and the St. Charles chapter of the National Committee for the Relief of German and Austrian Women and Children functioned in the name of humanitarian aid. Upon closing his appeal at one of their meetings, Father Weiner from St. Paul felt compelled to remind his audience, "funds to be collected will be used only to buy food and clothing for the victims concerned."[962]

Prohibition, feared by the defenders of German *Kultur* for the previous half century,

To increase the supply of food during the war, the Children's Community Gardening Contest was instituted. Each child, age nine to 14, was given seed, tools and a plot of ground at the corner of Benton and Monroe Streets. The children sold the produce they grew and received prizes for exceptional success. *John J. Buse Collection, 1860-1931, Western Historical Manuscript Collection-Columbia, MO*

was also a by-product of the war. With attacks on their culture at a peak, German-Americans were least able to resist. Taverns, breweries and wine garden closed in St. Charles County, as elsewhere, and drinking went underground. Stills located on islands in the Missouri River supplied individuals and taverns with whiskey.[963] Local enforcement of prohibition was half-hearted with prosecutions primarily in the federal court. In 1925 Jacob Fischbach, president of the former Fischbach Brewery, was fined $1,500 after federal agents found 180 barrels of beer in his brewery.[964] The sheriff of St. Louis County arrested a St. Charles man, Dowell Gross, when his still was found in a barn on St. Charles Rock Road.[965] Sheriff John Grothe arrested a "colored woman" for possession of alcohol on a complaint by a man that he had been short-changed in a transaction.[966] On two other occasions when arrests had been made, the evidence, in one instance $5,000 worth of "hooch," was stolen before the Grand Jury could indict anyone.[967] In 1927, deputy sheriffs Isidore Grothe and Lester Plackemeier raided the Guttermuth farm and seized a still and some alcohol. A few days later, on a anonymous tip, federal agent James Dillon raided the same farm and seized a second still, leading to speculation that the first still had been returned or a second still had been conveniently overlooked.[968] A few weeks later, Constable Kleeschulte reported that he had been warned by armed men not to interfere with the sale of "hooch" to the patrons of a dance in O'Fallon. Another police officer had a bomb thrown on the front porch of his home. These incidents led some citizens, including Robert Langenbacher, Guy Motley, and Dr. J.L. Roemer, president of Lindenwood College, to call a "law and order" meeting where a resolution was passed calling on law enforcement officers to enforce the law. One participant at the meeting stated, "there is no hope of enforcing the prohibition laws in this county as the large majority of the people are opposed to such a law," but he believed that, "open violations can be curbed through the officers if their attention is called to it."[969]

Pressure to conform to traditional American norms increased when the Ku Klux Klan was resurrected in the 1920s. The Klan was politically powerful, especially within the Democratic Party, as politicians often sought its support, especially in the South and Midwest. The scope of the Klan's hatred had now grown to include Catholics, Jews and all immigrants. The Democratic *Banner-News* was non-judgmental when it reported a "stunt" by Klan members in November 1923. It stated, "The sign of the Ku Klux Klan was in evidence again last night for a third time within two weeks. This time the burning cross flared in brilliant outline on the hill south of Adams between Second and Third Streets." The article went on to describe the size of the cross and the crowd that observed it but failed to mention that it was burning directly across the street from the home of the Weils, a prominent Jewish family in the city. The article went on to mention, "On Friday night of this week one of the crosses was burned adjacent to West Clay St., opposite the Kaplan property," but it again failed to mention that the Kaplans were also Jewish.[970]

Because of the immigrant past of so many St. Charles County families, along with the large percentage of Catholics in the community, the Klan did not prosper in the county. Nevertheless, the KKK made several brief appearances in St. Charles, including several donations in 1923 to needy families and worthy causes, including the school district. In January 1924, a member of the Klan appeared before the County Court seeking permission to use the circuit courtroom for a Klan meeting. Republican Presiding Judge John H. Sandfort denied the request on behalf of the court. Police Judge A.F. Regot had accompanied the Klan representative to the meeting but later denied being a Klan member. However, he did say, "there are a number of citizens in St. Charles like myself who would like to hear a lecture on the ideals and principles of the Klan."[971] The St. Charles City Council was not as direct when it received a petition from the Klan to allow a meeting at the city hall. The council tabled the petition on a technicality since no person had signed the petition. Thus the city avoided giving the Klan the type of unofficial endorsement it sought and thereby avoided upsetting the Jewish, Catholic and black communities in the city.[972] Since Jewish families were few, many of the Catholics sent their children to parochial schools and the African-Americans were politically powerless, the Board of Education was not as circumspect. The school board accepted an American flag that had been sent by the Klan and hung it from the balcony of the auditorium at the dedication ceremonies of the new high school in 1924.[973]

Eventually a Klan meeting was held at the Opera House on Main Street and 300 people attended. Local Protestant minister C.H. French, when called on to speak, said he had nothing to say regarding the Klan, "but if they wanted to hear of Jesus Christ and his teachings he did not mind saying a few words." The newspaper reported, "he bewailed the rottenness of this city as he saw it and quoted the scripture to substantiate his views." It was reported that another speaker criticized the lack of enforcement of prohibition:

> The 18th amendment is a part of the Constitution of the United States, he declared. "It is a moral as well as legal law and every citizen of the United States should be compelled to obey it. Who is at the bottom of all this disregard of law? I will tell you. It is the foreign element and you Americans back them up."[974]

Sheriff John Grothe (right) and his deputy with a moonshine still confiscated in a raid to enforce prohibition. *John J. Buse Collection, 1860-1931, Western Historical Manuscript Collection-Columbia, MO*

That same year, the Klan was an issue in state politics as well. The Democratic gubernatorial candidate, Arthur Davis, admitted he had attended a Klan rally and refused to sign an affidavit stating that he was not a member. Republican candidate Sam Baker, while promising to "get Missouri out of the mud" with a giant highway bond issue, signed the affidavit and spoke against the Klan. He was elected governor.[975]

On one issues the German-Americans and their neighbors could agree. Both resisted the influences of modern science. The theories of Charles Darwin had been discussed since the publication of *On the Origin of Species* in 1859, and was yet another area of disagreement between the German Liberals and the church-going Germans. A contemporary had described Arnold Krekel's views on the origin of man as "somewhat peculiar," stating, "He doubtless still believes in the natural and scientific theory of the creation of man rather than the scriptural."[976] In 1925, the conflict between religious fundamentalism and science, demonstrated at the "Scopes Monkey Trial," was covered in the local papers. Defense attorney Clarence Darrow called Winterton C. Curtis, University of Missouri zoology professor, as a witness for defendant Scopes, a Tennessee teacher who had taught evolution in spite of a state law prohibiting its teaching. Prosecuting the case for the State of Tennessee was William Jennings Bryan, who died shortly after the conclusion of the trial in which Scopes was found guilty and fined $100. All religious denominations in St. Charles County agreed with the result. Many Republican Lutherans, who had voted against William Jennings Bryan three times in presidential elections, agreed with Reverend Frederick Niedner of Immanuel Lutheran Church, when he editorialized in 1925:

> The Scopes Trial has ended. William Jennings Bryan, the bold confessor of truth, is dead. Mr. Darrow has gone back to Chicago, where many murders are committed and he is sorely needed. But "John Brown's body lies a moldering in the grave. His soul goes marching on!" The discussion of evolution has not ended, and it is still agitating the minds of people.[977]

Niedner went on to lament the way evolution was presented in academia and the popular media. He continued, "It is stated in such an appealing manner, and decorated with so many literary flourishes, that the student and the reader often lose sight of the fact that no proof is being offered, and that innumerable contradictions abound, and that many scientists are anti-evolutionists."[978] Nevertheless, it does not seem to have created much disappointment in St. Charles County in 1927 when an anti-evolution bill was defeated in the Missouri legislature.[979]

William Weinrich, state representative from St. Charles County, described his constituents in 1925, stating, "From the few remarks you will see that we are great financiers, real producers of agriculture, and able to get the very best education. But above all these I desire to add that our people are religious and God-loving. Everybody goes to church and it makes no difference what church you belong to we have it in our midst."[980] Nevertheless, the "sexual revolution," sparked by the writings of Sigmund Freud and stoked by newfound independence afforded young people by the back seats of automobiles, reached St. Charles by 1923. A local newspaper described the sexual activity between some local teenagers as a "most abominable, depraved and demoralized condition." The county prosecuting attorney, after a hearing on the subject, stated, "I wished that there had never been an automobile manufactured."[981] While certain Victorian practices were clearly being challenged, the family unit remained strong. Nationally, in 1920 slightly more than 60 percent of people over the age of 15 were married, with less than one percent listing their status as divorced.[982] While the divorce rate went up in the 1920s, divorce was so rare in St. Charles County that when it occurred it was often reported in the local newspapers.

While the "roaring twenties" did not roar as loudly as in the large cities, the social conservatism and economic prosperity made St. Charles County a great place to raise children; children who became the "Greatest Generation."[983] Representatives of local churches met and formed the Community Film Association in 1917. This organization, along with a St. Charles branch of the National Committee for Better Films, worked to secure appropriate films for the children of the community and to protect them from "morally objectionable" movies.[984] Nine years after the Boy Scouts had been founded in Europe, a troop was organized in St. Charles. Some of the leading men in town were active in the troop that existed independently of the St. Louis Area Council from 1919 until 1928. Then, as now, the scouts purchased their uniforms and equipment at Thro's Clothing on Main Street.[985] In the rural parts of the county, there were 64 Boys and Girls Clubs with 526 members in 1916. Created with the cooperation of the county superintendent of schools, they were the forerunners of the 4-H Clubs, that officially began in 1927 as extra-curricular activities in the county schools.[986] Boys Week, sponsored by Rotary, was observed in 2,000 towns around the country, including St. Charles, in 1925. Activities were planned for the entire week including a "Boys Night at Home" during which every boy was supposed to be home with his father "talking over real problems of life."[987] By this time Calvin Castlio observed that the young folks, "were more willing to mingle with 'other kinds' than earlier generations had been: farmers with townies, Presbyterians with Catholics, Germans and Southerners, locals and folks from far away."[988]

After the First World War, things did not change much for the African-Americans who continued to face discrimination and segregation. Whites of all ethnic backgrounds experienced social change as religious influence and ethnic identifications diminished within St. Charles County. Secular and professional associations became more important as the Chamber of Commerce was chartered in 1918 and J. Edward Travis was elected president of the new St. Charles Country Club that had leased about 40 acres for a golf course and clubhouse near Black Jack School in 1924. By 1925 St. Charles had Rotary, Lions, Exchange and Optimists clubs, where religion and ethnicity were not as important.[989] The greatest social adjustment was required of the German-Americans, who were forced to assimilate to an extent undreamed of before the war. Those whose social life continued to revolve around ethnic and confessional organizations now read English language papers and drank in the privacy of their homes. A younger generation would be educated entirely in English. Having gained a position of prominence in the community and having proved their loyalty, the German-Americans lost their hyphens and became simply "Americans."

B. Republican Ascendancy

Within a year after the second election of Grover Cleveland, the country was in the throes of a terrible financial depression. The people expressed their discontent in St. Charles County in the mid-term elections of 1894. The Republican Party became the majority party in St. Charles County and the nation for the next 38 years. The key to Republican success was their economic message and the mainstays of Republican strength in St. Charles County were the Protestant German-Americans. They dominated politics in the county as long as the industrial society, with which the Republican Party was identified, continued to create new wealth and prosperity.

The political debate was reflected in the newspapers of the county. Among the German language papers, the *Demokrat* continued to promote the Democratic Party, and the *Republicaner* continued its Republican prejudices. Among the English press, the *Cosmos*, later the *Cosmos-Monitor*, had published from 1872 until 1877 as a Republican paper. In 1877, it had become independent, and even purchased the Democratic *St. Charles Journal* in 1883. The paper later returned to its Republican roots. Published by E. Lee Renno, it was the official Republican newspaper of the Ninth Congressional District by 1908. In 1885 the *St. Charles News* had a circulation of 2,000 and was Democrat in its leanings. James C. Holmes, a Catholic, was its editor. Ronald M. Thompson came to St. Charles in 1905 and founded the *Banner-News*, which became the predominant Democratic newspaper in St. Charles County. His competition included the *Wentzville Union*, founded in 1891 by W.S. Dickey.[990]

By 1890, the bad news for the Democratic Party in St. Charles County was that non-Germans had been declining as a percentage of the population of St. Charles County since the Civil War. The good news was that German Catholics continued to look to the Democratic Party to protect them from their long time foe, the German Protestants. Since the Reformation, no other European people had been more divided by religion than the Germans. The heritage of religious wars had made hatred for other religions the standard and religious conformity patriotic. The animosity continued in the United States where German Catholics avoided contact with other German-Americans, maintaining their own parish schools, orphanages, hospitals and press.[991]

This was certainly true in rural St. Charles County, where German Catholics not only established their own institutions, but usually lived in small farming communities comprised primarily of their co-religionists. The predominantly Catholic communities were Portage des Sioux, St. Peters, O'Fallon, St. Paul, Josephville and Dardenne. The predominantly Lutheran communities were Orchard Farm, Cave Springs, Harvester and New Melle. There was an Evangelical church in Friedens, Weldon Spring, New Melle and Femme Osage. Of all the small villages in the county in 1890, only Augusta and Cottleville had Catholic and Protestant German congregations. According to Walter Schroeder, in the one-church Lutheran and Catholic communities, "Allegiances to the local community develop from multi-generation marriage linkages, a conservative religious faith, religious homogeneity in the community and a sense of separateness from others, and a vigorous social life built around church support groups and parochial schools."[992] Among the Catholic church-supported groups were the Knights of America, founded in 1874, to which many prominent Catholics in the county belonged. The Knights of Columbus, a Catholic fraternal organization, was founded in 1882. James Lawyer helped organize a branch of the Knights of Columbus in St. Charles and was the first person locally elevated to grand knight of that organization.[993]

After 1890, the Republican Party in St. Charles County continued to get support from Lutherans, as they had since the Civil War. Lutherans were the second largest voting group in St. Charles County, and their distrust of Catholics remained strong. Some opposed the Democratic Party simply because they considered it the Catholic party.[994] In 1889, seven years after the death of his first wife, Lutheran farmer Johann Dietrich Bruns, was remarried at St. Peter's Catholic Church to Mary Elizabeth Rinsche, a Catholic. According to Robert Sandfort, "This marriage caused a rift between Johann Dietrich Bruns and the Immanuel Lutheran church. His case was the topic of discussion at several Voter's Assembly meetings, and led eventually to his excommunication."[995] By 1890 the threat to the Lutherans was no longer the nativists, who had discriminated against them when they were a minority, but those in the Democratic Party who would reverse the results of the Civil War, in which their fathers had sacrificed much.

In the 1890s, the temperance movement still elicited strong opposition from German-Americans, as seen in the following excerpt from the *Demokrat*:

> If the Germans were united, indeed if even just most of them were united, what all they could do! How they could make themselves felt and respected! How they could be present in politics, in everything that makes life good! In the biggest state of the union they have the edge, or would have if they acted together. There would be no trace of bigots, simpletons, know-nothings; Kansas, Iowa and Maine would be as free as all other states, and none would be threatened with losing its freedom and having to deprive its citizens of their personal freedom.[996]

Lutherans who opposed temperance now found it easier to support the Republican Party in Missouri, where the temperance issue had been defused by the passage of the Wood Local Option Law of 1887. Although the WCTU had committed itself to legislation rather than persuasion, it found that the legislators in Jefferson City liked the "money and votes of the saloons." Therefore, a compromise was reached which gave each county the option of banning alcohol. Efforts to ban alcohol in St. Charles County were defeated three times, and existing liquor regulations were often disregarded. As a result, the temperance issue receded from importance until the temperance forces were strong enough to force a statewide prohibition vote in 1916. While 81 Missouri counties had prohibited alcohol by local option, the statewide initiative did not pass, due largely to the efforts of the German-American Alliance. In 1917 the urban counties of Jackson, Buchanan, St. Charles, Green, and St. Louis had 3,504 licensed saloons, while rural counties with large German populations, like Osage, Warren, Jefferson, Perry, Gasconade and Franklin refused to adopt prohibition.[997] Thelen points out that seven-eighths of the counties supporting prohibition the most in 1916 were those with the heaviest concentrations of Baptist, Methodist, Disciples of Christ, and Presbyterians. None of the most prohibitionist counties contained significant numbers of Catholics, Lutherans, or German Evangelicals.[998]

Going into the 1894 congressional elections, social issues such as prohibition diminished in importance as the country was in the midst of a serious depression. The *Demokrat* reported, "…the year 1893 was probably one of the worst in human memory. The panic which the year brought us was the harshest the United States ever suffered. The number of unemployed and needy rose to a height never before reached, and also the bankruptcy numbers exceeded those of all previous years."[999] Democrats, badly shaken by the depression, tried to return to the cultural battles of the 1880s and to unite the liturgical groups against the Republicans. The Republicans, who had learned their lesson, avoided those issues. Led by Governor William McKinley of Ohio, they reached out for the immigrant vote and focused strictly on economic issues, promising prosperity and opportunity.[1000]

An example of the new tone can be seen in the *Cosmos-Monitor* from February 1894:

Those who urge a division of the school funds, for denominational schools, are honest in their zeal, but dreadfully mistaken in their judgement of what would be best for the public good. A full fair and candid discussion of the question however, should not only be tolerated, but also invited. It is by discussion and argument on these subjects that the truth is discovered. Bigotry on one side and zeal without wisdom or knowledge on the other has much to do with the misunderstandings on these subjects.[1001]

When the issue of parochial schools next came up in the General Assembly, it was a Democrat from Shelby County who introduced a bill to curtail parochial education and put religious colleges under the State Board of Education.[1002]

Because of this refocusing, 1894 was a good year for the Republicans nationally, and also in Missouri, where they won ten of the state's 15 congressional seats.[1003] In St. Charles County, while they had controlled only 30 percent of countywide offices in 1892, the percentage jumped to nearly 80 percent in 1894. Democrat H.F. Knippenburg, a farmer from Femme Osage, was replaced by Republican Rudolph W. Mueller, from Augusta, as state representative from St. Charles County. Mueller served as speaker pro tem of the House of Representatives in the 38th General Assembly. When not a single Democratic candidate won in St. Charles County in 1894, the *Demokrat* reported:

In the election held Tuesday the Democrats suffered a tremendous defeat.... The storm was forecast for months, and the party leaders have to blame themselves.... The "hard times" led to the political swing. But whoever believes that a personnel change will bring an improvement in economic conditions must have a childish spirit....[1004]

The Republican percentage of the vote in St. Charles County jumped from just under 50 percent to nearly 55 percent, initiating a Republican predominance that lasted until 1932.

In the national election of 1896 William Jenning Bryan was the Democratic nominee for president and the reversal of roles for the two political parties became complete. Kleppner explains:

In the hands of William Jennings Bryan, the democracy was not the "traditional democracy," not the party of the "saloon interest" and the Catholics, but a vehicle through which those groups interested in a moral reconstitution of society could pursue their goals. The Republican Party of McKinley was not the agency of rabid evangelical Protestantism that it had been for the temperance, sabbatarian, and abolitionist crusaders of the 1850's. Instead, it was an integrated mechanism whose leaders overtly and primarily sought to minimize the latent cultural animosities among its sub-coalitional elements in order to broaden its social base of support.[1005]

The Democrat presidential candidate became the favorite of the pietistic forces. Although not officially for prohibition, Bryan became the favorite of the temperance movement because of his own personal disdain for alcohol.[1006] His stand on social issues contrasted with the high tariff economic approach adopted by McKinley and the Republicans. McKinley, who had led efforts to reach out to German-American voters in Ohio ten years earlier by toning down the party's image on divisive social issues, was very popular in St. Charles County. Not even the *Demokrat* could support the Bryan monetary policies calling for the unlimited coinage of silver at the ratio of 16 to one.[1007] The county went solidly for McKinley in 1896 and in no Democratic precinct, save Defiance, did Bryan do as well as Cleveland had done four years earlier. Defiance was a typical pietistic area, containing no Lutheran, Evangelical, or Catholic congregations and having a small percentage of German-Americans. It followed the rest of the state, which voted for Bryan and elected Democrats to 12 of 15 congressional seats. In the county, the Populist crusade had little appeal and the entire Republican ticket was elected again. In March 1898 William F. Bloebaum was reappointed postmaster of St. Charles, having served in that capacity from May 1889 until February 1894. He served in the post for a total of 20 years through several Republican administrations.[1008]

The German language press in St. Louis criticized American involvement in the war with Spain in 1898 and their St. Charles counterparts followed suit. The *Demokrat* editorialized, "to stop our jingos' mad cries for war one need only stick each of them into the shoes of the President or Minister of the Navy for just 24 hours. Putting on the sailor's jacket would have the same effect."[1009] As war approached the *Demokrat* concluded: "If the United States declares war on the Spanish dons, as an American patriot we wish a U.S. victory. But because of developments until now we must doubt the United States is absolutely right in this case."[1010]

Although couched in the terms of anti-imperialism, historian Audrey Olson believes this criticism, coupled with German praise a few years later for the Boers' struggle in South Africa, reflected a concern that imperialistic ventures would wed the United States to Great Britain at the expense of its relations with the German Empire. She also suggests that the German-Americans equated the British with their tormentors in the United States – the nativists and the temperance advocates. While individual

Germans had aided the Americans in the Revolutionary War, Great Britain had sympathized with the Confederacy during the Civil War. Worst of all the descendants of the Puritans were attacking their right to drink beer.[1011] Not all German-Americans shared this view as half of the 39 men from St. Charles who joined Company C of the Missouri All-Volunteer Infantry at Camp Columbia in Havanna, Cuba, had German surnames.[1012] The war was short, lasting only four months, and when the election of 1900 came around it appears that St. Charlesans were more interested in the "full dinner pail" than any concerns about imperialism raised by German Liberals. McKinley did even better in St. Charles County, again defeating Bryan in the 1900 presidential election. In that same year, John Henry Stumberg, a physician from St. Charles, was elected as the county's state representative and served in that post until 1906.[1013]

As in the nation and state, African-Americans in St. Charles County continued to vote Republican and continued to be an important part of that party's success. In 1880, Democrat John Jay Johns had complained, "It is a sad commentary on popular elections to see the ignorant negroes and low whites that in great measure control these elections."[1014] A tongue-in-cheek letter to the editor appeared in the *Demokrat* supporting Walter C. Brown, an African-American, for the Republican nomination to the office of constable of St. Charles Township. It pointed out that Republican success depended on the black vote and asked, "will the Republicans repay a little part of the obligation which they owe the Negro for his loyalty and constant support of their party?"[1015] Of course the prejudice was too strong for an African-American to be elected, even running as a Republican in St. Charles County. A more direct attack on African-Americans and their support of the Republican Party appeared in the *Demokrat* which lamented, "On Monday the Blacks celebrated emancipation, and yet they have so little cause to do so. Formerly, they were the slaves of their masters; now they are the slaves of all vices and, above all, of the ward politicians."[1016]

In the 1904 election, Theodore Roosevelt did very well in the Protestant/Republican precincts of St. Charles County. He had very little support, however, within the Catholic/Democratic areas. Roosevelt won the state of Missouri, as the Republicans gained control of the state legislature. They won nine of 16 congressional seats, and elected William Warner, a noted leader of the G.A.R. in Missouri, as the state's first Republican U.S. senator in 34 years. In spite of all that, Joseph Folk, a Democrat running for governor as a "progressive," outpolled even Roosevelt.[1017] Some have suggested that many Republicans, rather than back the Republican nominee Cyrus Walbridge, supported both Roosevelt and Folk.[1018] In St. Charles County, most Republicans did not. Walbridge got virtually the same majority as President Roosevelt. In 1908, President Roosevelt did not run for re-election. The Republican nominee, William Howard Taft, addressed a large crowd at the St. Charles County courthouse on October 6, 1908. His Democratic opponent, William Jennings Bryan, did no better than before in St. Charles County and was defeated in a third attempt to win the presidency. This time the Republicans were carrying the progressive banner with their gubernatorial candidate, Herbert Hadley, who did just as well as Taft in St. Charles County.

Republican dominance in St. Charles County continued in 1912, although Democrat Woodrow Wilson won the presidency. Taft received a larger percentage in the

Though he never carried St. Charles County in his three runs for the presidency, Democrat William Jennings Bryan spoke at the Chautauqua in St. Charles in 1915. The man pictured on the far right is Carr Edwards. *John J. Buse Collection, 1860-1931, Western Historical Manuscript Collection-Columbia, MO*

county than Theodore Roosevelt, now a third-party candidate who received more votes than Taft nationally. Republican R.C. Haenssler, a lawyer from St. Charles, was elected state representative to replace another Republican lawyer, Robert Silver, who had replaced Dr. Stumberg in 1906. Carr Edwards, who had first been elected county highway engineer in 1892, was reelected. He was one of the few successful local Democrats during this period. President Wilson appointed Albert Iffrig postmaster of St. Peters, a post he then held for 43 years.[1019]

According to Jo Ann Brown, the priests at St Charles Borromeo shared the preference of many of their parishioners for the Democratic Party. The *Historia Domus* of that parish notes that they attended Chautauquas and occasionally expressed their views on issues. One of the Jesuits noted on Election Day, 1896, "Father Wolters was very much pressed to vote and did vote in the afternoon, [Democratic ticket]."[1020] While support by German-American Catholics for the Democratic Party reached a peak in 1928 when Al Smith became the first Catholic nominated for president, the relationship was well established in St. Charles by the 1890s. Only the coming of World War and its aftermath challenged the German-Catholic allegiance to the Democrats.

As the 1916 presidential election approached, a debate had been raging since the outbreak of the First World War in August 1914. German-Americans resented President Woodrow Wilson's preferential treatment of Great Britain. Anti-war feeling was strong in St. Charles and the *Cosmos-Monitor* consistently advocated neutrality. In January 1916 the newspaper argued against conscription to produce a standing army in case of war, saying:

> There seems to be an unnecessary fear retained by some of the majority in Congress that some great nation of Europe or Japan is going to be dropped down on us and eat us all alive before breakfast with every nation's help. With millions of men falling in Europe and the wealth of those nations being wiped away, it is hardly likely that any of them will be looking for another war with this country when they get through with the one on hand.[1021]

A few months later, the St. Charles County Catholic League charged that the Wilson administration was not pursuing true neutrality.[1022] Some believe that Theodore Roosevelt's saber rattling about the war hurt Republican chances among German-Americans in Missouri, where Wilson barely beat Hughes in the 1916 election. They point out that Wilson ran better in German wards in St. Louis than he had four years earlier, and only slightly worse in rural German areas.[1023] St. Charles County was the exception as German-Americans gave Republican Charles Evans Hughes a large majority. Wilson's percentage in the county dropped from 37.3 percent in 1912 to 34.9 percent in 1916, as almost every precinct voted for Hughes. Nationally, Americans of German birth voted disproportionately more for Republicans in 1916.[1024] On Election Day in 1916, the *Banner-News* reported the following conversation, which took place at a Chamber of Commerce luncheon where election results were reported as they came in. "We sold out to the Kaiser," said one loyal Democrat, after a report showed that Hughes had a big lead in New York, "But President Wilson carried London," remarked a staunch Republican.[1025] The same day a *Banner-News* editorial attributed Hughes' strong showing to the hyphenated vote.[1026]

Having been elected in November on the slogan "he kept us out of war," Woodrow Wilson asked Congress for a declaration of war the following April. The federal government instituted war measures almost immediately. Some foods were rationed and everyone was urged to economize to prevent food shortages. The newspapers offered the following advice:

> Buy less, Serve small portions
> Preach the Gospel of the clean plate
> Don't eat a fourth meal
> Don't limit the food of growing children
> Watch out for waste in the community
> Full garbage pails in America mean empty dinner pails in America and Europe[1027]

Republican nominee William Howard Taft delivered a campaign speech from the balcony of the courthouse in October 1908. *John J. Buse Collection, 1860-1931, Western Historical Manuscript Collection-Columbia, MO*

A War Industries Board was established by the Wilson administration to impose control over those industries considered vital to the war effort, including the American Car and Foundry plant that produced more than 2,500 escort wagons and numerous parts for artillery vehicles during the war.[1028]

President Wilson also established a Committee on Public Information, headed by George Creel, charged with presenting to the public the government's view of the war. The propaganda efforts of the committee reached St. Charles County where "Four-Minute Men" gave four-minute speeches promoting the war effort. A friend of Creel had initiated the concept by asking colleagues to make speeches in movie houses, where it took about four minutes to change the reels during the showing of a movie. Creel turned the concept into a national movement and supplied the material, as the Four-Minute Men gave over 755,190 speeches across the nation.[1029] Creel's committee financed and produced movies including *Pershing's Crusaders* and *Under Four Flags*. By the spring of 1917, the Opera House in St. Charles was showing films depicting "war's most terrible side," and stating, "we must prepare to protect our mothers, wives and sweethearts from the ravages of war." An advertisement for the films continued, "no children will be permitted under 16 years of age unless accompanied by parents."[1030]

President Wilson signed a Selective Service Act in May 1917. St. Charles County had one of the 166 local draft boards in the state, each of which had to meet quotas and could subtract enlistees from their quota. On June 5, 1917 all men age 21 to 30 were required to register with their local board and the first batch of 687,000 men were drafted in July. Physical examinations were given in August and the first St. Charles County draftees, Walter Wegener and Frank Billing, bid farewell at the Wabash depot on September 5, 1917. A much larger group left on September 21 when 3,000 people showed up to see them off. One reporter explained, "St. Charles wants to show the drafted boys that we appreciate their service and will give them a farewell that they will long remember. Everyone should join in making the demonstration one of the greatest ever held in the county. It is in honor of the boys who are going to make the world safe for democracy."[1031]

In the Ninth Congressional District, Bernard H. Dyer opposed Champ Clark, the Democratic Speaker of the House of Representatives in 1918. Dyer polled 63 percent of the votes in St. Charles County. Clark came to St. Charles County to make two speeches; one at Howell, a non-German area, and the other at Harvester, heavily German. Thinking he was at Howell and wishing to play on the anti-German sentiment aroused by the war, he told the voters in Harvester, "I don't need the votes

The stage at the St. Charles Opera House is set for a speech by Congressman Champ Clark, whose picture appears at the right of the stage. The poster at center depicts William Jennings Bryan and his running mate in the 1908 presidential election. *John J. Buse Collection, 1860-1931, Western Historical Manuscript Collection-Columbia, MO*

of those Dutchmen down here in St Charles."[1032] Such an ill-timed pronouncement cost him a great number of votes in St. Charles County. However, he was very popular elsewhere in the heavily Democratic Ninth Congressional District and he easily won re-election.[1033] St. Charles County remained solidly Republican as John C. Parr, a retired farmer from just outside St. Charles, was elected state representative.

The war brought the culmination of women's struggle for the vote. In 1872, Virginia Minor, first president of the Missouri Women's Suffrage Association, had brought suit

One of the 2,500 Army Escort Wagons built by American Car and Foundry at St. Charles during the First World War. *John J. Buse Collection, 1860-1931, Western Historical Manuscript Collection-Columbia, MO*

after her registration to vote in St. Louis was not accepted. The United States Supreme Court ruled unanimously that it was too late to claim the right of suffrage by implication in the Constitution. The court looked at the original intent of the founders and refused to "update" its interpretation. Missouri women had tried unsuccessfully to get the 1875 Constitutional Convention to approve the female franchise. They were likewise unsuccessful in getting language in the St. Louis City Charter to exempt the property of women from state taxes as long as they were disenfranchised.[1034]

In 1914, women's suffrage was presented to Missouri voters by initiative petition. Disagreement on the issue was not along partisan lines. Champ Clark believed women's suffrage was "as inevitable as the rising of tomorrow's sun." He threw his considerable weight in favor of a suffrage amendment to the state constitution. U.S. Senator James Reed, also a Democrat, was a vocal critic. In the end, its ballot position, the 13th amendment voters had before them that year, proved unlucky for Missouri women. St. Charles County voted against the amendment 3,277 to 526. The Republican *Cosmos-Monitor* said, "we feel the ladies of Missouri will never place any more confidence in men's promises. In St. Charles many of the men promised the ladies to vote for them and then forgot all about it at the polls."[1035]

Given the split on the issue within the Democratic Party and the way the 1914 initiative had been trounced in St. Charles County, it is amazing that the 1918 elections saw the first female candidate for election in St. Charles County. "Mrs. Irwin Ehlmann" was on the ballot as Democratic candidate for county clerk. The *Banner-News* stated, "in placing Mrs. Ehlmann on the ticket, the Democrats have shown themselves to be in the vanguard of the coming movement for equal suffrage. They're not waiting until

Congressman Champ Clark delivering an address at Blanchette Park in September 1916 to the Great Home Coming and Old Settlers Reunion. *John J. Buse Collection, 1860-1931, Western Historical Manuscript Collection-Columbia, MO*

sentiment forces them to put up women for office but they are showing the world in advance that they have faith in a popular idea that is sweeping through every state in the union." The *Cosmos-Monitor* never mentioned Mrs. Ehlmann or attacked her directly. Nevertheless it was surely intending to send a subliminal message when it used "men" or "man" five times and claimed, for her incumbent opponent, that "no other man has a cleaner record in office." The editorial concluded, "The Republican ticket is composed of excellent men."[1036]

Women had always played an important role in the history of St. Charles County. Catherine Collier, Phillipine Duchesne and Mary Easton Sibley made important contributions to education in the early history. Mary E. Jewel was president of Lindenwood College from 1876 until 1880 and Kathryn Linnemann founded the public library. But in this first attempt at elective office, Nell Ehlmann received only 27 percent of the vote. Of course, this was a vast improvement on the 14 percent the 13th Amendment had received four years earlier. Her total was only 28 votes short of the male Democratic candidate for probate judge and 66 votes shy of the male Democratic candidate for prosecuting attorney in an election where women were not yet allowed to vote. What might appear today as a stunning defeat was probably a great moral victory in 1918.[1037] Of the precincts studied, only Portage and Dardenne gave her a slight majority. Generally, the more German an area, the lower the totals for Mrs. Ehlmann. This was in keeping with the German attitude that the scope of a woman's activities should be limited to the three k's - *Kinder, Kirche, und Kueche,* - (Children, Church, and Kitchen). Many German-Americans continued to hold the view expressed by the

Demokrat when Virginia Minor had filed her lawsuit 46 years earlier characterizing the suffragettes as, "…half-crazed women, seeking their professions everywhere except in their natural spheres of activity…."[1038]

The suffragists, however, kept pushing their cause. In January 1918 President Wilson, who had opposed a federal suffrage amendment at the 1916 Democratic Convention in St. Louis, announced his support for it as a "war measure." The next day the House of Representatives approved the 19th Amendment by one vote. In the summer of 1919, the Senate, by a large Republican majority and a small Democratic one, passed the amendment. In St. Charles County, "There was a parade when women got the vote," one woman recalled, "but not many women were in it. Most of them just came out to watch."[1039] Nationally, women at first did not exercise their franchise in the same proportion as men. This seems to have been particularly true in immigrant communities, where large numbers of women did not vote until 1928, when Al Smith, son of an immigrant, was on the ballot.[1040] These trends were reflected in the returns from St. Charles County, where 5,484 men voted in the 1916 presidential election, but only 9, 217 men and women voted in the 1920 election and only 7,898 men and women voted in 1924. The *Cosmos-Monitor* addressed itself to reluctant female voters before the Republican primary in 1924, stating, "It is the duty of every Republican, woman as well as man, to go to the polls." The newspaper warned, "a woman voter should use her own mind and not be influenced by anyone, not even her husband."[1041] Matching the national trend in immigrant communities, the total number of voters in St. Charles County rose to 10,534 for the Smith vs. Hoover presidential election of 1928, still short of double the 1916 total.

Even though they had gotten the vote, there remained a great deal of pressure on women to continue in their traditional roles and professions. Men, and not just men from German families, continued to patronize women. In 1924 the *Banner-News*, reporting on an assault trial at the courthouse, explained, "Due to the smutty nature of the testimony, Judge Woolfolk advised all women to stay out of the courtroom and instructed the sheriff to carry out the request."[1042]

Prohibition also became the law of the land as a "wartime measure." By 1917, 96 of Missouri's 114 counties were totally or partially dry. St. Charles County voters defeated prohibition for the county in 1910, 1916 and 1918. In the first state referendum held on the issue in November 1918 St. Charles had voted 3,005 to 592 against the referendum, which lost statewide as well.[1043] But the prohibitionists triumphed at the national level when Congress passed the 18th Amendment to the Constitution, with 12 of 15 Missouri Congressmen voting for the amendment. It passed 22 to 10 in the Missouri Senate and 104 to 36 in the Missouri House on its way to ratification in 1919.[1044]

As the 1920 election approached, Democrats preferred talking about issues like race, rather than the war or the prohibition amendment. A few days before the election, the *Cosmos-Monitor* accused the Democrats of starting a rumor that the Republican presidential candidate, Warren Harding "is tainted with negro (sic) blood." The *Banner-News* responded that the alleged genealogy of Harding was sent out "wholly by private citizens."[1045] But having gone to war against Germany and having passed the 18th Amendment, President Wilson and the Democrats had to answer to the German-American voters in 1920. The Democrats won only 34 percent of the national vote, and did even worse in St. Charles County, garnering a mere 27 percent. The German Catholic precincts of St. Peters, O'Fallon and Dardenne voted Republican for the only time between 1890 and 1940. The historian of the Catholic Archdiocese of St. Louis, writing in 1922, expressed additional reasons for the disillusionment of Catholics with President Wilson:

> The Archbishop's (Glennon's) faith in President Wilson's honesty of purpose was rudely shaken by the cold reception of his appeal for justice to the nations, great or small, and especially "the oldest, most oppressed and most deserving of them all, the Irish nation." Then, came the exclusion of the Pope, the true Prince of Peace, from the Peace Conference at Versailles. And finally the Treaty of Versailles embodying the Covenant of the League....[1046]

Not only in St. Charles County, but also throughout the Midwest, there were dramatic shifts away from the Democrats in German areas.[1047] In 1924, German-Americans were still reluctant to support Democrats. Many who refused to vote Republican voted for Robert LaFollette, a third-party candidate. LaFollette enjoyed their support in 1924 because of his previous opposition to American involvement in World War I.[1048] In October 1924, the *Banner-News* reported, "quite a sprinkling of St. Charles people were in the audience of Senator LaFollette at the coliseum, St Louis last night," at which, "he charged that Wilson was unneutral in favor of the British and that Coolidge under a slight disguise was carrying out the same policies."[1049] In St. Charles County LaFollette won 11 percent of the vote as a third party candidate. This did not equal the 16 percent he received nationally, but was much better than the third party showing by Teddy Roosevelt in 1912 as the "Bull Moose" Party candidate. The week before the election, the Republican *Cosmos-Monitor*, ran the following story titled, "Trying to Fool the Germans:"

> Our friend Mr. Cannon (9th District Congressman Clarence Cannon) is reportedly trying to fool some of the Germans - not so much up in Lincoln, Callaway, Audrain, Pike or Ralls county but down in St. Charles, Warren, Gasconade and Franklin. He loves the German vote down along the Missouri River but up in the other counties he talks in a different key . . .[1050]

Both parties were aware that German-American voters were motivated by their own set of issues.

Coolidge carried St. Charles County easily and the Republican Party even won a majority in the Missouri House of Representatives. Representative William Weinrich from St. Charles County was mentioned as a candidate for speaker, but was reported by the *Banner-News* to have withdrawn his name in return for support of his efforts to end the toll on the Highway 40 Bridge.[1051] Republican influence in St. Charles County remained at an all-time high in 1926, when the Democratic Party failed to file a slate of candidates, due to an oversight by party officials.[1052]

African-American support continued to be part of the Republican electoral coalition and Jim Crow never came to the county the way it did to other parts of rural Missouri. Because it was a Republican county where the politicians courted them, black political action, coordinated through a men's organization called the City Club, was sometimes successful. In March 1926, it was reported that, "The colored people of St. Charles will have a mass meeting in anticipation of the coming election." The article concluded, "It is said that the colored population resents certain practices, and that they will support candidates pledged to policies in harmony with their ideas."[1053] Later that year another news story explained how the management of the local bus line had announced that "colored people" would be allowed to ride the buses. Under earlier management by the Lowe line African-Americans had not been allowed to ride, a fact which, "…created a resentment which worked out in the political channel through threats of the colored voters to throw their support against certain councilmen who were upholding the Lowe line. It is even said that some of the defeated candidates of the last city election have the Negro population to thank for the trip they took up Salt River."[1054] Patronage bolstered Republican support in the community. The *Cosmos-Monitor* reported in 1927 that, "Mr. Ringe [Republican state representative from St. Charles County] also secured the appointment of James Davis, one of our well known colored citizens, as assistant door keeper in the House and he has taken up his duties there."[1055]

A precinct by precinct examination of the voting patterns in St. Charles County after 1924 shows a reversion to previous patterns where large numbers of German Catholics voted Democratic, while German Protestants continued to vote Republican. As the parties were realigned along economic, rather than social lines, there were new reasons for the attraction of Catholics to the Democratic Party. By the 1880s, about two-thirds of the membership and a substantial part of the leadership of organized labor had been Catholics, including Terrence B. Powderly, president of the then prominent Knights of Labor. While Archbishop Kenrick disapproved of the Knights as a "secret society," Cornelius O'Leary, a parish priest serving in DeSoto, Missouri was a strong supporter of the Knights of Labor during a railroad strike in that town. Powderly wrote "no man in or out of the organization did greater service to the men than Father O'Leary."[1056] When Archbishop James Gibbons went to Rome in 1886 to become a Cardinal, he was able to persuade Pope Leo the XIII that the Knights should be tolerated. When the Knights of Labor lost influence and the American Federation of Labor assumed leadership of the labor movement, Catholics were also a large part of their membership.[1057]

Meanwhile, Republican Calvin Coolidge made his national reputation by breaking the Boston police strike in 1919, while governor of Massachusetts. During the

1920s, the Republican Party became solidly identified as the party of business. In 1926, Republican Governor Baker allowed the Missouri prison system to lease convicts to a mining interest causing 140 union miners to lose their jobs. He also vetoed a "scaffold law," and proposed a regressive amusement tax. As a result more and more working people turned to the Democratic Party. As early as 1922, Congressman Cannon, speaking to a Labor Day gathering in St. Charles stated:

> I hold no brief for organized labor. I have not always agreed with its policies, but I prefer it infinitely to organized and predatory capital. The fight between the two can never be a fair fight. Capital is fighting for profits. Labor is fighting for bread. To one it means merely a few more shares of stock, a few more trips to Europe, another ocean-going yacht. To the other its means food and clothing and shelter and medicine, school for the children and a contribution to the church and the opportunity to rear his family in that comfort and decency which is the right of every industrious citizen....[1058]

The 1928, presidential election was the first in which a major political party nominated a Catholic, Al Smith. The major issue of the campaign was Prohibition. The Republican nominee, Herbert Hoover, was in favor of its continuation while Al Smith favored repeal of the Eighteenth Amendment. The candidates' position on Prohibition undoubtedly influenced many German-Americans to vote Democratic in 1928.

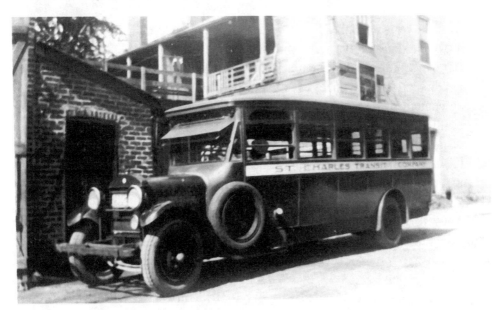

A bus of the St. Charles Transit Company, that began operating in May 1925. After complaints by the African-American population, the City Council passed an ordinance allowing blacks to ride the busses. *John J. Buse Collection, 1860-1931, Western Historical Manuscript Collection-Columbia, MO*

An editorial in the *Banner-News* on the eve of the 1928 election, titled "Herbert Hoover will be the next President," stated that the Democrats were going to vote for Hoover because Smith was not "a true Democrat," since he was not running upon the platform adopted at the Houston Convention.[1059] The reference is to the battle that took place at their Houston Convention over Prohibition. Many Democrats, including the author of this editorial, were opposed to Smith's position on Prohibition and, to please these people, the language in the Democratic Party platform had been left ambiguous and did not take a clear stand on the issue. Meanwhile, an editorial in the *Cosmos-Monitor* warned:

> The St. Charles Republican who votes for Smith in hopes of getting back beer is just as foolish as the St. Charles Republican who voted for Senator Jim Reed six years ago is. "IT CAN'T BE DID." The President of the United States can't give you beer. The Constitution of the United States will tell you plainly how Amendments to the Constitution can be made or repealed.[1060]

An editorial in the *Banner-News* supported Smith and showed the strength he had among many German-Americans. It stated, "The German-American Smith-for-President League has just sent out a bulletin declaring that 150,000 voters of German-American ancestry who voted for Coolidge in 1924 will vote for Smith this time."[1061] The same newspaper published excerpts from an interview with Clarence Cannon in which he made an obvious play for the German vote by pointing out:

> Mr. Hoover's refusal to admit food to Germany before the signing of the Treaty of Versailles was in keeping with his opposition to the bill to alleviate famine conditions pending negotiations on reparations. It was merely a step in Mr. Hoover's policy of starving Germany into signing the reparations agreement. Certainly his printed official statement in opposition to the bill before the committee leaves no doubt as to his attitude and effectively disposes of all attempts to gloss over his record by claiming he favored this bill or any other proposal for relief legislation for German women and children in the sixty-eighth Congress or any subsequent Congress.[1062]

The 1928 election results show large majorities for Al Smith in precincts with Catholic churches: West Alton - 68 percent, O'Fallon - 81 percent, St. Paul - 83 percent, Josephville - 86 percent, Dardenne - 90 percent, Portage - 90 percent, and St. Peters - 94 percent. Nevertheless, Smith did not do nearly as well nationally among German-Americans as had Robert LaFollette in 1924. The anti-Catholicism of German Lutherans kept many of them from voting for Smith in 1928.[1063] The Republican National Committee's summary of returns pointed out, "there was a line of demarcation between German Catholics and German Lutherans, the former being divided and the latter being almost solidly Republican."[1064] In St. Charles County precincts with Lutheran or Evangelical Churches - Friedens, Harvester, Black Jack, New Melle and

Augusta - were solidly Republican in 1928. The Lutheran opposition to Smith was influenced by the Protestant press including the following statement of the Convention of Lutheran Editors, whose publications reached over two million readers:

> The claims, teachings and principles of the Roman Catholic Church are antagonistic to, and irreconcilable with, the fundamental principles set forth in the Constitution of our Country concerning the separation of church and state. Such is the opposition by this Church to the toleration by the State of any religion other than the Roman Catholic; this denial of the right of individual judgment, liberty of conscience and freedom of worship; that the worldly government is in duty bound not only to assist, support and protect exclusively the Roman Catholic Church, but to suppress, if necessary, by force every other religion.[1065]

The Prohibition question allowed some people to oppose Al Smith when the real source of their opposition was his Catholicism. By focusing on Prohibition, Protestant opponents were able to engage in rhetoric opposing his disrespect for the law without raising the religious question.[1066]

Even in 1928, not all German Catholics voted Democratic. Some Catholic voters were voting Republican. Indeed Archbishop Glennon was known to support the Republican Party.[1067] Some of the most successful Republican politicians in St. Charles County during this period were Catholic. Anton Mispagel had been Republican Central Committee chairman in the 1880s. Henry Pieper was presiding judge at the beginning of this period, and Henry Ohlms held the same office at the end. Bernard Dyer was a candidate for Congress and later was elected circuit court judge. All were Catholic Republicans. Nevertheless, the 1928 election is generally considered to be significant in that large numbers of Catholics solidified their allegiance with the Democratic Party. The identification of the Catholics with the Democratic Party in St. Charles County did not begin in 1928 but actually dates back to the 1870s. It was not merely the result of the Democrats nominating a Catholic for President, but was the result of a series of cultural and historical circumstances.

In the end, Hoover was elected, as all Republican presidents since 1896, because the nation was enjoying economic prosperity. Prohibition and religion had become important issues in the 1928 election only because a consensus had been developing since the late 1890s that industrial capitalism was the engine of progress that had given the American people the highest standard of living in the world. Progressive voices bemoaned this fact even in St. Charles, as when the *Banner-News* reported the remarks of a guest speaker at Lindenwood College:

> Discussing the American governmental party system, Dr. Devine said and showed how the question of the Ku Klux Klan, the Protective Tariff, Anti-lynching law, Income Tax, the Soldier Bonus and Immigration legislation

189

pending before Congress (in 1924) and how vague and uncertain the spokesmen of both the Democratic and Republican Parties were on those important issues, and that the actual differences between the two parties are slight indeed.[1068]

The wealthy were influential in the leadership of both parties. The businessman was well respected throughout the country, and generally credited with the prosperity the country was experiencing. Neither party was criticizing the economic system. Historian Robert S. McElvaine observes:

> Thus by the end of the twenties, Raskob seemed to be close to the mark when he said that the only difference between the two parties was that the Democrats were wet and the Republicans were dry. He might have added that the Republicans favored shifting taxes from the rich to the poor by means of a national sales tax, while the Democrats would try to achieve the same end by taxing beer. The conservative era had reached its zenith – or nadir, depending on one's point of view.[1069]

C. Industrialization and Urbanization

In 1860, the United States had not surpassed Great Britain, France or Germany in industrial output. By 1900, U.S. industrial production had surpassed the total of all three.[1070] The northern victory in the Civil War had not only insured the triumph of free labor, but also the triumph of industry, as Republicans raised tariffs to protect American industry. Not all industrialization took place in the large cities. In the Midwest, 50 percent of all industrial workers resided in the region's largest cities, while the other 50 percent resided in smaller communities like St. Charles, with a population of 6,161 by 1890.[1071] The industrial workers coming from the farms had to make significant adjustments as their jobs moved from field to factory. As industry expanded, cities like St. Charles grew. While the population of the county grew very little during this period, the population of St. Charles grew from 6,161 in 1890 to 10,491 in 1930. As cities like St. Charles grew, they provided more municipal services for residents while their industries provided the manufactured items that gave Americans the highest standard of living in the world.

While a number of small towns served as railroad depots for farm produce, in 1890 St. Charles was the only urbanized area in St. Charles County. The *St. Charles Journal* wrote in 1881:

> It is becoming more patent that St. Charles County must depend for her future growth on manufactures and industries within herself. The area of county for which this is now a supplying and shipping point is comprised within a radius of six or eight miles, and the prospect is, that it will constantly diminish instead of increase.[1072]

In a series of articles in 1882, the *Cosmos-Monitor* gave a good overview of the St. Charles economy. Crops had been good the year before and business was better than at any time since the crash of 1873. The city had three dry goods stores, eight grocery stores, three drug stores, eight shoe sales and repair stores, three banks, three stove and tinware stores, ten saloons, eleven hotels and boarding houses, five blacksmith shops, five millinery shops, two lumber dealers, six butchers, two hardware stores and two furniture stores. There were also five mills that employed from five to eight people each and one factory that employed 600. A water works had been erected and the city maintained 55 hydrants to dispense the water that came from the Missouri River. The *Cosmos-Monitor* went on to state, "the works likewise afford a fine opportunity for developing the manufacturing interest of St. Charles."[1073]

Before 1890, the only substantial industry in St. Charles County was the St. Charles Car Company. During the 1860s the North Missouri Railroad had been one of the major employers in St. Charles. After the city and the company had a dispute over where to build the railroad bridge the company had moved its maintenance plant from St. Charles to Moberly in the fall of 1867. The loss was devastating to the local economy and in 1872 a Citizens Association was established to start a new business venture. At one hundred dollars per share, almost 1,200 shares of stock were sold to local residents and farmers, in the St. Charles Manufacturing Company that would manufacture railroad cars. The City Council agreed to release the proposed company from municipal taxes for 35 years and the grounds formerly occupied by the North Missouri Railroad shops were chosen as the site for production. In 1874 the first contract for 50 cars was received from the St. Louis Iron Mountain and Southern Railway. The following year the car company began to construct the bridge that the county built over Dardenne Creek.[1074]

The late 1870s were difficult years for railroad car manufacturing since railroads could not pay cash because of the depression of 1873. Instead, they gave notes to the car manufacturing company that would have to be sold to a bank in order to maintain working capital. Stockholders received no dividends and the value of the St. Charles Manufacturing Company stock plummeted. At this point Henry B. Denker, a local merchant who was vice president, rescued the company until it began to prosper again in 1879, when T. C. Salveter was hired to run the shop. In his first year on the job, the company's stock went from five to 25 cents a share in value. In 1881 the company reorganized, changed its name to the St. Charles Car Company and expanded its facilities and workforce.

The company had so much work that the president went to New York to try to recruit German immigrants as plant workers.[1075] By 1900, more than 80 percent of America's industrial labor force were foreign-born workers and children of the foreign-born.[1076] While the Civil War and economic difficulties in the 1870s had reduced the influx of immigrants, the return of prosperity in the late 1870s brought 4,000,000 immigrants in the 1880s, more than in the previous 25 years. Immigrants and their children, made up 78 percent of the St. Louis work force in the 1880s.[1077]

The largest untapped source of labor, however, continued to be the local countryside, as the excess agricultural population moved to the city. The 1890 census revealed that St. Charles County's population had declined by 68 since 1880 to 22,977. Startup costs were increasing to the point that the average cost for farm equipment of $750 in the 1890s was several times the average 30 years earlier.[1078] Not only were equipment costs higher, but the farmer was constantly forced to buy ever more sophisticated equipment. Land prices in the county had also increased. While improved farms in 1873 ranged in price from $30 to $100 per acre, by 1904 unimproved farmland sold for $80 to $125 an acre. The total value of St. Charles County land in 1865 was $8 million. In 1904 the number had risen to over $11 million.[1079] To make matters worse, inflation in land prices was occurring during an over-all deflationary period during which the farmer received less and less for his crops.

Steam tractors came into use in the 1890s, followed by gasoline tractors after 1912. While most small farmers continued to use horses and mules, mechanization of agriculture continued, creating less need for the labor of farm children. In the period from 1910 to 1920 farm morale was further weakened by serious depletions in the fertility of the soil, causing St. Charles County Extension Agent Robert Langenbacher to comment, "A general discouragement could easily be detected wherever groups of farmers gathered and the general tendency was for young men to leave the farm for what they believed more encouraging fields of endeavor."[1080] These factors, along with their diminished prospects of a farm of their own, caused many young adults to move from the farm to the city to work in manufacturing.[1081] These internal immigrants preferred small and medium-sized towns, like St. Charles, to large cities like St. Louis. Many sons and daughters, raised on the farm, went to St. Charles seeking industrial jobs.[1082]

The exodus from the farms required major lifestyle adjustments. John Buse noted at the time that:

> The farmer's life was, of course, tied to the seasons and each season brought its own set of chores. In the spring, summer and fall, farm work revolved around cultivating and harvesting the crops. Winter chores, however, revolved around maintaining life until the spring came again as winter gave the farmer a chance to catch up.[1083]

The new industrial workers did not have to worry about droughts, floods or pestilence; they did have to worry about boredom, recession and injury. When the farmer moved to the city and engaged in manufacturing he had to adjust to an entirely different regimen. While farm work was not any easier, it afforded some diversity over the course of the year and the farmer was his own boss. It was sometime difficult for new industrial workers to adjust to the "tyranny of the clock," which required a person to be at a particular place at a particular time every day throughout the year and to perform the same, often very monotonous, work throughout the day. In 1860, one artisan performed 67 different steps to make a shoe and it took 1,025 hours at a labor cost of $256.33 to make 100 pairs of cheap women's shoes. By 1895, 85 unskilled workers did 95 operations with each worker tending the same machine all day. The new process, performed in a factory, took less than 81 hours at a labor cost of $18.59. With the increased productivity, the number of boot- shoemaking establishments in Missouri shrank from 114 in 1869 to 73 in 1919, while the capitalization of the average plant rose from $1,000 to $997,000 and the number of workers at the average plant increased from two to 324. The *History of St. Charles County* complained in 1885:

> Formerly Mr. Fuhr carried on the manufacture of boots and shoes quite extensively, and worked from ten to fifteen men. Now, however, the protective tariff upheld by Republican rule has had the effect to place the boot and shoe manufacturing industry, as almost every other industry has been placed, in the hands of a few large manufacturing capitalists, who have crowded all men of limited means out of the different manufacturing industries, and forced them to go to work at daily labor in large factories, or to engage in other pursuits.[1084]

As wages and prices became more dependent on national and international market conditions, workers became more concerned about periodic wage cuts and lay-offs during hard times. While the farmer could, to some extent, revert to subsistence farming to survive, the industrial worker was totally at the mercy of the business cycle. The largest employer in the city was the car shop and during the depression of the 1890s at least a fifth of the workers were laid off in Missouri's railroad car industry.[1085] Likewise, the new machines greatly increased the likelihood of accidents on the job. The Missouri industrial accident rate rose from four percent in 1905 to 14.1 percent in 1913. The accident rate for railway car shopmen, the largest single occupation in St. Charles, was 34 percent.[1086] While at a greater risk of injury, many of the workers at the car shops were skilled carpenters rather than assembly-line workers, and thus were spared the monotony of the machine and could at least take some pride in making their product.

Industrialization affected interaction of family members. On the farm, men worked with their sons and women worked with their daughters. Fathers taught the boys everything they needed to know to be a farmer and the mother taught the girls all they needed to know to be a farmer's wife. Both parents spent a lot of time with their children and had plenty of time to teach them their value system. Parents softened the consequences of failure by providing a supportive environment.[1087] After moving to the city and taking a manufacturing job, the father saw much less of his family.[1088] At the International Shoe factory men worked 60 hours a week during most of the year. It was a front-page news story when the workers were given Saturday afternoon off. In an expression of gratitude to the shoe company the *Cosmos-Monitor* noted that the employees worked "only 55 hours each week," and now had adequate time for recreation on Saturdays. When winter came, children again had much less time to spend with their fathers as the 520 workers began working again on Saturday afternoons at the factory.[1089]

This picture was taken as part of the investigation of an injury suffered by a worker at American Car and Foundry in 1908, when the wagon ran over his foot. Railway car shopmen experienced high accident rates. *John J. Buse Collection, 1860-1931, Western Historical Manuscript Collection-Columbia, MO*

An industrialized society required more formally educated workers, but farmers needed their children to work in the fields, and some worried that, if their children got too much education, they would leave the farm.[1090] County school superintendents in the 1860s and 1870s had complained about parents, "who cling to the time-honored ways of their fathers, and refused to advance." [1091] In 1873, Dr. John Henry Stumberg had reported that average school attendance at St. Charles County's 89 elementary schools was 50 percent, while the attendance at the rural schools was 40 percent.[1092] In 1875 there had been some 53 schools located in the six townships of St. Charles County. Many of these were one room, where all grades were taught by the same teacher, who was required to teach a balance of subjects and was responsible to the school board. The school term centered on the winter months, since young men and boys were required to plant and harvest crops.[1093]

Efforts began in the last decade of the nineteenth century to pass a compulsory attendance law in Missouri. In 1905, a new law required children between six and 14 to attend school for at least one-half of the year. Children between 14 and 16 had to attend if they were unemployed or had not completed eighth grade. Governor Folk, as part of his Progressive agenda, convinced the legislature to require children between six and 16 to attend school for the entire term after 1907.[1094] Better attendance did not guarantee better graduation rates. There were 2,677 children attending school in St. Charles public schools in 1909. However, the graduating class that year consists of only three girls and six boys. [1095] Nevertheless, compared to an earlier time, children were spending more time at school and away from their home and family.

Finally, the work of women changed considerably with industrialization, usually for the better. The farm wife kept the house and cared for the children. In addition, the farm wife tended the garden, milked cows, fed poultry, cooked for family and farm hands during threshing time and, if need be, worked in the fields to make sure the harvest was completed.[1096] In the industrial sector, the father became the sole breadwinner among all but the most unskilled workers. Families usually lived on the income of male heads of families alone and the female did not leave her home and domestic duties.[1097] While wives rarely worked outside the home, depending on the economic situation of the family, they continued many of the subsistence farming habits of an earlier age, even after they had moved to the city. Homemakers had summer gardens and they "canned" or preserved fruits for winter use. Households stocked cellars with fruits and vegetables, and had cow barns, pigpens, smokehouses, and chicken houses, even on city lots.[1098] In St. Charles, older citizens continued some of these practices into the 1960s.

In the new industrialized society, children usually postponed full-time gainful employment until formal schooling ended. Single women often worked in the factories until they married. This was quite common at the International Shoe factory in St. Charles, which employed a good number of female workers in its later years. Generally speaking, the wages and annual earnings of all workers rose by nearly 50 percent between 1860 and 1890; easily the greatest percentage increase during the century. Real daily wages rose from $1 a day to $1.50 a day, and real cash earnings rose from under $300 to over $425 a year. Some of this was due to the deflationary spiral that caused so many problems for the highly mortgaged farmer.[1099] A family had to stay in a single community over several decades and be extremely frugal to save the $1000 or so required for the purchase of a small house. In St. Louis, 22.8 percent of the families owned their residences in 1900. However, St. Charles had more than its share of working class homeowners, as residents owned 75 percent of the homes in the city in 1916.[1100]

By 1900, many industries were entering a new phase of the industrial revolution, characterized by larger, bureaucratically managed, multi-functional and capital intensive corporations, that marketed mass-produced items nationally and even internationally. This "Second Industrial Revolution," was a huge departure from earlier entrepreneurial capitalism. Railroads were the first to introduce scientific management and bureaucratic principles of management with clear lines of authority and very explicit rules and regulations to control all aspects of operations. Corporations could now produce products on a much larger scale. Average shop size jumped from six to over 20 workers between 1860 and 1890, and the larger businesses now had their main offices in metropolitan centers and branch plants throughout the country.[1101]

Such a company was the Robert, Johnson and Rand Shoe Company of St. Louis that was looking in 1905 to build a plant outside St. Louis. State Representative R.C. Haenssler and others worked to raise private funds to entice the company to locate in St. Charles. The group gave the company $25,000 and property worth another $10,000, being the city block bounded by Fifth, Jackson, Fourth and Tompkins Streets, where a new factory was built. Shoe production began in January 1906, with the facility employing about 500 men and women.[1102]

Likewise, in 1899, the American Car and Foundry Company of New Jersey purchased the St. Charles Car Company. The company continued to thrive and grow but decision making and control shifted to the east. The old buildings were torn down and the present brick structures were built, as the company began constructing steel railroad cars to be sold around the world. ACF, the largest industry in St. Charles, extended over almost half of the city and employed about 1,600 men.[1103] This was almost three times as many people as the next largest factory in town. It reported yearly earnings of $10,310,871 in 1917. The following year, the *Cosmos-Monitor* reported that a new and modern machine shop would be erected which would give St. Charles, "a machine shop equal to any other in the United States, equipment for modern work of any kind."[1104]

In 1913 the Citizens Association began negotiations with St. Mary's Machine Co. of St. Mary's, Ohio to relocate in St. Charles. The following year the city provided a 28,000 square foot factory at a cost not to exceed $30,000, paid the cost of relocating the company and provided all utilities and access to railroad facilities. To finance this, the voters approved a $64,000 bond issue that enabled them to fulfill their obligations.[1105] The company's plant was located on North Fourth Street, just north of the railroad-bridge. The Fairbanks Engine Company of New York purchased St. Mary's Oil Engine Company and improvements were made to the plant. The infusion of capital was beneficial and on September 19, 1914 Fairbanks announced that the capacity and equipment in the plant would be enhanced and more men would be put to work as soon as the improvements were completed.[1106] But, as with the car shop, control was with a large impersonal corporation on the East Coast.

The substitution of foremen for contractors was part of a larger managerial change that followed the increase in plant size and mechanization of production. There was also a substitution of professional managers for entrepreneurs. At ACF, James Lawler was such a professional manager. He had started working at the carshops in 1879 as a blacksmith at $2 a day. Before long he was foreman of the blacksmith shop and later superintendent of the entire works. He was finally appointed to the honored position of district manager in 1899, a position he held until his death in 1922. The *Cosmos-Monitor* wrote, "under his control the local plant has grown to be one of the best equipped plants of that great corporation."[1107]

As St. Charles County became more industrialized, it also became more urbanized as well. St. Peters formed a volunteer fire department in 1904 and was incorpo-

The Robert Johnson and Rand Shoe Company, which began manufacturing shoes in this new building in January 1906, became the second largest employer in St Charles. *John J. Buse Collection, 1860-1931, Western Historical Manuscript Collection-Columbia, MO*

rated by the county court in 1910. While it assessed taxes and passed ordinances, its main expenditures were for gravel streets, oil streetlights and levee improvements. O'Fallon also organized a fire department in 1906 and was incorporated in 1912 as a fourth-class city. Wentzville was still the second largest municipality in St. Charles County but only St. Charles provided significant municipal services.[1108]

In 1870 the population of St. Charles had been 5,570, making it the fifth largest city in Missouri.[1109] An 1885 description of the city had proclaimed, "The city is well lighted, the streets are graded and macadamized, and water works have been constructed which supply an abundance of water."[1110] At that time, over 100 private homes were equipped with gas service and the town had 59 street lamps.[1111] Great changes that had begun in the 1870s, like running water, electricity, telephone service and sidewalks, increased at an even faster pace as the new century began.[1112] All these changes were necessary if the city was going to control disease and fire; provide power to light homes and run factories; and provide transportation and communication within the city and to the rest of the nation.

As with most municipalities, the water works was built in response to public health concerns, rather than consumer demand for water.[1113] Diseases that have since been brought under control by modern medicine had plagued St. Charles during its early history. Cholera epidemics had appeared in St. Charles in 1849, 1854 and 1867. Dysentery, a very common malady that could be fatal to children, was often the result of bad drinking water or poor sanitation.[1114] By 1876, most cities with populations of more than 10,000 had installed a municipal water supply system and St.

Charles' first waterworks opened in 1867. By the 1880s, the water was pumped from the Missouri River into a first, and then a second settling basin, each with a capacity of 500,000 gallons.[1115]

It was common for towns to construct a water tower, usually the community's tallest public structure and frequently emblazoned with the community's name, at the highest point in the community. The water was pumped to this tower and, from here gravity dispatched water through wooden, iron, and steel pipes to homes and businesses.[1116] The water tower in St. Charles was located on the Lindenwood campus, where it can still be seen today.[1117] Homeowners were reluctant to hook up to the new system and there was bad management. So, after ten years, the company was sold to the Water Improvement Company of St. Charles, which was incorporated in January 1894. But health problems persisted, including a typhoid epidemic in 1899 that claimed 90 lives in the city during a single month in 1900. People blamed the water supply that was extracted from the river at a point close to the sewer outlet. Ironically, a man named Mudd led the campaign for clean water in St. Charles. Having had three children stricken with typhoid, Councilman James R. Mudd ran for mayor on a platform of "pure water," guaranteed by municipal ownership of the water plant. Dr. Mudd was elected in 1901 and, when the city's contract with the company was about to expire, the people approved a $150,000 bond issue to build a new municipal water plant on the river.[1118]

A municipal water supply was no guarantee of sanitary sewers, and sewer construction lagged behind water supply. The city's first sewer system was constructed in 1907 after the voters approved an $80,000 bond issue. The sewer pipe was laid some 20 feet below the street surface and the system provided for 46 flush tanks. John Buse, a resident at that time, believed, "this was one of the most important improvements made in St. Charles from a standpoint of health."[1119]

A hospital was also necessary. Located at what became Jaycees Park, Summit Gardens, the St. Charles County asylum, had originally been constructed in 1868 to isolate smallpox victims. It later served as a nursing home and finally as the County Poor Farm to care for needy individuals.[1120] The Sisters of St. Mary moved St. Joseph Hospital to its present site at the corner of Second Street and First Capital in 1891, dedicating a new facility containing 35 beds. In earlier decades hospitals were primarily to provide inexpensive care for the indigent. Middle-class patients were cared for at home by their family. By 1890, the American hospital had become the site of events in the life cycle, such as birth, sickness and death, events that had previously taken place at home.[1121] St. Joseph hospital had gained widespread acceptance. Although run by the Sisters of St. Mary, the entire community supported it. In 1923 a full-scale campaign to fund a 21-room addition, headed by J.C. Willbrand, collected $45,000 in ten days. The St. Charles papers ran the following appeal on August 7 of that year,

This facility was opened in 1891 by the Sisters of St. Mary on the site of the present St. Joseph Health Center in St. Charles. *John J. Buse Collection, 1860-1931, Western Historical Manuscript Collection-Columbia, MO*

Who will carry the load? Have you, citizens in St. Charles or vicinity, considered the importance of St. Joseph Hospital to all of us? If you're sick, this is the only place where you can receive professional care under proper surroundings in St. Charles County. More than that, you will receive the same tender and efficient care as your neighbor, whether you are Protestant or Catholic, Jew or gentile, rich or poor. Charity abounds in St. Joseph's. Where else can the lame and halt, the sick and afflicted, who are without money, receive as one of God's children needing help? Here, too, no question as to belief is asked.[1122]

With a new wing in 1924 and another addition in the 1930s, the hospital had a total of 100 beds. St. Joseph continued its charitable work, and many early financial records had the letters "ODL" next to the patient's name. The letters stood for "Our Dear Lord's."[1123]

One of the greatest threats to community health occurred in 1910 when the company that collected the garbage for St. Louis built a garbage processing plant in St. Louis County, directly across the river from St. Charles. The stench emanating from the plant proved to be unbearable. John J. Buse explained:

The premises about the plant were kept in a most filthy condition. Small heaps and particles of garbage were permitted to accumulate here and there, decomposing where they lay. Loaded railroad cars of garbage, containing all the imaginable refuse of a swill barrel, decayed vegetables and even carcasses of dead animals (which were already several days old before loading them in cars at receiving stations in St. Louis) were permitted to stand on tracks near the plant for days. Drippings from these cars saturated the ground along the tracks and created an unbearable stench.[1124]

When promises by St. Louis to rectify the problem went unfulfilled, St. Charles sued the owners of the plant. A St. Louis County judge eventually ordered the plant closed but the relief from the odor did not erase the hard feeling that had developed toward St. Louis.[1125]

To provide for the energy needs of home and industry, gaslight had become an alternative to kerosene illumination by the mid-nineteenth century. It was first available only in mansions of the wealthy, upscale stores, public buildings and factories rather than private residences.[1126] The St. Charles Gas Company had only 153 private consumers and 50 public street lamps in 1871. In 1899, approximately 75 percent of the gas produced across the nation was being used for illumination. By 1919, though it continued to be used for heating and cooking, the amount used for lighting had shrunk to 21 percent. Gas lighting had lost out in the "energy wars" of the late nineteenth century to Edison's incandescent light bulb, invented in 1879.[1127]

Across the nation, towns were electrified using steam or water-powered dynamos. The St. Charles Incandescent Light and Power plant was built in 1894. It received a franchise to use the city's poles to string wires throughout the corporate limits that provided an incandescent lighting system. The power was generated by a Stanley dynamo propelled by a 30-horsepower engine, and the capacity of the system was 2,000 incandescent lamps of 16 candlepower each. The St. Charles Electric Light and Power Co. began providing electricity to the city in October 1901 stressing better and more reliable service. Later, electricity was obtained from sources outside the state, such as the Keokuk hydroelectric project on the upper Mississippi River.[1128] Mayor Olson of St. Charles was quoted in 1914 as saying, "these lights are fed from the Keokuk dam. The current comes up from St. Louis. I tried to get those dam people to run their wires to St. Charles, but they left us to one side."[1129] The high-voltage lines ran through the Mississippi and Missouri River floodplains crossing St. Charles County and extending to St. Louis. The current then had to be brought back to St. Charles.

A new power source was now available for industry. While less that ten percent of power in industry was electrical in 1905, 80 percent of power used by industry came from electricity by 1930. Electricity provided a surge in industrial productivity in the 1920s and improved the standard of living as new home appliances were invented and marketed. With the advent of these appliances the use of electricity doubled during the 1920s. During the decade the percentage of urban dwellings wired for electricity in the country grew from 47 to 85 percent. Companies began to mass-produce, and St. Charles County newspapers began to advertise washing machines, sewing machines, vacuum cleaners and other popular kitchen appliances. Among the "scrubby Dutch" of St. Charles County these improvements increased the expectations of cleanliness by the family.[1130] Studies in the 1920s showed that women continued to spend between 51 and 60 hours per week on housework, even with the new appliances.[1131]

Electricity was the forerunner of a communications revolution. By the end of the first decade of the twentieth century the motion picture had become a part of American life, allowing people to see the world without ever leaving their hometown. By 1923 the United States had 15,000 movie theatres with a weekly attendance of 50 million. St. Charles had its movie theatres, including the Lyric Airdome Theatre, built in 1909. The Strand Theatre, built later on the site of the present city hall, announced in 1929 that it would have talking pictures and the *Banner-News* bragged that the St. Charles moviegoer, "will be able to see and hear the same productions that are being given in the best theatres in St. Louis."[1132]

Radio also became an important source of information and entertainment in the 1920s. RCA began manufacturing the Radiola in 1922 and, by the end of that year, there were 508 radio stations and some 3 million receivers in use. In June 1924 the *Banner-News* thought it newsworthy that, "Radio fans of St. Charles are taking in the Democratic Convention at New York, listening to the speeches, the hilarious demonstrations, the bands, and vivid descriptions of the crowd broadcasted by the radio operator."[1133] The National Broadcasting Company (NBC) was formed in 1926 and the Columbia Broadcasting System (CBS) the following year. The first car radio was invented in 1928 and the popularity of radio continued to grow.[1134] Like the cinema, radio made the world a smaller place and alleviated the isolation of rural and small-town life. There were over 1,500 radios on the farms of St. Charles County and many farmers listened each Monday and Wednesday at noon to the farm hour broadcast on KMOX radio.[1135] Calvin Castlio commented, "In short years to come we on the prairie would listen to folks talking, making music, and playing baseball, from New York to San Francisco. We would listen to presidents and preachers, songsters an' newsies."[1136]

The most important element of the ongoing communications revolution was the telephone. Alexander Graham Bell had invented the telephone in 1876 and the first telephone exchange, serving 21 subscribers, started in 1878 in New Haven, Connecticut. When American Telephone & Telegraph's patent expired, independent local exchanges proliferated. Telephone service, like electric service, was local in character initially, with local exchanges managed by local companies. Like electric companies, phone companies began expanding and consolidating in the 1920s.[1137] The first telephone exchange in St. Charles appeared about 1896. After it burned, the Kinloch Telephone Company purchased the franchise and rebuilt the exchange. While competition lowered rates, it also caused inconvenience. After the Bell Telephone Com-

These towers, built through the northern part of St. Charles County in 1912, supported the lines that transmitted electricity from the Keokuk Dam to St. Louis. The towers were erected in pairs and were 400 feet apart. *John J. Buse Collection, 1860-1931, Western Historical Manuscript Collection-Columbia, MO*

pany came to St. Charles in 1899, a person needed to have two different phones if they wanted access to everyone in town. You could not talk to someone on the Bell exchange with a Kinloch phone and vice versa.[1138] Bell gave the best service and gained ground on its competitor. The company operated all night with more operators at all times.[1139] The population of St. Charles grew from 8,503 in 1920 to 10,391 during the prosperous 1920s. During the same period, the Bell and Kinloch companies merged and more than doubled the number of phones in St. Charles from 736 to 1,887. In 1929 the company promised, "up to date telephone service in keeping with the steady growth of St. Charles will be one of our goals during the 1930s."[1140]

Smaller, independent companies continued to exist nationwide and locally, as thousands of telephone companies sprang up in small towns. The Vine Hill Telephone Exchange was set up in 1898 to connect the communities of Defiance, Femme Osage, Cappeln, Schluersburg, Matson and New Melle.[1141] There was a St. Charles County Telephone Co. in 1904, with 64 miles of line, 30 public phones and ten private phones, but it was destroyed by the tornado of 1915.[1142] Throughout the rural areas of the country, it was common for farmers to pool resources, cut some poles, buy wire, insulation, phones and switchboards, and install their own telephone system.[1143] Around the turn of the century, a group of farmers strung wire between the farms in the Orchard Farm area. One of the farmers, John Wilke, bought out the other members of the Farmer's Cooperative Telephone Company in 1905 and renamed it the Orchard Farm Telephone Company. The switchboard was in the family home until electronic switching arrived in the 1950s and the Wilke family continued to own the business until

The first streetcar crossed the new highway bridge at St. Charles in April, 1904. The last streetcar crossed in January, 1932. *John J. Buse Collection, 1860-1931, Western Historical Manuscript Collection-Columbia, MO*

1988. In 1930, the Machens-West Alton Telephone Company closed in Machens and the New Haven Phone Company opened in Portage des Sioux, providing phone service to that area until the company was purchased by Bell Telephone.[1144]

In 1909, a Centennial Week was observed to mark the 100th anniversary of the incorporation of St. Charles as a town.[1145] The census of the following year put the city's population at 9,437. As St. Charles grew so did the level of municipal services that were offered. While a volunteer fire department had existed in the city since before the Civil War, by the turn of the century the city had a professional department. It purchased a horse-drawn fire engine in 1900 and a motorized hook and ladder truck in 1921.[1146] In 1914, the voters approved a $90,000 bond issues so the city could buy the county fair grounds and establish Blanchette Park. In 1922 the city created a nine-member Park Board appointed by the mayor in an attempt to keep city politics out of decisions affecting the parks.[1147] Kathryn Linnemann established the first library in St. Charles in 1914. The Board of Education provided some of the books, the rest she acquired from friends. The library, located in a small room at Jefferson School, was destroyed when the school burned down in 1918. A Library Board was formed in 1920, and in 1928 the voters approved a public library tax in St. Charles. In 1931 the public library moved into an old home at 572 Jefferson.[1148]

After 1890, transportation improved as it had not since the coming of the railroad. On June 1, 1890 a pontoon bridge opened across the Missouri River at St. Charles. The bridge was 1500 feet long, wide enough for carriages to pass, and lit

Before it closed in 1932, kids in St. Charles could walk to this station at Second and Adams Streets, take the streetcars all the way to Sportsman's Park and get into the Cardinal baseball game free as members of the "Knot-Hole Gang." *John J. Buse Collection, 1860-1931, Western Historical Manuscript Collection-Columbia, MO*

with gaslights. The bridge did not make it through the first winter as ice and rising waters caused the cables holding the pontoons together to break.[1149] In 1894, discussion began about a new bridge to carry pedestrians and vehicles across the river. Congress chartered a corporation in 1896 to build a highway bridge at St. Charles. The bridge was completed in December 1903, at a cost of $400,000 and the lives of four workmen. In 1899 J. E. Housman Jr. began building a streetcar line connecting St. Charles to Wellston. It was known as the St. Louis, St. Charles and Western Electric Railroad and ran every one-half hour until 8 p.m. and then on the hour until midnight. Until the bridge was completed, the ferry known as the *Peerless* continued to cross the river until it sank when struck by river ice in the winter of 1903. For a short time, travelers had to rent fishing boats and row themselves across the river to catch the streetcar. When the bridge was completed, the streetcar crossed the river and turned around at the terminal at the corner of Second and Adams Streets.[1150] In 1909 Mayor Olson commented, "The next time you come here maybe you can ride around town on streetcars. I am after Captain McCulloch to build us a line by continuing this St. Louis-St. Charles line, instead of stopping it where you get off at that dandy new station."[1151]

The old wooden bridge that had been built in 1874 over Dardenne Creek at St. Peters (background) had to be replaced by a steel structure with the coming of the automobile. *John J. Buse Collection, 1860-1931, Western Historical Manuscript Collection-Columbia, MO*

The new bridge opened in time for the St. Louis World's Fair and brought St. Charles County much closer to St. Louis and its growing suburbs.[1152] By 1923, the streetcar had competition. The Walters Transit Co. began running two buses between St. Charles and the St. Louis City limits. For 35¢ the bus took you from the foot of the bridge to the streetcar barn in Wellston, where patrons could transfer to St. Louis streetcars. The commuting time was 35 minutes compared to 50 minutes on the streetcar. A second bus company got into the competition in 1924 and cut the commute to 30 minutes.[1153] Streetcars, because they were privately financed but highly regulated, could not compete with the bus lines. Buses, also privately financed, were actually subsidized by government road building. To get the contract to provide the streetcar transportation, companies often had to enter into long term contracts in an inflationary period. It kept costing more and more to provide the nickel streetcar ride, and it was not politically popular to provide relief to the companies. Meanwhile, cheap gasoline also made the buses more economical.[1154] It was soon clear that St. Charlesans preferred rubber tires to rails and the streetcar made its final run in January 1932, a victim of the internal combustion engine.[1155]

The people pressured city, county and state for new road and bridge projects. Someone at the time predicted wrongly that, "other electric lines will be built," but correctly that, "it is no idle fancy to see in the future another bridge at the upper end of town."[1156] Cities, including St. Charles, spent public monies to improve local streets.

**St. Louis Mayor Kiel (center) and St. Charles Mayor May (right) at the opening
of St. Charles Rock Road as a new concrete highway in November 1921.** *John J.
Buse Collection, 1860-1931, Western Historical Manuscript Collection-
Columbia, MO*

In 1908, the city purchased road-building equipment including a first-class steam-
roller, resurfacer, and later a modern road oiling machine. The streets of St. Charles
were first oiled in 1911 and, in 1922, the city reconstructed the business portion of
Main Street. Pressure for street improvement came from special interest groups,
including tire manufacturers and dealers, parts suppliers, oil companies, service station
owners, land developers and road builders. Merchants argued that roadway improvements paid for themselves by increasing property tax revenues from businesses along the
route.[1157] St. Charles County also improved its roads and built new bridges to handle the
automobile traffic. The county had 35 road districts with the same number of road overseers. In 1920 the voters of the county passed a $1 million bond issue for road improve-
ments.[1158]

By 1916, St. Charles had more than 200 automobiles, while Missouri had more
than 76,000.[1159] By 1921, there were 2,108 cars in the city and over 297,000 in the
state. In that year Congress passed the Federal Road Act that offered funds to states
that established highway departments. Missouri did so and was able to take advantage of the Federal Road Act of 1921 that made 200,000 miles of highways eligible
for matching federal funds. The act also established a Bureau of Public Roads to plan
a highway network to connect the major cities of the country.[1160] States began adopting gasoline taxes to pay their share of the construction costs. Nationally, highway
construction projects exceeded $1,000,000 in value for the first time in 1925. It fell

below that mark only at the depth of the Great Depression and during WWII.[1161]

Missouri followed suit in 1920 when the voters of the state approved a $60 million bond issue for the construction of roads in every county of the state. The following year, the legislature passed the Centennial Road Law that put a State Highway Commission in charge of county road systems as well as the state system.[1162] In 1921 St. Charles Rock Road became a concrete highway, an important transportation link between St. Charles and St. Louis. In that same year, construction began on State Highway 94 that started in West Alton and went through St. Charles, Harvester, Weldon Springs, Hamburg, Defiance, Matson and Augusta, before connecting to Highway 47 in Warren County. State expenditures averaged over $44 million per year in the period from 1923 through 1928. In January 1923, work began on what became U.S. 40, then called the "Victory Highway." Concrete was poured to replace the bricks on Second Street from Clark Street to Clay Street. In 1927, as a result of national coordination, the highway was renamed U.S. 40, even though it was a state highway.[1163] In 1923 the St. Charles Chamber of Commerce proposed that the State Highway Commission purchase the privately owned U.S. 40 Bridge. By 1926 agitation to reroute U. S. 40 to avoid the toll prompted an agreement whereby the bridge was turned over to St. Charles and St. Louis Counties for $1.25 million, with the money to be recovered by continued tolls until 1931.[1164]

In the 1920s, the "rush hour" in St. Charles continued to be the many workers walking on the sidewalks of the city before seven o'clock each morning on their way to the car shop or the shoe factory; but the automobile had made it easier for local workers to commute to jobs in St. Louis. The automobile accelerated change in a period that had seen tremendous change already. As the automobile industry became the basis of prosperity in the 1920s, St. Charles had five automobile dealerships by the end of the decade.[1165] According to historian Paul Johnson, the boom of the 1920s was based essentially on the automobile. In the late 1920s America was producing almost as many cars as it would in the 1950s. One of the biggest growth stocks of the 1920s was General Motors: anyone who had bought $25,000 of GM common stock in 1921 was a millionaire by 1929.[1166] Before the market crashed in 1929, GM stock was at 73. By July 1932, it had fallen to 8.[1167] Everyone's world had changed.

CHAPTER V
Depression and War
1929-1945

In January 1941, the federal government broke ground for a new ordnance plant at Weldon Spring in St. Charles County. Ten months later, the immense project was completed and began manufacturing explosives. It was a peacetime federal government project on a scale that would have been unthinkable eight years earlier. But much else had changed in the previous eight years. From the pinnacle of prosperity in 1929 to the depth of depression in 1933, GNP had dropped 29 percent, while spending dropped 18 percent, construction 78 percent and investment by 98 percent. Unemployment rose from 3.2 to 24.9 percent.[1168] The experience of the Great Depression changed the view of many Americans. Faith in free markets, strong in St. Charles County since the coming of the first American settlers, was severely shaken. Not since the common field system had the social consequences of economic decisions been given importance as they were during the New Deal. Politically, both nationally and locally, the Democrats replaced the Republicans as the majority party, as people looked to the federal government to solve their economic problems like they never had before. The New Deal could not end the depression, but it did alleviate some of the suffering, reformed many of our economic institutions and showed that government could mobilize people and materials on a scale never before imagined. But it would take war production to actually end the Great Depression. As construction commenced on the Weldon Spring Plant at the beginning of 1941, the unemployment rate for the country was still 9.9 percent, with 5.6 million still jobless. By the end of that year, industrial production had exceeded 1929 levels by 30 percent.[1169]

A. Depression Memories and the Home Front

In March 1925, the following was included in a radio broadcast from Jefferson City by State Representative William Weinrich:

> With perhaps the wealthiest per capita and most contented people of the state, St. Charles has been developed to the highest state of commerce and agriculture. We have 18 banks with total assets of $8,677,000 or $400.00 for each man, woman and child. This paradisiacal county has an assessed valuation of over $35,000,000 or about $1600 per capita.[1170]

Weinrich described the county as, "a land that floweth with milk and honey."[1171]

This equipment floated in Dardenne Creek as the shovel dug a new straighter channel. *Calvin & Helen Iffrig*

The stock market crash of 1929 and the ensuing Great Depression of the 1930s destroyed paradise as the industrial expansion of the previous half-century ended. As the milk and honey stopped flowing, significant political and economic changes took place in the nation and in St. Charles County. Individuals and families were affected differently and dealt differently with the Great Depression. While many retained their jobs and their confidence in the system, others could get by only with the help of private charity. For others, relief did not come until provided by the federal government and many of these individuals lost, and never recovered, their faith in free markets. While people dealt with the economic emergency, little social change occurred. When war came, so did social changes including the addition of large numbers of women to the work force.

The extent to which an individual was impacted by the national crisis depended upon where he lived, where he worked, where he saved his money, and many other factors. [1172] The effects of the depression were often not as severe in the country where, so long as a farmer could keep his farm, he could at least grow food to feed his family. Unfortunately, bad economic conditions had begun long before 1929 for the American farmer. The golden age of American agriculture had been during the World War, when the demand was high for food to feed the armies and agricultural production in Europe had fallen drastically. Responding to the demand, American farmers had increased wheat acreage by nearly 40 percent and output by almost 50 percent. The St. Charles County Council of Defense asked the federal government to pressure

As the new channel was dug, water filled it and floated the equipment forward, including floating quarters for the crew. *Calvin & Helen Iffrig.*

the Burlington Railroad to widen an opening in its embankment to allow better drainage so that an additional 300 acres could be put into production during the war.[1173] In 1915 farmers in the Dardenne Creek watershed formed a drainage district and straightened the course of the creek to bring more acres into production. When European competition returned, overproduction dictated low prices throughout the 1920s.

Decades of single cropping with corn and wheat had left the soil low in humus and too acidic to grow legumes profitably. The corn yields on this "clover sick" soil had declined from an average of 37.3 bushels per acre in 1910 to 33 bushels in 1920, while wheat declined in the same period 18.6 to 12.8 bushels per acre.[1174] Because of its proximity to urban markets, dairy farming should have been profitable in St. Charles County; but dairy farming required clover and alfalfa and the acreage in such legumes decreased by 1,512 acres between 1910 and 1920. To increase the acreage on which these crops could be raised, large doses of agricultural limestone had to be spread on the soil.[1175] County Extension Agent Robert Langenbacher recognized, "The present farmers are largely of the sturdy industrious German class, rather slow to adapt to new ideas but regular in practices that they find profitable."[1176] Slow to recognize the benefits of lime, fertilizers and modern machinery, Langenbacher concluded, "Even though the German farmers were as a rule better tillers of the soil than many others, yet they had a few of these ideas that held them back."[1177]

After a decade-long public relations campaign by Langenbacher, most St. Charles County farmers adopted the improved farming methods and soil fertility improved by 1929. But they had not shared in the general prosperity of the 1920s. Democratic Ninth District Congressman Clarence Cannon had protested lack of congressional action on farm problems in 1926:

> You have jammed through the House the foreign debt settlement demanded by organized business – nothing for the farmer but millions for Mussolini. You have completely forgotten the farmer. You have not reduced his taxes. You have not reduced his freight rates. You have not enforced his rights in the packer's decree. You have not reduced the price of fertilizer or the price of any other item entering into his costs of production. You have not reduced the tariff on the necessities of life he must buy. You have not increased the price of farm products.[1178]

Not only farm income, but also the number of farmers declined during the 1920s. In the 1920 census the urban population of the United States, people living in communities of 2,500 or more, exceeded the rural population for the first time. Not only the number of farmers, but their status was on the decline. According to one historian, during the 1920s, "Farmers and small-town residents, long accustomed to being hailed as the backbone of the nation, now found themselves ridiculed as hayseeds and hicks. An urban-industrial society that they neither liked nor understood was engulfing them."[1179] Calvin Castlio stated that farmers in St. Charles County wanted more for their children, "But they surely didn't want to lose them from the land. Some feared that very thing if their children became too educated."[1180]

Farmers did not share in the higher standard of living experienced by urban Americans. Often there was no running water, no sewers and no modern appliances since there was no electricity. Rural women understood from mail-order catalogues and magazines what they were missing without electricity.[1181] In 1920 only 1.6 percent of U.S. farmhouses had electricity. By 1930, that percentage had only increased to ten percent, compared to 85 percent of urban homes. St. Peters got electric service in 1927, Harvester in 1934, Hamburg and Howell in 1935 and Defiance in 1936. But as the 1930s ended many farms in St. Charles County did not have electricity and thus none of the appliances that were improving the quality of life for others.[1182] While transportation and communication were improving for others, Calvin Castlio commented during that decade in rural St. Charles County, "our roads were still just a sea of mud whenever it rained or the snow melted."[1183]

In 1920, farm families represented 22 percent of the population and received 15 percent of the nation's income; by 1928 their percentage of income had shrunk to nine percent.[1184] When the Great Depression hit things went from bad to worse. Prices of farm products fell more than 50 percent while prices of materials and services the farmer had to purchase declined only 32 percent. Heavily mortgaged farmers, many of whom had purchased more land and equipment during the World War, were unable to make mortgage payments and lost their farms. Weather added to the economic problems of St. Charles County farmers as the county experienced severe drought in 1930. Drought returned in 1934 and 1936, greatly reducing crop yields and creating soil erosion problems.[1185]

While things were bad for the farmer, things were even worse for the unemployed industrial worker during the Great Depression. Without assistance, such a person could end up in one of the quickly constructed shantytowns that became known as "Hoovervilles" around the country. The Hooverville in St. Charles was located near the railroad tracks along the Missouri River. Men often "rode the rails," looking for work. Called "bums" or "hobos," some had actually left their families hoping that their absence would qualify their children for more local charity.[1186] The Wabash Railroad ran behind Blanchette Park and the train slowed there as it approached the bridge over the Missouri River, thus providing a chance to jump on the train. Transients set up makeshift shelters in what became known as "bum's hollow."

Private relief organizations including churches, civic clubs, businesses and student organizations provided food, fuel and other relief to the unemployed. In St. Charles, the Red Cross began serving soup each weekday to grade school children. The Ladies' Guild of Trinity Episcopal Church quilted and sewed to raise the $16.50 per week necessary to provide 180 bottles of milk per day to needy public school children. In the initial weeks of the program it was reported that, "the weights of children receiving the milk have consistently increased from one to five pounds."[1187] A chapter of the St. Vincent dePaul Society had been founded in 1927 at St. Charles Borromeo to assist the poor. Within three years, it was forced to meet the needs of the numerous parish families who were unemployed. "The scenes were pathetic," wrote Pastor Sommershauser as he described the plight of many of his parishioners in 1931. In July the parish announced, "considering the condition of the finances at this time and realizing that members of the parish are experiencing serious problems brought about by the present business depression, we have decided to defer the building of the school for the present."[1188]

By the end of 1930, the *Cosmos-Monitor* editorialized, "people are very liberal in St. Charles," pointing out that the Junior Chamber of Commerce drive had raised $2,600, rather than the normal $1,700. It then added, "While it is not as much as had been hoped for ($4,000), the business men and others who have made the contributions are to be congratulated on what has been done – contributing more money than ever in the history of St. Charles."[1189] About the same time, the *Banner- News* was more pessimistic, questioning the ability of the private sector to handle the emergency. A deputy sheriff was assigned in December 1932 to investigate the plight of children who no longer attended school. The students, many of whom were black, lacked descent clothing in many cases.[1190] *The Cosmos-Monitor* chided those who had neglected to go through their clothes closets and urged all to, "wake up and help to care for our unemployed until prosperity gets around that big corner."[1191] A local committee on unemployment composed of civic club representatives, organized in 1932 to assist those who were unemployed, was quickly spending over $1,200 per month on unemployment assistance.[1192]

Private charity across the nation in 1932 rose to its highest levels in history but it was not enough. The head of the Association of Community Chests and Councils was warning that their funds were "altogether inadequate" to meet the emergency.[1193] When people turned to governments for help, public spending for welfare more than doubled 1920s levels. Still it amounted to only $1.67 per resident of the United States.[1194] In Missouri, where responsibility for the poor and aged rested with the county government, the State Board of Charities and Corrections reported in 1932, "The social burden of counties of Missouri, where old age is receiving necessary support, is growing each year. Missouri is taking better care of her indigent than formerly and more persons are depending on counties for support."[1195] Many adults now ended up in badly financed poor houses, along with handicapped individuals and healthy children. In St. Charles County, the "Poor Farm" was located on Elm Street in St. Charles, on the site of the present Jaycees Park. With relatives and charities no longer able to help them, more people now went to the poorhouse and more government support was required while tax revenues were down. County governments lacked the means to meet the needs of the unemployed and would not raise taxes during a depression.[1196]

In 1932, only eight states provided any form of unemployment insurance and Missouri was not one of them. To make matters worse many state constitutions, including Missouri's, did not allow deficit spending.[1197] Where the state could not help directly it could sometimes help indirectly. In 1936, St. Theodore's, the Catholic school in Flint Hill, was made a public school. As a result, the state paid for the use of the school building and the salaries of the nuns that taught in the school.[1198]

With the State unable to provide relief, people looked to the federal government. However, the Hoover administration was opposed to direct federal relief. Secretary of War Patrick J. Hurley argued in June 1932, "to give a gratuity to an individual, is divesting men and women of their spirit, their self-reliance. It is striking at the very foundation of the system on which the nation is builded."[1199] As hard as it was for charities to raise money, and for the Hoover administration to ask Congress to appropriate relief funds, it was even harder for some people to take a handout. Even those who kept their jobs could be ruined financially by the Great Depression. Across the nation, more than 2,000 banks failed in 1931. Despite efforts by the Hoover administration to prop up the banks, the entire system was near collapse by the beginning of 1933. People who still had money in banks rushed to get it out, causing still more bank failures.[1200] The banks in St. Charles were robbed 12 times between May 15, 1930 and December 19, 1933, resulting in a loss of almost $100,000. Of the five banks in St. Charles when the depression began, two had closed by the time it was over. Small banks in Portage des Sioux, Defiance, Hamburg, Wentzville, Augusta and New Melle also failed.[1201] Many middle class people were ruined by the failure of these banks.[1202] The employed also had to deal with wage cuts. In the summer of 1932, the International Shoe Company, one of the two major employers in St. Charles, announced a wage reduction of 10 to 15 percent.[1203] When the "Roosevelt recession" occurred later in the decade the company instituted a ten percent wage reduction.[1204]

In addition to dealing with the depression, small businessmen had to compete against the rise of national chain stores. With seven different independent stores on Main Street in St. Charles, the grocery business was very competitive. Traditionally, merchandise had been kept behind the counter to be fetched by a clerk with a grocery list prepared by the customer. The first "self-service grocery stores" began to appear after 1916. Still, most people expected to go to several different stores when shopping for food. However, by the late 1920s, "supermarkets," containing everything under one roof, were opening.[1205] When the first supermarket chain came to St. Charles in 1929, the independent grocers called a series of meetings. Stressing the danger of chain-store monopoly and the need to educate housewives on the value of buying from local merchants, at one meeting the local merchants discussed treating the ladies of the town to a free luncheon at Blanchette Park.[1206] There were 33 grocers listed in the city directory in 1931. While there were still 33 in the 1941 directory, only 12 of them had been in business ten years earlier. General stores had to meet chain store competition when the J.C. Penney Company announced in 1938 that it would open the first department store on Main Street in St. Charles.

As businesses struggled, the local Chamber of Commerce was inactive until 1939 when James Duggan, Abe Hess, Dr. J. M. Jenkins, Ed Travis, Dave Weil and Saul Wolf reestablished the chamber. It immediately became active in promoting economic development in St. Charles.[1207] Another sign of returning vitality was the founding of the Kiwanis Club in 1935 to, "promote the adoption and application of higher social, business and professional standards."[1208]

The Great Depression profoundly affected the everyday lives of the people in an economic sense and led to important political changes. There were not, however, great social changes. The arrival of immigrants had always posed new challenges to the social status quo in St. Charles County. However, in 1924 the nation had restricted immigration, reducing the flow of newcomers to St. Charles County from Germany or elsewhere. The county's population increased only slightly during the depression decade, from 24,354 to 25,562. In the 1930s the movement of people from farm to city stopped, and the number of farms in St. Charles County actually increased from 2,021 to 2,190, a gain attributed to St. Louisans purchasing property in the county.[1209]

Social trends that had started in the 1920s, such as more women in the work force, were interrupted by the depression. Women lost jobs to men who had to support a family. By 1933 many states, cities and school boards discriminated against married women seeking employment. A federal law in 1932 ordered personnel cutbacks be applied first to married persons whose spouses were also on the federal payroll. More than 80 percent of Americans expressed the belief that a woman's place was in the home. Even the AF of L passed resolutions opposing the hiring of married women whose husbands were employed.[1210] However, the League of Women Voters, active in St. Charles County, called for a federal minimum wage law, applicable to men and women alike.[1211] The St. Charles Business and Professional Women's Club was formed in 1937. But the advances of women in the work place would not proceed until prosperity returned. Women in the county continued the charitable activities they had been involved with for years. In 1935 the St. Joseph Hospital Auxiliary was formed and women of all faiths volunteered to assist the hospital in its mission. The local Red Cross chapter, that had been so active during the World War, continued to attract female volunteers, as did the women's organizations in the various churches.[1212]

The "noble experiment" also came to a halt and the country returned to its traditional drinking habits after Franklin Roosevelt, in one of his first acts as president, called for and obtained the legalization of 3.2 percent beer. The Democratic Congress had begun the process that led to the repeal of Prohibition even before Roosevelt's inauguration. Missouri ratified the amendment repealing Prohibition in August 1932 by a three to one margin, as St. Charles County supported ratification 15 to one.

Ethnic differences persisted, as the margin for ratification in the Anglo-American Howell community was 23 to 19, while the margin of victory among neighboring German-Americans was 46 to two in Hamburg and 48 to one in Weldon Spring.[1213] Repeal became effective in December 1932 after sufficient states had ratified the amendment and the state legislature had authorized sale by package or the drink.[1214] St. Charles voters approved liquor by the drink the following April by a 14 to one ratio.[1215] Jacob Fischbach, having purchased the Schibi Brewery in 1907 and the Moerschel Springs Brewery in 1922, merged the two and began brewing again.[1216]

The end of Prohibition meant a return to the "continental Sunday" tradition among the German-Americans, as every weekend during the summer there was a church picnic in St. Charles County. Chicken dinners, bingo, beer gardens and a dance usually constituted the day's program. Lindenwood College continued to uphold the traditional Anglo-American values against the Teutonic element in the town. Cordelia Stumberg, a Lindenwood student during this period, writes that:

> Each dormitory had a "black list" which named the young men in the community we were not allowed to date. When I saw the list I thought it described the reputation of all the young men in town and vowed I would never date a lad from St. Charles, and I relayed this information to my mother in a phone call. We had to dress for dinner every evening, no smoking allowed, and the smell of liquor on one's breath would mean the next trip home on the train.[1217]

The people continued to enjoy traditional pastimes during this time of economic problems. Bridge was popular among the middle class of the county and the working classes and farmers, especially the German-Americans, played card games like Pinochle or Euchre. Bowling remained popular in St. Charles. The sport had been popular even before the German-Americans arrived and the city council had felt the need to license bowling alleys in 1835 because of the gambling associated with the sport. The German immigrants made the sport even more popular and the American Bowling Congress, founded in 1895, standardized the equipment and rules and worked to eliminate the gambling. As the sport became more respectable, bowling alleys like Schultes, and later St. Charles Lanes, became very popular. Bowling became respectable enough in St. Charles that alleys were built in the basements of St. Peter's Catholic and Immanuel Lutheran church halls. Depression youth set pins at the alleys for ten cents an hour.[1218]

Baseball had long been popular in St. Charles County. As early as 1890, the *Demokrat* observed that, "Everyday is baseball day. Daily, Sunday being no exception, the American national game is played by hundred and thousands. Daily the English-language press fills numerous columns, often entire pages, with reports about a single game and with chat and trivia about the players."[1219] Local historian Ben L. Emmons pointed out that the dispute over proper behavior on Sunday extended even to the baseball diamond, explaining, "In those days (1870s) there were two classes of

This picture of the St. Charles Browns baseball team was taken around 1874 at a ballfield located at Eighth and Jefferson Streets. *John J. Buse Collection, 1860-1931, Western Historical Manuscript Collection-Columbia, MO*

players, those who could only play ball on Saturdays or weekdays, and those who played on Sunday."[1220] Emmons also relates the following story,

In 1876 there was an exciting political election, Hayes and Wheeler vs. Tilden and Hendricks. As most of you know, it was impossible for Bill (Bloebaum) to stay out of politics, so he organized a nine at the Jefferson School in 1876, called the Hayes and Wheeler Club. Then another boy organized the Tilden and Hendrix Club. The score of the first game played on the lot at Fourth and Jefferson was 5 to 4, in favor of Hayes, a queer coincident as that was the (vote in the) decision in which Hayes was declared elected president. In that game Harry Fowler played right field for the Hayes and Wheeler nine, but on the following Saturday he switched over to the Democrats.[1221]

In August of 1939, a celebration honoring 100 years of Baseball in America was held at Blanchette Park. Former players who had played as early as the 1880s were introduced, and Stephen Boehmer was awarded a large basket of flowers as the oldest ballplayer at the event. A team from the city beat a team from the county 12-4 in the "old timers" game, while St. Charles beat Washington, Missouri in the Trolley League game.[1222]

The 1930s and 1940s were the heyday of amateur baseball in St. Charles County. Before the advent of television, fans had to go to the park to see baseball. The East Missouri Hardroad League featured two teams from the city and teams from almost every town in the county. Ken Heintzelmann from St. Peters and Ham Schultenhenrich from St. Charles made it to the major leagues, and others played in the minors. Every young boy's dream was to escape the hardship of the depression by signing a professional baseball contract. While football and basketball were also popular, every good athlete played baseball because it, along with boxing, were the only established professional sports. The success of the St. Louis Cardinals added to the popularity of baseball in the St. Louis area. The Cardinals won nine pennants and six World Series between 1926 and 1946. During the early 1930s young boys from St. Charles walked down to Second and Adams Streets to catch the street car that would take them down to Sportsman's Park in St. Louis. As members of the "Knothole Gang" they would be admitted to the ballpark free of charge. Others listened to the games on the radio and a few were even St. Louis Browns fans.

As the 1930s began, girls in St. Charles County were still playing baseball. The American Softball Association was formed in 1933 and most high schools, reflecting the social conservatism of the decade, adopted softball as a more appropriate game for female students. The same attitude led to the banning of women's intercollegiate sports at the college level during the decade. At St. Charles High School, girls continued to play basketball, but only as an intramural program.[1223] When baseball was reinstated in 1934, after a ten-year absence, the boys had a full complement of sports at St. Charles High School. High school sporting events were well attended at the new gymnasium at St. Charles High, where St. Peter's High School also played their games. A new gymnasium was also built

In the period before World War II women's sports were popular in the local high schools. *St. Charles County Historical Society*

217

at Franklin High School in 1938 and the school had some very successful teams during this period. The St. Charles High School football team played its first game under the lights in 1931, and went undefeated in the 1940 season.

On summer evenings, people took walks around the neighborhood and visited with neighbors sitting on the front porch. On Saturday nights families would go down on Main Street, whether they had money to spend or not. People would drive their car downtown and park it in the afternoon so they could sit in it and visit with passersby in the evening. Elaine Goodrich Linn describes other aspects of growing up in St. Charles during the depression. After touching on such day-to-day concerns as canning, coal-burning stoves, Sears catalogues, sponge baths, streetcars, Zeisler's orange soda and school picnics at Blanchette Park, she concludes, "Some of the good thing to remember about the Depression were that children were not plentiful and all were valued highly."[1224] Indeed, members of the "greatest generation" were going through adolescence during the 1930s and McElvaine observes:

> Although the loss of any appreciable portion of one's childhood is tragic, there were some compensations for the youth of the thirties. The work thrust upon children in the Depression was likely to instill in them what industrial society commonly considers to be virtues; dependability, self-reliance, order, awareness of the needs of others, and practice in managing money.[1225]

Educational opportunities expanded slowly. In 1937 Wentzville High School became a three-year high school and the following year it became a full four-year school. Nevertheless, while nationally almost 50 percent of 18-year-olds graduated from high school in 1940, triple the percentage of 20 years earlier, only 35 percent of eligible students even attended high school in rural St. Charles County. In 1930 the state recommended that Francis Howell High School close, due to declining enrollments. Third year teacher C. Fred Hollenbeck actively recruited student to make sure that the school stayed open. In the 1929-1930 school year, there were only 17 students from St. Charles County enrolled at the University of Missouri.[1226] Nationally, college enrollment increased by 400,000 during the Great Depression. By 1938 there was an active Missouri Alumni Association of St. Charles County and community leaders like Ed Travis, H.K. Stumberg and Robert Niedner served as officers.[1227] Nevertheless, college remained too expensive for all but an elite few. Those with higher education, like doctors and lawyers, continued, to be the important leaders in the community. Dr. T.L. Hardin, for example, served on the St. Charles School Board from 1920 until 1953.

While their parents struggled to make ends meet, the adolescents of St. Charles County went through all the rites of passage associated with being a teenager. If life in a small town seemed boring, at least some excitement occurred in June 1935 when runaway train cars on the Wabash spur crashed into the highway bridge on Main Street. A span of the bridge fell onto Main Street causing some injuries but no deaths.[1228] The teenagers of depression St. Charles would soon have more excitement in their lives than anyone imagined.

As the depression ended and full employment returned, young men had another concern – the military draft. The *Cosmos-Monitor* reported in July 1940 that few favored the peacetime draft that was being debated by Congress. Most of the opposition centered on the belief that married men would not be able to support their families on $21 a month. A report that married men would be exempt from the draft was said to, "cause a rush here over the weekend in the marriage business."[1229] In September 1940 Congress passed the Selective Service Act, requiring each adult male between the ages of 21 and 35 to register for the draft. When registration began in October 1940 the St. Charles county clerk estimated that 3,587 men would register.[1230] The first draft lottery occurred later that month and the local paper contained the names of the 150 men with the lowest numbers. After these men were informed of their draft numbers, those with children were allowed to appeal to the local draft board for a deferment.[1231] For the next year, even though the country was not yet at war, draft notices appeared in the county newspapers. Never popular, when it came up in Congress for re-authorization a year later, the draft passed by only a single vote in the House of Representatives.

When war came following the attack on Pearl Harbor, the *Banner News* reported;

> Mayor (Adolph) Thro said today every precaution would be taken to guard against sabotage since this country is actively involved in war. While no statements were forthcoming from officials of American Car and Foundry it was expected to be only a question of time until troops are brought here to guard the plant where small 12 t tanks are being manufactured. It was anticipated that guards would be placed on the Lewis and Clark, Weldon Spring, and Highway bridges across the Mississippi and Missouri Rivers in this county.[1232]

Within a few days, Governor Forrest Donnell announced that the only bridge that the army would be able to guard in the St. Louis area was the Daniel Boone Bridge. Although soldiers would later also guard the Lewis and Clark Bridges, St. Charles County took out one of the first sabotage insurance policies in the Midwest to cover those bridges.[1233] By the end of December, members of the American Legion were taking turns guarding the Wabash and Highway Bridges in St. Charles.[1234] The U.S. Coast Guard had taken over the Palisades Yacht Club in Portage des Sioux as a repair base and a barracks in 1941.[1235]

There were concerns over possible air attack or sabotage. The 1942 Rose Bowl was canceled in Pasadena, California and moved to Durham, North Carolina because of fear of air attack by Japanese planes or sabotage by Japanese aliens. As late as April 1942, Henry L. Stimson, Secretary of War, exhorted all Americans to be ready because an attack on the continental United States was "inevitable."[1236] The Office of Civil Defense had been created in May 1941 to instruct Americans on what to do in the event of an air raid or enemy attack.[1237] When, a month after Pearl

Harbor, the St. Charles County Civilian Defense Committee called for volunteers to help with the war effort, 1,000 St. Charlesans registered within a week. Meanwhile, Lindenwood College held its first air raid drill in January. In that same month Robert Langenbecker, veteran agricultural agent for the county, speaking before an audience at the Lutheran Hall in St. Charles, warned that there was danger of an air attack.[1238] The aircraft warning service trained volunteers on how to alert the population in the event of an attack. Three hundred people attended a program at St. Charles High School in which certificates were handed out to those who had completed civil defense courses. Elmer "Jocko" Bruns, master of ceremonies, pointed out, "the efficiency of the trainees was measured by the success of the blackout in St. Charles last Monday night."[1239] The most likely target for an air attack in the county was the ordnance plant at Weldon Spring, where pilots in unidentified aircraft reported being fired upon.[1240]

Sabotage remained a concern throughout the war. In 1945 there were German prisoners of war working as farm laborers in Chesterfield, across the river from the ordnance plant. Walter Winchell mentioned in his radio broadcast one night that "nothing is to prevent them from blowing up the Weldon Spring plant," prompting plant officials to reassure everyone that the area was secure.[1241] The issue of German aliens came up again as it had in the First World War. The number of German aliens was a fraction of what it had been in 1917, and significant numbers of them were Jews who had fled Germany and other areas under German control. Only a small number of German-Americans sympathized with the Nazi regime, as membership in the German-American Bund in the St. Louis area had peaked at 200 in 1939. While they distributed Nazi propaganda from 1937-1940 and collected information on local war plants for German authorities, there was no evidence that they even attempted sabotage.[1242] Nevertheless, after Pearl Harbor aliens were again required to register, and this time they were ordered to turn in any radios in their possession that could have enabled them to communicate with the enemy. However, as of January 14, 1942, not one radio had been turned in by any of the 135 aliens, most of them German, who where registered in St. Charles County.[1243]

While the St. Charles High School *Deutscher Wanderbund*, a club whose activities "are always carried out in American style but are usually tinted with characteristic German habits," had fewer members than the Latin Club, it was disbanded as the schools got behind the war effort. Students purchased 5¢ and 10¢ stamps to fill-up savings bonds booklets. When their booklets were full, the students redeemed them for savings bonds.[1244] St. Charles High School, which began its war stamp drive in January 1942, sold more bonds than any other school in the county. To prepare students for future military service, the "Victory Corps" provided military drill and calisthenics. Extracurricular activities were cut back at all high schools because of strained transportation facilities and gas rationing.[1245]

The Office of Price Administration (OPA) established ration boards in town and cities across the country. After February 1942, no more automobiles were built for

St. Peters was the first town in the county to start a scrap-iron drive to assist the war effort. *Calvin & Helen Iffing*

civilian use, and gas was rationed to save rubber as well as fuel for the war effort.[1246] Service stations advertised that readers should, "sell the scrap and slap the Jap," and offered to pay 1¢ for each pound of rubber.[1247] In November 1942, the owners of approximately 3,000 automobiles in St. Charles, registered their cars at one of several schools. The children had been given the day off so that the teachers could process the registrations and issue gas ration cards to each car owner. Gas rationing did not apply to trucks and other service vehicles, but tire rationing did.[1248] The *Agricultural History of St. Charles County* tells us:

> In 1944, there was a severe shortage of tires. One had to have special permission from the rationing board to buy a tire. Alfred Ehlmann was one of many farmers who used a truck to haul wheat to the elevators or to store in the granaries. One day, while he was threshing wheat, one of his tires blew out and he put on his spare. It wasn't long before the spare blew as well. He and Oscar Boenker went to the ration board but were refused a permit to purchase two tires. Oscar Boenker, who owned a garage, said

he had the tires and that if they weren't given a permit to buy the tires they would simply have to dump the wheat on the ground. Horses and wagons couldn't haul it away fast enough as there was an overabundance of wheat in that year. There was also a severe manpower shortage as most of the young men were in the Army. They finally gave Alfred Ehlmann a permit to buy two new tires.[1249]

Landlords had to register their dwellings by August 15, 1942 and were subject to rent controls. Tenants could be awarded treble damages against landlords who tried to raise their rent.[1250] There were plenty of jobs as everyone rolled up their sleeves and went to work. St. Charles Country Club closed in 1942 and the land was used as a farm for grazing cattle. With everyone working but nothing to buy, people supported the war effort by purchasing war bonds. In November 1945, the county was third in the state in total bond sales and first in percentage of quota subscribed. When the totals came out at the end of the year, it was announced that the Victory Loan sales in St. Charles County had hit 335 percent of the county's quota.[1251]

Butcher shops collected waste fat from which glycerin was extracted and used in manufacturing explosives. A popular poster of the period urged housewives to "save waste fats to help stop Japs."[1252] St. Peters, the first town in the county to start a scrap-iron drive, was also the first to start a drive to salvage fats and nylon or silk stockings. The *Banner-News* pointed out that many farm homemakers had habitually used waste fats in making their own soap and added, "any fats not so used are of critical importance to the war effort."[1253] A local drive to collect 200 tons of scrap iron and steel in August of 1942 was sponsored by the St. Charles Salvage Committee and the material was collected on the used car lot of Pundmann Ford on Second Street.[1254]

Pearl Harbor created such outrage against the Japanese that many St. Charles men volunteered for the armed services. When the Selective Service registration age was lowered to 18 many more men volunteered before they were drafted. Civil War veteran George Washington Tainter, resident of St. Charles, wrote on February 18, 1942:

It is a proud day for me. I accompanied my grandson George Tainter III when he enlisted in the Navy as a hospital apprentice first class. He is the son of Dr. and Mrs. George W. Tainter of 130 McDonough Street, St. Charles. I am one hundred years old and I wore my original ensign uniform. True it is faded and worn but I wore it to St. Louis where George enlisted. I told the recruiting officer, "We licked them once we can do it again."[1255]

By the summer of 1942, large numbers of local men were being processed into the armed forces. As during World War I, the local chapter of the Red Cross prepared kits for the soldiers as they left the community. Again, as in WWI, there were rallies to support the war effort as almost 12,000 people attended a "Hero's Day" celebration at Blanchette Park in August that summer. After a parade, dignitaries in-

In 1945 a "Liberty ship" was named S.S. Lindenwood. Students at the school raised money for a library on the ship. *Lindenwood University*

cluding the Mayor of St. Louis and Congressman Cannon, made speeches designed to boost the morale of the people at a time when most of the news from the battle-fronts was not encouraging.[1256]

With more and more men leaving for war, a manpower shortage developed locally, as it did throughout the country. Most of the single women had been hired and only the married women remained. While sentiment was against such a step, even married women now went to work.[1257] In 1939 the St. Charles School District would not hire a married women, and as late as 1942, long time Board of Education member George M. Null was vehemently opposed to hiring married women; but the war had created a shortage of teachers and Cordelia Stumberg, whose husband H.K. Stumberg had entered the armed services, was hired to teach.[1258] Women also went to work in defense industries. Darlene Hahn of St. Charles worked the second shift as a riveter at the Curtis Wright Aircraft Factory in St. Louis County. She remembered, "It was hard work but we all felt like we were doing something for the country. I can't remember how much we were paid, but it seemed like big money at the time."[1259] Actually, women's pay was 51¢ an hour, about one-half of the men's pay. Top pay for women was 59¢ an hour and the minimum wage was lowered from 18 to 16¢ an hour in mid-1942. After May 1942, women also had the opportunity to enlist in the WAAC's or the WAVE's.[1260]

Not only women, but also African-Americans were hired in the defense industries. By the end of 1942 St. Louis area defense firms had hired 8,000 black workers, although five times that many African-Americans remained unemployed. While the Weldon Spring ordnance plant hired African-Americans, they worked in segregated production units, just as black GI's fought in segregated units during the war. Blacks were also used to address a shortage of farm workers. At the beginning of the war sons of farmers could get a deferment from the draft, based on a point system that used acreage and number of livestock to determine eligibility. Later, the selective service began deferring only one son in each family until 1944, when deferments were given only if the son was the sole support of the family.[1261] To meet the resulting demand for agricultural labor, the Army ordered a contingent of black soldiers to set up camp at Blanchette Park. When they arrived on July 13, 1943, the *Banner-News* noted that more than 50 area farmers had already applied for assistance. The newspapers reported no racial tension between them and the community.[1262]

One local commentator suggests that the town's race hatred was directed against the "Japs." He states, "While editorial cartoons depicted Germans as unfortunate dupes and victims of the Nazi government, they pictured the Japanese as buck teeth barbarians deserving of a rain of American bombs."[1263] He further points out that on May 8, 1945, when victory was announced in Europe, the *Banner-News* described local reaction as "quiet," reporting, "1,000 people attended services in their churches…in thanksgiving for victory." By contrast, when the people heard the news of Japan's defeat on August 15, 1945 they crowded into the streets and celebrated. Cars, with clanging tubs and tin cans fastened to the bumpers, paraded down the street. The despised Japanese General Hideki Tojo was observed hanging in effigy on at least two trucks, as businesses, offices and factories closed while the city celebrated.[1264]

St. Charles County supplied 1,487 men and women to the armed services during World War II, of whom 47 men were killed.[1265] The propaganda throughout the war had, indeed, used racial themes against the Japanese and St. Charlesans were no less affected than the nation as a whole. One must also remember that the Germans did not bomb Pearl Harbor, and until December 7, 1941, a majority of Americans were opposed to going to war against them. Americans did not yet know of the horrors of Nazi concentration camps but they did know about the Bataan Death March. VE Day was long anticipated and came at a time when there was much fighting still to do in the Pacific. VJ Day came unexpectedly, after atomic bombs were dropped on Japan, and marked the end of all hostilities. The American soldiers of German ancestry from St. Charles County did not enjoy fighting Germany for the second time in 35 years, but did their duty. The list of those killed in the Second World War from the county shows 60 percent had German surnames. [1266]

World War II guaranteed the final assimilation of German-Americans in St. Charles County and around the country. The changes spurred by World War I continued through the 1930s. In 1932 the German Methodist disbanded their school and congregation; most of their members joining the First Methodist Church. Ethnic and religious barriers were beginning to break down. In 1933 civic-minded citizens formed the Wentzville Community Club, composed of individuals from all ethnic and religious groups. In 1935 it began sponsoring annual homecomings to promote the city.[1267] In 1938, after a very successful St. Charles Pageant of Progress, Reverend Lloyd Harmon, pastor of the Presbyterian Church, said, "one of the greatest values of the production was the fact that so many people of all classes and all religious beliefs were brought together and worked with one common interest as citizens of our community."[1268] The war extinguished the last vestiges of German separatism in St. Charles. In 1941 Immanuel Lutheran Church dropped the German language from its early morning Sunday service.

By the end of 1945, the "Greatest Generation" had now made it through the Great Depression and World War II. While social changes had been few during the depression, the war had brought significant changes. Returning soldiers wanted a country fit for heroes but feared a return to pre-war depression.

B. Revolution and Restoration

In 1894, severe financial depression had allowed the Republicans to become the majority party in St. Charles County. In the 1930s the country would experience the Great Depression and, this time, the Democrats would turn the tables on the Republicans, becoming the majority party. As more people went back to work by 1938, many also returned to the Republican ranks. They stayed there as talk of war prompted isolationist sentiment and preparation for war brought 1,000 new jobs to St. Charles County. While politics took a back seat to the war effort, by 1945 the state and country, with depression and war now behind them, were becoming more conservative and the Democratic monopoly on power was weakening.

The first election after the stockmarket crash was not encouraging for President Hoover and the national Republicans. After the 1930 congressional elections, a little more than a year after the crash, the Republicans remained the majority party in the country, gaining 54.1 percent of the vote, down from 57.4 percent two years earlier. They retained their control of both houses of Congress, but by very narrow margins. In St. Charles County, the Republicans did much better than they did nationally, winning 16 elected offices, to only two for the Democrats. In the next six years the positions of the two parties would be reversed. By 1936 the Democrats, rather than the Republicans, held 16 of 18 elected offices in St. Charles County.

On June 11, 1930 Anna Weinrich, widow of former county judge and state representative William Weinrich, filed for state representative. The *Cosmos-Monitor* observed on June 11, 1930:

> Mrs. Weinrich is perhaps one of the best known women in this county as she was the first lady to go out into the county to organize the Republican women voters and she was also one of the active lady workers during the World War and visited almost every community in St. Charles County, if not all of them. As to her ability to fill the office there is no dispute among her friends who know her well. She is well posted on all political matters and has been an ardent Republican worker since the women were given the franchise of suffrage.

St. Charles County was obviously not yet ready for women in elected office, as she was defeated in the Republican primary by the incumbent, Louis J. Ringe, by a margin of 4,006 to 1,237.

By 1932, public opinion was running strongly against President Hoover. In June of that year, Secretary of War Patrick Jay Hurley spoke to a gathering at Blanchette Park, promoting completion of a project to deepen the Missouri River channel as an aid to agriculture in St. Charles County. He also spoke in support of the administration's public works policy, stating, "There are persons who are offering to spend the government's money in pork barrel legislation for votes, but there are men in Washington standing in their way who are more interested in the future of the nation than in their own political future."[1269] In spite of this rhetoric, the Hoover administration had spent $700 million in 1931 on public works projects to create jobs, but the president remained adamantly opposed to any direct relief to the unemployed.[1270] It appeared that he was willing to help corporations and banks but not the common people. These Hoover programs had not been effective and it was becoming clear that the majority favored a more active federal role in alleviating the suffering caused by the depression, and they did not want men in Washington "standing in their way." St. Charles County Democrats had already begun in 1930 to organize for the November 1932 election. While not accustomed to political success, they believed that political beliefs were changing in the county.[1271] While 1,800 people showed up for a Democratic rally at Blanchette Park during the summer of 1932, the Democrats were not the only party showing increased activity in St. Charles County. Socialist organizers spoke

This get-together of incoming and outgoing public officials after the 1930 election reflects the fact that, even though women had received the vote ten years earlier, men continued to dominate politics in St. Charles County. *St. Charles County Historical Society*

at the St. Charles County courthouse and, on one occasion, they challenged Republicans meeting in the adjacent room to a debate.[1272]

The 1932 election was a disaster for the Republicans nationally and locally. President Hoover, who won 42 percent of the vote nationally, received only 25 percent in St. Charles County. Only the most loyal Republican precincts voted for Hoover: Augusta - 51 percent, Harvester - 59 percent, New Melle -62 percent, and Weldon Spring -69 percent. The Democrats took majorities in both houses of Congress, swept into the county courthouse and elected Frank Iffrig the first Democratic state representative from the county in over 40 years.[1273] The day after the November election the *Banner-News* stated:

> … the Democrats, unable previously to elect an entire ticket for the last 40 years, have put their candidates over by majorities that compare favorably with those on which Republican officeholders are accustomed to ride into office … Local politicians are cogitating on the meaning. The fact that the average man was badly dissatisfied with his economic conditions and voted for Roosevelt to obtain relief, and further that many Republicans voted a straight Democratic ticket to avoid making a mistake, only partially explains it."[1274]

The election of 1932 was, like 1860 and 1896, one in which the entire political landscape was reordered. FDR was a master of the new medium of radio and, after his election, the people seemed especially reassured by Roosevelt's "fireside chats." The Democrats completed their take-over of urban workers that had begun in 1928, while holding on to the traditional Democratic constituencies. Influenced by local and national political developments, organized labor in Missouri allied with the Democratic Party and become an important part of the "Roosevelt Coalition."[1275]

There was little demand in St. Charles County for radical measures. On June 8, 1932, speakers from St. Louis had urged the unemployed to form a St. Charles chapter of the Unemployed Council, a national Communist organization. About 300 people attended the meeting and 100 joined the organization.[1276] However, Roosevelt's election later that year, and the introduction of direct relief in 1933, blunted any appeal that radical groups might have had in the county.

At his inauguration, President Franklin D. Roosevelt stated, "This nation asks for action, and action now." He called Congress into extraordinary session and, in the first "hundred days," Congress passed a series of measures to deal with the emergency. A "bank holiday" was declared, during which all the nation's banks closed. They were opened again only after federal regulators had determined that they were solvent. This approach was taken with the full support and cooperation of the banking community and, like many of the original New Deal programs, was actually conservative in nature. Many of the hastily conceived and implemented relief programs did not work particularly well, but the country seemed relieved that someone was trying to do something.

As the 1934 general election approached, the Democratic *Banner-News* reported that $462, 000 had been allotted for work on the Missouri River while men were being employed on other federal government projects like the Alton Dam, state highway projects, and municipal public works projects in St. Charles and Wentzville. Farm subsidies totaling $150,000 had been distributed to St. Charles County farmers and various forms of government relief were now available. The repeal of Prohibition had created new demand for glass bottles and sand from the Klondike quarry to make them. Relying on these facts, the paper proclaimed, "Let the pessimist and the objector to New Deal policies consider facts as they actually exist in this city and county, and then say, if he can, that the prosperity outlook in this community is not better than it has been for many a day."[1277] Democratic Senator Bennett C. Clark addressed 400 people in St. Peters and told them, "The crisis came in 1929 and although Hoover had the remedies at hand the same as Roosevelt, he refused to use them."[1278]

Nationally, the 1934 mid-term elections would be a referendum on Roosevelt and the New Deal. Local Democratic politicians tried to create Roosevelt "coattails" even though the president was not on the ballot. One of them suggested in a speech, "By putting your own officers in the Court House you are voting for the greatest president that ever held office."[1279] Two weeks before the election, 1,518 checks totaling $59,000 were mailed to St. Charles County farmers participating in the wheat program.[1280] Nationally, Democrats' piled up a 69-25 majority in the U.S. Senate and a 322-103 margin in the

House of Representatives, increasing their margins in each.[1281] A number of New Deal opponents were beaten at the polls in 1934, sometimes by previously obscure Democrats such as Harry S. Truman.[1282] In the primary, St. Charles County Democrats were solidly behind Truman's opponent, Congressman John Cochran. The *Banner-News* reported, " Cochran is by long odds the most popular candidate in the U.S. Senatorial race in this city and county. Milligan and Truman, if conditions are to be judged on very convincing evidence, are attracting very small minorities among local voters."[1283] A few days before the primary election, Catherine Lawler, in charge of the Truman headquarters, announced that the headquarters would close, "due to lack of response because of the many inconsistent statements made by County Judge Harry Truman, the candidate of "Boss" Pendergast of Kansas City." Lawler stated, "the residents of St. Charles County showed absolutely no interest in his candidacy…"[1284], a fact that was born out on primary election day when Truman received only 125 votes compared to Cochran's 1380 and Jacob Milligan's 494. Truman won the general election in November even though he lost St. Charles County by two percentage points.

While the Democratic candidates in St. Charles County continued to do well in 1934, winning 14 of 18 contested seats, the Republicans took heart from the fact that they had done much better than in 1932.[1285] In addition, the Republicans won back a majority on the County Court. Two years earlier, after nearly 40 years out of power, the Democratic judges had filled all appointed positions with Democrats. When the Republicans took the court in 1934, they returned the favor, leading to indignant charges of patronage by both sides in the local newspapers as the 1936 elections approached.[1286] The best local patronage job, postmaster of St. Charles County, went to Hugh Holmes, who was appointed by FDR on December 1, 1935 and would serve in the post for over 25 years.[1287]

Nationally, the election of 1936 was shaping up as another referendum on the New Deal. As the election approached, to meet the challenges on the left, FDR launched an all-out attack on big business. While opposed to the Wagner Act guaranteeing collective bargaining for unions in 1934, FDR saw that it was going to pass in 1935 and got behind it, alienating the business community.[1288] Congress passed the Social Security Act in the same year. The president also called for a soak-the-rich tax bill that would have included inheritance taxes, high rates in the upper income brackets and a graduated corporate income tax. While the bill that finally passed was extremely watered down and raised only 250 million dollars, FDR had made it clear that he was for the "forgotten man" and against the "unjust concentrations of wealth and power."[1289] Taking up the theme, the *Banner-News* editorialized in August of 1936 saying:

> Some of our critics are heads of corporations that are now able to make their ledger entries in black that had been in red ever since the stock market crash of nearly seven years ago. What are they complaining about? Trimmed down to simple words, it is that having been placed again on their financial feet, they are now seeking a return to the old processes that made millionaires of them and bankrupts of most of the rest of us.[1290]

In the summer of 1934, New Deal opponents had formed the Liberty League, a pro-business group led by former Democratic presidential candidate Al Smith. Obviously encouraged by this development, the Republican *Cosmos-Monitor* advocated a coalition ticket in 1936. It stated, "This is not a contest between Democrat and Republican Parties but is a contest between the New Deal outfit against all true Americans."[1291] It further pointed out that, in spite of ten billion dollars of expenditure, the depression continued with 12 million unemployed and 20 million more on relief.[1292] Democrats replied, "while members of the Liberty League took billions from the treasury no mention was made of the Constitution," and regretted that the same men were complaining that taking money from the treasury for the common man was unconstitutional.[1293] Speeches and editorials throughout the campaign continued to remind the people about "Charles Dawes, Andrew Mellon and the rest of the millionaires."[1294]

The "New Deal outfit" did very well in November as FDR carried every state except Maine and Vermont, while increasing already large Democratic super-majorities in Congress. Much of their support came from the people – presumably poor – who had not even voted in 1932. Approximately 6 million more people cast ballots in 1936 and 5 million of them supported the New Deal.[1295] Among the poor voting Democratic for the first time were large numbers of African-Americans. Before 1932, both nationally and locally, they had remained loyal to the party of Lincoln. After 1932, more and more black voters deserted the Republican Party as FDR included them in the "Roosevelt Coalition." Nationally, 1934 was the first election in which a majority of African-Americans voted Democratic, and efforts to recruit them extended to St. Charles County. Announcing the windup to the 1934 Democratic campaign with a rally

State Representative Frank Iffrig complains on the floor of the Missouri House of Representatives that the low per-diem received during the special session of the legislature meant that he could not afford to wear a suit. *Herbert Iffrig*

at the Knights of Columbus Hall, the *Banner-News* announced, "Both colored and white people are urged to be present to hear Congressman Cannon and former Governor Major tonight, but for those who prefer to hear a Negro orator, arrangements have been made for a special Negro rally at the Odd Fellows Hall near Blanchette Park this evening."[1296]

The same paper reported the next day that the "Negro orator" related to the crowd that a local Republican leader had insisted, "Negroes who voted the Democratic ticket were convicts, imbeciles and Judas Iscariot. It had been said that a colored person who voted a Democratic ticket ought to be sent to Fulton." The black speaker suggested, "it would do no good to take a Negro who voted a Republican ticket to Fulton. He was so crazy that the only cure possible would be to take him out and shoot him."[1297] The effort to recruit St. Charles County African-Americans continued in the 1936 campaign when black Democrats from St. Louis spoke in St. Charles. They reminded the crowd that the Republican administration in that city had built a new facility to house primates at the zoo and declared, "Monkeys are better off than Negroes in St. Louis under the Republican Administration," and "people earning less than $1,000 would be idiots to vote for Landon."[1298]

Roosevelt earned 62 percent of the national vote, but only 54 percent in St. Charles County in 1936. Democratic sheriff candidate Joe Borgmeyer received 83 percent and FDR's coattails were long enough for the Democrats to win back the County Court. While the appeal of the Populists and the Progressives had been minimal, the majority of the voters in St. Charles County voiced their approval for the New Deal's promise of relief, recovery and reform. It seemed inconsistent to many at the time that the Democratic Party, which since the days of Jackson had sought to keep the federal government weak lest those with economic power use it to the disadvantage of the common man, now proposed to strengthen that federal government to serve "the forgotten man." No man personified the change better than Missouri's junior senator, Harry S. Truman. Perhaps this explains the "inconsistent statements" that Catherine Lawler referred to as the reason for his lack of support in St. Charles County during the primary. Nagel states that Truman, "found himself obliged to accept the exercise of governmental power in behalf of citizens dwarfed by business consolidation within the Republic's economy." He concludes, "In this spirit Truman learned to use political power in a fashion appropriate for a Missouri Jeffersonian."[1299]

Families in St. Charles County received direct assistance from the government like they had not received since the Spanish authorities granted common field lots to those who requested them and could show a need. The federal government initiated public improvements on a scale that former Whig and Radical Republican politicians would never have imagined. The National Recovery Act, which set up local and national committees to set prices and wages, placed cooperation for the public good ahead of the free market. The common law, Supreme Court decisions, and constitutional amendments that had bolstered capitalism at the beginning of the nineteenth century were now used as precedent to overturn certain key legislative enactments of the New Deal. When the NRA was declared unconstitutional, the *Cosmos-Monitor's* headlines proclaimed, "The decision is the unanimous opinion of the United States Supreme Court – Liberty of the people saved by the Supreme Court – Way now open for revival of business under laws made by Congress not code writers."[1300] Liberal opinion did not agree and attacked the outdated thinking of the "nine old men." Senator Truman backed the president when he attacked the Supreme Court and proposed appointing additional justices to the conservative court for each justice that reached a particular age. Under the threat of such a plan the members of the Supreme Court moderated their positions and began upholding New Deal measures, ignoring nineteenth-century precedents. But Roosevelt had overplayed his hand by this attempt to "pack" the Supreme Court and a conservative coalition of Republicans and southern Democrats developed in Congress.

There was also a backlash against the "sit down strikes" used by organized labor in 1937. In August 1937, the stock market collapsed again and unemployment reached 20 percent. As a result, in the 1938 elections, the Republicans gained 13 governorships, eight seats in the Senate, and 81 seats in the House of Representatives.[1301] In 1938, Republicans in St. Charles County also came storming back. Claiming that the Democratic County Court had spent $22,236.65 more than the previous Republican court, and that the Democrats had awarded contracts to the *Banner News* without competitive bids, the entire Republican ticket was elected. Robert Linnemann was elected state representative and Robert Niedner was elected prosecuting attorney. Both would continue to be leaders in the community for years to come.[1302] The remaining Democratic office holders in St. Charles County were defeated in 1940 as the County Court became entirely Republican. Omar Schnatmeier became sheriff and Alf Oetting became assessor as the Republicans regained the dominance they had enjoyed before 1932. The Democrats did not return to power in St. Charles County for almost twenty years.[1303]

During the 1930s, even when the Democrats had a majority on the County Court, Republican Henry F. Ohlms was the presiding commissioner of St. Charles County. During his tenure, maintenance of county roads was taken away from overseers, who were usually patronage appointments, and given to full-time county employees. The county enjoyed an excellent credit rating during these years because of the conservative spending habits of Republicans and Democrats; but even county government responded to the popular demand for government action. In 1936, the County Court voted unanimously to purchase the Lewis and Clark Bridges from private interests that had originally built the structures. The *Cosmos-Monitor,* nevertheless, was compelled to explain to its readers that:

> Judge Ohlms said that the county would make purchase of the property with twenty-year revenue bonds. Judge Ohlms said that interest and principal and all expenses of maintenance and upkeep on the bridge would be borne entirely by toll from the bridge. He said the purchase of the bridge will not cost the taxpayers of the county one cent of tax money."[1304]

Of course, that was not entirely true since the county lost $5000 worth of taxes on the two bridges annually. The prediction that the bonds could be retired in as little as ten years did not come to pass. The county collected a toll on the bridges until the bonds were paid off in 1951 and they became free bridges maintained by the State of Missouri.[1305]

City politics in St. Charles in the 1930s was contentious and often reflected national philosophical debates. In 1925, after years of study and debate, the voters had turned down by a large margin a proposal to adopt a city manager form of government.[1306] Having retained their mayor-council structure, the city voters elected Henry J. Broeker mayor in 1927 by only 39 votes over Joseph H. Lackland. Broeker had survived a lawsuit to oust him from that position that alleged he could not serve because was in arrears on his city taxes.[1307] There had been heated debates over private versus municipal utilities and whether the city should grant a franchise to one bus company or allow competition among several.[1308]

In March 1933, the city government moved into the building at Main and Jefferson Streets that now houses the St. Charles County Historical Society. As the city fathers moved into the new city hall they were already embroiled in a debate over municipal ownership of electric power generating facilities that would make earlier controversies seem minor. This debate mirrored the national debate that was going on across the country, where there were 13 utility holding companies by 1932 that produced no electricity themselves, but controlled 75 percent of the nation's private electrical power. In 1936 President Roosevelt backed the Wheeler-Rayburn Bill that would have ordered the dissolution of these holding companies. Although it passed the Senate, the bill failed in the House after the electric industry generated a quarter of a million telegrams and five million letters to congressmen. The federal government also went into the electricity generating business with the creation of the Tennessee Valley Authority that competed with the private companies. The TVA eventually sold electricity at $2.00 to $2.75 a kWh, against a national average of $5.50.[1309] In 1931, Union Electric was selling electricity in St. Charles at the rate of $3.27 a kWh, well below the national average, but well above what TVA would later charge.[1310]

On the state level, during a special session of the General Assembly in 1934, Democratic Governor Guy Park, with the support of organized labor, had tried to pass legislation exempting bonds used to finance municipal utilities from the bonded indebtedness limit placed on cities by the Missouri constitution. Had it passed, it would have encouraged cities to build their own electric generating facilities.[1311] The debate in St. Charles began long before the TVA was generating any electricity; before President Roosevelt and Governor Park were even elected. In November 1930 a committee of citizens and City Council members reported that a municipal power plant was feasible. In three years the 20-year franchise granted on March 8, 1913, of which Union Electric was the assignee, would expire.[1312] The city continued to study the issue, and in May 1932 another committee reported that a municipal plant would be profitable and recommended that a $300,000 bond issue be presented to the voters for their approval. The fighting began immediately. Two councilmen voted against receiving the report and pointed out that the vote of the committee had taken place when a quorum was not present, and that Union Electric and the press had not been allowed into the meeting.[1313]

Those in favor of public ownership, now organized as the Municipal League, were able to get their man, Harry Kienker, elected in a special City Council election in October and the question was put on the ballot for the January 6, 1933, election.[1314] The debate heated up considerably and remained intense until Election Day. The *Cosmos-Monitor*, which had remained uncommitted at first, came out against the bond issue. It was taking the position that a five, rather than 20-year franchise should be granted to Union Electric. It not only claimed that the city would not be able to pay off the debt without raising current rates, but that the proposed plant would not even meet the current needs of the city.[1315]

The *Banner-News* stated, "We shall leave no effort unattended to awaken the public to a sense of the type of propaganda this private utility aggregation is sponsoring."[1316] Over the next four months, the *Banner-News* made the case for municipal ownership. It argued that Union Electric's profits were excessive;[1317] that publicly owned facilities can be built and operated more cheaply since they can get lower interest rates and do not have to pay property taxes;[1318] and that city officials had promised to employ only local labor to build the public plant, thus reducing local unemployment.[1319]

On Election Day, the $300,000 bond issue failed the two-thirds majority needed by 427 votes. Since it carried a simple majority by 428 votes and passed in all but one precinct in St. Charles, the Municipal League immediately called for another election. The issue did not go away, and remained a bone of contention for the remainder of the decade. The *Cosmos-Monitor* repeatedly ran comparisons of St. Charles rates with other areas of the state; provided information about how much Union Electric paid in taxes; and warned of the corruption that would be inherent in public ownership. The *Banner-News* continued to push for a municipally owned power plant and made it an issue at every municipal election.[1320]

In the 1937 municipal election, Municipal League candidate Charles Kansteiner opposed incumbent Mayor Edward Schnare, who favored private ownership. Kansteiner won the election by 248 votes, but the Municipal League lost a position on the council when Clarence Westerfeld defeated Fred Mintrupp, so the stalemate continued.[1321] In January 1939, a SEC investigation disclosed that a *Cosmos-Monitor* reporter was being paid by Union Electric while he wrote articles against public ownership. Union Electric also paid liberally for advertising in the paper. William Waye, attorney for Union Electric, also admitted he had been reimbursed by the company for contributions he had made to political campaigns, including the reelection campaign of Mayor Schnare, a violation of Missouri's Corrupt Practices Statute.[1322] On May 4, 1940, the $600,000 bond issue for a municipal electric plant was again put to the voters. The campaign had the same issues, same arguments and same result as the earlier attempt.[1323] These elections demonstrated, as did the 1936 presidential election, that the majority of the voters in St. Charles favored an expanded role for government, even if not the two-thirds majority required to pass a bond issue. The members of the Municipal League got the last laugh when Union Electric was fined $175,000 by a local circuit judge for violating the Corrupt Practices Act.[1324] David A. Dyer, the young prosecuting attorney of St. Charles County, brought the prosecution. He had been elected vice-president of the Missouri Young Republicans in 1937 and prosecuting attorney in 1940, and was considered to be one of the Republican Party's rising stars.[1325]

The presidential election of 1940 would be completely different from its predecessor. First of all, the Republican candidate Wendell Wilkie accepted many of the reforms of the New Deal and argued only against its excesses. Secondly, by 1940 the Second World War had started in Europe and many Americans had strong isolationist feelings, wanting America to stay out of the European war. Disillusionment following World War I had surfaced in the 1920s and did not dissipate in the 1930s. The German Republic had defaulted on its reparations payments required by the Treaty of Versailles, and the French army occupied the Ruhr industrial areas in 1923 to collect its debt. As a result, articles like the following, entitled "Letter from Germany Tells of French Deeds," had appeared in the *Banner-News*:

> A letter from Germany sent to this office for examination contains among others the following passage giving some idea of the French occupation of the Ruhr: "All the people living in districts occupied by the French are unemployed, nobody knows where to live on the next day. Bands of men and women are plundering the shops. Can you imagine it? I can. Have you ever seen your parents and relatives with pale faces dried out by hunger, your children weeping and crying for only a bit of bread? If you have already seen such dreadful scenes you can understand many a revolt in Germany. But you can never imagine that here are cultivated people, as the French call themselves, who are pleased with such poverty and misery. Right or wrong that is all the same to these self-conceited rascals and white and black brutes. The English always talk about fair play, but where are their fair deeds."[1326]

Some St. Charles Countians had heard presidential candidate Robert M. LaFollette charge in 1924, "The war was fought in order to save Morgan's millions."[1327] Theories like that gained additional adherents when the U.S. Senate charged a committee under the chairmanship of North Dakota Republican Senator Gerald Nye, with investigating the relationship between the international arms trade and America's involvement in the World War. The committee found that the arms trade had prodded the U.S. into war. In response, Congress passed a series of neutrality acts between 1935 and 1939 to avoid the entanglements that had led to our involvement in the First World War. When the Second World War began in September 1939, Congress allowed arms to go to the belligerents only on a "cash and carry" basis. The strategic effect of the policy was to put Great Britain at a tremendous advantage over Germany since it had naval superiority in the North Atlantic. The political effect was to make many, including most German-Americans, fearful of being drawn into another European war against Germany.[1328]

President Roosevelt received only 41 percent of the vote in St. Charles County in 1940. Such a drop-off was not unusual for a community with a large majority of German-Americans, among the most isolationist of American ethnic groups. Nationally, Roosevelt lost seven percent of his strength between 1936 and 1940. In 20 counties across the country his loss exceeded 35 percent, which was five times the national average. Nineteen of those counties were predominantly German-American.[1329] St. Charles County was not one of the 20, but Roosevelt's margins had dropped 24 points from 1932 to 1940. Undoubtedly, isolationist sentiment was alive and well in St. Charles County and played a part in Republican successes in 1940. On September 11, 1940, the *Cosmos-Monitor* criticized the destroyer deal Roosevelt had made with Great Britain, in which the Americans gave 50 old destroyers to the British in return for some bases in the Caribbean.[1330]

Isolationist sentiment alone does not explain the Republican resurgence in St. Charles County. Support for the New Deal continued to weaken. A poll by the American Institute of Public Opinion conducted after the 1940 election found that, nationwide, 80 percent of those on relief voted for Roosevelt, as did 60 percent of those who said they would be able to survive a month or less if unemployed. Those who said they could survive at least three years without relief voted 61-39 for Wilkie.[1331] In 1929, St. Charles factories had produced $10,354,008 worth of products. In 1931 that number shrank to $4,701,195. The number of people employed went from 1,576 to 929, and these numbers explain the Roosevelt landslide in 1932. The inability of county Democrats to make their majorities permanent may be found in the production numbers for 1933, when manufacturing increased from $4,701,195 to $5,233,165 and employees increased from 929 to 1224. Before the New Deal could even get started, the manufacturing sector of the local economy had begun to improve.[1332] The country would not surpass 1929 levels of production until 1941, and then would exceed those levels by 30 percent in that same year. By the 1940 presidential election, construction was about to begin on the Weldon Spring ordnance plant and people were finding more job opportunities in St. Charles County.[1333] Paul Johnson explains, "The New Deal earth-movers became the creators of the Arsenal of Democracy," and adds "The war economy, with the state the biggest purchaser and consumer, was the natural sequel to the New Deal and rescued it from oblivion."[1334] The military build-up that would finally bring the entire country out of the Great Depression by 1941 had gotten a head start in St. Charles County in 1940 and that fact was reflected in the election results in November.

With the economic emergency over, the county reverted to its previous political habits in 1940, where social issues and ethnic history had more to do with voting patterns than economic class. Traditionally Republican precincts like Augusta, New Melle, Harvester, Weldon Spring, Friedens, Black Jack, and Wentzville reverted to voting as Republican as they had before the depression. Dardenne went from being heavily Democratic to become a swing precinct. Only Cottleville, along with the first and fourth wards in St. Charles, did not return to their previous Republican percentages.[1335]

In 1940, every Republican vote was needed in St. Charles County, where Republican gubernatorial candidate Forrest Donnell received a 2,771 vote majority, only 852 votes less than his majority in the entire state. Several Democratic leaders decided to take advantage of language in the Missouri constitution requiring the Speaker of the House to tabulate the vote in the presence of the House of Representatives and Senate and declare the winner. They proposed to look behind the returns from the individual counties, hoping to find irregularities in at least 3,613 votes, Donnell's margin of victory. The Democratic candidate was Lawrence McDaniel, liquor commissioner of St. Louis, who had been severely criticized by a Grand Jury for his handling of that office the month after the election.[1336] Since many of those attempting this maneuver were also members of the big-city machines who had a poor reputation when it came to voter fraud, their was an outcry across the state against those involved. The *Cosmos-Monitor* reported, "The Dickmann and Pendergast political machines are trying, by unconstitutional, back-door methods, to seat McDaniel, the defeated Democratic candidate on the face of returns, in the Governor's office."[1337] The Democrats split on this strategy as Governor Lloyd Stark and Senate Majority Leader Philip Donnelly denounced the move. The *Banner-News* supported the move stating, "Now lets be fair about it all. In all of these proceedings the Democrats have played in the open. Every move has been a legal move – in no instance has the spirit or letter of the constitution been violated."[1338] All seven Democrats on the State Supreme Court disagreed with the *Banner-News*, voting unanimously to order the speaker to declare Donnell the winner.[1339] No one from St. Louis has been elected governor of Missouri since.

The Republicans, while opposed to the urban political machines, were not opposed to a little patronage in the county courthouses. In April 1941, it was announced that as many as 35 state jobs would be created in St. Charles County under a plan released by Republican Governor Forrest Donnell. That plan gave one job for every 225 votes Donnell received in the county the previous November. Under the plan each of the 65 Republican state representatives could name one person for a $200 per month job, subject to the approval of the Republican County Committee. Donnell pointed out that the total number of jobs would be less than the number under the previous Democratic administration and local Republican party chairman, H.K. Stumberg observed, "many of the state jobs are of minor importance but this county would receive some of the better appointments."[1340]

While military preparedness and Lend-Lease alleviated the problem of unemployment, America's entry into the Second World War after December 7, 1941 created a whole new series of political problems for the Roosevelt administration. In October 1942, Congress passed a flat five percent gross income tax on annual incomes over $624.00. This regressive tax would force many workers to pay income tax for the first time, and the administration had also imposed price controls about the same time. While both these measures were necessary to halt inflation, neither was politically popular at a time when American troops had not begun turning back the Axis tide in either the Pacific or European theatres of war. Pollsters predicted 1942 would not be a good election for the Democrats, and it was not. In St. Charles County, Republicans held 16 of the 17 county offices after the 1942 election. Theodore Bruere Jr. defeated a 30-year incumbent Democrat for circuit judge in the 11th Circuit that included the Democratic counties of Lincoln and Pike. Although he lost St. Charles County by more than 1,000 votes, Clarence Cannon easily won re-election in the heavily Democratic Ninth Congressional District. However, nationally the Republicans gained 44 seats in the U.S. House of Representatives, only six seats short of a majority. The Republicans also added seven seats in the Senate and picked up some governorships. With the southern Democrats, there was now a strong conservative majority in Congress that would disagree with the Roosevelt administration often during the next two years.[1341]

Democrats began experiencing setback as 1943 began. D. Oty Groce, a St. Charles Democrat, lost to Roy D. Miller, a Columbia Republican, in a special election for a vacant seat in the Missouri Senate. The victory gave the Republicans a 17-17 tie. On the national level, Congress passed a bill, over the president's veto, giving the government the power to seize factories necessary to the nation's defense. Congress also outlawed political contributions by unions and the House Un-American Activities Committee began investigating radicals in the Roosevelt administration. To provide relief to taxpayers whose taxes were withheld after 1943, Congress passed the Current Tax Payment Act of 1943, which forgave 75 percent of tax liability for 1942. Congress blocked an administration initiative that would have provided a federal ballot to servicemen in 1944, making them request a ballot through their state of residence.[1342]

As the 1944 presidential election neared, both parties sensed the conservative shift of the country and opted for less liberal candidates. The Republicans turned from Wendell Wilkie to Thomas Dewey. The Democrats dropped the ultra-liberal Henry Wallace as their vice-presidential candidate for the more moderate Harry S. Truman. Senator Truman had gained national attention as the chairman of a Senate Committee investigating corruption in the defense industry. In 1944, several employees of the Weldon Spring ordnance plant filed affidavits that told of gambling and idleness at the plant; of employees scrubbing swimming pools while they should have been producing bombs. Upon preliminary investigation, the charges lacked merit and Truman declined to bring his committee to St. Louis to investigate the charges.[1343]

While expanding New Deal measures was out of the question, President Roosevelt was able to get Congress to provide increased social benefits to servicemen in the form of the GI Bill. In 1944, FDR featured this and his leadership during the war, while Dewey stressed the president's poor health and alleged the presence of Communists in the Democratic Party. The result was a fourth term for Roosevelt.[1344] The big city vote was decisive in 1944. In cities of 100,000 people, FDR received 61 percent of the vote. The Democrats made small gains in the Congress, but not enough to affect the conservative majority of Republicans and southern Democrats. St. Charles County gave the losing candidate Dewey 59 percent. On April 12, 1945, shortly after being inaugurated for a fourth time, President Roosevelt died and Harry Truman became president of the United States.

From 1932 to 1945, the State of Missouri, continued to be controlled by the Democratic Party that had been popular in the rural parts of the state since 1896 because of its conservative social values and progressive positions on economic issues. It had become popular with the urban working class because of the party's pro-labor stance. This coalition of conservative and liberal elements created an unbeatable coalition in the country, state and even traditionally Republican St. Charles County. While the Roosevelt coalition lost in St. Charles County in 1938, on the state and national level, it would not start to unravel until the 1968 presidential election. After 1932, except for short periods after 1946, 1952, and 1980, the Democratic Party controlled both houses of Congress until 1994 and both houses of the General Assembly until 2000.

C. New Deal and War Production

At the beginning of the nineteenth century, the Americans had replaced traditional mercantilist and monopolist features of the fur trade with a free market approach. They had done away with the commons of the Spanish agricultural system, allowing the land to be sold or leased to farmers who were now part of a market-driven system of privately owned farms. While the Spanish system had some entrepreneurial aspects and the Americans were usually more pragmatic than ideological, capitalism became the dominant economic philosophy for the next 100 years. During the Great Depression, the justice of capitalism was seriously questioned. New laws were passed to correct the injustices of the market and protect the collective good against the abuses of individuals. The New Deal came to St. Charles County and the federal government became involved in the everyday lives of people as it never had before. That expanded federal government was better prepared to fight the Second World War, the event that would really increase the size of the federal budget and bureaucracy.

The collapse of the stock market and the depression that followed paralyzed the private sector of the American economy during the 1930s, and there was very little private investment, either in St. Charles County or the country during the decade. The Missouri-Kansas pipeline, built in 1930 to provide natural gas for St. Charles, would be the last major private investment for some time. When International Shoe Company needed to expand its operations in St.Charles later in the decade, it did so only after local businessmen collected enough money to buy 8.8 acres next to Blanchette Park and donate it to the company for a new heel plant. Other than these two projects, government rather than private interests would fund all or part of every other major construction project in St. Charles County during the 1930s.

In 1937 the new highway bridge over the Missouri River at Weldon Spring became an important link to St. Louis County. *Missouri State Archives*

Transportation continued to be as important to St. Charles County as it had been in the 1920s, but now government stepped in to accomplish what the private sector could not. In the late twenties, a private corporation had begun construction on the Lewis and Clark Bridges across the Missouri and Mississippi Rivers, linking St. Louis County with Alton, Illinois. After the stock market crash, the corporation did not have the capital to complete the project so the county purchased the company's interest and completed the bridges in 1936, imposing a toll to retire the bonds that had been sold to finance the project.

By the 1930s, local leaders looked primarily to Jefferson City for roads and bridges. In 1928, Missouri voters had amended the constitution to allow the State Highway Department to add the lettered highways in each county to the system of roadways maintained by the state. A statute allowing the transfer was enacted and upheld by the State Supreme Court in 1929. By 1930 farm groups and the Highway Commission were promoting the building of additional "farm-to-market" roads to boost agriculture and the rural standard of living.[1345]

In the previous decade, U.S. 40, a major east-west artery in the nation's highway system, had been built through St. Charles. During the early years of the Great Depression, children would sit on a wall at the northeast corner of Sixth and Clay (now First Capitol) on Saturday evenings and identify the license plates on the cars as they stopped at the stoplight. Many of those traveling from New York to San Francisco would pass through this intersection.[1346] It was not surprising therefore, that merchants in the city became concerned when it was proposed that a new bridge be built over the Missouri River at Weldon Spring, with U.S. 40 redirected at Wentzville to cross it, by-passing St. Charles. As early as November 6, 1929, the *Cosmos-Monitor* opined that Highway 40 should remain over the St. Charles Rock Road Bridge.[1347] Even though the toll was removed from the Rock Road Bridge in January 1932, the city fathers could not keep the U.S. 40 route through the city.[1348] While deciding the route the highway would follow through St. Louis County, a Page Avenue extension was discussed but rejected.[1349] On January 11, 1933, the last hurdle was removed and construction of the $3 million project through the "Gumbo Flats" of St. Louis County began. The loss for St. Charles was a gain for the western parts of St. Charles County and everyone benefited from the jobs created by construction of the new bridge and highway.[1350] When the bridge was completed in June 1937, it was the most expensive bridge built by the State Highway Department up to that date. Governor Lloyd Stark dedicated the "Daniel Boone Bridge" on June 30, 1937 and promised the crowd more "farm-to-market" roads in the future.[1351]

In the 1930s, trains were still more important than automobiles and the old North Missouri Railroad, now the Wabash, planned to replace the bridge that had been built in St. Charles in 1871 with a new steel structure. The old bridge went through the northern part of St. Charles, with the depot at the end of Fifth Street. The proposed new route would have skirted the edge of the city and put the new depot at Elm Point, outside the city limits. The city was successful in keeping the station within its limits, largely because a state statute required trains to stop within all county seats.[1352] Construction of the bridge began in 1930, but was halted for three years because of the railroad's financial problems. The St. Louis and Hannibal Railroad, that connected to the Wabash at Gilmore, was controlled by John Ringling, one of the owners of the Ringling Circus. Abandonment was authorized in 1932 after the railroad showed an operating deficit for four of five years.[1353]

Federal involvement in the economy increased rapidly after Franklin D. Roosevelt's inauguration in March 1933 and was felt in St. Charles County immediately. With the banking system in crisis, President Roosevelt proclaimed a nationwide "bank holiday" on March 4, and rushed through an emergency banking bill that gave Washington control over the reopening of the banks. A Federal Deposit Insurance Corporation was also created to guarantee bank deposits.[1354] By March 15, 1933, every bank in St. Charles County had been given a permit to do business.[1355]

Congress also passed the National Industrial Recovery Act (NIRA) that set up national and local boards under the National Recovery Administration (NRA) to set wages and prices. This act called for business, labor and government to work together and, like many of the New Deal measures, gave the administration broad powers. The goal was to introduce rational planning to the economy, giving business relief from the anti-trust laws and labor increased influence. Codes were established for each industry that set prices and prohibited anyone from selling below that price. At the same time, labor was guaranteed minimum wages and maximum hours, an end to child labor and the right to collective

The swimming pool in Blanchette Park was built with the help of a $40,000 WPA grant and provided relief from the warm summers for over 60 years before it was replaced. *St. Charles County Historical Society*

bargaining. NRA Compliance Boards were elected to enforce the NRA codes where no local code had been adopted. The members of the local board in St. Charles County were: John Fischbach, representing industrial employers, Frank Rauch, representing retailers and wholesalers, Phil Rupp, representing industrial workers, Fred Janning, representing retail employees, Mrs. Douglas V. Martin representing consumers, and Judge B.H. Dyer, attorney for the board.[1356] Participation was voluntary, but even the *Cosmos-Monitor* showed the "blue eagle", symbol of the NRA, on its masthead. Other than a small jolt to the economy in the summer of 1933, the NRA did not bring about prosperity. When the Supreme Court declared the NRA unconstitutional, the *Cosmos-Monitor* editorialized, "With the scrapping of the NRA we believe the whole country will be benefited and prosperity will be revived. Thank God we have a Supreme Court to protect our liberty and save our Constitution."[1357]

The New Deal meant direct relief and jobs for individual citizens and new facilities for their communities. Within a month of its inception, the Civil Works Administration (CWA) had hired 2.6 million people, and by January 1934 had hired 4 million, paying an average salary of over $15 per week.[1358] It spent in excess of $22 million in Missouri and employed nearly 105,000 in the state at its peak in 1934.[1359] More than 2,000 registered for work with the CWA in St. Charles County. In the fall of 1933 local businessmen Edwin Ell and J. Ed Travis went to Jefferson City, where they secured approval of four CWA projects for St. Charles County. Three projects, that employed a total of 134 people, involved street work in the cities of St. Charles, O'Fallon and Wentzville. The fourth project involved jobs cleaning the county court house that would, according to the *Cosmos-Monitor*, "be given to colored women."[1360] Providing so much relief so fast, it was inevitable that here would have been "petty graft" and "politics," in the program. Therefore, in the spring of 1934 President Roosevelt ordered the CWA phased out.[1361]

The Public Works Administration (PWA) under Harold Ickes was a more efficient New Deal employment program. Ickes saw the program not only as a means to bring about recovery, but also as a way to build valuable public infrastructure. It also took longer to get geared up.[1362] In March 1935 the St. Charles school board applied for a PWA loan to build a new junior high school and gymnasium adjacent to the high school, a new gym at Franklin School and other school improvements. In January 1937 the voters approved a $130,000 bond issue by a better than four to one majority. Forty-five percent of the costs of the buildings would be covered by the PWA grant.[1363] The addition was built and is still in use at St. Charles High School today. With the assistance of the WPA, work on the new Wabash Railroad Bridge resumed in April 1935. The new bridge opened to traffic on October 13, 1936. Having providing many jobs, it was finished in 17 months rather than the projected two years.[1364]

Because of the New Deal, federal relief and jobs came to the workers and families of St. Charles County. By September 1935, 464 families in St. Charles County were receiving government relief.[1365] The total amount of federal assistance to the county from September 1932 until November 1935 was $528,436. Still, as Gary McKiddy points out, "during most years there were 75 to 100 heads of households in St. Charles County who had applied for federally sponsored jobs, but for whom no work was available."[1366]

The State of Missouri, under the authority of a 1932 amendment to the state constitution, provided a $30 per month pension to each Missourian over 70 who had, "no income or an income inadequate to provide a reasonable subsistence compatible with decency and health." The number of people who qualified turned out to be three times the original estimate of 20,000 and the funds were provided from a one percent general sales tax that was raised to two percent in 1937.[1367] Congress passed the Social Security Act in the same year and the elderly in St. Charles County became the recipients of large-scale direct relief from the state and national governments.

In 1935, part of the nearly $5 billion appropriated for relief, went to the National Youth Administration to help two million high school and college students stay in school by giving them part-time jobs. It also helped 2.6 million young people who were not in school, such as the 26 young men who were hired to tear down the old Lincoln School in January 1941. The NYA project lasted for about four months and paid $2,489 to workers and supervisors, with the school having to spend $370 for tools and equipment.[1368] Mary McLeod Bethune, a black woman who had founded Bethune-Cookman College, was the assistant secretary of the NYA that became a model federal assistance program for African-Americans.[1369] While the old Lincoln School had originally been the grade school for black children in St. Charles, newspaper accounts do not indicate whether any African-Americans were hired to raze the building.

Roosevelt took $1.39 billion of the $5 billion appropriation to create, by executive order, the Works Progress Administration (WPA) under the direction of Harry Hopkins. In October the President approved a $166,963 grant for WPA work in St. Charles County. The grant included $40,000 for a swimming pool in Blanchette Park, conditioned on city voters approving a $25,000 bond issue, which they did on August 28, 1935.[1370] O'Fallon passed a bond issue in 1940 in order to qualify for a $74,000 WPA grant to build a municipal water plant.[1371] The WPA had built almost 90 miles of roads, highways, streets and bridges in St. Charles County by 1941.[1372] In 1941 a surplus commodities lunch program was started in the schools to feed the children of WPA workers. This was the beginning of school lunch programs at schools like St. Charles Borromeo, where parents who could afford it paid ten cents per week so the school could continue to purchase surplus food items. That same year the parish sponsored a WPA garden to raise vegetables for the lunch program. WPA workers tended the garden and canned the vegetables.[1373]

Across the country, the percentage of unemployed on WPA rolls hovered around 30 percent between 1935 and 1940.[1374] At the beginning of 1938 there were still 882 totally unemployed, 582 underemployed and only 216 working on government emergency programs in St. Charles County.[1375] Full employment, brought on by the defense build-up in 1940, made the WPA no longer necessary and, when it was terminated in December 1942, it was employing only 40 people in St. Charles County.[1376]

One of the most popular New Deal programs was the Civilian Conservation Corps (CCC). Established in 1933, it was administered by the U.S. Army and the Soil Conservation Service. The CCC camps helped 2.5 million young men survive the depression. A man had to be 17 to 23 years of age and unemployed to be accepted into the program. He had to agree to send $25 out of his $30 monthly salary back to his family or, if he had no family, to have the money put into savings for him. The CCC, working on public and private lands, promoted soil conservation, developed recreational facilities and supplied emergency aid. By 1937 the CCC had 37 camps in Missouri including one near Wentzville, in St. Charles County. By 1940, the CCC had planted 18,000 trees in the county to fight soil erosion.[1377] The CCC was popular because the jobs aided the unemployed in the city, while the project aided the farmer in the countryside. While some criticized the military nature of the camps, others believed the regimentation in the camps was "probably little worse than the practice sessions of high school football teams."[1378]

During the 1932 presidential campaign, Roosevelt had maintained that insufficient farm income was at the root of the depression. Between Election Day in November, and Inauguration Day in March, Roosevelt had rejected any offers from the out-going administration for cooperative efforts. Therefore, by the time he became president, many farmers, especially in the South, had already planted their crops. To have any impact on that growing season Congress had to act quickly. In the spirit of cooperation, and to shield himself from criticism if it did not work, Roosevelt got all the major farm groups to agree to a farm bill before he gave it his blessing. Congress approved the Agricultural Adjustment Act (AAA) on May 12, 1933. Its goal was to

This St. Peters post card shows how a building had been raised to keep it above flood waters. *Herbert Iffrig*

restore farm purchasing power by raising farm prices. Those prices would rise because of government enforced scarcity, achieved by paying farmers to take acreage out of production. The money to pay the farmers came from a tax on the processing of food products. The late date of passage meant that many crops had to be plowed under, while people were going hungry.[1379]

Locally, the AAA was handled through the Agricultural Extension Service, which had offices in the county courthouse. Robert Langenbacher was the county agent, Doris Abling Johnson the secretary-treasurer and Henry S. Hoffman the president of the council. In 1935 the Department of Agriculture established farm committees to administer the programs. Under the committee system among the first to serve were Martin J. Hollrah, chairman, with Edgar Borgelt and Rudolph G. Kessler. To assist the county committee, community committees of three farmers were elected in each of the county's six townships.[1380] The program, along with the effects of the Dust Bowl, did reduce production and raise prices by 50 percent during FDR's first term. However, farm income did not reach its 1929 level until the Second World War created a demand for American agricultural products.[1381]

When the Supreme Court declared the AAA unconstitutional, Congress passed the Soil Conservation and Domestic Allotment Act in February 1936 that paid farmers to shift production from soil-depleting grain crops into soil conserving and enriching crops such as grasses and legumes. Farmers had to fill out paperwork showing the 1935 crop acreage and other information pertaining to the use of their land. This was to establish a "soil depleting base" for the farm, which would determine the amount of the check the farmer would receive from the government. By June 10, 1936 over 2,000 worksheets covering 96 percent of the farm ground in St. Charles County had been completed.[1382] These programs not only aided the farmer but also helped to aid the unemployment problem, since the new programs required measurement of acreage, necessitating the hiring of approximately 30 men called reporters. They measured with wooden wheels in the fields while an additional 14 office clerks computed the acreage. As the years passed this crude method was replaced by steel tape and eventually by aerial photography. An amendment to the Farm Act was approved February 6, 1938 combining the 1936 programs, and substituting marketing controls for production controls. In addition, the Ever-Normal Granary Plan made possible the storage of supplies by providing non-recourse loans to farmers.[1383] Under the new program, St. Charles County had the largest wheat allotment of any county in the state in 1939.[1384]

Another New Deal program popular in the agricultural community was the Rural Electrification Authority (REA). The market was going to bring electricity to outlying farms in St. Charles County only after everyone else had it, and at a much higher cost. Rural electrification required federal assistance. Unfortunately it did not come to the county until 1941, when a program to serve 750 families in St. Charles, Warren and Lincoln counties was proposed. A committee began signing up subscribers with a lifetime membership fee of five dollars. Minimums of 340 customers and 150 miles of line were met before the newly chartered Cuivre River Electric Cooperative received aid from the REA.[1385] When a contract was let to start work in October 1941, St. Charles County had 198 of the planned 466 miles, and 400 of the 700 subscribers for the multi-county project. When completed, one half of the farms in the county would have electrical service. Work was scheduled to begin in O'Fallon, and they hoped to have power by Christmas.[1386] But the country went to war and in February 1942, the project was cancelled "for the duration," as Washington needed copper wire for the war effort.[1387]

Aside from the direct financial aid, local farmers also approved of New Deal flood control measures. Flooding on the Missouri and Mississippi Rivers had always been a problem. In 1875, the *Demokrat*, reporting the devastation experienced by farmers in the bottoms when the Missouri River flooded their crops, had asked the question, "Will they now wake up and finally persuade Congress to intervene and grant the monies to somewhat control the brutal fellow."[1388] Flooding particularly affected the small communities of Defiance, West Alton, Portage des Sioux and St. Peters. In the spring of 1881, a flood on the Missouri had wiped out Brotherton, directly across the river from St. Charles and had done extensive damage in St. Charles County.[1389] The *Journal* had claimed that a four-foot high levee over a distance of one-third mile would have kept the waters out of thousand of acres around *Marais Crouche* and *Maire Temp Claire*. It added that such a levee could be built with, "an expenditure small, not only in comparison with the value of the result, but actually small."[1390]

When the Army Corps of Engineers began draining the swamps in the Bootheel, the Missouri legislature had passed a measure allowing the creation of levee and drainage districts. Several levee districts were created and their supervisors built levees in the Hancock, Greens Bottom, Cul de Sac, Dardenne and St. Peters Districts of St. Charles County. While the federal government had taken major responsibility for flood control in 1917 and had built additional levees, they had proved inadequate during the 1927 flood on the Mississippi. The Corps of Engineers then conducted a study of the entire Mississippi River System, leading Congress to pass a Flood Control Act in 1928 that appropriated funds for Mississippi River levee improvements and authorized surveying and planning on the Missouri River.[1391] President Roosevelt's strong personal interest in resource management and flood control measures encouraged the district engineer of the Army Corps of Engineers in Kansas City to propose a comprehensive plan in 1933 for the Missouri River. The plan would improve navigation, waterpower, flood control and irrigation on the river. Construction actually began on a Fort Peck dam and reservoir, on the upper Missouri, as a PWA project in 1934.[1392]

The Missouri River flooded in 1935, and St. Charles County was particularly hard hit. On June 12, 1935, the Rock Road Bridge had to be closed when water covered a section of U.S. 40 just east of the bridge approach. A break in the Black Walnut Levee kept motorist from using Highway 94 through West Alton as an alternate route. To get to work in St. Louis, St. Charlesans had to walk across a section of railroad right-of way to catch a bus to work. About 50,000 acres of farmland north of St. Charles, along with 7,000 acres near Weldon Spring had flooded.[1393] This event and similar disasters throughout the Missouri River valley generated additional pressure for action from Washington. Farmers in the county established committees from each levee district, as well as a general county committee, to push for a unified levee system in the county.[1394]

The 1936 Flood Control Act gave the federal government responsibility for flood control and congressional action in 1938 reduced local cost sharing requirements. The Corps became a very active builder and repairer of levees.[1395] This was a radical departure from the past, when levees were the responsibility of local levee districts established under state law. When the federal government took over responsibility for levees many of the levee districts in St. Charles County and elsewhere became dormant. The president's proposed budget for 1937 included $27 million in water resource improvements for Missouri and Illinois towns along the Mississippi River.[1396] Congress also appropriated $16 million to implement the comprehensive plan on the Missouri, but construction was not completed by the time of U.S. entry into WWII.

In 1942, 80,000 acres of cropland in St. Charles County were under water again, and residents of the Cul de Sac and Mullanphy Slough Levee Districts appeared before the County Court. They asked the County Court to petition the Corps of Engineers to make a survey for a continuous levee running from St. Charles down the Missouri River and then back up the Mississippi River to Machens.[1397] Severe flooding in April, May and June 1943 caused considerable damage in the county. As usual, the Missouri left its banks just past St. Charles where the only levee protection was that afforded by the embankment of the MKT Railroad. The water ran with such force across the peninsula to the Mississippi River that it cut a swath in the area of Highway H. This area, known as "Grau's cut," retained water when the flood subsided and became a permanent lake.

There was also a lot of flood damage in Kansas City disrupting industrial production important to the war. Responding to this, Colonel Lewis A. Pick, of the Kansas City Corps of Engineers, hurriedly developed a plan that emphasized levees, dams and reservoirs through the entire length of the Missouri River. It also emphasized navigation, the original responsibility of the Corps. Groups on the upper reaches of the river and the Bureau of Land Reclamation thought the plan did not address the need for irrigation or hydroelectric power. They put forward a plan developed by a bureau official, W. Glenn Sloan. Battles raged in Washington over the two plans, along with a third plan, designed to develop a Missouri Valley Authority, (MVA), on a scale similar to the TVA, that would have been responsible for all water resources. Fearful that they could lose jurisdiction over the river to a MVA, the Corps of Engineers and the Bureau of Land Reclamation agreed on a compromise that became known as the Pick-Sloan Plan, which Congress endorsed as part of the Flood Control Act of 1945. The following year they appropriated money to establish a nine-foot navigational channel.[1398]

The St. Louis Corps of Engineers, whose jurisdiction included the Mississippi River, was also busy during this period. In 1933, it announced that a navigational dam would be built at Alton, Illinois. The lake to be created by the dam would inundate 6,000 acres of ground in St. Charles County and be two miles wide at its widest point, where the Illinois River flowed into the Mississippi River.[1399] The lake would be 62.5 square miles in size, the size of St. Louis, and extend 38 miles up the Mississippi River. The Alton Dam would be the southernmost of 26 dams between St. Paul, Minnesota and Alton, Illinois.[1400] The dam was finished in May 1938 at a cost of $13,131,230.[1401] In the litigation over damages caused by the inundation of lands between Machens and West Alton, it became obvious that Frederick Bates, while confirming title to the Spanish land grant in the early nineteenth century, had acted beyond his authority. Judge B.H. Dyer made a trip to Washington D.C. and convinced Congressman Clarence Cannon and Senator Bennett C. Clark to support legislation to clear the title on the 9,753 acres involved.[1402]

The New Deal's most permanent contribution to the interests of working people was the Wagner Act, which guaranteed workers the right to collective bargaining and outlawed unfair labor practices. In 1929 the only two labor unions listed in the *St. Charles City Directory* were the Barber's Union, Local No. 861 and the Carpenter's Union, Local No. 1987. When the American Federation of Labor (AF of L), who represented primarily skilled workers, appeared unwilling to organize unskilled factory workers, the Congress of Industrial Organizations (CIO), emerged to fill that role. Originally a committee of the AF of L, it became an independent organization in September 1936. Under the leadership of John L. Lewis, the CIO staged a series of

The Alton Dam provided much needed jobs during the Great Depression. It has aided river transport and provided recreational opportunities ever since. In the 1980s this lock and dam was replaced by a new facility just down stream. *St. Charles Journal*

successful 'sit down strikes" in 1937, where workers quit working but refused to leave the factory. While successful in gaining concessions from employers, the tactic's disregard for the employer's property rights, and the resort to violence by strikers and strikebreakers, led to a loss of support among some Americans who had been generally supportive of unions during the 1930s.[1403]

Against this backdrop, St. Charles County experienced its first union labor dispute. In December 1937, the War Department announced that 300 men would be needed to clear the trees from the land to be flooded by the Alton Dam. When work on the dam had begun a few years earlier the members of an Illinois union were paid 67.5¢ per hour, while Missouri workers were paid 37¢ per hour. The workers from St. Charles County quickly formed their own union, an American Federation of Labor (AF of L) affiliate, in order to receive the same union wage. Fifty members of the union, which eventually became Laborer's Local 660, under the leadership of Owen L. Femmer and Wilbert Scheffer, appeared at the timber clearing project and announced their intent to unionize that project. The federal government had rejected all six private bids to clear the timber and announced that the Corps of Engineers would be doing the $400,000 project and paying 44¢ per hour for common labor. Union representative Owen L. Femmer stated, "They paid our men 67 and ½ ¢ an hour for labor on the dam and now they want to pay only 44¢ an hour for clearing the land behind the dam." He promised a "showdown," and shortly thereafter some of the 200 union pickets assaulted three men who claimed to be simply bystanders.[1404] Union picketers were also the victims of violence as two men were injured when struck by vehicles believed to have been occupied by U.S. engineers, workmen and special St. Charles County deputies. Angered by the incident, union picketers smashed the car windows of many workmen as they left the job site.[1405] One-hundred-fifty picketers also marched to the county courthouse and threatened to arm themselves if Joseph Wentker, prosecuting attorney, did not shut down the job.[1406] On February 14, Joseph Feltes, one of the two injured union picketers, died of his injuries and tempers got even shorter. Sheriff Joseph Borgmeyer insisted that none of his deputies had been in the car that hit Feltes, as union members continued to pressure Wentker to seek an arrest warrant.[1407]

As the impasse continued, the St. Louis Building Trades Council voted to shut down all federal projects employing union labor, including several school projects in St. Charles County, in protest over the government's treatment of the St. Charles union. Members of the St. Louis area congressional delegation were sent a telegram complaining, "The Army Engineers devised ways and means to defeat the purposes of organized labor in this locality…."[1408] The next day the Corps of Engineers suspended the timber clearing project citing the "wave of violence" and explaining that the timber clearing was only being done to enhance the recreational purposes of the Alton pool and was not necessary for navigation, the primary purpose of the project. The Trades Council called off its threatened strike and the dam opened that spring with the trees around West Alton still uncut.[1409]

The State Highway Department announced in December 1937 that Massman Construction Company was the successful bidder on a $389,000 project to repair the U.S. 40 Bridge in St. Charles, with work to begin on February 1, 1938. The union was happy with the wage scales but wanted Massman to recognize the union and a "closed shop."[1410] Massman announced that it would not recognize the union as the sole bargaining agent for all its employees on the bridge and would retain an "open shop." St. Louis County deputies had to escort 11 Massman workmen through 100 picketers at the east approach of the bridge. When the men got to the west end, St. Charles County deputies had to protect them as they walked a block to the St. Charles Hotel where they were paid. The next day, one of the 11 non-union workmen was beaten at his home and two suspects were arrested. Work on the bridge was suspended.[1411]

In early March, a new group, called the Independent Workers Organization, (I.W.O.), announced that its members would accept common labor jobs at prevailing wage scales in order to keep the jobs in St. Charles County. One of its spokesmen told the *Banner-News,* "There was plenty of work in St. Charles County until it was suspended because other union men would not accept the wage scale and picketed the jobs. Our organization believes that men willing to work at a prevailing wage should be permitted to work."[1412]

On March 25, Massman, which had contracted with the I.W.O., resumed work on the bridge. Fifteen hundred AF of L members again picketed the project on April 2 and union leaders were arrested. Work was halted again as 6,000 AF of L men walked off PWA projects around the St. Louis area under instructions from the St. Louis Building Trades Council. On April 18, violence broke out between union and I.W.O. workers at the junior high and Lincoln School projects in St. Charles. Bricks were thrown and nine men, three from the I.W.O. and six from the union, were injured. Ten days later the parties, meeting at the St. Charles Hotel, reached a settlement on all outstanding issues. Local 660 of the AF of L got the bridge contract but some I.W.O. men were hired. The AF of L continued the work on the school buildings but agreed not to interfere with the land clearing at the Alton Pool should it resume.[1413]

The local response to these labor conflicts varied as the *Banner-News* reported:

Clashes between workmen and pickets caused much concern during the past few months. A number of misdemeanor and felony cases against members of both sides are still pending. As a result, the labor situation in the last few weeks developed into the main topic of discussion. News of the situation was read in every part of the county.[1414]

George Helfert, Anton Brush, Clem Echele and Raymond Sammelmann, speaking for the laborer's union, told a *Banner-News* reporter that the public did not understand the viewpoint of the local union, and announced a series of public meetings. The *Banner-News* wrote: "In this way the local union plans to educate St. Charles County people in their cause. Helfert said the program of the union is merely to see that St. Charles County men are hired on the land clearing and highway-bridge projects. The union opposes the importation of out-of-county labor."[1415]

Public support for the union did not keep all 24 special police, who were given the option of turning in their badges, from agreeing to serve when summoned by Mayor Kansteiner to help keep order on the bridge. Likewise, the Democratic Sheriff, Joseph Borgmeyer, had nearly 100 special deputies.[1416] Although organized labor had already formed alliances with both state and national Democratic parties, the dispute in St. Charles County did not appear to revolve around political parties. Prosecutor Wentker, Sheriff Borgmeyer and the majority of the County Court were Democrats but did not take the side of the union. Republican attorney David Dyer represented the three union men charged with assaulting the Massman employees. Democratic Circuit Judge Woolfolk believed that there was enough public criticism of the unions in the county that Dyer's clients could not get a fair trial and transferred the case to Lincoln County.[1417]

The differing loyalties of the two newspapers were also expressed only subtly. The *Banner-News* reprinted an editorial from a St. Louis labor publication:

Glance at any small town newspaper where civil liberties are being flouted and labor organization being bitterly fought, and you will more often than not find the town journal on the side of reaction and oppression and advertising. This is due to the fact that the small town publisher is dependent to a larger degree upon limited community advertising and subsidization from public utility and other sources than are our metropolitan papers. Yet here and there you will find a country newspaper which is fair and courageous and inclined to give labor an even break. The two newspapers in St. Charles, *The Daily Banner-News* and the *Cosmos-Monitor*, have naturally taken a realistic approach to this serious labor controversy which is financially hurting the business interests of the community. The *Daily Banner-News* takes a restrained, moderate stand in the three-cornered battle being waged.[1418]

The editorial continued stating, "To deliberately confound and confuse the public as the *Cosmos-Monitor* is doing is neither constructive public service nor honest journalism."[1419]

A group of "business and professional men," never identified by name, met in a closed meeting, urged completion of the bridge, and pledged their support to the I.W.O. From these closed meetings came reports of statements such as, "We don't want any labor racketeers telling us how to run our businesses. We'll have to quit if they get control here."[1420] Among the business community the *Banner-News* reported, "The general impression left was that there is a fear that organized labor will next attempt to unionize shoe workers, carshop workers, truck drivers and all other businesses if the union here is permitted to get a foothold."[1421] Indeed the new Congress of Industrial Organizations (CIO) was working hard to organize the shoe and car shop industry throughout Missouri, including St. Charles.[1422] An unsuccessful sit-down strike closed the International Shoe factory in St. Charles in November of 1940. Almost 1,000 workers were laid off pending settlement of the dispute with 53 employees of the finishing room.[1423] Shortly thereafter the United Shoe Workers of America, a CIO affiliate, began organizing and by March 1941 had nearly signed up the 51 percent needed to become the sole bargaining representative.[1424] In that month, a St. Louis labor leader addressed the International Shoe workers and explained:

A number of years ago many factories were moved from large cities to small cities so that lower wage scales would prevail. In recent years.... organized labor has found its way into every part of the country. And if a factory is moved now by the management to escape having to bargain with its employees, the National Labor Relations Board steps in immediately.[1425]

The union eventually received the needed support and became the bargaining agent for the workers at the plant. The steelworkers, also a CIO affiliate, became exclusive bargaining agent for the employees at ACF in June 1941. By that time, approximately 85 percent of the workers had voluntarily joined the union at ACF where they were working on 30 new railroad coaches, as well as a government defense contract for 1,000 tanks.[1426]

The union movement not only had to overcome non-union workers, hostile business interests and an apprehensive public, but also had to survive the rivalry between the AF of L and the CIO. On December 13, 1940 the Corps of Engineers announced that the 5,000 workmen to be hired to build the ordnance plant at Weldon Spring would be hired without reference to union affiliation. In addition, no one hired would be forced to join or contribute to a union. [1427] Within a few days the National Defense Commission in Washington D.C. forced the Corps to drop the rule and an AF of L official announced that only AF of L members would be hired. This action prompted efforts by the United Construction Workers, a CIO affiliate, to reinstate the previous policy. On December 31 it was made official when the construction company building the $20 million plant announced that members of the AF of L would be hired first because "it is the most reliable source of competent workmen."[1428] As the hiring began the CIO complained to the War Department that the AF of L was blacklisting local labor. An affidavit signed by B.H. Jolly, county superintendent of schools, noted this statement by the AF of L:

> St. Charles County labor was black-listed because St. Charles County businessmen had not assisted the American Federation of Labor organization in previous labor trouble in and around St. Charles, that it didn't matter to him whether St. Charles County laborers became affiliated with the American Federation of Labor or not, they would in no case be employed at the said Ordnance Plant.[1429]

Further allegations by the CIO charged the AF of L with job racketeering and charging exorbitant dues. In the end, the AF of L preserved its closed shop and many St. Charles County workers did get work at the plant.

Other groups were upset as well by the Weldon Spring construction. In October 1940, Newton McDowell, acting for the federal government, began purchasing options on approximately 700 parcels of land in the Hamburg-Howell area, for the construction of the ordnance plant. Many landowners were opposed to a five percent commission that they would have to pay McDowell in addition to the cost of clearing title.[1430] The first purchases took place in December 1940. Some landowners were paid $92 per acre and agreed to pay McDowell his commission. The War Department approved the options taken by McDowell and, as the government began paying, people held auction sales and moved off the land.[1431]

Everything was going well until the War Department began to question whether McDowell had paid too much for some of the land and whether his commission was too high. Half of the landowners had been compensated by the time payments were halted. While the U.S. attorney filed a lawsuit to determine whether there had been criminal fraud, the landowners suffered. They had sold their livestock simultaneously, creating a buyer's market, and they had used the proceeds to make down payments on new farms, assuming the remainder of the money would be forthcoming. [1432] Local people wondered why the government had to go across the state to find real-estate agents. Senator Bennett C. Clark pressed the War Department to explain why a Kansas City contractor had been granted such "fat fees." Although the War Department discontinued payments to McDowell a month later, it was estimated that he made more than $50,000 in commissions. [1433]

While the government had expected to acquire the site for about $1 million, exercising the options would have cost $3 million. So the federal government exercised their options on only 121 parcels and filed condemnation suits on the 146 parcels where the options were too high, and on another three because no options had been granted. Forty-five landowners retained attorney Samuel M. Watson to represent them. According to Calvin Castlio, "Sam Watson expressed the opinion that the contract[s] held [are] legal and binding and would finally be so decided... He said we had to be prepared to go all the way to the Supreme Court of the United States if necessary." [1434]

Construction on the ordnance plant began in January 1941 and was completed in ten months. Twenty-seven cemeteries, including an Indian burial ground, were fenced; the villages of Howell, Hamburg and Toonerville were evacuated; 13 miles of railroad track was laid and 50 miles of road was built; a major pipeline was relocated; and five deep wells were sunk to produce 17 million gallons of water a day. The project consumed 8.5 million board feet of lumber, 1,500 tons of structural steel, and 40,000 cubic yards of concrete. Francis Howell High School had to move to the new Central Elementary School from 1942 until 1946, when the school moved back to buildings at the abandoned ordnance plant. [1435]

In December 1940, J. Ed Travis, newly elected president of the Chamber of Commerce, urged businesses in St. Charles not to over expand because of wartime contracts. He did not want St. Charles to become a "ghost town" after the war. He was also concerned about social problems that could be created by the influx of 8,000 to 12,000 workers at Weldon Spring. [1436] The plant was creating a housing shortage for the construction crews and for prospective workers. Fifteen houses were built near the site for plant officials and a 36-acre tract of land located in St. Charles provided for 200 additional units of public housing. The 36-acre tract became the Village of Weldon Spring Heights and the project in St. Charles was named "Powell Terrace," after Ludwell E. Powell, the city's first mayor. The city had to run water to the project and the government did the rest. Seventy-four housing units were built in O'Fallon and Cottleville. [1437] Father William Pezold, pastor of St. Joseph Parish, supported the public housing in Cottleville, known as the Village of All Saints. Having learned that the Bank of O'Fallon owned a 35-acre plot, Pezold induced its officers to divide it into 42 lots to be sold for $50 to families working at the ordnance plant. He had new homes built with the wreckage of temporary buildings being torn down at the plant, and soon had 24 homes under construction. [1438] To meet the need for additional housing, St. Charles Mayor Adolph Thro issued a proclamation asking the people to remodeled suitable quarters and rent them out.[1439] Nevertheless, the housing shortage continued in St. Charles throughout the war.

The Weldon Spring plant opened two months before Pearl Harbor and became the largest high-explosives plant in the country. Eventually producing 880 tons of TNT per day, it became known as the "TNT Plant." In February 1945 the U.S. Supreme Court ruled, in a 5-3 decision, in favor of the landowners. Nevertheless, many remained bitter toward the federal government for decades. Weldon Spring was only a small part of an unprecedented mobilization for war. The Navy built one of the best flight-training facilities in the Midwest near Portage des Sioux. There were eight 800-foot runways crisscrossing each other in the shape of an eight-pointed star, where American and British pilots practiced takeoffs and landings. When the war came, the field was named Smartt Field, after Ensign Joseph Gillespie Smartt, a former trainee who was killed at Pearl Harbor.[1440]

Defense orders would unleash the full production potential of American industry. A year after Pearl Harbor, the U.S. had equaled the industrial output of the three Axis Powers combined. It then doubled that figure by 1944 while putting 16 million men into uniform. The first order given to American Car and Foundry was for 329 light tanks, each with 2,800 different parts, not counting the engine and each weighing 12 tons.[1441] U.S. factories turned out 102,000 tanks, 17.2 percent of which were built by ACF plants, 1,800 of which were built at the plant in St. Charles. In St. Louis County, McDonnell Aircraft grew significantly during the war and employed over 5,000 people, 60 percent of them women. They worked primarily on subcontracts for other companies, including Boeing, and became the largest supplier of airplane parts by the end of the war. The company also experimented with its own aircraft designs, including a jet fighter for the Navy, but it was not ready for production by 1945. St. Charles County companies acquired nearly $235 million worth of war contracts, with the bulk going to ACF, International Shoe and the TNT Plant. In addition to light tanks, ACF also built highly specialized hospital cars at the rate of one per day in late 1944, while International Shoe produced boots for military personnel. Owing to the extensive defense work in St. Charles County, the Sisters of St. Mary were able to get a $130,000 federal grant to expand St. Joseph Hospital by 55 beds.[1442]

When the war started unions wanted a "closed shop," where everyone in the factory was forced to join the union if there was one. Of course management wanted an "open shop," where membership was optional. Under a compromise, each worker hired in a union shop had 15 days to resign from the union. If he did not, he would have to pay union dues for the duration of the contract. With the increase of overtime pay, average weekly earnings for workers rose 70 percent during the war.[1443] Labor strikes prompted Congress to pass a bill in 1943 giving the government the power to seize factories necessary to the nation's defense and making it illegal to strike in those factories. Nevertheless, a strike dragged on for several weeks at International Shoe Company in 1945 that could have affected the war effort since, at its peak, International Shoe produced 35,000 pair of shoes per day for the military at its plants.[1444]

Believing that there was a sufficient stockpile of bombs to win the war, the War Department shut down the TNT plant in the spring of 1944. The estimate was wrong and the plant reopened the following winter. Thousands of laid-off workers at the plant wondered what would happen when the war ended and the troops came home.[1445] One of the speakers at a meeting on post-war employment at Kiel Auditorium in St. Louis stated, "Competition between returning vets and civilian workers for jobs in the postwar era may lead to civil war, if there are not jobs for all."[1446]

Working through the Farm Bureau Federation and others, farmers were able to gain "parity" for farm prices, based on the ratio between agricultural and overall commercial prices in the 1910-1914 period. In 1942, Congress set a ceiling on farm prices at 110 percent of parity, a bonanza for the farmers. After 20 years of hard times, the farmers in St. Charles County and across the country were enjoying prosperity. They were enjoying a prosperity based on government subsidies; the businessmen were enjoying an industrial recovery based on war production, and workers were enjoying full employment based on 13 million Americans being in the military. When the war ended in August 1945, everyone wondered whether the prosperity would continue.

VI
Post-War Period
1945-1964

In August 1958, Congressman Clarence Cannon was the speaker at the dedication of the Interstate Highway Bridge that crossed the Missouri River at St. Charles and put that city within 30 minutes of downtown St. Louis. A lot had changed in the county since the end of World War II. The previous year an article entitled "Path of Progress for Metropolitan St. Louis," announced, "Much of St. Charles County will soon be connected by expressways with the central parts of St. Louis City and County. In terms of travel time St. Charles will be brought close to the business centers of the metropolitan area. This will stimulate a county which up to now has grown very slowly."[1447] The 1950s are usually considered a conservative period in American history. However, the post-war period was a time of transition and change in St. Charles County. In many regards, the returning veteran found St. Charles County no different than when he left it in 1942. The Republican Party was still dominant, there was still not enough housing and the schools were still segregated. By 1964, things had changed significantly and, the community was considerably different. Usually seen as a time of retrenchment by the federal government after the New Deal and before the Great Society, this period saw two pieces of legislation passed by Congress that would be very helpful to the residents of the county. At the beginning of the period the GI Bill provided opportunities to veterans for education and housing. At the end of the period the Interstate Highway Act created the interstate highway and bridge that Congressman Cannon helped dedicate and that spurred population growth in the county. After 1945, a very stable, homogeneous, racially segregated, Republican-controlled, small town gradually turned into a fast growing, more diverse, racially integrated, Democrat-controlled, suburban community.

A. Growth and Prosperity

As veterans returned, many feared that economic depression, which had troubled their fathers before the war, would also return. Instead the U.S. industrial complex, untouched by the devastation of World War II, now produced wealth at an unprecedented rate. In the 1950s the economy boomed and the country enjoyed prosperity. The population of the county, 29,834 in 1950, increased to 52,970 in 1960 according to the federal census. As people moved to St. Charles County, new housing was built. Old industries disappeared and new economic opportunities presented themselves. The Interstate Highway Act brought about demographic changes, and the automobile created lifestyle changes, as people moved to the county seeking the "American dream."

Farmers had prospered during the Second World War and agriculture continued to be an important part of the St. Charles County economy after 1945. Newspapers continued to report fully on agricultural issues. Less than a month after the end of the war, more than 200 men attended a farm program near Josephville conducted by the county agent, Robert Langenbacher, who reported that local farm income was much higher than before the war.[1448] From 1940 to 1950 the average Missouri farm more than doubled in value and its income more than tripled.[1449] In 1947 the county had a record wheat crop due to fair weather and an absence of floods. The bumper crop, that boosted the county into the top position in the state, yielded an average of 30 bushels per acre in the bottoms and about 20 bushels per acre in the hills. With a price of $2.25 to $2.30 per bushel, the value of the St. Charles County wheat crop topped $2 million.[1450]

A number of factors contributed to the increased productivity. Mechanization advanced as the percentage of farms with tractors in the state leaped from 27.8 in 1945 to 43.6 in 1950 and continued to rise in the early 1950s. Between 1945 and 1952, Missouri farmers increased their use of commercial fertilizers from 135,140 to 847,284 tons.[1451] In St. Charles County, where fertilizers were driving up crop yields, some farmers were getting more than 70 bushels of wheat per acre by the early 1950s. Five years earlier a yield of 50 bushels per acre had been a rarity in the county.[1452] Hybrid corn and soybeans were also introduced.[1453] While the assistance of federal, state and local agencies allowed farmers to improve and conserve the soil, the GI Bill provided agricultural training to veterans.[1454] In 1958 more than 25 county farmers entered the Soil Bank Program. Chairman Joseph A. Simon, of the County Agricultural Stabilization and Conservation Committee, announced that under the program the farmers would reduce cultivated crops under a three-year contract and the government would share the cost of carrying out soil and water conservation practices on the land.[1455] In July 1956, the *Cosmos-Monitor* stated:

> The importance of agriculture as an industry in St. Charles county is sometimes not realized by people in urban areas. Figures compiled by the Extension Office from the 1954 farm census report indicate that farming in

the county is indeed "big business." The total value for all farm products sold from our farms in 1954 exceeded $8 million dollars and this despite the fact that 1954 was a very dry year and the corn crop was cut very short. A breakdown of the figures shows that approximately $3 million of the total came from the sale of crops, fruits and vegetables, the major portion being from corn, wheat and soybeans. St. Charles ranks among the top three Missouri counties in wheat production. Sale of livestock and livestock products came to 5 and 1/4 million dollars, with dairy products accounting for one-fifth of the livestock income.[1456]

The paper reminded readers that, since most of the gross income of farmers was spent locally, farm prosperity was good for the entire community.[1457]

The St. Charles County Fair, held every year at Blanchette Park in St. Charles, demonstrated the importance of agriculture in the county. As early as 1948, the *Ban-*

The St. Charles County Fair underscored the importance of agriculture in the county as farmers and rural residents flocked to the fair and showed off their skills and wares. *St. Charles County Historical Society*

ner-News suggested that it was time to look for new fairgrounds as the county fair had outgrown Blanchette Park. In 1952 a committee began to study prospective sites for new fairgrounds and to explore ways of financing one of the few remaining free fairs in the state.[1458] Stockholders of a private corporation, the St. Charles County Fairgrounds Association, met in April 1953 and elected Otto Wilke president.[1459] The association then purchased land on the south side of what would become I-70 at the Fairgrounds overpass. The St. Charles County Fair moved to that site where it grew and prospered.

The floodplain was a significant part of the agricultural area of St. Charles County. Forty-three percent of the county was floodplain and an increasing share of the county's agricultural acreage was located there. Therefore, levee protection was essential to the county's agricultural prosperity. After the war, landowners resurrected their proposal for a levee from St. Charles to Portage des Sioux.[1460] In the summer of 1947, 20,000 acres were inundated as both the Missouri and Mississippi Rivers flooded again, causing about $575,000 worth of damage to crops.[1461] In the wake of this flood, farmers sought a $420,000 federal appropriation in 1949 for the construction of a levee from St. Charles to Machens, which would eventually extend to Portage des Sioux. It would be four feet higher than the MKT railroad embankment, which had provided the only levee protection in some areas. In 45 years there had been 13 major floods on the Missouri River, inflicting damage in excess of $330 million. During the past seven years floods had inflicted damages of $230 million.[1462] When a delegation of Missourians appeared before a Senate subcommittee on March 7, 1950, and urged construction of the 40-mile levee project, elected officials observed that the Corps of Engineers had declared the project feasible, but inadvisable at that time. As a result, no appropriation was approved.[1463]

In the spring of 1951, during the Korean War, the Mississippi Valley Association, a powerful midwestern and southern organization with headquarters in St. Louis, announced that all levee construction with the exception of the St. Charles-Portage de Sioux Levee could be postponed until there was less demand for men and materials for defense purposes. The president of the organization pointed out that the area was important because the MKT and CB&Q railroads traversed the area, which was very important to food production, and added, "this Levee should be built without further delay."[1464] Before action could be taken another flood occurred in the summer of 1951. The Missouri River topped all the levees and some 45,000 acres were inundated by the second highest river stage recorded up to that time.[1465]

The flood not only affected the farmers, but also anyone from St. Charles County who worked across the river. At a level of 35.71 feet, the water washed out St. Charles Rock Road in St. Louis County, (now Earth City). This meant that workers had to take the train across the river and catch a bus to get to work. Even that option disappeared when the flood weakened four piers on the east end of the railroad bridge and the bridge had to be closed. Commuters were forced to take the 25 mile detour over Highway 94-South to cross over into St. Louis County on the Daniel Boone Bridge at Weldon Spring.[1466] The flood did $250,000 in damage to clubhouses on

Alton Lake, with a like amount to county roads. Paul Niedner, Chamber of Commerce president, estimated $1 million in damage to the local economy, with more than 500 farms, 50 homes and 25 businesses flooded.[1467] The farmers renewed their complaint that the flooding was due to the Alton Dam. The *Cosmos-Monitor* reported: "Army engineers are quoted as having said that the Alton Dam helped immeasurably to diminish flood damages at Cairo and other places on the lower Mississippi. Farmers in the area agree with that, but they contend they are the victims when engineers back water over their land to protect farmers on the lower stretches."[1468] There had been very few floods in the early part of the century but seven major floods in the 14 years after the Alton Dam was built. Some St. Charles County farmers also charged that the Corps of Engineers had manipulated the Winfield Dam in a manner that had prevented Congressman Clarence Cannon's Lincoln County farms from being flooded. Someone pointed out at a meeting of the Alton Pool Protective Association that floods had occurred in all 26 pools on the Mississippi River, except No. 25 in Lincoln County. It was also reported that, "[Otto]Wilke expressed the opinion that landowners can accomplish more by getting on the good side of the engineers [and Congressman Cannon] than they can by criticizing them."[1469]

After the floods of 1947 and 1951 did considerable damage on the St. Louis riverfront, the Corps of Engineers built a floodwall.[1470] St. Charles County received no additional flood protection and prospects for future relief diminished for several reasons. As St. Charles was a Republican county in a heavily Democratic Ninth Congressional District, the personal attacks against Congressman Cannon probably made a bad situation worse. Secondly, future flooding would not affect commuters from St. Charles as it had in 1951. Planning had begun for a new bridge into the county, carrying a super highway built high enough to keep it open during floods. Once this was completed, St. Charles lost interest in flood protection issues. Thirdly, after the 1951 flood the federal government began providing low-interest loans to flood victims, a private flood insurance program backed by the government in the same way the government insured banks, and a rehabilitation program to assist farmers.[1471] It was argued that the flood insurance program would allow people to continue to reside in the floodplain without building levees. Finally, the lack of a unified plan also continued to haunt levee-building efforts. Asked whether he favored the Pick-Sloan plan or the proposed Missouri Valley Authority, Congressman Cannon replied, "Each has its merits," but he had not yet decided which he favored.[1472] St. Charles County got two more floods in the decade, in 1952 and 1958, but no federal levees.

The population of St. Charles grew significantly after the war and reached 14,314 by 1950. A major source of growth was an internal migration from farms in St. Charles County. In the 1950s, mechanization continued to push people off the land, while easing the labor of farmers. Tractors were replacing horses and mules, and corn farmers were turning to mechanical corn pickers. There was no new land available for sons who wanted to farm and the children of farm families moved to cities for work. Many new residents of St. Charles in the 1950s had grown up on nearby farms.

People from other rural areas in Missouri and adjacent states also contributed to the growth of the city. Evidence of this primarily Protestants migration can be seen in the

During the 1951 Flood the Missouri River washed out St. Charles Rock Road, shown here, and forced commuters to St. Louis County to take the 25-mile detour through Weldon Spring. *Missouri State Archives*

expansion of Protestant denominations in St. Charles. Some of those arriving from Southern Missouri and Arkansas took up residence in the area that had become known as "frogtown." Some, undoubtedly, because the cost of housing there was lower. Others, perhaps, because of the restrictive racial covenants that kept African-Americans from living in the area. Long after the Supreme Court declared such racial covenants unconstitutional in 1948, black St. Charlesans knew it was a neighborhood to avoid.[1473]

People were also moving to St. Charles County from St. Louis City and County, a trend that had begun 20 years earlier when the automobile made it easy to live in St. Charles and work in St. Louis. Others left St. Louis County because the cost of housing there had risen, due to rising land costs and construction costs, the result of zoning and other governmental regulation. Development costs were much lower in St. Charles County. By August 1954, 183 lots in High Point Acres, a subdivision along Jungermann Road, had been sold. The developer reported that 90 percent of the buyers were St. Louis Countians trying to get away from zoning restrictions and building regulations.[1474]

With the veterans returning from the war and so many new people moving to the county, the challenge would be finding them places to live, to work and to shop. Historian Kenneth T. Jackson, in his book *Crabgrass Frontier, The Suburbanization of the United States*, opines that, in 1945, "The United States was no better prepared for peace than it had been for war when the German Wehrmacht crossed the Polish frontier in the pre-dawn hours of September 1, 1939."[1475] Not much housing had been built during the Great Depression and military necessity had taken priority over consumer needs during the war in all areas, including housing. Almost one million people had migrated to defense areas, including St. Charles County, during the early 1940s. The marriage rate, after a decade of decline, had begun a steep rise in 1940, spurred by the threat of war and the additional $50 per month allotment received by married servicemen. The birthrate climbed to its highest point in two decades, reaching 22 per 1,000 in 1943.[1476]

During the war, some of the nation's best architects pictured their "dream houses" in a series in the *Ladies' Home Journal*. Electrical living shows were held at Memorial Hall in Blanchette Park, where admission was free, and local appliance dealers demonstrated their new appliances. In 1947 the electrical living show attracted over 3,000 people, and many new houses in St. Charles County became "all-electric."[1477] The combination of decreased supply and increased demand meant that there were virtually no homes for sale or apartments for rent at wars end. In an address to the Rotary Club in 1948, Mayor Homer Clevenger called attention to the housing needs in St. Charles, pointing out that the population of the city in 1890 was only 6,161. In the next 50 years the population had increased by only 4,642. In the next seven years the population had increased 4,347. In 1940 there were 3,041 dwelling units in St. Charles for 10,803 residents. In 1947 there were 3,404 housing units for 15,150 residents.[1478] Across the country six million families were doubling up with relatives or friends by 1947, and another 500,000 were occupying Quonset huts or temporary quarters, including Powell Terrace in St. Charles.[1479]

With the end of the war, the city remained under federal rent control provisions designed to keep landlords from gouging their tenants. As late as November 1949 a member of the St. Louis area Rent Advisory Board called for a thorough investigation of rental practices in St. Charles, explaining that tenants were paying exorbitant rents, primarily because they were afraid of being evicted if they complained. He promised, "If a landlord tries to evict a family that reveals information showing they have paid excessive rents, I will have a federal attorney issue an injunction to prevent the action." He charged that many landlords were extracting rents 100 percent above the legal levels, and stated, "St. Charles, without doubt, has the most serious housing shortage in the St. Louis area."[1480] In 1949, Congress passed legislation allowing local governments to lift rent controls. St. Charles delayed this action until October 1, 1950. In St. Louis County and City controls remained for an additional six months.[1481]

Where were these internal and external immigrants and their children to live? In St. Charles, Powell Terrace was the largest temporary housing project. The project consisted of 200 units in 51 concrete block buildings, and 24 newer units in 62 buildings with wood exterior walls. In November 1946, the federal government announced its intention to dispose of Powell Terrace, and established priorities for its sale. The first priority was sale or transfer to government agencies for public uses, including low-rent public housing. This option was never seriously considered after city officials decided that, under Missouri law, the city did not have the authority to operate public housing.[1482]

The second option was to sell to a mutual ownership association where present occupants would have preference over new buyers and veterans would have preference over non-veterans for future occupancy. A housing committee appointed by the mayor reported in February that 191 residents of the project intended to form such a mutual homeowner's association. The third option, which eventually occurred, was to sell on the open market to the highest bidder, while protecting the rights of present occupants and affording veterans priority during the housing emergency.[1483]

St. Charles took the position that the homes should be sold to individuals rather than to investors under the theory that individual holders would maintain the area better than absentee landlords. The problem was that the individuals living there could not afford to buy a building with multiple units. Therefore, a group plan was adopted where not less than three veterans could combine assets to buy a building. The six-family buildings ranged in price from $15,000 to $16,500 depending on the number of rooms. Half the applicants in January 1949 were St. Louis veterans.[1484] Non-veteran residents of Powell Terrace who had worked at the TNT plant attempted to halt the sale of the homes in the "temporary" government-owned housing area where they had established permanent residences. Two hundred of these non-veteran residents met and discussed the revival of a mutual corporation, appointed a committee and raised $200 to hire a lobbyist in Washington D.C. to change the policy. Veterans, unhappy with the high price of the housing, announced that the Veterans of Foreign Wars planned a "two fisted" fight on the Public Housing Administration's program and would carry its arguments directly to President Truman and other officials in Washington.[1485] Apparently, neither $200 worth of lobbying nor the complaints of a lone VFW post carried much weight in Washington. The first 37 homes were sold at a drawing on February 16, 1949, to resident veterans of World War II.[1486]

It was clear that rent control and making temporary housing permanent were not going to solve the housing shortage in St. Charles. In 1946 permits were issued to developers to build 43 new homes.[1487] That number increased to 90 permits in 1947 and 126 in 1950, after which building slowed a little because of the restrictions on certain materials because of the Korean War.[1488] Twenty five-room bungalows were built in the area bound by Oak, Perry, Ninth and Tompkins Streets, for which veterans received a priority.[1489] A more upscale development was the High Prairie (Prairie Haute) subdivision, just west of Lindenwood College on Sibley Street, also laid out in 1946, containing 30 lots served by city utilities.[1490] In 1947, the Vatterott Company built 30 new homes on Bainbridge, off Fourth Street in the north end of town.[1491] In 1948, after a 100-lot subdivision was platted between Highway 94 and Powell Terrace, the *Banner-News* asked the question, "Can St. Charles Double Its Present Population in Three to Five Years?"[1492]

While other smaller projects were completed, the city's infrastructure had been pushed to its limit and in 1949 the City Council asked the city engineer to prepare plans for a sewer trunk line to serve the Boschert Creek watershed. There were reports that the Vatterott Company had wanted to develop in St Charles 15 years earlier but had not because of the lack of sewers. Instead they built what eventually became St. Ann, Missouri. While only 24 percent of the voters showed up, those who did approved, by an 83 vote margin, the $100,000 bond issue to build the sewer trunk line.[1493] When completed, it allowed development of a square mile of area, 60 percent the size of the city at that time.[1494]

This improvement gave St. Charles room to grow in the next decade. Frank Rauch developed Blanchette Hills, west of Kingshighway, between Gallaher and Park Streets. In 1955, The Kaplan Corporation developed a subdivision at the end of Sibley Street.[1495] In these early subdivisions the developers sold lots on which small contractors built custom homes. Kenneth T. Jackson notes, "Residential construction in the United States had always been highly fragmented in comparison with other industries, and dominated by small and poorly organized house builders who had to subcontract much of the work because their volume did not justify the hiring of all the craftsmen needed to put up a dwelling."[1496] While before 1945 the typical contractor built fewer than five houses per year, in 1959 the median single-family builder erected 22 structures per year.[1497] Subdivisions accounted for more than 75 percent of all new housing in metropolitan areas by 1955.[1498] St. Charles County followed the national trend. In 1955 the method and scale of development changed forever in St. Charles County when the Vatterott Company bought 70 acres from the Boschert Estate and announced that they would build 350 homes. A year later they opened the first homes in what was called Borromeo Hills subdivision.[1499] This exceeded any previous development in quantity and quality. The *Banner-News* reported:

> Charles F. Vatterott, President, stated that he was particularly pleased with the project, not only because it made an attractive addition to the fine old community of St. Charles, but because it represents the latest thinking in community planning. "A community, besides providing modern homes, streets and sewers, etc., must, as Borromeo Hills does, afford other conveniences. Our project affords the local residents the convenience of both public and parochial schools, high schools, churches and in the near future, a shopping center."[1500]

Jackson identifies five characteristics of post-war subdivisions, all of which can be seen in the development of St. Charles County. The first was the peripheral location of the subdivisions. By 1950, the suburban growth rate nationally was ten times that of central cities.[1501] While St. Louis had grown by only five percent in the previous decade, the fastest growing cities in the St. Louis area at mid-century were University City, Clayton, Ferguson, Kirkwood, Webster Groves and St. Charles, all of which had grown by more than 20 percent.[1502]

The second major characteristic of the post-war subdivisions was their relatively low density. Nationally, between 1946 and 1956, about 97 percent of single-family

The area north of Lindenwood College, shown here as it looked from Roemer Hall in the 1920s, was developed after the war as Blanchette Hills and Borromeo Hills subdivisions. Notice the Missouri River and Illinois bluffs in the distance. *Lindenwood University Archives*

homes built were detached with yards on all four sides. That percentage was probably higher in St. Charles County. Like the nation as a whole, typical lot size was between one-tenth and one-fifth of an acre, larger than the lots in the older parts of St. Charles.[1503]

The third major characteristic was architectural similarity. Developers, in order to simplify their production methods and reduce design fees, offered a limited number of house plans. The new subdivision could look especially stark until individual owners made modification in later years.[1504] The Borromeo Hills subdivision gave buyers a choice between only two "ultra modern" homes: the larger "Monterey" that sold for $16,290, and the smaller "Mary Ridge" that sold for $13,990. Both were one level ranch style structures that suggested, "...spacious living and easy relationship with the outdoors," where mothers with small children did not have to contend with stairs.[1505] Most importantly, the post World War II house represented newness. In 1945, the *Saturday Evening Post* reported that only 14 percent of the population wanted to live in an apartment or a "used" house.[1506] This attitude was strong in St. Charles, where many of the beautiful old houses in the older part of town became rental property during the 1950s and 1960s. The new houses had no porches and the new neighborhoods had no sidewalks. People in the older part of town continued to sit on their front porches and visit with neighbors who walked by. In the new subdivisions, if not watching TV, residents were in the back yard on the patio with friends. Perhaps once a year, the traditional neighborhood camaraderie would be resurrected at a neighborhood block party.

The fourth characteristic of post-war housing was its affordability. Four hundred homes were built in the Steeple Chase subdivision near St. Peters in 1959. They sold for as little as $10,500, requiring a $350 down payment and $75 per month mortgage payment. The thresholds of home ownership were lowered in truly revolutionary ways, as income groups that had never thought of ownership were buying new homes in the suburbs. The vast timber resources of the United States made the use of two-by-four inch wooden studs a lot less expensive than older construction techniques. The use of brick veneer rather than full brick decreased cost, as did the use of drywall rather than plaster. Mass production techniques brought down the price of individual units.[1507] Another contributor to low housing cost was inexpensive land.[1508] In St. Charles County, the often marginal, less expensive, hill ground was available at a reasonable price for development. The thick deposits of loess soil, common in the area, could be graded inexpensively. Many farmers sold their farms for subdivisions and retired from farming, while others took the proceeds and purchased more land.

Another contributor to low costs was federal policy. FHA and VA mortgage insurance, the federal highway system, the financing of sewers, and various decisions by federal agencies including the Department of Defense, encouraged suburban development. St. Charles County had a federal highway running through it, public housing after 1959, an Atomic Energy Plant in Weldon Spring, municipal bonds for sewers that were tax exempt and many returning veterans eligible for VA loans. Federal tax policy also favored home ownership, since owners were able to deduct their mortgage interest payments from their taxable income. This was a significant tax break since federal income tax rates had gone up considerably during the war.[1509]

Another characteristic of post-war housing was its accommodation of the automobile. Unaffordable during the depression and unavailable during the war, so many people wanted to buy a new car that one had to get on a waiting list. New homes in the 1940s had garages that were detached and in the back yard. By the 1950s, garages had become part of the main house structure, first as an attached unenclosed structure called a carport, but eventually as an attached garage.[1510] While almost everyone now had a car, the new subdivisions were close enough to the older neighborhoods that a family did not need two cars because the children could ride their bikes to schools, parks and stores.

The second great challenge of the post-war era was to provide jobs for everyone. Initially, most St. Charles Countians involved in non-agricultural pursuits continued to be employed by local industries. The number of women in the workforce declined after the war but began to increase again by the 1950s. The impetus for a wife to take a job now was not to "Beat the Axis," but to add a second family income to guarantee the middle-class life-style. Nationally, from 1950 to 1960 the percentage of the work force composed of women rose from 17 to 30 percent. In 1950 the first women were named to serve on the Lindenwood College Board of Directors. The St. Charles club, active since 1937, sponsored a Wentzville Business and Professional Women's Club in 1958.[1511]

More and more employees were members of unions. The electricians organized and affiliated with the AF of L, while the employees of the two local papers formed a union that became a CIO affiliate.[1512] In 1946 a strike by the telephone operators in St. Charles was narrowly averted. On March 17, 1948 the vice-president of the International Shoe Company spoke in St. Charles in praise of the Taft-Hartley Act, passed by Congress, which he thought had restored some balance to labor-management relations. He stated it was, "the intention of International Shoe to work under existing law and not to take advantage of any of them to break up unions."[1513] The company employed 1,000 at the main plant and 160 at the heel plant. The two plants turned out 8,000 pairs of mens' and boys' shoes and 10,000 heels daily. By 1948, $30 million in wages had been paid in St. Charles, and the future of the plants looked good.[1514]

Nevertheless, in November 1949, the company laid off its 900 employees for three weeks. They drew only $20 per week unemployment compensation during the layoffs. On another occasion, 600 workers were out of work when nine employees conducted a wildcat strike that the union did not support.[1515] The plant closed on September 16, 1953. In August, the personnel department at American Car and Foundry had said it would take applications for jobs from employees laid off by International Shoe and the Chamber of Commerce tried to acquire the plant and find another industry to relocate there.[1516] One hundred of the employees were transferred to the company's Madison Street plant in St. Louis. As of December 23, 1953 there were 250 former shoe workers still without jobs, mostly women.[1517]

While individual lives were affected, the plant closing did not ruin the economy of the area, as most workers moved to other industries or into the service sector. The company pointed to a high rate of labor turnover, more than double the average for other International Shoe plants, as its reason for closing the plant. The company could not keep workers because the average industry wage for the St. Louis area was $1.39 an hour and was still lower in the St. Charles factory. Only the textile industry paid a lower average wage of $1.27 an hour in 1952, and the food industry average was $1.83 per hour.[1518] New job opportunities became available when, 15 months after the shoe factory closed, the Sterling Aluminum Corporation announced construction of a $3 million manufacturing plant employing 600 workers in St. Charles, just north of the Wabash Bridge. On the same day the Ford plant in Hazelwood announced its plan to hire 1,500 new workers for a second shift.[1519]

After the war, safety experts decontaminated the TNT plant in Weldon Spring and converted it to civilian use. Since future uses would not require the vast expanse of land that surrounded the plant, 18,000 acres were put up for sale by the federal government. An application by the St. Charles County Court to acquire the TNT area

The TNT Plant became a uranium processing plant and employed 1500 workers in 1957. *St. Charles County Journals*

was denied.[1520] In April 1947, 7,000 acres were approved for sale to the Missouri Conservation Commission, for $250,750. The payment included a $70,000 gift from Mrs. Alice Busch in honor of her late husband, August A. Busch, former chairman of Anheuser-Busch Inc. The area was set aside as a game refuge and recreational area and named the Busch Wildlife Area.[1521] The University of Missouri accepted transfer of approximately 7,900 acres in December 1948, with the federal government retaining the right to repossess the land in the event of a national emergency. As a condition of the transfer, the university had to utilize the property for research and educational purposes for 20 years.[1522]

Upon the signing of the United Nations Charter on June 26, 1945, one of the first decisions that had to be made was where to locate the organization's headquarters. Former Secretary of State Edward R. Stettinius wanted the headquarters to be in the center of the nation and picked the Weldon Spring ordnance plant as the site. In spite of lobbying by Missouri Governor Phil Donnelly, St. Louis Mayor Aloys Kaufmann and Chamber of Commerce president George Smith, New York City was chosen.[1523] The area was also considered as the location for the United States Air Force Academy, but the choice was delayed by the Korean conflict.[1524] The Atomic Energy Commission eventually constructed a $33 million uranium processing plant at the Weldon Spring location. The Mallinckrodt Chemical Works operated the uranium plant, employing 2,000 at the peak of construction in 1955. An operating force of 1,500 permanent personnel was employed by May 26, 1957 processing uranium ore concentrates and a small amount of thorium.[1525]

ACF continued to be the major employer in St. Charles. Upon the death of James Lawler in 1922, his son J.W. Lawler had replaced him as district manager of the plant. The facility expanded and prospered under the leadership of J.W. Lawler, until his retirement in 1948. In March 1949, ACF observed a half-century of railroad car building in St. Charles, but the company was "too busy to stop for any fanfare."[1526] With some of the most skilled craftsmen in the world, 95 percent of the private railroad coaches built in the country were turned out at the St. Charles plant, where skills had been handed down from fathers to sons for three generations.[1527] When the plant started building the fuselage section of the B-47 bomber for Boeing Aircraft, new orders insured work well into 1955. In February 1954 the company's payroll was $250,000 a week due to the company's ability to perform diversified work.[1528]

On October 24, 1956, union members returned to work after a seven-week strike by 400 members of Steelworker's Local 2409 at St. Charles. It was the first authorized strike in the history of relations between ACF and the United Steelworkers.[1529] Throughout 1957, the company's earnings remained high.[1530] Nevertheless, by 1958 the plant was operating with a skeleton crew and the company had to deny persistent rumors that the plant would be sold to an aircraft company. Most of its employees had sought employment elsewhere, with many of them already employed by McDonnell Aircraft Corporation in St. Louis County. The *Cosmos-Monitor* reported that the reduction in workers resulted from labor-management difficulty at the St. Charles plant.[1531] But the closing was due primarily to the decline in passenger traffic on U.S. railroads as the airline industry grew.[1532]

By 1959, both of the major hometown employers were gone. While other factories opened in St. Charles County, more and more workers were driving to jobs in St. Louis County each day. In 1940, there had been 25,562 people in St. Charles County and three and one-half lanes of traffic to St. Louis County. (The Daniel Boone Bridge had a middle lane for passing in either direction.) Before the opening of the Veterans Memorial (Page Avenue) Bridge in 2004, the county was approaching 300,000 people and had ten lanes of traffic to St. Louis County. In the immediate post-war period the commute was easier and less expensive with low gasoline prices. American gasoline consumption doubled in the 1950s and the cost of operating a car in the U.S. remained lower than in any other developed country.[1533] St. Charles County "gas wars" were not uncommon, and in December 1950 regular gasoline sold for 21.9 cents a gallon.[1534]

After the opening of the Daniel Boone Expressway in the early 1940s, highway construction had not been a big issue for the next ten years and it was news when the St. Charles City Council voted in January 1946 to install electric stoplights along U.S. Highway 40 in the city.[1535] The main battles with the State Highway Department were

Newly-poured pavement ends at the western approach to the Interstate 70 Bridge over the Missouri River. *Missouri State Archives*

to get them to resurface Clay Street, which carried Highway 94, referred to by locals as "Washboard Avenue."[1536] In October 1950, a Bi-State Development Agency committee, on which St. Charles businessman Ed Travis served, announced a long-range highway plan for the area. It contained what became the scenic highway between Alton and Grafton, Interstate 270, (except it used the Lewis and Clark Bridges to get to Illinois), and Interstate 70 (called "the Defense Highway").[1537] In May 1953, the State Highway Department approved funds to plan a new six-lane bridge just south of the St. Charles city limits.[1538] The plans for the $13.5 million bridge were completed the following year, while a dual divided highway had already been completed between St. Charles and Wentzville, eliminating "Dead Man's Curve" and cutting driving time 20 percent between the two cities.[1539]

Financing for the new bridge was still uncertain and it appeared that a bond issue might be necessary to finance the project.[1540] That problem was solved when Congress passed the Interstate Highway Act in 1956, providing for a 41,000-mile, (eventually a 42,500-mile) system, with the federal government paying 90 percent of the cost.[1541] The bridge and its approaches were opened in August 1958 at a ceremony featuring Congressman Clarence Cannon as the speaker. The western approach to the bridge was the first section in the country built under the Interstate Highway Act, and it reduced to 30 minutes the driving time from St. Charles to downtown St. Louis.[1542]

Many of the commuters worked at McDonnell Aircraft, a big contributor to the local economy by 1955, when it paid over $7.5 million in payroll to its 1,371 employees who lived in St. Charles County.[1543] In January 1959, the company was awarded a contract to design and construct the Mercury spacecraft for the National Aeronautical and Space Administration. At that time the Mercury project was estimated to cost $15 million and its goal was to put a man into orbital space flight and return him safely.[1544] By the following December, there were 1,600 McDonnell employees working to deliver 20 capsules to NASA.[1545] The capsule that Alan Shepard flew into space in May 1961 had approximately 4,000 suppliers and sub-contractors including Artra Aluminum Foundry of St. Charles, where aluminum castings for the capsule were manufactured.[1546]

By this time, the automobile culture not only dictated where people lived and worked, but how they shopped. A standardized gasoline station that all Americans could identify reinforced the mass marketing techniques of the big oil companies. These were usually operated by local businessmen and were an important part of the local community.[1547] While St. Charles County had many of these full-service stations, most were converted to auto repair shops or used-car lots after the energy crisis of the 1970s. One such facility still in use is Budde Brothers Sinclair on the corner of Fifth and First Capitol in St. Charles.

The first drive-in restaurant in St. Charles was A&W Root-Beer on West Clay Street. *St. Charles High School Yearbook*

Likewise, the local movie theater in the 1950s had to compete with drive-in theaters, where people sat in their cars and watched double or triple features on a giant screen at bargain prices. In 1948, the *Banner-News* printed a story entitled, "Facts Concerning New Airway Drive-in Theatre Built in St. Ann Village."[1548] By 1958, there were more than 4,000 drive-in theaters across the country, including the

Plaza Drive-In that had opened in St. Charles in 1954.[1549] St. Charles got its first drive-in restaurant when the A&W opened on West Clay Street. The Union Savings Bank was the first in town to install a drive-up window and opened a "Drive-In Bank Facility" in 1960 at 615 Clay Street.[1550]

With the opening of the interstate highway, there were no longer interstate travelers stopping in St. Charles. There had been an old fashion motel along the route for several years on the edge of town across from Lindenwood College. J. Edgar Hoover, in 1940, had declared that most of these old motels were "assignation camps and hideouts for criminals."[1551] However, motels after World War II were larger and more expensive than the earlier cabins. The traveling public could depend on major chains to set standards and by 1960 there were 60,000 modern motels and old hotels were closing all over America.[1552] The St. Charles Hotel eventually closed and modern motels sprouted up along I-70. Jackson bemoans this development because, "To a considerable extent, the hotel was the place for informal social interaction and business, and the very heart and soul of the city." [1553] This was certainly the case with the St. Charles Hotel, which had been the favorite venue for all sorts of meetings and get-togethers in previous decades.

With the exception of the people of West Alton, who might shop in Alton, and the people in Augusta, who might shop in Washington, everyone else in the county over the years had shopped on Main Street in St. Charles. In 1946 the first new construction on Main Street in many years, the Denwol Building, was erected at 114 North Main Street, and downtown St. Charles continued to be the place to shop in St. Charles County.[1554] But reliance by shoppers on the automobile was creating multiple problems as fewer individuals were now using the local bus service and the downtown business district did not have enough parking places to accommodate the increased number of automobiles. Totally misreading the *Zeitgeist*, a *Cosmos-Monitor* editorial suggested that, rather than increase parking, the merchants should underwrite free bus service downtown on Friday and Saturday nights. What shoppers wanted was the convenience of parking their cars in a giant parking lot in front of the store. The concept of the shopping center had been around for years, with the Nichols Country Club Plaza in Kansas City, built in 1925, the best-known example. But the Great Depression and the war had a chilling effect on private construction of shopping centers and in 1946 there were only eight in the entire United States, including Hampton Village in St. Louis.[1555] In October 1955, plans to build a $1.5 million shopping center on a 20-acre tract at the corner of old U.S. Highway 40 and Droste Road were announced. [1556] Its opening as the Plaza Shopping Center in 1958 accelerated the decline of downtown St. Charles. Jackson regrets, "the automobile swept everything and everybody before it, however, and it was not until the first oil boycott of 1973, that Americans would ponder the full implications of their drive-in culture."[1557]

The deconcentration of population in the St. Louis area meant growth and prosperity for St. Charles County as inner-city residents arrived, seeking the "American Dream." In the beginning, no one in St. Louis minded as that city, with 856,796 residents in one of the smallest geographical areas of any major city, was terribly overcrowded in the post-war years. In the 1960s no one in the inner city complained since the entire metropolitan area was growing along with St. Charles County. St. Charles would no longer be a small town, but would now become a suburb of St. Louis and, even more than before, the economic wellbeing of the county would be linked with the economic health of the entire metropolitan area.

B. Homecoming and Baby Boom

The period from 1945 until 1964, usually considered conservative compared to the periods before and after, was a time of social change in St. Charles County. The society envisioned by the Radical Republicans had been rejected in St. Charles County 90 years earlier because of ethnic identification, religious antagonism and racial animosity. By 1945 German ethnicity had disappeared. By 1964 the final major battles of the "culture war" that had been going on between Catholics and Protestants had been fought. Indeed, by the 1950s the public school system envisioned by the Radicals had become a reality and chances had greatly improved for the realization of another of their goals – racial equality.

In July 1946, 20,000 people witnessed the fireworks display at the "Heroes Homecoming," sponsored by the American Legion at Blanchette Park.[1558] German-American members of the "greatest generation," whose parents had been taught in German, had themselves been taught in English. They were returning triumphantly from the second war in 30 years against Germany and the defenders of German *Kultur* had all but disappeared. In 1948, the Evangelical Church in Femme Osage, founded by Reverend Garlichs in 1831, discontinued services in German.[1559] By 1951 the German language had also disappeared from the worship services of the Lutheran churches in New Melle and Augusta.[1560] Any sense of German identity in St. Charles County had largely disappeared, not only from politics, but from the culture as well. As the 1960s began, one of the few remaining reminders of the German heritage was the American Legion Schnippeled Bean Soup Dinners. The *Banner-News* stated, "many area residents have never heard of Schnippeled beans and some have never tasted them; but a good many others have become acquainted with the old German delicacy at one of the Schnippeled bean suppers sponsored by American Legion Post 312."[1561] Many families of German descent still hung their stockings as part of the German celebration of St. Nicholas Day. In the words of Daniel Patrick Moynihan, German-Americans in St. Charles and elsewhere carried out an "ethnic disappearance."

While German influence is to be seen in virtually every aspect of the City's life, the Germans as a group are vanished. No appeals are made to the German vote, there are no German politicians in the sense that there are Irish or Italian politicians and, generally speaking, no German component in the structure of the ethnic interest of the City.[1562]

While religion continued to be important, the conflict caused by religious differences reached a climax in the 1950s and then began to abate. Protestant churches grew and prospered in St. Charles County. The Presbyterians, having been split into northern and southern congregations for over 100 years, were reunited in 1948 and moved to a new church and facility on Sibley Street, adjacent to Lindenwood College. When the Methodist Church at Fifth and Washington was destroyed by fire in 1953, the members built a beautiful new church and expanded facilities at 801 First Capitol. By 1964, the Calvary Evangelical Methodist and Faith Methodist congregations had opened their doors. At least ten other Pentecostal and evangelical denominations, which for years had been active in the Ozarks and other rural areas, were established in St. Charles by 1964.[1563] The Baptists, having built a new church at Adams and Kingshighway in 1916, expanded that facility in 1961, by which time the congregation counted 700 members.[1564] By 1964 there were five other Baptist congregations in the city, including Ridgecrest Baptist, established in 1955. The First Baptist Church of O'Fallon was founded in 1957 as a mission of the First Baptist Church of Winfield, and Landmark Missionary Baptist was established in 1959. The First Assembly of God Church in St. Charles, started in 1925, had conducted services in a basement at Sixth and Franklin Streets in St. Charles until the late 1940s, when a building was erected on the basement. The congregation built a new church in 1964 and soon reported 521 people attending Sunday school. The First Assembly of God Church in O'Fallon dates from 1962. In 1964 an independent St. Charles branch of the Church of Jesus Christ of Latter-Day Saints was established.[1565]

Members of these congregations sent their children to public schools, which continued to reflect Protestant social values. When Irv Obermark returned from the war, he took a job as assistant football coach at St. Charles High School for the 1946 season. From a German Catholic north St. Louis family, he saw nothing wrong with stopping at Red Meier's tavern after the game to have a beer. The next Monday morning he was in the office of Superintendent Stephen Blackhurst, who informed him that teachers were not supposed to drink in public. The next season he returned to his *alma mater* Beaumont High School where he had a very successful coaching career and the administrators appreciated a little *Gemuetlichkeit*.

Catholic congregations, institutions and schools in the county were prospering as well. The Carmelite Home built a new addition that served 96 senior citizens. A new parish was established in New Melle (Immaculate Heart of Mary) in 1945. In 1959 St. Joseph Hospital broke ground for a 100-bed expansion in St. Charles, with Saul Wolff serving as fundraising chairman.[1566] In 1947 the School Sisters of Notre Dame celebrated 100 years in the United States and almost that long in St. Charles. The Sisters of the Most Precious Blood built an infirmary in 1949 and a new gymnasium in 1955 at the Motherhouse in O'Fallon, where they operated St. Mary's Institute as a branch of the St. Louis University until 1961.

Before 1962 the Catholic Church had changed little since the arrival of French and German Catholics in St. Charles County. Until 1957 St. Charles Borromeo was still a "mission" church of the Jesuit Order. Devotional Catholicism, including its Marian piety, flourished in the county. Jo Ann Brown relates that Borromeo students continued to participate in traditional devotions:

> October 24, 1950 was a Children's Sodality day of prayer, marked by the praying of the rosary throughout the day and the formation of the "living rosary" in the evening.... Forty Hours devotion usually involved the whole school, and many children took part in the Corpus Christi procession and May crowning. Eighth graders had their own day of recollection at the end of the school year. Visiting Jesuits sometimes gave special missions just for the schoolchildren.[1567]

Philippine Duchesne had been beatified by the Catholic Church in 1940 and the *Banner-News* reported crowds of 3,000 to 6,500 each year for the annual pilgrimage to the shrine of Blessed Philippine Duchesne that had been erected on the convent grounds. In August 1950 a shrine to Our Lady of Fatima was dedicated on the front lawn of St. Joseph Hospital.

During the flood of 1951, it appeared that the Mississippi River might reach the homes of Portage des Sioux for the first time in the history of the town. The *Banner-News* relates:

This statue was erected along the Mississippi River at Portage des Sioux after the town narrowly escaped the Flood of 1951. *St Charles County Journals*

While the streets of many riverbank communities disappeared beneath the rising waters, something important was happening in Portage des Sioux, Mo. Father Edward B. Schlattmann, pastor of St. Francis Church, called upon his parish Legion of Mary to pray to the Blessed Virgin. For the first time anywhere, Mary's protection was sought under the appellative, "Our Lady of the Rivers." The surging current swept over the roads leading into Portage and lapsed hungrily toward the town. Isolated and frightened, Portage people watched helplessly as the water inched nearer their homes. After two weeks, when the flood finally crested, their community was still high and mostly dry.[1568]

In thanksgiving, the parish erected a statue on the banks of the river, dedicated to "Our Lady of the Rivers." Ten thousand people came to the small town of Portage des Sioux for the unveiling and blessing of the 25-foot high statue.

During this period, new parochial grade schools were built in Portage des Sioux, (St. Francis Parish), and Wentzville, (St. Patrick Parish).[1569] St. Peter's Parish built a new school building and had 640 students by 1959. In 1958 St. Charles Borromeo moved into their new school that had 729 students within two years.[1570] In late 1953, the Pastors of St. Charles Borromeo and St. Peter's parishes announced a fund drive for a new Catholic high school in St. Charles. Although St. Peter's High School had only 200 students at that time, the new school would have a capacity of 400 students.[1571] Eight months later, Assumption Parish in O'Fallon announced it intention to build a new Catholic high school for 250 students, with surrounding parishes paying a portion of the cost for their students to attend.[1572] St. Dominic High School in O'Fallon was dedicated in late 1955 and opened with 215 students.[1573] Duchesne High School, in St. Charles, opened with an enrollment of 380 in September 1956.[1574]

The churches continued to exert significant influence in the post-war era in St. Charles County. Religious differences persisted on issues, like parochial schools, gambling and Sunday observance. These disagreements came to a head during the post-war period. Protestants, except for the Lutherans, continued to send their children to the public schools.[1575] After the war, those schools went through significant reorganizations and saw significant increases in their enrollment. Three-director common school districts had largely replaced township school districts after 1874 and by the turn of the century there were 10,000 such districts in Missouri. By 1947, 8,000 of them still existed but, under a recently passed statute, all school districts that did not have $500,000 assessed property valuation, or 100 students, had to consolidate.[1576] Consolidation was controversial in the rural portions of St. Charles County. In July 1948, the county superintendent of schools called a meeting of the members of the boards of education of all school districts in the county. At this meeting a County Board of Education was elected to make a comprehensive study and prepare a plan of reorganization. After the plan was approved by the State Board of Education, the county superintendent called an election for approval by the voters.[1577]

Under the board's proposal, only two public high schools would be maintained; one in St. Charles and the other in the western part of the county. There would be four school districts with a fifth elementary district in the area that is now the Orchard Farm School district. The other four would become the school districts of St. Charles, Central, Francis Howell, and Wentzville. [1578] The only area where consolidation was approved by the voters was the Central School District, which was renamed Fort Zumwalt R-II in 1966.[1579] The Wentzville consolidation proposal was defeated by a three to one margin.[1580] The Francis Howell district, that had expanded over the years as the patrons of small districts voted to join, extended from the St. Charles city limits all the way to Warren County by 1951. In that year the Board of Education formally reorganized the district as Francis Howell R-III, covering 140 square miles of predominantly rural St. Charles County.[1581]

The St. Charles School District announced in January 1959 that it would no longer accept high school students from rural districts.[1582] Shortly thereafter, the State Board of Education approved the consolidation of the 15 school districts north and east of St. Charles. The voters approved the R-V school district and passed a bond issue to build a high school near Orchard Farm.[1583] That left Black Jack School District as the only remaining common school district in the county and it joined the School District of the City of St. Charles on January 1, 1961.[1584] In 1965, the voters of the Augusta R-I School District voted to join the Washington School District in Franklin County, thereby establishing the contemporary boundaries of the five school districts in St. Charles County.

More than 9,000 students were enrolled in St. Charles County public schools in 1957. *Lindenwood University*

During the 1940-41 school year, there had been 528 white students registered at St. Charles High School and 59 black students at Franklin High School. In 1950-51, there were 544 at SCHS, but only 38 at Franklin. Francis Howell High School, which had opened in 1942 and moved to the site of the former TNT plant in 1950, had an additional

192 students.[1585] While the county grew by 5,000 during the 1940s, there had been very little impact on high school enrollment. The elementary grades were a different story. The *Cosmos-Monitor* stated in 1952 that, "the biggest problems facing school officials is what to do with the 'war baby' classes that will reach the third grade this year."[1586] In 1953 public school enrollment in St. Charles increased by 13.5 percent, with the largest increase in the kindergartens, which had grown from 206 to 273.[1587] In May the St. Charles School District announced that a new junior high and high school gymnasium would be built behind the existing high school facility. The *Cosmos-Monitor* stated, "the increased birth rate, which has resulted in crowding of the lower elementary schools is about to make its impact on the junior high school, and will soon reach the senior high school."[1588] By 1960 the county had a total of approximately 14,400 children between the ages of six and 20 years, and it was predicted that by 1962 the St. Charles schools would have an enrollment in excess of 8,000 pupils requiring approximately 30 additional teachers.[1589] As this growth was occurring, Stephen Blackhurst, who had been named superintendent in 1926, was still leading the district. In a city where so many children went to parochial schools, he had been very conservative with expenditures. In October 1958, the St. Charles school board honored Stephen Blackhurst by naming their new elementary school after him. But when the growth began the district was not ready to deal with it and the voters were not ready to finance it.

By 1955, there were many new schools built or under construction throughout the county, including a new auditorium-gymnasium and lunchroom in Augusta. The Fort Zumwalt District, under Superintendent J.L. Mudd, built an elementary school in O'Fallon. The Central and Daniel Boone Elementary schools were built in the Francis Howell District, where Robert W. Barnwell was now the superintendent. There were also new elementary school buildings at Elm Point, West Alton and Kampville, all rural districts at the time.[1590] Meanwhile, C. Fred Hollenbeck, county superintendent of schools, emphasized the need for proper planning to meet even greater challenges after the I-70 Bridge was completed.[1591] The 1956 school year saw nearly 9,000 students in St. Charles County Schools.[1592]

The battle between public and parochial schools had been relatively quiet for over a generation. While parochial school attendance remained high in St. Charles County, nationally, one-half of all Catholic children were in public schools by 1959. The two systems had learned to co-exist. The St. Charles School District allowed St. Peter's Catholic High School free use of the St. Charles High School gymnasium.[1593] A few nuns from the Precious Blood Order in O'Fallon were employed by local school districts as teachers. C. Fred Hollenbeck, who had become superintendent of the Francis Howell School District in 1936, believed that Father William Pezold, Pastor of St. Joseph Parish in Cottleville, was a pioneer in pupil transportation. In the mid-1930s, he drove a parish school bus to pick up students. According to Hollenbeck:

Father Pezold never allowed a youngster to stand on the roadside if he could accommodate them. This was regardless of whether they were going to his school or one of the public schools. This was just his philosophy. In those early days of transportation we had a number of agreements with Father Pezold. He would pick up all of the pupils on one road and the public school bus on another. As the busses met, the ones going to the parochial school would get on his bus and the ones attending public school would change to their bus.[1594]

When free transportation for schoolchildren was initiated by the state in 1938, it had not been restricted to public school students. In the Francis Howell School District, "limited incidental transportation," had been provided to parochial school students.[1595] The state aid to parochial schools issue reappeared in April 1951 when Republican State Representative Omar Schnatmeier from St. Charles County criticized a bill in the Missouri House that would have barred parochial pupils from riding public school buses.[1596] When a meeting of Catholic men discussed this legislation, the pastor of All Saints Parish stated, "the injustice of this move stems from the fact that Catholics pay an equal share of taxes to maintain public schools and busses and therefore have the constitutional privilege to their use."[1597] In 1952, a petition signed by 500 patrons of the Francis Howell District, including many public school parents, demanded equal bus service for all students. According to Daniel T. Brown, historian of the school district, board members said, "We feel the petition would be a violation of the [Missouri] Constitution, and, as we have taken an oath to support the Constitution we could not grant the petition."[1598] Parochial school children were still being transported in the surrounding districts and the *Cosmos-Monitor* editorialized that this approach, "is the one most neutral observers will applaud as being more typical of the general attitude that has always prevailed in our county."[1599] Parochial parents filed a lawsuit to overturn the district's decision. But before it could be heard, the State Supreme Court ruled that the Missouri constitution forbade the transportation of parochial students on public school busses.[1600] Because of the controversy, efforts to pass a bond issue to build a new elementary school in New Melle failed four times. The bussing issue, along with a split between patrons of the eastern and western portions of Francis Howell School District, led to a petition to dissolve the district. In April 1954 the bond issue, including construction in the eastern and western ends of the district, passed with the necessary two-thirds, while the proposal to dissolve the district, that also needed two-thirds, received only ten percent of the votes cast.[1601]

Nuns taught in the public schools in Flint Hill and Josephville. In those communities, any parent who objected to a nun teaching could have their child bussed to a different public school. Things began to change at St. Theodore's in the Flint Hill by the late 1940s. Catechism had to be taught before school or in the church, rather than in the classroom. No "holy pictures" were allowed in the school. Even though the populations of Flint Hill and Josephville were almost entirely Catholic, the state imposed increased regulations on prayer and convent garb.[1602] In 1953, the State Supreme Court confirmed a Franklin County circuit judge's decision that nuns could not be employed by public schools, since the educational policies of the Catholic Church and the State of Missouri are "utterly inconsistent and mutually exclusive."[1603]

As if to assure everyone that all this was not a war against religion in the schools, but merely against parochial schools, the PTA held a meeting at St. Charles Junior High in November 1953. Reverend Roy Schaffer, vice-president and program director of the PTA, pointed out that public grade school classes opened with a prayer and that religious songs were sung in the high school. Superintendent Stephen Blackhurst said he favored teaching religion and teaching God, but said, "we cannot cross the line and teach sectarian religion."[1604] The Supreme Court had given the public schools a major victory. Thereafter, a constitutional amendment was introduced annually in Jefferson City to allow use of public funds to transport parochial school pupils. In 1963 a large delegations of residents from Portage des Sioux, Flint Hill, Dardenne and O'Fallon were among more than a 1,000 persons who packed the legislative chamber in Jefferson City for a hearing on that year's parochial school bill. A Lutheran minister, a Catholic priest, lawyers and representatives of the parents emphasized the health welfare and safety advantages of bus transportation.[1605] To increase the pressure on the legislature, parochial school supporters across the state tried to get parochial parents to register their children for public schools for the 1963 school year. That effort bogged down in the St. Charles after only 16 such children were registered in the school district.[1606] Referring to the divisive issue, the *Banner-News* wrote:

> It is unfortunate that at a time when real efforts and some progress are being made toward better understanding between people of various religious beliefs that the school bus argument must be raised. But be raised it must, as both proponents and opponents of the school bus transportation are apparently very sincere about a matter on which they have deep conviction…. We just wonder how much rancor could be avoided if the transportation of all schoolchildren were made the responsibility of their parents or guardians.[1607]

While the school bus decision increased the cost of parochial education, another source of funds for those schools was under attack. Cultural antagonism between Catholic and Protestant surfaced in a renewal of the debate over gambling. Dr. Laura Nahm offered the following recollection about church picnics in the early 1900s, "Unique at the Catholic picnic was a wheel of fortune and raffles. Schoolgirls, 12 to 14, and young women went around the crowd saying 'Take a chance!' The price was 10 or 25¢. I don't remember what the chances were for, maybe quilts, but it was nothing of interest to children."[1608] By the 1930s, Catholic leaders had pronounced that gambling was not a sin. Rather, according to the chancellor of the diocese of Cincinnati, gambling was "a legitimate amusement or recreation because it is intended as a necessary relaxation of the mind."[1609] Throughout the 1930s, Catholic Churches had sponsored bingo, raffles, and Monte Carlo casino nights as fundraisers. A Gallup poll in 1938 had shown that more people gambled at church-sponsored events than at any other legal or illegal forum.[1610] This position was attacked from two sides. Writing in the *Christian Century*, one Protestant minister said, "I find it impossible even in my weakest moments, when the financial needs of the church are most pressing, to imagine St. John, St. Paul or St. Peter running a bingo party or our Lord sending out his disciple to sell chances."[1611] Proponents of legalized gambling attacked the hypocrisy of local prosecutors, stating, "you can do it (gambling) behind a cross but not behind a beer case."[1612]

The Missouri Supreme Court had defined a lottery in 1927 as, "every scheme or devise whereby anything of value is for a consideration allotted by chance." While people caught with slot machines and other gambling devises were prosecuted, during the 1930s lotteries at picnics in St. Charles County had been largely ignored.[1613] Because of gas rationing, most picnics were discontinued during the war.[1614] When picnics resumed after the war, the public was more aware of the influence of organized crime in gambling activities, primarily because of the Kefauver Hearings in the early 1950s. Local politicians had to take a tougher stance toward gambling. In June 1946 St. Charles County Prosecuting Attorney Robert Niedner informed all organizations in the city and county planning a future picnic that the awarding of money prizes on games of chance was illegal. The *Cosmos-Monitor* explained, "Up until a few years ago merchandise prizes were awarded players at such games and concessions and since that type of entertainment was generally acceptable in the community, law enforcement officials felt that to prohibit such activity would be unreasonably harsh application of the law." The editorial suggested that outside influences were becoming involved and the proceeds no longer being used solely "for the financial benefit of the local organization sponsoring the picnic."[1615] A month later, Sheriff Lester Plackemeier warned tavern owners that there would be "No punch boards, no pay-offs on machines, no craps or professional card playing – in fact no gambling." A state liquor inspector was now making regular inspections with a sheriff's deputy.[1616] In August of 1948 raids led to the arrest of four individuals and the seizure of 18 punchboards.[1617]

In March 1948, a member of the Park Board said, "We haven't forgotten the cry that went up when a fraternal organization ran everything from bingo to crap games on the park grounds." The Park Board announced, for the second year in a row, that organizations having picnics should restrict themselves to amusements that have merchandise as the prize. It then warned, "This may be a violation of existing statutes and ordinances which you must determine and for which you will be held responsible."[1618] Trying to strike a balance between the letter of the law and the spirit of the community, Prosecuting Attorney H.K. Stumberg and Sheriff Les Plackemeier called a meeting in 1949 of 75 representatives of organizations and churches to discuss "games of chance that are actually gambling but are accepted by the general public." A St. Louis County Grand Jury report, which was to serve as a guide for picnics in St. Charles County, was handed out to all in attendance. It stated, "As we recognize that the American people seek the milder forms of taking a chance as an inducement to contribute to charities, we believe that the giving of groceries and prizes other than cash should be tolerated." At the meeting, the Mayor of Wentzville insisted that big-time gambling never made its way into Wentzville picnics and reminded everyone that if you, "cut out games you cut down on the financial success of the picnics." The Pastor of All Saints Parish in St. Peters expressed his opposition to gambling for big stakes but saw nothing wrong in 10¢ stakes, adding, "at his picnic money taken in on gambling wouldn't enable him to hire a good lawyer."[1619]

Prosecutors continued to walk a fine line and, as long as no one filed a formal complaint, no one was prosecuted. Andrew McColloch took office in 1956 and, as a Catholic, he was not anxious to prosecute those trying to raise money for a church or fraternal organization. Like his Republican predecessors, the Democrat McColloch had to balance his duty to the law and to the people who elected him; always a difficult job. It became even more difficult for McColloch when his wife won a car at the St. Peter's parish picnic and he was sent a $100 check for selling her the winning ticket.[1620]

A third area of historical tension between Catholics and Protestants was the Puritan Sunday. In 1961, the Missouri Supreme Court overruled a constitutional challenge to the state's "Blue Laws."[1621] Even the Supreme Court suggested, "it would seem to be time to modernize our Sunday statutes," but stated, "that is a matter for the Legislature." Echoing arguments heard in the past, State Senator Francis X. Reller called the laws, originally passed in 1837, "Archaic, obsolete and antiquated." The statute read:

> Every person who shall either labor himself, or compel or permit his apprentice or servant, or any other person under his charge or control, to labor, or perform any work other than household offices of daily necessity, or other works of necessity or charity, or who shall be guilty of hunting game or shooting on the first day of the week, commonly called Sunday, shall be deemed guilty of a misdemeanor and fined not exceeding fifty dollars.

Another statute made it a crime to engage in, "horse racing, cockfighting, or playing at cards or games of any kind, on the first day of the week."[1622] Senator Reller feared that by playing amateur or professional baseball, basketball, golf tennis and football many adults and youngsters would be law-breakers. People would also be unable on a Sunday, "to attend the games of our St. Louis Hawks basketball team, our St. Louis Cardinals, Kansas City Athletics and St. Louis Cardinal Football teams."[1623] Since County Prosecuting Attorney Donald Dalton and State Attorney General Thomas Eagleton had threatened enforcement of the law Senator Reller called on the governor to call a special session of the General Assembly to amend the law.[1624]

Before that could happen, the Missouri Supreme Court ruled that the old prohibition on Sunday sales was "vague and unenforceable" in the case of *Harvey v. Priest*.[1625] As a result, a number of discount stores immediately began opening for business on Sunday, and some smaller retailers were forced to do the same. The

Missouri Retail Association told local businesses that they would be forced to open Sundays if the new law forbidding Sunday sales was not passed. The St. Charles County Council of Churches endorsed the proposed stiffening of the Sunday closing law. With the support of church groups and the Missouri State Labor Council, AFL-CIO, the legislature passed a compromise bill forbidding most businesses from opening on Sunday. While traditionally a cultural issue, "Blue Laws" had become largely an economic issue, as small businesses did not want to be open seven days a week. The Missouri Supreme Court upheld the bill over the protest of giant chain stores.[1626]

With the vanishing of German ethnicity during the war, hyphenated Americanism disappeared. During the 1950s, accommodations or legal settlements resolved some of the issues that had separated Catholic and Protestant. At the Second Vatican Council in late 1962, the Catholic Church adopted a more ecumenical spirit. According to one Catholic historian, "Suspicion disappeared overnight. Catholic and Protestant clergy began to talk to one another more frequently and more cordially. Local dialogues took place among clergy of various churches, and soon interdenominational worship services became commonplace. Religiously mixed marriages became more frequent and less scorned."[1627] After Vatican II, non-Catholics who married Catholics no longer had to sign papers promising to raise their children in the Catholic faith. By 1950, the Pastor at Immanuel Lutheran no longer denied Communion to those who had married non-Lutherans.[1628]

In addition to more "mixed marriages," secular institutions came to play larger roles in everyday life. Veterans from German-American families joined veteran's organizations with other WWII veterans. The Veterans Service Committee announced that Walter Horst had been appointed assistant state service officer for veterans in St. Charles County. American Legion Post 312 had purchased the Denker Home at Third and Washington Streets in St. Charles in October 1944 and Horst's office was located there. Office expense and a full-time secretary's salary were paid for by the Community Chest. The reemployment committeeman of the Selective Service office at the courthouse assisted veterans wanting their old jobs back and the United States Employment Service helped veterans get new jobs.[1629]

The social life of many returning veterans revolved around the veterans' organizations and the activities they sponsored. In addition to Post 312, there were smaller American Legion posts in Portage des Sioux, St. Peters, O'Fallon, Wentzville, Cottleville-Harvester and Augusta. The Kohl-Jeck Post 2866, Veterans of Foreign Wars, paid $6,000 for the former Jefferson Junior High School at the corner of Fourth and Jefferson Streets in 1945. The membership of the post had grown from 50 members in 1943 to 250 members in December 1945.[1630] The Hinkel-Kleeschulte-Westhoff VFW post in O'Fallon was chartered in 1945 and named after the three men from that community who had lost their lives in the two world wars.

Not only did "mixed marriages," involving persons of different faiths, increase among veterans, but marriages generally were on the rise.[1631] The national marriage rate, that in 1926 had been 26 per 1,000 women, peaked in 1946 at 118 per 1,000 women.[1632] While there had been only 237 babies born in St. Charles in 1937, as

Many returning veterans like Harold Barklage and Erich Ehlmann became active in American Legion Post 312's Green Mules Drum and Bugle Corp.

early as November 1942 the *Banner-News* reported 67 births in a single month in the county. This was more than twice the number in the same month two years before.[1633] After the war, the "baby boom" was chronicled each month in the *Cosmos-Monitor*. In July 1946, the paper found it noteworthy that there were 34 births in June, 75 births in July, 63 births in August, 58 births in September and 79 births during December. For all of 1947 there were 812 births, topping all previous records.[1634]

Secular youth organizations expanded and developed to provide recreational opportunities and guidance primarily to boys. There were American Legion baseball programs for high school age boys by the late 1940s.[1635] In 1949, the VFW Post began Khoury League baseball in O'Fallon. The same year the Optimists Club of St. Charles began sponsoring a Junior Baseball League that by 1952 had 570 boys playing on 38 teams in three age divisions. Efforts to start a Khoury League program in St. Charles City were rebuffed. One of the reasons was that the Khoury League was segregated and the Optimists had allowed black youths to compete in their league.[1636] The "Hot Stove League" combined with the Optimists to form a countywide Junior Baseball Association for the 1958 season with teams from St. Peters and Harvester as well as St. Charles.[1637]

The first Soapbox Derby, sponsored by the *Banner-News*, *Cosmos-Monitor*, Moose Club and St. Charles Motors, was run in 1954. Homemade miniature racecars, powered only by gravity, raced down Kingshighway between Bennett and Morgan Streets, as thousands waved from the sidewalk. Girls participated only by competing in the Soapbox Derby Queen Contest.[1638]

Ninth-District Congressman Clarence Cannon addressed a gathering at the dedication of the first Boys' Club in St. Charles in 1955. *St Charles Boys & Girls Club*

The Boys' Club of St. Charles Missouri Inc. met for the first time on September 21, 1955 at the Benton School auditorium. Joseph T. Hepp was elected president. That same month about 50 men attended a public inspection of the renovated home at the club's location on the corner of Sixth and Clark Streets.[1639] The facility was dedicated at a ceremony in December of that year, where Congressman Clarence Cannon spoke.[1640] In October of the following year, J. Edward "Brick" Travis led a drive to raise the $1,000 per month that it took to keep the club open.[1641] The Boys' Club Board of Directors conducted a campaign in 1961 to raise money for a new Boys' Club building in Blanchette Park. Local businessman Ted Schoetker, chairman of the building committee, led the effort as businesses, labor unions and approximately 400 volunteer laborers worked to build the facility. Completed in November 1962, Representative Clarence Cannon again spoke at the dedication ceremony in December.[1642] Scouting and 4-H Clubs in the rural areas remained important youth activities serving both girls and boys.

The March of Dimes was also important for the welfare of youngsters. Two cases of Infantile Paralysis were reported in O'Fallon in August 1946 and a third case at the Baptist Children's Home in Bridgeton, leading the Parks Department to close the swimming pool at Blanchette Park to children under 12.[1643] Many new cases reported in the summer of 1949 caused a 50 percent drop in attendance at Blanchette Park Pool that summer.[1644] In 1955, free polio vaccinations were given to first and second grade students as the first step in checking the deadly disease.[1645] The "March of Dimes" sponsored an annual "Mother's March" to raise money to fight polio. In

1957, Henry Elmendorf, chairman of the St. Charles County chapter of the National Foundation for Infantile Paralysis, announced that there were 68 former victims of both paralytic and non-paralytic polio in St. Charles County.[1646]

Ethnic identification and religious antagonism, factors that had thwarted the social revolution of the Radical Republicans 90 years earlier, were now greatly reduced. Indeed, the public school system envisioned by the radicals had become a reality and chances had greatly improved for the realization of the second goal of the Radicals – racial equality. The Catholic Church, an enemy of the Radical Republicans, actually led the way in what historians came to call the "Second Reconstruction." Since the early 1930s black children had attended St. Charles Borromeo School, although they were denied participation in social events, and were required to sit with their family in the last two pews during church services.[1647] This Jesuit parish was far ahead of the rest of the Archdiocese of St. Louis, where segregation remained the norm throughout the Second World War. Jesuits at St. Louis University and Webster College opened those institutions to African-Americans in 1944, even though Archbishop John J. Glennon opposed integration of Catholic elementary and secondary schools.[1648]

As the war ended, it was doubtful that race relations would improve. Veterans, with a love of music and nostalgia for military drill, joined the "Green Mules" drum and bugle corps of American Legion Post 312 in St. Charles. In August 1947, having already won the Missouri championship, they flew to New York for the national competition.[1649] To raise money for the trip, they had put on their annual minstrel show at the high school auditorium. African-Americans, who had served in segregated units during the war, had a separate American Legion post. African-Americans could not go to the public library, play on "white" athletic fields, swim in the public swimming pool or attend the same public schools; but things were changing.

Some improvement in racial attitudes had begun even before the war. By the 1930s, it had become common in St. Charles County for local black jazz bands like "Sylvester Dryden and the Virginia Night Hawks" to play at dances attended exclusively by whites. Throughout the 1930s and 1940s, Franklin High School had good basketball teams that attracted large crowds of both races. After the war African-Americans began to work for desegregation of those public facilities that the state constitution did not require to be segregated. In August 1946, after meeting with a committee from the Negro Advancement Association, the St. Charles Library Board resolved, "The Negro population of St. Charles, Mo. will be granted privileges of the St. Charles Public Library beginning Sept. 16, 1946." It was an important first victory in the struggle for integration in St. Charles County.[1650]

In June 1948, spokespersons for the local Negro Advancement Association asked the St. Charles Park Board to grant one-day-per-week swimming privileges to young African-Americans at the Blanchette Park Pool. The board took the matter under advisement and a year later the group asked the park board to provide more convenient hours for African-Americans to use the tennis courts at Blanchette Park, and to allow inter-racial baseball games in the park. The Bombers, a local black baseball team, had wanted to schedule contests with white clubs. While there was no rule against such contests, neither had there been any precedent for them, so the Association wanted a ruling from the board before proceeding. Both requests were granted. The Park Board announced, "the No. 3 court, in the future would be allotted to Negros all day every Saturday." In approving the inter-racial baseball games, they reserved the right to cancel should, "any difficulties arise due to the policy."[1651] It was not just in St. Charles County that the first effort at racial integration took place on the baseball diamond. The Brooklyn Dodgers had broken the color barrier in baseball by bringing Jackie Robinson to the major leagues in 1947. On February 23, 1949, the Brooklyn Dodgers signed Jim Pendleton of St. Charles. Pendleton was a 25 year-old African-American athlete who had first attracted attention as a member of the Franklin High School basketball team. He was chosen the Most Valuable Player at a national basketball tournament for black high schools in Durham, North Carolina in 1942.[1652]

In 1951, Reverend William D. Edwards, Pastor of the Mount Zion Baptist Church at Fifth and Clay Streets, wrote the following letter which appeared in the *Cosmos-Monitor*.

Dear Editor,

This is an appeal to the white people of St. Charles for justice-for human consideration - for a chance to work - for living wages, and for houses in which to live, for the colored people of St. Charles.

The plight of the colored people of St. Charles is an indictment against the Christianity and Americanism of the white people of this city. About one half of the Negro population of St. Charles is packed in hovels and shacks unfit for cattle. And these people, who are Americans thru and thru, live in such shacks because the miserably low wages paid them for their work. (when they can find work), they are unable to buy and build homes for themselves. There seems to be a general agreement by the real-estate dealers not to build any houses for Negroes. Not only that, but many pieces of property that were used by Negroes have been bought from under them by whites despite the vast number of new houses available to them. If the Negro housing conditions are deplorable, and they are, his chances to find work in St. Charles, and the wages he is paid are worse. Except for the American Car and Foundry and one or two coal companies, those places and private homes that do hire Negroes pay them less than the minimum wage law stipulates - pay them less than 75¢ an hour. Many St. Charles Negroe's works six days a week - 48 hours, for $18.

The Negro deserves to be treated as Full Americans everywhere. He has paid thousands and thousands of times the price of American citizenship - paid it in blood. He was the first to die for American independence; the first to die that America might live. Negroes are dying now in Korea for America, and St. Charles.

In the Name of God and America I appeal to the white people St. Charles for equal opportunity for my people - hours, jobs and pay.[1653]

In that same year, a black welder named Oliver Brown, living in Topeka, Kansas, objected to the fact that his daughter was bussed to a black school 22 blocks away when there was a white school within seven blocks. He sued the Board of Education when they refused to admit his daughter to the white school.[1654] Public schools in Missouri were also segregated. Melvin Washington was principal of Franklin High School from the spring of 1943 until June 1955. Under his leadership, the school had an excellent student-teacher ratio, and its athletic teams excelled, winning four state basketball championships in six years in the 1940s. However, the school offered only 17 units in high school, which included only two electives. Melvin Washington later stated, "the black students just didn't have as many courses to choose from as the white students."[1655] The schools were separate but not equal. In the early 1950s St. Charles High School began sharing its vocational shop facilities with Franklin. A white speech therapist, a white English teacher and two white visiting band instructors were assigned to teach at Franklin. Washington later commented that with the arrival of white faculty, "I knew integration was just around the corner."[1656] Locally, the political influence of the black community, whatever it had been, was declining as the black population of St. Charles County dwindled to 1.5 percent in 1950. In 1953 there were only 117 black students from all of St. Charles County at Franklin School, compared to 1,554 white students in St. Charles alone. [1657]

The U.S. Supreme Court, on May 17, 1954, ruled in the case of *Brown vs. Board of Education of Topeka, Kansas*. Earl Warren read the unanimous opinion of the court stating, "We conclude that in the field of public education the doctrine of separate but equal has no place. Separate educational facilities are inherently unequal."[1658] Three weeks later, six black youths swam at Blanchette Park Pool with about 400 white patrons. The Park Board had decided the pool should be made available now to all citizens regardless of race, but were uncertain about how this would affect pool attendance. On June 6, 1954, the *Cosmos-Monitor* reported, "the colored people were accepted by the white patrons without question park officials said there was no noticeable diminishing in the amount of patronage."[1659] When, at the end of that summer, it was announced that attendance at the pool was down 20 percent, Park Superintendent Norbert Wappelhorst was quick to explain that it was due to cool evenings through most of the summer. He added that some segregated private pools in the area had experienced even greater losses in attendance. He concluded, "operation of the pool on an integrated basis for the first time was a negligible factor in the small patronage."[1660]

There was little opposition when the St. Charles School Board announced in August 1954, that grades one through six would be integrated in the upcoming school year. State Attorney General John Dalton had offered an opinion that Missouri's segregation laws were unenforceable. Local school boards acted accordingly.[1661] Franklin School, which could accommodate 150 students, helped alleviate the overcrowding at the district's white schools. Only 20 of the 72 high school students at Franklin were residents of the St. Charles School District. The rest were from the county, and would attend other county high schools.[1662] Franklin High School's last graduation in 1955 drew a mixed response from the black community. Superintendent Stephen Blackhurst noted:

> Although integration was, for the most part, considered desirable by the Negro citizens, nevertheless, when integration was about to become a reality, emotions broke loose and the closing days and hours of the school year were filled with moments of tenderness and even sadness. But through their tears, the pupils faced the future with a hope and faith that the new era would bring to them greater opportunity than they had known before.[1663]

Faculty of Franklin High School in St. Charles. *St. Charles County Journals*

The following school year, St. Charles High School was desegregated with little fanfare. In March 1957, the basketball team won the Class L Missouri State Championship with a combination of white and black stars. Kenny Clarke was named to the first team of the St. Louis All-District basketball team, and Frank Williams, another former Franklin player, was named to the second team.[1664] The thrill of winning the championship certainly made desegregation less controversial at St. Charles High School. Another reason suggested by Judge Joseph Briscoe for successful desegregation in St. Charles was, "Everyone had a great deal of respect for Mel Washington."[1665] Nevertheless, only three of the seven black teachers at Franklin School were retained to teach in the integrated schools, and Principal Washington was assigned to teach mathematics at the junior high school.[1666]

St. Charlesans did not always agree with the civil rights leadership as racial tensions flared in the South. During the desegregation crisis in Little Rock at the beginning of the 1957 school year, a *Cosmos-Monitor* editorial entitled, " Louis, You Hit the Wrong Note," regarding Louis Armstrong's statement, "the way they're treating my people in the south, the government can go to hell," stated,

All thinking men can only be saddened by what has happened in the South recently. But in a matter so complex, the best thing that any representative of the colored race could do would be to set a good example of faith in a government which is trying to solve a difficult problem justly. Satchmo has long been known and admired as an artist at blowing a horn. We like him much better that way than we do when he starts blowing his top and saying things which will hurt the cause of his race and the cause of the nation. We think Louie should stick to music, a field in which he excels.[1667]

Not all vestiges of segregation disappeared immediately. While St. Joseph Hospital began admitting black patients, it was not until 1964 that Dr. Oliver W.H. Tyler became the first black physician to practice at the facility. He had begun his practice in St. Charles in 1927 when most of his patients were African-Americans from around the county. When he retired 47 years later, about 90 percent of Dr. Tyler's patients were white.[1668]

The housing front began to show signs of improvement for African-Americans in March 1955 when Mayor Henry Vogt and three St. Charles City Council members met with the Brotherhood of St. Johns A.M.E. Church. They discussed a proposed federal housing program that would build new housing in the black neighborhood around Blanchette Park.[1669] Two months later, a Land Clearance for Redevelopment committee was formed to make a recommendation to the City Council.[1670] In July 1956, $717,418 was allotted by the federal government to build 48 housing units in 18 buildings in the area bounded by Gallaher, Pine, Randolph and Lindenwood Avenues.[1671] The city submitted a $28,000 bond issue proposal to the voters in November 1958. If approved, the bonds would have financed the city's share of the project. The proposal carried, 2,496 to 2,366, but was far short of the two-thirds majority necessary for passage. On the same day, the voters gave a two-thirds majority to a $222,000 sewer bond issue. Federal housing for the black community was clearly not as popular as sewers, but it did have majority support so the city leaders proceeded. The day after the election, the mayor announced that the project would be built and St. Charles would pay its share of the project costs from general revenue over the next three years.[1672]

Progress toward full racial integration was slow and African-Americans were not guaranteed the right to eat in St. Charles County restaurants, drink in local bars or sleep in local hotels until Congress passed the Public Accommodations Act of 1964, forbidding discrimination in public accommodations. In the period 1946 to 1964, much progress had been made toward racial integration.

C. Politics of Prosperity

A Republican General Assembly and Republican Congress were elected in 1946 and, going into 1948, President Harry Truman was considered the underdog for re-election. In that year, Truman temporarily reversed the conservative trend, winning even in St. Charles County. But after Truman, the Republicans rebounded with Dwight D. Eisenhower, and continued to win in St. Charles County through 1956. But large numbers of new voters with new dreams were moving to the county and they gave the Democrats total victory in the 1958 election. The county voted Democratic in 1960 and the Democrats reached the peak of their popularity in 1964.

In 1945, the voters of Missouri adopted a new constitution that contained few radical changes, but did reflect some recent legal and social developments in Missouri. Women were no longer disqualified from jury duty, collective bargaining for non-government workers was guaranteed and freedoms of speech and press were extended to radio. The new constitution contained new powers for cities wanting to reclaim blighted areas, but the two-thirds majorities required to incur bonded indebtedness remained. The convention retained certain Jeffersonian prejudices against African-Americans and cities. The convention did nothing to remove the constitutional ban on integrated schools and called for separate schools for "white and colored." Although it did contain a provision whereby school districts with small black populations could, with a vote of the people, integrate.[1673] Nagel states, "Dominated by the certainty of members that any innovative document was doomed, the delegates carefully steered away from issues which might enlarge the bitter relationship between the two cities and the countryside," after which he concludes, "Missouri's Jeffersonian mistrust of government was evident in the new constitution, which proved to be a classic restatement of nineteenth-century political philosophy."[1674]

Yet the Constitutional Convention did not completely follow the tradition of the Jeffersonians, who had worked for direct election of public officials 100 years earlier. Instead, the elected office of state superintendent of schools was abandoned, and replaced by an eight-member board appointed by the governor with advice and consent of the Senate. The board then appointed a commissioner of education as the state's chief educational administrator. Changes in policy now required a new governor and several appointments to the State Board of Education. Similarly, the Non-Partisan Court Plan was instituted in St. Louis, St. Louis County and Jackson County for the appointment of circuit judges. The same plan was used for the selection of all appellate judges. A commission recommended three candidates, one of which the governor appointed.[1675] These important aspects of education and the judiciary were substantially removed from politics and popular pressure, and handed over to "non-partisan" experts.

The Convention did not bring about needed change in the make-up of the House of Representatives, retaining the one-county one-seat provision, thereby perpetuating the flagrant over-representation of rural areas. However, it did pass a plan for the Senate that made possible some increase in urban strength. Before 1945, it was not unusual for St. Charles County voters to see their choice for the Missouri Senate defeated because of Democratic strength outside St. Charles County. In the period from 1901 until 1943, the county had consistently given large majorities to the Republican candidate for the 20th District State Senate seat. However, the district also included Warren, Montgomery, Callaway, and eventually Boone County. Callaway and Boone consistently gave the Democratic candidate even larger majorities that overcame the Republican strength in St. Charles and Warren Counties and insured the election of a Democrat.[1676] In 1945 the Senate lines where redrawn so that the 20th District included Lincoln, St. Charles, Warren and Montgomery. But instead of Callaway and Boone, Republican Franklin and Gasconade counties were included. As a result, Representative Robert Linnemann from St. Charles County, who had been elected to the Missouri House of Representatives three times beginning in 1940, won the Republican nomination and was elected to the Missouri Senate in 1946; the first St. Charles Countian in that body in over 60 years.[1677]

As the 1946 elections approached and returning veterans became involved in politics, the *Banner-News* reminded its readers:

> Service men were told that when they got back from the army they would run this country and should be running it. Not only should they vote for service men running for county offices whether Democratic or Republican but they should see that the right congressman and the right U.S. Senator go to Washington and the right State Representative and the right State Senator go to Jefferson City. These jobs are purely political and unlike county jobs which are by nature non-partisan and for whom the people should vote in favor of the man and not for the party.[1678]

St. Charles County Republicans were without one of their best young leaders in the post-war period. David A. Dyer, son of Judge Bernard Dyer and former prosecuting attorney of St. Charles County, was killed in action as a naval officer in World War II. H.K. Stumberg, who had taken Dyer's place as prosecuting attorney for a few months in 1942 before going to war himself, was elected prosecuting attorney. The Democrats attacked Linnemann and the Republican candidate for state representative, Ben Borgelt, for their opposition to "Old Age Pensions," and suggested that they would also be against the Soldier's Bonus. The Missouri General Assembly had passed resolutions favoring the payment of a bonus to World War II servicemen and women, proposing that the state issue bonds sufficient to pay veterans $10 a year for each month of service in the United States and $12.50 a year for each month of overseas service.[1679] In October 1946 veterans interested in the Missouri bonus met at the VFW headquarters. Democrats ran a slate of young veterans against the middle-aged Republicans on the County Court, and formed a veteran's organization to promote their election.

Nevertheless, the election turned out well for Republicans, with all St. Charles County offices remaining in GOP hands, as in the previous six years.[1680] While the highly educated or financially successful continued to provide leadership in politics and elsewhere, military experience now also became a political asset. On the state and national level, the 1946 mid-term elections marked a high point for Republicans as they took control of both houses of the 80th Congress. In Missouri, Republican James P. Kem beat incumbent Senator Frank P. Briggs, who had been appointed to replace Senator Truman when he became vice-president, giving the Republicans both U.S. Senate seats. They also won nine of Missouri's 13 congressional seats and strengthened their hold on the General Assembly.[1681]

Dr. Franc McCluer had been a delegate to the Constitutional Convention in 1943-44, while serving as president of Westminster College in Fulton, Missouri. Born in O'Fallon, he was very active in Democratic circles when he returned to St. Charles County as president of Lindenwood College in 1947. He became an important leader in the community until his retirement in 1966.[1682] He used his political connections to give the people of St. Charles County a foretaste of the 1948 presidential campaign. Forty-three universities sent delegates to mock political conventions at Lindenwood College during the first week of April. Wyoming Senator Joseph C. O'Malley addressed the Democratic Convention, while Ohio Senator Robert Taft addressed the Republicans. Their speeches were broadcast nationally and the event created quite a bit of excitement, especially when some students from Washington University showed

up wearing Wallace buttons. Henry Wallace, former vice-president and candidate of the far left, was not popular with the more conservative Democratic voters and the *Banner-News* warned, "It was also rumored that the printed matter on the platform, that was circulated, was tainted with Wallace ideas."[1683]

Republican hopes to return to the White House in 1948, after a 16-year absence, were dashed by President Harry S. Truman, who led the Democratic ticket in Missouri, getting 58 percent of the vote. Running against the "do nothing" Republican Congress, he won big in the cities and outstate, "nearly duplicating the Roosevelt pattern of support in 1936."[1684] The Democrats defeated eight of the nine Republican congressmen, swept all state-

Elected prosecuting attorney in 1948, H. K. Stumberg was one of many WWII veterans that became community leaders after the war. *St. Charles County Historical Society*

wide offices and regained control of the state legislature. About 40 percent of the Democratic vote came from the two major cities and included many African-Americans and blue-collar workers. Historian Richard Kirkendall notes, "Democrats were quite weak, on the other hand, in the northwest, the western prairie, the western and southeastern Ozarks, and the counties near the lower Missouri River, as well as among people whose origins lay in Germany...."[1685] St. Charles County fit into those last two categories and, although Truman carried the county by 73 votes, local Republicans did very well. While Bernard Brockgreitens was elected public administrator by a 6-vote majority to become the first Democrat to hold county office in ten years, Republicans won every other county office.[1686] Sheriff Lester Plackemeier and Prosecuting Attorney H.K. Stumberg[1687] each received over 1,000 more votes than the president, as the GOP retained solid control of county government, and elected Ellis Ellerman to the Missouri House of Representatives.[1688] But, with the strength of the Democratic Party in the Ninth Congressional District, Democrats won all multi-county contests. Incumbent Circuit Judge Theodore Bruere Jr., although one of the leading vote-getters in St. Charles County, was not able to get the 3,000 votes needed to overcome the Democratic majorities in Lincoln and Pike Counties, losing to Democrat B.R. Creech of Troy.[1689] Clarence Cannon beat local attorney Robert Niedner, the Republican candidate, by 677 votes in St. Charles County on the way to his re-election in the Ninth Congressional District.[1690]

By 1950, labor unions were beginning to have a greater influence within the local Democratic Party. The St. Charles United Labor Council held regular monthly meetings and endorsed the entire Democratic ticket. Robert Niedner, who the *Banner-News* referred to as the "local GOP boss," reportedly referred to the labor leaders as "Communists", "racketeers" and "self-styled labor leaders" who "were not able to speak for their members."[1691] Without Truman leading the ticket in 1950, the Republicans again swept all the county offices, carrying 26 of 38 precincts. The only Democrat to win a majority in St. Charles County that year was Congressman Clarence Cannon. State Senator Robert Linnemann was re-elected by 1,800 votes over fellow St. Charlesan Frank Lawler, the Democratic candidate. However, it was reported that the Republicans did begin to notice more "ticket splitters" in the county.[1692]

If 1950 was a good year for Republicans in St. Charles County, 1952 would be even better. State Representative Omar Schnatmeier was re-elected in 1952. He had been sheriff from 1941 to 1945; had served on the Republican State Committee from 1944 to 1948; and had been a delegate to the Republican National Convention in 1948. He sold the *Cosmos-Monitor* to Darby Tally in December 1948. He was a member of the delegation that approached retired General Dwight D. Eisenhower about being the Republican nominee for president in 1952. In that year, Republican dominance in St. Charles County continued as 3,200 Republicans voted in their primary compared to 1,900 in the Democratic primary. After 20 years of Democratic dominance, the Republicans were back in the White House. Eisenhower received 57 percent of the vote in St. Charles County against Adlai Stevenson, the Democratic nominee, making it nearly impossible for the Democrats to make gains in local contests. He was almost as popular nationally, and if a normally Democratic precinct like St. Peters gave Eisenhower 73 percent, it probably had as much to do with his war record as the fact that he had a German surname. The war in Korea had bogged down and candidate Eisenhower had promised that he would "go to Korea" to end the war in which eight men from St. Charles County were killed and another eight were wounded fighting Communist aggression.[1693] After the beginning of the Korean conflict in June 1950, the St. Charles newspapers began running more articles on Communism. A series of articles appeared in the Democratic *Banner-News* entitled "100 Things You Should Know About Communism in the U.S.A."[1694]

Omar Schnatmeier used his connections with the Eisenhower campaign to get the appointment as U.S. marshal of the Eastern District of Missouri from 1953-1961. He later served two more terms in the Missouri House in the early 1970s and was a typical Republican politicians of the time. He was partisan but not ideological. Politicians like Schnatmeier were more conservative than most urban Democrats from St. Louis and Kansas City, but often not as conservative as some Democrats from outstate Missouri. After 20 years out of power they were not looking to undo the New Deal, but to slow the growth of government and make it more efficient. In St. Charles County they relied on the groups that had traditionally supported them and the individual relationships they had developed with the electorate, rather than a set of ideas.[1695]

While they gained a short-lived majority in the Missouri House in 1952, Republican fortunes in the State of Missouri otherwise continued to decline as Stuart Symington, a member of the Truman Administration, easily defeated incumbent Republican Senator Kem. Eisenhower carried only 50.7 percent in Missouri, compared to 55 percent nationally. Richard Kirkendall notes, "The Democrats remained strong in St. Louis, Kansas City and St. Joseph, had some success in St. Louis County, largely because of the recent migration of blue-collar workers to the suburbs."[1696] During the next four years, that migration would reach St. Charles County. Until it did, the Republican domination continued and reached a peak in 1954 when the Democrats did not even offer candidates for five St. Charles County offices.[1697] Clarence Cannon was the only Democrat to receive a majority in the county that year. State Senator Linnemann was re-elected and State Representative Alf Oetting, who had won a special election the previous spring to fill an unexpired term, was re-elected to the House of Representatives from St. Charles County.[1698] Nationwide, the Republicans lost control of the House of Representatives, and they would not win it back until 1994. Statewide, they lost the House of Representatives, and would not win it back until 2002.

It was municipal elections in St. Charles that first reflected the demographic changes taking place in the 1950s. In March 1949, incumbent Alderman Frank Lawler withdrew his re-election petition, leaving Marcela Wilson as the only candidate in the Fourth Ward. Wilson had taken the leading role some months earlier when residents of several subdivisions appealed to the city to improve the sewers. She became the

Andrew McColloch moved to St. Charles after the war and was elected prosecuting attorney in 1956 as a Democrat.

first woman to hold elective office in St. Charles. Two years later, Andrew McColloch defeated Paul Niedner in the race for city attorney.[1699] As Omar Schnatmeier was typical of Republican politicians of the time, Andrew McColloch's career helps explain the resurgence of the Democrats in St. Charles County. McColloch, originally from Monroe County, united the traditional Democratic constituencies in the county, with the labor union members from St. Louis County and conservative Democrats from rural Missouri, who began moving to St. Charles County in the 1950s. McColloch, a New Deal Democrat, was a marine pilot during World War II. He married Mary Dyer, from one of the leading Republican families. He became an attorney in the law office of Judge Bernard Dyer, who failed to convert him to the GOP. His first electoral victory was for the post of St. Charles city attorney. He remembers that people voted for him on the theory, "Whatever he didn't know Judge Dyer would teach him." McColloch sparked a comeback for the Democratic Party, and in January 1954 the Republican *Cosmos-Monitor* announced that a new organization had been incorporated in St. Charles County to, "foster and perpetuate the ideals and principles of the Democratic Party."[1700]

New attitudes had begun to emerge in St. Charles by 1950, when Glen Goellner, city editor of the *Banner-News* wrote:

> St. Charles today seems to be on the threshold of a new and progressive era following a glorious but nevertheless ultra-conservative history of almost two centuries. Evidence that a transition is taking place is visible on every hand. One of the important forward steps taken was approval of new sewers, which automatically enable the city to grow beyond the narrow confines of the existing system. … The administration, while it has proceeded cautiously since the responsibility of raising funds to finance new ventures is in its lap, has also shown a progressive attitude in initiation of forward-looking projects. The planning and zoning commission is an example of its valuable contributions.[1701]

A planning and zoning ordinance had first been passed in New York City in 1916. St. Louis had passed such an ordinance two years later. In theory, zoning was designed to protect the interest of all citizens by limiting land speculation and providing for orderly growth. Although it greatly expanded municipal power, it had become quite common. By 1936, 85 percent of cities in the country had zoning ordinances.[1702] Representative Robert Linnemann passed a city planning bill in the House in 1945, but when Mayor Homer Clevenger decided not to seek reelection in April 1951, St. Charles still did not have planning and zoning. Henry Vogt, by a margin of five to one, won the race to replace Clevenger and, a few years later, signed an ordinance that had passed the City Council by a unanimous vote, creating planning and zoning in the city.[1703] Opposition to zoning came from conservative property owners concerned that their property rights would be diminished. Later, criticism of zoning came from liberals, concerned that zoning was a device to keep obnoxious industries, poor people and minorities out of affluent areas.[1704] The St. Charles zoning ordinance infringed minimally on property rights, a fact made obvious by the lack of green space surrounding commercial development and the roads from the new subdivisions that were not required to matchup. With regard to exclusionary zoning, the St. Charles ordinance merely prescribed physical dimensions of structures in the various zoning areas, causing the *Cosmos-Monitor* to report that the ordinance was expected to have the greatest impact on persons dividing corner lots for construction of a second residence. It is doubtful that zoning had any appreciable impact on the availability of low-income housing before 1965.[1705] When urban renewal came to the city, the Park Ridge Apartments were built right across the street from the mayor's home, and inhabited almost exclusively by African-Americans. When Sterling Aluminum moved to the city, its plant was built within walking distance of residential neighborhoods. Finally, the first rezoning applications the St. Charles City Council had to deal with were a 36 unit "Trailer Camp" on Cunningham Street and a 144 unit "Trailer Camp" on old U.S. Highway 40 at Droste Road. Both were approved and still existed in 2004.

In April 1959, Dr. F. L. Harrington, an osteopathic surgeon, defeated incumbent Mayor Henry Vogt. In the First Ward council race in that same year, in what was one of the closest races ever, Gene Wolf received 23 of 29 absentee votes to overtake Mel Plackemeier, the apparent winner with a 15-vote lead on election night.[1706] In April 1963 Harrington did not run for re-election and Henry Vogt was again elected mayor of St. Charles.[1707]

In the 1954 general election the voters of St. Charles County also passed planning and zoning by a 275-vote majority. Eleven of the 12 precincts in the city favored the measure, while 11 of 19 in the county were opposed to planning and zoning.[1708] Missouri's attorney general issued an opinion in October 1955 that a county was not authorized to have zoning unless it was adjacent to a city of at least 70,000, (St. Louis or Kansas City). Efforts to change the statute in the General Assembly eventually succeeded in 1957.[1709] A new election was required and a committee was formed to educate the voters on zoning questions. Farmers had to be reassured that the state zoning statute did not apply to agricultural uses and property owners had to understand that existing structures were exempt.[1710] In October, with only 1,000 voters casting ballots, county zoning passed 326 to 53 in St. Charles, and passed by a one-vote majority in the rest of the county. In Defiance the vote was one yes and 55 no.[1711] While the majority of voters had approved planning and zoning there was much resistance in the rural areas, causing the *Banner-News* to editorialize:

> We believe it is in the interest of this county that a zoning authority be established as soon as possible. We do not believe that the delaying tactics of a minority group should be allowed to thwart the will of the majority or to bring about a delay on adoption or watering down of the proposed ordinance that is not in the interest of the majority.[1712]

The Planning and Zoning Commission, chaired by Carl Rohlfing, recommended that the County Court appoint a Board of Adjustment. Despite continuing opposition, by the end of the year zoning was in effect in the county.[1713]

As the 1956 presidential election neared, President Eisenhower appeared to be a shoo-in for re-election. His conservative fiscal policies were popular in St. Charles County and across the country. The style of politics would change in 1956 as television dominated the campaigns. Locally, fewer political rallies took place and politicians gave fewer speeches as voters started getting more of their information from media sound bites. Nationally, one historian suggests, "No more whistle-stops; no more rallies in huge auditoriums. The networks made time available, and the viewing public obliged by watching a toned-down Stevenson try to pry votes away from Ike, who was now a father figure for the nation."[1714]

In 1956, Eisenhower won St. Charles County by about the same margin as in 1952, but lost Missouri and he had very short coattails, even in St. Charles County. Three Democrats broke the Republican hold on the county. Andrew McColloch won the race for prosecuting attorney; Joseph T Mahon, incumbent Eastern District county judge, was re-elected; and Joe Haake was elected county clerk. On the state level, the Democrats swept all the statewide offices, with James T. Blair elected governor and Thomas C. Hennings returned to the U.S. Senate.[1715] Observers in St. Charles County wondered how the Republicans would do in two years without Eisenhower at the top of the ballot.

On September 27, 1957, *The Banner-News* ran an editorial entitled "County Politics, 1958." It stated:

> Politically, there are some healthy signs in St. Charles County. Both parties are actively working to organize support for elections in 1958. What does this mean?
>
> It means that the County GOP knows that the Democrats have been slowly, but very definitely gaining strength in this county. It means that the

long enthroned Republican regime here realizes that it can no longer expect to consider everything finished after the primary elections. This is good, for a party too long unchallenged becomes slothful. Its members, in public office, often feel so sure of their positions and that they forget that they are servants of the people and become, "Empire Builders" in their own small way. The County GOP can have no such assurance for 1858.

The Democrats, organizing now, are looking to 1958 with enthusiasm long absent from their ranks in St. Charles County. They have noted the gain in Democratic voting strength in this county, and now feel there is something to work for. With both parties getting ready to really work for offices, the people will benefit regardless of the outcome. This was not true here for many years.[1716]

By 1958, Democrats were blaming Republicans for unemployment and lack of military preparedness. They criticized Republicans in the North on Taft-Hartley's "right to work" clause, and in the South on their responsibility for integration.[1717] It was ironic that the Republicans would be blamed for forced integration since the exodus of African-Americans to the Democratic Party for economic reasons had continued after the New Deal and by 1944, 80 percent of the black vote was going to the Democrats. As a result, Eisenhower and the Republicans showed little interest in pushing a civil rights agenda for African-Americans. However, the president did his duty and sent federal troops to Little Rock in 1957 to force integration of the public high school. Given recent history and Eisenhower's military background, it is also surprising that the Republicans were perceived as weak on defense. However, in October 1957 the Russians had launched the first space satellite Sputnik, leading to soul-searching about U.S. education and fear of a "missile gap" between the U.S.A. and the U.S.S.R.[1718]

Locally, things began going wrong for the Republicans from the beginning of the campaign cycle. The Democrats recruited good candidates, including Omer Dames, a retired rural mail carrier, who filed for and won the nomination for state representative. His job had kept him out of politics and the inevitable accumulation of enemies that can accompany a political career, while it allowed him to meet a lot of people. He was attempting to be only the second Democrat to hold the office in 66 years and the first since Frank Iffrig was state representative from 1932 to1940.[1719]

Meanwhile, the Republicans were self-destructing. Robert Linnemann, Senator from the 20th District for 12 years, was running for re-election. A Republican from Gasconade County had already filed against him in the primary, when Judge Theodore Bruere Jr. filed as well.[1720] In July, *Banner-News* headlines announced, "Once Considered Safe for GOP, 20th District Could Go to Democrats." The article pointed out that, not only St. Charles, but also Franklin, Montgomery and Osage counties were starting to elect some Democrats. If Linnemann and Bruere split the St. Charles County Republican primary vote, the third candidate could win. Without a St. Charles

County Republican on the ballot in November, Democratic nominee, Frank X. Reller from St. Charles County, might win.[1721]

In May 1958, 1,000 people signed a petition addressed to the Republican controlled County Court, asking it to name the new Interstate 70 Bridge after Harry S. Truman. When, quite predictably, the court tabled the proposal permanently, the *Banner News* called it a "dictatorial stand," and claimed they were "ignoring the wishes of the people."[1722] Republicans began to see the handwriting on the wall after the August primary, when two-thirds of the voters took Democrat ballots. The Democratic primary vote had doubled in four years.[1723] As predicted, in the Republican primary, Judge Bruere out-polled incumbent, Senator Linnemann, but could not beat C.W. Toedtmann, of Hermann.[1724]

The next disaster for local Republicans involved Arlie Griewe, county collector. On October 9, 1958, the *Banner-News* revealed that the state auditor had discovered "irregularities" in the collector's office. The fact that missing money had been repaid was out-weighed by the fact that the County Court had tried to sweep the matter under the rug six months earlier and that the collector's office had apparently burned some of the records without the Circuit Court's authorization.[1725] The *Banner-News* editorialized, "Somehow, the courthouse 'inner guard' seems to have thought it politically expedient to keep the facts from the people. How very close they came to actually succeeding should give pause to every voter, regardless of his normal political allegiance."[1726] During this time, new families were moving to St. Charles County every day in anticipation of the opening of the new Interstate 70 Bridge which would make downtown St. Louis 30 minutes away. Many of these newcomers were blue-collar workers and union members loyal to the Democratic Party.

The Republican Party lacked a strong ideological base locally and nationally. Liberalism was dominant, and the Democratic Party's liberal agenda had captured the imagination of a majority. Republicans had abandoned many of their conservative ideas and seemed to offer only the promise that they could run the welfare state more efficiently than the Democrats. Locally, the Republicans offered no new ideas to meet the challenges of growth in St. Charles County.

To make matters worse, as the 1958 election neared, 1,900 persons were reported to be unemployed in St. Charles County during what the Democrats nationally were calling the "Eisenhower Recession." A Democratic speaker in West Alton, referring to the unemployment, stated, "Someone is going to get beat this year and beat bad and it's not going to be the Democrats."[1727]

When Election Day came, the Republicans did get "beat bad." The only Republican left standing was Ernie Paule, recorder of deeds. Leading the Democrats was Andrew McColloch. Omer Dames defeated Alf Oetting for state representative. Francis X. Reller, who earned the nickname "landslide" that day, became the new state senator by a margin of five votes.[1728] In four years, the Republicans went from controlling every office in St. Charles County to controlling only one. The Democratic Party, that had been in power only eight years out of the last 64, was again the majority party in St. Charles County. In January 1959 the *Cosmos-Monitor*, the Republican voice in St. Charles County for generations, quit publishing.[1729]

While a political era in St. Charles County had ended, and a new one was beginning, the changes were not always that dramatic. Conservative Democrats still had a place, within the Democratic Party on every level. The Democratic presidential candidate in 1960 ran on a platform calling for a tax cut and claimed that the Republicans had allowed a "missile gap" to develop with the Soviet Union. Their candidate, Senator John F. Kennedy of Massachusetts, became the second Catholic to run for President of the United States. In response to concerns about his religion he contended that, given the separation of church and state, a president's religion was a private affair and stated, "I am not the Catholic candidate for president, I am the candidate who happens to be Catholic."[1730] In the election the traditional Catholic precincts in St. Charles County gave Kennedy large majorities, but not nearly as big as they had given Al Smith in 1928. One reason for this was that the small towns had new inhabitants and were not as homogeneous as in the past. A second was that, since 1932, political loyalties had come to depend more on economic than social issues. Thirdly, religious affiliation was not as important as it had been in the past. The 91 percent Democratic vote in Portage des Sioux in 1928 was only 64 percent in 1960. The 90 percent Democratic majority in St. Peters in 1928 was reduced to 65 percent in 1960. Smith's 87 percent in O'Fallon was down to 64 percent for Kennedy. In all but one precinct in St. Charles County, Kennedy did better than Stevenson four years earlier. On the other hand, in no precinct in the county did Kennedy do as well as Stuart Symington had done in his re-election victory of 1958. Of course Senator Symington's opponent was no Richard Nixon, and Symington was not Catholic. Nevertheless, Kennedy beat Nixon 52 percent to 48 percent in the county, a better percentage than he received nationally.

The Kennedy administration's greatest achievements were in the area of foreign policy, and its finest hour was the peaceful resolution of the Cuban missile crisis in October 1962. With the threat of nuclear war looming, the *Banner News* reported that area citizens were seeking information on bomb shelters. St. Charles civil defense director, Lawrence Boschert, reported that there were shelters in the area for 1,800 people.[1731]

Lindenwood College continued to be an important asset to the community as nationally known speakers visited the campus including United States Senator Margaret Chase Smith, Republican from Maine. Speaking at the 1961 Lindenwood commencement, she said, with regard to America's problems, "The greatest danger that exists is not from outside our country, it is not the communist threat. It is the growing softness of our people and consequently the growing softness of our nation."[1732] In the same vein, as the 1962 elections approached, local Republican leader H.K. Stumberg pointed out that Democratic policies were reducing individual freedom with encroaching federal power.[1733]

In May 1961, Francis X. Reller filibustered in the Missouri Senate for one-and-one-half hours against a $4,000-per-year pay raise for judges. The *Banner News* reported that apparently, "defeated in all his attempts to beat the pay boost measure or to submit it to a vote of the people, Senator Reller later collapsed in his office and was rushed to a hospital. He was later reported resting comfortably, apparently having suffered an attack of acute indigestion."[1734] Locally, the Republicans were taking aim at "Landslide" Reller. In the Republican primary Don Owens, from Franklin County, defeated William Baggermann of Augusta, even though Baggermann had won by a wide margin in St. Charles County.[1735] In the general election Reller lost to Don Owens, who swept four of the six counties in the district to pile up a 4,000-vote majority. While Reller had won St. Charles County by almost 2,200 votes in 1958, he led by only 708 votes in 1962. Nevertheless, the Republicans elected only one other candidate in St. Charles County, as the strongest of the Democratic candidates was again Clarence Cannon.

In 1964, 13 candidates filed for the Democratic nomination for the Ninth District congressional seat that had become vacant with the death of Clarence Cannon. Andrew McColloch, former St. Charles County prosecuting attorney, mounted a strong effort in the crowded race. On July 29 the *Banner-News* wrote, "There are several well-qualified candidates in the Democratic Primary race, but none, we feel, more qualified than Mr. McColloch."[1736] Andrew McColloch came in second to William Hungate.

After the primary, Erwin Davis, the very capable Democratic county chairman for the previous two years, resigned to devote more time to his private law practice.[1737] Nevertheless, the Democrats prevailed in November, concentrating much of their fire on the Republican presidential nominee, Barry Goldwater. The *Banner-News* deplored the influence of the John Birch Society on Goldwater and said:

> To us Goldwater represents a not too wonderful part of the past. We recall the days of Laissez faire, "rugged individualism", "rights" for the select few and the philosophy of every man for himself. There is a choice in this election. It is a choice between hope and fear, progress or retreat, compassion or bigotry, a unified quest for peace or misunderstanding that could lead to obliteration of civilization. Let those who are afraid of the future walk in the shade of the Goldwater-Wallace-Birch past.[1738]

Goldwater's supporters elected a slate of delegates at the St. Charles County Republican Convention pledged to support Goldwater at the Ninth District and State Republican Conventions.[1739] Internal division in the party persisted into the August primary, where the insurgent Goldwater group gained seats on the County Central Committee. The "moderates" prevailed, despite being blamed for the Democratic gains in recent years. The moderates labeled the insurgents as "John Birch oriented" and accused them of being more interested in Goldwater for president than the political situation at the county level.[1740] Goldwater eventually won the Republican nomination, but Sheriff Lester Plackemeier was the only victorious Republican in county races in November. While the Kennedy-Johnson ticket had carried St. Charles County by 1,002 votes in 1960, in 1964 Johnson carried the county by 5,002 votes, sweeping most of the local Democratic candidates into office as well.[1741] Nationally, the Congress now had a liberal majority as well as a Democratic majority.[1742]

Like the Americans and Germans before them, a whole new group of people moved to St. Charles County in the late 1950s and early 1960s. The newcomers included conservative Democrats from rural Missouri and labor union Democrats from north St. Louis County. Like earlier arrivals, they altered the political make-up of the county. No one knew it at the time, but Democratic prospects in St. Charles County had peaked, and the Democrats have not since enjoyed the electoral majorities they achieved in 1964.

VII
Challenges of Growth
1965-1980

In July 1970, Senator Thomas Eagleton and Congressman William Hungate attended the opening of an industrial park in Wentzville. They both congratulated the people of Wentzville for their foresight in seeking industrial development.[1743] Both men were Democratic politicians and the years between 1965 and 1980 were good years for the Democratic Party in St. Charles County. Senator Eagleton would serve as the Democratic nominee for vice-president for a few weeks in 1972 until disclosure of health problems forced him to withdraw from the ticket. Congressman Hungate would gain national attention as a member of the House Judiciary Committee considering articles of impeachment against Richard Nixon following the Watergate scandal. They were in Wentzville to open something for which there was a great need in St. Charles County - an industrial park. These were times of tremendous job creation nationally, and St. Charles Countians shared in that prosperity; but their jobs were not in St. Charles County. More roads and bridges had to be built to get the workers to their jobs in St. Louis County. County school districts did not have sufficient assessed valuation to serve the increased number of students without raising taxes. The new industrial park was in Wentzville, one of several small towns beginning to grow due to the many new families moving to St. Charles County. Those families could move all the way out to Wentzville because Interstate 70 put them within commuting distance of their jobs. Ten years later, politicians would return to Wentzville to dedicate a new General Motors plant, a major step in the county's throwing off the label of "bedroom" community. As families dealt with good and bad economic times, they also had to adjust to unprecedented social changes that were taking place in American society.

A. New Cultural Conflicts

The social and cultural changes occurring nationally after 1964 arrived a little bit late in St. Charles County. But when they did come, they had a great impact on the conservative mid-western communities of the county. As the "counter culture" emerged after 1964, the "sexual revolution", school discipline, race relations, crime and breakdown of the traditional family became new social issues dividing the people and widening the "generation gap."

By 1965, most of the old German customs and traditions had disappeared. Nationally, the percentage of foreign born in the population bottomed out at 5 percent in 1970. David Frum notes that one still heard foreign languages only in poor urban neighborhoods, remote coal-mining towns, and "old-folks' homes." He points out that Americanization had become so complete that social critics of the 1950s worried that the country was becoming too homogeneous.[1744] Some traditions, like the free band concerts provided by the Municipal Band of St. Charles, remained. Long a tradition in the city, the band had been supported by a two-cent property tax since 1929 that was netting the city about $20,000 a year by 1977. In that year the tax was found to be illegal, but Mayor Frank Brockgreitens quickly reassured residents that loss of the tax would not mean the end of the band.[1745] At the same time, some of today's traditions were in their infancy. In 1969, St. Charles celebrated its bicentennial. The year-long celebration was so well received and enjoyed that it was repeated the following year and evolved into the annual "Festival of the Little Hills," held every August in the South Main Street historical district.

While some were still opposed to beer gardens, it was now no longer likely to be for religious reasons. In August 1975, following the Festival of the Little Hills, a group of South Main residents and shop owners complained about the unruly crowd and vandalism at the festival and asked that beer gardens be banned from future festivals. Fond memories of *Gemuetlichkeit* were still strong enough to overcome these complaints, although the beer gardens were eventually moved from Main Street to Frontier Park on the riverfront. Reluctance to enforce every statute and ordinance regarding alcohol apparently survived as news reports suggested that minors had been served beer at the festival.[1746]

While the debate over public funding of parochial schools subsided, the public schools of St. Charles County faced the most challenging period in their history. The launch of Sputnik by the Soviet Union in October 1957 caused a national concern that the country had not been spending enough on its schools, especially in the areas of math and science. Complacency was magnified in a conservative community like St. Charles where the large number of families with children in parochial schools made it difficult to raise taxes for the schools. Stephen Blackhurst had retired in 1961 after 35 years as superintendent of schools in St. Charles. As more new families moved to St. Charles, the no-frills district had to build new schools. With enrollments rising and insufficient tax base to meet the demand, the Board of Education was forced to go to the voters for tax increases. In April 1963 the voters of the St. Charles School District failed to give a two-thirds majority for a bond issue, and returned a narrow majority for increasing the tax levy from $3.58 to $3.93.[1747] In 1964, with 400 new pupils, the board proposed a $500,000 bond issue to build an addition to the high school.[1748] Despite a record turnout, neither that proposal nor a tax rate increase received even a simple majority from the 3,277 voters who voted in February 1965. After this defeat advocates criticized the nay-sayers, prompting the *Banner-News* to write, "the *Banner-News* endorsed the tax increase proposal and we too are 'appalled' - not by those who voted it down - but by those who feel the voters who voted against the proposition had no right to vote as they did."[1749] A 26 ¢ increase to $4.19 was finally passed in a fourth attempt in May.[1750]

A 65¢ tax increase failed in February 1968 with little more than a third of the vote, and a "no tax increase" bond issue was defeated. It was announced that without a new junior high school, double sessions at the existing junior high school would be required. Three of the four issues were resubmitted in March 1968. All three were defeated again, prompting the Commission on Christian Social Concerns at the First Methodist Church to unanimously endorse a $5.35 school tax levy proposal in May.[1751] At that time the voters gave narrow approval to a bond issue but defeated the tax increase for the fourth time.[1752] Voters defeated a 99¢ increase in June, but finally approved an increase of 59¢ in July, allowing the district to begin hiring teachers.[1753]

These events repeated themselves in 1969 with the first tax levy going down in March. The same anti-tax attitudes were widely shared. On April 1, 1969, voters rejected tax levy increases in all five districts in St. Charles County. In addition to Fort Zumwalt and St. Charles, Francis Howell voted down a 78¢ increase; Orchard Farm voted down a 94¢ increase; Wentzville voted down 9¢ increase.[1754] In St. Charles, the proposed levy was rejected for a sixth time in June 1969 and did not pass until August.

The new decade brought more of the same problems in St. Charles County, as the St. Charles voters rejected a $5.94 tax levy in February 1970. But on the same day the Orchard Farm voters approved a $3.82 levy and the Francis Howell voters approved a $4.98 levy.[1755] When smaller increases were again rejected in July, the board announced that there would be no school until a levy was passed.[1756] In late September a $5.53 levy was approved and the schools opened almost a month late, with the junior high school operating on a "split-shift," where half the students attended in the morning and the other half in the afternoon.[1757]

There were several reasons why the School District of the City of St.Charles was having financial problems. Many parochial school families remained reluctant to support higher taxes when state funds could not even be used for the transportation of their children; but there were new political and economic problems. Before 1965, urban school districts were allowed to expand their boundaries at the expense of rural districts and the St. Charles District had been expanding along with the city to bring in more industrial areas and more tax revenue.[1758] In October 1965, a new state law

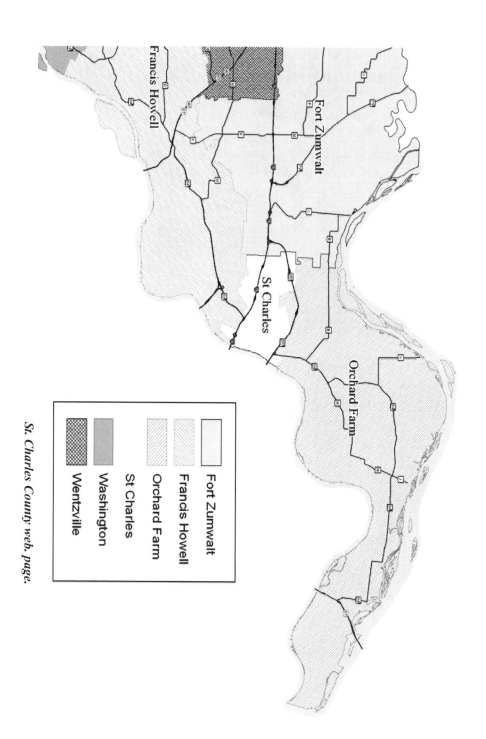

St. Charles County web. page.

308

kept school districts from expanding their boundaries. Now the only way to increase assessed valuation in a district was more industrial development within district boundaries. In January 1967 St. Charles Mayor Henry Vogt was asked to explain why earlier City Councils had not attracted more industrial development that would have given the city a tax base capable of supporting its schools.[1759]

School finances were also becoming more dependent on property taxes because state aid had fallen from 31.9 percent to 29.2 percent of the school budget between 1966 and 1970.[1760] The only new properties coming on the tax rolls were new homes, including many mobile homes. Older homes were usually under-assessed because they were not reassessed until they changed owners. Many new homeowners had high-rate mortgages and simply could not afford higher taxes.[1761] The schools received some relief when the Missouri Constitution was amended in November 1970 allowing the existing levy to remain in effect if a new one was not approved. At the same time, the rate of population growth in St. Charles was easing.

In 1973, with a new junior and senior high school open or under construction already decided on, the enrollment dropped, a fact that reportedly "astounded" the superintendent of schools.[1762] He would have not been so astounded if he had been examining housing starts in St. Charles. There were 231 housing starts in the first 11 months of 1973, compared to 329 in 1972 and 407 in 1971. The slowdown was attributed to the high cost of land, bridge congestion and high interest rates.[1763] A few years after the opening of St. Charles West High School in 1976, the district had fewer students in two high schools than they had in one a few years earlier. By 1978, the district had suffered a net loss of more than 700 students since 1974 and enrollment continued to decline.[1764]

The other school districts in St. Charles County were now having growing pains. The Wentzville Schools also did not open on time in 1970, as the voters, by 81 votes, turned down a $5.43 levy for the fifth time in August.[1765] They did not open until October 2 that year.[1766] Meanwhile, with large enrollment increases, Francis Howell went to a year-round school calendar for elementary and junior high students in July 1971.[1767] Fort Zumwalt's proposed 39 ¢ levy increase was defeated in September 1971. The district borrowed to make it through the year, warning of the impending closing of the schools.[1768] By 1980 Fort Zumwalt High School's enrollment had increased from 587 in 1968 to 1,700 students, reflecting the tremendous growth in the St. Peters area. In that year a bond issue was approved to construct Hawthorne Elementary School, the district's seventh elementary school.[1769]

Some students in St. Peters attended schools in Francis-Howell instead of in the Fort Zumwalt district. Several families petitioned to form a new school district for St. Peters. A Francis Howell School District survey in 1980 showed that 80 percent of the Francis Howell constituents in St. Peters wanted to stay in the Francis Howell district. The *St. Charles Post* reported, "Those forty who favored formation of a new St. Peters district said that Francis Howell Schools are too far away from their homes, that St. Peters needs a sense of community and they prefer a nine-month school schedule. Some said that new growth in the St. Peters area would produce a richer district."[1770]

There was substantial cooperation on educational issues in St. Charles County. In 1968, the Lewis and Clark Vocational Technical School was built with federal assistance by the School District of the City of St. Charles to serve students throughout the county.[1771] By 1980, the St. Charles schools, realizing that they had more in common with the growing districts of St. Charles County, quit participating in St. Louis County athletic conferences and joined the Gateway Athletic Conference, composed of Duchesne, Fort Zumwalt, Francis Howell and Wentzville High Schools. In 1975, GROWTH INC completed a feasibility study for a junior college district. William Weber was the chairman of the committee looking at the question.[1772] The voters of the county elected a Board of Directors, but defeated the bond issue and tax levy necessary to build the facilities and open the school.[1773]

Not only schools, but also child welfare organizations, grew and prospered for girls as well as boys. While the Soapbox Derby was discontinued, St. Charles Junior Baseball added girls' softball in the mid-1960s and the Boys' Club became the Boys' and Girls' Club of St. Charles County in the late 1970s. Other youth sports leagues were started and Scouting continued to be popular with boys and girls in the county. In 1963 St. Charles voters approved a bond issue to purchase the land for what became McNair Park.[1774] In 1975 a five-acre site east of St. Peters was purchased for construction of a YMCA. St. Peters agreed to develop the land adjacent to the "Y" as a municipal park. The facilities were located in what became the population center of the county in 1980, the Cave Springs area.[1775]

In spite of the many youth activities and organizations, St. Charles County had its share of juvenile crime and youth related social problems. During the Great Depression, most mothers in St. Charles County were married, were housewives and were generally responsible for their own children. St. Charles was still a small town and so not a lot of attention was paid to juvenile delinquency. In January 1946 the county Grand Jury, which had discovered that the sheriff was detaining juveniles in the county jail in contravention of state law, ordered him to find separate facilities.[1776] By the mid-1960s the family structure began to weaken, with increasing numbers of children raised in one-parent families. Nationally the number of never-married mothers between age 18 and 34, which had been 73,000 in 1960, increased to 1 million by 1980.[1777] In 1964, a committee of city and county officials was formed to deal with juvenile problems. At a Community Council meeting, the chairman stated, "we hope to get a cross-section of community feeling on the problems of youth, with everyone who wishes participating in the program, we should find out what citizens feel are our most pressing juvenile problems and what they want to be done about them."[1778]

To deal with juvenile delinquency the St. Charles City Council adopted a curfew in 1967, starting on the first holiday weekend of summer. Youths under 17 could not be in any commercial place of amusement between the hours of 12:30 a.m. and 6:00 a.m. Saturday and Sunday, or between 11:30 p.m. and 6:00 a.m. during the rest of the week. Youths accompanied by parents were not subject to the curfew and a warning was to be given for the first violation. The *Banner-News* reported that the ordinance was passed because of, "the rising incidence of juvenile crime in the city."[1779] Shortly after the ordinance was passed, a so-called "Battle of the Bands" teen dance at Memorial Hall turned into a brawl. When police ordered the hall closed, some of the teen-agers sat down on the floor, refused to leave and had to be forcibly removed. Parents were concerned because a police officer had fired a shot in the air when one of the fleeing teenagers failed to stop when ordered to. It was also reported that many of the youths involved were from St. Louis and St. Louis County.[1780] As the 1960s came to an end, the *Banner-News* wrote in April 1969:

> The really outstanding factor about America's young people is that so many of them have kept their balance, perspective and their sense of values despite the pressures which have been exerted on them by some of their peers. Worst of all, leverage comes from some of their seniors who certainly should know better. We also owe it to you to avoid that permissiveness that will only breed contempt for society as well as for parents. The older generations are challenged to match the good judgment shown by the majority of our young adults.[1781]

While not a single drug case had been referred to the county juvenile office in 1968, there were 128 drug cases involving juveniles in 1969. The discovery of widespread use of drugs by high school students led to an extensive investigation by the St. Charles police and county sheriff's department. When undercover agents made arrests after a $40,000 drug transaction, it made front-page news in November 1970. A Youth in Need (YIN) house was established in St. Charles in 1974 to house runaway children and a satellite house was established in Wentzville in 1976 to serve the western end of the county.[1782] The authorities were vigilant about gatherings of young people. In 1974, the prosecuting attorney got an injunction against a rock concert at which Ike and Tina Turner were supposed to perform. When their agent was contacted, he knew nothing about it but the injunction was still granted.[1783] Efforts were made by adults to provide activities such as the Silo Youth Center that opened in 1972.[1784]

In 1972, the Supreme Court held that it was unconstitutional for a state to differentiate between sexual relations inside and outside of marriage. In 1977 it took the logical next step and held that children conceived out of wedlock could not be discriminated against by the state, which had no legitimate interest in promoting "legitimate family relationships."[1785] In December 1974 the *Banner-News* said, "The breakdown of the family unit is largely responsible for many of the ills of today's society, and a report showing divorce and separation on the increase is of little comfort."[1786] The paper lamented that single mothers headed 6.6 million families in 1973, representing 12 percent of all families in the U.S. and a 47 percent increase in 13 years.[1787] In 1977, the Center for the Prevention of Disease Control found that children born out of wedlock were 250 percent more likely to be abused than children born to married parents. In 1975 the state had ordered the Division of Family Services to investigate every abuse and neglect complaint and created a state abuse and neglect registry.[1788] The *Banner-News* reported an increase in child abuse in St. Charles County and quoted an official with Division of Family Services as saying, "Most people still think there's a small-town flavor to the population and people just don't do this to their children."[1789] Clearly, St. Charles was not a small town anymore.

The churches continued to meet the needs of their youth as private and parochial schools expanded and changed their missions. St. Robert Bellarmine (1963) and St. Cletus (1965) parishes in St. Charles and St. Barnabas in O'Fallon were established, along with parish schools. Old parishes like All Saints and Assumption grew as new residents flocked to the new subdivisions. In 1969, Lindenwood College announced that 50 males would be admitted in the fall, joining the 600 women.[1790] In 1972, the Academy of the Sacred Heart, having closed its high school to concentrate on its 260 elementary school students, announced that it would admit boys for the first time in the pre-primary and primary grades. St. Mary's College in O'Fallon, on the grounds of the Sisters of the Most Precious Blood, became accredited in 1962 and began offering associates degrees in 1963.[1791]

Long-established congregations, Catholic, Lutheran, Evangelical (now United Church of Christ)[1792], Presbyterian and Methodists remained conservative in their response to most of the social changes. The Catholics and Lutherans continued to support parochial schools, while Presbyterian, Methodist and United Church of Christ congregations established youth activities to shield their children from secular society and preached against the decline of morality from the pulpit. These denominations continued to grow in St. Charles County because of the overall population growth of the county. However, nationally Lutheran membership dropped five percent, United Methodist, ten percent, Northern Presbyterians 12 percent, United Church of Christ 12 percent from 1965 to 1975. From 1957 to 1975 the percent of Catholics claiming to have attended Mass in the previous week dropped from 75 percent to 54 percent.[1793]

The growing number of Evangelical Christians in the county would be in the front lines of the "culture wars." While other denominations were declining nationally during this period, Church of the Nazarene, eight percent, Southern Baptist, 18 percent, Seventh-Day Adventists, 36 percent, and Assembly of God, 37 percent, were growing rapidly. There were only a handful of these congregations in St. Charles County in 1960. By 1981 congregations from these denominations, along with Christian, Evangelical Methodists, Church of Christ, Disciples of Christ and Pentecostal, numbered 47 in the county.[1794] Interfaith Tent Crusades were held at the county fairgrounds in 1966 and 1967. In 1968 the Christian Men's Fellowship was organized for weekly prayer and fellowship, and the St. Charles Christian Women's Club began holding monthly luncheons and Bible study in 1975. The first St. Charles County "Crusade for Christ," held at the county fairgrounds in August of 1966, was billed as "the largest Protestant religious event that St. Charles has ever known."[1795] In 1976, the "Crusade for Christ" met at Jefferson Junior High with Dr. Moody Adams as the evangelist. It was reported that chairman James Fitz was "very encouraged by the turnout."[1796]

Nationally, respondents claiming that religion was "increasing its influence on American life" tripled between 1970 and 1978, from 14 percent to 44 percent.[1797] According to John Clecak, "tens of millions of Americans were able to discover or rediscover a fuller sense of the possibilities of life through their encounters with Evangelical and Neo-Pentecostal modes of worship during the sixties and seventies."[1798] Lisa McGirr explains that the counter-culture of the 1960s showed deep dissatisfaction among the nation's youth with the materialistic, affluent, middle-class lifestyle of their parents. The growth of evangelical Christianity also reflected a search for meaning in the modern consumer society.[1799]

Evangelical Christians, around the country and in St. Charles County, would be among the first to speak out against the "sexual revolution," with its greater sexual freedom or promiscuity, depending on one's point of view. Pornography was one manifestation of the change, and obscenity was one area where Evangelicals would protest the loudest. A Supreme Court opinion in 1962 had made obscenity prosecutions more difficult and in 1964 the Court held that obscene material must be without "redeeming social value" to be censored.[1800] In June 1972 the sheriff closed the Roxy Theatre in Wentzville, that had been in operation for three weeks as an X-rated movie theatre. A short time later, a St. Charles County jury found the film that had been playing there, "Sex Acts of Sweden," to be obscene based on local community standards.[1801] In 1974 a "massage parlor" was shut down after the prosecuting attorney charged the owner with "maintaining a bawdy house…within 100 yards of a church."[1802]

At the same time, culture wars were being fought out in the schools. McGirr points out that conservatives believed that schools reflected "the will and power of the state vis-à-vis the nation's public culture" and they fought against secularism, scientific rationalism, and the liberal values held by many educators.[1803] The first move to protect morality in the county had come in 1963, when prosecuting attorney Donald Dalton announced an investigation of sex crimes in St. Charles. The prosecutor revealed that the local scandal involved not only statutory rape, but also forcible rape and perversion. It was reported that 15 St. Charles High School students were to be suspended because of their alleged involvement in the sex scandal. The school board blocked the suspensions and expulsions because the action taken was based on information made available to the board illegally. Apparently, the juvenile officer had given the confidential information to the school board.[1804]

In response to such incidents, school districts instituted sex education in the schools. Many Evangelical Christians believed, as one pamphlet of the day proclaimed, that sex education, "drives a wedge between the family, church and school, bolstering the authority of the school while casting doubts on the moral teachings of the home or church."[1805] As with most social issues of the time, sex education had surfaced first in California, where conservatives were able to get a law passed requiring parental permission before a child could enter a sex education class.[1806] The issue emerged in St. Charles when C. Ben Basye, a school board member, called for the resignation of the superintendent because of a sex-education workshop held for secondary teachers. He complained that three admitted homosexuals were present, and birth control and abortion were discussed. No action was taken by the board.[1807]

Evangelical Christians, and probably a lot of other Christians as well, had been outraged by the Supreme Court's decision in 1962 outlawing prayer in public schools. They also became concerned in 1972 when a dispute arose at St. Charles High School over whether witches should be allowed to speak at the school. The *Banner-News* described the showdown as follows, " In this corner, Dr. and Mrs. Gavin Frost, better known as the witches and in this corner about 60 religious fundamentalists, many with Bible in hand."[1808] The issue received nationwide publicity as many who did not agree with the witches thought it was a freedom of speech issue. In an ironic twist, the religious fundamentalists argued that the witches believed they practiced a religion and thus the separation clause of the First Amendment required that they be excluded from the curriculum. On another occasion, a group of businessmen objected to the book "Promise of America'" because of obscene language and unpatriotic commentary.

There was also concern about the breakdown of discipline in the schools. In 1971, the Eighth Circuit Federal Court of Appeals found that St. Charles High School had no right to suspend a male student for having long hair. The court said that the school's dress code, "seeks to restrict a young person's liberty to mold his own lifestyle."[1809] In a 1980 poll, 80 percent of residents responding in the St. Charles School District preferred that discipline be tightened, while 86 percent of students said it was too strict or about right.[1810] Ironically, some of the parents of those students had been students at St. Charles High School in 1948 when the student body had staged a two-day strike over the firing of a teacher.[1811]

After 1965, the Civil Rights Movement moved into issues of economic equality and became increasingly associated with the anti-war movement. More importantly, between 1964 and 1968, there were 329 racially inspired riots in 257 cities, with the most famous in Los Angeles, Newark and Detroit.[1812] Many in St. Charles County who had supported the non-violent stance of Dr. Martin Luther King now became suspicious of the Civil Rights Movement. The tension of the times often led to speculation that any fight between students of different races was racially motivated.[1813] There were complaints against violent incidents at the Parkridge Apartments, where the majority of tenants were African-Americans. Nineteen residents signed a petition asking, "for an immediate positive solution to the lawbreaking attitudes of some of the citizens of St. Charles. The lack of police protection is a violation of our rights as taxpaying citizens of St. Charles."[1814] The police chief responded that the violence was the result to a feud between two families living in the apartments, and he could not justify 24-hour patrols even though residents were reporting windows being shot out and verbal abuse.[1815] The victims of these crimes were black but the result in the community when crime was reported in the public housing project was to reinforce negative racial stereotypes. The "law and order" issue in St. Charles was also fed by a real increase in crime by members of all races. In December 1968 Governor Hearnes' Citizen Committee on Delinquency and Crime issued a report stating, "Missouri has a serious and increasing crime problem," that would, "require the expenditure of substantial funds."[1816] In St. Charles, statistics showed a jump in crime from 1968 to 1969. Burglaries showed the greatest increase, going from 168 in 1968 to 331 in 1969, as complaints handled by the police rose from 9,661 to 12,000 in that same time period.[1817]

Prejudice against African-Americans did not disappear. In the summer of 1967, Suntan Beach, a privately owned swimming area north of St. Charles, agreed to admit African-Americans after a complaint was filed with the Missouri Human Rights Commission.[1818] Discrimination also remained in housing as the St. Charles City Council turned down a request by St. John AME Church to rezone five acres from single family to multi-family zoning. One resident explained, "as a 'poor workingman of the white race,' he is opposed not only to new apartment zoning, but to any more apartment construction at all." Reverend Frank Cummings pointed out that the city had applied for funds to build public housing for the elderly and suggested prejudice against "black developers." Support for public housing eroded further in August of 1980 when HUD set a deadline for the St. Charles Housing Authority to improve its rent collection. At the time, it had the worst rent collection record in its region with 74 percent of its monthly charges uncollected.[1819] Such stories did not help the cause of subsidized housing in St. Charles County. In April 1980, the St. Charles City Council approved plans for the Fox Hill Apartments, a subsidized housing project that was opposed by the surrounding neighborhood. The attorney for the developer suggested, "The only reason to vote no against this ordinance is because of bias against minorities or the economically disadvantaged." The three councilmen voting no insisted that race had nothing to do with their vote.[1820] That project later proved to be a model for subsidized housing in the county.

Women also made great strides during the 1970s in their quest for equality. A big lift came in 1971 when Congress passed, and President Nixon signed, Title IX, mandating that schools receiving federal funds provide equal programs, including sports programs, for men and women. Women's interscholastic sports returned to the local high schools. The Missouri General Assembly never ratified the Equal Rights Amendment. While the amendment never became part of the constitution, opportunities for women increased. Women began sitting on the boards of St. Charles County banks in the mid-1970s, and more women-owned and-operated businesses appeared. Developer Robert McKelvey suggested that there was greater demand in the county for upscale housing in 1977 since, "total family incomes are up because more wives are working."[1821]

The mentally handicapped also made great strides in the late 1970s. The Handicapped Facilities Board, (later renamed the Developmentally Disabled Resources Board), a public taxing entity, was established in 1977 when the voters approved a 10¢ levy to provide funds to those agencies providing support and services to the disabled. In 1978 the Mental Health Council of Lincoln, Warren, and St. Charles Counties was incorporated under the leadership of Jane Crider. In 1979 the organization, later renamed Four County Mental Health, hired Karl Wilson as a part-time executive director and began providing services in 1979. Nevertheless, as the decade ended residents continued to oppose group homes for developmentally disabled adults.

During the late 1960s, a new *Kulturkampf* had begun in St. Charles County. Older cultural issues now took a back seat as conservative forces confronted the forces of the counter-culture. Ethnic and religious differences paled when compared to the generation gap. From the "War on Poverty" at the beginning of this period, to the "War on Drugs" at the end, St. Charles County grappled with the same social problems as other suburbs in the St. Louis area and the country.

B. Political Parity

From 1965 to 1980, the two-party system was particularly strong in St. Charles County. The Republicans staged a long slow comeback after 1964, aided by discontent created by the "War on Poverty," the Vietnam War and extremism within the Civil Rights Movement. As the Republicans were about to overtake the Democrats, the Watergate Scandal dealt them a severe setback in 1974. The differences between the two parties focused primarily on economic issues in St. Charles County. On social issues, conservatives in both parties predominated. Because of that fact, there were many Reagan Democrats in St. Charles County in 1980 and Reagan had long coattails. As the period ended, the Republican Party was again the majority party in St. Charles County.

That comeback began in 1965. With 52,970 people according to the 1960 census St Charles County, by the narrowest of margins, had failed to qualify for a second representative in the Missouri House of Representatives. By 1964, it was the fastest growing county in Missouri. With an increase of 24.5 percent since the census of 1960, its population was more than 66,000.[1822] As the county continued to grow, its under-representation in the Missouri House of Representatives became even more glaring. After the Supreme Court announced the "one-man one-vote" principle, the state redistricted, giving the county a second representative. In 1965 the new legislative maps made St. Charles and the floodplain areas to the north a separate district from the rest of St. Charles County.

At the St. Charles County Lincoln Day dinner in February 1965, Republican State Representative R.J. "Bus" King spoke against the factionalism that had divided the party in 1964 and said, "we must unite under the banner of Republicanism or face the possibility of being reduced to several splinter groups."[1823] In May of that year, Harold Rayfield resigned as chairman of the County Central Committee. Joseph Briscoe, president of the Junior Chamber of Commerce, who was serving his second term as councilman in St. Charles, replaced him.[1824] Republicans reunited and their prospects improved through the remainder of the decade.

As the 1966 elections approached, Democrats continued to express concern about the influence of the John Birch Society on the Republican Party. The new Democratic County Committee chairman, Herbert Stewart, announced that John Birch Society members would not be welcome in the Democratic Party. However, the Democrats could no longer rely on disunity in Republican ranks. Between 1964 and 1966, many white Americans had begun to have second thoughts about the Civil Rights Movement after the eruption of race riots in Watts, Chicago and Newark. The war in Vietnam had begun to cost American lives and treasure while inflation was becoming a threat to the middle class. By November 1966, the mood of the country had changed significantly and in November 1966 the GOP gained 47 seats in the U.S. House of Representatives and three in the Senate, enough to revive the conservative coalition that the Johnson landslide of 1964 had temporarily overcome.[1825]

Republicans made similar advances in state and local races as they swept all but two contests in St. Charles County. The entire County Court and the county treasurer's office went Republican, and Republican Arlie Meyer defeated Democrat William Goellner for the new state representative seat. Republican Ed Stone of Chesterfield was able to hold off Democratic nominee William Corrigan to enable the Republicans to hold on to the state senate seat as well. Local Democrats attributed the Republican sweep to what some called, "a Johnson backlash, inflation, the war in Vietnam, and hidden but real anti-Civil Rights sentiment on the part of some voters."[1826]

Indeed, the Great Society was never intended to benefit prosperous white suburbs and Johnson's popularity had eroded in those areas since 1964. The *St. Charles Journal* reported in 1965 that 85 city and county officials, upon hearing plans for the "War of Poverty," gave the programs a "lukewarm reception." Applications for the Youth Corps, a jobs program for impoverished youngsters, were below the county's quota. Federal domestic spending and increased military expenditures were creating deficits and spurring inflation.[1827] In December 1965, Marine Corporal Robert John Wilkins became the first St. Charles Countian killed in the Vietnam conflict.[1828] Draft calls increased throughout 1966, with 33 from the county inducted in December.[1829] In 1967, the local Realtors Association charged that the Civil Rights Bill attacked, "a basic right of all citizens considered unassailable since the founding of this nation. I refer to the human right to sell or rent private real estate - or refuse to sell or rent – to whomever the owner chooses for whatever reason without any coercion or dictation from the government."[1830]

Democrats were aware that the "law and order" issue was hurting them. Appearing before 400 people in St. Charles in April 1968, Governor Warren Hearnes condemned the rioting in Detroit and Washington D.C., stating that, "There will be law and order, and we are going to have respect for law and order."[1831] Rioting and lawlessness continued right up to the Democratic Convention in Chicago, where Hubert Humphrey was nominated. In his campaign against Humphrey, Republican nominee Richard Nixon appealed to the middle class; "the forgotten Americans, those who did not indulge in violence, those who did not break the law, people who pay their taxes and go to work, people who send their children to school, who go to their churches, people who are not haters, people who love this country."[1832] That was a good description of most people in St. Charles County, Republican and Democrat. The "silent majority" responded by voting for Nixon in 1968.

On the statewide level, Republicans made some gains with the election of John Danforth as attorney general in 1968; making him the first statewide Republican officeholder in some time. Democrat Thomas Eagleton was elected to the U.S. Senate. Locally, the Democrats actually made gains by stressing local issues and espousing conservative ideas. The St. Charles County Democratic platform criticized the Republican County Court for raising taxes, deficit spending and purchasing an old bowling alley for expansion of county government.[1833] Nixon's percentage in the county had gone from 48 percent in 1960 to 52 percent in 1968, despite 19.4 percent voting for third-party candidate George Wallace. Nixon won German-Catholic St. Peters, Dardenne and O'Fallon even though each of those communities gave George Wallace over 23 percent. In *The Emerging Republican Majority*, Kevin Phillips, writing shortly after the 1968 election, identified two voting trends that converged in St. Charles County. Phillips stated that Nixon could not have won Missouri without a strong showing among St. Louis area German Catholics. In fact, he turned a 10,000 loss in the still quite German area around St. Louis, (St. Louis, St. Charles, Osage and Perry Counties) into a 20,000-vote edge. While Nixon's gains in the suburbs of St. Louis also rested on general suburban behavior as well, the ethnic factor was definitely at work[1834] At the same time, Phillips points out that the percentage of the statewide vote cast in St. Louis had slipped from 22 percent in 1948 to 12 percent in 1968, leading to a decline in the importance of the old central cities, a factor which aided the cause of both conservatism and Republicanism.[1835]

The new Republican administration embarked on a policy called the "New Federalism," in an attempt to return resources and power back to states and communities through "revenue sharing."[1836] In February 1970, House Republican Minority leader R.J. "Bus" King made the New Federalism the topic of his Lincoln Day address in St. Charles. He outlined Republican efforts in Jefferson City to allow Missouri to benefit from the new policy of revenue sharing, that was replacing some of the block grant programs.[1837]

County government was growing and in 1969 the county budget topped $2 million for the first time.[1838] In March 1970, Democratic County Chairman Glennon Bishop filed as a candidate for Presiding Judge. Neither Republican Presiding Judge Charles Kinnamore nor Western District Judge Curtis Burkemper chose to run for reelection. Douglas Boschert was elected presiding judge while Democrat Leo Luetkenhaus was elected to represent the Western District. Republican Darby Tally was reelected to the Eastern District seat, allowing the Republicans to maintain their majority.[1839] The new court moved into the new County Administration Building on Second Street that included 20,000 square feet of office space for the county offices, leaving the courthouse entirely for the courts.[1840]

In 1969, Representative Omer Dames was killed in a tractor accident and Republican Fred Meyer won a special election to replace him. In November 1970 Omer Dames' son, George Dames, defeated Meyer to take back the seat held by his father. At the same time, in the 105th District in eastern St. Charles County, incumbent Arlie Meyer defeated Andrew McColloch, who had given up his office as prosecuting attorney to run for the House of Representatives.[1841] County Assessor Robert Bauer was unable to unseat incumbent State Senator Ed Stone, a resident of Chesterfield. After redistricting following the 1970 census, St. Charles County became part of a different Senate district in which the county contained over one-half of the voters. The district also included Florissant and Spanish Lake in St. Louis County, and was expected to be slightly Republican. After redistricting St. Charles County had three state representative seats as well.[1842]

Things were looking good for the Republicans on every level as the issues of 1968 continued to be important as the 1972 presidential election approached. After the 1968 convention the Democratic Party had changed many of its rules to allow new, more liberal, groups greater influence, making possible the nomination of George McGovern, a candidate who was as far to the left in 1972 as Goldwater had been to the right in 1964. The growing influence of liberal leaders in the local Democratic Party created friction with the more traditional Democrats. Erwin Davis probably typified those traditional Democrats as well as anyone in St. Charles County. Having moved to St. Charles from rural Arkansas in 1948, he earned his undergraduate and law degrees by attending night school while working full time to support his family during the day. His progressive economic thinking and social conservatism were typical of most Democrats in St. Charles County and, while he did not often seek political office, he was the most influential Democrat in the county. He called the social liberals who were becoming more numerous in the local party's leadership the "Lindenwood crowd."[1843] Many traditional Democrats were unhappy with the party's move to the left and Richard Nixon later recalled, "McGovern's perverse treatment of the traditional Democratic power blocks … made possible the creation of a New Republican Majority as an electoral force in American politics."[1844] The majority definitely existed in St. Charles County where Nixon received a huge majority. Christopher "Kit" Bond and Jack Danforth received large majorities as well while the Republicans won the governorship and retained the attorney general's office. While Fred Dyer was elected state representative for the first time, Nixon's coattails were not long as St. Charles County also gave large majorities to Democrats James Spainhower for treasurer and James Kirkpatrick for secretary of state. Leo Luetkenhaus and several other Democrats were re-elected on the county level.

The shallowness of the new Republican majority became apparent two years later. The quadrupling of oil prices in 1973-74 led to the worst recession since WWII.[1845] As the election approached, President Nixon was embroiled in the Watergate scandal. Reporting on the November 1974 elections, the *Banner-News* stated, "St. Charles County Republicans did not escape the wrath of Watergate and its aftermath as Democrats swept key county offices in Tuesday's general election, scoring major upsets in County races and popping surprises in other contests that were odds-on favorites (for the Republicans) as polls opened."[1846] Incumbent Judges Boschert and Talley were unseated as an all-Democrat county court was elected comprised of Charles Schwendemann, presiding judge, John C. Hanneke, eastern district judge, and Joseph Graves, western district judge. Democrat Robert Bauer carried St. Charles County, but lost the new state senate seat to Republican Joseph Frappier, a state representative from Florrisant. Democrat Grace Nichols, running against incumbent State Representative Omar Schnattmeier for the second time, barely lost. All incumbent Democrats were reelected and Democrat Fred Rush won the new circuit judgeship that had recently been created for the 11th Circuit, comprising St. Charles, Lincoln and Pike Counties.[1847] Democratic fortunes were at their highest point in the county since 1964.

In the previous ten years, county government had dealt with the challenges created by the rapid development of St. Charles County. Some of the most controversial zoning decisions made by the County Court involved mobile home parks. Mobile homes had become popular in the 1950s. In the 1960s 12 and 14-foot widths were introduced. After 1967, doublewides were available.[1848] Kenneth Jackson states that mobile homes, "provided a suburban alternative to the inner-city housing that would otherwise be available to blue collar workers, newly married couples, and retired persons.[1849] In 1962, neighbors opposed the expansion of the Trio Mobile Home Park at Zumbehl Road and I-70 because the sewerage lagoon that served the park was emitting foul odors.[1850] At about the same time, the County Court approved several other trailer parks just outside the limits of St. Charles.

One of the most controversial proposals was what became Fox Run Mobile Home Park, located at the intersection of what is now Little Hills Expressway and Boschertown Road. After the County Court approved the rezoning in November 1965, the *Banner-News* said, "It appears the trailer court case has been bobbled badly and the worse bobble of all in our opinion, was when the Democratic County Court 'blew the bit' by overruling the zoning commission when the zoning commission denied rezoning for the proposed trailer court."[1851] The editorial went on to state, "It cannot be denied that the Democrats face political repercussions as the result of what has transpired."[1852] St. Charles filed lawsuits to challenge the decision and it was two years before the matter was back before the County Court for plat approval. St. Charles then filed a remonstrance, meaning that all three commissioners had to approve the plat.[1853] When they did, the County Court's excuse was that it had only recently established a designated classification for trailer courts but had neglected to amend the old ordinance allowing the courts in areas designated "light industry."[1854] The County Court claimed it could not stop the development and that people should blame St. Charles for agreeing to provide sewer and water to the project.[1855]

As additional mobile home parks were approved on North Highway 94, just outside the city limits, St. Charles was concerned about county decisions on land use in areas into which the city wanted to expand. In October 1976, the City Council passed resolutions expressing "dismay and displeasure" with the county's rezoning of 36 acres on Elm Point Road for a mobile home park, even though the county Planning and Zoning Commission had recommended against it. Residents opposed that rezoning because it was in their neighborhood; environmentalists, because it was in the floodplain; Orchard Farm School District because it would not generate sufficient revenue to educate the students who would live there; and St. Charles because it wanted to use the land for industrial development.[1856]

By the 1970s, people had begun to question the suitability of the County Court system because of incidents like the one described above. The system was 150 years old and designed primarily for small rural counties. In a fast-growing county like St. Charles, where the population had increased to 92,986 by 1970, an unpopular measure could be passed with the vote of the judge from the other district, and the vote of the presiding judge, who ran countywide. At the Lincoln Day dinner in 1970, William T. Davis, the Republican county chairman, pointed out that the St. Charles County Court lacked legislative power, meaning that the county was dependent on the General Assembly to pass the legislation it needed.[1857] In February 1974, a petition signed by almost 8,000 registered voters called for the appointment of a Charter Commission. Circuit Judges William Turpin and Donald E. Dalton, along with Probate Judge Webster Karrenbrock named a 14-member panel, chaired by H.K. Stumberg, to draw up a charter to present to the voters for their approval.[1858] Municipal officials were afraid that municipal taxpayers would end up paying more taxes to provide municipal services to unincorporated area, as had happened with the development of south St. Louis County.[1859] Another reluctant group was the elected county officials. To get them on board and blunt any criticism that charter government was less democratic, the proposed charter kept all county offices elected.[1860] At a special election in May 1975, the charter failed by a mere 126 votes. The *Banner-News* lamented that voters failed to consider the advantages of home rule, which would have allowed the county to pass its own laws without going to the legislature every time it wanted a change. Instead:

> City dwellers, who generally went against the proposal, live in areas governed by city councils or aldermen and are not as directly affected by some of the problems with which county residents must deal, such as roads, health and the like. City streets are maintained, the local police departments provide adequate protection in most instances, whereas county residents, especially those living in subdivisions in unincorporated areas, want the same type of services as the cities which for obvious reasons the county cannot provide. So those in these subdivisions generally backed the charter, while the cities backed away from it.[1861]

By 1974 property assessment had become a big political issue. As early as 1958, the Democrats had used the inequality in property assessment as a campaign issue. At that time, all the new housing had been recently assessed, while older homes, unless recently sold, had assessments that had not kept pace with inflation. A reassessment program begun in 1952 had not yet produced any results. The Democratic court received a petition from some mid-county residents requesting that a reassessment program be initiated and the court contracted with an appraisal company from St. Louis County to revalue all property in the county. It was argued that, by hiring a private firm, politics would be kept out of the process. However, after the private company had completed its work the County Court and the assessor agreed that the new numbers were not acceptable and all the figures would have to be reviewed by the elected officials. This left them open to the charges of political influence they had hoped to avoid. Others argued that the County Court should not have spent $152,000 to hire the private appraisers, whose conclusions they were not going to accept. Another controversy surrounded the assessment of agricultural land. Farmers wanted land assessed on its agricultural productivity, not on the amount a land speculator was willing to pay to develop it.[1862]

Aside from the local pressure, reassessment also became a statewide issue. In September 1974, the county assessor reported receiving an "extremely strong" directive from the State Tax Commission to assess values upward 11 percent, as required by a law passed by the General Assembly the previous spring. The law required that property be taxed at 33 percent of actual value. The county had been putting the assessed value at only 30 percent of actual value. The effect was to raise the tax burden on homeowners and make the inequities of the assessment process even more controversial.[1863] Because property was only reassessed when it changed hands, a house in which a family had lived for 30 years could have an assessed value of one-fifth of the identical house that had just been purchased next door.[1864] Immediately after the general election of 1976, the county assessor announced that he was beginning to plan a complete reassessment of property because he believed that either the legislature would legislate it or the courts would order it. This was no small matter since the estimated cost for the state to reassess all property was $55 million. Since school districts collected 80 percent of the revenue, they would have to bear 80 percent of the cost.[1865] The following August, St. Charles County assessor Robert Bauer announced that a St. Louis County judge had ordered reassessment in that county and that would probably lead to the passage of a law requiring it statewide.[1866]

Watergate took its toll even on the Democrats as Congressman William Hungate, a very visible member of the House Judiciary Committee during the impeachment hearings, announced his retirement from Congress. He was quoted in the *Banner-News* as saying that since he was first elected to Congress, "politics has gone from the age of Camelot, when all things were possible, to the age of Watergate, when all things are suspect."[1867] When the Democrats had their convention in 1976, they were hopeful that the Watergate backlash would continue. Unfortunately for St. Charles County

Democrats, another issue was coming to the fore that greatly affected the Democratic Party in St. Charles County and the State of Missouri. In 1973, the Supreme Court had decided the case of *Roe v. Wade* greatly restricting the ability of state legislatures to regulate abortion. By 1976, the abortion issue was causing rifts within the Democratic Party in Missouri. At the national convention, the Missouri delegation attempted to change the plank opposing a constitutional amendment giving the states the right to regulate abortions. Delegate Kenneth Worley from O'Fallon stated, "I would have preferred to see it left totally out of the platform. Apparently, unless they can find some other maneuver, that position is in the platform."[1868] While most local Democratic officials remained pro-life, their party embraced the pro-choice position. Eventually, the issue caused many Democrats to vote for Republicans on the national and state levels.

The split in the Republican Party between moderates and conservatives that had been defused by the election of Richard Nixon, reappeared after his departure. In 1976, conservatives favored Ronald Reagan, former governor of California, while Republican moderates favored incumbent President Gerald Ford. Reagan supporters prevailed at the St. Charles County Convention as they did at the State Convention, even though Governor Bond was supporting Gerald Ford, who had assumed the presidency when Nixon resigned. While President Ford got the nomination at the Republican National Convention in Kansas City, he was plagued by the fact that he had given Nixon a presidential pardon. 1976 was a Democratic year as Jimmy Carter and Joseph Teasdale carried the state for president and governor respectively. Ford polled over 54 percent in St. Charles County and Governor Bond got nearly 53 percent in his losing effort. Jack Danforth defeated former Governor Hearnes, with 60 percent in the race for the U.S. Senate. The legislative delegation from the county continued to be three Republicans and one Democrat, as Douglas Boschert was elected to replace the retiring Omar Schnattmeier. However, the Democrats continued their near-total control of county government, where the social issues were not as important. Although they had criticized the Republicans for buying the bowling alley in 1968 for more office space, the Democratic court in 1977, with increased population demanding more county services, bought the old Fischbach Hotel building for additional office space.[1869]

The 1978 elections were a great victory for the Democrats. In 1977, the National Right-To-Work Committee targeted Missouri. An attempt to send a proposal to the voters that would have outlawed union shop agreements was defeated in the legislature. In the summer of 1978, supporters collected enough signatures to put the proposal on the November ballot. Early polls showed support for the measure, prompting the Greater St. Louis Labor Council to launch a massive grassroots effort to turn out voters in November. Their efforts succeeded as the proposal was defeated by a three to two margin.[1870] The increased turnout meant defeat for several Republican candidates including incumbent Representative Fred Dyer.

St. Charles County voters also elected Republican Peggy Coppage as western district judge and Democrat Barbara Walker as collector in 1978. They had elected

Melvin Washington was the first African-American elected to public office when he was elected to the St. Charles School Board.
St. Charles County Journals

Democrat Loretta Debrecht county treasurer in 1968 and Marsha Duncan public administrator in 1976. Nationally, the number of women holding public office doubled in the second half of the 1970s, rising from 7,242 (or about 4.7 percent of officeholders) to 17,782 (or about 10.9 percent). Between 1971 and 1981, the number of women lawyers nationally rose from four percent to 14 percent.[1871] In 1981, Ronald Reagan appointed Sandra Day O'Connor as the first woman member of the United States Supreme Court and in 1982 the voters elected the first female judge in St. Charles County when they elected Lucy Rauch as associate circuit court judge.

In the 1970s, two African-Americans, Thomas Stephenson and Paris Brown, ran for the St. Charles City Council but lost. Melvin Washington was appointed to the Missouri Commission on Human Rights by Governor Bond and was a member of the Land Clearance for Redevelopment Authority. Other African-Americans served on appointed boards, but it was not until 1979 that Melvin Washington became the first African-American elected to public office in St. Charles County. He was the leading vote getter in the St. Charles school board election, as he was when re-elected in 1982.[1872]

Politics on the municipal level continued to be non-partisan. There was a discussion of a Home Rule Charter in St. Charles after a survey by the Junior Chamber of Commerce showed that the residents were not happy with street maintenance, transportation or gas rates in 1966.[1873] In April 1967, the voters favored appointment of a Charter Commission and in January 1968 the City Council voted reluctantly to put the proposed charter on the ballot.[1874] The commission adopted a charter that featured a Mayor-Council form of municipal government, which the voters turned down.[1875] Twelve years later, a Charter Commission composed of Ed Pundmann, Shirley Lohmar, Henry J. Wussler, David L. White, George Clemmons, Cleo Holiday, Leo F. Bahr, William T. McCoy, F. Arlene Williams, Mary Jane Schaberg, Frank Niccoli, Earl Roberts and Charles K. Webb, drew up a charter which the voters approved, making St. Charles the first charter city in the county.[1876]

In April 1971, Mayor Henry Vogt, who had not filed for re-election after 16 years as the Mayor of St. Charles, endorsed Frank B. Brockgreitens for that office. The long time city clerk defeated Glennon Bishop and William Shea in the election.[1877] After serving eight years as the city's first full-time mayor, Brockgreitens did not run for re-election. Douglas Boschert was elected mayor of St. Charles in April 1979, vacating his seat as state representative.[1878] In August 1973 the voters approved a $2 million bond issue for a new city hall in downtown St. Charles, designed to blend in with the new Main Street Mall.[1879] The city staff moved into the new city hall in April 1976.[1880]

By now, St. Charles was no longer the only thriving municipality in the county. Six months earlier, St. Peters had also moved to a new city hall in the Cave Springs area. The *Banner-News* commented that, "Like many other communities in St. Charles County, as well as the general St. Louis metropolitan area, St. Peters has felt the pangs of growth, expanding from a sleepy little town of only a few hundred to an up and coming community of several thousand."[1881] Not only was St. Peters growing in population, the assessed valuation in 1972 had grown to $4.7 million from $2.8 million the year before. This allowed the Board of Aldermen to cut the tax-rate 20 cents and still raise almost twice the revenue as the year before.[1882] By the end of the decade the city had 11 parks in use and another under development. In April 1980 Gary Turner was elected to a second term as Mayor of St. Peters.

O'Fallon was also growing, if not as fast as St. Peters. Under the leadership of Mayor Delbert Peters, the residents passed a one-cent sales tax on the fourth try in December 1974,[1883] and the budget for the following year reflected a 50 percent increase.[1884] O'Fallon was laying a good foundation for the rapid growth it experienced in the 1990s. While Lake St. Louis was established in the decade of the 1970s, older communities like Wentzville, Cottleville and Weldon Spring had not yet begun to grow in 1980.

As the 1980 presidential election approached, the *Banner-News* reported that interest rates had reached 15.5 percent, while the people were weary of gas lines, the hostage situation in Iran and high federal taxes.[1885] A large majority of the Evangelical Christians in St. Charles County were now solidly in the Republican camp.[1886] When the Republican platform endorsed the Pro-Life cause, many Democrats began supporting Pro-Life Republicans, at least on the state and national levels. As a result, Republican presidential candidate Ronald Reagan got 63.5 percent in St. Charles County and had extremely long coattails. Christopher Bond returned to the governor's mansion and John Ashcroft was elected attorney general. In the county legislative delegation, Fred Dyer easily regained his old seat and Thomas Barklage retained the seat he had won in a special election when Representative Boschert resigned to become mayor of St. Charles. Veteran Democratic State Representative George Dames narrowly avoided defeat, winning by 60 votes. On the county level, the Republicans picked up the assessor, sheriff and public administrator offices. After twenty-two years of Democratic preeminence with the Republican Party in loyal opposition, the Republican victories in 1980 began a period of Republican predominance in St. Charles County.

C. Building the American Dream

From 1965 to 1980, St. Charles County was one of the fastest growing counties in the nation. No one expected it to grow from 52,970 in 1960 to 144,107 in 1980, requiring new sewer, water, telephone and electric service and roads. The growth was unprecedented and unanticipated by a generation of leaders who had come of age during the Great Depression, when St. Charles was still a small town. No one had a long range plan to meet these needs and there was no consensus on how development should take place. There were a variety of options open to developers who could keep their land unincorporated or be annexed into a city. As a result, each governmental entity had to work with the development community who, theoretically, were reflecting the desires of the public in a free market.

In 1965, most of the land in the county was still dedicated to agriculture. As more and more farms were converted to residential subdivisions, the floodplains represented an ever-increasing percentage of the agricultural land. In October 1965, the Army Corps of Engineers revealed plans for a 45 mile, one million dollar project, to become known as the L-15 Levee, that would extend from St. Charles down the Missouri to the confluence and then up the Mississippi to Portage des Sioux.[1887] In 1967 more than 500 owners of 27,000 acres signed a petition asking the Circuit Court to form the North County Levee District. While the federal government would pay for levee construction, the district was necessary to finance the right-of-way costs for the L-15 and maintain the completed levee.[1888] The landowners elected Herbert Wappelhorst, Stanley Mintert, Ruben Alfred, James Beckman and Marvin Meyer to the first Board of Directors.[1889] In May 1968, Congressman Hungate asked the House of Representatives to include funding in the budget for the L-15 project.[1890] The project was close to being funded until budgetary constraints, brought on by the Vietnam War, caused cancellation of the project in 1972.[1891]

Not only was there no federal assistance for flood protection, but now the federal government began to make it more difficult for farmers to finance and build their own levees. The National Flood Insurance Act became law in 1968 and in 1973 Congress passed another Flood Disaster Protection Act, finding that development was occurring, "…largely as a result of the accelerating development of, and concentration of population in, areas of flood and mudslide hazards. This development was being encouraged by federal agencies and by the availability of federally insured loans, grants and guarantees for land acquisition and construction of floodplain areas."[1892]

There was also a finding that local zoning boards were encouraging development in the floodplain by disregarding flood hazards, such as when the St. Charles County Court had rezoned large areas within the floodplain for trailer parks. Likewise, St. Charles had rezoned an area that had flooded 15 times in ten years even after the city planning department had stated, "it is doubtful whether threatened trailers could be evacuated ahead of a rapidly rising river."[1893] Having enticed people into the flood plain with its loan programs, the federal government now instituted another program to

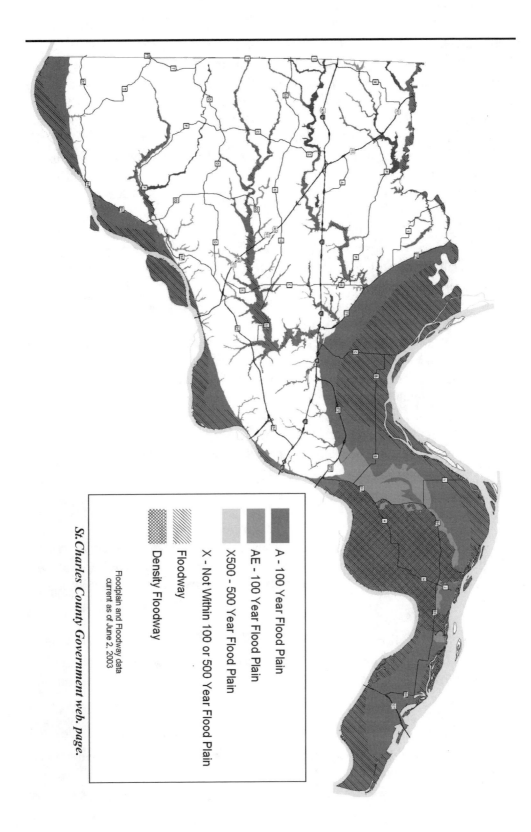

St. Charles County Government web. page.

insure developments against flood loss, and yet another set of regulations to decide what counties would qualify for that insurance program. To become eligible, St. Charles County had to adopt maps designating the 100-year floodplain and a floodway along each river and creek. Anything built within the 100-year floodplain had to have the first floor elevated above the level of the 100-year flood elevation, and within the floodway no building at all, including levees, was allowed. In October 1976, the Corps of Engineers completed the flood hazard maps placing 43 percent of St. Charles County within the 100-year floodplain. When the floodways were drawn, all of the levees in St. Louis County were outside the floodway, while all the levees in St. Charles County were inside the floodway.[1894] As a result, higher levees could be built in St. Charles County only by building new levees outside the floodway, thus increasing the costs of the L-15. At the same time, the levees would now protect fewer acres, thus decreasing the net benefits to be derived from the levees, and significantly altering the cost-benefit ratio.[1895]

If the county did not enforce its ordinance, it could be denied federal flood assistance, including the flood insurance program.[1896] Some homeowners had already become quite attached to the flood insurance program that allowed them to purchase a policy five days before the water got into their homes and still collect on the policy. In February 1977 a committee of the St. Charles City Council recommended that the city also adopt floodplain ordinances as well, which it soon did.

Since this was a tremendous expansion of federal power in the area of land use that had previously been a state and local matter, the St. Charles County Court waited until pushed by FEMA before it passed an ordinance putting the regulations into effect. In September 1979, a *Post-Dispatch* editorial stated:

> By its failure to adopt floodplain building codes, St. Charles County's administrative court is subverting the obvious public interest in the ready availability of flood insurance. For absent codes controlling construction in the floodplain, the federal flood insurance program will be unavailable to residents of the county's unincorporated areas and existing policies will not be renewed.[1897]

After the 1973 flood, there was the usual flurry of activity and talk by the levee district about not waiting for the federal government but raising the levees itself. Counsel for the North County Levee District, Theodore Bruere Jr., stated, "We've been depending on the government all these years, and we can't do that anymore."[1898] The *Banner-News* announced in April 1974 that the L-15 levee plan was still alive in Congress, even though the previous February the Corps of Engineers had indicated that a new cost-benefit analysis had indicated that the cost of the project made it unfeasible.[1899] While farmers fought for flood protection, another flood of people was inundating St. Charles County. McDonnell Aircraft continued to employ many of them. In 1963, expanded work on the Gemini and Phantom programs were expected to in-

In 1980 General Motors announced plans to built this assembly plant in Wentzville.
St. Charles County Journals

crease the total work force at "Mac" to 29,500, record employment up to that time.[1900]
Two years after Sterling Aluminum moved its operations to Malden, Missouri, McDonnell
Aircraft moved a large number of employees to Sterling's former facility in St. Charles.[1901]
In 1973, McDonnell Aircraft hired an additional 200 employees at the facility, which was
heavily involved in flight simulation.[1902] By 1974 the payroll stood at 1,000 and the facility
was in the third year of a contract with the military to build missiles.[1903]

By 1970, many industries were leaving St. Louis and building new facilities in the
suburbs. As part of this national trend, as early as 1963, more than half of the industrial
employment in the U.S. was in the suburbs. By 1981, two-thirds of industrial production
took place in "industrial parks" in the suburbs where, because of improvements in communications, companies no longer had to have their entire operation centralized.[1904] With
political and business leaders going to great lengths to attract new industry, the St. Charles
County zoning ordinance was amended in 1970 to allow for District M-3, Planned Industrial Park District.[1905] The St. Charles Industrial Development Corporation was formed to
help attract and finance industrial development in the county, and by 1966 three new companies had been established employing 245 persons with a $1 million payroll. Twenty-five
local business people formed the Crossroads Economic Development Corporation in 1976.
With Norbert Wappelhorst as its president, Crossroads teamed with local banks to provide the local financing for federal Small Business Administration loans.[1906]

A bigger boost for economic development in the county came in 1980 when General Motors rejected an offer from St. Louis Mayor James Conway to keep its assembly plant in St. Louis, opening the way for the plant's move to a site near Wentzville.[1907] Under the leadership of co-chairmen Henry J. Elmendorf and Charles W. Boswell, "St. Charles County Citizens for GM" raised $90,000 from local business people to promote the passage of a bond issue to build sewers and roads for the plant. The voters gave the proposal 80 percent approval,[1908] and construction of the 500-million dollar plant began just west of what had been the town of Gilmore. With regard to Gilmore, the *History of St. Charles County* had stated in 1885, "One or two business houses and a few dwellings comprise the town. The location is excellent, and in time Gilmore will undoubtedly become quite a thriving place."[1909] Even though the railroad had been abandoned in 1932, the prophesy came true when General Motors completed its plant, increasing the assessed valuation of St. Charles County by almost a third.

This success yielded the first grumbling from St. Louis that perhaps St. Charles County's success was hurting them. *The Post-Dispatch* wrote:

> By chance, groundbreaking for the new $300 million General Motors assembly plant in St. Charles County coincided with the announcement by Hunter Packing company that it intends to close its 75-year old East St. Louis plant - evidently as part of a plan to build a new facility in St. Charles County. GM is abandoning a 59-year old plant in St. Louis. So in each case, exurban St. Charles County stands to expand its tax base and economy at the expense of the two long-developed communities.[1910]

These complaints intensified when the 1980 census showed that the entire St. Louis Region, including St. Charles County, had experienced a net out-migration approaching 200,000 individuals. The region was no longer growing, only spreading out.

Not only was industry moving to St. Charles County, but the nature of the economy was changing. Daniel Bell first published *Coming of the Post Industrial Society* in 1976. He predicted the emergence of an economy based on information instead of goods, characterized by the growth of a knowledge class, a new emphasis on services, and the emergence of the university, over the business firm, as a source of technical innovation. In St. Charles County, a major step in this transformation took place in 1974, when the Board of Curators announced that the University of Missouri would develope a research park on land at Weldon Springs. It marked the beginning of what would become a "high-tech corridor" along Highway 40 between Weldon Spring and Wentzville.

In St. Charles County, 100-acre farms, that had been carved out of the 1,000-acre "plantations" 100 years earlier, were now further sub-divided into residential lots. The infrastructure had to be provided to these subdivisions. In some cases the law was clear how that was to be accomplished. When the volume of mail justified it, a new Post Office was dedicated in St. Charles in 1964.[1911] The federal government also provided millions indirectly through road, sewer and water project grants that were administered through state and local governments. But direct federal involvement was minimal.

The state, through its Public Service Commission, regulated electric and telephone utilities. Southwestern Bell now had a regulated monopoly in eastern St. Charles County, except for the few hundred customers served by the Orchard Farm Telephone Company. The Continental Telephone Company, with its headquarters in Wentzville, had a regulated monopoly in the western part of the county. Union Electric and Cuivre River Electric Cooperative provided electricity to St. Charles County under the supervision of the PSC. These companies all had exclusive franchises and were mandated to provide service when a new residential development was built. They built the infrastructure needed and the PSC authorized them to recover the costs in their rate structure. To meet the increased demand for electricity, Union Electric let the first contract on a new $70 million coal-burning power plant in Portage des Sioux in April 1963.

The state also regulated the building of health care facilities. In the early 1970s the Missouri Office of Health Planning denied the Sisters of St. Mary permission to build a satellite hospital in the western part of the county. The request was denied a second time in July 1974 and Christian Northwest was also turned down for a facility in the same area.[1912] St. Peters Community Hospital, a for-profit facility, was approved and opened its door on March 1, 1980, even though critics insisted that the additional 120 hospital beds were not needed.[1913] St Joseph's conducted a major renovation and expansion of its St. Charles facility, raising the total beds at that facility to 403 when completed in 1978.[1914] Parkside Meadows, a retirement village next to Blanchette Park, sponsored by St. John United Church of Christ, was also approved by the state.

Roads and bridges were another important infrastructure need, making highway decisions by the state very important to the future of St. Charles County. As residential growth continued with most of the jobs still in St. Louis County, "rush hour" traffic became a nightmare. The situation worsened in 1963 when the City Council allowed St. Charles Transit Company to discontinue bus service.[1915] Ten years later, Mayor Frank Brockgreitens urged the Norfolk and Western Railroad to build a rapid transit line from St. Charles to the McDonnell Aircraft facilities near Lambert Airport. But the railroad's freight lines were highly profitable and it did not wish to get into the mass transit business. Nevertheless, Brockgreitens stated, "you simply cannot build enough highways to take care of the future needs of automobiles, you can't concrete the whole world. The right-of-way is here and we think it should be utilized."[1916] Nevertheless, the county was left out of the mass transit plan adopted by the East-West Gateway Coordinating Council in January 1974.[1917]

A lot more of St. Charles County was concreted as residential growth in the area west and south of St. Charles made road improvements necessary. While a section of I-70 finally opened between the cities of St. Charles and St. Peters, Highway 94

South was still a two-lane road with an almost-continuous traffic jam. Protests to the State Highway Commission intensified for speedy completion of a widened highway, and the commission approved a $2.97 million highway plan for St. Charles County in 1964. The contract for the work on Highway 94 between I-70 and Weldon Spring was awarded to Bernard McMenamy Contractors of St. Charles in July 1968. Once completed it attracted even more residential growth to the Highway 94 corridor.[1918]

In 1973, the State Highway Commission approved construction of a second I-70 bridge, a Brown Road extension from St. Louis County, and "tentative location approval" for a Page Avenue extension into St. Charles County.[1919] However, by 1976, the last two projects were running into trouble. In April 1976, Page and Brown Road were dropped from the active planning program of the highway department for, "lack of funds and negative comments resulting from an 'unprecedented action' by the East-West Gateway Coordinating Council in reviewing the proposed project." Presiding Judge Lee Schwendemann complained about being outvoted on these projects for St. Charles County, as the rest of the region was becoming concerned about growth in St. Charles County.[1920] East-West Gateway actually recommended that, "the number of lanes and access be reduced to control development."[1921]

The Missouri River Bridges Committee, originally formed in 1973 to lobby for bridges, was reactivated in 1977 when the County Court passed a resolution calling for the completion of the Page Avenue Bridge before the Brown Road Bridge. Interests in St. Charles then formed a committee to lobby for Brown Road, pointing out it would help bring industrial, as well as residential, development to the county. They also pointed out that it was estimated by East-West Gateway that Brown Road Bridge would take 26 percent of the traffic off I-70 in 1995, as opposed to 17 percent for a Page Avenue Bridge.[1922] In 1978, the Missouri River Bridges committee was commissioned to compile facts about the two bridges and the relative merits of each. The committee, chaired by Representative Douglas Boschert, raised $10,000 for the study that concluded the Brown Road was preferable without actually endorsing it. Actually, the next bridge built across the Missouri River in St. Charles County was a companion bridge to the Highway 40-61 Bridge at Weldon Spring, which entered its initial design stage in 1978.[1923]

Local road improvements were also needed in St. Charles County. In May 1975 county voters turned down a $10.3 million bond issue for road improvements that would have been built primarily in St. Peters and the newer neighborhoods of St. Charles. Needing a two-thirds majority, the issue failed, receiving only 46.3 percent countywide. The *Banner-News* explained:

> The road bond issue appeared to be decided strictly along parochial lines, with the St. Peters area for the most part going for the proposal, while west, north and south county areas, along with St. Charles, said no. The proposal called for sale of the $10.3 million in bonds to finance numerous major projects. A majority of the projects were in the city limits of St.

Peters. St. Charles, as the largest city in the county, was to receive about $2 million of the total in benefits, while obviously paying the larger share of taxes to retire the bonds[1924]

While paved highways, telephones and electric service had not even existed 60 years earlier, the state had procedures for their orderly establishment. Sewer and water utilities had been around for a much longer time but there was less state regulation and a number of ways for the new subdivisions to obtain these utilities. Federal regulations became stiffer with regard to sewers in the 1960s and cities like St. Charles were forced to quit dumping raw sewage into the Missouri River. In 1965 the city planned to build a $2.27 million sewage treatment plant on the Mississippi River, for which the federal government would provide 30 percent of the funding.[1925] A smaller treatment plant north of town handled sewage in the Missouri River drainage area. When, after three tries, a sewer bond issue failed to pass, the state Water Pollution Control Board ordered that no new connections be made to the existing system that was pouring sewage into a lagoon at Elm Point. The ban on new development was not lifted until the bond issue was finally approved in April 1967.[1926] In 1972, St. Charles began pumping water from three new wells in the Elm Point area that produced 4.5 million gallons of water per day. They were part of a $1.25 million water works improvement program.[1927]

St. Charles had solved its sewer and water problem. However, by 1963 new residential construction in unincorporated St. Charles County was fast approaching the $6.5 million in residential building in St. Charles.[1928] Who would provide sewer and water to the growing areas surrounding the city? There were five options. The first was to incorporate new subdivisions as new municipalities. A second was for St. Charles to annex the new residential areas and extend its sewers and water to those areas. The third option was to have the county or special use districts provide utilities to subdivisions in unincorporated areas. The fourth option was for private companies, supervised by the Public Service Commission, provide sewer and water. The final option was for smaller towns like St. Peters and O'Fallon to build their own sewer and water systems, extending them to the surrounding residential growth areas after annexation.

In August 1959, it seemed that new incorporations might occur. Residents of Westwinds Subdivision, responding to a proposal to triple the size of St. Charles by pushing its boundaries to Friedens Road on the south, Zumbehl Road on the west and the Wabash Railroad on the north, presented the County Court with a petition to incorporate as a village. Two days later, it denied the petition, finding it not "reasonable."[1929] The court then denied a similar petition to incorporate Hi-Point Acres as a village.[1930] These types of defensive incorporations had been common in St. Louis County in the late 1940s and early 1950s, when over 50 incorporations took place over a seven-year period, most of them to avoid annexation by a larger municipality.[1931] Aware of this precedent, the *Banner-News* warned against the "feudal-like patchwork of municipalities present in St. Louis County now."[1932] By denying these small incorporations, the County Court allowed existing municipalities to grow sufficiently to provide real municipal services, including professional planning departments.

Defensive incorporations were discouraged further by the state legislature in 1973 when it prohibited new incorporations within two miles of an existing city limit.[1933] Nevertheless, the developers and residents around a large lake that had been formed by damming Peruque Creek at I-70 were afraid O'Fallon or Wentzville would involuntarily annex them. However, only a small commercial development on that lake, Harbor Town, was more than two miles from either of those municipalities so they filed a petition to incorporate Harbor Town. After the court approved the incorporation in 1975, Harbor Town annexed the residential property around the lake in April 1976 and changed its name to Lake St. Louis in July of that year. By 1977 the city achieved fourth-class status and George Heidelbaugh was elected the first mayor. Within a year the city developed Freymuth Park, adopted a comprehensive zoning ordinance and hired a city manager.[1934]

In 1964, Missouri statutes allowed incorporation only of an unincorporated "city," "town," or "village." Case law made it clear that some sort of community had to exist or the area could not be incorporated.[1935] St. Charles, St. Peters, Portage des Sioux, Cottleville and others had existed as communities before they were incorporated. In 1978 the General Assembly amended section 72.080 RSMo. to also allow incorporation of "other areas." The Missouri Supreme Court made it clear that, "This section is no longer limited to incorporation of unincorporated cities or towns."[1936] Among the "other areas" that now sought incorporation was Dardenne Prairie, where the residents, wanting large lot zoning and fearing annexation by O'Fallon, incorporated the Town of Dardenne Prairie. As the 1970s ended, the question was whether new municipalities like Lake St. Louis and Dardenne Prairie would become communities and grow to sufficient size to function as full-service municipalities.

As the 1960s began, it looked as though most residential growth in St. Charles County would occur, not through new incorporations, but by St. Charles annexing new subdivisions and providing them sewer and water. The *Banner-News* published an editorial entitled, "St. Charles Must Expand." It stated, "Subdivisions located around the city didn't just happen to be built there by accident. They were built there because the city was here. Residents are close enough to the city to utilize advantages of the city."[1937] The same attitude, that municipal citizenship was something granted by the city, whether the residents of the area to be incorporated wanted it or not, had led to statutes that required that a city had only to pass an ordinance to annex a tract of land. In 1953 the General Assembly had passed the Sawyer Act requiring a municipality to prove in a Circuit Court proceeding that the annexation was "reasonable and necessary to the proper development of said city," and that it could "furnish normal municipal services" within "a reasonable time."[1938] While a circuit judge could now provide some protection for the people living in the area to be annexed, they still were not allowed to vote on their fate. If the court approved the annexation, only a majority of city voters voting in the election were needed for approval.

In February 1961, St. Charles had annexed a large portion of the Cole Creek drainage area and proposed a bond issue to build sewers and a treatment plant. Showing some concern for the residents in the newly annexed area, the *Banner-News* editorialized that, since the people of the newly created fifth ward would be retiring the bonds and they had yet to elect a member to the City Council, perhaps the election should be put off until they did.[1939] Annexation became controversial in December 1965, when St. Charles proposed to annex an area bounded by Highway 94, Highway B, Mueller Road and Ehlmann Road. The proposal would have nearly doubled the city's size and brought in potential industrial areas that the city would make attractive to industry by providing sewers and water.[1940] The North St. Charles Improvement Association opposed annexation to the north, wondering why the city did not expand in non-floodplain areas to the south. Alluding to the fact that Mayor Vogt was the owner of the St. Charles Golf Course, its leader asked, "Could it be that some of the city officials and other very influential people in the community live, or own property in these areas in the southern part of the county."[1941] In October 1967, the city agreed to take sewage from the area south of I-70 to be treated in the plant on the north end of the city, allowing a sewerage lagoon that had become a nuisance because of its odors, to be eliminated.[1942] Then, in November 1967 Councilman Joseph Briscoe made a motion to annex areas south of the city, comprising about 30 subdivisions and 6,000 to 7,000 people. The motion failed by a five to four vote. The *Banner-News* reported that Mayor Vogt "was obviously dismayed at the proposal," and that, "Some councilmen have expressed fear that there is a change in state law that would make annexation of the populated area south of the city impossible if it is delayed until 1970 as recommended."[1943] The change that they feared, giving the people in the area to be annexed the right to vote, was not passed by the general assembly for another ten years.[1944]

Annexation controversies resumed in 1970 when St. Charles decided to annex St. Charles Hills, Mark Twain and Mamelle Hills, all established subdivisions, as part of a 5,843-acre annexation. Opponents threatened to take the issue of their disenfranchisement all the way to the State Supreme Court.[1945] Not only did they oppose additional municipal taxes, but there was another factor at work. The *Banner-News* described the opposition of one man as follows:

> He explains that he left Florissant for an unincorporated area at least partly because he didn't like restrictive ordinances. Fourth of July fireworks and sparklers are forbidden in Florissant, he says. He notes another ordinance that would forbid parking pick-up trucks on city streets. "They try to pass these silly little ordinances and they don't mean anything," he says.[1946]

While St. Charles had often been reluctant to annex in the 1960s, by the 1970s the city was ready but it had waited too long, as other options had opened to developers. Cities no longer grew block by block and the interstate highway allowed commuters to skip over high-priced land and go further out with only a slightly longer commute. By the 1970s developers were not building on the outskirts of St. Charles but were developing new subdivisions in St. Peters, O'Fallon, Lake St. Louis or unincorporated areas of the county.

New residents of those areas did not come into St. Charles to shop, unless it was for antiques on South Main Street. In 1829, Hezekiah Simmons, a St. Louis merchant, had invested $17,000 to open a store in St. Peters. By 1981, St. Louis companies had invested a lot more to build Mid-Rivers Mall in St. Peters. The mall and the additional development it encouraged made St. Peters the commercial heart of the county. As much of St. Charles County's industrial development during the 1970s occurred in O'Fallon, it became clear that the county would eventually have several cities as big, or bigger, than St. Charles.[1947] Unfortunately, this had not been obvious to the St. Charles leadership in the early 1960s. They believed that the older residential neighborhoods, as they had in the growth of industrial cities earlier, would give way to multi-family and commercial development. Many old homes were divided into apartments or, worse yet, torn down for commercial strip malls.[1948] This unfortunate trend accelerated during the energy crisis in 1973 when many Victorian homes with their high ceilings were no longer profitable as apartments and were torn down to make way for commercial strip centers or gas stations.[1949] The timing was unfortunate as St. Charles was just beginning to appreciate the importance of its historical buildings.

The St. Charles Historical Society, formed in 1956 to call attention to the city's heritage, had established its first permanent quarters at 515 South Main in 1962.[1950] In April 1964, the Historical Society unanimously passed a resolution, offered by Dr. Homer Clevenger, Chairman of the History Department at Lindenwood College and chairman of the First State Capitol Commission, urging the creation of an historic district in the vicinity of the First State Capitol.[1951] In 1965, the city renamed Clay Street "First Capitol Drive" and the following year an historic district was established. Demolition or alteration of buildings in the district was prohibited without approval.[1952]

Inspired by the restoration of the First State Capitol on South Main Street, many individuals began restoring the beautiful old homes of the city.[1953] Since 1921, when an historical marker had been placed on the old building as part of the state's centennial celebration, various organizations had kept alive the idea of restoration. In 1959 the state purchased the three original capitol buildings for $39,000 and a First Capitol Commission was formed. After almost a decade of lobbying and construction, the restored First State Capitol was opened to the public in the early 1970s.[1954]

In September 1975, the Planning and Zoning Commission of St. Charles recommended a landmarks ordinance that would have required approval by a Landmark Preservation Board before changes could be made to a building. However, under the ordinance the board could not take jurisdiction without the owner's agreement, which reduced its power.[1955] Finally passed in 1976, an ordinance covering all historic structures gave the board the necessary power, but stilled allow owners to appeal decisions to the City Council. One of the first actions by the board was to conduct a survey of the entire city to determine what structures were historically significant.[1956] Before all this was in place, many historic structures were lost to the wrecking ball. The Land Clearance for Redevelopment Authority even tore down some homes for a parking lot for the city hall.

When a redevelopment plan for North Main was proposed in 1977 that would have turned the street into a pedestrian mall, one-half of the Main Street merchants opposed it and the other half favored it.[1957] The mall was completed in October 1979, with parking in a city hall garage and along Riverside Drive.[1958] This did not bring shoppers back to Main Street, even after the city advertised to assure downtown visitors that the garage was a convenient and safe place to park.[1959]

While St. Charles was rediscovering its historical past, the rest of the county continued to boom. The county's assessed valuation reached $300 million in 1974, qualifying it as a first class county. In January 1975 the county's population had risen 20.4 percent since the 1970 census.[1960] During the 1970s at least four large developments, each incorporating single, multi-family and commercial components, were built in unincorporated areas of the county. They included the St. Charles Hills, Heritage and Park

Douglas Boschert served as presiding judge of the county, state representative, and mayor of St. Charles. *Manual of the State of Missouri*

Charles subdivisions. The largest and most ambitious was Lake St. Louis, a 3,000-acre plus development by R.T. Crow. To meet the needs of these developments either the county, special districts or private companies would have to respond.

The county formed Water District No. 2 in 1967 to serve the southwest portion of the county. The county bought the Weldon Spring water plant and contracted with Missouri Cities Water Company to extend water services to the county. In 1972, 82 percent of those voting authorized the creation of a Regional Sewer District to develop a master plan to build sewers in St. Charles County. The Board of the RSD put a $12.8 million bond issue on the ballot and worked with the municipalities to get their support for the bond issue.[1961] Two weeks before the election, RSD reached an agreement with St. Peters, allowing the municipality to serve the parts of the Dardenne Creek drainage area that were in the city's growth pattern. The city agreed to use the Dardenne Creek treatment plant to be built by RSD.[1962]

RSD and St. Charles disagreed about the Duckett Creek watershed, currently being served by a privately owned facility. RSD wanted to build a regional plant for the watershed while St. Charles wanted to serve the area from its Missouri River plant north of the city. The proposed compromise was to leave the future of the Duckett Creek watershed up to the Missouri Clean Water Commission and to sell back to the city its sewer lines at cost, and remove any charges against the residents, should the area they serve be annexed into the city. Of course there was a dilemma for the cities; once people had sewers, why would they agree to be annexed? Therefore, St. Charles and O'Fallon came out against the proposal. RSD supporters asked:

> Should a few officials jeopardize the position of all other cities in the District who have much to gain, many of which cannot afford to build the plants that RSD will build? Should a few officials jeopardize RSD's grant application and the public's chances to get $29,000,000 and let it go down the drain or better yet – into the lagoons? …Let those who want to defeat this project be accountable to the public for ultimate increased costs if they are successful in killing this project. Let them be accountable for disease or building moratoriums if this happens![1963]

The Banner-News endorsed the proposal and pointed out that as little as $7 million would be needed to meet the county's one-fourth share, with the state and federal government paying the balance.[1964] Presiding Judge Douglas Boschert tried to assure voters in St. Charles that their rates would not go up. Opponents distributed literature claiming they would, and the bond issue lost by a two-to-one margin in November 1973. The next day the *Banner-News* stated, "St. Charles County is the fifth fastest growing county in the entire country. This tremendous influx of people is not going to stop, and problems of increasing density in population are not going to get any better. Our county is polluted – and we must clean it up or face more serious threats in the future."[1965]

Douglas Boschert warned in 1974 that the biggest task confronting St. Charles County was to achieve cooperation between the county and its cities to avoid duplication of services and improve efficiency. He said, "We must unite. We are jealous of each other. The real problem, however, is that there is a duplication of services."[1966] Ambulance service was one example. In 1974 the local mortuaries announced that they would be discontinuing ambulance service. Residents filed a petition with the county clerk asking that a tax-supported ambulance district be formed. After the filing, but before its approval in November 1974, St. Charles began providing ambulance service through its fire department. To this day, the taxpayers of St. Charles pay twice for ambulance service.[1967]

There was much better cooperation on other issues. Since the city and county library districts both charged the same tax rate, on October 1, 1967 the two entered into a reciprocal agreement where patrons of each district could use the resources of the other. Later the two merged into the St. Charles City-County Library District.[1968] Special districts met the need in the area for fire service. The St. Charles Fire Protection

District had been organized in 1947 to protect the area surrounding St. Charles. In 1971 the St. Peters Volunteer Department petitioned the County Court to hold an election to create a tax-supported fire district. The St. Peters Fire Protection District was created, hiring its first full-time professional fire fighter in 1980. Fire Protection Districts were also formed in Wentzville (1971), Cottleville (1972), O'Fallon and Lake St. Louis.[1969]

Where public agencies failed, private utilities met the developer's needs for sewer and water. The *Banner-News* reported in 1974, "Private utility companies have grown up in St. Charles County because of the inability of the public sector to provide services to outlying areas. There were 16 private sewer and water utilities in the county last year."[1970] Disputes often arose between these utilities and the municipalities. In 1972, when St. Charles tried to annex the Cave Springs area, property owners and the Missouri

Another member of the "Greatest Generation," Henry Elmendorf, was an effective civic, charitable and church leader.

Cities Water Company intervened and held the matter up for two years until the city withdrew its petitions in November 1974.[1971] At the same time, the Missouri Cities Water Company appealed a Circuit Court opinion that allowed a municipality to provide utility services into an area served by a private corporation. In 1972, the County Court created the Duckett Creek Sewer District, and in October 1977, 11 percent of the eligible voters in the Harvester area turned out to vote for a Duckett Creek Sewer District bond issue by a ten-one margin. Most of the $2.5 million bond issue was used to purchase the privately owned St. Charles County Utilities and St. Charles County Water and Waste. The private utilities had no future since they were not eligible for state and federal funding grants. With a public district the customers would be eligible for up to 90 percent federal and state funding. With a public district tap-on fees dropped from $800 to $400.[1972]

Where new incorporations, St. Charles, county government, private utility or special district failed, St. Peters and O'Fallon met the challenges of growth. Federal funding was important to the development of St. Peters. Developer Robert McKelvey said in 1977, "St. Peters had the foresight to begin applying for grants to expand water and sewer facilities a long time ago."[1973] St. Peters had voted to become a fourth-class city in August 1959. In January 1964 the city had annexed 100 acres.[1974] Having grown from 900 in 1955 to 2000 in 1959 and expecting to double the size of the

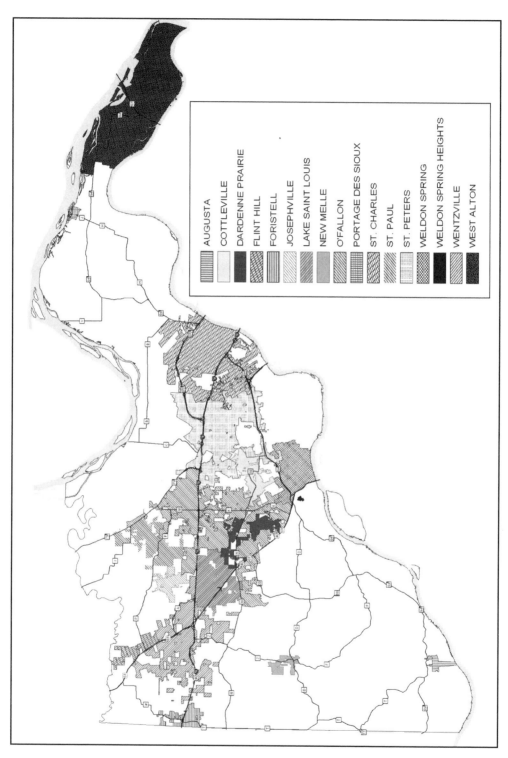

The legend includes:
AUGUSTA, COTTLEVILLE, DARDENNE PRAIRIE, FLINT HILL, FORISTELL, JOSEPHVILLE, LAKE SAINT LOUIS, NEW MELLE, OFALLON, PORTAGE DES SIOUX, ST. CHARLES, ST. PAUL, ST. PETERS, WELDON SPRING, WELDON SPRING HEIGHTS, WENTZVILLE, WEST ALTON

The process of annexation has created the above municipal corporate boundaries in St. Charles County in 2004. *St. Charles County Web Page*

city through annexation, O'Fallon had passed a bond issue in 1959 to expand its sewer and waterworks facilities.[1975]

O'Fallon, already a fourth-class city, had annexed 430 acres in 1959, and another 890 acres in 1967.[1976] It also took over the management of 27 private sewer facilities serving subdivisions in the Peruque Creek area, prompting a growth spurt south of I-70 that continued into the 1980s.[1977] When Lake St. Louis was developed, R.T. Crow and Citizens Mortgage Investment Trust built and owned the sewer system with a contract that allowed the county to buy the facilities. When the county threatened to exercise its option, the residents of Lake St. Louis passed a $3 million bond issue to purchase the sewers.[1978] St. Peters became the boomtown of St. Charles County in the 1970s, growing from 600 residents in 1970 to 10,500 in 1979. In 1977, 1299 building permits were issued by St. Peters, compared to 94 building permits issued by St. Charles, 132 by Lake St. Louis, 132 by Wentzville and 39 by O'Fallon.[1979]

As in St. Charles, involuntary annexations were often unpopular. In 1978 O'Fallon tried to annex 16,000 acres of farmland to the northeast. A judge ruled in favor of the opposing landowners but he was reversed on appeal. O'Fallon voters, responding to the resistance of the farmers in the area to be annexed, failed to give the measure the majority it needed at the election.[1980] Municipal growth was greatly expedited when, in 1973, the General Assembly enacted legislation allowing voluntary annexations if property owners and city were in agreement. Under this statute St. Charles annexed land in its commons in 1974 by petitioning itself, since the city was the fee simple owner of the land.[1981] A developer could now agree to annexation in return for the city agreeing to provide sewer and water. The Missouri Cities Water Company failed in court to have the statute declared unconstitutional because it applied to only three counties.[1982] Thereafter, St. Peters, O'Fallon and Wentzville used this approach almost exclusively, rarely resorting to the involuntary process of Section 71.015.

Many were concerned that annexations had become less a matter of who was going to provide sewer and water, than who was going to control land use and get the tax revenue from existing and future commercial development. Citizens formed a committee in 1974 to fight "land grabbing" by municipalities and discussed a model statute with State Representative Fred Dyer. Since the statute allowing voluntary annexations went into effect the previous year, St. Peters had annexed 2,100 acres. Efforts by St. Charles to annex St. Charles Hills, Mark Twain Hills and the St. Andrews Shopping Center and golf course met resistance.[1983] In 1979, St. Charles tried again to annex land down to Jungs Station Road, citing the rapid development in the South 94 corridor.[1984] *The Post-Dispatch* applauded,

> Beyond that, the crazy-quilt municipal development that is so distressing a feature of St. Louis County's appearance, particularly along Natural Bridge Road, is a living museum of the kind of urban development that the City of St. Charles, by intelligent use of the annexation statutes, can help St. Charles County to avoid. Perhaps an ideal pattern for development of that exurban

county would be one in which its unincorporated territory would be composed largely of a few contiguous incorporated municipalities. That way, the cost of strictly municipal functions would be charged only to those property owners who lived in the cities and benefited from the services that each provided. Everyone in St. Louis County pays the cost of servicing that county's built up unincorporated areas; which of course is unfair.[1985]

Residents of unincorporated areas complained that only in first class charter counties like St. Louis and Jackson were residents allowed to vote on whether they should be annexed. Residents of Belleau Lakes Estates, Sunny Meadows and Dardenne Lakes Estates subdivisions combined to challenge annexation by St. Peters, claiming it was unconstitutional since they did not get to vote on the matter. A bill before the General Assembly required a majority vote in the area to be annexed. A compromise bill passed in which annexation was allowed if majorities were obtained in the city and the area to be annexed on the first vote. If not, a second combined two-thirds vote of municipal residents and those in the area to be annexed would authorize the annexation. While Mayors of both St. Peters and St. Charles criticized the bill, Mayor Douglas Boschert said, "If you can't convince a majority of those people to be annexed that it will be a benefit to come into the city, then I don't think they should be forced into the city." St. Peters Mayor Gary Turner predicted that the growth of the city would be "seriously hampered," by the bill.[1986]

Before 1980, developers, who survived in business only by giving purchasers what they wanted, had several options in developing raw ground. Neither cities nor county anticipated the extent of the growth, and both lacked a clear vision of how to control it. Even if they had, it would have been difficult to impose it so long as the developer had other options. Professor E. Terrence Jones, in his work *Fragmented by Design*, discusses the theories of Charles Tiebolt, Vincent Ostrom and Robert Warren, who believe, "multiplicity of governments promotes choice, a value exceedingly compatible with American individualism."[1987] Jones continues, stating, "The ability of citizens to select locations within a metropolitan region causes the many governments to compete to have them live, work, and shop within their jurisdictions. Multiplicity engages the forces of the market place and the outcome is a greater public good. Instead of generating chaos, fragmentation creates choice."[1988]

Some argue that the fragmentation in St. Louis County was so extreme that many of the municipalities were too small to function. In St. Charles County, with most of the municipalities of sufficient size, this dynamic certainly kept the cities and county more responsive to the marketplace. If there was a demand for high-density development and the county was not receptive, the developer could volunteer to be annexed into a city that might be more amenable. At the same time, elected officials had to be responsive to the wishes of residents who were already there and interested in how new development would impact their property. The lawsuits and political disputes, in the end, generally gave the people what most of them wanted, even if it was imperfect.

One reason St. Charles was reluctant to annex in the 1960s was the investment in infrastructure required by the city. Residential development often did not generate enough tax revenue to pay for those investments. What early leaders did not realize was that commercial development would follow and sales taxes generated would more than pay for the initial infrastructure. In 1975, St. Peters announced a $20 million development plan for the Cave Springs area that included a 150-room hotel.[1989] Construction activity for the first six months of 1977 equaled total construction in 1976. By 1977, 4900 acres had been annexed to the city's original 166 acres and commercial enterprises were following the residential growth. *The Banner-News* reported,

> These figures represent the highest concentration of building activity in the county. The only area that approaches that kind of activity is in the Harvester area, and the reason seems to be availability of land and utility services, coupled with public willingness to buy after the construction doldrums of 1974-75."[1990]

In 1978, the May Company planned to build a regional shopping mall in St. Peters.[1991] A successful $3.5 million bond issue in 1978 paid for roads leading to the site, including Mid-Rivers Mall Drive. In 1981 Famous-Barr opened a store in the mall. The St. Peters water plant's capacity was doubled to 6 million gallons per day in 1980. Discussions began about flood protection for the city's old town. The 1980 census put the population of St. Peters at 15, 691, an increase of over 3,100 percent since the 1970 census count of 486.[1992]

While St. Charles was rediscovering its history and St. Peters was expanding, the most significant regional debate in the 1970s involved the future of Lambert International Airport. In 1971, a study authorized by the Missouri legislature looked at potential sites for a new airport. Of the eleven sites considered for study, five were in St. Charles County. A similar study had already recommended the Waterloo, Illinois site to the Metropolitan Airport Authority. Several of the county sites were promising because they did not require construction of additional roads.[1993] When environmentalists objected to the expansion of Smartt Field, the study chose a site on Dardenne prairie, in what became southern O'Fallon, as the best for a new airport in Missouri. Although 25 miles from downtown St. Louis, the site was served by 40-61 and I-70.[1994] While the *Banner-News* endorsed the concept, the East-West Gateway Coordinating Council voted 13-7 to recommend the Illinois site, even though 15 million of the 17.5 million annual passengers using the facility would be from Missouri.[1995] The Columbia-Waterloo site was favored by Mayor Alfonso Cervantes of St. Louis, even though 77 percent of the users lived in Missouri, and users' dollars paid for airport improvements.[1996] So when Atlanta, Dallas-Fort Worth, and even Kansas City were making the decision to build new airports on the outskirts of their cities,

St. Louis was trying to move the airport to Illinois and others were fighting to expand Lambert. The Citizen's Committee to Save Lambert was chaired by August A. Busch Jr., and Henry Elmendorf, Chairman of the Missouri Airport Authority, endorsed its efforts.[1997]

In November 1972, when a non-binding referendum asked the voters in St. Charles County whether they preferred an expansion of Lambert Field or a new airport in Illinois, 97 percent voted for expansion.[1998] Planners in 1970 had anticipated 23.6 million passengers through Lambert by 1995, but a new forecast predicted 11.2 million passengers instead. Expansion backers argued that, with bigger planes, the number of flights would not increase significantly.[1999] However, a committee of the Regional Commerce and Growth Association (RCGA) predicted that Lambert Airport would be obsolete within 14 years rather than the 25 years previously reported.[2000] In 1975 the *Banner-News* pointed out:

> During this time, some have continually pointed to the new Kansas City Airport as the example we should follow- a new modern, large airport which is certain to make Kansas City a major transportation center. It is also interesting to note that the airport was built in Missouri, not Kansas. There is a good lesson there.[2001]

On September 1, 1976, the federal Department of Transportation ruled in favor of the Columbia-Waterloo site, stating that the Illinois site, "will have substantially less adverse environmental consequences in terms of noise than would an expanded Lambert alternative or even the present alternative."[2002] Henry Elmendorf stated,

> It is absurd to have a federal czar from Washington come to St. Louis and expect the airport users of this region to accept the fact that their airport is moved from Missouri to Illinois, and in the same breath tell them this is not what they want to hear but that it is good for them and expect the people to swallow this type of Washington bureaucracy.[2003]

Lawsuits were filed but the courts upheld the secretary's action. In March 1977 the new Carter administration reversed the previous decision and halted funding for the Illinois airport. Elmendorf pointed out that 25 percent of the people who worked at the airport lived in St. Charles County and he maintained that the loss of Lambert would have been a disaster for the local economy.[2004] Lambert Airport was expanded instead of building a new airport.

In 1980, the economic future of St. Charles County seemed bright. It continued to have the advantage of a major metropolitan airport ten minutes from the county seat. St. Charles had become a leader in historic renovation while St. Peters was the fastest growing city in the state. Because of its soils, transportation and local governments, the county was becoming the favorite location for new development over other collar counties in the St. Louis metropolitan area. Continued growth over the next two decades brought benefits and new challenges to St. Charles County.

VIII
Recent Developments

Since 1981, some of the issues of the previous two hundred years have been resolved, while others continue to divide the people of St. Charles County. In addition, new issues have arisen. While historical perspective can inform our views on the issues we face today, their newness and our personal involvement makes analysis more difficult, especially by anyone who has been involved in political decisions made during the period. Nevertheless, it is possible to identify some of the important developments, since 1981, especially when they represent the continuation of older historical trends in St. Charles County, and leave it to future historians to judge the wisdom of those decisions.

The ethnic differences that once divided the people of St. Charles County are now being celebrated. During Portage des Sioux's bicentennial celebration, the role of Native Americans in the history of the county was recognized. The most common reminder of their former presence is when construction crews find Indian artifacts, usually arrowheads, on a construction site. Federal law often requires an archeological evaluation of the site before construction can continue.[2005]

While the 2000 census identified only 5.6 percent of the county's population as of French or French-Canadian descent, the annual "Festival of the Little Hills" recalls the original French name of St. Charles, *Les Petite Cotes*. Efforts are ongoing to find a "sister city" for St. Charles in France. Only a few descendants of the original French-Canadian families who settled St. Charles remain. Many of those, who live in the old clubhouses along the Mississippi River, approximate the easy-going lifestyle of the *voyageurs*. Some even work on barges, as the *voyageurs* worked on the keelboats plying the rivers. Some of their clubhouses are on federal flowage easements, where their continued presence is subsidized through the National Flood Insurance Program, much as the Spanish government subsidized French settlers by giving them common fields.[2006]

Other aspects of certain modern lifestyles are reminiscent of the French and Indian period. With the emergence of the counterculture in the late 1960s, Victorian mores have continued to break down in St. Charles County and the rest of the country. Like the Osage Indians that once hunted in St. Charles County, some young adults today are having their bodies tattooed, often to the consternation of their parents. Cohabitation without benefit of marriage is much more common today, as it was among the French trappers and Indians of the eighteenth century. Likewise, there are many more interracial marriages. The 2000 census lists 3,049 individuals in St. Charles County as multi-racial, a statistic that was not even kept in previous censuses.

The Portage des Sioux commons is still inhabited primarily by the descendants of the German-Americans who arrived in the nineteenth century. They continue to chafe under the perpetual leases that allow Portage des Sioux to collect rents and allow the farmers to use the land only for "agricultural purposes." The hunting habits of the French and Indians are carried on today in the floodplain by hunters of every ethnic background. The Mississippi River floodplain continues to boast some of the best hunting and nicest hunting lodges in the Midwest. Like the Indians almost 200 years ago, the hunters have organized to protect their hunting grounds from the encroachment of residential and commercial development.[2007]

Recently, St. Charles Borromeo Parish and Portage des Sioux have sponsored bicentennial events celebrating their French heritage. At the Academy of the Sacred Heart, French language instruction is an important part of the curriculum. Catholicism, introduced in St. Charles County by the French, is prospering as the Catholic Church canonized Philippine Duchesne in May 1988. While the Spanish administered the St. Charles District for 40 years, not many Spanish came to the area in the late eighteenth century. That has changed in the last decade, especially in St. Charles where the St. Charles Borromeo Parish conducts an outreach effort to the Hispanic community.

The annual Lewis and Clark Festival recognizes the contributions of the primarily Scotch-Irish pioneers who were, according to the German immigrants, "ashamed of their ancestry if they were still aware of it."[2008] Only 1.6 percent of St. Charles Countians identified their ancestry as Scotch-Irish; although Scotch-Irish were undoubtedly among the 1.5 percent that identified their ancestry as Scottish or the 10.4 percent that identified themselves as English. To celebrate the bicentennial of the Corps of Discovery, a boathouse and nature center was erected, with the help of a federal grant and local contributions, to house models of the boats used by Lewis and Clark. The Anglo-American legacy also continues to thrive. Lindenwood College, after nearly closing in 1988, is prospering as Lindenwood University under the leadership of President Dennis Spellmann. Taking advantage of the growing population of St. Charles County, it has expanded its physical facilities and greatly increased the size of its student body. The university has purchased the historic Boone property in the Femme Osage area and developed an academic program around the frontier experience in St. Charles County.[2009]

Each August at Blanchette Park, the African-American Legion Post in St. Charles continues to hold a picnic, the successor to the St. Charles Relief Association picnic. While the black population is up to 2.5 percent, the larger community has not yet acknowledged the picnic as a way to recognize the historical role of African-Americans in St. Charles over the last 200 years. The legacies of racism and "white flight" remain in St. Charles County. As many of the new residents of the county came from St. Louis City and County since 1980, it is also necessary to know the history of St.

Louis to understand race relations in the county.[2010] More African-Americans have been elected to public office as Herman Elmore served on the St. Charles City Council and Sherman Parker was elected to the Missouri House of Representatives.

Another significant ethnic group continues to be the Irish. In the 2000 census, 17.5 percent of St. Charles Countians listed Irish as their ancestry. St. Patrick's Day celebrations are not, however, confined to the Irish.

German-Americans continued to be the largest ethnic group as 38.7 percent in the county reported German ancestry on the 2000 census and the German cultural legacy is celebrated throughout the county. St. Charles is involved in the "Sister Cities" program with Ludwigsburg, in Germany, while New Melle has a similar relationship with Melle in Hanover. St. Charles has a German-American club that sponsors the *Burgermeister's* Ball each year, and there is an *Octoberfest* as well. The wine gardens of Augusta offer a taste of the Rhineland throughout the year in the best German tradition. The St. Paul Picnic, the largest of several parish picnics that survive, is famous for its *Gemuetlichkeit*, and the St. Charles Municipal Band still plays every Thursday night in the summer on the riverfront. Old German Catholic parishes like Immaculate Conception in Dardenne, St. Patrick in Wentzville, and St. Joseph in Cottleville have expanded to meet the population growth in St. Charles County.

As in the rest of the country, the role of women in the workforce and elsewhere has continued to evolve. Not only are more women working outside the home, the number of women entrepreneurs has increased greatly and women are well represented on corporate, banking and not-for-profit boards. In 2004, two of the five largest cities in the county had women mayors. At the same time, two of the nine state representative, two of eight judges and one of seven County Council members were women.

Only faint murmurings of the cultural battles of the first half of the twentieth century remain, usually disguised as a different issue. Alcohol abuse is still a problem as it was during the "alcoholic republic." However, the German-Americans won the culture war over alcohol. In St. Charles County and the state, only those who so choose observe the Puritan Sunday. Alcoholic beverages, sporting events, theatre and shopping are all available on Sunday. The only remnant of the Blue Laws is that establishments selling alcohol cannot open until noon, unless there is a football game at the Edward D. Jones Dome. Opposition to alcohol is now expressed in the name of health and safety, not religion. [2011]

The debate over gambling was renewed when the people voted to legalize lotteries. Then, in 1991 "Riverboat Gambling" was placed on the ballot for approval. To gain support for legalized gambling, supporters reminded people of the riverboat era and sold the proposition as something that would promote tourism. The "Riverboat Gambling" proposition passed and, in 1994, the General Assembly clarified the law so that riverboats had to cruise the river, unless it was "unsafe" to do so. The legislature had apparently forgotten that there were 273 steamboat accidents between the mouth of the Missouri and Kansas City in the heyday of the steamboat. As a result, the boats no longer cruised and the voters eventually approved "dock-side casinos," one of which is in St. Charles.

Efforts to make English the "official language" continue as they did before the First World War. Interest in the debate is minimal in St. Charles County, where Hispanics make up the largest group of non-English speakers, and constitute only 1.58% of the population. In the county only 1,245 children age 5 to 17 spoke Spanish at home according to the 2000 census.

The tension between public and parochial schools has resulted in an overwhelming victory for public schools. As St. Charles County continues to grow, 31.6 percent of the population is under age twenty, compared to 28.9 percent for the St. Louis Metropolitan Region. Eighty-three percent of school age children attend the constantly expanding county public schools. Both Francis Howell and Fort Zumwalt School Districts now have three high schools; Wentzville and St. Charles each have two. Seventeen percent of students are enrolled in private or parochial schools, and others are "home schooled." Catholics need public support more than ever as the number of religious teaching in the schools has drastically declined.[2012] The issue of state support for the parents of parochial school children remains alive in Jefferson City only as part of the "school choice" movement, propelled largely by poor public schools in the inner cities. While that movement received a boost when the Supreme Court upheld the school voucher program in Cleveland, the question remains as to whether the Missouri constitution, as amended in 1870, has built a higher wall of separation between church and state.[2013]

The new cultural issues and social problems that emerged in the late 1960s continue to challenge the county. Adequate public school funding was addressed when the General Assembly passed a new foundation formula in 1993 that equalized school funding, regardless of the assessed valuation of the district. Those areas of St. Charles County that were still "bed-room communities" received equal funding. To provide greater access to higher education, the voters of St. Charles County created a Community College District in 1986. Within a few years a beautiful new campus was built in Cottleville, where 9,610 students attended credit classes during the 2003-2004 school year. More than 24,000 students participated in non-credit continuing education activities. By 2000 there were 15,745 students from St. Charles County enrolled in college; 18.5 percent of the population had at least a bachelor's degree; and another 33.2 percent had some college but no degree.[201]

Parents remain concerned about the effects of popular culture on the moral values of their children. Scouting continues to provide moral guidance to the youth of St. Charles County. Sports organizations that began in the 1950s can now be found in every community. The YMCA and the Boys and Girls Club have opened new facilities in O'Fallon. The county has built a skate park in the western area of the county. The Children and Family Services Authority was created to oversee the mental health concerns of children.[2015] The D.A.R.E. program has been established in all the schools to fight drug use. When drug abuse was reported at an event at the Family Arena, the county executive invoked a clause in the county's contract with the arena management company requiring that his office approve events. The County Council backed him.

Religion continues to exert influence on the community. While existing parishes have grown and prospered, St. Joachim and Ann has been established as a new Catholic parish. Its Care Center has been an advocate for workforce housing in the community. The Salvation Army has built expanded facilities for the homeless in O'Fallon, while many other faith-based organizations continue to serve the poor. The county now has a Jewish congregation, B'nai Torah, with a synagogue in St. Peters. Protestant congregations also continue to grow and multiply. Prayer breakfasts have become popular and the annual Businessman's Prayer Breakfast has drawn a thousand people. Catholic organizations like the Knights of Columbus continue to serve the community, and there is an active Catholic Business and Professional Persons Association that meets twice a year. While St. Peters Community Hospital is now part of the BJC system, and Crossroads Hospital operates in Wentzville, the Sisters of St. Mary continue to serve a large portion of the county's health care needs at St. Joseph Hospital and St. Joseph Hospital West in Lake St. Louis. The Emmaus Home continues to operate in St. Charles, as the St. John congregation has also sponsored Fairgrounds Village, a residence for senior citizens.

The people of the county also continue to be very patriotic. Just as Nathan Boone and his neighbors volunteered for ranger companies to protect the frontier from Indian attack, St. Charles County residents have continued to serve their country in the armed forces. Fourteen percent of those over 18 years of age are veterans.[2016] In 2000, 204 were serving in the armed forces and many more were serving in the Missouri National Guard. The armory of Company B of the 203rd Battalion of the Missouri Army National Guard is located in St. Peters. County and city governments have worked with veterans' organizations to erect several impressive veterans' memorials. The Page Avenue Bridge across the Missouri River has been named the Veterans Memorial Bridge.

St. Charles County has significantly increased its political influence by picking up seats in each of the last three redistricting of the Missouri General Assembly. After 1981, the county had its own State Senate seat held by Fred Dyer. In 1990, the county's population reached 212,907, according to the census, entitling it to one complete senatorial district and half of another. After 2000, the county was entitled to almost two complete districts. The number of state representatives went from five in the 1980s, to seven in the 1990s, to nine after 2000. But the county is a minority part of two different congressional districts, making it difficult for a St. Charles County candidate to win election to Congress. In 1992, 60 percent of the electorate voted for a County Charter. To eliminate potential opposition from elected officials, most county offices were kept elected.[2017] The voters expressed their Jacksonian attitudes when they later voted to keep the sheriff and several other county offices elected directly by the people. Likewise, the county has shown no interest in adopting the Non-Partisan Court Plan, preferring to elect its judges.

In politics, the county has had a Republican majority since 1980. The one exception was in 1990, when Republican enthusiasm was diminished after George Bush broke his "no new taxes" pledge, and two Democrats were elected to the three-member County Commission. As of 2004, the county executive, all members of the County Council and all but one of the elected county officials were Republican. Republicans generally have a 6000 to 7000 vote margin on straight party voting at a major election. Talented Democratic candidates, who are conservative on social issues, are still able to get elected. In 2004, eight of the nine state representatives and both state senators were Republicans. With Republican majorities in both the House and Senate for the first time in 46 years, the political influence of St. Charles County was further enhanced. As in other areas, doctors and lawyers do not dominate the political leadership of the county as they once did. There is not a single lawyer in the county legislative delegation; only one lawyer among the elected county officials not required to be lawyers; and only two lawyers on the county school boards. No doctors from the county served as elected officials in 2004 and their leadership role has greatly diminished. Higher education and financial success are not as important for political success as they once were. The rhetoric of the Jacksonian Democrats is now matched by the facts.

The average St. Charles County Republican today differs from the Radical Republicans of the 1860s. They also differ from the Republicans of the 1890-1932 era and are closer to the Liberal Republicans of the 1870s, led by Carl Schurz and B. Gratz Brown. The Liberal Republicans favored re-enfranchisement of the former Confederates, low tariff, civil service reform, tax reduction and opposition to government land give-aways to private corporations. They believed that all adult males should have the right to vote even if the resulting majority could not be trusted to follow the reconstruction policies of that day. Today's Republicans tend to support the Hancock Amendment to the state constitution, requiring that people vote on tax increases. While Republicans of the 1890-1932 era supported high tariffs to protect American industry, today's Republican platform supports free trade, as did the Liberal Republicans.[2018] The charter approved by the voters of St. Charles County established a merit system for county employees in the spirit of Carl Schurz' civil service reform efforts on the national level. Finally, as the Liberal Republican disliked the abuses of the railroad building era, when government, rather than the market, picked the winners by giving certain people subsidies, some modern Republican leaders in St. Charles County, while pro-business, have questioned public subsidies to individual retail businesses.

In today's Republican Party, social issues no longer split Catholic from Protestant. Disagreements over alcohol, gambling and parochial schools can be ignored because of agreement over other social issues that have evolved since 1965. Opposition to abortion and support of pro-family issues unite various Christian groups in the Republican Party and there is a strong presence of what some have termed the "Christian right," in St. Charles County.

At the state level, the Democratic Party has, on some issues, taken the position of the Radical Republicans, defending the public schools from attempts to divert state funds to competing educational alternatives and pushing increased funding for education.[2019] Like the Radical Republicans, the national Democratic Party has led the struggle for the civil rights of African-Americans, often referred as the "Second Reconstruction." That has not translated into electoral success in St. Charles County because the percentage of African-Americans remains low; although it is growing faster than the overall population. Like the Radical Republicans, Democrats today tend to be more protectionist on trade issues, owing largely to the influence of organized labor in the party since the New Deal. The state and national Democratic Party have taken liberal positions on most social issues, including abortion. Successful St. Charles County Democratic candidates have gone against their party on these issues, and have often been leaders in the Pro-Life movement, while supporting other socially conservative causes. As a result, they have been popular in St. Charles County but have not been able to advance within the Democratic Party statewide.

While residents owned 75 percent of the homes in St. Charles in 1916, 83 percent of the housing units in St. Charles County were owner occupied by 2000.[2020] Many individuals were able to own their homes because of the gains made by organized labor over the last 60 years. There is now a broad consensus, that includes all but the most die-hard conservatives, that most of the New Deal programs that benefited the middle class are good and should be retained. The same may even be said of middle-class entitlements like Medicare and Medicaid, passed as part of the Great Society in the 1960s. The same cannot be said for other federal government programs like the National Flood Insurance Act and the Clean Water Act, both passed by Congress in 1968. As later amended by statute and rule, and as interpreted by the courts, these acts have been very controversial in St. Charles County, where many inhabitants of the floodplains have not welcomed increased federal regulation. Authority to enforce floodplain regulations through city or county ordinances comes from state statutes. The Federal Emergency Management Agency required St. Charles County to enforce its regulations against public, as well as private land. St. Charles County was required to enforce zoning regulation against another political subdivision, the Consolidated North County Levee District. Since the concept of government immunity from zoning had been well established in Missouri, the attorney general ruled they could not do so.[2021] The Missouri Supreme Court held, in the case of *St Charles County v. Dardenne Realty Co.*, that land used for agricultural purposes was exempt from county zoning requirements, including the county floodplain ordinance. The entire federally inspired, but locally enforced, regulatory program appeared unenforceable.[2022]

After two years of quarreling with the St. Charles County legislative delegation, and after threatening to withhold flood insurance from the entire state, FEMA got the state law changed. A few years later FEMA required St. Charles County to enforce a "density floodway" that allows development of only 18 percent of the land in the floodway, and allows "no continuous fill." With the changes to the state statute, FEMA could force the county to enforce the density floodway ordinance preventing the Consolidated North County Levee District from raising its levees.[2023]

Meanwhile, the Clean Water Act was being used to delaying the construction of the Page Avenue Bridge over the Missouri River. Since the bridge approaches in St. Louis County were to be built through a floodplain, wetland permits had to be issued by the St. Louis Corps of Engineers and a floodplain permit had to be issued by St. Louis County. These permits involved years of hearings and reviews by various state and federal agencies. After the permit was issued, including a mitigation plan that provided hundreds of acres of land for Creve Coeur Park, environmental groups filed lawsuits challenging the permit. The suit dragged on for nearly two years, until the federal courts eventually upheld the permits.

While subdivisions had replaced cornfields and bridges were more important than levees, 43 percent of the county is floodplain and many of the people living there were disturbed in November 1987 when the Corps of Engineers announced that the L-15 project would not be built. The decision came right after the devastating flood of 1986. Federal law now required the local public entity to contribute 20 percent of the cost of repairs, a major departure from federal policies from the previous 60 years. The Consolidated North County Levee District filed a Plan of Reclamation which was approved by the Circuit Court, and prepared to float a $2.5 million bond issue to finance the levee improvements that the federal government had refused to do.[2024] At this point leaders realized that FEMA regulations made it impossible to raise the existing levees in this area of St. Charles County. The levee district board decided it would take an act of Congress to fix the problem, and began working with their congressman and U.S. senators to effect a change in the law. In the fall of 1996, the federal statute was changed to allow a maximum 20-year level of protection on both sides of the Missouri River from St. Charles to the confluence with the Mississippi River. In addition, the district was able to get federal assistance to build a 20 year agricultural levee.[2025]

The event that led to better levee protection was the Great Flood of 1993, an event which devastated the floodplains. The Mississippi floodwaters had come within inches of closing Interstate 70, when Missouri River flooding in Chesterfield had already closed Interstate 64. This would have crippled transportation in the entire Middle West. Therefore, the Corps of Engineers approved the Old Town levee project to protect the interstate, old town St. Peters and adjacent industrial development sites. Better levee protection, something that the county had been working toward for 60 years was becoming a reality.

During the Flood of 1993, West Alton was under eight feet of water and Portage des Sioux flooded for the first time in its history. Dissatisfaction with FEMA intensified after the water receded. Portage des Sioux enforced its own floodplain ordinances and very few of its homes were condemned pursuant to the "51 percent rule." This required that any structure requiring improvements costing 51 percent or more of the market value of the structure before the start of construction could not be rebuilt unless raised above the 100-year flood level. St. Charles County, under the watchful eye of FEMA enforced the letter of the law and almost all the homes in West Alton were condemned. In Region VII of FEMA, including St. Charles County, all jurisdictions were instructed to use pre-flood market value to determine whether the structure was damaged more than 50 percent. Across the Mississippi River, in the State of Illinois, which is in Region V of FEMA, replacement cost was used to enforce the 51 percent rule. When this was brought to the attention of FEMA they were forced to back down and allow jurisdictions to use replacement cost in figuring the 51 percent rule. This meant that many structures that had previously been condemned could now be rehabilitated and reoccupied. In West Alton it meant the difference between almost every structure having to be torn down and almost every structure being eligible for rehabilitation. The people of West Alton then incorporated as a municipality so that, in the next flood, they would be able to administer the FEMA regulations themselves.

Another area of contention with the federal government was the clean up of the former uranium processing plant at Weldon Spring. Waste generated at the plant between 1958 and 1966 was stored in four open-air lagoons called raffinate pits. Uranium residue had also been stored in a quarry on the site. The Department of Energy took control of the site in 1985 and began an extensive clean up of the site that has only recently been completed.[2026]

Because of the amount of pollution in the air, St. Charles County, along with the entire St. Louis metropolitan area in Missouri, has been designated a "modified non-attainment" area by the federal Environmental Protection Agency. To avoid further penalties from the federal government that would significantly curtail industrial production in counties like St. Charles, the state has imposed measures like reformulated gasoline and emissions testing to reduce pollution. Two of the 12 monitoring stations in the area are located at Orchard Farm and West Alton.

While waging political battles against the federal government, the main battles with state government have been over new roads and bridges. In 2000, with 87.1 percent of those commuting to work driving alone and the mean travel time to work 26.4 minutes, better roads and bridges were essential to the growth of the county.[2027] In 1992 the Highway 370 Discovery Bridge over the Missouri River was opened to traffic after the State Highway Department received bridge-replacement funds from Washington and the old Rock Road Bridge was torn down. In 1994, the voters of the county barely rejected a tax increase for mass transit that would have provided the local share, if federal funds had become available, to extend Metrolink to St. Charles County. One of the proposed alternatives for Metrolink would have brought the light rail over the old Rock Road Bridge that had carried streetcars in the period between 1904 and 1931; but the key to transportation for St. Charles County was the ten-lane Page Avenue Bridge. While the St. Louis County Council passed an ordinance to accept the wetland mitigation acres for the bridge, opponents of the project collected enough signatures to put the ordinance to a vote of the people. The Missouri River Bridges Committee assisted the effort to pass the St. Louis County ordinance via the ballot box. That vote took place, the ordinance passed and the bridge was opened to the public in December 2003.

Success in most of these political battles had insured continued economic growth in St. Charles County as the economy continue to evolve. While the population of the county grows, eight percent of the people are still classified as "rural population" by the 2000 census. However, only 869 persons are identified as living on farms. While the total value of livestock went down 57 percent from 1990 to 2000, the value of crops produced in the county increased 32 percent.[2028] The County Fair, having moved to Wentzville in the 1970s, now has a new home at Rotary Park, developed by the Wentzville Rotary and Lions Clubs, Wentzville and the County Fair Board.[2029] Because of residential growth, most of the agricultural production of the county is in the floodplains.

Likewise, railroads are no longer as important to the national economy as they were in the nineteenth century. The MKT "Katy" Railroad abandoned its right-of-way under the federal "Rails-to-Trails" statute, and the Missouri Department of Natural Resources maintains the Katy Trail State Park along the abandoned right-of-way. The two remaining railroads in St. Charles County carry only freight, but the Amtrak trains from St. Louis to Kansas City are on the Missouri Pacific directly across the Missouri River from Augusta and can be boarded at the Washington, Missouri depot. The federal and state governments continue to subsidize that Amtrak route, as they subsidized railroads in the nineteenth century.

The state legislature passed a telecommunications bill in 1998 designed to return competition to the telecommunications industry by allowing competitors into the market. The theory was to provide the kind of competition that formerly existed between Bell Telephone Company and the Kinloch Telephone Company, without duplication of phones or wires. Similar debates continue over the proper relationship between the public and private sector. While there is a general consensus that the state government should spend money to encourage economic development, to whom and for what projects the money should go continues to be debated. It took several lawsuits and a statutory change to clarify which businesses in the University of Missouri Research Park doing research and development were required to pay property taxes. The Economic Development Center of St. Charles County was formed in 1990 and took over the role of Crossroads on federal SBA loans. Since 1992, with financial assistance from county and municipal governments, the EDC has formed a Small Business Incubator, hired a recruitment specialist, and opened a small business development center. It also formed Partners for Progress in 2000, a group of chief executive officers working to support quality growth in St. Charles County.

Today, more than 47 percent of St. Charles Countians work in the county. New jobs are being created, especially in the High Tech Corridor along Highway 40. According to the 2000 census, the number of firms in the county increased by 177 percent from 1980 until 1999. In December 2003, the Bureau of Labor Statistics reported the growth rate of employment in St. Charles County at 4.6 percent, making it the fourth highest of any county in the nation. By 2004, while the General Motors Assembly Plant was still the number two employer in the county, other top employers indicated the maturation of the post-industrial society in St. Charles county. The other employers in the top ten were Citigroup (5,000), SSM Healthcare (2,500), Ameristar Casino (2,456), Mastercard International (2,330), MEMC (1,175), Barnes-Jewish St. Peters Hospital (850), Central States Coca-Cola (750) and SBC Communications (500). The county had become the economic engine of the St. Louis region. With all the new business activity in St. Charles, in 2004 the only businesses still around from 1929 were Pundmann Ford, St. Charles Savings Bank, Thro Clothing, Hackmann Lumber, Parkview Gardens and the Mutual Fire Insurance Co. of St. Charles, a company that has existed since the Civil War.

After the 2000 census, the population of St. Charles County was 283,883, up 47.8 percent in the 1980s and 33.3 percent in the 1990s. Since 1980, the county government has been able to build a number of new buildings. Upon approval of the voters, it built a new jail on the same block where the Spanish Fort had housed the jail immediately after the Louisiana Purchase. In addition, after approval of a Capital Improvements Tax, the county built a county administration building; restored the 1903 courthouse to provide a legislative chamber and offices for the County Council, and built a Youth Activity Park. It built a new courthouse for the courts of the 11th Circuit that, after 1991, contained only St. Charles County, a new circuit having been formed with Lincoln and Pike Counties.[2030] The county that was still using the county jail to house juvenile detainees in 1946, also built a new state-of-the-art Juvenile Justice Center in 2002. A county park system, purchased with Capital Improvement Tax revenue, and built and maintained with revenue from a Use Tax passed by the voters, provides passive use parks for the residents of the county. One of the parks is located at the site of the old Klondike Quarry, and features a magnificent view of the Missouri River. Voters also approved a one-tenth-of-one-percent tax to be part of the Metropolitan Parks and Recreational district. That organization has worked with the Missouri Department of Natural Resources to develop a park at the confluence of the Missouri and Mississippi Rivers in St. Charles County. The County, with some financial assistance from St. Charles, built the Family Arena, a 10,000-seat entertainment facility. The voters of St. Charles County approved a Transportation Tax in the mid-1980s, reapproved it for another ten years in the mid-1990s, and re-approved it again in 2004. A County Road Board, made up of individuals representing the municipalities and the unincorporated areas of the county, make recommendations to the county concerning which roads are to be improved. This source of revenue, along with transportation taxes approved in county municipalities, mean that many of the farm-to-market roads, named for the German families that farmed the vicinity in the nineteenth century, are now three to five lane boulevards.

The achievements of county municipalities are equally impressive. St. Charles, with 60,321 people, has a gambling casino, numerous renovated historic structures including St. Charles High School, and a revitalized North Main Street, the result of tearing out the pedestrian mall and opening up the street to traffic. In 1991 the city tore down its 55-year old swimming pool in Blanchette Park and built knew aquatic facilities in each of its parks. The city, as it did in 1910, had to fight off another possible landfill site. This one was not across the river but at an abandoned quarry south of the city limits. The industrial development envisioned since the 1950s for the Elm Point area materialized in the Fountain Lakes development in the Highway 370 corridor. While many of its residents had been in favor of airport expansion in 1980, St. Charles opposed unsuccessfully the W-1-W runway expansion plan for Lambert Airport that brought the end of the runway closer to the city. The New Town development, in the area that was previously the St. Charles common fields, features "new urbanism," neighborhoods built as they were before the 1950s. Debate continues on whether to tear down the "temporary" housing built by the federal government in Powell Terrace in 1941. The St. Charles County Convention and Sports Authority, in conjunction with the city, began building a convention center and hotel in 2003 at the old county fair grounds.

St. Peters, with a population of 51, 381, has avoided many of the zoning mistakes made by St. Charles and O'Fallon. With the Rec-Plex facility, a new police station, city hall and senior citizen's center, the city was a model of progress for the county. City parks grew by 153 acres in the 1980s and the city aggressively tackled environmental issues in the 1990s. It has attracted retail business by the use of Tax Increment Financing and continues to be a commercial center of the county.

O'Fallon, with 46,169 people, is the fastest growing municipality in the state and seems destined to be the largest municipality in St. Charles County. Its commercial growth has allowed it to build facilities like T.R. Hughes Field, a minor league baseball park that houses an Amateur Sports Hall of Fame that honors baseball and bowling stars from the 1930s, 1940s and 1950s. The city renovated several buildings acquired from the Sisters of the Precious Blood for a new city hall. In 1992 the city advanced the Missouri Department of Transportation (MoDot) the money to widen and rebuild Highway K, leading to tremendous growth in that area. Wentzville, with a population of 6896 in 2000, was next to experience extensive growth as new subdivisions were built north and south of I-70. County Road Board projects in the city have created opportunities for commercial development.

Annexations continued to be controversial. In 1991, the entire county legislative delegation supported an amendment to the annexation statute granting St. Charles County residents what the people in the St. Louis and Jackson County already had, the right to determine by majority vote whether they would be annexed. Cities complained that the amendment would stop their growth while supporters of the amendment said it ensured majority rule. To guarantee municipal support for the County Charter, language had been inserted keeping the county government from filing lawsuits in court challenging the legality of an annexation, a right enjoyed by every other county in the state. Believing that some annexations were violating the legal requirement that they be "contiguous and compact," in 2004 the County Council put an amendment before the voters giving the county the power to, once again, challenge annexation they believe to be illegal. The measure passed with a 70 percent majority.

According to the 2000 census, the median family income for St. Charles County was $57, 258, with the county passing St. Louis County in that category for the first time. By 2002, the median income was estimated to be $62,292, an 8.8 percent increase in two years. The county was losing its blue-collar image as more upscale housing was being built. Some of the defensive incorporations had become exclusive residential areas. Lake St. Louis was large enough to provide real municipal services efficiently. In the 1980s Weldon Spring incorporated with some very exclusive residential neighborhoods. Cottleville, long incorporated, grew and annexed, lest St. Peters surround it. As both municipalities continue to grow, they are providing more extensive municipal services. Dardenne Prairie has grown in population. While it is dissected by O'Fallon, it has shown new vitality. Residents south of Highway 40, following the example of Wildwood in St. Louis County, petitioned the County Council to incorporate the Town of Boone's Trails. Residents were interested in controlling their own zoning and protecting the rural nature of the area. The County Council was not convinced that the town would have the ability to provide the needed municipal services and turned down the incorporation.[2031]

The net out-migration from the St. Louis Metropolitan Region slowed during the 1980s, but still approached 90,000 individuals. In the 1990s, the net out-migration declined to just fewer than 36,000 and the region is thought to be nearing a no-migration population, where population change is attributable only to births or deaths. Nevertheless, as the situation improved the debate over "urban sprawl" became more heated as St. Charles County added 71,000 people during the 1990s, with 55 percent coming from St. Louis County. Attempts to legislate growth boundaries did not pass, but those who would stop growth in St. Charles County continue to work through the bureaucracies at Missouri Department of Natural Resources, Missouri Department of Transportation and others to put up roadblocks to further development. Groups within the county are questioning unlimited growth, especially in the floodplain.

St. Charles County continues to grow, it continues to be an important crossroads, as new people move to the county who will make their mark just as previous newcomers have done. While certain families have asserted influence over several generations - Dyer, Howell, Lawler, Rauch, Stumberg, Bruere, Sandfort, Ohlms, Machens, Thro, Weinrich and others come to mind – each generation has provided new leaders, often from the newest arrivals to the county. The future looked bright and the people of St. Charles County were optimistic as they entered the twenty-first century. While the charges of "urban sprawl" continue to be heard from the county's critics, St. Charlesans try to ensure "smart growth." History will determine if they are succeeding.

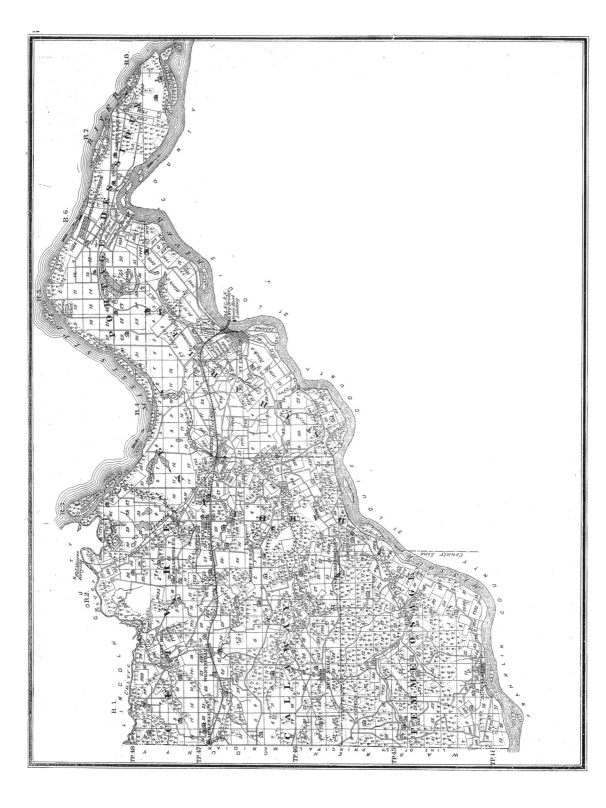

OUTLINE MAP OF

St. Charles County

MISSOURI.

1905.

Scale 2 Inches to 1 Mile.

COPYRIGHTED

COMPILED FROM

OFFICIAL RECORDS, RECORDS & SURVEYS

BY J. F. DUNN, M. E.

Clinton, Iowa.

EXPLANATION

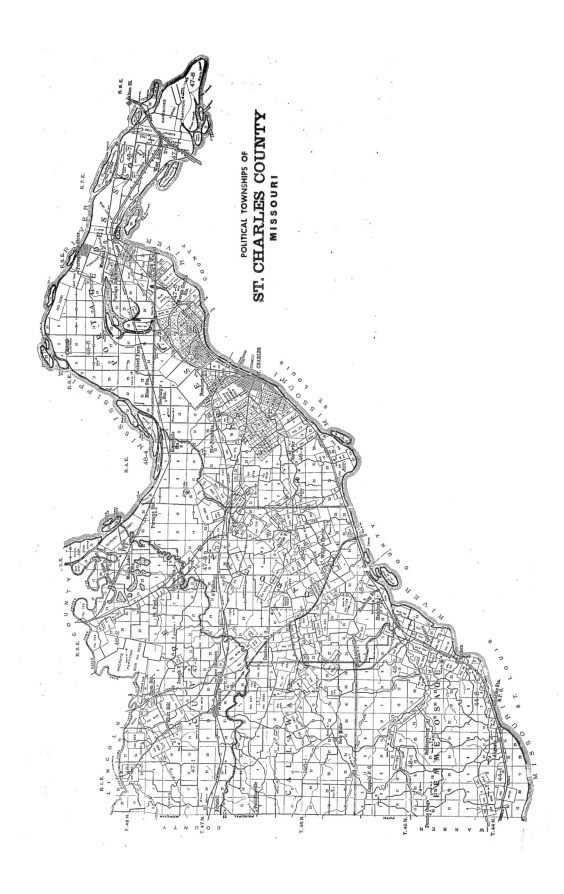

POLITICAL TOWNSHIPS OF
ST. CHARLES COUNTY
MISSOURI

Chapter I
End Notes

[1] Hiram Martin Chittendon, *The American Fur Trade in the Far West*, (Lincoln: University of Nebraska Press, 1986), p. 79.

[2] Paul C. Nagel, *Missouri, A History,* (Lawrence: University Press of Kansas, 1977), p. 50. *The Later Letters of Ralph Waldo Emerson, 1843-1871,* Edited by Ronald A Bosco and Joel Myerson, (Athens: University of Georgia press), p. 286.

[3] Walter Schroeder, *The Environmental Setting of the St. Louis Region,Common Fields, An Environmental History of St. Louis,* (St. Louis: Missouri Historical Society Press, 1997), p. 13.

[4] *History of St. Charles County, Missouri,1765-1885,* (Reprint from *History of St. Charles, Montgomery, and Warren Counties,* with an introduction by Paul R. Hollrah, n.p: Patria Press 1997,) p. 145.

[5] Schroeder, *Environmental Setting,* p. 26.

[6] *History of St. Charles County*, p.131.

[7] Schroeder, *Environmental Setting,* p. 26. Donald Mincke, *The History of Portage des Sioux Township, The Land Between the Rivers,*(Portage des Sioux: Land Between the Rivers Historical Society), 1999, p.3.

[8] *History of St. Charles County*, p. 134. Edna McElhiney Olson, *Historical Articles, St. Charles, Missouri,* Vols. 1-4, (St. Charles: St. Charles Genealogical Society, 1993), Vol. I, p. 44-45.

[9] Schroeder, *Environmental Setting,* p. 27.

[10] Daniel K. Richter, *Facing East from Indian Country,* (Cambridge: Harvard University Press, 2001), p. 5.

[11] Ibid.

[12] Edna McElhiney Olson, *Historical Articles,* Vol. 1, p. 93.

[13] Schroeder, *Environmental Setting,* p. 27.

[14] *History of St. Charles County*, p. 146.

[15] D.W. Meining, *The Shaping of America, The Geographical Perspective on 500 Years of History, Vol.2,* "Continental America, 1800-1867," (New Haven: Yale University Press, 1993), p. 240.

[16] Ibid.

[17] Jeffrey S. Adler, *Yankee Merchants and the Making of the Urban West, The Rise and Fall of Antebellum St. Louis,* (Cambridge: Cambridge University Press, 1991), p. 2.

[18] Nagel, *Missouri*, p. 54.

[19] Schroeder, *Environmental Setting,* p. 28. The MKT "Katy" Railroad abandoned its right-of-way under the federal "Rails-to-Trails" statute, and the Missouri Department of Natural Resources maintains the Katy Trail State Park along the abandoned right-of-way.

[20] Donald Mincke, *History of Portage de Sioux*, pp. 13-14.

[21] Schroeder, *Environmental Setting*, p. 32.

[22] Ibid.

[23] Nagel, *Missouri*, p. 50

[24] Anita M. Mallinckrodt, *From Nights to Pioneers, One German Family In Westphalia and Missouri,* (Carbondale: Southern Illinois University Press, 1994), p. 235.

[25] *A 1795 Inspection of Missoui,* trans. and ed. by Jack D.L.Holmes, *MHR*, October 1960, p. 14.

[26] R. Douglas Hurt, *Nathan Boone and the American Frontier*, (Columbia: University of Missouri Press, 1998), p. 40.

[27] Mincke, *History of Portage des Sioux*, p. 4. Blackhawk's village was on the Rock River in Illinois.

[28] *History of St. Charles County*, p. 117.

[29] Edna McElhiney Olson, *Historical Articles, Vol. I*, p. 111.

[30] *The Agricultural History of St. Charles County*, edited by Stephen D. Livingston, (St. Charles: American Revolution Bicentennial Committee of St. Charles County, 1976), pp. 113-114.

[31] Edna McElhiney Olson, *Historical Articles*, Vol. I, p. 103.

[32] Mincke, *History of Portage des Sioux,* p. 52.

[33] Walter D. Kamphoefner, *The Westfalians, From Germany to Missouri,* Prinecton: (Princeton University Press, 1987), p. 122.

[34] *History of St. Charles County*, p. 134.

[35] Fields, Jean, "A Season of Fear, San Carlos Del Misury, 1792-1793," *St. Charles County Heritage*, Vol. 9, No. 1, January, 1991, p. 8.

[36] Jo Ann Brown, *St. Charles Borromeo, 200 Years of Faith*, (St. Louis: Patrice Press, 1991), p. 2.

[37] Ibid.

[38] William E. Foley, *A History of Missouri, 1673 to 1820, Volume I,* (Columbia: University of Missouri Press, 1971), pp. 9-14.

[39] Ibid. p. 16.

[40] John Francis Bannon, "The Spanish in the Mississippi Valley, an Introduction." *The Spanish in the Mississippi Valley*, ed. by John Francis McDermott, (Urbana: University of Illinois Press, 1965), p. 12.

[41] Ibid. See also Mincke, *History of Portage des Sioux*, p. 93.

[42] Bannon, "The Spanish in the Mississippi Valley," p. 12. O'Reilly was Spain's top General and had joined the Spanish army because Irish could advance more readily than they could in the British army. James Neal Primm, *Lion of the Valley*, St. Louis, Missouri, (Boulder: Pruett Publishing Company, 1981), pp. 22-26. See also Michael O'Laughlin, *Irish Settlers on the American Frontier, 1770-1900*, Vol. 1, *(Gateway West Through Missouri*, Specially Commissioned Patrons' Issue, Kansas City: Irish Genealogical Society), p. 16

[43] Brown, *St. Charles Borromeo*, p. 3.

[44] Ibid. p. 4

[45] *Banner-News*, December 17, 1948. Three stories high and thirty feet wide, with walls thirty inches thick, the fort was constructed by French-Canadian workers sometime between 1770 and 1776. Ibid.

[46] Bannon, "The Spanish in the Mississippi Valley, an Introduction." p. 12.

[47] Foley, *A History of Missouri*, p. 25.

[48] Ibid., p. 26.

[49] Ibid., p. 32.

[50] Ibid., p. 41.

[51] Ibid. pp. 158-161.

[52] "A 1795 Inspection of Spanish Missouri," p. 13.

[53] Fields, *Season of Fear*, p. 17.

[54] Ibid. Actually, the Osage after 1794 did not attack the settlements anywhere. See Primm, *Lion of the Valley*, pp. 60-61.

[55] "A 1795 Inspection of Spanish Missouri," p. 13.

[56] Hurt, *Nathan Boone*, pp.41-43.

[57] Jack D.L. Holmes, "Spanish Regulation of Taverns and the Liquor Trade in the Mississippi Valley," in *The Spanish in the Mississippi Valley*, ed. by John Francis McDermott, (Urbana: University of Illinois Press, 1965), pp. 156-157.

[58] Edna McElhiney Olson, *Historical St. Charles, Missouri*, (St. Charles: St. Charles County Historical Society, 1967, reprinted 1998), p. 4.

[59] Foley, *A History of Missouri, 1683-1820*, p. 48.

[60] Stewart Banner, *Legal Systems in Conflict, Property and Sovereignty in Missouri, 1750-1860*, (Norman: University of Oklahoma Press, 2000), p. 30.

[61] Ibid. p. 31.

[62] Jo Ann Brown, *St. Charles Borromeo*, p. 20.

[63] William C. Lloyd, *A History of the City of St. Peters*, (St. Peters: City of St. Peters, 1999), p. 25.

[64] Ibid.

[65] Ibid.

[66] Jo Ann Brown, *St. Charles Borromeo*, p. 20.

[67] *History of St. Charles County*, pp. 262-63. Because it was on higher ground Portage did not flood until the Flood of 1993, though it was routinely cut off by lesser flooding events.

[68] Banner, *Legal Systems in Conflict*, p.32.

[69] Jo Ann Brown, *St. Charles Borromeo*, p. 6. Primm, *Lion of the Valley*, p. 83.

[70] Foley, *A History of Missouri*, p. 62.

[71] Jo Ann Brown, *St. Charles Borromeo*, p. 6. However, in 1798, a lieutenant governor ordered that the $700 collected that year from the village's drinking establishments be given to the poor. Ibid. See also Holmes, "Spanish Regulation," p. 154.

[72] Banner, *Legal Systems in Conflict*, p. 93.

[73] John Francis McDermott, "Captain de Leyba and the Defense of St. Louis in 1780" in *The Spanish in the Mississippi Valley*, (Urbana: University of Illinois Press, 1974), p.363.

[74] Banner, *Legal Systems*, p. 35.

[75] Ibid. p. 50.

[76] Jo Ann Brown, *St. Charles Borromeo*, p. 6.

[77] Lloyd, *History of the City of St. Peters*, pp. 31-32.

[78] Holmes, "Spanish Regulations," p. 169.

[79] Jo Ann Brown, *St. Charles Borromeo*, p. 18. One of the problems was an acute shortage of priests caused by France's 1763 suppression of the Society of Jesus, which had forced most of the Jesuit missionaries to leave North America.

[80] Jo Ann Brown, *St. Charles Borromeo*, pp. 197, 23.

[81] Ibid.

[82] Ibid.

[83] *History of St. Charles County*, p. 310.

[84] Foley, *A History of Missouri, 1683-1820*, p. 44.

[85] Janet Lecompte, "Introduction," *French Fur Traders and Voyageurs in the American West*, ed. by Leroy R. Hafen, (Spokane: The Arthur Clark Company, 1995), p. 19.

[86] Jo Ann Brown, *St. Charles Borromeo*, p. 21.

[87] Richard White, *The Middle Ground, Indians, Empires, and Republics in the Great Lakes Region, 1650-1815*, (New York: Cambridge University Press, 1991), p.16.

[88] Ibid. p. 52. Between 1649 and the mid-1660s, the Iroquois, looking for better hunting grounds, had disrupted what would become known as the Illinois Country. This would be the last time native Americans would fight each other with such intensity. Geographically, the Iroquois would push the Algonquians further west; politically, they would push them into an alliance with the French. In the 1690s the French and Algonqian forces put the Iroquois on the defensive. Their success led to the Grand Settlement of 1701, which established a general peace at about the same time French trappers and traders were first moving up the Missouri River. The Iroquois abandoned hunting territory west of Detroit, agreed to allow the French governor to arbitrate conflicts between the tribes allied to France and promised to remain neutral in all future Anglo-French wars. Ibid.

[89] Mincke, *History of Portage des Sioux*, pp. 7-8.

[90] White, *Middle Ground*, p. 65.

[91] Ibid.

[92] Ibid. p. 75.

[93] JoAnn Brown, *St. Charles Borromeo*, pp. 23-24.

[94] White, *Middle Ground*, p. 76.

[95] Fields, "Season of Fear," pp. 15-16.

[96] Judith A. Gilbert, "An Indian Named Angelique," *St. Charles County Heritage*, Vol. 16, No. 1,

January 1998, p. 7.

[97] Ibid. p. 10. Angelique's and her husband continued to live in St. Charles until he died in 1816, at which time she bought a farm for herself on Dardenne Creek north of St. Peters where she lived until 1822. Ibid.

[98] Burma Wilkins, "The Trial of Little Crow," in Mincke, *History of Portage des Sioux*, p. 36.

[99] Ibid. p. 37. With few new settlers coming to the St. Charles District, there was not the level of conflict with the Indians that would occur later, when Americans would begin migrating across the Mississippi River. Additionally, the Spanish authorities ordered early officials to protect the land rights of the Indian tribes, passing laws clearly stating that, "Indians shall be protected in their holdings." The Spanish made a distinction between Christian and non-Christian Indians, with the former holding land the same as anyone else, while the letter could sell his or her land only with the approval of the governor. C. Richard Arena, "Land Settlement Policies and Practices in Spanish Louisiana," In *The Spanish in the Mississippi Valley*, ed. by John Francis McDermott, Urbana: University of Illinois Press, 1965. p. 56.

[100] James H. Knipmeyer, *"Denis Julien, Midwestern Fur Trader." MHR*, April 2000, pp. 251-252. Of the 25 biographical sketches of fur traders of French extraction, three had roots in St. Charles County and were undoubtedly of the *bourgeois* or *commis* classification. *French Fur Traders and Voyageurs in the American West*, ed. by Leroy R. Hafen, (Spokane: The Arthur Clark Company, 1995).

[101] Janet Lecompte, "Jean-Baptiste Chalifoux," *French Fur Traders and Voyageurs in the American West*, p. 63.

[102] Kenneth L. Holmes, "Joseph Gervais," *French Fur Traders and Voyageurs in the American West*, pp. 144-145.

[103] John Dishon McDermott, "James Bordeaux," *French Fur Traders and Voyageurs in the American West*, pp. 42-43.

[104] James H. Knipmeyer, "Denis Julien," p. 252.

[105] *Valley of the Mississippi*, edited by Louis Thomas, (St. Louis: Hawthorne Publishing Co., 1841), p. 42.

[106] White, *Middle Ground*, pp. 97-98.

[107] Ibid.

[108] Ibid. p. 103.

[109] Ibid. pp. 112-119.

[110] Bannon, "The Spanish in the Mississippi Valley, an Introduction." p. 13. Foley, *A History of Missouri, 1683-1820*, pp. 30-31.

[111] Lecompte, *French Fur Traders*, p. 22.

[112] Edna McElhiney Olson, *Historical Articles*, Vol. II, p. 322.

[113] Nagel, *Missouri*, p. 58.

[114] Jo Ann Brown, *St. Charles Borromeo*, p. 3.

[115] Ibid. p. 13

[116] Ibid. p.13.

[117] Ibid. p. 29.

[118] Ibid. p. 21.

[119] Ibid. p. 19.

[120] Ibid. p. 25. Edna McElhiney Olson, *Historical Articles*, Vol. I, p. 117.

[121] Foley, *A History of Missouri, 1683-1820*, p. 47.

[122] *History of St. Charles County*, p. 272.

[123] JoAnn Brown, *St. Charles Borromeo*, pp.22, 38. Indians had practiced slavery since the arrival of the French. Ibid.

[124] Foley, *A History of Missouri, 1683-1820*, p. 51.

[125] Ibid., pp. 52-53.

[126] Jo Ann Brown, *St. Charles Borromeo*, p. 3.

[127] Lloyd, *History of the City of St. Peters*, p. 33.

[128] *St. Charles, Missouri, Bicentennial Historical Program Book*, (St. Charles: St. Charles Bicentennial Committee, 1969), p. 20

[129] Jo Ann Brown, *St. Charles Borromeo*, pp. 27, 37. Edna McElhiney Olson, *Historical Articles*, Vol. I, pp. 37-39.

[130] Patricia Cleary, "Environmental Agendas and Settlement Choices in Colonial St. Louis", *Common Fields, An Environmental History of St. Louis*, (St. Louis: Missouri Historical Society Press, 1997), p. 62.

[131] Primm, *Lion of the Valley*, p. 66. Nicolas de Finiels recorded that, in the late 1790s St. Charles had 300 head of cattle and 60 horses; harvested 400 bushels of wheat, 400 bushels of corn, and 2,000 pounds of tobacco annually. Nicolas de Finiels, *An Account of Upper Louisiana*, ed by Carl J. Ekberg and William E. Foley, (Columbia: University of Missouri Press, 1989), p. 77.

[132] Nagel, *Missouri*, p. 37.

[133] Arena, "Land Settlement Policies," p. 59.

[134] Banner, *Legal Systems in Conflict*, p. 67.

[135] Arena, "Land Settlement Policies," p. 53.

[136] Banner, *Legal Systems in Conflict*, pp. 68-69.

[137] Ibid., p. 69.

[138] Ibid.

[139] Arena, "Land Settlement Policies," p. 54.

[140] Banner, *Legal Systems in Conflict*, p. 69.

[141] Ibid. pp. 68-70.

[142] Ibid. p. 72. Nicolas de Finiels identified additional obstacles to agriculture including the inhabitant's sloth, the uncertainty of the harvests and the ignorance and inexperience of the *Voyagers*. Finiels, *Account of Upper Louisiana*, p. 134.

[143] Banner, *Legal Systems in Conflict*, p. 72.

[144] Ibid.

[145] Ibid. 148

[146] Ibid. pp. 78-79

[147] Ibid. pp. 73-74. Much as the common ground in a condominium today.

[148] Ibid. pp. 75-76

[149] Ibid. p. 76.

[150] Ibid.

[151] Ibid. p. 77

Chapter 2
End Notes

[152] Malcolm C. Drummond, *Historic Sites in St. Charles County, Missouri,* (St. Louis: Harland Bartholomew and Associates, 1976), p. 22.

[153] John Francis Bannon, "The Spaniards in the Mississippi Valley, An Introduction," *The Spanish in the Mississippi Valley*, 1762-1804, ed by John Francis McDermott, (Urbana: University of Illinois Press, 1974), p. 11.

[154] Foley, *A History of Missouri, 1683-1820*, p. 34.

[155] *History of St. Charles County*, p. 96.

[156] Ibid., p. 97.

[157] Robert M. Sandfort, *Hermann Heinrich Sandfort, Farmer and Furniture Maker from Hahlen, Germany*, (St. Charles), p. 262. Griffith visited with Lewis and Clark at their Wood River encampment and was mentioned in Clark's journal. Like his neighbors of the period, he was litigious and fought against the Indians between 1806 and 1815. Ibid.

[158] Paul Spellman, "Zadock and Minerva Cottle Woods, American Pioneers," (Austin: 1987), Manuscript in author's possession, pp.40-41.

[159] Sandfort, *Hermann Heinrich Sandfort*, p. 101.

[160] Foley, *A History of Missouri, 1683-1820*, p. 68-73. See also Peg Tucker, "A Rendezvous with America's Future Greatness," *Times Past, Vol. 1*, No. 1, spring, 1984. p.14. *St. Louis Post-Dispatch*, February 18, 2004, Metro Section.

[161] Foley, *A History of Missouri,* p. 90.

[162] Ibid., p. 88.

[163] *History of St. Charles County*, p. 196.

[164] *Banner-News*, December 17, 1948.

[165] Foley, *A History of Missouri, 1683-1820*, p. 95.

[166] Ibid., Meigs had previously served as a judge in the Northwest Territory and chief justice of the Ohio Supreme Court. He later served as governor, a United States senator and postmaster general of the United States. Ibid.

[167] Dennis J. Hahn, "Rufus Easton, Attorney, Public Servant, and First Postmaster," February 27, 2000., p.4, Manuscript in possession of author.

[168] Foley, *A History of Missouri, 1683-1820*, p. 94.

[169] Ibid., p. 122. Primm, *Lion of the Valley*, p. 115.

[170] Foley, *A History of Missouri, 1683-1820*, p. 127.

[171] Ibid., pp. 150-151.

[172] *History of St. Charles County*, p. 188. Benjamin Emmons, senior member of the first Council, was a native of New England, while James Flauherty was a native of Virginia. John Pittman had gained fame as a colonel in the 15th Missouri State Militia. His family came from Pennsylvania, by way of Virginia. The fourth member, Robert Spencer, was an early pioneer to the county and the first judge of the Court of Common Pleas for the District of St. Charles. Ibid.

[173] *History of St. Charles County*, p. 188. Primm, *Lion of the Valley*, p. 116.

[174] Foley, *A History of Missouri, 1683-1820*, p. 92.

[175] Ibid., p. 94.

[176] *History of St. Charles County*, p. 150.

[177] Foley, *A History of Missouri, 1683-1820*, p. 115.

[178] Hurt, *Nathan Boone*, p. 54.

[179] Ibid., pp. 54-55

[180] Ibid., p. 59.

[181] Ibid., p. 76.

[182] Ibid., p. 78. The principle forts were Boone's Fort in Darst Bottom, Howell's Fort on Howell Prairie, Pond Fort on the Dardenne Prairie, White's Fort on Dog Prairie, Kountz Fort on the Booneslick Road, Zumwalt's Fort in what is now O'Fallon and Castlio's Fort near Howell Prairie. *History of St. Charles County*, p. 152.

[183] Richard White, *Middle Ground*, p. 512.

[184] Hurt, *Nathan Boone*, p. 78.

[185] Ibid., p. 79. Tenskatawa rose to power after 1809 by exploiting the hostility that had been developing and resurrecting the doctrine of the common ownership of land. He threatened village chiefs with death for their cessions to the Americans and preached a return to the old ways. Richard White, *Middle Ground*, p. 18.

[186] Hurt, *Nathan Boone*, p. 81.

[187] Foley, *A History of Missouri, 1683-1820*, p. 152.

[188] *History of St. Charles County*, p. 164.

[189] Hurt, *Nathan Boone*, p. 91.

[190] Ibid.

[191] Foley, *A History of Missouri, 1683-1820*, p. 153.

[192] In August 1832 President Jackson commissioned Boone captain of dragoons, and during

President Polk's administration he was promoted to major. In 1850 he was again promoted to lieutenant colonel of dragoons by President Fillmore. He died October 16, 1856, at age 76. See Hurt, *Nathan Boone.*

[193] Foley, *A History of Missouri, 1683-1820*, p. 158.

[194] Lori Breslow, *Small Town*, (St. Charles: The John J. Buse Historical Museum, 1977), pp. 195-196.

[195] Ruby Matson Robbins, "The Missouri Reader," *MHR*, Vol.47, January 1953, p.160.

[196] Hurt, *Nathan Boone*, p. 95.

[197] Spellman, *American Pioneers*, p. 57. A troop was recruited and fought with General Jackson at the Battle of New Orleans. Ibid.

[198] Hurt, Nathan Boone, pp. 102-105.

[199] Edna McElhiney Olson, *Historical Articles*, Vol. II, p. 322.

[200] Hurt, *Nathan Boone,* p.164

[201] Richard White, *Middle Ground*, p. 517.

[202] Foley, *A History of Missouri, 1683-1820*, p. 161.

[203] *History of St. Charles County*, p. 164.

[204] Ibid.

[205] Foley, *A History of Missouri, 1683-1820*, p. 198.

[206] *History of St. Charles County*. pp. 206-7.

[207] *Missourian*, August 5, 1820, p. 3.

[208] Foley, *A History of Missouri, 1683-1820*, p. 202.

[209] Perry McCandliss, *A History of Missouri, 1820 -1860*, Volume II, (Columbia: University of Missouri Press, 1971), p. 5. and Spellman, *American Pioneers*, p. 65.

[210] *History of St. Charles County*, p. 99. Benjamin Emmons of St. Charles was the only delegate to the Convention to vote against the slavery clause in the constitution. George R. Lee, *Slavery North of St. Louis*, (Lewis County Historical Society) p. 13.

[211] Michael J., O'Brien, *Grassland, Forest, and Historical Settlement, An Analysis of Dynamics in Northeast Missouri*, (Lincoln: University of Nebraska Press, 1984), p. 81.

[212] Nagel, *Missouri*, p. 47. Primm, *Lion of the Valley*, pp. 121-122.

[213] *Bicentennial Historical Program*, p. 51.

[214] Ibid., p. 22.

[215] *Valley of the Mississippi*, p. 41.

[216] Nagel, *Missouri*, p. 104. This provision concerned Missourians who knew how Jefferson's old foe, Chief Justice John Marshall, had talked of the threat to order and progress if state legislatures were unrestrained by judicial review. Ibid.

[217] Jo Ann Brown, *St. Charles Borromeo*, pp. 34-36 Uriah Devore would serve as sheriff of St. Charles County, *History of St. Charles County* p. 203.

[218] Perry McCandless, *A History of Missouri, 1820 -1860*, Volume II, (Columbia: University of Missouri Press, 1971), p. 71.

[219] Ibid., p. 91. *History of St. Charles County*, p. 194.

[220] *History of St. Charles County*, pp. 198-99.

[221] Louis Gerteis, *Civil War St. Louis*, (Lawrence: University Press of Kansas, 2001), p. 40.

[222] Elizabeth Snapp, "Government Patronage of the Press in St. Louis, Missouri," *MHR,* January 1980, p. 215. Charles T. Jones, *George Champlin Sibley: The Prairie Puritan 1782-1863,* (Independence, Missouri: Jackson County Historical Society, 1970), p. 260.

[223] *History of St. Charles County*, pp. 195-197.

[224] Ibid., p. 197.

[225] Primm, *Lion of the Valley*,p. 76.

[226] Marvin R. Cain, *Lincoln's Attorney General, Edward Bates of Missouri*, (Columbia: University of Missouri Press, 1965), p. 50.

[227] *History of St. Charles County*, pp. 206-207. "Three Missouri Statehood Fathers," *MHR,*

January 1980. p. 267. Cain, *Lincoln's Attorney General,* pp. 7,19.

[228] Richard White, *Middle Ground*, p. 384. The settlers coming through St. Charles came "almost exclusively from the states south of the Potomac and the Ohio." Accounts further asserted "scarcely a Yankee has moved into the country this year." Harrison Trexler, *Slavery in Missouri, 1804-1865, (Baltimore:* The John Hopkins Press, 1914), p. 103.

[229] *History of St. Charles County,* p. 112.

[230] Ibid.

[231] Ibid., p.108.

[232] McCandless, *A History of Missouri, 1820 -1860,* p. 35.

[233] *History of St. Charles County*, p. 109.

[234] Ibid. pp. 169-70.

[235] Ibid., p. 310-311. Edna McElhiney Olsen, *Historical Articles* Vol. I, p. 39.

[236] Mallinckrodt, *Knights to Pioneers*, p. 191.

[237] Dick Stewart, *Duels and the Roots of Violence in Missouri*, (Columbia: University of Missouri Press, 2002), p. 89.

[238] Early Irish settlers included James Flaugherty, justice of the peace in 1804, James Murdoch and his seven children, Katherine Kennedy, a schoolteacher, Abraham Kennedy, who built a fort and was a member of Nathan Boone's rangers in 1812. Michael O'Laughlin, *Irish Settlers on the American Frontier, 1770-1900*, vol. 1.

[239] McCandliss, *History of Missouri, 1820-1860*, p. 18 (for Flint quote). *History of St. Charles County*, pp. 98-99.

[240] Charles T. Jones, *George Champlin Sibley*, p. 221.

[241] *Cosmos-Monitor*, Sept. 22, 1937. *History of the First Presbyterian Church of St. Charles1818-1942*, (n.p.n.d.) p. 9.

[242] Charles Sellers, *The Market Revolution, Jacksonian America 1815-1846*, (New York: Oxford University Press, 1991), p. 160.

[243] *O'Fallon Centennial, Celebrating 100 Years of Progress*, 1856-1956, (n.p.n.d.), p. 17.

[244] Ibid.

[245] *Cosmos-Monitor*, September 22, 1937.

[246] Edna McElhiney Olson, *Historical Articles*, Vol. II, p. 222. By 1830 the congregation had become dormant but was reconstituted in 1832 by the Reverend William Hurley. Ibid.

[247] Ruby Matson Robbins, "Missouri Reader," p. 160.

[248] Edith Freeman McElhiney, *My Hometown, St. Charles, Missouri*, (St. Charles: School District of the City of St. Charles, n.d.), p. 25. William Schiermeier, *Cracker Barrel Country*, Vol. III, (Washington, Missouri: Missourian Publishing Company, 1996), p. 144.

[249] Edna McElhiney Olson, *Historical Articles*, Vol. I, p. 79.

[250] The Masons were unpopular across the country at this time because of their secrecy. A rumor spread that Masons had murdered William Morgan, a disgruntled member of the Masons who had written a book revealing the secrets of the organization. An anti-Masonic political party emerged and efforts were made in some states to prohibit Masons from holding pubic office. Gerteis, *Civil War St. Louis,* p. 7.

[251] Edna McElhiney Olson, *Historical Articles*, Vol. I, p. 79. Lynn Dumenil, "Masonry" *World Book Online American Edition*, http.//www.worldbook online.com. February 12, 2003. The movement had its origins in England in 1717 and was popular in the early nineteenth century in America. Ibid.

[252] W.J. Rorabaugh, *The Alcoholic Republic, An American Tradition*, (New York: Oxford University Press, 1979), p. 55.

[253] Ibid., p. 10.

[254] Ray Donald Cook, "History of St. Charles, Missouri 1816-1840," (Master's thesis, Washington University, 1965), p. 64.

[255] Rorabaugh, *Alcoholic Republic*, p. 217.

[256] Mark Poindexter, "A Right Smart Little Town," manuscript at Kathryn Linnemann Library, p. 39.

[257] Rorabaugh, *Alcoholic Republic*, p. 193.

[258] William Thomas, *History of St. Louis County, Missouri*, (St. Louis: The S.J. Clarke Publishing Co., 1911), p. 63.

[259] Poindexter, "A Right Smart Little Town," p. 40.

[260] *History of St. Charles County*, p. 199.

[261] Poindexter, "A Right Smart Little Town," p. 38.

[262] Cook, "History of St. Charles," p. 18, quoting letter from Timothy Flint to Reverend Abel Flint, August 3, 1817.

[263] Ibid.

[264] Ibid., p. 75.

[265] Stewart, *Duels*, p. 17.

[266] Meining, *Shaping of America*, pp. 275-276.

[267] R. Douglas Hurt, *Agriculture and Slavery in Missouri's Little Dixie*, (Columbia: University of Missouri Press, 1992), p. 50.

[268] Primm, *Lion of the Valley*, pp. 35, 80.

[269] *History of St. Charles County*, p. 121.

[270] Archives of the St. Charles County Circuit Court for 1822.

[271] Banner, *Legal Systems in Conflict*, p. 92.

[272] Ibid.

[273] Ibid.

[274] Meining, *Shaping of America*, pp. 16-17.

[275] Archives of the St. Charles County Circuit Court for 1822.

[276] Cook, "History of St. Charles," p. 70, quoting letter from Hamilton P. to his cousin, Mrs. Joseph Stanwood, Feb. 18, 1830.

[277] Nagel, *Missouri*, p. 37.

[278] Jo Ann Brown, *St. Charles Borromeo*, p. 19.

[279] Ibid., p. 53.

[280] Ibid., p. 70.

[281] Ibid., pp. 46, 60. Phillipine Duchesne died on November 18, 1852.

[282] McElhiney, *My Hometown*, p. 35.

[283] Jo Ann Brown, *St. Charles Borromeo*, p. 46. This system of a "select" school for the wealthy supporting a free school for the poor originated in America in the nineteenth century. The first to promote these schools side by side was Sr. Elizabeth Ann Seton, whose select school in Emmitsburg, Maryland supported her adjacent school for the poor. Ibid.

[284] Edna McElhiney Olson, *Historical Articles*, Vol. II, p. 177.

[285] Poindexter, "A Right Smart Little Town," p. 25.

[286] Richard White, *Middle Ground*, p. 384.

[287] *Cosmos-Monitor*, April 21, 1938.

[288] Richard White, *Middle Ground*, p.389. In the summer of 1789, Patrick Brown of Kentucky, out to revenge Indian raids, attacked friendly bands of Indians. His men killed nine Indians and stole horses. The Indiana militia refused to act against the Kentuckians. The Kickapoo Indians then attacked an American army convoy and inflicting heavy casualties. These events escalated the violence and were typical. Ibid. p. 430.

[289] *History of St. Charles County*, pp. 306-307. "The point" refers to the area at the confluence of the Missouri and Mississippi Rivers. As late as the 1880s the author of the *History of St. Charles County* referred to "characteristic Indian perfidy." Ibid. p. 150.

[290] Richard White, *Middle Ground*, p. 392.

[291] Hurt, *Nathan Boone*, p. 107.

[292] Wilkins, *"Trial of Little Crow,"* p. 37.

[293] McCandless, *History of Missouri, 1820-1860*, p. 53.

[294] Meinig, *Shaping of America*, Vol. 2, p. 78.

[295] Ibid. p. 81.

[296] Jo Ann Brown, *St. Charles Borromeo*, p. 71.

[297] Foley, *A History of Missouri, 1683-1820*, p. 175.

[298] Ibid., In 1810 there were 600 free blacks in the territory of 20,000 inhabitants. By 1820 there were only 375 out of 66,000 inhabitants. Ibid.

[299] Lloyd, *A History of the City of St. Peters*, p. 73.

[300] Cook, "History of St. Charles," pp. 55, 75. Hurt, *Agriculture and Slavery*, p. 247. After capturing a runaway, the sheriff of St. Charles County, when no one responded to the notice in the newspaper, sold the slave at auction for $200. After his expensees were paid, there was no money left to send to the state. Lee, *Slavery p. 80.*

[301] Foley, *A History of Missouri, 1683-1820*, p. 175.

[302] There were 20 counties in Missouri that had a higher percentage of the population in slavery, including Howard (59%), Saline (50%), Lafayette (47%), New Madrid (44%), Callaway (36%), Boone (35%), and Lincoln (25%).

[303] Gerald Dunne, *The Missouri Supreme Court, From Dred Scott to Nancy Cruzan*, (Columbia: University of Missouri Press, 1993), pp. 17-22.

[304] Hurt, *Agriculture and Slavery*, pp. 255-256. By 1860 the escape rate in Missouri was one out of every 1,457 slaves, while the average for all slave states was 1 out of every 4,919. In 1841, a statue made it a crime to aid the excape of a slave, even if it was unintended. Ibid. Sandfort, Hermann *Heinrich Sandfort*, p. 267. Lee *Slavery,* p. 89, Siting Trexler, *Slavery in Missouri* p. 231, n. 89.

[305] *History of St. Charles County*, p. 206.

[306] McCandless, *History of Missouri, 1820-1860*, p. 6. Slaves, however, were treated as more than mere chattels in St. Charles, where they were required, like everyone else, to "work on the streets." Trexler, *Slavery in Missouri* p. 63, n-25.

[307] McElhiney, *My Hometown* p. 25. Hurt*, Agriculture and Slavery*, p. 247. Lovejoy's criticism centered on Judge Luke Lawless who had encouraged the grand jurors not to indict and was a Catholic. Showing his nativist tendencies, Lovejoy attacked Lawless Irish birth and Catholicism, seeing in his actions, " the cloven feet of Jesuitism, peeping out from under the veil of almost every paragraph." Primm, *Lion of the Valley*, p. 184.

[308] Gerteis, *Civil War St. Louis*, p. 22.

[309] Ibid., p. 21.

[310] Ibid., pp. 23, 27-28. While the jury, sitting at the federal courthouse in St. Louis, decided against Scott on the merits of the case, what was significant was that Judge Robert W. Wells had allowed the trial to take place at all. Under the Fugitive Slave Law of 1850, fugitives had no right of *habeus corpus* in state courts. If Scott had the right to be tried before a jury in a federal court, any alleged fugitive slave could also request a federal jury trial to decide his fate. Ibid.

[311] Kevin Phillips, *The Cousins'War*, (New York: Basic Books, 1999), p. 384. *History of St. Charles County*, p. 346. In 1867 a new church was built at Fifth and Madison, called the First Presbyterian Church and was the home of the Southern Presbyterians, while the Northern Presbyterians attended the Jefferson Street Presbyterian Church at Jefferson and Benton. Edna McElniney Olson, *Historical Articles*, Vol. IV, p. 779.

[312] *History of St. Charles County*, p. 349. In 1870, the northern branch had a church that was attended primarily by workmen on the Railroad Bridge. When the bridgework was complete and the men moved on, the congregation at Third and Franklin disappeared and the Franklin Street African-American Baptist Church took its place. Ibid.

[313] Lloyd, *History of St. Peters*, p. 73. In 1852 Captain Andrew Harper of St. Charles turned his 24 slaves over to the colonization society on the condition that they "be immediately colonized to Africa." All but 2 reached Liberia. Trexler, *Slavery in Missouri*, p. 230.

[314] Stewart, *Duels*, p. 133.

[315] Ibid. p. 50.

[316] *Banner-News*, December 17, 1948.

[317] Stewart, *Duels*, p. 126.

[318] Ibid. pp. 43-44.

[319] Ibid. pp. 106-107.

[320] Ibid. p. 124.

[321] Edna McElhiney Olson, *Historical Articles*, Vol. I, p. 29.

[322] Hurt, *Agriculture and Slavery*, p. 203.

[323] Ibid.

[324] Mallinckrodt, *Knights to Pioneers*, p. 199.

[325] Ibid.

[326] McElhiney, *My Hometown*, p. 31.

[327] Daniel T. Brown, *Small Glories*, (St. Charles, Howell Foundation, Inc., 2003), p. 74.

[328] Edna McElhiney Olson, *Historical Articles*, Vol. I, p. 29.

[329] David L. Colton, "Lawyers, Legislation and Educational Localism," *MHR*, January 1975, p. 144.

[330] Alphonse, Wetmore, *Gazetteer of the State of Missouri*, p. 166, Cook, "History of St. Charles," p. 69.

[331] Sara M. Evans, *Born for Liberty*, (New York: The Free Press, 1989), pp. 70-72. In the 1820s and 1830s, numerous schools offering higher education for women were founded in the eastern United States. Ibid.

[332] Lindenwood College Alumni Directories 1986 and 1991.

[333] Primm, *Lion of the Valley*, p. 153.

[334] Chittenden, *American Fur Trade*, p. 3.

[335] Frederick E. Voelker, "The French Mountain Men of the Early Far West," in *The Spanish in the Mississippi Valley*, ed. by. John Francis McDermott, (Urbana: University of Illinois Press, 1965), p. 95.

[336] Hurt, *Nathan Boone*, p. 30.

[337] Stephen E. Ambrose, *Undaunted Courage, Meriwether Lewis, Thomas Jefferson, and the Opening of the American West*, (New York: Simon and Schuster, 1996), p. 138.

[338] Edna McElhiney Olson, *Historical Articles*, Vol. II, p. 257. *St. Charles County Portrait and Biographical Record*, (St. Charles: Chapman Publishing Company, 1895), p. 67. Primm, *Lion of the Valley,* pp. 128-132.

[339] Chittenden, *American Fur Trade*, p. 16.

[340] Ibid., pp. 19-20.

[341] Ibid., p. 30.

[342] Ambrose, *Undaunted Courage*, p. 138.

[343] Ruby Matson Robbins, "Missouri Reader," p. 155.

[344] Lloyd, *History of the City of St. Peters*, p. 31.

[345] Banner, *Legal Systems in Conflict*, p. 95.

[346] Ibid. p. 97.

[347] Foley, *A History of Missouri, 1683-1820*, p. 109.

[348] Ibid. p. 104.

[349] Ibid. p. 95.

[350] Ibid. p. 99.

[351] Hurt, *Nathan Boone*, pp. 111, 50.

[352] Ibid. p. 173.

[353] Meining, *Shaping of America*, Vol. 2, pp. 243-244.

[354] Ibid.

[355] O'Brien, *Grassland, Forest, and Historical Settlement*, p. 82.

[356] Meining, *Shaping of America*, Vol. 2, pp. 242-243.

[357] McCandless, *History of Missouri. 1820-1860*, p. 85.

[358] Banner, *Legal Systems in Conflict*, p. 8.

[359] Ibid.

[360] Ibid.

[361] Ibid.

[362] Ibid.

[363] Ibid.

[364] Ibid. p. 138.

[365] Ibid.

[366] Ibid., pp. 86-87.

[367] Mo. Rep. Vol. 1, p. 2. The case was a writ of error from a Circuit Court judgement on the petition of plaintiffs to have dower assigned to them.

[368] Banner, *Legal Systems in Conflict*, p. 103.

[369] *History of St. Charles County*, p. 205.[370] Sellers, *Market Revolution*, p.48.

[371] Sellers, *Market Revolution*, p. 47.

[372] Ibid., p. 159. Opposition to this in New Orleans led to Congress accepting the Code Napoleon in that area. Ibid.

[373] Ibid., p. 50.

[374] James Neal Primm, *Economic Policy in the Development of a Western State, Missouri 1820-1860*, (Cambridge: Harvard University Press, 1954), pp. 48-49.

[375] Ibid., pp. 38-39.

[376] Ibid., pp. 50-51.

[377] Sellers, *Market Revolution*, p. 54.

[378] Dunne, *The Missouri Supreme Court*, pp. 18-21. Cook, "History of St. Charles," p. 42.

[379] Atherton, "Missouri Society and Economy in 1821," *MHR*, October 1998, p. 6.

[380] Hurt, *Nathan Boone*, pp. 33-34.

[381] Bruce Laurie, *Artisans into Workers, Labor in Nineteenth-Century America*, (New York: Hill and Wang, 1989), p. 16.

[382] Sellers, *Market Revolution*, p. 9.

[383] Ibid.

[384] Ibid. p. 117.

[385] Ibid. p. 18.

[386] Ibid., p. 13.

[387] Atherton, "Missouri Society and Economy in 1821," *MHR*, October 1998, pp. 7-8.

[388] David Thelen, *Paths of Resistance, Tradition and Dignity in Industrializing Missouri*, (New York: Oxford University Press, 1986), p. 14.

[389] Cook, "History of St. Charles," p. 7.

[390] The woolen mill now houses the Lewis and Clark microbrewery and restaurant.

[391] Lewis E. Atherton, *The Frontier Merchant in Mid-America*, (Colombia: University of Missouri Press, 1971), p. 52.

[392] Rorabaugh, *Alcoholic Republic*, p. 78.

[393] Ibid., p. 83.

[394] Ibid.

[395] Sandfort, *Hermann Heinrich Sandfort*, pp. 266-267.

[396] Rorabaugh, *Alcoholic Republic*, pp. 160-161.

[397] Kamphoefner, *Westfalians*, pp. 128-129. James Judge owned 200 horses, 40 mules, 24 oxen and 17 slaves. Lee, *Slavery*, p. 58.

[398] Atherton, "Missouri Society," p. 11.

[399] Atherton, *Frontier Merchant*, p. 140.

[400] Kamphoefner, *Westfalians*, p. 127.

[401] Sandfort, *Hermann Heinrich Sandfort*, pp. 266-67.

[402] Edna McElhiney Olson, *Historical Articles*, Vol. III, p. 519. Dr. McElniney was also a delegate to the 1860 Democratic convention that nominated Breckenridge, and served as a Curator of the University of Missouri. Ibid.

[403] Kamphoefner, *Westfalians*, p. 127.

[404] Hurt, *Agriculture and Slavery*, pp. 83-87. Primm, *Economic Policy*, pp.116-118.

[405] Edna McElhiney Olson, *Historical Articles*, Vol. I, p. 114.

[406] Meining, *Shaping of America*, p. 335.

[407] *Valley of the Mississippi*, p. 42.

[408] George Rogers Taylor, *The Transportation Revolution 1815-1860*, (New York: Holt, Rinehart and Winston, 1995), p. 166.

[409] McElhiney, *My Hometown*, p. 2.

[410] Minke, *History of Portage des Sioux Township*, pp. 55, 69.

[411] McCandless, *History of Missouri, 1820-1860*, p. 139. Meining, *Shaping of America*, p. 318.

[412] Nagel, *Missouri*, p. 65.

[413] Drummond, *Historic Sites*, p. 55.

[414] *History of St. Charles County*, p. 115.

[415] Kamper, Ken, "Trail to the Village of the Missouri Indians," in Donald Minke, *The History of Portage de Sioux Township Missouri, The Land Between the Rivers, Portage des Sioux*: (Land Between the Rivers Historical Society, 1999), p. 6.

[416] Kamper, Ken, "The Boone Family," in *Donald Minke, The History of Portage de Sioux Township Missouri, The Land Between the Rivers*, (Portage des Sioux: Land Between the Rivers Historical Society, 1999), pp. 18-19.

[417] Floyd Calvin Shoemaker, *Missouri and the Missourians*, Vol.1 (Chicago: The Lewis Publishing Company, 1943), p. 589.

[418] Taylor, *Transportation Revolution*, p. 176.

[419] Cook, "History of St. Charles," p. 44.

[420] Ibid., p. 36.

[421] Daniel T. Brown, *Small Glories*, p. 35.

[422] Edna McElhiney Olson, *Historical Articles*, Vol. II, p. 295.

[423] Cook, "History of St. Charles," p. 12.

[424] *Missourian*, July 1, 1820, p. 3. Nevertheless, the National Road directed many settlers to the St. Louis area, and was the only federal effort before 1830 other than a few military roads. In that year Congress finally passed a federal road bill, but President Andrew Jackson vetoed it claiming it was unconstitutional.

[425] Hahn, *Rufus Easton*, p. 7. Alton, Illinois was promoted by Easton who named the town after his oldest son Alton Rufus Easton. Ibid.

[426] "A 1795 Inspection of Spanish Missouri," p. 14.

[427] Drummond, *Historic Sites*, p. 17.

[428] Mallinckrodt, *Knights to Pioneers*, p. 126.

[429] O'Brien, *Grassland, Forests and Historical Settlement*, p. 91.

[430] Drummond, *Historic Sites*, p. 226. Other early settlers included George Huffman from Kentucky, Aaron Rutger from Holland, Nathaniel Simons from New England and Nicholas Countz, a Pennsylvania Dutchman. Ibid.

[431] Meining, *Shaping of America*, Vol. 2, p. 252.

[432] Ibid.

[433] *Cosmos-Monitor*, August 24, 1938.

[434] Minke, *History of Portage des Sioux Township*, p. 74.

[435] *History of St. Charles County*, pp. 29, 142.

[436] Adler, *Yankee Merchants*, p. 175.

[437] Edna McElhiney Olson, *Historical Articles*, Vol. III, p. 423.

[438] *Valley of the Mississippi*, p. 42-43.

Chapter III
End Notes

[439] Attorney General Edward Bates had defended Colonel John Muldrow in his trial in St. Charles and gained his acquital on assault charges. The fight had ensued in 1836 when Muldrow had suggested raising money to buy the freedom of Missouri slaves, Trexler, *Slavery in Missouri, p. 120*. Bates was the vice president of a colonization society and favored sending freed slaves back to Africia. Ibid. p. 231.

[440] *History of St. Charles County*, pp. 173-174.

[441] Ibid., p. 197.

[442] Nagel, *Missouri*, pp.115-117.

[443] Gerteis, *Civil War St. Louis*, p. 59.

[444] Ibid. .

[445] H.K. Stumberg, "Duden Tells of Advantages in the Area," in *Historical Articles St. Charles County*, Vol. II, pp. 232-240.

[446] Kamphoefner, *Westfalians*. p. 86. St. Charles and Warren counties formed part of a "German belt" extending up the Missouri River from St. Louis where German culture predominated. Ibid.

[447] John A. Hawgood, *The Tragedy of German-America: The Germans in the United State of America During the Nineteenth Century and After,* (New York: 1970), p. 45. See also Kenneth M. Stamp, *America in 1857. a Nation on the Brink*, (New York: Oxford University Press, 1990), p. 77. M.A. Gienapp, "Nativism in the Creation of a Republican Majority Before the Civil War." *Journal of American History. LXXII*, 1985, p. 547.

[448] Poindexter, "A Right Smart Little Town," p. 42. Pope Pius IX had given the nativists plenty of ammunition when, between 1846 and 1878, he condemned in a series if documents, representative government, freedom of the press, and separation of church and State. William Barnaby Faherty, *The St. Louis Irish, an Unmatched Celtic Community*, (St. Louis: Missouri Historical Society Press, 2001), p. 65.

[449] Dan Brown, *Small Glories*, p. 133.

[450] Stamp, *America in 1857,* p. 102. Gienapp, "Nativism and the Creation of the Republican Majority Before the Civil War," p. 131. Hawgood, *Tragedy of German-America*, p. 299.

[451] In Great Britain, the Liberal Party had gained its first parliamentary majority in 1832 and outlawed slavery throughout the British Empire.

[452] Anita, Mallinckrodt, trans. "Augusta," *Demokrat*, October 7, 1860, in *A History of Augusta, Missouri and its Area*, Vol. 1, p. 48. Friedrich Muench was born on June 25,1799 in Nieergemuenden in the German State of Hesse. While studying theology at the University of Giessen he adopted rationalist religious and democratic political ideas. After the failure of the Liberal Revolutions in 1830, he and his brother-in-law formed the Giesen Society and led 500 Germans to Missouri. *Dictionary, of Missouri Biography,* ed. by Lawrence O. Christensen, William E. Foley, Gary P. Kremer, and Kenneth H. Winn, (Columbia: University of Missouri Press, 1999), p. 562.

[453] Gary McKiddy, "St. Charles During the Civil War," *St. Charles County Heritage*, Vol., 15, No. 4, October 1997, p. 131.

[454] Anita Mallinckrodt, trans. "Democrats are Enemy of Immigrants," *Demokrat*, April 26, 1860, in *A History of Augusta*, Missouri and its Area, Vol.1, p. 41.

[455] *Cosmos-Monitor*, March 12,1941, "This day in Missouri History." After his appointment to the federal District Court of Western Missouri he lived the rest of his life in Jefferson City and Kansas City, where he died on July 14th, 1888, after a distinguished career as a jurist. Lawrence H. Larsen, *Federal Justice in Western Missouri, The Judges, the Cases, the Times*, (Columbia: University of Missouri Press, 1994), pp. 49-73.

[456] Poindexter, *A Right Smart Little Town,* p. 31.

[457] Ibid. p. 39.

[458] Gerteis, *Civil War St. Louis*, pp. 74-75.

[459] Hawgood, *The Tragedy of German-America*, p. 248. Gerteis, *Civil War St. Louis*, pp. 76-77.

[460] Bob Schultz, "Some Civil War Politics in St. Charles County," *St. Charles County Heritage*, Vol.20, No.1, January 2002, p.11.

[461] Anita Mallinckrodt, trans. "Freedom or Slavery Will Be Decided,"*Demokrat*, October 7, 1860, in *A History of Augusta, Missouri and Its Area*, Vol. 1, p. 49.

[462] Schultz, "Civil War Politics," p. 13.

[463] Ibid.

[464] Anita Mallinckrodt, trans. "Two Americans Driven from House and Farm Because They Voted for Lincoln," *Demokrat*, November 29, 1860, in *A History of Augusta, Missouri and Its Area*, Vol. 1, p. 50.

[465] *Excerpts from the Diary of John Jay Johns 1860-1899 and Allied Papers*, Florence Johns, ed. December 13, 1860, Lindenwood University archives.

[466] Schultz, "Civil War Politics," p. 15. Frayser was a farmer who owned 16 slaves in the 1852 state census. He owned 608 acres in Dardenne prairie, and was a member of the Dardenne Presbyterian Church, having joined as an adult in 1855. Ibid., p. 16. It was said that, in Dardenne Prairie slavery was "a name rather than a condition" and that slaves "had all things in common with thier master including the virtues and manners." *History of North East Missouri*, Vol. 1(Chicago: Lewis, 1913), p. 567.

[467] Gerteis, *Civil War St. Louis*, p. 88.

[468] Walter D. Kamphoefner, "St. Louis Germans and the Republican Party, 1848-1860," *Mid-America*. Vol. 57, No. 2, April 1975, p. 87. For a review of the historical debate, Ibid. p. 69.

[469] *History of St. Charles County*, pp. 180-181.

[470] Ibid., pp. 179-180.

[471] Gerteis, *Civil War St. Louis*, pp. 111-112.

[472] *History of St.Charles County*, p. 183.

[473] Gerteis, *Civil War St. Louis*, p. 114. The Federal forces pursued Governor Jackson and the remnant of his government as they fled southwest from Jefferson City. While in exile, the members of the legislature who fled with him, passed an Ordinance of Secession and ratified the Constitution of the Confederate States of America.

[474] Ibid. pp.133-134. The company organized at the courthouse that evening was under the leadership of Captain Richard Overall and First Lieutenant David Schultz and numbered about fifty men. Ibid.

[475] McKiddy, "*St. Charles During the Civil War*," pp. 137-138. Conrad Weinrich, an officer in the Home Guard, wrote the following in a letter to his family on July the 26th, 1861: ... "Heinrich also wanted to know if we'd gotten U.S. arms. We didn't have them yet at the time, but a week ago we received 80 pieces in Cotlevill [Cottleville] and another company got 40, that makes 120 in our area, and in Cotlevill 60 and in St. Peters 60, that makes 220 altogether, apart from St. Charles where they received 100. Mr. A. Krekel is the commander of the Union Guard of St. Charles County. Last Saturday 400 men from the Union Guard assembled with Captain Woodson near Dr. Talley's. Capt. Heine's Company was drilling with U.S. weapons, and then the *Fire eaters* came and wanted to take them away, but they got a hot *Brackfeest* [breakfast] instead with *Muskets, Rifles, & Shottgunns*. They'd gotten 400 men together, but if they'd had 1,000 we still would have beaten them up all right. I don't know what will happen now." *Deutsche im Amerikanischen Burgerkrieg: Briefe von Front and Farm, 1861-1865,* ed. Wolfgang Helbich and Walter Kampkoefner, (Schoening: Paderhorn, 2002), pp. 392-396.

[476] *History of St. Charles County*, p. 183, Adele Achelpohl Barton, *The John F. Dierker Story* (St. Charles: manuscript available at Kathryn Linnemann Library)

[477] McKiddy, "St. Charles During the Civil War," pp. 143-144. Bushwackers were prevalent in the Wentzville area and on Dog Prairie. In 1864 they plundered the stores of union people and, on one occasion, appeared at the home of Carl Groeblinghoff, a farmer at Elm Prairie, and called him

out, at which time they shot him for his pro-union sympathies. Anita Mallinckrodt, trans. "Bushwackers in the County," *Demokrat*, in *A History of Augusta, Missouri and its Area,* Vol. 1, pp. 117-119.

[478] McKiddy, "St. Charles During the Civil War," p. 133.

[479] Gerteis, *Civil War St. Louis*, p. 132. The practice was declared unconstitutional by a unanimous Supreme Court in 1866, after the war was over. Ibid.

[480] *History of St. Charles County*, p. 407.

[481] Gerteis, *Civil War St. Louis*, p. 171.

[482] Missouri's Union Provost Marshal Papers, Missouri Archives, Examination of Dougherty, Joseph H, 5-19-1863 f1304. George P. Strong was also involved in the McPheeters case where President Lincoln had to intervene to keep Strong and the provost marshall from prosecuting a Presbyterian minister because he baptized an infant named Strerling Price. Strong would also later be a delegate to the 1865 Constitutional Convention.

[483] Ibid.

[484] Ibid. Krekel, Arnold, A general report on William Chambers, 8-17-1862, F1236.

[485] Larson, *Federal Justice*, pp. 51-52.

[486] *History of the First Presbyterian Church*, p. 10.

[487] McKiddy, "St. Charles During the Civil War," p. 136.

[488] Minke, *History of Portage des Sioux Township*, pp. 62-63.

[489] Provost Marshall Papers, Missouri Archives, Mary S. Dines to Major General Merrill, She asks on what conditions her husband may return from prison, 01-05-1863, F1304.

[490] Ibid.

[491] Ibid. Humphreys, James, Sworn statement about R.B.Keeble helping rebels, 01-17-1863, F1405. Krekel, Arnold, Asking to give a shotgun to R. Keeble, 3-18-1863, F1355.

[492] Ibid. Mason, A.S., Order for arrest harboring Bushwackers, 01-20-1865, F1484.

[493] Edna McElhiney Olson, *Historical Articles*, Vol. II, p. 282. Schiermeier, *Cracker Barrel Country*, Vol. II, p. 126.

[494] Mallinckrodt, *Knights to Pioneers*, p. 320.

[495] McKiddy, "St. Charles During the Civil War," pp.137-144. Conrad Weinrich wrote, "Some 4-5,000 secessionists have gotten together in Lincoln County and are after our hides, but I don't think these guy's have any *Spunch* and we are ready for them anytime." *Deutche in Amerkanischen,* pp. 392-396.

[496] Edna McElhiney Olson, *Historical Articles*, p. 442.

[497] Anita Mallinckrodt, trans. "Elected Germans in the Legislature," *Demokrat*, November 20, 1862, in *A History of Augusta, Missouri and its Area,* Vol. 1, p. 82. The same oath was required of all civil servants, professors and curators at the University, bank employees, public school teachers, employees of state chartered corporations, priests and ministers.

[498] Provost Marshall Papers, Missouri Archives, Krekel, Arnold, Asking to give a shotgun to Richard Keeble, 3-18-11863, F1355.

[499] Anita Mallinckrodt, trans. "Dissolution of Krekel's Battalion, Missouri State Militia," *Demokrat*, November 27, 1862, in *A History of Augusta, Missouri and its Area,* Vol. 1, p. 83.

[500] Gerteis, *Civil War St. Louis*, pp. 152-153.

[501] Ibid., p. 157.

[502] *History of St. Charles County*, p. 182. Three of the companies were honorably discharged and a fourth was attached to the First Missouri Militia infantry for three years. Ibid. On occasion they conducted raids in Northern Missouri under command of General Merrill. Hennington, Moses, Sworn statement about J.M. Tebbetts and his oats, 7-7-1863, F1403 During one of these campaigns Moses Henntington filed a report with the provost marshal estimating that "Merrill's Horse" expropriated 500 bushels of oats worth 50 cents per bushel while the regiment was encamped at the farm of J.M. Tebbets near Pond Fort, July 9, 1862. Ibid.

[503] Provost Marshall Paper, Missouri Archives, Trexler, *Slavery in Missouri,* p. 237, n-116.

[504] Michael Feldman, *"Emancipation in Missouri,"* *MHR*, October 1958, p.42.

[505] McKiddy, "St. Charles During the Civil War," p. 143. Callaway County had given Lincoln just 15 votes out of 2632 in 1860 and seceded from the Union as the Kingdom of Callaway, with its capitol in Kingdom City.

[506] Ibid.

[507] Anita Mallinckrodt, trans. "The Infamy Against Krekel and the Germans Becomes Greater," *Demokrat*, December 4, 1864, in *A History of Augusta, Missouri and its Area*, Vol. 1, p. 84.

[508] Ibid.

[509] Blassingame, John W., "The Recruitment of Negro Troops in Missouri During the Civil War," *MHR* vol. 58, p. 326-329.

[510] Ibid.

[511] Gerteis, *Civil War St. Louis*, p. 283.

[512] Schultz, "Civil War Politics," p.18, Cain, *Lincoln's Attorney General*, p. 280.

[513] Blassingame, "The Recruitment on Negro Troops," p. 332.

[514] Ibid.

[515] Gerteis, *Civil War St. Louis*, p. 283. Dennis Naglich, "The Slave System and the Civil War in Missouri," *MHR*, April 1993, p. 270.

[516] *St. Louis Daily Missouri Democrat,* January 21, 1864. quoted in Blassingame, *"The Recruitment of Negro Troops,"* p. 338.

[517] Anita Mallinckrodt, *Freed Slaves*, (Missouri Research Roundtable Occasional Paper, 1999), p. 5.

[518] Lorenzo J. Greene, Gary R. Kremer, Antonio F. Holland, *Missouri's Black Heritage,* (Columbia: University of Missouri Press, 1993), p. 80.

[519] Edna McElhiney Olson, *Historical Articles*, Vol.III, p. 520.

[520] Ibid.

[521] Blassingame, "The Recruitment of Negro Troops," p. 337.

[522] Ibid., pp. 336-337.

[523] William E. Parrish, *A History of Missouri, 1860-1875*, Volume III, (Columbia: University of Missouri Press, 1973), p. 112.

[524] Anita Mallinckrodt, trans. "St. Charles County Under Arms," *Demokrat*, October 6, 1864, in *A History of Augusta, Missouri and its Area*,Vol. 1, p. 118.

[525] Anita Mallinckrodt, trans. "General Order No. 107," *Demokrat*, July 14, 1864, in *A History of Augusta Missouri and its Area*, Vol. 1, p. 113.

[526] Members included Krekel, Joseph Maher, Theodore Bruere, Robert Bailey, Phillip Peuster, John Orf, Friedrich Weinreben, Ben Emmons, Jr., W.H. Martens, Joseph Barwise, John Nahm, J.H. Besser, Dr. Gerling.

[527] *History of St. Charles County*, p. 200.

[528] William E. Parrish, *A History of Missouri, 1860-1875*, Volume III, (Columbia: University of Missouri Press, 1973), p. 114.

[529] Ibid.

[530] Edna McElhiney Olson, *Historical Articles*, Vol. II, p. 370.

[531] McKiddy, "St. Charles During the Civil War," p. 144.

[532] "Reminiscences of Lindenwood College, 1827-1920," *Lindenwood College*, Vol. 89, No. 12(b), May, 1920, p. 64.

[533] *Bicentennial Celebration Program,* p. 37.

[534] *Banner-News*, March 8, 1950.

[535] Larson, *Federal Justice*, p. 50. The Krekel family remained involved in county politics through Frank Bezzenberger, who had married Emma Krekel, daughter of Nicholas and niece of Arnold Krekel. He was elected county collector in 1882. *History of St. Charles County*, pp. 360-361.

[536] Schultz, "Civil War Politics," p. 19.

[537] *History of St. Charles County*, p. 200.

[538] Parrish, *History of Missouri*, 1860-1875, p. 121.

[539] Anita Mallinckrodt, trans. "The Loyalty Oath," *Demokrat*, September 21, 1865, in *A History of Augusta, Missouri and Its Area*, Vol. 1, p. 136.

[540] Schiermeier, *Cracker Barrel Country*, Vol. III, p. 96. Boswell Randolph was related to the famous Randolphs of Virginia. Ibid.

[541] Ibid. p. 95.

[542] Parrish, *History of Missouri*, 1860-1875, p. 119.

[543] Ibid. 127.

[544] Schultz, "Civil War Politics," p. 19. See also Gerteis, *Civil War St. Louis*, p. 311.

[545] *History of St. Charles County*, p. 406.

[546] Larsen, *Federal Justice*, p. 62.

[547] Anita Mallinckrodt, trans. "Riot in Wentzville Attempt to Drive Out Lincoln Supporters and Germans," *Demokrat*, September 27, 1866, in *A History of Augusta, Missouri and Its Area*, Vol. 1, p. 153.

[548] Schultz, "Civil War Politics," p. 21.

[549] Kamphoefner, trans in *Deutsche im Amerikanischen Bürgerkrieg: Briefe von Front und Farm, 1861-1865,* ed Wolfgang Helbich and Walter D. Kamphoefner, (Schöningh: Paderborn, 2002), pp. 392-396. *The Demokrat* continued to support Radical Republicanism, strongly opposed the lenient policies of President Andrew Johnson, and heartily endorsed Radical efforts in Congress to impeach and remove him. Anita Mallinckrodt, trans. "The People Were Not Asked," *Demokrat,* January 4, 1866, in *A History of Augusta, Missouri and Its Area,* Vol. 1, pp. 140-141.

[550] Mallinckrodt, *Freed Slaves*, pp. 6-7.

[551] Anita Mallinckrodt, trans. "Negro Equality," *Demokrat*, August 6, 1868, in *A History of Augusta, Missouri and Its Area*, Vol. 2, p. 173.

[552] Walter Kamphoefner, trans *Anzeiger des Westens*, November 1, 1866, in *Deutsche im Amerikanischen Bürgerkrieg: Briefe von Front und Farm, 1861-1865,* pp. 392-396. African-American suffrage gained majorities of 74 and 68 percent in two German precincts in St. Charles County. Ibid. Nevertheless, it carried in only 41 of Missouri's 114 counties, largely the radical strongholds in the Southwest and along the northern border. In St. Louis County it was defeated by nearly three to one. Connecticut, Wisconsin Minnesota, Kansas, Ohio, Michigan, Nebraska and District of Columbia had also rejected similar constitutional referenda, often out of fear that if it granted the vote when the rest of the states did not, that blacks would rush to that state. Parrish, *History of Missouri, 1860-1875*, pp. 246-247.

[553] Rothensteiner, John, *History of the Archdiocese of St. Louis*, Volume 2, (St. Louis: Blackwell Wielandy Co., 1928), p. 218.

[554] Parrish, *History of Missouri, 1860-1875*, pp. 131-134. The majority held that the oath constituted a bill of attainder and ex post facto legislation. Ibid.

[555] Ibid. pp. 237-238.

[556] Ibid. p. 251. They later discovered that in their haste, they had ommitted the second section of the amendment, so they had to repeat the entire process when they reconvened the following January.

[557] Ibid. p. 256.

[558] Anita Mallinckrodt, trans. "The Fifteenth Amendment," *Demokrat*, January 27, 1870, in *A History of Augusta, Missouri and Its Area,* Vol. 2, p. 208.

[559] Parrish, *History of Missouri, 1860-1875,* p. 256.

[560] Anita Mallinckrodt, trans. "The Liberal Republican Party," *Demokrat*, September 8, 1870, in *A History of Augusta, Missouri and Its Area,* Vol. 1, p. 214.

[561] Parrish, *History of Missouri, 1860-1875,* p. 263. The Democrats employed a "possum policy," whereby they did not run candidates for statewide office but only local races.

[562] *St. Charles News*, November 24, 1870. William Bryan founded the *St. Charles News* in Wentzville in 1863 and moved the paper to St. Charles in 1870. *Wentzville Centennial Program,* 1955, p. 34.

[563] *History of St. Charles County*, pp. 377, 406. A. H. Edwards had been admitted to the bar after

studying under his brother, W.W. Edwards, who became a circuit judge. Ibid.

564 *St. Charles News*, November 24, 1870.

565 Ibid., January 19, 1871.

566 Ibid., February 2, 1871.

567 Ibid., January 5, 1871.

568 Ibid., January 12, 1871.

569 Ibid., May 18, 1871.

570 Anita Mallinckrodt, trans. "The Germans in Missouri," *Demokrat*, October 19, 1871, in *A History of Augusta, Missouri and Its Area,* Vol. 2, p. 232.

571 Ibid. p. 252.

572 Paul Kleppner, *The Cross of Culture, A Social Analysis of Midwest Politics, 1850-1900*. (New York: The Free Press), p. 17.

573 Ibid.

574 *History of St. Charles County*, pp. 200-203.

575 Anita Mallinckrodt, trans. "Horace Greeley Meeting in New Melle," *Demokrat*, October 3, 1872, in *A History of Augusta, Missouri and Its Area*, Vol. 2, p. 246. Among those listed were Col. Conrad Weinrich, T. Borberg, M. Doelling, Capt. Heinrich Koelling, Goltermann, Tuepker, Meier, who "go hand in hand with the Liberals and want to know nothing of the Grant fraud." Ibid.

576 Anita Mallinckrodt, trans. "About the Political Situation," *Demokrat*, July 18, 1872, in *A History of Augusta, Missouri* and Its Area, Vol. 2, p. 243.

577 Anita Mallinckrodt, trans. "United Opposition against the Grant Ring." *Demokrat*, July 18, 1872, in *A History of Augusta, Missouri and Its Area*, Vol. 2, p. 243.

578 Parrish, *History of Missouri, 1860-1875*, p. 281.

579 Hans L.Trefousse, *Carl Schurz,* (New York: Fordham University Press, 1998), pp. 187-188, 204-206. Friedrich Muench was disappointed with the Greeley candidacy and returned to the Republican Party. *Dictionary,* p. 563.

580 Lawrence O. Christensen and Gary R. Kremer, *A History of Missouri*, Vol. IV, 1875 to 1919, (Columbia: University of Missouri Press, 1997), p. 7.

581 Anita Mallinckrodt, trans. "Mass Meeting in St. Charles, Mo." *Demokrat*, August 20, 1874, in *A History of Augusta, Missouri and Its Area,* Vol. 2, p. 279.

582 *History of St. Charles County*, p. 223.

583 Anita Mallinckrodt, trans. "Our Liberals and Independents," *Demokrat*, November 23, 1876, in *A History of Augusta, Missouri and Its Area*, Vol. 2, p. 353. Carl Schurz became Secretary of the Interior in the Hays Administration.

584 Thelen, *Paths of Resistance*, p. 23.

585 *History of St. Charles County*, p. 201. Judge W.W. Edwards, State Senator A.W. Edwards and Major James Edwards were all brothers. Ibid. p. 285.

586 Leading Anglo-American Democrats at that time were A.H. Buckner and Andrew King, both of whom moved away from the county after being elected to Congress. State Senator A.H. Edwards, served in the General Assembly for 12 years, Theodorick McDearmon, ran unsuccessfully for the Eastern District Court of Appeals, H.C. Lackland was a member of the Constitutional Convention in 1875 and chairman of the Judiciary Committee in the House. As used hereafter, the term "Anglo-Americans" refers to English-speaking Americans, even though the families of most such people in St. Charles County were Scots or Scots-Irish rather than English.

587 *History of St. Charles County*, pp. 396-397.

588 Colonel Benjamin Emmons, a lawyer who served as circuit court clerk was one of the few Anglo-American Republican leaders. See *History of St. Charles County* and *St. Charles County Portrait and Biographical Record*, (St. Charles: Chapman Publishing Company, 1895).

589 *St. Charles County Portrait and Biographical Record.*

590 R. Hal Williams, *Years of Decision, American Politics in the 1890's*, (Prospect Heights, IL: Waveland Press, Inc. 1978), p. 46.

[591] Ibid.

[592] Kleppner, *Cross of Culture*, p. 45.

[593] Ibid., p. 46.

[594] Ibid., p. 43. Generally, in the Midwest, the more Calvinistic a denomination when it came to ritual, the more likely it was to be Republican. Ibid.

[595] Phillips, *Cousins' War*, p. 438.

[596] Ibid.

[597] *St. Charles County Portrait and Biographical Record.*

[598] Kleppner, *Cross of Culture*, p. 47.

[599] Ibid., p. 50.

[600] *Diary of John Jay Johns*, March 3, 1877. George Brown Tindall and David Shi, *America*, (New York: W.W. Norton and Company, 2004),pp. 753-754. Voter fraud decreased when, around 1890, states went to the Australian Ballot, a government printed ballot cast in private, instead of the old party printed ballot cast in public. Johns wrote in 1890 that, "The Australian system is a great improvement." *Diary of John Jay Johns,* November 4, 1890.

[601] *St. Charles County Portrait and Biographical Record*

[602] Phillip Gleason, *Conservative Reformers, German-American Catholics and the Social Order,* (South Bend: University of Notre Dame Press, 1968), p. 327. In the month of May in 1873, 1874 and 1875, under the direction of Adalbert Falk, Prussian Minister of culture and Education, a number of laws were passed which are collectively known as the May Laws. They instituted civil marriage, withdrew state support from recalcitrant clergy, placed all clerical education and appointments under the state and dissolved most religious orders. Marshall Dill, *Germany: A Modern History*, (Ann Arbor: University of Michigan Press), p. 152.

[604] *History of St. Charles County,* p. 180.

[605] Kleppner, *Cross of Culture*, pp. 38-42.

[606] Mallinckrodt, *Knights to Pioneers*, p. 230. This organization was a more immediate threat to the Evangelical Churches in the Femme Osage area. Paul Nagel states they, "sought to infiltrate and dominate the organization of German Evangelical congregations being formed in the neighborhood. They argued loudly that pastor Garlichs was in fact trying to impose the same sort of authority upon the worshippers in St. Charles and Warren Counties that many had deplored in Germany. Also Garlichs was charged with being an "obscurantist," meaning that he was seeking to withhold enlightenment from his parishioners and that he was opposed to freedom of thought. Paul C. Nagel, *The German Migration to Missouri, My Family's Story*, (Kansas City: Kansas City Star Books, 2002), p. 61.

[607] *Dictionary*, p. 563.

[608] *Cosmos-Monitor*, March 12, 1941, "This Week in Missouri History." Krekel, "embraced liberal views in religious matters at a very early age, and although perhaps not an infidel in the real meaning of that word, he does not believe in the divine origin of the Bible or the Biblical account of creation." *History of St. Charles County,* p. 107.

[609] Jo Ann Brown, *St. Charles Borromeo*, p. 77. The Freeman's Society was founded to combat "American religious, social, and political prejudices, including slavery, Temperance, the manipulations of organized religion, and social political and economic injustice. Members gathered to discuss politics, participate in dramatic presentations, attend lectures and debates and drink at the society's bar." Stephen J. Ross, *Workers on the Edge, Work, Leisure, and Politics in Industrializing Cincinnati,* 1788-1890, (New York: Columbia University Press, 1985), p. 175.

[610] James M. McPherson, *Battle Cry of Freedom: The Civil War Era,* (New York: Oxford University Press, 1988), p.122.

[611] Ibid. p.137.

[612] Jo Ann Brown, *St. Charles Borromeo*, p. 77.

[613] Ibid., p. 88. *History of St. Charles County*, p. 72. Peter Verhaegen was born in Belgium in 1800 and came to this country in 1823. He also served as Vicar General of St. Louis and held a similar

position in Maryland. He served in St. Charles from 1851 to 1868. Jo Ann Brown, *St. Charles Borromeo*, p. 90.

[614] Thelen, *Paths of Resistance*, p.23.

[615] Richard Jensen, *The Winning of the Midwest: Social and Political Conflict 1888 to 1896.* (Chicago: University of Chicago Press, 1971), p. 153. The Evangelical Synod of North America was Lutheran in its external appearance. The majority of its members worshipped in German. The religious organization operated more than 300 schools and maintained a Seminary in Marthasville, Mo. Frederick C. Luebke, *Bonds of Loyalty, German-Americans in World War*, (Dekalb: Northern Illinois Press, 1974), p. 39.

[616] *Diary of John Jay Johns,* July 14, 1886.

[617] Jensen, *Winning of the West,* pp. 70-71.

[618] *Diary of John Jay Johns*, July 4, 1880.

[619] Kamphoefner, trans. in *Deutsche im Amerikanischen Bürgerkrieg: Briefe von Front und Farm, 1861-1865,* pp. 392-396. Throughout the decade of the 1880s voting precincts in Nebraska identifiable as German Catholic regularly gave 65 to 90 percent of their votes to Democrats. In these Nebraska counties there was also a close connection between church affiliation and politics. Jensen, *Winning of the Midwest,* p. 96.

[620] Anita Mallinckrodt, trans. "Wine Licensing," *Demokrat*, April 8, 1869, *A History of Augusta, Missouri and Its Area,* Vol. 1, p. 183. Senator Theodore Bruere was born in Cologne, Germany and came to St. Charles County in 1852 to become county surveyor and later worked for the *Demokrat* paper. He was admitted to the Missouri bar in 1855 by Arnold Krekel and became city attorney in 1863 and Missouri senator in 1866. He was a member of the St. Charles school board for 21 years. Edna McElhiney Olson, *Historical Article*, Vol. III, p. 559.

[621] Anita Mallinckrodt, trans. *"Sunday Blue Laws,"* *Demokrat*, December 22, 1855, in *A History of Augusta, Missouri and Its Area*, Vol. 1, p. 17.

[622] Anita Mallinckrodt, trans. "Oppose the Fanatics," *Democrat*, August 14, 1873, in *A History of Augusta, Missouri and Its Area,* Vol. 2, p. 256.

[623] *St. Charles Journal*, February 11, 1881, p. 3.

[624] *Ibid.,* March 4, 1881, p. 4.

[625] *St. Charles news*, February 8, 1872.

[626] Anita Mallinckrodt, trans. "Temperance Folks Against Pres. Arthur," *Demokrat*, May 24, 1883, in *A History of Augusta, Missouri and Its Area*, Vol. 3, p. 483. Democrat John Jay Johns had equal dislike for Arthur and wrote, "What a sad condition of things that such devils are abroad in the land." *Diary of John Jay Johns,* July 2, 1881.

[627] Anita Mallinckrodt, trans. "For Which Presidential Candidate Will the Germans Vote?" *Demokrat*, October 21, 1880, in *A History of Augusta, Missouri and its Area*, Vol. 3, p. 449.

[628] Carol Berlin and Leonard Wood, *Land of Promise* (Glenview, Illinois: Scott, Foresman and Company, 1987)p. 458.

[629] Ibid. Two weeks after the election, the defeated candidate Blaine was in Augusta to give a speech. Trefousse, *Carl Schurz,* pp. 261-263.

[630] Kleppner, *Cross of Culture*, pp.78-79.

[631] J. Michael Hohe, "Missouri Education at the Crossroads: The Phelan Miscalculation and the Education Amendment of 1870," *MHR*, 1999, p. 388. Nationally about 25 to 30 percent of German immigrants were Catholic. Many of the Catholic Germans would not come to St. Charles County until after the unification of Germany in 1870. Jay P. Dolan, *The American Catholic Experience, A History from Colonial Times to the Present*, (New York: Doubleday & Company, 1985), p. 168.

[632] Dolan, *American Catholic Experience*, p. 270.

[633] *Diary of John Jay Johns*, November 22, 1887.

[634] Christensen and Kremer, *A History of Missouri, 1875-1919*, p. 242. Williams, *Years of Decision*, pp. 46-47. Walter Kamphoefner " Learning from the 'Majority-Minority' City," *St Louis in the Century of Henry Shaw*, ed. by Eric Sandweiss, (Columbia University of Missouri Press 2003)

p. 97. Republicans had sponsored the Bennett Law in Wisconsin and the Edwards Law in Illinois requiring the use of the English language in schools.

[635] Anita Mallinckrodt, trans. "Complete Report of the Election in St. Charles County," *Demokrat*, November 8, 1892, in *A History of Augusta, Missouri and Its Area*, Vol. 3, p. 586.

[636] Jensen, *Winning of the Midwest*, p. 153.

[637] Primm, *Lion of the Valley*, p. 236.

[638] Ibid. p. 231. Control of the North Missouri Railroad quickly passed to St. Louisans like John O'Fallon. 1.2 million in stock subscriptions came from St. Louis city and county, 1.04 million from St. Charles, Boone, Warren, Audrain, Randolph, Macon and other counties; $307,500 from individuals. Ibid.

[639] Robert W. Jackson, *Rails Across the Mississippi, A History of the St. Louis Bridge* (Urbana: University of Illinois Press, 2001), p. 26.

[640] Kamphoefner, *Westfalians*, p. 86.

[641] Ibid., p. 13. Not only did Germans immigrate to the United States, but also went to South America and the Caucuses region of Russia.

[642] *History of St. Charles County*, p.106.

[643] Kamphoefner, *Westfalians*, p.124. They lived up to their reputation as skilled artisans. Occupations dominated by the Germans were restricted to the artisan sector. Including common tradesmen, weaving, tin smithing, brewing, watchmaking, distilling, baking and woodworking. Ibid.

[644] Interview with Robert Sandfort.

[645] Kamphoefner, *Westfalians*, p. 123.

[646] Ibid., p. 124.

[647] Ibid. p. 131. Interview with Robert Sandfort.

[648] Ibid., p. 134.

[649] Anita Mallinckrodt, trans. "First Years of Immigration," *Demokrat*, June 14, 1860, in *A History of Augusta, Missouri and Its Area*, Vol. 1, p. 43.

[650] Kamphocfner, *Westfalians*, p. 120.

[651] Ibid.

[652] Ibid., p. 134. Indian maize had not been grown at all in Germany. While expressing dismay at first the immigrants quickly adapted and grew the crop. Ibid.

[653] Ibid., p. 116.

[654] McKiddy, "St. Charles During the Civil War," p. 132.

[655] Eric Foner, *Reconstruction, America's Unfinished Revolution 1863-1877*, (New York: Harper & Row, 1988), p. 235.

[656] Anita Mallinckrodt, trans. "Immigration," *Demokrat*, January 14, 1864, in *A History of Augusta, Missouri and Its Area*, Vol. 1, p. 108.

[657] Sandfort, *Hermann Heinrich Sandfort*, pp. 273-274.

[658] Edna McElhiney Olson, *Historical Articles*, Vol. III, p. 520.

[659] *History of St. Charles County*, p. 446. Robards moved to St, Charlse where he latter serve as postmaster during the 1870s and 1880s. Ibid.

[660] Meining, *Shaping of America*, p. 246. Twenty-one years after arriving in St. Charles County, Zaddock Woods led a group of settlers to Texas in 1823. Spellman, *Zadock and Minerva Cottle Woods*, p. 80. Others from St. Charles County migrated to Texas and three men with St. Charles County ties died at the Alamo. Brown, *Small Glories*, p. 95. The wife of the owner of the King Ranch had moved with her family from Wentzville to Texas. *Cosmos-Monitor*, A number of St. Charles Countians left for the gold fields of California in 1849-50. *History of St. Charles County*, pp. 228-229.

[661] Interview with Robert Sandfort

[662] Edna McElhiney Olson, *Historical Articles*, Vol. I, p. 93. See also Primm, *Lion of the Valley*, p. 349.

[663] Daniel T. Brown, *Small Glories*, p. 160. Mittelbuscher, Barbara Eisenbath, "Wentzville's 406 Elm Street Placed on National Register of Historic Places," *Newstime*, October 7, 1990, p. 28. The

decline in the tobacco industry was also caused by the "Great Plug War," in which James Buchanan Duke engaged in predatory pricing to drive smaller competitors out of the market and establish a monopoly for the American Tobacco Company. Ibid.

[664] Kamphoefner, *Westfalians*, p. 172.

[665] Anita Mallinckrodt, trans, "German and American Farmers," *Demokrat*, May 6, 1886, in *A History of Augusta, Missouri and Its Area*,Vol. 3. p. 517.

[666] Anita Mallinckrodt, trans, "Germans Increase Land Holdings," *Demokrat*, October 2, 1879, in *A History of Augusta, Missouri and Its Area*, Vol. 2, p. 405. Muench was a pioneer in viticulture in Missouri and his *School for Grape Culture* appeared in German and English. He was a frequent contributor to the German edition of the *American Agriculturist. Dictionary*, p.563.

[667] *History of St. Charles County*, p. 136.

[668] Kamphoefner, *Westfalians*, p.108-109. The Homestead Act had less effect than hoped for since 160-acre farms did not support families on the Great Plains. By 1900 most of the land had been acquired by cattle farmers. Interview with James Neal Primm.

[669] Walter Licht, *Industrializing America, The Nineteenth Century*, (Baltimore: Johns Hopkins University Press, 1995), p. 97.

[670] Edna McElhiney Olsen, *Historical Articles*, Vol. I, p. 78. *History of St. Charles County*, p. 440.

[671] Thelen, *Paths of Resistance*, pp. 37-38. From 1870-1875 he exported millions of phylloxera-resistant cuttings to France where the insect was destroying the vineyards, thus saving the French wine industry. Ibid.

[672] Anita Mallinckrodt, trans, "Vineyards and Orchards," *Demokrat*, September 10, 1957, in *A History of Augusta, Missouri and its Area*, Vol. 2, p. 404.

[673] *Agricultural History*, p.156.

[674] Christensen and Kremer, *A History of Missouri, 1875-1919*, p. 32-33. The St. Charles County Agricultural Extension Service, though the University of Missouri did not come into being until 1915. *Agricultural History*, p. 128.

[675] Edna McElhiney Olson, *Historical Articles*, Vol. III, p. 561. The bank was located on the northeast corner of Main and Jefferson for over 125 years. Not only was there opposition to National Banks, drafters of the original Missouri Constitution forbade the creation of more than one state bank and held the investors personally liable for the debts of that institution. Gerteis, *Civil War St. Louis*, p. 37.

[676] Foner, *Reconstruction*, p. 379.

[677] McCandless, *History of Missouri, 1820-1860*, p. 145. The railroad-building craze had begun on February 28, 1827, when the Maryland legislature passed an act chartering the Baltimore & Ohio Railroad. The charter had given the company sole right to build the line, the power of eminent domain and exemption from state taxation. Ibid.

[678] *Cosmos-Monitor*, 1937.

[679] *History of St. Charles County*, p. 196. Allen was first elected to the legislature in 1846. Four years later he was elected to the State Senate. He was a slaveholder and landowner, from an old well-known Virginia family. Ibid.

[680] McCandless, *History of Missouri, 1820-1860*, pp. 246-7.

[681] Primm, *Economic Policy*, pp. 112-113.

[682] Anita Mallinckrodt, trans. "Railroad Finished to St. Charles," *Demokrat*, September 8, 1855, in *A History of Augusta, Missouri and Its Area*, Vol. 1, p. 16-17.

[683] Larson, *Federal Justice*, p.54. Federal District Judge Arnold Krekel was unsympathetic to counties in the 17 bond cases involving attempts by Missouri counties to default on their bond obligations, most of which were incurred under the provisions of the 1865 Constitution that he helped write. Ibid.

[684] Primm, *Lion of the Valley*, p. 232. Parrish, *History of Missouri, 1860-1875*, pp. 208-209.

[685] Parrish, *History of Missouri, 1860-1875*, pp. 208-209.

[686] Edna McElhiney Olson, *Historical Articles*, Vol. III, p.441.

[687] *The Bridges at St. Charles, Missouri,* (program for the dedication of the Page Avenue Bridge, December 13, 2003), p. 4. The bridge was 6535 feet long, had 8 river piers with spans over 300 feet in length, and was the longest cast iron bridge in the United States. Ibid.

[688] Jo Ann Brown, *St. Charles Borromeo*, p. 87.

[689] Ibid.

[690] Michael O'Laughlin, *Irish Settlers on the American Frontier, 1770-1900*, p. 65. One of the leading Irish families was that of Peter McMenamy who came to the county in 1852 from Ireland. *History of St. Charles County*, p. 519.

[691] Sara M. Evans, *Born for Liberty*, p. 100. Mary Yates Villert, "Orphan Trains from Portage des Sioux Township," in Mincke, Donald, *The History of Portage de Sioux Township Missouri, The Land Between the Rivers*, (Portage des Sioux: Land Between the Rivers Historical Society, 1999), p. 101. See also Marilyn Holt, *The Orphan Trains, Placing Out in America, (*Lincoln: University of Nebraska Press, 1992).

[692] Lloyd, *History of the City of St. Peters*, p. 71.

[693] John O'Fallon was born in Kentucky and raised by his uncle, Missouri Territorial Governor William Clark. He was the wealthiest merchant in St. Louis in the 1830s and a leader in the Whig Party there in the 1840s. He became a Democrat upon the demise of the Whigs in the mid-1850s. He donated eight million dollars to found O'Fallon Polytechnic Institute in 1865. Gerteis, *Civil War St. Louis*, p. 15.

[694] O'Fallon Centennial. p. 47.

[695] Ibid.

[696] Drummond, *Historic Sites*, p. 162.

[697] Thomas Gilmore, for whom the town was named, had fought the Indians at Rock Island in the 1830s. Drummond, *Historic Sites*, p. 206.

[698] David J. Russo, *American Towns, An Interpretive History*, (Chicago: Ivan R. Dee, 2001), p. 69. Daniel T. Brown, *Small Glories*, p. 134. Schiermeier, "Wentz of Wentzville" *Cracker Barrel Country,* Vol. IV, p. 101.

[699] *Agricultural History*, p. 39.The tobacco business declined in the area when the Meyers company moved to St. Louis. Drummond, *Historic Sites,* pp. 206, 208. H*istory of St. Charles County*, pp. 412, 432. Edna McElniney Olson, *Historical Articles*, Vol. I, p. 92. Mittelbuscher, "406 Elm Street," p. 28.

[700] Edna McElhiney Olson, *Historical Articles*, Vol. III, p. 441.

[701] Ibid.

[702] Drummond, *Historic Sites*, p. 207.

[703] Ibid. p. 98.

[704] Daniel T. Brown, *Small Glories*, p. 214.

[705] Licht, *Industrializing America*, p. 86. In June 1852, Congress granted to the state all the even numbered sections of land in a strip six sections in width on each side of the Hannibal and St. Joseph and Pacific Railroads. Ibid.

[706] McCandless, *History of Missouri, 1820-1860*, p. 148.

[707] Primm, *Lion of the Valley*, pp. 234-235.

[708] *History of St. Charles County*, p. 227.

[709] Christensen and Kremer, *A History of Missouri, 1875-1919*, p. 31.

[710] Ibid.

[711] Ibid., p. 48.

[712] Ibid. p. 49.

[713] *Cosmos-Monitor*, February 2, 1938.

[714] Kleppner, *Cross of Culture*, p. 121.

[715] Interview with Robert Sandfort.

[716] *History of St. Charles County,* p.227. *Agricultural History,* pp. 32, 96. Daniel T. Brown, *Small Glories*, pp. 222-224.

[717] Edna McElhiney Olson, *Historical Articles*, Vol. IV, p. 782.

[718] Drummond, *Historic Sites*, p. 27.

[719] Ibid., p. 133.

[720] Ibid.

[721] *History of St. Charles County*, pp. 143-144. S.M. Watson recalled in 1925 that, prior to the 1870s, there were only four bridges in the county: over the Femme Osage near the Missouri, over the Dardenne at Cottleville, over the Peruque north of O'Fallon and one over Scott's Branch on the Booneslick Road. *Banner-News,* February 26 1925

[722] Schiermeier, *Cracker Barrel Country*, Vol. II, p. 20. Christensen and Kremer, *A History of Missouri, 1875-1919*, pp. 34-35.

[723] *Agricultural History*, p. 73. In the early 1900s the use of lime increased crop yields. Lime trains brought in the material and special trains traveled around the state promoting its use. Later, chemical fertilizers came into use, greatly increasing crop yields. Ibid.

[724] Anita Mallinckrodt, trans. "Good Implements," *Demokrat*, October 2, 1879, in *A History of Augusta, Missouri and Its Area*, Vol. 2, p. 404.

[725] Christensen and Kremer, A *History of Missouri,* 1875-1919, p. 35.

[726] *Agricultural History*, pp. 58-59.

[727] Christensen and Kremer, *A History of Missouri, 1875-1919*, p. 35.

[728] *Agricultural History*, p. 71. Interview with Robert Sandfort.

[729] Paul Johnson, *A History of the American People*, (New York: Harper-Collins, 1997), p. 361.

[730] *Agricultural History*, p. 52.

[731] Thelen, *Paths of Resistance*, p. 40.

[732] *Agricultural History*, p. 83. By 1918, some farmers had milking machines and the trend to automated operations was accelerated when electricity became available in certain rural areas. Ibid.

[733] Thelen, *Paths of Resistanc*e, p. 16.

[734] Laurie, *Artisans into Workers*, p. 14.

[735] Thelen, *Paths of Resistance*, p. 16.

[736] Ibid., pp. 31-32.

[737] Foner, *Reconstruction*, p. 365.

[738] Anita Mallinckrodt, trans. "Protest Meeting at Augusta," *Demokrat*, March 26, 1863, in *A History of Augusta, Missouri and Its Area*, Vol. 1, p. 92.

[739] Bonnie J. Krause, *"German –Americans in the St. Louis Region 1840-1860." MHR,* April 1989, p. 302.

[740] Ibid., p. 304. Pope Gregory XVI had issued an Apostolic Letter condemning both slavery and the slave trade. Kendrick would later become archbishop of St. Louis. Ibid.

[741] Ibid, pp. 304-305.

[742] Ibid.

[743] Schultz, Bob, "Some Civil War Politics in St. Charles County," *St. Charles County Heritage,* Vol. 20, No. 1, January, 2002, p. 10.

[744] Kamphoefner, *Westfalians*, p. 116.

[745] Ibid.

[746] Ibid., p. 130. Friedrich Muench was an exception and was a member of the "Charcoal" radical emancipationist faction in the Missouri Senate in 1862-1866. *Dictionary,* p. 563.

[747] Lorenzo J. Greene et. al., *Missouri's Black Heritage*, p. 68. Reverand J.M. Peck wrote from St. Charles in 1835, "I am happy to find among the slave holders in Missouri a growing disposition to have the blacks educated, and to patronize Sunday Schools for the purpose." Trexler, *Slavery in Missouri*, p. 83, n.4.

[748] Jo Ann Brown, *St. Charles Borromeo*, p. 47.

[749] Drummond, *Historic Sites*, p. 31. Parrish, *History of Missouri*, p. 158. Edna McElhiney Olson, *Historical Articles*, Vol. I, p. 178. The first African-American teacher in St. Charles was Sina

Simmonds, a free mulatto woman who taught at Mrs. Collier's school. She purchased many slaves over the years and granted them their freedom. Edna McElhiney Olson, *Historical Articles*, Vol. I, p. 178.

[750] Parrish, *History of Missouri, 1860-1875*, pp.160-161.

[751] Ibid., p. 162.

[752] *Cosmos-Monitor*, June 15, 1955.

[753] Anita Mallinckrodt trans. "Negro Schools" *Demokrat,* October 3, 1867 in *A History of Augusta, Missouri and Its Area,* Vol. 1, p. 164.

[754] Parrish, *History of Missouri, 1860-1875,* p. 163, *Cosmos-Monitor*, June 15, 1955 Statewide, 59 percent of white children were enrolled in school. See also Stephen Blackhurst, "One Hundred Years of Negro Education in St. Charles, Missouri." Copy on file at the Board of Education, St. Charles School District.

[755] *Cosmos-Monitor*, June 15, 1955.

[756] Anita Mallinckrodt, trans, "Negro Schools," *Demokrat*, October 3, 1867, in *A History of Augusta, Missouri and Its Area*, Vol.1, p. 164.

[757] Barbara Eisenbath Mittelbuscher, *Flint Hill, 150 Years, 1836-1986*, (Bridgeton: Lineage Press, 1986), p. 15.

[758] O'Fallon Centennial, p. 23. It operated until 1949, after which it was closed and the children transported to Franklin School in the City of St. Charles. Ibid.

[759] Anita Mallinckrodt, *Freed Slaves*, p. 6., *Keen v. Keen.* 527, *Cosmos-Monitor*, October 12, 1941. Benjamin F. Keen, a farmer from Portage des Sioux Township, was educated at Lincoln Institute. *History of St. Charles County,* p. 281.

[760] Anita Mallinckrodt trans. "The Social Position," *Demokrat,* February 15, 1872, in *A History of Augusta, Missouri and its Area,* Vol. 2, p. 238.

[761] Thelen, *Paths of Resistance*, p. 111.

[762] Hohe, *"Phelan Miscalculation,"* p. 377.

[763] Edna, McElhiney Olsen, *Historical Articles*, Vol. I, p.52.

[764] *Cosmos-Monitor*, May 6, 1949. Edna McElhmey Olson, *Historical Articles* Vol 3., p. 534.

[765] Sandfort, *Hermann Heinrich Sandfort*, p. 272.

[766] *History of St. Charles County*, p. 199.

[767] Ibid., p. 340.

[768] Ibid., pp. 314-316. There are conflicting versions over whether the case was settled with the War Department because of the intervention of Congressman Champ Clark, according to a 1903 *Banner-News* Article, or because of the ruling of alumnus, and then Federal District Judge Arnold Krekel, in a federal court case brought by the college. Brad Edwards and Gary McKiddy, "St. Charles College vs. The War Department, *St. Charles County Heritage,* Vol. 10, No. 3, July, 1992, p. 66.

[769] "Reminiscences of Lindenwood College, 1827-1920," p. 6.

[770] Ibid.

[771] Ibid., p. 116.

[772] Edna McElhiney Olson, *Historical Articles*, Vol. II, p. 284.

[773] *History of St. Charles County*, pp. 104-107.

[774] Ken Luebbering and Robyn Burnett, *German Settlement in Missouri*, (Columbia: University of Missouri Press, 1996), p. 93. Muench found time to conduct a local school and also carried on a lively intellectual life as a journalist, an anti-slavery campaigner and a state senator. Daniel T. Brown, *Small Glories,* p. 91.

[775] Mallinckrodt, *Knights to Pioneers*, p. 148.

[776] Kamphoefner, *Westfalians,* p.94.

[777] Ibid., p. 100, quoting F. Muench,"Die Duden'sche Niederlassung," p. 199; Bek, "Followers of Duden," 18:575.

[778] Ibid., p. 171. Faherty, *St. Louis Irish*, p. 92.

[779] *History of St. Charles County*, p. 106.

[780] Kamphoefner, *Westfalians*, p. 96.

[781] Ibid., p. 89.

[782] Ibid., p. 88.

[783] Ibid., p. 101. The immigrants often brought place names with them. The towns of New Melle and Cappeln are only six miles apart in St. Charles County while Melle and Wester Kappeln are 20 miles apart in Osnabruck. Schluersburg was not a source of chain migration, but was the birthplace of local storekeeper, Wilhelm Horst. Hamburg, once a village in St. Charles County, was the port of embarkation for many German immigrants to America, although the majority of those who came to St. Charles County probably departed from the port of Bremen. Ibid., p. 89.

[784] Ibid., pp. 106-07, quoting *Demokrat*, August 2, 1852.

[785] Ibid., p. 107. Germans were ambivalent about dancing. While most enjoyed their waltzes and polkes. St. John German Evangelical Church in St. Charles did not allow dancing on church grounds until the late 1930s. "One Hundredth Anniversary of the St. John Church," p. 26.

[786] Kamphoefner, *Westfalians,* p. 101.

[787] Ibid., p. 108.

[788] Ibid., quoting *Demokrat*, January 10, 1857, December 13, 1857.

[789] Ibid.

[790] Ibid., 108-109, quoting diary of Adelheide Garlichs, 1835-1840.

[791] Ibid., p. 109.

[792] Ibid.

[793] Ibid., p. 108.

[794] Donald M. Lance, "Settlement Patterns, Missouri German-Americans and Local Dialects." *The German-American Experience in Missouri*, n.d. p. 125.

[795] Kamphoefner, *Westfalians,* p. 112-113. "One Hundredth Anniversary of St. John Church," p. 26. "Immanual Evangelical Lutheran Church 100th Annivarsary." p. 22.

[796] Daniel T. Brown, *Small Glories,* p. 103

[797] Anita Mallinckrodt, trans. "Mixed-Culture Marriages Rare," *Demokrat*, October 2, 1879, in *A History of Augusta, Missouri and Its Area*, Vol. 2, p. 405.

[798] Kamphoefner, *Westfalians*, p. 172.

[799] "St. Charles, Missouri, Bicentennial Historical Program Book," (St. Charles: Bicentennial Committee, 1969) p. 79. The company is still in business today.

[800] Drummond, *Historic Sites*, p. 132. "Bicentennial Celebration Program," p. 73. Because of the marshy land the road was often impassable in wet weather. As a result, a toll road was constructed about 1865 under a franchise from the County Court to cover the two-and-one-half miles beginning at Tecumseh Street in St. Charles. The name of the road was changed to Boschert Road and the name of the town was changed to Boschertown in 1876. The toll was removed and the road came under ownership of the county in 1886. Drummond, *Historic Sites,* p. 132.

[801] Ibid., p. 100.

[802] Ibid., p. 256.

[803] Ibid., p. 134.

[804] Daniel T. Brown, *Small Glories*, p. 89.

[805] Mallinckrodt, *Knights to Pioneers*, p. 272.

[806] Drummond, *Historic Sites,* pp. 283-284.

[807] Kamphoefner, *Westfalians,* p. 118.

[808] Anita Mallinckrodt, trans. "St. Charles County – Overview," *Demokrat,* November 20, 1873, in *A History of Augusta, Missouri and Its Area*, Vol. 2, pp. 260-61.

[809] Kamphoefner, *Westfalians,* p. 134.

[810] Daniel T. Brown, *Small Glories*, p. 160.

[811] Anita Mallinckrodt, trans. "German Language," *Demokrat*, October 17, 1861, in *A History of Augusta, Missouri and Its Area*, Vol. 1, p. 64.

[812] Anita Mallinckrodt, trans. "Instruction in the Public Schools," *Demokrat*, June 22, 1882, in *A History of Augusta, Missouri and Its Area*, Vol. 2, p. 474.

[813] Anita Mallinckrodt, trans. "Danger for the German Language," *Demokrat*, September 29, 1877, in *A History of Augusta, Missouri and Its Area*, Vol. 3, p. 532.

[814] Kamphoefner, *Westfalians*, p.115

[815] Nagel, *German Migration*, p. 16.

[816] Thelen, *Paths of Resistance*, p. 20.

[817] Mallinckrodt, *Knights to Pioneers*, p. 229. The German Evangelical Synod was the former Church of Prussia. It was considered more liberal than the Missouri Synod Lutherans. Audrey L. Olson, *St. Louis Germans, 1850-1920*, (New York: Arno Press, 1980), p. 117.

[818] Mallinckrodt, *Knights to Pioneers,* p. 259.

[819] Nagel, *German Migration*, p. 154. The curriculum at Eden Seminary was not changed to English instruction until 1924. Ibid.

[820] Edna McElhiney Olson, *Historical Articles, Vol. I*, p. 134. An Evangelical congregation was established in the previously American community of Defiance in 1906. Ibid., p. 150.

[821] *History of St. Charles County*, p. 348. Interview with Robert Sandfort.

[822] *Cosmos-Monitor*, July 20, 1940, *Cosmos-Monitor*, Vol. 116, No. 39. Mallinckrodt, *Knights to Pioneers,* p. 275. See also "Anniversary Booklet" of Immanuel Evangelical Lutheran Church.

[823] "Wentzville Centennial Program," 1955.

[824] *History of St. Charles County,* p. 289.

[825] Rothensteiner, *History of the Archdiocese*, pp. 562-563.

[826] *History of St. Charles County,* p. 349. Rothensteiner, *History of the Archdiocese,* pp. 423-424. Father Christian Wappelhorst replaced the first pastor, Father Joseph Rauch, in 1857, who was replaced by Father Phillip Vogt in 1865. Ibid. When German Catholics had problems with the Church hierarchy, Peter Cahensley urged the establishment of diocese in the U.S., not along geographical lines, but along lines of nationality and culture. Ibid., p. 159. In 1916 there were over 200 Catholic parishes that used German in their sermon and songs. Nearly 2000 others used some German in their services. Luebke, *Bonds of Loyalty,* p. 35.

[827] Barbara Eisenbath Mittelbusher, "Josephville in Allen Prairie," *Bulletin*, Vol.18, No.4, October 2000.

[828] Rothensteiner, *History of the Archdiocese,* p. 427.

[829] Mittelbuscher, *Flint Hill,* pp. 15-17.

[830] Edna McElhiney Olson, *Historical Articles,* Vol. IV, p. 689. There was a parochial school from 1843 to 1878 and the present church structure of Immaculate Conception parish was dedicated in 1901. During the Civil War a man named Joseph Shade took sanctuary from confederate sympathizers in the rectory of the parish. Ibid.

[831] Sandy Hense, "Beginnings of St. Joseph's Parish, Cottleville," *St. Charles County Heritage,* Vol. 13, No. 1, January 1995, p. 4-11. In 1914 a brick church was finally completed. Ibid.

[832] Ibid. See also Rothensteiner, *History of the Archdiocese,* pp. 430-431.

[833] "Program to Commemorate the Sesquicentennial of St. Francis of Assisi Parish," (St. Louis: The Archdiocese of St.Louis, 1964).

[834] Lloyd, *History of St. Peters,* p. 50.

[835] Drummond, *Historic Sites,* p. 167.

[836] Lloyd, *History of St. Peters,* p. 82.

[837] Dolan, *American Catholic Experience,* p. 169.

[838] Kamphoefner, *Westfalians,* p. 174.

[839] *History of St. Charles County,* pp. 226, 345. By comparison, while 80 percent of German children attended parochial school in the City of St. Louis in 1864, by 1887 80 percent were attending public school. Kamphoefner, "Majority-Minority," p. 97.

[840] "O'Fallon Centennial," pp. 40-41. For information on the *Kulturkampf* see Arthur Rosenburg, *Imperial Germany, the Birth of the German Republic 1871-1918,* pp.10-15. The order also taught

in the parochial schools in Cottleville, Josephville, St. Peters, St. Paul and Wentzville.

[841] Kleppner, *Cross of Culture,* p. 78.

[842] Brown, *Small Glories,* p. 180.

[843] "The Phelan Miscalculation," p. 388.

[844] Anita Mallinckrodt, trans. "Religious Schools," *Demokrat,* May 13, 1875, in *A History of Augusta, Missouri and Its Area,* Vol. 2, p. 292.

[845] Dolan, *American Catholic Experience,* p. 270.

[846] Rothensteiner, *History of the Archdiocese,* p 172. In 1844 C.F.W. Walther published *Der Lutheraner* as a weekly newspaper for the Missouri Synod Lutherans.

[847] Interviews with Wayne Hoffmann and Pastor Allan Schade from Immanuel Lutheran. For several decades during the pastorate of Reverend Niedner at Immanuel beer was not served in the church hall or at the church picnic. However an exception was made for ushers and Men's Club meetings where each members was allowed two glasses of beer. Ibid.

[848] On the Fourth of July St. John sponsored a parade of decorated floats and held a public dinner in Blanchette Park each year from 1889-1951, with the exception of 1932. That year the question of the church selling beer became an issue.

[849] *History of St. Charles County,* p. 359.

[850] "Program for dedication of St. Joseph's Church," September 16, 1962.

[851] Anita Mallinckrodt, trans. "Sunday in St. Charles," *Demokrat,* June 27, 1878, in *A History of Augusta, Missouri and Its Area,* Vol. 2, p. 375.

[852] *Diary of John Jay Johns,* June 24, 1878.

[853] Anita Mallinckrodt, trans. "Old Sunday Law Revised," *Demokrat,* August 30, 1883, in *A History of Augusta, Missouri and Its Area,* Vol. 3, p. 486. The Grand Jury did bring charges against salon-keepers W. Fitch, E. Schaeffer, H. Bruns, of St. Charles and Charles H. Haferkamp of Augusta. Anita Mallinckrodt, trans. "Charges Brought," *Demokrat,* September 8, 1883, in *A History of Augusta Missouri and Its Area,* Vol. 3, p. 486.

[854] Anita Mallinckrodt, trans. "About Temperance and Sunday Restrictions," *Demokrat,* July 29, 1884, in *A History of Augusta, Missouri and Its Area,* Vol. 3, p. 498.

Chapter IV
End Notes

[855] The level of taxation in the 1880s suggests that, whatever their political affiliation, most elected officials in the county where fiscal conservatives. In 1880 the county was twentieth in population and fifth in wealth among Missouri counties, but paid taxes at a lower rate than every other county in the state with a smaller population. *History of St Charles County,* pp. 140-141.

[856] *Banner-News,* March 5, 1926.

[857] Nagel, *German Migration,* p. 131. German racism in its African colonies during this period was deplorable.

[858] Daniel T. Brown, *Small Glories,* p. 253.

[859] *Diary of John Jay Johns,* November 7, 1880.

[860] *Cosmos-Monitor,* January 15, 1882.

[861] *History of St. Charles County.* Only three of those listed were French. The vast majority of the remaining hailed from Virginia, many by way of Kentucky and Tennessee. There were many from Pennsylvania and Ohio, with a few from New England.

[862] Robertus Love, "Newspaper Feature Captures Essence of 'Wide Awake' St. Charles in 1914," *Past Times,* Vol.1, No. 1, spring, 1984. p. 26.

[863] Anita Mallinckrodt, trans. "Excerpts from Mr. Schurz Recent Speech," *Demokrat,* September 17, 1897, in *A History of Augusta, Missouri and its Area,* Vol. 3, p. 637.

[864] Anita Mallinckrodt, trans. "German Day" *Demokrat*, October 8, 1891, in *A History of Augusta, Missouri and Its Area,* Vol. 3, p. 575.

[865] Anita Mallinckrodt, trans. "A Really German Celebration," *Demokrat*, October 12, 1893, in *A History of Augusta, Missouri and Its Area,* Vol. 3, p. 595. In 1987, October 6 was officially named German-American Day by President Reagan, almost 100 years after it was first celebrated in Missouri. Anita Mallinckrodt, "St. Charles County-100 Years Ago," *St. Charles County Heritage,* Vol. 17, No. 3, July 1999, p. 111.

[866] Elbert R. Bowen, "German Theatre in Rural Missouri," *MHR*, January 1952.

[867] Breslow, *Small Town,* pp. 164-165. "Bicentennial Celebration Program," p. 80. Schiermeier, *Cracker Barrel Country,* Vol. IV, pp. 39,75. Edna McElhiney Olson, *Historical Articles, Vol. III,* p. 536. *The St. Charles Band's History 1810-2004,* (St. Charles: St. Charles Municipal Band Inc., 2004) pp. 1-13. In 1913, Rummel's Military Band became the St. Charles Military Band under a new director, Donato La Banco II, who also directed the American Legion Drum and Bugle Corps. formed in 1930. *Cosmos-Monitor,* June 18, 1930.

[868] Russo, *American Towns,* pp.196-197.

[869] 1906 Hackman and St. Charles City Directories. See also Richard Lowell Vinson, ed. *The St. Charles, Missouri Citizen Improvement Association, 1905-1907,* reprint, (St.Charles: Frenchtown Museum Corp., 1993).

[870] Ibid.

[871] Ibid. Schiermeier, *Cracker Barrel Country,* Vol. III, pp. 24, 66.

[872] *Cosmos-Monitor*, July 31, 1940. F. X. Willmes was born in Schmallenberg, Westphalia on September 25, 1852. He came to this country in 1875 during Bismarck's *Kulturkampf* in Germany. He entered St. Francis Seminary at Milwaukee, Wisconsin where he was ordained June 24, 1877. He became monsignor in May 1923 and was appointed dean of the St. Charles Deanery February 1, 1924. Ibid.

[873] Sr. Inez Kennedy, "St. Joseph Health Center and the Franciscan Sisters of St. Mary," *St Charles County Heritage,* Vol. 16, No. 2, April 1998, pp. 53-59.

[874] "Bicentennial Celebration Program," p. 48. And http://carmelitedcjnorth.org/history.htm

[875] *Cosmos-Monitor*, May 11 1938.

[876] Ibid. The Notre Dame Order, which also taught at Immaculate Conception School in Dardenne, was originally established in 1847 in Baltimore, after which convents were opened in Milwaukee, Mankato, Minn. and St. Louis in 1883. The order comprised 2,752 women by 1900. *Cosmos-Monitor*, November 5, 1947. Dolan, *American Catholic Experience,* p. 277.

[877] Jo Ann Brown, *St. Charles Borromeo,* p. 170. The school was accredited by the state of Missouri in 1934. Ibid. Parochial education grew because the number of nuns in the U.S. increased from 1,344 in 1850 to 40,340 in 1900. Dolan, *American Catholic Experience,* p. 277.

[878] Interview with Robert Sandfort. Architects of Immanuel were Griese and Wylie of Cincinatti, Ohio. The revival of the Gothic style was part of the ecclesiological movement and was most at home with those denominations that had a liturgical service like the Catholic and Lutheran. Osmund Overby, "German Churches in the Pelster Housebarn Neighborhood," *The German-American Experience in America,* (Missouri Cultural Heritage Center, 1986), p. 93.

[879] Jo Ann Brown, *St. Charles Borromeo,* p. 93. The Sisters of Lorretto taught in the parish school until 1932, when the School Sisters of Notre Dame took over. The brick church was destroyed by a tornado in 1915 and replaced with the present romanesque structure. Ibid.

[880] "Bicentennial Celebration Program," p.6. Breslow, *Small Town,* pp. 202-203. *History of St. Charles County,* pp. 355, 520.

[881] Edna McElhiney Olson, *Historical Articles,* Vol. 3, p. 407.

[882] "Bicentennial Celebration Program," p.70.

[883] *The St. Charles Missouri Citizen Improvement Association, 1905-1907,* reprint, ed. by Richard Lowell Vinson, (St. Charles: Frenchtown Museum Corp. 1993), p. 13.

[884] There are conflicting versions over whether the case was settled with the War Department

because of the intervention of Congressman Champ Clark, according to a 1903 *Banner-News* article, or because of the ruling of Federal District Judge Arnold Krekel, in a case brought by the college. Brad, Edwards, and Gary McKiddy, "St. Charles College vs. The War Department," *St. Charles County Heritage,* Vol. 10, no. 3, July, 1992, p. 66.

[885] Poindexter, "A Right Smart Little Town," p. 106. "Bicentennial Celebration Program," p.44. "Lindenwood Alumni Directory," 1986.

[886] The Lutherans believed that the purchase of insurance showed a lack of faith that God would provide. Interview with H. K. Stumberg.

[887] David E. Kyvig, *Daily Life in the United States, 1920-1939: Decades of Promise and Pain,* (Westport, CT: Greenwood Press 2002), p. 124-125. World War I caused great concern regarding public education. The war was the first opportunity to do nationwide testing and it was discovered that many men were unfit for military service because of lack of education. Ibid.

[888] *Agricultural History,* pp. 14-17.

[889] Edna McElhiney Olson, *Historical Articles,* Vol. II, p. 180. Brown, *Small Glories,* p. 199-201. Schiermeier, *Cracker Barrel Country,* Vol. II, p. 126.

[890] "Relax in Modern O'Fallon," a publication of the O'Fallon Chamber of Commerce, 1984.

[891] Breslow, *Small Town,* p. 151.

[892] *History of St. Charles County,* p. 142. *Cosmos-Monitor,* September 6, 1916.

[893] The 1929 "Polk's City Directory" list 1510 parochial and 1200 public school students. This is obviously based on numbers gathered earlier in the decade since the directory for the next year lists 2308 parochial and 1960 public.

[894] *Cosmos-Monitor,* September 6, 1916.

[895] "1906 St. Charles City Directory." Edna McElhiny Olsen, *Historical Articles,* Vol. 3, pp. 394-395. Daniel T. Brown, *Small Glories,* p. 181.

[896] *History of St. Charles County,* pp. 467-468. The history does not identify his religion, Jewish businessmen Julius and Sigmund Baer were also born in Baden about a decade after Simon Baer and immigrated to St. Louis in the late 1870s and were also in merchandising, eventually becoming partners in Stix, Baer and Fuller Department Stores. Simon Baer also married Jennie Steinberg from St. Louis. Steinberg was a prominent Jewish name in St. Louis at the time. Walter Ehrlich, *Zion in the Valley, The Jewish Community of St. Louis,* Volume I, (Columbia: University of Missouri Press, 1997), pp. 267, 308.

[897] Frank was a prominent Jewish name in St. Louis. Nathan Frank was elected to Congress in 1889 and later served on the World's Fair Commission. Ehrlich, *Zion in the Valley,* p. 341.

[898] Edna McElhiney Olson, *Historical Articles,* Vol. II, p. 367.

[899] Ida Kaplan was three years old when she came to St. Charles in 1907 with her parents, Mr. and Mrs. R. Willner, who had immigrated to St. Louis from Russia. Her father had worked in a sweat shop in St. Louis. Interview with Ida Kaplan, October 2002.

[900] Ehrlich, *Zion in the Valley,* p. 349, Interview with Ida Kaplan. All eastern European Jews, including Polish, Rumanian and others were lumped together as "Russian" by the census bureau.

[901] Ibid., pp. 354-355, and interview with Ida Kaplan.

[902] St. Charles city directories and interview with Ida Kaplan.

[903] Nagel, *German Migration,* p. 131. In addition to its restrictive covenant against blacks, the 1943 deed for Lake Shore Subdivision, located on Alton Lake, stated, "neither shall any lot in this subdivision be sold, leased, let or rented to be used by any people of Jewish or Hebrew descent." Deed in possession of author.

[904] Ehrlich, *Zion in the Valley,* p. 279.

[905] *Diary of John Jay Johns,* February 4, 1990.

[906] Edna McElhiney Olson, *Historical Articles,* Vol. II. p. 258. These arguments were still posited as late as 1963 by an elderly Edna McElhiney Olson, whose ancestors had been slaveholders. Ibid.

[907] Mallinckrodt, *Knights to Pioneers,* p. 381.

[908] Anita Mallinckrodt, trans, "City's Black Population Grow More Presumptuous and Impudent," *Demokrat*, August 10, 1893, in *A History of Augusta, Missouri and its Area,* Vol. 4, p. 593.

[909] Daniel T. Brown, *Small Glories,* p. 158.

[910] As late as 1910 African-Americans in Missouri owned 3800 farms worth an estimated $27.7 million. Greene, *Missouri's Black Heritage,* p. 107, 115. See also Primm, *Lion of the Valley,* pp. 331-32. "O'Fallon Centennial," p. 23.

[911] Primm, *Lion of the Valley,* p. 441. The overall population of St. Charles County increased by only 221 in the ten years prior to the 1910 census, according to which St. Charles County had 24,695 population.

[912] Lorenzo J. Greene et. al., *Missouri's Black Heritage,* p. 115. They not only went to Missouri cities. From 1900 to 1910 the African-American population of Missouri declined 2.3%. Ibid.

[913] Primm, *Lion of the Valley,* p. 331.

[914] Edna McElhiney Olson, *Historical Articles,* Vol. II, p. 197.

[915] Interview with Melvin Washington.

[916] Interview with Melvin Washington. The City of St. Louis passed a segregation ordinance by referendum by a 3 to 1 vote in 1916 that was later declared unconstitutional. Greene, *Missouri's Black Heritage,* p. 117.

[917] *Cosmos-Monitor*, July 21, 1937.

[918] Poindexter, "A Right Smart Little Town," p. 130. Interview with Melvin Washington.

[919] Ibid. Franklin had been the boys' school operated by the Jesuits at Borromeo until bought by the school district in 1870 for the education of white students.

[920] Ibid., See also Christensen and Kremer, *A History of Missouri, 1875-1919*, p. 59. Sumner High School, named after the famous Radical Republican leader in the U.S. Senate, Charles Sumner, was the first high school for blacks west of the Mississippi, when it opened. Ibid.

[921] *Keen v. Keen,* 184 Mo. 358, 83 SW 526, (Sup. Ct.1904), Primm, *Lion of the Valley,* p. 319. The "Whiskey Ring" bribed tax collectors to rob the federal government of millions in revenue. President Grant's secretary had been involved in the scheme. Tindall, *America,* p. 750. D.P. Dyer later served as judge in St. Louis and declared the Residential Segregation Ordinance, passed in that city in 1916, unconstitutional. Interview with James Neil Primm.

[922] Keen v. Keen, 184 Mo. 358, 83 SW 526, (Sup. Ct.1904), pp. 526-530. The Circuit Court had found, "While it was known in the community in which they lived that Eli Keen and Phoebe were living together, and cohabiting and raising a family of children, as above detailed, it was the reputation of the community that they were so living together and cohabiting without the sanction of marriage. The reputation was that they had never been married." Ibid.

[923] E. Terrence Jones, quoted in Amy Stuart Wells and Robert L. Crain, *Stepping over the Color Line, African-American Students in White Suburban Schools,* (New Haven: Yale University Press, 1997), p. 31.

[924] Interview with Melvin Washington.

[925] Breslow, *Small Town,* p. 147.

[926] Poindexter, "Right Smart Little Town," p. 86.

[927] Breslow, *Small Town,* p. 148.

[928] Douglas E. Abrams, *A Very Special Place in Life, The History of Juvenile Justice in Missouri,* (Missouri Juvenile Justice Association, 2003), p. 11.

[929] Christensen and Kremer, *A History of Missouri, 1875-1919,* pp. 179-180.

[930] Anita Mallinckrodt, trans. "Lynching," *Demokrat*, January 13, 1898, in *A History of Augusta, Missouri and Its Area,* Vol. 3, p. 644.

[931] Breslow, Small Town, pp.144-145.

[932] Interview with Ozzie Maher, long time resident and civic leader of O'Fallon. John O'Fallon, for whom the town was named, had been selected foreman of the Grand Jury in St. Louis that failed to hand up an indictment when it looked into the lynching of Francis L. Macintosh, a free Mulatto boatman, in 1836. Gerteis, *Civil War St. Louis,* p. 15.

[933] Brown, *Small Glories,* p. 253.

[934] Mincke, *History of Portage des Sioux,* p. 118.

[935] Anita Mallinckrodt, trans. "Puritanical Sunday," *Demokrat,* January 31, 1895, in *A History of Augusta, Missouri and Its Area,* Vol. 3, p. 615.

[936] Ibid.

[937] Christensen and Kremer, *A History of Missouri, 1875-1919,* p. 131.

[938] Poindexter, "A Right Smart Little Town," p. 87

[939] Ibid.

[940] Audrey Olson, *St. Louis Germans,* pp. 150-151. Dr. Benjamin Geret had served as a surgeon in the German forces during the Franco-Prussian War before coming to America in 1871 and practiced medicine in St. Charles. *History of St. Charles County,* p. 383.

[941] Anita Mallinckrodt, trans. "Protection for the Immigrants," *Demokrat,* June 3, 1869, in *A History of Augusta, Missouri and Its Area,* Vol. 1, p. 185.

[942] Judy Sigmund, *Dog Prairie Tales,* (St. Charles: Goellner Printing, n.d.), p. 45.

[943] Christensen and Kremer, *A History of Missouri, 1875-1919,* p. 201. *Cosmos-Monitor,* October 12, 1214. Primm, *Lion of the Valley,* p. 459.

[944] Breslow, *Small Town,* p. 101.

[945] Ibid. See also "O'Fallon Centennial," p. 27.

[946] Daniel T. Brown, *Small Glories,* p. 253. In January 1920 the parochial school at St. John in St. Charles announced it would no longer teach in German. *Cosmos-Monitor,* January 12, 1920.

[947] Breslow, *Small Town,* pp. 103, 154-155.

[948] Luebke, *Bonds of Loyalty,* p. 10.

[949] Breslow, *Small Town,* p. 154.

[950] *St. Charles County in the World War,* (St. Charles: The Honor Roll Association of St. Charles County, St. Louis: Peters and Mann, 1919), p. 4.

[951] Breslow, *Small Town,* p. 153.

[952] *St. Charles County in the World War,* p 86.

[953] Gary Mead, *Doughboys,* (New York: The Overlook Press, 2002), p. 368.

[954] Bryan Brewer, "Amber Waves of Grain: St. Charles County Farmers During World War I," *St. Charles County Heritage,* Vol. 12, No. 3, July 1994, pp. 90-91.

[955] Missouri Council of Defense Papers, St. Charles County, No. 24953, Western Manuscript Collection, University of Missouri. The signatures were gathered by the Family Food Enrollment Organization of St. Charles County, under Herbert Hoover, Federal Food Administrator, Celeste Rauch, Chairman, Ibid.

[956] Kim Oellschlager, "St. Charles County Chapter of the American Red Cross, Then and Now," *St. Charles County Heritage,* Vol. 12, Number 3, July 1994, pp. 82-89.

[957] *St. Charles County in the World War,* p. 75. Established in 1917 with 50 members, The St. Charles chapter of the Red Cross was the first in Missouri outside St. Louis. Edna McElhiney Olsen, *Historical Articles,* Vol. I, p. 78.

[958] *St. Charles County in the World War,* p. 98.

[959] Breslow, *Small Town,* p. 155.

[960] Anita Mallinckrodt, *Augusta Magazine,* November/December, 1993, p. 17.

[961] *Cosmos-Monitor,* May 18, 1920.

[962] *Banner-News,* June 21, 1923. As late as 1929 the "Polk's St. Charles City Directory" lists the German Benefit Union among the fraternal organizations in the city.

[963] Poindexter, "A Right Smart Little Town," p. 108.

[964] *Banner-News,* January 20, 1925.

[965] Ibid., March 5, 1925.

[966] Ibid., December 10, 1925.

[967] Ibid., November 12, 1925. The booze was actually stolen from the courthouse in the case of *State v. Hoffmann.* See also, *Banner-News,* May 19, 1926.

[968] Ibid., February 24, 1927. Sheriff John Grothe had first been elected in 1917, was succeeded by his brother Isidore Grothe in 1921, but was re-elected in 1925. He died in office and was buried from St. Peter's Church in July of 1927 at one of the largest funerals ever had at that church up to that time. *Banner-News*, June 28, 1927.

[969] *Cosmos-Monitor*, February 28, 1927. *Banner-News*, March 3, 1927. Guy Motley became secretary of Lindenwood College in 1918, assistant to the president in 1938 and Acting President in 1940. One of the founders of Rotary, he was chairman of the Democratic Central Committee and presidential elector in 1937. "Lindenwood College Bulletin," February, 1950, p. 17.

[970] *Banner-News*, November 22, 1923.

[971] Ibid., January 17, 1924.

[972] Grant Toten and Carrie Waldvogel, "The KKK in St. Charles in the 1920's," *St. Charles County Heritage*, p. 38-41. William Joseph Simmons revived the Klan in 1915 on Stone Mountain in Atlanta, Georgia. It reached the height of its power in the 1920s when it had a membership of 4 to 6 million. It was particularly strong in Indiana. Ibid.

[973] "Bicentennial Celebration Program," p. 65.

[974] *Banner-News*, January 17, 1924.

[975] Lorenzo J. Greene et. al., *Missouri's Black Heritage*, p. 150.

[976] *History of St. Charles County*, p 107. German Liberals like Emil Mallinckrodt were obviously influenced by Social Darwinism based on his statement about race. See above.

[977] *Banner-News*, September 10, 1925. The reference to Chicago is regarding the Leopold and Loeb case in which Darrow represented two teenage boys who had killed another child and saved them from the death penalty.

[978] Ibid.

[979] Linda Brown-Kubisch and Christine Montgomery, "Show Me Missouri History: Celebrating the Century Part 2", *MHR,* April 2000, p. 318.

[980] *Banner-News*, March 5, 1925.

[981] *Cosmos-Monitor*, July 28, 1923.

[982] Kyvig, *Daily Life in the United States, 1920-1939,* p. 8.

[983] Tom Brokaw, *The Greatest Generation,* (New York: Random House, 1998).

[984] Lisa Politt, "Quality Family Programming for the Silent Screen," *St. Charles County Heritage,* January, 1993, pp. 52-53.

[985] In the late 1920s the Knights of Columbus became very interested in scouting. Up to that time it had been considered a Protestant organization. Faherty, *St. Louis Irish,* p. 176. From its inception, as today, scouting supplies and uniforms were purchased a Thro's Clothing.

[986] *Agricultural History,* p. 139. Nationally, there were 750,000 young people in 4-H Clubs by 1929. The clubs taught social skills and moral values, while encouraging participation in county fair competitions. Ibid.

[987] *Cosmos-Monitor*, April 14, 1925.

[988] Daniel T. Brown, *Small Glories,* p. 364.

[989] "Bicentennial Celebration Program," p. 50. *Cosmos-Monitor*, February 12, 1924. John J. Buse, *In His Own Hand, A Historical Scrapbook of St. Charles County, Missouri, 1998,* p. 29. The orginal country club is now Bogey Hills Country Club. The initiation fee in 1924 was $75 and the annual fee was $25. Ibid.

[990] *History of St. Charles County,* p. 393. *Banner-News*, January 15, 1953. "Wentzville Centennial Program," 1955, p. 3. Schiermeier, *Cracker Barrel Country,* Vol. III, p, 164.

[992] Walter A, Schroeder, *"Rural Settlement Patterns of the German-Missourian Cultural Land-scape," The German Experience in Missouri,* (Missouri Cultural Heritage Center, 1986), p. 40.

[993] Olson, *Historical Articles,* Vol. I, p. 79. Breslow, *Small Town,* p. 109. Faherty, *St. Louis Irish,* p. 112.

[994] Kleppner, *Cross of Culture,* p. 110.

[995] Sandfort, *Hermann Heinrich Sandfort,* p. 230.

[996] Anita Mallinckrodt, trans. "United Against Temperance Efforts," *Demokrat*, September 11, 1884, in *A History of Augusta, Missouri and its Area,* Vol. 3, p. 493.

[997] Christensen and Kremer, *A History of Missouri, 1875-1919,* p. 200. Eighty-one Missouri counties had voted to become dry. Ibid.

[998] Thelen, *Paths of Resistance,* p. 155.

[999] Anita Mallinckrodt, trans. "1894," *Demokrat*, January 4, 1894, in *A History of Augusta, Missouri and its Area,* Vol. 3, p. 600.

[1000] Richard Jensen, *Winning of the Midwest,* p. 209.

[1001] *Cosmos-Monitor*, February 28, 1894.

[1002] Faherty, *St. Louis Irish,* p. 133. The legislation was introduced by Representative E.J. Simmons in 1901 but failed to pass. Ibid.

[1003] Christensen and Kremer, *A History of Missouri, 1875-1919,* p. 145.

[1004] Anita Mallinckrodt, trans. "Political Flood," *Demokrat*, November 8, 1894, in *A History of Augusta, Missouri and Its Area,* Vol. 3, p. 609.

[1005] Kleppner, *Cross of Culture,* pp. 338-39.

[1006] Ibid., p. 124. Even the Irish-Catholics may have softened their stance on prohibition. The St. Louis based Knights of Father Mathew was founded in 1881 and preached total abstinence for young men. The organization had 3,000 members in 1898. Before the Catholic Total Abstinence Union held its convention in St. Louis in 1904, membership had grown to 6,000 members and by 1906 the organization had a parish council in St. Charles. Martin G. Towey and Margaret Loicollo Sullivan, "The Knights of Father Mathew: Parallel Ethnic Reform," *MHR*, Vol. LXXV, No. 2, January 1981, p. 173.

[1007] Anita Mallinckrodt, trans. *"A Piece of History,"* *Demokrat*, October 8, 1896, in *A History of Augusta, Missouri and Its Area,* Vol. 3, p. 625.

[1008] Edna McElhiney Olsen, *Historical Articles,* Vol. I, p. 59.

[1009] Anita Mallinckrodt, trans. "Jingoists and War," *Demokrat*, March 3, 1898, in *A History of Augusta, Missouri and Its Area,* Vol. 3, p. 646.

[1010] Ibid.

[1011] Audrey Olson, *St. Louis Germans,* p. 174. St. Louis Congressman Richard Barthold supported the McKinley foreign policy and was elected by a 12,000-vote plurality even though threatened with defeat by powerful German language paper editor Emil Pretorius. Ibid., p. 175.

[1012] Edna McElhiney Olson, *Historical Articles,* Vol. IV, p. 668.

[1013] Carl Schurz remained the consistent nineteenth century Liberal to the end. He opposed imperialism to the extent that he supported Bryan in the 1900 election, even though he vehemently disagreed with his monetary policies. Trefousse, *Carl Schurz,* pp. 285-286.

[1014] *Diary of John Jay Johns,* April 6, 1880. Eight years later he wrote, "At the election down town today I witnessed disgusting scenes – a lot of noisy whites and blacks- profane – totally ignorant of political questions." Ibid., November 6, 1888.

[1015] Anita Mallinckrodt, trans. "A Word for the Negro," *Demokrat*, October 25, 1888, in *A History of Augusta, Missouri and its Area,* Vol. 3, p. 547.

[1016] Anita Mallinckrodt, trans. "Industry in the South," *Demokrat*, August 1, 1889, in *A History of Augusta, Missouri and Its Area,* Vol. 3, p. 555.

[1017] Christensen and Kremer, *A History of Missouri, 1875-1919,* p. 178.

[1018] Ibid.

[1019] Edna McElhiney Olson, *Historical Articles,* Vol. III, p. 735. Schiermeier, *Cracker Barrel Country,* Vol. III, p. 168. Edwards was the cousin of W.W. Edwards, A.H. Edwards and Major James Edwards. He served as highway engineer until 1922 and was a leader in the Democratic Party, serving as a delegate to the Chicago Convention where William Jennings Bryan was nominated. Ibid.

[1020] Jo Ann Brown, *St. Charles Borromeo,* p. 109.

[1021] Poindexter, "Right Smart Little Town," p. 93.

[1022] Ibid., pp. 93-94.

[1023] Christensen and Kremer, *A History of Missouri, 1875-1919,* p. 206.

[1024] Luebke, *Bonds of Loyalty,* p. 190.

[1025] *Banner News,* November 9, 1916.

[1026] Ibid.

[1027] Breslow, *Small Town,* p. 152.

[1028] Edward Kaminski, *American Car and Foundry Company, A Centennial History,* (n.p., n.d.,) p. 19.

[1029] Mead, *Doughboys,* p. 376.

[1030] Poindexter, "Right Smart Little Town," p. 99.

[1031] Breslow, *Small Town,* p. 152. Mead, *Doughboys,* p. 70.

[1032] As related to the author by H. K. Stumberg, a life-long resident of St. Charles and former Republican activist.

[1033] Official Manual of the State of Missouri (Blue Book). All election data after 1890 is taken from these bi-annual publications by the Missouri Secretary of State.

[1034] Steve Ehlmann, "Victory in Defeat," *St. Louis Post-Dispatch,* March 26, 2001, p. B7.

[1035] Ibid.

[1036] Ibid.

[1037] Ibid. Nell Ehlmann's son, Winston Ehlmann, later served as assistant attorney general of Minnesota.

[1038] Anita Mallinckrodt, trans. "Women Suffragettes," *Demokrat,* May 11, 1871, in *A History of Augusta, Missouri and Its Area,* Vol. 2, p. 223.

[1039] Poindexter, "A Right Smart Little Town," p. 107.

[1040] Kyvig, *Daily Life in the United States, 1920-1939,* p. 19.

[1041] Poindexter, "A Right Smart Little Town," p. 106.

[1042] *Banner-News,* November 1, 1923.

[1043] Poindexter, "A Right Smart Little Town," Ibid., p. 107.

[1044] Richard S. Kirkendall, *The History of Missouri, 1919 to 1953,* Volume V, (Columbia: University of Missouri Press, 1986), p. 26.

[1045] *Banner-News,* November 1, 1920.

[1046] Rothensteiner, *History of the Archdiocese,* pp. 713-714.

[1047] Luebke, *Bonds of Loyalty,* p. 325.

[1048] Allan Lichtman, *Prejudice and the Old Politics, the Presidential Election of 1928,* (Chapel Hill: University of North Carolina Press, 1979), p. 105.

[1049] *Banner-News,* October 16, 1924.

[1050] *Cosmos-Monitor,* October 29, 1924, p. 4.

[1051] *Banner-News,* January 8, 1925. William F. Weinrich was born at New Melle on October 21, 1874 and educated in the public and parochial schools of New Melle. He was the son of Representative Conrad Weinrich. An insurance salesman, he was a member of the St. Charles City Council for six years. He served as chairman of the Committee on Building and Loan. Blue Book

[1052] *Banner-News,* October 21, 1926.

[1053] Ibid., March 4, 1926.

[1054] Ibid., April 21, 1926.

[1055] *Cosmos-Monitor,* January 17, 1927, p. 2. Republican Representative Louis J. Ringe, was born December 21, 1869 at St. Charles and was president of Good-Will Lubricating Company of St. Louis. Elected to the House in 1926, his father was a Civil War veteran. Blue Book.

[1056] Faherty, *St. Louis Irish,* p. 122.

[1057] Will Herberg, *Protestant, Catholic, Jew: An Essay in American Religious Sociology,* (New York: Doubleday Company, 1935), p. 160.

[1058] Gary M. Fink, *Labor's Search for Political Order,* (Columbia: University of Missouri Press, 1973), p. 116.

[1059] *Banner News,* November 1, 1928.

[1060] *Cosmos-Monitor*, June 27, 1928.

[1061] *Banner News*, November 1, 1928.

[1062] Ibid. Hoover had been in charge of food relief for Germany after the Armistice. *The Cosmos-Monitor* ran an article during the same week entitled "Urges German-Americans to Vote for Hoover" citing "the wonderful work that he (Hoover) did for the women and children in Germany, both during the war and after the armistice was signed." *Cosmos-Monitor,* Oct. 31, 1928.

[1063] Lichtman, *Prejudice and the Old Politics,* p. 116.

[1064] Ibid., p. 51.

[1065] Ibid. p. 60.

[1066] Ibid. p. 89.

[1067] Faherty, *St. Louis Irish,* p. 177.

[1068] *Banner-News*, September 25, 1924.

[1069] Robert McElvaine, *The Great Depression,* (New York: Three Rivers Press, 1993), p. 24.

[1070] Licht, *Industrializing America,* p. 102.

[1071] Ibid., p. 125.

[1072] *Journal*, January 14, 1881, p. 4.

[1073] *Cosmos-Monitor*, January-February 1882, Licht, *Industrializing America,* p. 127.

[1074] Breslow, *Small Town,* p. 137.

[1075] Ibid. *Portrait and Biography,* pp. 123-124.

[1076] Ibid.

[1077] Laurie, *Artisans into Workers,* p. 123.

[1078] Ibid., p. 124.

[1079] Breslow, *Small Town,* pp. 23-24.

[1080] Langenbacher, R.A. "St. Charles County, Missouri in the Agricultural Limestone Contest," No. 23226, Western Manuscript Collection, University of Missouri, Columbia.

[1081] Ibid., p. 32.

[1082] Licht, *Industrializing America,* p. 124.

[1083] Breslow, *Small Town,* p. 38.

[1084] *History of St. Charles County,* p. 245. Thelen, *Paths of Resistance,* p. 48. One of the 73 boot-making establishments was the shoe factory that was built in the City of St. Charles in 1905.

[1085] Ibid., p. 46.

[1086] Ibid., p. 49.

[1087] Ibid., p. 19.

[1088] When the author's grandfather, who worked at the shoe factory for fifty years, walked home everyday for lunch with his wife and two children as long as he lived 3 blocks away. When he moved six blocks away he had to take a lunch.

[1089] Poindexter, "A Right Smart Little Town," p. 88.

[1090] Daniel T. Brown, *Small Glories,* p.281.

[1091] Thelen, *Paths of Resistance,* p. 114.

[1092] Anita Mallinckrodt, trans, "St. Charles County Schools," *Demokrat*, October 30, 1873, in *A History of Augusta, Missouri and its Area,* Vol.2, p. 259.

[1093] *Agricultural History*, pp. 8-10.

[1094] Christensen and Kremer, *A History of Missouri, 1875-1919*, p. 113.

[1095] Poindexter, "A Right Smart Little Town," p. 89.

[1096] Breslow, *Small Town,* pp. 40-41.

[1097] Evans, *Born for Liberty,* p. 86.

[1098] Russo, *American Towns,* p. 148.

[1099] Laurie, *Artisans into Workers,* p. 127.

[1100] Ibid. p. 128. Primm, *Lion of the Valley,* p. 358.

[1101] Licht, *Industrializing America,* pp. 116, 131, 133-134.

[1102] "Bicentennial Celebration Program, " p. 41.

[1103] Poindexter, "A Right Smart Little Town, p. 91-92. *Cosmos Monitor,* April 19,1950

[1104] Breslow, *Small Town,* p. 138.

[1105] Ibid.

[1106] Ibid., p. 139.

[1107] Ibid., pp.109-110.

[1108] "O'Fallon Centennial, Program" and http://www.stpetersmo.net

[1109] Breslow, *Small Town,* p. 180.

[1110] Ibid., p. 79.

[1111] Ibid.

[1112] Ibid., p. 211.

[1113] Thomas J. Schlereth, *Victorian America, Transformations in Everyday Life, 1876-1915,* (New York: Harper-Collins, 1991). p. 111.

[1114] Breslow, *Small Town,* p. 52.

[1115] Schlereth, *Victorian America,* p. 111, Breslow, *Small Town,* p.52.

[1116] Schlereth, *Victorian America,* p. 112.

[1117] Breslow, *Small Town ,* p. 52.

[1118] Ibid. Edna McElhiney Olson, *Historical Articles,* Vol. I, p. 168.

[1119] Breslow, *Small Town,* p. 52. 1120 Jennifer Broeker, "For Holding One in Bondage," *St. Charles County Heritage,* Vol. 13, No. 2, April 1995, pp. 63-65.

[1121] Schlereth, *Victorian America,* p. 287.

[1122] Breslow, *Small Town,* p. 134.

[1123] Kennedy, "St. Joseph Health Center and the Franciscan Sisters of St. Mary," pp. 53-59.

[1124] Breslow, *Small Town,* p. 140.

[1125] Ibid., p. 141.

[1126] Schlereth, *Victorian America*, p. 114.

[1127] Ibid. p. 115. Breslow, *Small Town,* p. 213.

[1128] Kirkendall, *History of Missouri, 1919 to 1953,* p. 23.

[1129] Love, "Newspaper Feature," p.23.

[1130] Kyvig, *Daily Life in the United States, 1920-1939,* pp. 50-54.

[1131] Ibid.

[1132] Ibid., p. 79. Breslow, *Small Town,* p. 211. Politt, "Quality Family Programming for the Silent Screen," p. 53.

[1133] *Banner-News*, June 24, 1924.

[1134] Kyvig, *Daily Life in the United State, 1920-1939,* p. 62. Tindall, *America,* pp. 1092-93.

[1135] Langenbacher, R.A., *"A Soil Improvement Program for St. Charles County, Missouri, 1921-1929,* No 2677 Western Manuscript Collection, University of Missouri, Columbia, p. 61.

[1136] Daniel Brown, *Small Glories,* p. 269.

[1137] Russo, *American Towns,* p. 168.

[1138] Breslow, *Small Town,* p. 215.

[1139] Edna McElhiney Olson, *Historical Articles,* Vol. III, p. 463.

[1140] Breslow, *Small Town,* p. 215.

[1141] Daniel Brown, *Small Glories,* p. 230.

[1142] Edna McElhiney Olson, *Historical Articles,* Vol. III, p. 536, Vol. IV, p. 646.

[1143] Schlereth, *Victorian America,* p. 189.

[1144] Mincke, *History of Portage des Sioux,* p.130.

[1145] Breslow, *Small Town,* p. 174.

[1146] "Bicentennial Celebration Program," p. 61. Smaller communities in St. Charles County provided fire protection through volunteer fire departments founded in St. Peters (1904), Augusta (1905), Cottleville (1908) and Wentzville (1928). Edna McElhiney Olsen, *Historical Articles,* Vol. I, p. 55.

[1147] Edna McElhiney Olsen, *Historical Articles,* Vol. I, p. 78.

[1148] Kristina Korth, "Kathryn Linnemann," *St. Charles County Heritage,* Vol.16, No. 3, July 1998, p. 111-115. Her brother, Robert Linnemann, served as state representative and senator.

[1149] McElhiney, *My Hometown,* p. 4.

[1150] Breslow, *Small Town,* p. 222. "The Bridges at St. Charles," p. 12. In 1916 the wooden floor of the bridge burned and was replaced with reinforced concrete. Ibid.

[1151] Love, *"Past Times,"* p. 23.

[1152] "Bicentennial Celebration Program," p. 32.

[1153] Breslow, *Small Town,* p. 223.

[1154] Kenneth T. Jackson, *Crabgrass Frontier: The Suburbanization of the United States,* (New York: Oxford University Press, 1985), p. 169. The number of electric street cars peaked in 1917, while total ridership crested in 1923 at 15.7 billion. It declined to 14.4 billion by 1929 and to 8.3 billion in 1940. Ibid., pp. 170-171.

[1155] Breslow, *Small Town,* p. 223.

[1156] Ibid.

[1157] Ibid. Jackson, *Crabgrass Frontier,* p.173.

[1158] Brown, *Small Glories,* p. 314.

[1159] Kirkendall, *History of Missouri,* 1919-1953, p. 85.

[1160] Breslow, *Small Town,* p. 217. Jackson, *Crabgrass Frontier,* p. 167.

[1161] Jackson, *Crabgrass Frontier,* p.167.

[1162] Kirkendall, *History of Missouri, 1919-1953,* p. 37. Ever since the lettered highways in the counties have been under the State Highway Department.

[1163] Schiermeier, *Cracker Barrel Country,* Vol. III, p. 209. Louis J. Launer, "Victory Highway," *St. Charles County Heritage,* Vol. 13, No. 1, January 1995, p. 25.

[1164] "The Bridges at St. Charles," p. 14.

[1165] "Polk's St. Charles City Directory" for 1929 lists Charles F. Gatzweiler Motors, Joseph H. Machens Motor Company, McGee Motor Company, Travis Motor Company and Pundmann Motor Company, as the auto dealers in St. Charles.

[1166] Johnson, *History of the American People*, p. 730.

[1167] Ibid. p. 735.

Chapter V
End Notes

[1168] McElvaine, *The Great Depression,* p. 75.

[1169] Ibid., p. 320.

[1170] *Banner-News*, March 5, 1925.

[1171] Ibid.

[1172] Poindexter, "A Right Smart Little Town," p. 114.

[1173] "Missouri Council of Defense Papers," St. Charles County, F. 1060, No. 24953, Western Manuscript Collection, University of Missouri, Columbia.

[1174] Langenbacher, "Soil Improvement Program," p. 18-19.

[1175] Ibid. p. 16, 19, 20. The legumes were plowed under or fed to livestock and the manure spread back on the fields. Ibid.

[1176] Ibid. p. 10.

[1177] Ibid. p. 17.

[1178] *Banner-News*, April 29, 1926.

[1179] McElvaine, *The Great Depression,* p. 19.

[1180] Daniel Brown, *Small Glories,* p. 281.

[1181] Kyvig, *Daily Life in the United States, 1920-1939,* p. 56.

[1182] Kirkendall, *History of Missouri, 1919-1953,* p. 121. Edna McElhiney Olson, *Historical Articles,* Vol. I, p. 150, Daniel Brown, *Small Glories,* p 397.

[1183] Ibid., p. 317.

[1184] McElvaine, *The Great Depression,* pp. 11, 21.

[1185] Breslow, *Small Town,* p. 58. Kirkendall, *History of Missouri, 1919-1953,* pp. 131-132.

[1186] Gloria P. Crail, "With Spading Fork and Popcorn They Survived," *We Had Everything but Money,* ed. By Deb Mulvey and Clancey Stock, (Greendale, WI: Country Books, 1992). p. 12.

[1187] *Cosmos-Monitor*, February 10, 1932.

[1188] Jo Ann Brown, *St.Charles Borromeo,* p. 147.

[1189] *Cosmos-Monitor,* December 3,1930.

[1190] Poindexter, "A Right Smart Little Town," p. 117, citing *Banner-News,* Dec. 1,1932.

[1191] *Cosmos-Monitor,* February 10, 1932.

[1192] Ibid., March 2, 1932.

[1193] Poindexter, "Right Smart Little Town," p. 117, citing *Banner-News*, December 1, 1932.

[1194] McElvaine, *The Great Depression,* p. 151.

[1195] David D. March, "Missouri's Care of Indigent Aged," *MHR,* January 1984, p.213.

[1196] Ibid.

[1197] McElvaine, *The Great Depression,* p. 80.

[1198] Mittelbuscher, *Flint Hill,* p. 26

[1199] McElvaine, *The Great Depression,* p. 80.

[1200] Ibid., p. 137.

[1201] Poindexter, "A Right Smart Little Town," p. 118, citing *Banner News,* December 19, 1933. Edna McElhiney Olson, *Historical Articles,* Vol. I, p. 150. Daniel T. Brown, *Small Glories,* pp. 372, 377.

[1202] Poindexter, "A Right Smart Little Town," p. 118, citing interview with Theodosia Rauch, St. Charles , Missouri, March 19, 1973.

[1203] Ibid. citing *Banner-News,* February 13, 1932.

[1204] *Banner-News*, April 7, 1938.

[1205] Kyvig, *Daily Life in the United States, 1920-1939,* pp. 100-101.

[1206] Breslow, *Small Town,* p. 229.

[1207] "Bicentennial Celebration Program," p. 49-50. Dave Weil was the son of Emil Weil. Saul Wolf was another prominent Jewish businessman who started the Standard Drug Stores in the early thirties. Another prominent Jewish business leader was Abe Hess, manager of The Famous ladies clothing store.

[1208] Ibid.

[1209] *Cosmos-Monitor*, July 24, 1940 and Vol. 105, No. 29. Population figures: St. Charles, 10,807, Wentzville 740, O'Fallon 612, St. Peters 248. Portage des Sioux 254, Augusta 252, West Alton 198 New Melle 185, Foristell 142, Howell 129, Hamburg 121, Defiance 98,St. Paul 83, Gilmore 42, and Josephville 16. Ibid.

[1210] Evans, *Born for Liberty,* pp. 201-202.

[1211] *Banner-News*, May 10, 1938.

[1212] Edna McElhiney Olson, *Historical Articles,* Vol. III, p. 523. In 1900 twelve women, graduates of the Sacred Heart Academy and Lindenwood College, had formed the "Thimble Club." They sewed and staged concerts at the Opera House to raise money for St. Joseph Hospital. Ibid.

[1213] Daniel T. Brown, *Small Glories,* p. 387.

[1214] Kirkendahl, *History of Missouri, 1919-1953,* p. 163. Democratic Congressman, Clarence Cannon, lined up with the drys in an attempt to send a state-control amendment to the voters. *Cosmos-Monitor,* March 16, 1932.

[1215] *Cosmos-Monitor*, April 11, 1934. The *Literary Digest* Prohibition Poll of 27 Missouri cities over 5,000 population in 1930 ranked St. Charles the most strongly opposed to the enforcement of Prohibition. *Cosmos-Monitor,* June 4, 1930.

[1216] Ibid., May 9, 1951. Jacob Fischbach was born in Alsace-Lorraine in 1863.and worked at three breweries in France before coming to America in 1892.

[1217] Cordelia Stumberg, *"My Sonata: Music in My Life,"* a manuscript in the possession of the author. Ironically, Cordelia Buck married H.K. Stumberg, from one of the leading German-American families in St. Charles.

[1218] Cook, *History of St. Charles,* p. 75. The sport had been popular in Germany going back to the Middle Ages when the bowlers were called "kegelers."

[1219] Anita Mallinckrodt, trans. "Baseball in the United States," *Demokrat,* July 10, 1890, in *A History of Augusta, Missouri and Its Area,* Vol. 3, p. 564.

[1220] *Cosmos-Monitor,* August 16, 1939.

[1221] *Ibid.*

[1222] *Cosmos-Monitor,* August, 23,1939, Former players attending included Ben L. Emmons, Wm. Bloebaum, Emmett Edwards, Stephen Boehmer, H.H. Steed, Edward Meyer, Wm. J. Hafer, and Geo. Wallenbrink, Wm Meyer, Herman Moelenkamp, John Platz, John Steinbrinker, John Vogel, Conrad Broeckelmann, Louis Hellrich, John Ruenzi, Barney Wessler, Joe Wessler, Claude Taylor, Edward Kister, Frank Pallardy, Charlie Fredenberg, Hy. Spinks, P.J. Costigan, Morris Murry, Oscar Blankenmeister, Charles Bartley, Emile Bueneman and Jimmy Feeney. Ibid.

[1223] Lisa Smith, ed. *Nike is a Goddess,* (New York: Atlantic Monthly Press, 1998), pp. 49, 296.

[1224] Elaine Goodrich Linn, "Depression Kids," *St. Charles County Heritage,* Vol. 15, No. 4, October 1997, p. 49-55.

[1225] McElvaine, *The Great Depression,* p. 185.

[1226] *Cosmos-Monitor,* November 13, 1929 and November 27, 1940.

[1227] *Banner-News,* May 20, 1938. Local businessman Ed "Brick" Travis had been an all-conference member of the University of Missouri Football team in 1919 and 1920.

[1228] "Bicentennial Celebration Program," p. 32.

[1229] *Cosmos-Monitor,* July 31, 1940.

[1230] Ibid., October 16, 1940.

[1231] Ibid., October 30, 1940.

[1232] Poindexter, "A Right Smart Little Town," p. 121.

[1233] *Cosmos-Monitor,* June 25, 1941.

[1234] Ibid., December 24, 1941. Betty Burnett, *St. Louis at War, The Story of a City, 1941-1945,* (St. Louis: The Patrice Press, 1987), p. 2.

[1235] Mincke, *History of Portage des Sioux,* p. 139.

[1236] Burnett, *St. Louis at War,* p. 9.

[1237] Robert Heide and John Gilman, *Home Front America, Popular Culture of the World War II Era,* (San Francisco: Chronicle Books, 1995), p. 44.

[1238] Poindexter, "A Right Smart Little Town," p. 122. Citing *Banner News,* January 8,10, 16, 1942.

[1239] *Banner-News,* December 18, 1942.

[1240] Burnett, *St. Louis at War,* p. 15.

[1241] Ibid., p. 134. They explained that TNT was shipped as fast as possible. Two climb-proof fences and an armed patrol protected the buildings that had been arranged so that extensive damage would be impossible in the unlikely event of sabotage. Ibid.

[1242] John Morton Blum, *V Was for Victory, Politics and American Culture During World War II,* (New York: Harcourt Brace Jovanovich, 1976), p. 172.

[1243] Ibid. *Banner-News,* January 26, 1942. 1941 Charlemo.

[1244] Heide, *Home Front* p. 43.

[1245] Poindexter, "A Right Smart Little Town," p. 124. German language instruction had been dropped during WWI and then reinstated. It was probably dropped because only ten students had taken it the previous year. *Cosmos-Monitor,* August 12, 1942.

[1246] Heide, *Home Front,* pp. 54-56.

[1247] Poindexter, "A Right Smart Little Town," p. 124.

[1248] *Banner-News*, November 18, 1942.

[1249] *Agricultural History,* p. 126.

[1250] *Banner-News*, July 30, 1942.

[1251] Ibid., January 9, 1946.

[1252] Heide, *Home Front,* p. 58.

[1253] *Banner-News*, December 12, 1942.

[1254] Ibid., August 25, 1942.

[1255] Edna McElhiney Olson, *Historical Articles,* Vol. III, p. 415.

[1256] Poindexter, "A Right Smart Little Town," p. 124, citing *Banner-News*, August 31, 1942.

[1257] Evans, *Born for Liberty,* p. 221.

[1258] Interview with Cordelia Stumberg. The St. Louis City School Board did not hire married female teachers, and dismissed single teachers that married until 1948, when the Missouri Supreme Court declared it was illegal. Anita Weis and Mildred Holmes initiated the case in 1941. See Sharon Pedersen, "Married Women and the Right to Teach in St. Louis, 1941-1948," *MHR,* January 1987, p. 141. George M. Null, born in 1884, married Florence Bloebaum in 1912. A successful businessman, he served on the St. Charles School Board from 1920-1953. *St. Charles Journal,* November 23, 1965.

[1259] Darlene M. Hahn, "A St. Charles WW II Rosie the Riveter," *St. Charles County Heritage,* Vol. 20, No. 2, April 2002, p. 66.

[1260] Burnett, *St. Louis at War,* p. 43.

[1261] Ibid., *Agricultural History,* p. 126.

[1262] Ibid. citing *Banner-News*, July 13, 1943.

[1263] Poindexter, "A Right Smart Little Town," p. 126.

[1264] Ibid.

[1265] Ibid. p. 127.

[1266] Pictures of the German concentration camps were shown at an exhibit at Memorial Hall in Blanchette Park on September 4 and 5. A plaque in the same hall honors those who died in WWII. *Banner-News*, August 8, 1945.

[1267] "Wentzville Centennial Program," p. 34.

[1268] Michelle Kramme, "A Progressive Pageant Like No Other," *St. Charles County Heritage,* Vol. 11, no. 3, p. 87.

[1269] *Cosmos-Monitor*, June 20, 1930, June 22, 1932.

[1270] McElvaine, *The Great Depression,* p. 88.

[1271] Poindexter, "A Right Smart Little Town," p.116.

[1272] Ibid. citing *Banner-News*, Dec. 3 and 9, 1932.

[1273] Blue Book. The last Democratic state representative had been H. F. Knippenburg, a farmer from Femme Osage. Frank J. Iffrig was born near St. Peters June 21, 1876 and educated in the public and parochial schools and Quincy College. He was a merchant in St. Peters, where he also served as mayor. Blue Book.

[1274] Poindexter, "A Right Smart LittleTown," citing *Banner-News*, November 9, 1932.

[1275] Fink, *Labor's Search for Political Order,* p. 127.

[1276] *Cosmos-Monitor*, June 8, 1932. The meeting was held at 608 South Fourth Street at the residence of Lester Sweazy, an unemployed blacksmith. The small home is located on a high bank from which the speakers were able to address the crowd. Ibid.

[1277] *Banner-News*, September 12, 1934. A new water works and sewage treatment system was built in Wentzville. "Wentzville Centennial Program."

[1278] Ibid., October 22, 1934.

[1279] Ibid.

[1280] *Banner-News*, October 19, 1934.

[1281] The party of a sitting president would not pick up seats in a mid-term election again until the 2002 elections.

[1282] McElvaine, *The Great Depression,* p. 229.

[1283] *Banner-News*, July 25, 1934.

[1284] Ibid., August 1, 1934.

[1285] *Cosmos-Monitor*, November 14, 1934.

[1286] Ibid., January 8, 1936.

[1287] Edna McElhiney Olsen, *Historical Articles,* Vol. I, p. 59. President Cleveland had appointed Holmes father, James C. Holmes, to the same post in 1886.

[1288] McElvaine, *The Great Depression,* pp. 258-259.

[1289] Ibid., pp. 260-261.

[1290] *Banner-News*, August 1, 1936.

[1291] *Cosmos-Monitor*, June 15, 1936.

[1292] Ibid., June 15, 1936.

[1293] *Banner-News*, October 22, 1934.

[1294] Ibid., October 20, 1936.

[1295] McElvaine, *The Great Depression,* p. 281.

[1296] *Banner-News*, November 5, 1934.

[1297] Ibid., November 6, 1934.

[1298] Ibid., October 20, 1936.

[1299] Nagel, *Missouri,* p. 158.

[1300] *Cosmos-Monitor*, May 29, 1935.

[1301] McElvaine, *The Great Depression,* p. 305.

[1302] *Cosmos-Monitor*, October 26, 1938.

[1303] Ibid. January 1, 1941.

[1304] Ibid., May 27, 1936.

[1305] Ibid., September 16, 1953, and May 27, 1936.

[1306] *Banner-News*, September 24, 1925.

[1307] *Cosmos-Monitor*, April 8, 1927.

[1308] *Banner-News*, January 7, 1926.

[1309] Johnson, *History of the American People,* p. 756.

[1310] *Banner-News*, December 12, 1932. Union Electric, in 1925 had purchased the hydroelectric dam at Keokuk, Iowa creating the largest power system in the Midwest. In the 1930s Union Electric built Bagnell Dam at the Lake of the Ozarks. *Banner-News*, October 8, 1925.

[1311] Fink, *Labor's Search for Unity,* p. 137.

[1312] *Cosmos-Monitor,* November 26, 1930. Union Electric had purchased plant and franchise from St. Charles Electric Light and Power Co. for $61,811 on August 23, 1923.*Banner-News*, September 8, 1932.

[1313] Ibid.,July 6,1932.

[1314] *Banner-News*, October 17, 1932.

[1315] *Cosmos-Monitor*, January 4, 1933.

[1316] *Banner-News*, September 8, 1932.

[1317] Ibid., September 17, 1932, and December 21, 1932.

[1318] Ibid.,September 30, 1932.

[1319] Ibid., December 30,1932.

[1320] *Cosmos-Monitor,* May 1, 1940.

[1321] Luke Garzia, "Electric Gate: A Home-Grown Political Scandal," *St. Charles County Heritage,* Vol. 16, No.3, July 1998. p. 89.

[1322] Ibid., p. 90.

[1323] *Cosmos-Monitor*, April 17, 1940.

[1324] Ibid., May 14, 1941.

[1325] Ibid., February 17, 1937.

[1326] *Banner-News*, January 3, 1924.

[1327] Ibid., October 16, 1924.

[1328] Johnson, *History of the American People,* pp. 774-776.

[1329] Richard O'Conner, *The German Americans: An Informal History,*(Boston, Little, Brown & Co., 1968), p.435.

[1330] *Cosmos-Monitor*, Sept. 11, 1940, p. 5.

[1331] McElvaine, *The Great Depression,* p. 319.

[1332] *Cosmos-Monitor*, May 29, 1935.

[1333] McElvaine, *The Great Depression,* p. 320.

[1334] Johnson, *History of the American People,* p. 781.

[1335] The city had four wards. The boundaries separating them ran perpendicular to the river, with the First Ward on the south side and the Fourth Ward on the north side of town.

[1336] *Cosmos-Monitor*, January 6, 1941.

[1337] Ibid., January 6, 1941.

[1338] *Banner-News*, January 27, 1941.

[1339] Dunne, *Missouri Supreme Court,* pp. 142-150.

[1340] *Cosmos-Monitor*, April 2, 1941.

[1341] Blum, *V - Was for Victory,* pp.230-234.

[1342] Ibid., pp. 241-242.

[1343] Burnett, *St. Louis at War,* pp. 104, 407.

[1344] Blum, *V – Was for Victory,* p. 295.

[1345] *Cosmos-Monitor*, August 29, 1930.

[1346] As related to the author by Erich Ehlmann.

[1347] *Cosmos-Monitor*, November 6, 1929.

[1348] Ibid., January 20, 1932.

[1349] Ibid., March 26, 1930.

[1350] Ibid., January 18, 1933.

[1351] Ibid., June 30,1937.

[1352] Ibid., November 5, 1930.

[1353] Ibid., April 20, 1932.

[1354] Kirkendall, *History of Missouri,* 1919-1953, p. 162.

[1355] *Cosmos-Monitor*, March 15, 1933. The 8 banks were First National Bank of St.Charles, Bank of St. Peters, Bank of St. Paul, Bank of O'Fallon, Bank of Foristell, St. Charles Savings, Union Savings of St. Charles and Bank of Wentzville.

[1356] Ibid., October 4, 1933.

[1357] Ibid., March 29,1935.

[1358] McElvaine, *The Great Depression,* p. 153.

[1359] Kirkendall, *History of Missouri, 1919-1953,* p. 164.

[1360] *Cosmos-Monitor,* November 29, 1933. The workweek consisted of thirty hours and the workers received their paychecks directly from the federal government.

[1361] McElvaine, *The Great Depression,* p. 154.

[1362] Ibid., p. 152.

[1363] *Cosmos-Monitor*, January 27, 1937, December 5, 1934 and October 14,1936.

[1364] Ibid.

[1365] Gary McKiddy, "Federal Relief in St. Charles County During the First Half of the Great Depression," *St. Charles County Heritage,* Vol. 11, No. 1, January 1993, pp. 16-17.

[1366] Ibid., pp. 18-19

[1367] March, "Missouri's Care," p.213.

[1368] McElvaine, *The Great Depression,* p. 265, *Cosmos-Monitor*, January 6, 1941.

[1369] Ibid., p. 191.

[1370] *Cosmos-Monitor,* March 25 and July 15, 1935.

[1371] Ibid., March 13, 1940.

[1372] Ibid., May 8, 1940, and June 4, 1940.

[1373] Jo Ann Brown, *St. Charles Borromeo,* p. 162. Even after the WPA was discontinued the school continued to provide hot lunches.

[1374] McElvaine, *The Great Depression,* p. 268.

[1375] *Cosmos-Monitor*, January 19, 1938.

[1376] Ibid., December 9, 1942.

[1377] Kirkendall, *History of Missouri, 1919-1953,* p. 164. *Cosmos-Monitor,* March 27, 1940.

[1378] McElvaine, *The Great Depression,* p. 155. One St. Charles youth who went to a CCC Camp was Douglas Boschert. Interview with Douglas Boschert.

[1379] Ibid., p. 149. 6 million piglets and 200,000 sows were killed. Ten million acres of cotton were plowed under. Ibid.

[1380] *Agricultural History,* p.147. Kirkendall, *History of Missouri, 1919-1953,* p. 164. *The Great Depression,* pp. 147-148.

[1381] McElvaine, *The Great Depression,* p. 150.

[1382] *Cosmos-Monitor,* June 10,1936.

[1383] McElvaine, *The Great Depression,* pp.147-148. *Cosmos-Monitor,* June 10,1936.

[1384] *Cosmos-Monitor*, Vol.43, No.31., 1939.

[1385] Ibid., March 26, 1941.

[1386] Ibid., October 1, 1941. Nationwide, even after REA had doubled the number in the previous three years, in 1940 only one-third of rural residences had electricity, while 91 percent of urban homes had been wired. Ibid.

[1387] Ibid., February 4, 1942.

[1388] Anita Mallinckrodt, trans. "From Augusta," *Demokrat*, July 15, 1875, in *A History of Augusta, Missouri and Its Area,* Vol. 2, p. 299.

[1389] McElhiney, *My Hometown*, p. 3.

[1390] *Journal*, May 6, 1881, p. 1, and May 13, 1881, p. 4.

[1391] Kirkendall, *History of Missouri, 1919-1953,* p. 83.

[1392] Ibid., pp. 165-66.

[1393] *Cosmos-Monitor*, June 12, 1935.

[1394] Ibid., July 3, 1935.

[1395] Kirkendall, *History of Missouri, 1919-1953,* p. 191.

[1396] *Cosmos-Monitor*, February 10, 1937.

[1397] Ibid., September 16, 1942.

[1398] Kirkendall, *History of Missouri, 1919-1953,* p. 280.

[1399] *Cosmos-Monitor*, September 27, 1933.

[1400] Ibid., February 2, 1938.

[1401] Ibid., May 4, 1938. The navigational projects of the Corps of Engineers like the Alton Dam not only provided jobs and strengthened unions but also made possible a steady stream of products plying the rivers during World War II. Other demands shifted the attention of the Corps away from the river during the war. The Corps constructed ordnance plants, built an airbase, and expanded Jefferson barracks. It also built an internment camp at which it used German prisoners to build a scale model of the upper Missouri River system that was used to model imaginary flood events for years until replaced by computer models. Ibid.

[1402] *Banner-News*, January 31, 1938.

[1403] McElvaine, *The Great Depression,* pp. 287-296. In early 1937 Goodyear Rubber, General Motors and even U.S. Steel had accepted CIO unions in their plants. The smaller steel companies were another story as violence erupted at the Chicago plant of Republic Steel, further polarizing public opinion. On Memorial Day 1937 picketing workers began throwing rocks at police, who opened fire and killed ten picketers. Union supporters claimed that the company fed the police and all ten fatalities were shot in the back, as they were trying to flee. Ibid.

[1404] *Banner-News*, February 1, 1938. Interview with Eugene Steinhoff.

[1405] Ibid., February 9, 1938.

[1406] There was also a bit of parochialism involved as the picketers also claimed that 43 Alton men had been given work wile St. Charles County men were refused jobs. *Banner-News*, February 9, 1938.

[1407] *Banner-News*, February 15, 1938.

[1408] Ibid., February 28, 1938.

[1409] Ibid., February 18 and 19, 1938.

[1410] Ibid., January 27, 1938.

[1411] Ibid., February 3 and 4, 1938.

[1412] Ibid., March 5, 1938.

[1413] Ibid., March 25, April 1, April 2 and April 18, 1938.

[1414] Ibid., April 28, 1938.

[1415] Ibid., February 4, 1938

[1416] Ibid., February 8, 1938.

[1417] Ibid., February 28, 1938. Organized Labor had become a part of the Roosevelt coalition by 1936. John L. Lewis had supported Hoover in 1932 and FDR had supported the Wagner Act in 1935 only when it became clear that it was going to pass even without his support. Organized Labor provided the national Democratic campaign $770,000 in 1936 but labor was not influential locally as 1938 approached.

[1418] Ibid., March 23, 1938. The *Banner-News* later claimed to be the first newspaper in the country to have an all-CIO work force. Ibid., January 15, 1953.

[1419] Ibid.

[1420] Ibid., March 11, 1938.

[1421] Ibid.

[1422] Kirkendall, *History of Missouri, 1919-1953,* p. 192.

[1423] *Cosmos-Monitor*, November 27, 1940.

[1424] Ibid., December 18, 1940. Union dues were 50¢ to join and 25¢ per week. Ibid.

[1425] *Banner-News*, March 8, 1941.

[1426] *Cosmos-Monitor*, June 18, 1941. Under the contract hourly wages, which had ranged from 40¢ to 80¢ per hour, were raised to 55¢ to 90¢ per hour.

[1427] *Banner-News*, December 13, 1940.

[1428] Ibid., December 31, 1940. A. D. Lewis, brother of CIO head John L. Lewis, headed the United Construction Workers Union.

[1429] Ibid., February 18, 1941.

[1430] *Cosmos-Monitor*, October 30, 1940.

[1431] Ibid., December 25, 1940.

[1432] Ibid., August 13, 1941.

[1433] Ibid.

[1434] Brown, *Small Glories,* p. 468. Samuel McCluer Watson had graduated from Francis Howell High School and gone on to become a condemnation lawyer for the City of St. Louis. Ibid.

[1435] Ibid., October 1, 1941. Edna McElhiney Olson, *Historical Articles,* Vol. I, p. 180.

[1436] *Cosmos-Monitor* December 4, 1940.

[1437] Ibid., May 21, 1940.

[1438] Edna McElhiney Olson, *Historical Articles,* Vol. I, p. 159.

[1439] *Cosmos-Monitor*, October 8, 1941.

[1440] Mary Yates Villert, "Smartt Field," in Donald Mincke, *History of Portage de Sioux Township Missouri, The Land Between the Rivers,* (Portage des Sioux: Land Between the Rivers Historical Society, 1999), p. 131.

[1441] Burnett, *St. Louis at War,* pp. 100-102.

[1442] Kirkendall, *History of Missouri, 1919-1953,* pp. 260-261, Kaminski, *American Car and Foundry,* p. 19. Johnson, *History of the American People,* p. 780.

[1443] John Morton Blum, *Years of Discord, American Politics and Society, 1961-1974,* (New York: W.W. Norton and Co., 199), pp. 140-141. Between 1941 and 1945, union membership grew from 10.5 million to 14.75 million. Ibid.

[1444] Burnett, *St. Louis at War,* pp. 132-133.

[1445] Ibid., p. 104.

[1446] Ibid., p. 108.

Chapter VI
End Notes

[1447] *Metropolitan St. Louis Survey, University City.* (St. Louis 8147 Delmar Blvd, August 1957).

[1448] *Cosmos-Monitor*, September 12, 1945. In June 1948 a group of nearly 300 persons attended a dinner in honor of County Extension Agent Robert Langenbacher to commemorate the 25th anniversary of his affiliation with the Extension Service in St. Charles County. *Cosmos-Monitor,* January 23, 1948.

[1449] Kirkendall, *History of Missouri, 1919-1953,* p. 303.

[1450] *Cosmos-Monitor*, July 14, 1948. The year before the crop had been below average because of infestation of the Hessian fly and warm weather. *Cosmos-Monitor,* July 17, 1946.

[1451] Kirkendall, *History of Missouri, 1919-1953,* pp. 301-101.

[1452] *Cosmos-Monitor,* July 14, 1948.

[1453] Kirkendall, *History of Missouri, 1919-1953,* p. 302.

[1454] *Cosmos-Monitor*, May 22, 1946.

[1455] Ibid., November 1958.

[1456] Ibid., July 4, 1956.

[1457] Ibid.

[1458] *Banner-News*, September 14, 1948 and *Cosmos-Monitor,* September 12, 1952.

[1459] *Cosmos-Monitor,* April 15, 1953.

[1460] Ibid., January 30, 1946.

[1461] Ibid., June 18, 1947.

[1462] Ibid., April 16, 1949.

[1463] Ibid., March 8, 1950.

[1464] Ibid., May 23, 1951.

[1465] Ibid., July 4, 1951.

[1466] Ibid., July 25, 1951.

[1467] Ibid.

[1468] Ibid., August 1, 1951.

[1469] Ibid., August 27, 1951.

[1470] Kirkendall, *History of Missouri, 1919-1953,* p. 363.

[1471] *Cosmos-Monitor*, July 18, 1951 and April 16, 1952.

[1472] Kirkendall, *History of Missouri 1919-1953*, p. 363.

[1473] Ibid., pp. 317-318., The case of *Shelley v. Kramer* originated in St. Louis and declared restrictive racial covenants unconstitutional. Jackson, *Crabgrass Frontier,* p. 208.

[1474] *Cosmos-Monitor,* August 11, 1954. While the lower development costs were attractive at the time, the neighborhood had no curbs, storm sewers or sidewalks. The homes were on septic tanks for a long time, and the area remained unincorporated because no municipality was interested in providing these services for the amount of tax revenue they would receive from the area.

[1475] Kenneth T. Jackson, *Crabgrass Frontier, The Suburbanization of the United States,* (New York: Oxford University Press, 1985), p. 232.

[1476] Ibid.

[1477] Ibid., Louis Launer, "Electrical Living Shows," *St. Charles County Heritage,* Vol. 18, No.1, January 2000, pp. 62-65.

[1478] *Cosmos-Monitor*, January 21, 1948.

[1479] Kenneth T. Jackson, *Crabgrass Frontier,* p. 232.

[1480] *Cosmos-Monitor*, November 2, 1949.

[1481] Ibid., May 16,1949 and October 1, 1952.

[1482] Ibid., November 20, 1946.

[1483] Ibid., December 4, 1946.

[1484] Ibid., January 19, 1949, The committee was composed of Frank Rauch, Osmund Haenssler, Otto Struckmann, Paul Diehr, Harold Decoster, Robert Niedner, Mayor Homer Clevenger and James Duggan.

[1485] Ibid., February 2, 1949.

[1486] Ibid., February 16, 1949. Only one contest for a home developed when John K. Barklage and Lyle Gillom, residents of the duplex, both registered to buy. Their wives, both of whom said they wanted to lose because they preferred another house, represented their families at the drawing. Mrs. Barklage won, or lost, depending how you look at it.

[1487] Ibid., December 15, 1946.

[1488] Ibid., January 10, 1951.

[1489] Ibid., March 26, 1946.

[1490] Ibid., July 24, 1946.

[1491] Ibid., July 30, 1947.

[1492] *Banner-News*, January 7, 1948.

[1493] *Cosmos-Monitor*, November 23, 1949.

[1494] Ibid., July 20, 1949.

[1495] Ibid., January 26, 1955. Jake Kaplan and his two sons owned the Kaplan Corporation. Ibid.

[1496] Kenneth T. Jackson, *Crabgrass Frontier,* p. 233.

[1497] Ibid.

[1498] Ibid.

[1499] *Cosmos-Monitor*, February 9, 1955 and February 22, 1956. The development was between Park Street and Elm Street in the area of Boschert Creek.

[1500] *Banner-News*, November 5, 1956. Of the 200 lots in Phase II, 77 lots were zoned for duplexes. Ibid.

[1501] Kenneth T. Jackson, *Crabgrass Frontier*, p. 238.

[1502] Kirkendall, *History of Missouri, 1919-1953,* p. 293. University City had replaced Joplin as the state's fifth largest city. St. Louis population had grown by only five percent to 856,000. Ibid.

[1503] Kenneth T. Jackson, *Crabgrass Frontier,* p. 239.

[1504] Ibid.

[1505] *Cosmos-Monitor*, August 23, 1957.

[1506] Kenneth T. Jackson, *Crabgrass Frontier,* p. 239.

[1507] *Banner-News*, June 26, 1959, Kenneth T. Jackson, *Crabgrass Frontier*, pp. 241, 292-293. Ninety percent of the homes built in the twentieth century were balloon frame. Ibid.

[1508] Ibid. p.291. This was in marked contrast to Europe and Japan. Ibid.

[1509] Ibid., p. 293.

[1510] Ibid., p. 252.

[1511] Evans, *Born for Liberty,* p. 252. "Lindenwood College Bulletin," February, 1950, p.4. *Banner-News*, October 10, 1974.

[1512] *Banner-News*, July 17, 1948.

[1513] *Cosmos-Monitor*, March 17, 1948.

[1514] Ibid.

[1515] Ibid., November 9, 1949.

[1516] Ibid., August 12, 1953.

[1517] Ibid., December 23, 1953.

[1518] Ibid., August 12, 1953.

[1519] Ibid., January 5, 1955.

[1520] Ibid., March 20, 1946.

[1521] Ibid., May 14, 1947.

[1522] Ibid., December 1, 1948.

[1523] Burnett, *St. Louis at War,* pp. 158-160.

[1524] *Cosmos-Monitor*, January 21, 1951. [1525] Ibid., May 26, 1957. It had been the largest new industry to locate in Missouri three years earlier. Ibid.

[1526] Ibid., March 23, 1949, *Banner-News*, May 6, 1948.

[1527] *Cosmos-Monitor*, January 16, 1952.

[1528] Ibid., February 1, 1954.

[1529] Ibid., October 24, 1956.

[1530] Ibid., July 19, 1957 and December 13, 1957.

[1531] Ibid., September 11, 1958

[1532] Kaminski, *American Car and Foundry,* p. 19.

[1533] Kenneth T. Jackson, *Crabgrass Frontier,* p. 292.

[1534] *Cosmos–Monitor*, December 29, 1950 and February 4, 1955.

[1535] Ibid., January 22, 1946. They were installed at Kingshighway and Clay, Second and Clark and Second and Adams Streets.

[1536] Ibid., June 15, 1949.

[1537] Ibid., December 11, 1950.

[1538] Ibid., May 3, 1953.

[1539] Ibid., September 22, 1954.

[1540] Ibid., January 27, 1954.

[1541] Kenneth T. Jackson, *Crabrass Frontier,* p. 249.

[1542] *Cosmos-Monitor*, August 29, 1958.

[1543] Ibid., August 15, 1956.

[1544] *Banner-News*, January 12, 1959.

[1545] Ibid., December 1, 1959.

[1546] Ibid., May 5, 1961 and May 13, 1962.

[1547] Kenneth T. Jackson, *Crabgrass Frontier,* p. 256.

[1548] *Banner-News*, August 31, 1948.

[1549] Kenneth T. Jackson, *Crabgrass Frontier,* p. 255.

[1550] Edna McElhiney Olson, *Historical Articles,* Vol. I, p. 107. By 1950 A&W had 450 franchises and was one of the first nationally franchised drive-in restaurants. By 1960 there were over 2,000 restaurants. www.aw-drivein.com

[1551] Kenneth T. Jackson, *Crabgrass Frontier,* p. 253.

[1552] Ibid., p. 254.

[1553] Ibid., p. 253.

[1554] *Cosmos-Monitor,* January 16, 1946. Standard drug store would occupy one half and Denning Appliance the other half.

[1555] Kenneth T. Jackson, *Crabgrass Frontier,* pp. 258-59.

[1556] *Cosmos-Monitor*, October 5, 1955.

[1557] Kenneth T. Jackson, *Crabgrass Frontier,* p. 270.

[1558] *Banner-News*, July 29, 1946.

[1559] Edna McElhiney Olson, *Historical Articles,* Vol. III, pp. 421, 431.

[1560] Kamphoefner, *Westfalians*, p. 176.

[1561] *Banner-News*, January 17, 1963. Schnippeled beans were sliced to a prescribed degree, with an old hand-operated German device. The beans were then placed in crocks to ferment. The beans were mixed with meat and potatoes and served as a thick soup. Ibid.

[1562] O'Conner, *German Americans*, p. 456.

[1563] Kirkendall, *History of Missouri, 1919-1953,* pp. 317-318. 1964 City Directory.

[1564] Edna McElhiney Olson, *Historical Articles,* Vol. II, p. 222.

[1565] "Dedication Program of the Fourth Phase Building St. Charles Chapel," September 20, 1981. Joseph Smith had recorded a visit to St. Charles in his journal and Mormons used the Booneslick Trail between 1831-1839 on their journey west to Jackson County, Missouri. *The History of St. Charles County* states that no one in St. Charles County was involved in the "Mormon War" that occurred in western Missouri. There was a plan to locate a Mormon congregation in St. Charles in 1855 but was abandoned when Young called the Mormons to Utah. Those who remained formed the Re-organized Church of Latter-Day Saints and had a congregation in St. Charles in the 1920s. Ibid. *Cosmos-Monitor,* October 22, 1923. *History of St. Charles County,* p. 184.

[1566] *Banner-News*, February 4, 1959. Before the decade was ended, another major expansion doubled the capacity again to 365. Ibid.

[1567] Jo Ann Brown, *St. Charles Borromeo,* p. 169. See also Dolan, *American Catholic Experience,* pp. 383-387.

[1568] *Banner-News*, June 18, 1957.

[1569] *Cosmos-Monitor,* March 2, 1955.

[1570] Jo Ann Brown, *St. Charles Borromeo,* pp.179-184.

[1571] *Cosmos-Monitor*, November 18, 1953.

[1572] Ibid., July 14, 1954.

[1573] Ibid., November 30, 1955.

[1574] Ibid., September 5, 1956. Catholic Day was celebrated annually in the St. Charles. It included a parade, Mass and afternoon devotions. Ibid. October 8, 1947.

[1575] In September 1956, Immanuel Lutheran grade school opened it doors for the 108th year with a record enrollment of 368 in greatly expanded facilities. Our Savior Lutheran congregation opened in 1961 but did not have a parochial school. Good Shepherd UCC also opened in the decade. None of the former Evangelical congregations had parochial schools since St. John closed its school in 1932.

[1576] David L. Colton, "Lawyers, Legislation and Educational Localism," p. 146. The township organization became irrelevant after the school lands had all been sold, having no correlation with population density, and often proving too large an area for a school district. Ibid., p. 145.

[1577] *Cosmos-Monitor*, July 14, 1948. and January 12, 1949.

[1578] Ibid., April 13, 1949.

[1579] Ibid., July 20, 1949.

[1580] Daniel T. Brown, *Small Glories,* p. 507.

[1581] *Cosmos-Monitor,* August 8, 1951.

[1582] *Banner-News*, January 13, 1959.

[1583] Ibid., January 19, 1959. In May of 1965 Orchard Farm High School held its first graduation, with Congressman William Hungate as graduation speaker. *Banner-News*, May 26, 1965.

[1584] Daniel T. Brown, *Small Glories,* p. 551.

[1585] *Cosmos–Monitor*, September 5, 1950.

[1586] Ibid., August 30, 1952.

[1587] Ibid., September 9, 1953.

[1588] Ibid., May 10, 1953.

[1589] *Banner-News*, June 7, 1961.

[1590] *Cosmos-Monitor*, October 14, 1958.

[1591] Ibid., March 2, 1955.

[1592] Ibid., August 22, 1956. In late 1954 Governor Phil Donnelly appointed Hollenbeck county superintendent of schools. He took office in January and was elected by the voters in April. Schiermeier, *Cracker Barrel Country,* Vol. II, p. 66.

[1593] Dolan, *American Catholic Experience,* p. 397. *Cosmos-Monitor,* April 27, 1949.

[1594] *Agricultural History,* p. 23.

[1595] Daniel T. Brown, *Small Glories,* p. 532.

[1596] *Cosmos-Monitor,* April 1951.

[1597] Ibid., July 25, 1951.

[1598] Daniel T. Brown, *Small Glories,* p. 532.

[1599] *Cosmos-Monitor,* November 12, 1952.

[1600] Ibid., June 10, 1953.

[1601] Daniel T. Brown, *Small Glories,* p. 537.

[1602] *Banner-News,* May 2, 1952. "St. Theodore's First 100 Years," p. 17.

[1603] *Cosmos-Monitor,* August 12, 1953.

[1604] Ibid., November 18, 1953.

[1605] *Banner-News,* April 4, 1963. The fiscal note attached to the bill, indicating an average cost of $360 per pupil and a total cost of $2.6 million for the entire state, made passage unlikely.

[1606] Ibid., May 16, 1963. President Kennedy failed to support low interest loans to private institutions in the 1961 Education Bill, sticking with his campaign promise to oppose any public funds for private schools. His supporters claimed that the president really believed the Constitution forbade it, while more cynical individuals suggested that he already had the Catholic vote and did not want to alienate the public school lobby.

[1607] Ibid., May 25, 1965. A "shared time" bill passed in the House committee, that would have allow parochial school children to attend special classes at the public schools. Rep. James Spainhower, (D-Marshall,) who would later serve as President of Lindenwood College, sponsored the measure. Ibid., February 17, 1967.

[1608] Mallinckrodt, *Augusta Magazine,* "Picnics" July/August, 1995, p. 15. Dr. Laura J. Nahm was chair of the Biology Department at Central Missouri State University. Ibid.

[1609] J. M. Fenster, "Americans Have Historically Accepted Gambling," *Gambling,* (San Diego: Greenhaven Press, 1998), p. 44.

[1610] Ibid.

[1611] Ibid. It was pretty clear whose side the Missouri Supreme Court was on in 1938 when it found that the awarding of cash attendance prizes to a patron at a business was a lottery, refusing to, "join hands with those who designedly devise ways and means to evade our lottery laws and thereby defeat the very purpose of our Constitution and the laws enacted in obedience thereto." *State v. Emerson,* 818 Mo. 633.

[1612] Fenster, "Americans," p. 44.

[1613] *Banner-News,* March 16, 1938.

[1614] The picnics at Blanchette Park, in St. Charles, within walking distance for many, continued even during the war.

[1615] *State v. Emerson,* 818 Mo. 633, *Cosmos-Monitor,* June 26, 1946.

[1616] *Banner-News,* July 12, 1946.

[1617] Ibid., August 17, 1948.

[1618] Ibid., March 9, 1948.

[1619] *Cosmos-Monitor,* April 27, 1949.

[1620] Interview with Andrew McColloch.

[1621] *State v Katz Drug Company,* 532 SW2d 678. The case held that " matters of immediate necessity" allowed to be purchased on Sunday must be necessary to people generally rather than to a specific person at a specific time.

[1622] *Banner-News,* January 23, 1962.

[1623] Ibid., January 23, 1962.

[1624] Ibid.

[1625] *Harvey v. Priest,* 366 S.W.2d 324 (1963).

[1626] *Banner-News,* March 26, 1963. *GEM Stores, Inc v. O'Brien,* 374 S.W.2d 109 (1964).

[1627] Dolan, *American Catholic Experience,* p. 433.

[1628] Interviews with Reverend Richard Tillman and Melvin Plackemeier.

[1629] *Cosmos-Monitor*, October 17, 1945. The local Veterans Service Committee was composed of local men and women representing all the civic labor and other organizations of the county.

[1630] Ibid., December 15, 1945. The St. Charles Chapter of the VFW was organizes in 1933 by 23 overseas veterans at the old Owls Club. Kohl and Jeck were two St. Charles boys who died in action in the First World War. Edna McElhiney Olson, *Historical Articles,* Vol. II, p. 341.

[1631] Although many older members continued to discourage it and the Catholic Church made the Protestant spouse sign papers agreeing to raise the children Catholic.

[1632] Evans, *Born for Liberty,* p. 237.

[1633] *Banner-News*, January 11, 1938 and November 7, 1942.

[1634] *Cosmos-Monitor*, July 10, August 13, September, 15 and October 8, 1947.

[1635] Interview with Oscar Waltermann.

[1636] Interview with Melvin Plackemeier.

[1637] *Cosmos-Monitor*, October 25, 1958, *Banner-News*, November 12, 1952.

[1638] Ibid., August 7 and 16th, 1957. The total cost of the car could not exceed 13.00 dollars. The width could not exceed 42 inches and the height could not exceed 28 inches. The car could weigh no more that 250 pounds with driver. Ibid.

[1639] Ibid., September 28, 1955. Other officers were Paul Blessing, Elder Holiday and Hugh I. Holmes. Other board members were Arthur Baue, John Becker, Homer Clevenger, Lester Plackemeier, Henry Vogt, James Siegler, Albert Ostmann, William Mayer, Ted Schoetker, Walter Trump, Andrew McColloch, Webster Karrenbrock, Earl Pryor, Brand Wilhelm, Francis Mueller, Omar Osiek and Forest Watts.

[1640] Ibid., December 21, 1955.

[1641] Ibid., October 10, 1956.

[1642] *Banner-News*, April 26, 1961, September 13, October 30 and December 14, 1962. In 1968 an indoor swimming pool was added to the Boys' Club facility.

[1643] Ibid., August 1, 1946.

[1644] *Cosmos-Monitor*, August 17, 1949. Nationally, only 4.8 percent of reported polio cases in 1953 were fatal, compared with a death rate of 11percent during the five-year period of 1938 to 1942. The Salk Vaccine became available from physicians. Ibid.

[1645] Ibid., March 16, 1955.

[1646] Ibid., September 11, 1957.

[1647] Jo Ann Brown, *St. Charles Borromeo,* p. 163.

[1648] Kirkendall, *History of Missouri, 1919-1953,* pp. 271-272. Cardinal Glennon died in 1946 and was replaced by Joseph Ritter, a leader willing to challenge the prevailing racial beliefs in the area. In 1947 he instructed the pastors of the archdiocese that there would be no racial discrimination in admissions to Catholic schools. Ibid. This had very little impact in St. Charles County because only about 1.5 percent of the population was now African-American, and very few of them were Catholic. But the Catholic Church had shown leadership in what would be the dominant issue of the next decade. Ibid.

[1649] *Cosmos-Monitor*, August 27, 1947.

[1650] Interview with Melvin Washington. Copy of Resolution in the author's possession.

[1651] *Cosmos-Monitor*, June 9, 1948.

[1652] Ibid., February 23, 1949. After graduation in 1943 Jim Pendleton went into the service and performed as a member of the 20th Air Force baseball team in the South Pacific. He played with the Chicago Giants in the Negro American League in 1948 where he batted better than .360 and hit more than 15 home runs. Interview with Melvin Washington.

[1653] Ibid., January 3, 1951.

[1654] David Halberstam, *The Fifties,* (New York: Villard Books, 1993), p. 413.

[1655] Poindexter, "A Right Smart Little Town," p. 132.

[1656] Interview with Melvin Washington.

[1657] Halberstam, *The Fifties,* p. 132.

[1658] Ibid. p. 423.

[1659] *Cosmos-Monitor,* June 6, 1954.

[1660] Ibid., September 12, 1954. Norbert Wappelhorst served as director of parks for St. Charles. He began working in the parks in 1939 before serving in the U.S. Army during WWII and retired in 1979. Wappelhorst Park in St. Charles is named in his honor.

[1661] Ibid., July 7, 1954.

[1662] Ibid., May 19, 1954.

[1663] Stephen Blackhurst, "One Hundred Years of Negro Education in St Charles." Copy on file at the Board of Education Office, St. Charles, Missouri.

[1664] *Cosmos-Monitor,* March 15, 1957. The remaining starters, were Lanny Larson of Webster Groves, Bob MacKinnon, St. Louis U., Sandy Pomerantz of University City, and Mike Shannon of C.B.C.

[1665] Interview with the Honorable Joseph Briscoe, Circuit Judge, St. Charles County Circuit Court.

[1666] Interview with Melvin Washington.

[1667] *Cosmos-Monitor,* September 19, 1957.

[1668] *Banner-News*, January 16, 1974.

[1669] *Cosmos-Monitor*, March 30, 1955.

[1670] Ibid. May 18, 1955. The committee was composed of Albert Kister, Chairman, Homer Plackemeier, Melvin Washington, Paul Walters and Earl Pryor.

[1671] Ibid. July 18, 1956.

[1672] Ibid. November 7, 1958.

[1673] Nagel, *Missouri,* p. 164.

[1674] Ibid.

[1675] Kirkendall, *History of Missouri, 1919-1953,* pp. 284-87.

[1676] Blue Book

[1677] *Cosmos-Monitor,* November 7, 1946. Senator Robert Linnemann was born in St. Charles on July 30, 1882. He was a product of the public schools and St. Charles College. He was an engineer and contractor by profession. A member of the Masonic Lodge, he was first elected to the House in 1940. Blue Book.

[1678] *Banner-News*, October 29, 1946.

[1679] *Cosmos-Monitor*, October 2, 1946.

[1680] Ibid., January 1, 1947. Those taking the oath of office on January 1, 1947 were: Circuit Clerk Earl Sutton, State Representative Ben Borgelt, Presiding Judge Henry F. Ohlms, Associate Judges Herman Sandhaus and Ben Dickherber, Probate Judge and Magistrate Webster Karrenbrock, County Clerk Pershing Borgelt, Prosecuting Attorney H.K. Stumberg, Recorder of Deeds Ernie Paule, and County Treasurer Simon Henke. County Collector Arlie Greiwe was sworn in on February 28, 1947.

[1681] Kirkendall, *History of Missouri, 1919-1953,* pp. 346-347. Ben Borgelt, elected to the Missouri House as a Republican, was born on May 11, 1881 in St. Charles County and educated in the public schools. He was a buyer and shipper of livestock before serving as county judge from 1938-1944. He resided in Wentzville and attended the Lutheran Church. Blue Book.

[1682] "Lindenwood College Bulletin," *Spring, 1966.* Franc "Bullet" McCluer was raised in Fulton and received his Ph.D. from the University of Chicago. He was president of Westminster College during the Churchill visit and Iron Curtain speech. Ibid.

[1683] *Banner-News*, March 25, 1948, April 1, 1948 and April 5, 1948. In the presidential election that year Henry Wallace received only 23 votes in the county running as the Progressive Party candidate.

[1684] Kirkendall, *History of Missouri, 1919-1953,* p. 347.

[1685] Ibid. p. 348.

[1686] Bernard Brockgreitens, a Democrat, was an employee of the Republican-leaning *Cosmos-*

Monitor. Cosmos-Monitor, January 5, 1949.

[1687] H.K. "Kriete" Stumberg was born in St. Charles in 1911 and attended the University of Missouri. He began practicing law in St. Charles in 1936.

[1688] *Cosmos-Monitor,* November 10, 1948. Ellis T Ellermann, Republican, defeated Alice Parker by 283 votes. Ellerman was born and educated in Cedar County. He moved to the county after marrying Mildred Archer of Wentzville and was a member of the Methodist Church. Blue Book.

[1689] *Banner-News,* November 3, 1948.

[1690] Robert Niedner received A.B. and L.L.B. degrees from the University of Missouri, was president of the student body in 1934, and was captain of the university debate team. He became active in Republican politics in 1937 and chairman of the county committee in 1946. He served as city attorney in St. Charles and prosecuting attorney in the county. He served as president of the St. Charles Chamber of Commerce. *Cosmos-Monitor,* February 4. 1948.

[1691] *Banner-News,* October 26, 1950.

[1692] *Cosmos-Monitor,* November 8, 1950. Frank Lawler was an employee of ACF, where his father and grandfather had been plant manager. He served as a St. Charles councilman for the Fourth Ward.

[1693] "Bicentennial Celebration Program," p. 40.

[1694] *Banner-News,* July 21, 1950.

[1695] Interview with Ron Kjar, former Republican Central Committee chairman in the 1970s.

[1696] Kirkendall, *History of Missouri, 1919-1953,* p. 352.

[1697] *Cosmos-Monitor,* April 28, 1954.

[1698] Ibid., November 3, 1954. Alf H. Oetting, Republican, was born on March 1,1893,in St. Charles County. He was a farmer before serving as county assessor. He served in WWI and was a member of John J. Pershing's Guard of Honor. He attended the Lutheran Church. Blue Book.

[1699] Andrew McColloch came to St. Charles after graduating from the University of Missouri School of Law. He had a distinguished record as a Marine Corps pilot during WWII.

[1700] *Cosmos-Monitor,* January 27, 1954 Charter members of the St. Charles County Democratic Club were Robert Arseneau, Clem A. Buergess, Homer Clevenger, George Dunivan, Lyle E. Gilliom. Clarence A. Goellner Jr., James W. Hamilton, Andrew McColloch and Louis Seabaugh. Ibid.

[1701] *Banner-News,* December 20, 1950.

[1702] Kenneth T. Jackson, *Crabgrass Frontier,* p. 242.

[1703] *Cosmos-Monitor,* December 19, 1945. Section 89.380 RSMo. Did not become law until 1963.

[1704] Ibid.

[1705] This is something that people had been doing for decades when they ran short of money. Jefferson Street has many small cottages that were built in between the larger homes.

[1706] *Banner-News,* April 19, 1959.

[1707] Ibid., April 3, 1963.

[1708] *Cosmos-Monitor,* November 3, 1954.

[1709] Ibid., October 12, 1955. The statute provides for zoning in of any area adjoining and extending from a city of 70,000 population. The county is within the forty miles, but is not adjoining. The "and" needed to be changed to an "or".

[1710] Ibid. September 13, 1957. Statute read. " The (Zoning Provisions) shall not be exercised so as to impose regulations, or require permits with respect to land used or to be used, for the raising of crops, orchards or forestry, or with respect to the erection, maintenance, repair, alteration or extension of farm buildings or farm structures." The "zoning power" shall not be construed so as to deprive the owner, lessee or tenant of any existing property or its use or maintenance for the purpose to which it is then lawfully devoted."

[1711] Ibid., October 21, 1957.

[1712] *Banner-News,* July 30, 1959.

[1713] Ibid., October 29, 1959 and December 9, 1959.

[1714] Robert Allen, Rutland, *The Republicans, From Lincoln to Bush,* (Columbia: University of

Missouri Press, 1996), p 215.

[1715] *Cosmos-Monitor*, November 7, 1956.

[1716] *Banner-News,* September 27, 1957.

[1717] Stephen E. Ambrose, *Eisenhower, Vol. 2,* "The President," (New York: Simon and Shuster, 1984),p. 487.

[1718] Ibid., p. 487. Rutland, *Republicans,* p, 216.

[1719] *Banner News*, April 30, 1958, and August 21, 1958. Omer J. Dames, Democrat, was born on May 8,1894 in St. Paul. He was educated in the parochial school and attended O'Fallon Public High School. He served in WWI, attended Assumption Catholic Church and was a fourth degree Knight of Columbus. Blue Book.

[1720] *Cosmos-Monitor*, Vol. 79, No. 76. Theodore Bruere Jr. served as prosecuting attorney from 1930-1932 and as Circuit Judge from 1942-1948, when B. Richard Creech of Troy, defeated him. He was executive secretary of the St. Charles Savings and Loan Association. A member of St. John Church, he served the local Red Cross for 30 years and was a member of the school board from 1949-1958.

[1721] *Banner News*, July 3, 1954.

[1722] Ibid., May 28, 1958.

[1723] *Cosmos-Monitor*, August 12, 1958.

[1724] *Cosmos-Monitor*, September 19, 1958. One of Senator Linnemann's last achievements was to get the state to establish a 45-acre park on the site of Fort Zumwalt.

[1725] Ibid., October 9, 1958.

[1726] Ibid., October 15, 1958.

[1727] Ibid., September 19, 1958.

[1728] Ibid., November 5, 1958. Webster Karrenbrock had been unopposed for the office of county magistrate. Francis X. Reller was born and educated in St. Louis. He owned movie theatres including the American Theatre in Wentzville. He served as city judge of Wentzville. BlueBook.

[1729] The month before the *St. Charles Journal* had begun publishing as a free paper with William Mullins as editor.

[1730] Blum, *Years of Discord,* p. 18.

[1731] *Banner-News*, October 15, 1962.

[1732] Ibid., May 29, 1961. In 1948 Alexander Kerensky, former president of the Russian Republic, was a guest speaker at Lindenwood College. Ibid., December 3, 1948.

[1733] Ibid., October 9, 1962.

[1734] Ibid., May 22, 1961.

[1735] Ibid., August 8, 1962.

[1736] Ibid., July, 29, 1964.

[1737] Ibid., August 18, 1964.

[1738] Ibid., September 25, 1964.

[1739] Ibid., April 28, 1964. While Don Boschert was elected chairman of the meeting at which the Goldwater slate was elected, the *St. Charles Journal* stated that, " a group of strangers to local political followers, dominated the meeting and named their slate." *St. Charles Journal.* October 17, 1965.

[1740] Ibid., August 5, 1964. Harold Rayfield replaced Howard Ellis as Republican Central Committee Chairman.

[1741] Ibid., November 4, 1964. The exception was St. Charles County Sheriff Lester Plackemeier who won a sixth consecutive term.

[1742] David Frum, *How We Got Here, The Seventies: The Decade that Brought You Modern Life* (For Better or Worse), (New York: Basic Books, 2000), pp. 276-77.

Chapter VII
End Notes

[1743] *Banner-News*, July 20, 1970.

[1744] Frum, *The Seventies,* p. 268.

[1745] *Banner-News,* October 31, 1977.

[1746] Ibid., August 18-19, 1975.

[1747] Ibid., April 3, 1963.

[1748] Ibid., February 20, 1964.

[1749] Ibid., March 2, 1965.

[1750] Ibid., May 3, 1965.

[1751] Ibid., March 11, 1968, and May 16, 1968.

[1752] Ibid., May 24, 1968.

[1753] Ibid., July 9, 1968, One can imagine the quality of the teachers that were left at that point.

[1754] Ibid., April 2, 1969.

[1755] Ibid., May 6, 1970.

[1756] Ibid., September 9, 1970.

[1757] Ibid., September 27, 1970. A few high school seniors had, by that time, decided to skip their senior years and had enrolled at Lindenwood College.

[1758] Ibid., October 4, 1965.

[1759] Ibid., January 16, 1967. Because of the change in the law, suburban school district boundaries would not correspond to municipal boundaries.

[1760] Ibid., September 24, 1970.

[1761] There was already some of the anti-property tax feeling in St. Charles County that would express itself in California with the passage of Proposition 13 in 1978, limiting local property taxation.

[1762] *Banner-News*, June 15, 1973.

[1763] Ibid., December10, 1973.

[1764] Ibid., January 27, 1978.

[1765] Ibid., August 27, 1970.

[1766] Ibid., October 1, 1970.

[1767] Ibid., August 18, 1970. The program was first initiated at Becky David Elementary School in the 69-70 school year.

[1768] Ibid., September 29, 1971.

[1769] *St. Charles Post*, January 31, 1980.

[1770] Ibid., June 30, 1980.

[1771] *Banner-News*, November 11, 1968.

[1772] Ibid., May 27, 1975.

[1773] Interview with Melvin Washington.

[1774] *Banner-News*, July 10, 1963.

[1775] Ibid., January 29, 1975.

[1776] Ibid., January 9, 1946. Douglas E. Abrams, *A Very Special Place in Life,* (Missouri Juvenile Justice Association, 2003), p 65.

[1777] Johnson, *History of the American People,* pp. 971-972.

[1778] *Banner-News*, January 30, 1964.

[1779] Ibid., May 8, 1967.

[1780] Ibid., October 2, 1967.

[1781] Ibid., April 28, 1969.

[1782] Ibid., November 1, 1976.

[1783] Ibid., August 30, 1974. Ike Turner's Kings of Rhythm played St. Louis venues in the 1950s and early 1960s Turner joined with sixteen year old Anna Mae Bullock and became the Ike and Tina Turner Revue. "Celebrating the Century," p. 456.

[1784] *Banner-News*, October 10, 1974. However, the silo closed in October of 1974, reportedly because of drop-off in activities.

[1785] Frum, *The Seventies,* pp. 94-95.

[1786] *Banner-News*, December 27, 1974.

[1787] Ibid., December 27, 1974.

[1788] Frum,*The Seventies,*p.95. Abrams, *Special Place,* p. 161.

[1789] *Banner-News*, April 5, 1978.

[1790] Ibid., February 11, 1969. Actually a new college, Lindenwood College II was incorporated for the men and the institution became known as Lindenwood Colleges.

[1791] Ibid., March 10, 1972.

[1792] Ibid., April 22, 1948. The Evangelical-Reform Synod had voted for merger in 1948 with the Congregational Christian Churches to become the United Church of Christ. Ibid.

[1793] Frum, *TheSeventies,* pp.148-49.

[1794] Ibid., p.153. 1981 Telephone Directory.

[1795] *Banner-News,* July 29, 1966.

[1796] Ibid., May 3, 1976. Note the founding dates for several congregations in O'Fallon: O'Fallon Church of Christ, 1953, First Baptist, 1957, First United Pentecostal, 1966,Church of Christ, 1959, Hope Bible Church, 1962, Church of the Nazarene, 1963, Landmark Missionary Baptist, 1959, Grace Church United, 1962, Calvary Baptist, 1969, First Assembly of God, 1962, Free Will Baptist, 1967. "O'Fallon Centennial," pp. 30-35.

[1797] Peter Clecak, *America's Quest for the Ideal Self, Dissent and Fulfillment in the 60s and 70s,* (New York: Oxford University Press, 1983), p. 128.

[1798] Ibid., p. 139.

[1799] Lisa McGirr, *Suburban Warriors, The Origins of the New American Right,* (Princeton: Princeton University Press, 2001), p. 242. "Youth for Christ" had been founded in 1948 as an interfaith organization for young people. Interview with James Fitz.

[1800] McGirr, *Suburban Warriors,* p. 226.

[1801] *Banner-News,* June 18, 1972.

[1802] Ibid., April 9, 1974.

[1803] McGirr, *Suburban Warriors,* p. 180.

[1804] *Banner-News*, October 18, 1963.

[1805] McGirr, *Suburban Warriors,* p. 230.

[1806] Ibid.

[1807] The schools had continued to participate in federal food programs, and at the beginning of the 1970 school year, schools began providing free and reduced lunches for children from low-income families. While the federal government had subsidized the milk program for years, now a family of three with annual income under $3120 received free lunches for their children.

[1808] Ibid., March 7, 1972.

[1809] Ibid., October 29, 1971. In 1975 the U.S. Supreme Court ruled that a public school student had a right to a hearing before being suspended, stating, "Young people do not shed their rights at the schoolhouse door," *Goss v. Lopez,* Frum, *The Seventies,* p. 231.

[1810] *St. Charles Post,* April 15, 1980.

[1811] *Banner-News*, March 23, April 9, 13, 1948. 458 students paraded with signs protesting the firing of Coach Ted Boyett. Boyett had stepped behind the desk of Superintendent Stephen Blackhurst and challenge him to go outside and fight, whereupon Blackhurst slapped the teacher in the face. The petition in favor of Boyett was signed by 1,632 people, but the school board refused to reconsider its decision to fire him. At the urging of Boyett the students returned to class after a two-day absence. Ibid.

[1812] Elizabeth Cohen, *A Consumer's Republic,* (New York: Alfred Knopf, 2003), p. 356.

[1813] There were several such incidents reported at local schools.

[1814] *Banner-News*, June 1, 1976.

[1815] Ibid., June 4, 1976.

[1816] Ibid., December 17, 1968.

[1817] Ibid., January 9, 1970.

[1818] Ibid., June 22, 1967. Suntan Beach was located at "Grau's cut," where the Missouri River had cut across the county to the Mississippi River during the flood of 1951, creating a permanent lake.

[1819] *Banner-News*, May 5, 1971. *St. Charles Post,* August 13, 1980, SC, p. 1-5.

[1820] Ibid., April 9, 1980 SC p. 1-1.

[1821] *Banner-News*, August 18, 1977. Smith, *Nike,* p. 299.

[1822] *Banner-News*, March 20, 1964.

[1823] Ibid., February 10, 1964.

[1824] Ibid., May 4, 1964.

[1825] Blum, *Years of Discord,* p. 270.

[1826] *Banner-News*, November 9, 1966. Arlie H. Meyer, Republican, was born August 12, 1905 in St. Charles. He was educated in the public schools and was a real estate salesman. A member of the United Church of Christ, he served on the St. Charles City Council and as county assessor for twelve years. Blue Book.

[1827] Blum, *Years of Discord,* p. 250.

[1828] *Banner-News,* December 21, 1965. Wilkins was a 1963 graduate of St. Charles High School where he had been an undefeated member of the school's wrestling team. Ibid.

[1829] Ibid., December 1, 1966.

[1830] Ibid., June 13, 1966.

[1831] Ibid., April 18, 1968. In 1967, the 11th Circuit, that included St. Charles County, received a new judgeship and the governor appointed Donald Dalton as circuit judge. The governor also appointed Andrew H. McColloch to take Judge Dalton's place as prosecuting attorney of St. Charles County.

[1832] Blum, *Years of Discord,* pp. 313-314.

[1833] *Banner-News*, October 14, 1968 and November 6, 1968. The Democrats picked up a majority on the County Court and won several other county offices.

[1834] Kevin P. Phillips, *The Emerging Republican Majority,* (New Rochelle, NY: Arlington House, 1969), p. 327.

[1835] Ibid., p. 317.

[1836] Blum, *Years of Discord,* p. 347.

[1837] *Banner-News,* February 9, 1970. The New Federalism did not check the growth of entitlements. Between 1968 and 1980 federal outlays for services rose from 93 to 602 billion in unadjusted dollars, while direct government transfer payments to persons rose from 21.6 billion in 1960 to 244.9 billion in 1980 unadjusted dollars. Between 1960 and 1978 the total of public and private expenditures for social welfare on health, education, welfare and other social services rose from 78.7 billion dollars to 548.9 billion dollars, or from 15.8 percent to 26.9 percent of gross national product. Clecak, *America's Quest,* p, 192.

[1838] *Banner-News*, January 14, 1969.

[1839] *Banner-News*, March 6, 1970, October 9, 1970 and November 4, 1970. Darby Tally had become the owner/editor of the *Cosmos-Monitor* in 1948 after returning from France where he had served in the U.S. Army during WWII. *Banner-News,* December 22, 1948.

[1840] Ibid., October 19, 1970. The building had previously been the site of St. Charles Lanes bowling alley.

[1841] Ibid.

[1842] Ibid., September 2, 1971.

[1843] Interview with Erwin Davis. Davis had been a classmate at St. Louis University Law School of Joseph Teasdale, who became Governor of Missouri in 1976. That relationship increased his already considerable influence in St. Charles County Democratic politics. Ibid.

[1844] Blum, *Years of Discord,* p. 421.

[1845] Frum, *The Seventies,* p. 301.

[1846] *Banner-News*, November 6, 1972.

[1847] Ibid., November 6, 1974. Nixon had resigned from office on August 9, 1974.

[1848] Kenneth T. Jackson, *Crabgrass Frontier,* p. 263. By that time only two percent of mobile homes were ever moved from their original site and many states began taxing them as real rather than personal property. Ibid.

[1849] Ibid., p. 262.

[1850] *Banner-News*, July 25, 1962.

[1851] Ibid., November 3, 1965.

[1852] Ibid., November 3, 1965.

[1853] Ibid., November 2, 1967.

[1854] Ibid., February 18, 1966.

[1855] Ibid., June 5, 1968 and July 26, 1968.

[1856] Ibid., October 21, 1976.

[1857] Ibid., February 9, 1970.

[1858] Ibid., March 1, 1974. The Democratic members were Louis E. Cottle, John Denny, Robert H. Bauer, Eugene E. Weathers, Robert A. Koester, Grace Nichols and Kennard Fenton. The Republican members were Russell Emge, George Beilsmith, Arlie Meyer, H.K. Stumberg, Bernice Holbert, Elder B. Holiday and Richard Alferman. Ibid.

[1859] Ibid., October 1, 1974.

[1860] Ibid., October 22, 1974.

[1861] Ibid., May 7, 1975.

[1862] Ibid., March 16, 1965. The General Assembly passed a law in 1975, requiring agricultural land be assessed based on its productivity, not fair market value.

[1863] Ibid., September 7, 1974.

[1864] Ibid., February 23, 1975.

[1865] Ibid., November 19, 1976.

[1866] Ibid., August 8, 1977.

[1867] Ibid., July 3, 1975.

[1868] Ibid., July 14, 1976.

[1869] Ibid., November 2, 1977. Harold Volkmer was elected to Congress from the Ninth District.

[1870] "Centennial History of the Greater St. Louis Labor Council, AFL-CIO," http://www.stlclc.org/History.htm

[1871] Frum, *The Seventies*, p. 250.

[1872] Interview with Melvin Washington.

[1873] *Banner-News*, June 17, 1966.

[1874] Ibid., January 10, 1968 Members of the commission included Edward J. Pundmann, Dr. Charles Linsenmeyer, Robert C. Buehrle, Ted W. Mittler, Cyril Echele, Cleo L. Holiday, William J. Mayfield, George R. Sturmon Robert E. Thomas, Paul G. Dolan Jr., Norman W. Freiberger and Doyle B. Suit. Ibid., April 5, 1967.

[1875] Ibid., July 7, 1967.

[1876] *Post-Dispatch*, November 5, 1980, p. SC1.

[1877] *Banner-News*, April 5, 1971.

[1878] *Globe-Democrat*, April 18, 1979.

[1879] *Banner-News*, August 8, 1973.

[1880] Ibid., April 19, 1976.

[1881] Ibid., September 5, 1975.

[1882] Ibid., July 17, 1972. That year a consolidated telephone calling system was worked out between Bell and Continental Telephone companies to allow residents within the city to call each other without long-distance charges. Ibid.

[1883] Ibid., December 11, 1974.

[1884] Ibid., February 7, 1975.

[1885] *St. Louis Post-Dispatch*, June 3, 1980, p. 1sc. In January 1980 consumer prices were rising nationally at 17 percent. The prime interest rate would pass 20 percent in December. Frum, The *Seventies,* p. 292. The average one-wage-earner, two children family, that had paid 5.6 percent of its income for federal income tax in 1955, was paying 11.4 percent by 1980. During the same period, Social Security contribution tripled from less than two percent to 6.15 percent, while the costs of Medicare doubled every four years between 1966 and 1980.

[1886] McGirr, *Suburban Warriors,* p. 259.

[1887] *Banner-News*, December 17, 1965. The first flood of the decade was in 1961, fast rising water on the Mississippi River threatened old town St. Peters, on the Dardenne Creek. Ibid.

[1888] Ibid., February 16, 1967.

[1889] Ibid., October 1, 1967.

[1890] Ibid., May 8, 1968.

[1891] Steve Ehlmann, "Conflict at the Confluence: The Struggle over Federal Floodplain Management," *North Dakota Law Review,* Volume 74, N0. 1, 1998, p. 61.

[1892] Ibid.

[1893] *Banner-News*, January 3, 1972.

[1894] Ibid., February 25, 1977.

[1895] Ehlmann, "Conflict at the Confluence," p 63. This created a new problem for the L-15, since the benefits of the project had to exceed its costs in order for it to be funded. Ibid.

[1896] *Banner-News*, October 8, 1976.

[1897] *St. Louis Post-Dispatch*, September 28, 1979 p. 2b.

[1898] *Banner-News*, February 21, 1974.

[1899] Ibid., April 15, 1974.

[1900] Ibid., April 12, 1963. The company had a contract for a docking trainer for the Gemini project to be installed in the Houston training facility. Ibid., March 27, 1964. The company also received research contract of 40 million dollars on a space reentry vehicle that would become the space shuttle. Ibid., November13, 1964.

[1901] Ibid., October 10, 1963, November 5, 1965.

[1902] Ibid., December 13, 1973.

[1903] Ibid., June 18, 1974.

[1904] Kenneth T. Jackson, *Crabgrass Frontier,* pp. 267-8.

[1905] Ibid., March 5, 1970.

[1906] Ibid., February 8, 1966. Under SBA 504 loans, Crossroads put up 10 percent of the loan and the local bank 50 percent. The SBA put up 40 percent and accepted a second mortgage on the property. Interview with Henry Elmendorf.

[1907] *Post-Dispatch*,February 21, 1980, p. A1.

[1908] Ibid., June 4, 1980, p. SC1-4.

[1909] *History of St. Charles County,* p. 461.

[1910] Ibid., July 8, 1980, p. c-2, and May 14, 1974.

[1911] *Banner-News*, March 20, 1964. The existing Post Office was located in the 100 block of S. Main Street and had been built in 1908.

[1912] Ibid., March 12, 1974 and July 3, 1974.

[1913] Ibid., December 31, 1980.

[1914] Ibid., August 3, 1976.

[1915] Ibid., August 29, 1963. Cities Service Bus Co. had begun providing local bus service in 1945.

[1916] Ibid., December 8, 1971.

[1917] Ibid., January 21, 1974.

[1918] Ibid., July 26, 1963, January 7, 1964, July 16, 1968, December 15, 1968.

[1919] Ibid., December 28, 1973.

[1920] Ibid., April 20, 1976.

[1921] Ibid., May 6, 1976.

[1922] Ibid., October 27, 1977.

[1923] Ibid., May 10, 1978.

[1924] Ibid., May 7, 1975.

[1925] Ibid., November 29, 1965.

[1926] Ibid., April 5, 1967 and April 21, 1967.

[1927] Ibid., July 20, 1962 and August 2, 1962.

[1928] Ibid., January 9, 1964.

[1929] Ibid., August 25 and 27, 1959.

[1930] Ibid., Vol. 80, No. 226.

[1931] E. Terrence Jones, *Fragmented By Design, Why St. Louis Has So Many Governments,* (St. Louis: Palmerston and Reed Publishing, 2000), pp. 32-34.

[1932] Ibid., March 17, 1972.

[1933] Ibid., November 2, 1973.

[1934] AnneWhite, *For all Seasons, Lake St. Louis, Missouri,* (Marceline, Missouri: Walsworth Publishing Company, 1985), pp. 58, 152.

[1935] *In re: Village of Lone Jack,* 471 SW2d 513 (Mo. App. 1971)

[1936] *Cherry v. City of Hayti Heights,* 563 SW2d 72, (Sup. 1978).

[1937] *Banner-News*, August 27, 1959.

[1938] E. Terrence Jones, *Fragmented by Design,* p. 32.

[1939] *Banner-News*, February 14, 1961.

[1940] Ibid., December 20, 1965. Much of this area actually came into the city only after I-370 went through. Earth City development on the St. Louis Side of the river made development less likely along with the lack of good roads to the area.

[1941] Ibid., November 15, 1967. A new St.Charles County Club had been formed in October 1956 and its clubhouse was built adjacent to the St. Charles Golf Course. The old St. Charles Country Club had reopened in 1962 as a nine-hole Bogey Hills Golf Club. In 1971 it became an 18-hole semi-private course and became a private course in 1980. The St. Andrews Golf Course was built in the late 1960s.

[1942] Ibid., October 25, 1967.

[1943] Ibid., November 10, 1967.

[1944] Ibid., August 14, 1959 and August 19, 1959. Only in first class charter counties like St. Louis County, did the majority of the voters in the area to be annexed have to vote for the annexation to take place.

[1945] Ibid., April 24, 1970.

[1946] Ibid., June 2, 1971.

[1947] Atherton, *Frontier Merchant,* p. 140. It was first seen in Orange County California where, by 1980, there were 26 cities, none with more than 225,000 people. Kenneth T. Jackson quotes the experience of an Orange Countian: "I live in Garden City, work in Irvine, shop in Santa Ana, go to the dentist in Anaheim, my husband works in Long Beach, and I used to be president of the League of Women voters in Fullerton." Kenneth T. Jackson, *Crabrass Frontier,* p. 265.

[1948] *Banner-News*, May 27, 1966, May 5, 1967. Owners presented a petition to rezone the corner of Elm and Houston before a service station was built there. Ibid.

[1949] Examples were at Fifth and Clark and Fifth and Jefferson Streets.

[1950] "Bicentennial Celebration Program," p. 24.

[1951] *Banner-News,* April 29, 1964.

[1952] Ibid., February 24, 1966.

[1953] A survey of the Harvard class of 1968 revealed that more than 60 percent were engaged in restoring old houses in 1976.

[1954] "Bicentennial Celebration Program," p. 23. The commission was comprised of fifteen individuals, including Dr Clevenger, chairman, Henry Elmendorf, Fred Baue and Lee White, the director of the State Historical Society, five state representatives and five senators.

[1955] *Banner-News*, September 30, 1975.

[1956] Ibid., December 6, 1976. There were often disagreements when an historic structure was restored as a commercial or office facility and the health and safety goals of the BOCA Code and historic preservation goals came into conflict. The First Board, appointed by Mayor Frank Brockgreitens, was Herbert Pundmann, Paul Scheer, Archie Scott, Mary Lou Ahmann, Reinhart Stiegemeier, Ellen Spears and Jean Baggermann.

[1957] Ibid., February 10, 1977.

[1958] *Globe-Democrat*, September 19, 1979. The First State Capitol Urban Renewal Project was first made public in February of 1978.

[1959] *Banner-News,* October 12, 1976.

[1960] Ibid., January 24, 1975.

[1961] Ibid., October 4, 1973.

[1962] Ibid., October 16, 1973.

[1963] Ibid., November 5, 1973.

[1964] Ibid., November 5, 1973.

[1965] Ibid., November 7, 1973.

[1966] Ibid., November 15, 1974.

[1967] http://www.scad.com/history.html

[1968] *Banner-News*, September 29, 1967.

[1969] http://www.org./fire/history/

[1970] *Banner-News*, November 29, 1974.

[1971] Ibid., November 13, 1974.

[1972] Ibid., October 19, 1977.

[1973] *Post-Dispatch,* January 1, 1977.

[1974] *Banner-News*, January 14, 1964.

[1975] Ibid., June 4, 1959.

[1976] Ibid., August 31, 1959 and October 13, 1967.

[1977] Interview with Robert Wohler. Eventually Wentzville would extend its sewers toward Foristell and obtain federal funding for a sewer treatment plant along Highway 61 serving the McCoy Creek area.

[1978] *Banner-News*, October 21, 1977.

[1979] *Post Dispatch*, January 1, 1977.

[1980] Interview with Robert Wohler.

[1981] *Banner-News*, November 20, 1974.

[1982] Ibid., July 16, 1974.

[1983] Ibid., September 10, 1975.

[1984] Ibid., February 19, 1979.

[1985] *Post-Dispatch*, 2c, March 14, 1979.

[1986] *Post-Dispatch*, April 29, 1980, SC1.

[1987] E. Terrence Jones, *Fragmented by Design,* p. 125.

[1988] Ibid.

[1989] *Banner-News*, September 19, 1975.

[1990] Ibid., August 18, 1977.

[1991] Ibid., May 19, 1978.

[1992] Ibid., December 31, 1980.

[1993] Ibid., May 11, 1971.

[1994] Ibid., May 14, 1971.

[1995] Ibid., May 17, 1971 and December 16, 1971.

[1996] Ibid., January 4, 1972.

[1997] Ibid., September 22, 1972.

[1998] Ibid., November 8, 1972.

[1999] Ibid., October 16, 1974.

[2000] Ibid., November 10, 1975.

[2001] Ibid., June 20, 1975.

[2002] Ibid., September 1, 1976, Coleman was appointed by President Ford after St. Louis complained that his first choice, John Robson, had served as a consultant to the Illinois group. Coleman was a lawyer with the NAACP, wrote a brief on the Brown Case and was president of the legal defense fund.

[2003] Ibid., September 2, 1976.

[2004] Ibid., March 31, 1977.

Chapter VIII
End Notes

[2005] When the Consolidated North County Levee District wanted to build a levee near Portage des Sioux they were not allowed to proceed until the district retained an archaeologist to walk the fields and catalog the many arrowheads that were present.

[2006] *St. Louis Post-Dispatch*, "Post-Flood Snags keep 'River Rats' Out of Homes," September 12, 1994, p. 3. See also "Gathering of Rivers," June 5, 1994, p. 1T, and "Upriver talk of going Back," July 16, 1993, p. 14A. People in the area complain that the leasees are not supposed to be eligible for government assistance in the event of a flood. Nevertheless, every time there is a flood the inhabitants of these clubhouses receive benefits from the government. Then FEMA complains about the number of flood insurance claims in the area.

[2007] The Great Rivers Habitat Alliance has opposed a leveed development in the 370 corridor and expansion of Smartt Field.

[2008] Kamphoefner, *Westfalians,* p. 108.

[2009] The program at the Boone home is the National Center for the Study of American Culture and Values.

[2010] Primm, *Lion in the Valley,* pp. 509, 513-514.

[2011] The strength of the brewing industry is apparent every time the General Assembly takes up the issue of an open container law. In 2001 the state adopted .08 percent, rather than .10 percent, as the presumed level of intoxication for Driving While Intoxicated.

[2012] Ibid.

[2013] The United States Supreme Court ruled that vouchers are constitutional under the U.S. Constitution, so long as the money goes to the parents rather than the church and allow parents to choose from other public schools, as well as private schools. Some Evangelicals now send their children to "Christian School" or Home School their children. They disapprove of the seculor nature of public education today.

[2014] 2000 Census

[2015] These concerns that are being addressed by organizations including Youth in Need, Crider Center for Mental Health, Bridgeway Counseling Services, the St. Charles Crisis Nursery and others. United Services serves the special needs children of the county along with several newer organizations including the Booneslick State School for the severely handicapped, the Children's Home society, specializing in care to children with serious medical conditions.

[2016] 2000 census

[2017] Members of the Charter Commission included seven Democrats: Don Boehmer, Fred Drakesmith, Richard Zerr, John Hanneke, Nancy Reynolds, Thomas Heinsz, Sue Schneider, and seven Republicans: Dr. Michael Conoyer, Jim Machens, Keith Hazelwood, Dee Pundmann,

Douglas Boschert, James Larkin, and Philip Ohlms.

[2018] While the platform and leadership have supported the North America Free Trade Agreement (NAFTA), many rank and file have followed Ross Perot and Patrick Buchanan and favored protection.

[2019] In 1993 the Democratic legislature and Democratic Governor Mel Carnahan pushed through a large tax increase, without sending it to a vote of the people, as part of an effort to equalize school funding.

[2020] Report by the Office of Social and Economic Data, U. of Missouri Outreach And Extension. U.S. Bureau of the Census File 1, 2000 Decennial Census.

[2021] Ehlmann, "Conflict at the Confluence," p. 65. Local zoning ordinances, such as floodplain ordinances, were not applicable to public uses of property where political subdivisions, (in this case a levee district), has the power to acquire lands by the exercise of the power of eminent domain.

[2022] Ibid., p. 75. See *St. Charles County v. Dardenne Realty Company et, al,* 771 S.W. 2d 828.

[2023] Ehlmann, "Conflict at the Confluence," p. 76.

[2024] Ibid., p. 64.

[2025] Ehlmann, "Conflict at the Confluence," p. 86.

[2026] http://www.em.doe.gov/wssrap/wsshist.html

[2027] Ibid.

[2028] 2000 Census.

[2029] Interview with Robert Wohler

[2030] The judge sitting in Division 3 was transferred to the new circuit in Lincoln and Pike Counties. Hon. Nancy Schneider was elected the new circuit judge for Division 3 in St. Charles County. Two new associate judgeships, Division 7 and 8, were also created due to increased population of the county since 1980.

[2031] Wildwood was composed of upper-income property owners in west St. Louis County who wanted spacious lots and wooded lots and were afraid that St. Louis County zoning would allow low and middle income development, so they incorporated a 67-square-mile city. E. Terrence Jones, *Fragmented by Design,* p 35. 72.080 had been amended by the legislature, allowing agricultural areas to exclude themselves from the incorporation of Boone's Trails. Since the incorporation was denied this was not necessary.

Bibliography

"A 1795 Inspection of Missouri," translated and edited by Jack D.L. Holmes, *MHR*, October 1960.

Abrams, Douglas E., *A Very Special Place in Life, The History of Juvenile Justice in Missouri*, Missouri Juvenile Justice Association, 2003.

Adler, Jeffrey, S. *Yankee Merchants and the Making of the Urban West, The Rise and Fall of Antebellum St. Louis*, Cambridge: Cambridge University Press, 1991.

The Agricultural History of St. Charles County, edited by Stephen D. Livingston, St. Charles: American Revolution Bicentennial Committee of St. Charles County, 1976.

Ambrose, Stephen, E., *Eisenhower, Vol. 2*, "The President," New York: Simon and Shuster, 1984.

Ambrose, Stephen E., *Undaunted Courage, Meriwether Lewis, Thomas Jefferson, and the Opening of the American West*, New York: Simon and Schuster, 1996.

Arena, C. Richard, "Land Settlement Policies and Practices in Spanish Louisiana," In *The Spanish in the Mississippi Valley*, ed. by John Francis McDermott, Urbana: University of Illinois Press, 1965.

Atherton, Lewis E., *The Frontier Merchant in Mid-America*, Colombia: University of Missouri Press, 1971.

Atherton, Lewis E., "Missouri Society and Economy in 1821," *MHR*, October 1998.

Banner, Stewart, *Legal Systems in Conflict, Property and Sovereignty in Missouri, 1750-1860*, Norman: University of Oklahoma Press, 2000.

Bannon, John Francis, "The Spaniards in the Mississippi Valley, an Introduction." In *The Spanish in the Mississippi Valley*, ed. by John Francis McDermott, Urbana: University of Illinois Press, 1965.

Barton, Adele Achelpohl, *The John F. Dierker Story*, St. Charles: manuscript available at Kathryn Linnemann Library.

Berkin, Carol and Leonard Wood, *Land of Promise*, Glenview, Illinois: Scott, Foresman and Company, 1987.

Blackhurst, Stephen, "One Hundred Years of Negro Education in St Charles," Copy on file at St. Charles Board of Education Office, St. Charles, Missouri.

Blassingame, John W. "The Recruitment of Negro Troops in Missouri During the Civil War," *MHR*, Vol. 58, p. 326.

Blum, John Morton, *V Was for Victory, Politics and American Culture During World War II*, New York: Harcourt Brace Jovanovich, 1976.

Blum, John Morton, *Years of Discord, American Politics and Society, 1961-1974*, New York: W.W. Norton and Co., 1991.

Bowen, Elbert R. "German Theatre in Rural Missouri," *MHR*, January 1952

Broeker, Jennifer, "For Holding in Bondage," *St. Charles County Heritage*, Vol.13, No. 2, April 1995.

Brokaw, Tom, *The Greatest Generation*, New York: Random House, 1998.

Brown, Daniel T., *Small Glories*, St. Charles: Howell Foundation, Inc., 2003.

Brown, Jo Ann, *St. Charles Borromeo, 200 Years of Faith*, St. Louis: the Patrice Press, 1991.

Breslow, Lori, *Small Town, St. Charles*: The John J. Buse Historical Museum, 1977.

Brewer, Bryan, "Amber Waves of Grain: St. Charles County Farmers During World War I," *St. Charles County Heritage*, Vol.12, No.3, July 1994.

Burnett, Betty, *St. Louis at War, The Story of a City, 1941-1945*, St. Louis: The Patrice Press, 1987.

Cain, Marvin R. *Lincoln's Attorney General, Edward Bates of Missouri*, Columbia: University of Missouri Press, 1965.

Chittendon, Hiram Martin, *The American Fur Trade of the Far West*, Lincoln: University of Nebraska Press, 1986.

Christensen, Lawrence O. and Gary R. Kremer, A History of Missouri, Vol. IV, 1875 to 1919, Columbia: University of Missouri Press, 1997.

Cleary, Patricia, "Environmental Agendas and Settlement Choices in Colonial St. Louis", in *Common Fields, An Environmental History of St. Louis*, St. Louis: Missouri Historical Society Press, 1997, p. 58.

Clecak, Peter, *America's Quest for the Ideal Self, Dissent and Fulfillment in the 60's and 70's*, New York: Oxford University Press, 1983.

Cohen, Elizabeth, *A Consumers' Republic*, New York: Afred A. Knopf, 2003.

Colton, David L. "Lawyers, Legislation and Educational Localism," *MHR*, January 1975.

Cook, Ray Donald, "History of St. Charles, Missouri 1816-1840," Master's thesis, Washington University, 1965.

Crail, Gloria P. "With Spading Fork and Popcorn They Survive," *We Had Everything But Money,* ed. By Deb Mulvey and Clancey Stock, Greendale, WI: Country Books, 1992.

Dictionary of Missouri Biography, ed. by Lawrence O. Christensen, William E. Foley, Gary P. Kremer and Kenneth H. Winn, Columbia: University of Missouri Press, 1999.

Dolan, Jay P. *The American Catholic Experience, A History from Colonial Times to the Present,* New York: Doubleday & Company, 1985.

Drummond, Malcolm C., *Historic Sites in St. Charles County, Missouri*, St. Louis: Harland Bartholomew and Associates, 1976.

Dunne, Gerald, *The Missouri Supreme Court, From Dred Scott to Nancy Cruzan*, Columbia: University of Missouri Press, 1993.

Edwards, Brad and Gary McKiddy, "St. Charles College vs. The War Department, *St. Charles County Heritage*, Vol. 10, No. 3, July, 1992, p. 66.

Ehlmann, Steve, "Conflict at the Confluence: The Struggle over Federal Floodplain Management," *North Dakota Law Review*, Volume 74, No. 1, 1998, p. 61.

Ehlmann, Steve, "Victory in Defeat," *St. Louis Post-Dispatch*, March 26, 2001, p. B7.

Ehrlich, Walter, *Zion in the Valley, The Jewish Community of St. Louis, Volume I*, Columbia: University of Missouri Press, 1997.

Evans, Sara M., *Born for Liberty*, New York: The Free Press, 1989.

Excerpts from the Diary of John Jay Johns 1860-1899 and Allied Papers, ed. by Florence Johns, December 13, 1960, Lindenwood University Archives

Faherty, William Barnaby, *The St. Louis Irish, An Unmatched Celtic Community*, St. Louis: Missouri Historical Society Press, 2001.

Feldman, Michael, "Emancipation in Missouri," *MHR*, October 1958.

Fenster, J.M., "Americans Have Historically Accepted Gambling," *Gambling,* San Diego: Greenhaven Press, 1998.

Fields, Jean, "A Season of Fear," *St. Charles Heritage*, Vol. 9, No. 1, January 1991, p. 6.

Finiels, Nicholas de, *An Account of Upper Louisiana,* ed. by Carl. J. Ekburg and William E. Foley, Columbia: University of Missouri Press, 1989. Fink, Gary M., *Labor's Search for Political Order*, Columbia: University of Missouri Press, 1973.

Foley, William E., *A History of Missouri, 1683 to 1820, Volume I*, Columbia: University of Missouri Press, 1971.

Foner, Eric, *Reconstruction, America's Unfinished Revolution 1863-1877*, New York: Harper & Row, 1988.

French Fur Traders and Voyageurs in the American West, ed. by Leroy R. Hafen, Spokane: The Arthur Clark Company, 1995.

Frum, David, *How We Got Here, The Seventies: The Decade that Brought You Modern Life (For Better or Worse),* New York: Basic Books, 2000.

Garzia, Luke, "Electric Gate: A Home-Grown Political Scandal," *St. Charles County Heritage,* Vol. 16, No.3, July 1998. p. 87.

Gerteis, Louis, *Civil War St. Louis,* Lawrence: University Press of Kansas, 2001.

Gienapp, M.A. "Nativism in the Creation of a Republican Majority before the Civil War." *Journal of American History,* Vol. LXX11, 1985, p. 547.

Gilbert, Judith A., "An Indian Named Angelique," *St. Charles County Heritage,* Vol. 16, No. 1, January 1998, p. 6.

Gleason, Phillip, *Conservative Reformers, German-American Catholics and the Social Order,* South Bend: University of Notre Dame Press, 1968.

Greene, Lorenzo J., Gary R. Kremer, Antonio F. Holland, *Missouri's Black Heritage,* Columbia: University of Missouri Press, revised and updated by Gary R. Kremer and Antonio F. Holland, 1993.

Hahn, Darlene M. "A St. Charles WW II Rosie the Riveter," *St. Charles County Heritage,* Vol. 20, No. 2, April 2002, p. 64.

Hahn, Dennis J. "Rufus Easton, Attorney, Public Servant, and First Postmaster," February 27, 2000.

Halberstam, David, *The Fifties,* New York: Villard Books, 1993.

Hawgood, John A., *The Tragedy of German-America: The Germans in the United State of America During the Nineteenth Century and After,* New York: 1970.

Heide, Robert, and John Gilman, *Home Front America, Popular Culture of the World War II Era,* San Francisco: Chronicle Books, 1995.

Hense, Sandy, "Beginnings of St. Joseph's Parish," *St. Charles County Heritage,* Vol. 13, No. 1, January 1995, p. 4.

Herberg, Will, *Protestant, Catholic, Jew: An Essay in American Religious Sociology,* New York: Doubleday Company, 1935.

History of St. Charles County, Missouri, 1765-1885. Reprint from History of St. Charles, Montgomery, and Warren Counties, with an introduction by Paul R. Hollrah, n. p: Patria Press, 1997.

Hohe, J. Michael, "Missouri Education at the Crossroads: The Phelan Miscalculation and the Education Amendment of 1870," *MHR,* 1999, p. 372.

Holmes, Jack D.L. "Spanish Regulation of Taverns and the Liquor Trade in the Mississippi Valley," In *The Spanish in the Mississippi Valley,* ed. by John Francis McDermott, Urbana: University of Illinois Press, 1965.

Holt, Marilyn, *The Orphan Trains, Placing out in America*, Lincoln: University of Nebraska Press, 1992.

Hurt, R. Douglas, *Agriculture and Slavery in Missouri's Little Dixie*, Columbia: University of Missouri Press, 1992.

Hurt, R. Douglas, *Nathan Boone and the American Frontier*, Columbia: University of Missouri Press, 1998.

Jackson, Kenneth T., *Crabgrass Frontier, The Suburbanization of the United States*, New York: Oxford University Press, 1985.

Jackson, Robert W. *Rails Across the Mississippi, A History of the St. Louis Bridge*, Urbana: University of Illinois Press, 2001.

Jensen, Richard, *The Winning of the Midwest: Social and Political Conflict 1888 to 1896*. Chicago: University of Chicago Press, 1971.

Johnson, Paul, *A History of the American People*, New York, Harper-Collins, 1997.

Jones, Charles T. *George Champlin Sibley: The Prairie Puritan 1782-1863*, Independence, Missouri: Jackson County Historical Society, 1970.

Jones, E. Terrence, *Fragmented By Design, Why St. Louis Has So Many Governments*, St. Louis: Palmerston and Reed Publishing, 2000.

Kaminski, Edward, "American Car and Foundry Company, A Centennial History, 1899-1999." n.p. nd

Kamphoefner, Walter, "Learning from the 'Majority-Minority' City," *St Louis in the Century of Henry Shaw* ed. by Eric Sandweiss, Columbia: University of Missouri Press 2003.

Kamphoefner, Walter, *The Westfalians, From Germany to Missouri*, Princeton: Princeton University Press, 1987.

Kamphoefner, Walter, "St. Louis Germans in the Republican Party, 1848-1860," *Mid-America*, Vol. 57, No.2, April 1987.

Kennedy, Sr. Inez, "St. Joseph Health Center and the Franciscan Sisters of St. Mary," *St. Charles County Heritage,* Vol. 16, No. 2, April 1998, pp. 53-59.

Kirkendall, Richard S., *The History of Missouri, 1919 to 1953*, Volume V, Columbia: University of Missouri Press, 1986.

Kleppner, Paul, *The Cross of Culture, A Social Analysis of Midwest Politics, 1850-1900*. New York: The Free Press, 1975.

Knipmeyer, James H., "Denis Julien, Midwestern Fur Trader." *MHR*, April, 2000, p. 245.

Korth, Kristina, "Kathryn Linnemann," *St. Charles County Heritage*, Vol. 16, no. 3, July 1998.

Kramme, Michelle, "A Progressive Pageant Like No Other," *St. Charles County Heritage*, Vol. 11, No. 3, p. 87.

Krause, Bonnie J. "German-Americans in the St. Louis Region, 1840-1860," *MHR*, April 1989.

Kubisch, Linda and Christine Montgomery," Show Me Missouri History: Celebrating the Century, Part II," *MHR*, April 2000.

Kyvig, David E. *Daily Life in the United States, 1920-1939: Decades of Promise and Pain*, Westport, CT: Greenwood Press, 2002.

Lance, Donald M. "Settlement Patterns, Missouri German-Americans and Local Dialects." *The German-American Experience in Missour*i, n.p. n.d.

Larsen, Lawrence H. *Federal Justice in Western Missouri, The Judges, the Cases, the Times*, Columbia: University of Missouri Press, 1994.

Launer, Louis, "Victory Highways," *St. Charles County Heritage*, Vol.13, No.1, 1995.

Launer, Louis, "Electrical Living Shows," *St. Charles County Heritage*, Vol. 18, No.1, January 2000, p. 62.

Laurie, Bruce, *Artisans into Workers, Labor in Nineteenth Century America*, New York: Hill and Wang, 1989.

Lecompte, Janet, "Introduction," *French Fur Traders and Voyageurs in the American West*, ed. by Leroy R. Hafen, Spokane: The Arthur Clark Company, 1995, p. 9.

Lee, George R. *Slavery North of St. Louis.* Lewis County Historical Society, n.d.

Licht, Walter, *Industrializing America, The Nineteenth Century*, Baltimore: The Johns Hopkins University Press, 1995.

Lichtman, Allan, *Prejudice and the Old Politics, the Presidential Election of 1928*. Chapel Hill: University of North Carolina Press, 1979.

Linn, Elaine Goodrich, 'Depression Kids," *St. Charles County Heritage*, Vol. 15, No. 4, October 1997, p. 49.

Lloyd, William C. *A History of the City of St. Peters*, St. Peters: City of St. Peters, 1999.

Love, Robertus, "Newspaper Feature Captures Essence of " Wide Awake" St. Charles in 1914," *Past Times,* Volume 1, No.1, spring 1984, p. 22.

Luebbering, Ken and Robyn Burnett, *German Settlement in Missouri*, Columbia: University of Missouri Press, 1996.

Luebke, Frederick C. *Bonds of Loyalty German-Americans in World War I,* Dekalb: Northern Illinois Press, 1974.

Mallinckrodt, Anita M., *A History of Augusta, Missouri and Its Area, vol. 1,1850s/1860s*,

Augusta, Missouri: Mallinekrodt Communications and Research, 1998.

Mallinckrodt, Anita M., *A History of Augusta, Missouri and Its Area, vol. 2, 1870s*, Augusta, Missouri: Mallinckrodt, Communications and Research, 1998.

Mallinckrodt, Anite M., *A. History of Augusta, Missouri and its Area Vol 3,* 1880s/1890s, Augusta, Missouri: Mallinckrodt, Communications and Research, 1998.

Mallinckrodt, Anita M., *Freed Slaves*, Missouri Research Roundtable Occasional Paper, 1999.

Mallinckrodt, Anita M. *From Nights to Pioneers, One German family in Westphalia and Missouri*, Carbondale: Southern Illinois University Press, 1994.

March, David D. "Missouri's Care of Indigent Aged," *MHR*, January 1984, p. 210.

McCandless, Perry, *A History of Missouri, 1820 -1860, Volume II*, Columbia: University of Missouri Press, 1971.

McDermott, John Francis, *"Captain de Leyba and the Defense of St. Louis in 1780"* in *The Spanish in the Mississippi Valley*, Urbana: University of Illinois Press, 1974, p.363.

McDermott, John Dishon, "James Bordeaux," *French Fur Traders and Voyageurs in the American West*, ed. by Leroy R. Hafen, Spokane: The Arthur Clark Company, 1995, p. 42.

McElhiney, Edith Freeman, *My Home Town, St. Charles, Missouri*, St. Charles: The School District of the City of St. Charles, n.d.

McElvaine, Robert S., *The Great Depression*, New York: Three Rivers Press, 1993.

McGirr, Lisa, *Suburban Warriors, The Origins of the New American R*ight, Princeton: Princeton University Press, 2001.

McKiddy, Gary, "Relief in St. Charles County During the First Half of the Great Depression," *St. Charles County Heritage*, Vol. 11, No. 1, January 1993, p. 16.

McKiddy, Gary, "St. Charles During the Civil War," *St. Charles County Heritage*, Vol. 15, No. 4, October 1997, p. 131.

McPhearson, James, *Battle Cry of Freedom: The Civil War Era*, New York: Oxford University Press, 1988.

Mead, Gary, *Doughboys*, New York: The Overlook Press, 2002.

Meining, D.W., *The Shaping of America, The Geographical Perspective on 500 Years of History, Volume 2*, "Continental America, 1800-1867", New Haven: Yale University Press, 1993.

Meining, D.W., *The Shaping of America, The Geographical Perspective on 500 Years of History, Volume 3*, "Transcontinental America, 1867-1915", New Haven: Yale University Press, 1993.

Mincke, Donald, *The History of Portage de Sioux Township Missouri, The Land Between the Rivers*, Portage des Sioux: Land Between the Rivers Historical Society, 1999.

Mittelbuscher, Barbara Eisenbath, *Flint Hill, 150 Years, 1836-1986.* Bridgeton: Lineage Press, 1986.

Mittelbuscher, Barbara Eisenbath, " Wentzville's 406 Elm Street placed on National Register of Historic Places," *Newstime,* October 7, 1990.

Mittelbuscher, Barbara Eisenbath,"Josephville in Allen Prairie," *St. Charles County Heritage*, Vol.18, No.4, October 2000.

Nagel, Paul C., *Missouri, A History*, Lawrence: University Press of Kansas, 1977.

Nagel, Paul C., *The German Migration to Missouri, My Family's Story*, Kansas City: Kansas City Star Books, 2002.

Naglich, Dennis, "The Slave System and the Civil War in Missouri," *MHR*, April 1993.

O'Brien, Michael J. *Grassland, Forest, and Historical Settlement, An Analysis of Dynamics in Northeast Missouri*, Lincoln: University of Nebraska Press, 1984.

O'Conner, Richard, *The German Americans: An Informal History*. Boston: Little, Brown & Co., 1968.

Oellschlager, Kim, "St. Charles County Chapter of the American Red Cross, Then and Now," *St. Charles County Heritage*, Vol.12, No.3, July 1994.

Official Manual State of Missouri, popularly known as the *Blue Book*, Jefferson City: Von Hoffman Press, published bi-annually by the Secretary of State.

O'Laughlin, Michael, *Irish Settlers on the American Frontier, 1770-1900, vol. 1*, Kansas City: Irish Genealogical society, 1984.

Olson, Audrey L., *St. Louis Germans, 1850-1920*, New York: Arno Press, 1980.

Olson, Edna McElhiney, *Historical Articles St. Charles, Missouri, Vols. 1-4,* St. Charles: St. Charles Genealogical Society, 1993.

Olson, Edna McElhiney, *Historical St. Charles, Missouri,* St.Charles: St.Charles County Historical Society, 1967, reprinted 1998.

Overby, Osmund, "German Churches in the Pelster Housebarn Neighborhood, *The German-American Experience in America*, Missouri Cultural Heritage Center, 1986, p. 93.

Parrish, William E., *A History of Missouri, 1860-1875, Volume III*, Columbia: University of Missouri Press, 1973.

Phillips, Kevin, *The Cousins' War*, New York: Basic Books, 1999.

Phillips, Kevin P. *The Emerging Republican Majority*, New Rochelle, NY: Arlington House, 1969.

Poindexter, Mark, "A Right Smart Little Town," manuscript, at Kathryn Linnemann Library.

Politt, Lisa, "Quality Family Programming for the Silent Screen," *St. Charles County Heritage*, January, 1993, p. 52.

Primm, James Neal, *Economic Policy in the Development of a Western State, Missouri 1820-1860,* Cambridge: Harvard University Press, 1954.

Primm, James Neal, *Lion of the Valley, St. Louis, Missouri*, Boulder: Pruett Publishing Company, 1981.

"Reminiscences of Lindenwood College, 1827-1920," *Lindenwood College*, Vol. 89, No. 12(b), May 1920.

Richter, Daniel K. *Facing East from Indian Country*, Cambridge: Harvard University Press, 2001.

Robbins, Ruby Matson, "The Missouri Reader," *MHR*, Vol.47, January 1953.

Rorabaugh, W.J., *The Alcoholic Republic, An American Tradition*, New York: Oxford University Press, 1979.

Ross, Stephen J., *Workers on the Edge, Work, Leisure, and Politics in Industrializing Cincinnati, 1788-1890*, New York: Columbia University Press, 1985.

Rothensteiner, John, *History of the Archdiocese of St. Louis, Volume 2*, St. Louis: Blackwell Wielandy Co., 1928.

Russo, David J., *American Towns, An Interpretive History*, Chicago: Ivan R. Dee, 2001.

Rutland, Robert Allen, *The Republicans, From Lincoln to Bush*, Columbia: University of Missouri Press, 1996.

Sandfort, Robert M., *Hermann Heinrich Sandfort, Farmer and Furniture Maker from Hahlen, Germany,* St. Charles: 2000.

St. Charles County in the World War, St. Charles: The Honor Roll Association of St. Charles County, St. Louis: Peters and Mann, 1919.

St. Charles County Portrait and Biographical Record, St. Charles: Chapman Publishing Company, 1895.

"St. Charles, Missouri, Bicentennial Historical Program Book," St.Charles: St. Charles Bicentennial Committee, 1969.

The St. Charles Missouri Citizen Improvement Association, 1905-1907, reprint, ed. by Richard Lowell Vinson, St. Charles: Frenchtown Museum Corp. 1993.

Schiermeier, William, *Cracker Barrel Country*, Vols. I - IV, Washington, Missouri: Missourian

Publishing Company, 1996.

Schlereth, Thomas J., *Victorian America, Transformations in Everyday Life, 1876-1915*, New York: Harper-Collins, 1991.

Schroeder, Walter A. "Rural Settlement Patterns of the German-Missourian Cultural Landscape," *The German Experience in Missouri*, Missouri Cultural Heritage Center, 1986.

Schroeder, Walter, "The Environmental Setting of the St. Louis Region," in *Common Fields, An Environmental History of St. Louis*, St. Louis: Missouri Historical Society Press, 1997.

Schultz, Bob, "Some Civil War Politics in St. Charles County," *St. Charles County Heritage*, Vol.20, No.1, January 2002.

Sellers, Charles, *The Market Revolution, Jacksonian America 1815-1846*, New York: Oxford University Press, 1991.

Shoemaker, Floyd Calvin, *Missouri and the Missourians, Vol.1*, Chicago: The Lewis Publishing Company, 1943.

Sigmund, Judy, *Dog Prairie Tales*, St. Charles: Goellner Printing, n.d.

Snapp, Elizabeth, "Government Patronage of the Press in St. Louis, Missouri," *MHR*, January 1980.

Smith, Lisa, ed. *Nike is a Goddess*, New York: Atlantic Monthly Press, 1998.

The Spanish in the Mississippi Valley, edited by John Francis McDermott, Urbana: University of Illinois Press, 1974.

Spellman, Paul N. *Zadock and Minerva Cottle Woods*, *American Pioneers,* Austin: 1987.

Stamp, Kenneth, *America in 1857, A Nation on the Brink*, NewYork: Oxford University Press.1990.

Stewart, Dick, *Duels and the Roots of Violence in Missouri*, Columbia: University of Missouri Press, 2002.

Stumberg, Cordelia, *My Sonata: Music in My Life,* manuscript in the possession of the author.

Taylor, George Rogers, *The Transportation Revolution 1815-1860*, New York: Holt, Rinehart and Winston, 1995.

Thelen, David, *Paths of Resistance, Tradition and Dignity in Industrializing Missouri*, New York: Oxford University Press, 1986.

Thomas, William, *History of St. Louis County, Missouri*, St. Louis: The S.J. Clarke Publishing Co., 1911.

"Three Missouri Statehood Fathers," *MHR,* January 1980.

Tindall, George Brown and David Shi, *America*, New York: W.W. Norton & Company, 2004.

Toten, Grant and Carrie Waldvogel, "The KKK in St. Charles in the 1920's," *St. Charles County Heritage*, Vol. 20, p. 38.

Towey, Martin G. and Margaret Loicollo Sullivan, "The Knights of Father Mathew: Parallel Ethnic Reform," *MHR*, Vol. LXXV, No. 2, January, 1981, p. 168.

Trefousse, Hans L. *Carl Schurz*, New York: Fordham University Press, 1998.

Trexler, Harrison, *Slavery in Missouri, 1804-1865*. Baltimore. The John Hopkins Press. 1914.

Valley of the Mississippi, edited by Louis Thomas, St. Louis: Hawthorne Publishing Co., 1841.

Villert, Mary Yates, "Orphan Trains from New York to Portage des Sioux Township," in Donald Mincke, *The History of Portage de Sioux Township Missouri, The Land Between the Rivers*, Portage des Sioux: Land Between the Rivers Historical Society, 1999.

Villert, Mary Yates, "Smartt Field," in Mincke, Donald, *The History of Portage de Sioux Township Missouri, The Land Between the Rivers*, Portage des Sioux: Land Between the Rivers Historical Society, 1999, p. 131.

Voelker, Frederick E. "The French Mountain Men in the Early Far West," *The Spanish in the Mississippi Valley*, ed. by. John Francis McDermott, Urbana: University of Illinois Press, 1965.

Wells, Amy Stuart and Robert L. Crain, *Stepping over the Color Line, African-American Students in White Suburban School*s, New Haven: Yale University Press, 1997.

White, Anne, *For All Seasons, Lake St. Louis, Missouri*, Walsworth Publishing Company, Marceline, Missouri, 1985.

White, Richard, *The Middle Ground, Indians, Empires, and Republics in the Great Lakes Region, 1650-1815*, New York: Cambridge University Press, 1991.

Williams, R. Hal, *Years of Decision, American Politics in the 1890s*, Prospects Heights, IL: Waveland Press, Inc., 1978.

INDEX

15th Amendment, 99
370 Discovery Bridge, 353

A

abolition of slavery, 41, 43, 57, 92, 94, 96, 108, 130, 131
abortion, 314
Academy of the Sacred Heart, 28
French language instruction, 346
Achelpohl, Wm. 151
Adair County, 104
Adams, John Quincy 43; John Quincy President 76; Moody Dr. 313
Adler, Jeffrey 77
AF of L, 268
Africa Hill, 159
African Church, 132
African School, 132
African-Americans, 45, 55, 56, 92, 99, 100, 130, 132, 136, 149, 158, 159, 224, 230, 231, 243, 262, 287, 298, 315, 347, 351
age of homespun, 71
agriculture, 21, 29, 31, 72, 77, 78, 114-119, 125-129, 135, 136, 163, 166, 168, 174, 176, 209, 226, 240, 245, 258, 259, 354
Agricultural Adjustment Act (AAA), 244
Agricultural Extension Service, 245
alcohol, 16, 17, 18, 19, 24, 49, 50, 63, 77, 96, 109, 110, 146, 168, 347
Alderson, Benjamin 153
Alfred, Ruben 326
Algonquian tribes, 12, 22, 23, 25, 37
All Saints Parish, 280
Allen, William 80; William M.

124; William, Senator 44; William State Senator 113
Alsace-Lorraine, 144, 155
Alsatians, 136
Alton Illinois, 11
Amateur Sports Hall of Fame, 356
Ambrose, Stephen 62
American Car and Foundry, 148, 161, 180, 196, 255, 268
American colonists, 5
American Federation of Labor, 248
American Legion, 287
American Protective League, 165
American settlers, 13, 46
American Softball Association, 217
Ameristar Casino, 355
Anderson, Bloody Bill 93
Andrew County, 104
Angelique, 23
Anglo-Americans, 107, 153, 346
Anheuser-Busch Inc., 269
anti-Semitism, 156
Anzeiger des Westens, 99
Archbishop of Havana Cuba, 19
Archbishop of Quebec, 19
Armstrong, Louis 290
Army of the West, 80
Arsenal of Democracy, 236
Arthur, Chester 111
Ashcroft, John 325
Ashley, William H. General 62
Association of Community Chests and Councils, 212
Assumption Parish, 277
Atchison, David R., 6, 80
Atchison County, 104
Atherton, Lewis Historian 68
Atomic Energy Commission, 270

Atomic Energy Plant, 267
Audrain County, 37, 103
Augusta, 83, 93, 97, 108, 119, 132, 136, 139, 142, 173, 175, 207, 213, 227, 236, 279
A&W, 273

B

B-47 bomber, 270
Baber, Hiram H. 41
Baden, 164
Baer, Simon 155
Baggermann, William 303
Bahr, Leo F. 324
Baker, Governor, 187
Ballantine Grange, 126
bank holiday, 241
Banner, Stuart Professor 15, 19, 29
Bannerman, Ernest 138
Banner-News, 95, 165, 169, 179, 182, 184, 185, 186, 188, 189, 201, 219, 222, 224, 228, 229, 231, 232, 234, 235, 237, 250, 251, 252, 259, 265, 272, 274, 276, 281, 285, 293, 294, 295, 296, 297, 299, 300, 301, 302, 308, 311, 312, 314, 319, 320, 321, 322, 325, 328, 332, 333, 335, 338, 339, 343
Baptist Church, 49
Baptists, 48, 106, 174, 275
Barber's Union, 248
Barklage, Thomas 325
barley, 28
Barnes-Jewish St. Peters Hospital, 355
Barnwell, Robert W. 279
Barton, David 35, 43, 65; David Senator 58; Joshua 45, 58; William 161
Baseball, 215
Basye, C. Ben 314
Bataan Death March, 225
bateau, 27

Bates, Barton 92, 114, 154; Cora 154; Edward 45, 81, 83, 85, 91, 114, 148, 154; Edward Congressman 65; Frederick 45, 52, 59, 248

Battle of the Bands, 311

Bauer, Robert 319, 320, 322

Bavaria, 164

Beaumont High School, 275

Beckman, James 326

Beck's Landing, 123

Bel Aire Plantation, 71, 117

Bell, Alexander Graham 201; John 84

Bell Telephone Company, 201

Benton, Thomas Hart 43, 63, 80, 81

Benton School, 154

Berlin Immigration Society, 134

Bernard McMenamy Contractors, 332

Bethlehem Church, 49

Bethune, Mary McLeod 243

Bethune-Cookman College, 243

Billing, Frank 181

birth control, 314

Bishop, Glennon 318, 325

Bishop of Havana, 53

Bismarck, 107; Otto von 163

bison, 11

Bitter, Carl 152

Black Codes, 27

black enlistments, 90

black farmers, 158

Black Hole of Calcutta, 9

Black Jack, 236

Black Jack Grange, 126

Black Jack School, 278

black population, 45, 158

black Republicans, 86

black slaves, 92

black soldiers, 82, 224

black stick, 128

black students, 132

Black Walnut Levee, 247

Blackhawk, 38, 40; Sac Chief 12, 40

Blackhawk War, 40

Blackhurst, Stephen Superintendent 275, 279, 281, 307

Blaine, 111

Blair, Frank 81, 102; James T. 299

Blanchette, Louis 15, 17, 23, 153

Blanchette Hills, 265

Blanchette Park, 118, 159, 167, 203, 214, 216, 218, 222, 224, 226, 231, 259, 260, 263, 286, 291, 331, 346, 356

Blessed Philippine Duchesne, 276

blockhouses, 15, 38

Blodget, Lorin 9

Blondeau, John Baptiste 17

Bloody Island, 58

blue eagle, 242

blue laws, 97, 146, 163, 284, 347

Blue Ville School, 132

B'nai Torah, 349

Board of Curators, 330

Bode, John Henry, 105, 152

Boenker, Hermann Dietrich 116; Oscar 221

Bond, Christopher "Kit" 319, 323, 324, 325

Boone, 75; Daniel 33, 41, 48, 55, 64, 133; Daniel Morgan 35; Morgan 20, 33; Nathan 38, 39, 41, 62, 64, 68, 69, 349; Nathan Captain 40

Boone County, 87

Boone family, 76

Boone's Lick, 76

Boone's Rangers, 38, 40

Boone's Survey, 64

Booneslick county, 76

Booneslick Region, 13

Booneslick Road, 70, 77, 127, 153

Booneslick trail, 7, 71, 76

Bootheel, 247

Bordeaux, James 24

Borgelt, Ben 293; Edgar 245

Borgmeyer, Joseph Sheriff 231, 250, 251

Borromeo, 23, 27; St. Charles patron saint of Charles VI the King of Spain 26

Borromeo Hills subdivision, 265, 266

Boschert, 320; Douglas 323, 325, 338; Douglas Judge 338; Douglas Mayor 342; Douglas Representative 325, 332; Lawrence 302

Boschert Creek, 265

Boschert Estate, 265

Boschertown, 18, 138

Boschertown Road, 320

Boston, 95

Boswell, Charles W. 330

bourgeois, 24

Boys Club of St. Charles Missouri, 286, 348

Boys Night at Home, 172

Braufman, Herman 155

Breckenridge, 84

Brecker, Louis 107

Briggs, Frank P. Senator 294

Briscoe, Joseph 316; Joseph Councilman 335; Joseph Judge 290

British America, 9

British forces, 39

British trading party, 15

Broadhead, James O. attorney 81, 86, 93

Brockgreitens, 325; Bernard 295; Frank Mayor 307, 325, 331

Brockhagen, Henry Father 144

Broeker, Henry J. mayor 233

Brooklyn Dodgers, 288

Brotherhood of St. Johns A.M.E. Church, 291

Brown, 103; Ann 54; Daniel T. 280; Gatz 81; Gratz 101, 103, 350; Jo Ann 178, 276; Oliver

289; Paris 324; Paul 124; Walter C. 177

Brown Club, 103

Brown Road extension, 332

Brown Tobacco Company, 124

Brown vs. Board of Education of Topeka, Kansas 289

Bruere, 80, 300, 357; Gustave 85; Gustave Captain 104; John 85, 152; John Surgeon 91, 94; Theodore 138, 148, 151; Theodore C. 151; Theodore Jr. 328; Theodore Jr. Circuit Judge 295; Theodore Jr. Judge 300, 301; Theodore State Senator 109

Bruns, Elmer "Jocko" 220; Henry 117; Hermann J. 116; Johann Dietrich 174

Brunswick, 114

Brush, Anton 251

Bryan, 176; Mary Emily 154; William Jennings 153, 171, 175, 176, 177

Buchanan, 174

Buckner, George Dr. of St. Charles to the Board of Cur 118; George Robards 117

Budde Brothers Sinclair, 272

buggies, 12

Bull Moose, 185

Bunker, Simeon General 89

Bureau of Labor Statistics, 355

Bureau of Land Reclamation, 248

Burger, Mary Odelia Sister 152

Burgermeister, 347

Burkemper, Curtis Judge 318

Burlington Railroad, 210

Busch, Alice 269; August A. 269; August A. Jr. 344

Busch Wildlife Area, 12, 269

Buse, John 162, 199

Bush, George 350

bushwhackers, 89, 91, 94

C

Cahokia, 7, 8, 21

Caldwell County, 104

Callaway, James Captain 39

Callaway County, 40, 91, 92, 103

Callaway Township, 136

Calvary Evangelical Methodist congregation, 275

Camp Jackson, 86

Camp Krekel in Cottleville, 86

Campbell, William 42, 44

Canada, 14, 15

Cannon, Clarence 248, 286, 295, 296, 303; Clarence Congressman 187, 210, 223, 231, 257, 261, 271, 286, 295

Cape Girardeau, 17, 35, 59, 152

capitalism, 61, 63, 67, 78, 189, 195, 231, 239

Caplan, Harry 155

Cappeln, 139, 142, 202

Car of Commerce, 74

Car of Commerce Chute, 74

Carmelite Home, 275

Carmelite Sisters, 152

Carondelet, 17; Baron 26

Carpenter's Union, 248

carriages, 12

Carroll County, 14

Carter, Jimmy 323

Cash crop, 73

Castlio, Calvin 172, 211, 254; Hiram 154; Hiram Beverly 124; Jasper Newton 152; Jasper Newton Dr. 82, 157; Nancy Callaway 60, 138

Catholic Church, 15, 18, 19, 20, 22, 106

Catholic Spain, 5

Catholic Watchman, 145

Catholicism, 13, 18, 19, 141

Catiche and Marguerite, 56

cattle, 11

Cave Springs, 71, 173

Centennial Farms, 117

Centennial Road Law, 207

Center for the Prevention of Disease Control, 311

Central Bank of St. Charles, 151

Central Elementary School, 254

Central States Coca-Cola, 355

Centralia Missouri, 93, 94

Cervantes, Alfonso Mayor 343

chain migration, 136

Chalifoux, Baptiste 24; Joseph 24

Chamber of Commerce, 179, 254, 268

Chambers, William 88

Chanley, Lacy 162

Chariton River, 17

chasseur, 15, 28

Chautauqua, 153, 178

Chicago, Illinois, 27

Chittendon, Hiram 5

Cholera, 197

Chouteau, 56; August of St. Louis 39; Auguste 34; Pierre 56

Christian Century, 282

Christy, William Jr. 44

Chronotype, 42

Church of God in Christ, 159

Church of Jesus Christ of Latter-Day Saints, 275

circuit riders, 49

Citigroup, 355

Civil Rights Movement, 314, 316

Civil War, 5, 12, 80, 96, 113, 140, 152

Civil Works Administration (CWA), 242

Civilian Conservation Corps (CCC), 244

Clarion, 42

Clark, 34; Bennett C. Senator 228, 248, 254; Champ 181,

182; Governor of Missouri
39; William 24, 26, 34, 35,
37, 38, 43, 55; William
Governor 36
Clark, Kenny 290
Clarksville, 122
Clay, Henry 42, 44
Clay Street, 271
Clean Water Act, 351, 352
Clecak, John 313
Clement, Archie 93
Clemmons, George 324
Cleveland, 104, 112, 176;
Grover 111, 172; Grover
President 119
Clevenger, Homer Mayor 263,
298
closed shop, 250
Clover, Henry A. 92
Coalter, John D. 45; Julia D.
45
Cochran, 229; John
Congressman 229
Cole County, 84
Cole Creek, 335
Colgin, Daniel 51
College of Agriculture, 129
Collier, Catherine 48, 49, 60,
131, 183; George 51, 60, 134
Collier v. Wheldon and Wife,
67
Collinsville, Illinois, 166
Collot, George Victor French
spy 26
Colman, Norman J. 119
Columbia, 177
Columbia Missourian, 92
Columbia-Waterloo, 344
commis, 24
**Commission on Christian
Social Concerns,** 308
commons, 28-31, 32, 52, 65,
66, 78, 239, 356
communism, 46, 130, 296
Community College District,
348
Community Film Association,

171
comunales, 28
Concord grape, 119
Concordia Verein, 150
Confederacy, 79, 85, 86, 94,
104
Confederate forces, 89
Confederate sympathizers, 98
**Congress of Industrial
Organizations,** 248, 252,
268
Conservatives, 90
**Consolidated North County
Levee District,** 351
Constam, Ike 155
Constitutional Convention,
41, 292
**Continental Telephone
Company,** 331
Conway, James Mayor 330
Cook, Ray Donald 70
Coolidge, Calvin 186
Coppage, Peggy Republican
323
cordelle, 74
corn, 28
Corps of Discovery, 34, 35
Corps of Engineers, 8, 253,
326
Corrigan, William 317
Corrupt Practices Statute,
234
Cosmos-Monitor, 149, 155,
161, 163, 164, 165, 173, 175,
179, 182, 183, 184, 185, 186,
188, 191, 193, 196, 212, 219,
226, 230, 232, 234, 236, 237,
241, 242, 243, 252, 258, 261,
270, 273, 279, 280, 282, 285,
289, 290, 295, 298, 302
Cotes Sans Dessein, 40
Cottle, Ira 34; Warren 34, 77
Cottleville, 34, 49, 76, 85, 94,
103, 132, 142, 143, 155, 173,
254, 325, 348, 357
counter culture, 307, 345
**County Agricultural
Stabilization and**

Conservation Committee,
258
County Board of Education,
277
County Charter, 349
County Fair Board, 354
Court of Common Pleas, 35
Court of Quarter Sessions,
75
Coutumes de Paris, 51
Craig, Delinda 51; James 51;
James P. 126
Craven's Band, 150
Creech, B.R. 295
Creel, George 180
Creoles, 27
**Crossroads Economic
Development Corporation,**
329
Crow, Jim 186; R.T. 337
Cruzat, Lieutenant Governor
27
Cruzatte, Pierre crewmember
34
Cuivre River, 34
**Cuivre River Electric
Cooperative,** 246, 331
Cul de Sac District, 247
Cummings, John A. 100
Cunningham, Thomas W.
Mayor 120
Curtis, Winterton C. 170
**Curtis Wright Aircraft
Factory,** 224

D

Dairy farming, 129
Dakotas, 22, 24
Dalton, Donald Attorney 283;
Donald E. Judge 321; John
State Attorney General 289
Dames, George 319; George
Representative 325; Omer
300, 319
Danforth, Jack 319, 323
Daniel Boone Bridge, 219,
241, 260, 270
Daniel Boone Elementary,

279

Daniel Boone expressway, 270

Dardenne, 17, 18, 76, 90, 107, 112, 139, 173, 237

Dardenne and Richfield hunting clubs, 9

Dardenne Creek, 17, 18, 64, 76, 122, 143, 144, 210, 337

Dardenne Creek floodplain, 158

Dardenne Drainage District, 247

Dardenne Grange, 126

Dardenne Prairie, 143, 343, 357

Dardenne Presbyterian Church, 48

Dardenne Temperance Society, 50

Dardenne Township, 117

D.A.R.E., 348

Darnell, Robert 89, 95

Darrow, Clarence 170

Darst, David 34

Darst Bottom, 49, 84

Darwin, Charles 170

Daudt, Carl 151; Charles 151; Charles Captain 104

Daughters of the American Revolution, 153

Davis, Arthur Democratic gubernatorial candidate 170; Erwin 303, 319; William T. 321

de Bourgmont, 14; Etiene Veniard commandant of the Missouri River 14

de Finiels, Nicholas 17

de jure, 161

de Lassos, Charles 29, 33

De Lemos, Manuel Gayosa 11, 17

de Leyba, Fernando Captain 19

de Leyba Captain, 19

Debrecht, Loretta Democrat 324

Decatur Streets, 27

Defiance, Missouri, 72, 176,

202, 207, 211, 213, 246

deforestation, 12

Dekalb County, 104

Democrats, 43, 44, 79, 96, 97, 104

Democratic Party, 33, 102

Demokrat, 83, 84, 85, 90, 91, 92, 94, 99, 100, 101, 102, 103, 104, 105, 109, 110, 111, 115, 116, 119, 120, 130, 131, 132, 136, 137, 138, 139, 140, 145, 146, 147, 150, 152, 157, 161, 162, 163, 172, 174, 175, 176, 177, 184, 215, 246

D'Englise, Jacques 24

Denker, Henry 85, 107; Henry B. 191

Denker Home, 284

Dennigmann, Hermann 116

Denwol Building, 273

Department of Agriculture, 118

Department of Transportation, 344

Deppe, H. 122

Des Moines River, 10, 17

Deschamps, Jean Baptiste 34

Deutscher Wanderbund, 220

Devore, Uriah 43; Uriah J. first sheriff 46

Dewey, 239; Thomas 238

Dickens, Charles 9, 78

Dickey, W.S. 173

Dickmann, 237

Didier, Don 19

Dierker, John F. 86; John H. Sheriff 162

Dillon, James 168

Dine, Mary S. 88

Dines, Tyson Reverend 88

Disciples of Christ, 174

Distillers, 49

District of St. Charles, 5

Divine Right of Kings, 13

Division of Family Services, 312

Dixie Guards, 86

Dog Prairie, 143

Donnell, 237; Forrest Governor 219

Donnelly, Phil Missouri Governor 269; Philip 237

Dougherty, Joseph D. 87

Drake, 97, 100; Charles 92, 96, 102

Drake Constitution, 97

Drive-In Bank, 273

Droste Road, 298

Drummond, James T. 124

Drummond Tobacco Company, 124

Dryden, Sylvester 287

du Lac, Francois Marie Perr 28

du Sable, Baptiste Point 27

DuBourg Bishop, 53, 54

Ducharme, Jean Marie 15

Duchesne, 310; Philippine 54, 55, 131; Philippine Mother 53, 183, 276

Duchesne High School, 277

Duden, 135; Gottfried 81, 82

Duggan, James 214

Dula, Caleb 124

Duncan, Marsha public administrator 324

Duquette, Francis 28, 35

Dutch, 86, 95

Dutch Planks, 83

Dutzow, 134, 136

Dyer, 293, 357; Bernard 189; Bernard H. 181; Bernard Judge 293, 297; B.H. 151; B.H. Judge 242, 248; David A. 235, 293; David attorney 251; D.P. 161; Fred 319, 323, 325, 349; Fred State Representative 341; Mary 297

E

Eagleton, Thomas 318; Thomas Senator 305; Thomas State Attorney General 283

Easton, Rufus 35, 36, 40, 41, 42, 52, 61, 77

Echele, Clem 251

Edna, 74
Edward, A.H. Democrat 103
Edward D. Jones Dome, 347
Edwards, A.H. 101; Carr 178; James Major 104; Ninian 52; Ninian Governor of Illinois 39; W.W. 85
Ehlmann, 117; Alfred 221; Hermann Dietrich 116; Irwin Mrs. 182; Nell 183
Ehrlich, Walter 156
Eighth Missouri Infantry, 89
Eintracht, 150
Eisenhower, 296; Dwight D. 292; Dwight D. General 295, 299
Eisenhower Recession, 301
Electoral College, 43
Electoral Commission, 106
Ell, Edwin 242
Elm Point, 241, 279
Elmendorf, Henry 287, 330, 344
Elmore, Herman 347
Elsah, Illinois, 77
emancipation, 96, 116, 117
Emancipation Proclamation, 92
Emerson, Irene 57; John Dr. 57; Ralph Waldo 6
Emmons, 216; Ben L. 153, 215; Benjamin 36, 41, 51, 77
engages, 24
English language, 13, 15, 21, 47, 53, 59, 96, 100. 104, 112, 137, 140, 142, 143, 144, 150, 152, 153, 155, 164, 165, 167, 172, 173, 215, 274, 348
Episcopalians, 48
Ermeling, Henry 117
European colonies, 13
European diseases, 22
European settlers, 12
European-made goods, 25
Europeans, 12, 13, 14
Evangelical Christians, 313, 325

Evangelical church in Femme Osage, 173, 274
Evangelical church in Friedens, 173
Evangelical church in New Melle, 173
Evangelical church in Weldon Spring, 173
Evangelical Synod, 141

F

Fairbanks Engine Company, 196
Fairview Institute, 134
Faith Methodist congregation, 275
Family Arena, 348
Family Services Authority, 348
Farm Bureau Federation, 256
farm-to-market, 240, 241
Farris, Robert P. Reverend 88
FDR, 230
federal budget, 239
Federal Deposit Insurance Corporation, 241
Federal Emeregency Management Agency, 328, 351, 352, 353
Federal Environmental Protection Agency, 9
federal government, 330
Federal Land Law, 64
Federal Road Act, 206
Federal Road Act of 1921, 206
Feltes, Joseph 250
Femme Osage, 34, 39, 49, 97, 119, 137, 139, 141, 142, 175, 202, 346
Femme Osage Creek, 33
Femme Osage Township, 135
Femmer, Owen L. 249
Ferney, Charles 72
ferry, 75
Festival of the Little Hills, 307, 345
Fielding, John H. Reverend 49,

134
Fields, Jean 17
Fillmore President, 45
First Assembly of God Church, 275
First Assembly of God Church in O'Fallon, 275
First Baptist Church of O'Fallon, 275
First Baptist Church of Winfield, 275
First Methodist Church, 308
First National Bank, 151
First State Capitol, 32, 33, 336
First State Capitol Commission, 336
First World War, 172
Fischbach, Jacob 168; John 242
Fischbach Brewery, 168
Fischbach Hotel, 323
Fitz, James 313
Flauherty, James 36
Fletcher, Thomas C. 94
Flint, Timothy 47, 48, 76, 131
Flint Hill, 46, 48, 49, 93, 117, 132, 280
Flood Control Act, 247
Flood Disaster Protection Act, 326
Florissant, 53, 319
Folk, Joseph 177
Follenius, Paul 134; Wm. 91, 103
Foner, Eric Historian 129
Ford, Gerald 323
Ford plant, 268
Foristell, 124; Pierre 124
Fort Chartres, 14
Fort Don Carlos, 15
Fort Leavenworth, 80
Fort Madison, 37
Fort Orleans, 14
Fort Peruque, 123
Fort Zumwalt, 49, 310
Fort Zumwalt School District, 278, 279
Forty-Eighers, 82

Forty-Ninth Missouri, 86
four-minute men, 180
Fox, 17, 37, 38, 39
Fox Run Mobile Home Park, 320
Fragmented by Design, 342
France, 5, 14, 103
Francis Howell, 278, 310
Francis Howell School District, 279, 280
Francis Howell High School, 154, 218, 254
Francis Howell Institute, 154
Francis Howell R-III, 278
Franco-Prussian War, 103
Frank, Julius 155
Franklin County, 125, 141
Franklin High School, 218, 288, 289
Franklin School, 160, 243
Frappier, Joseph 320
Frayser, 85; Robert B. 85
free African-Americans, 42, 55, 157
free navigation on the Mississippi, 20
Free Press, 42
Freeman, Will L. Dr. 165
Freemasonry, 82
Fremont, 91; John C. 87; John C. General 91, 92
French, 13, 27, 45; C.H. 169
French and Indian War, 5
French Canadians, 17
French common field system, 61
French culture, 13
French customs, 21
French explorers, 14
French fur traders, 14
French merchants, 25
French Revolution, 82
French settlers, 5, 20
French trappers, 346
French-Canadian, 5
Freymuth Park, 334
Friedens, 142, 236
Friedens Road, 333

Friedensbote, 146
Friedrich, Jules Reverend 152
Friends of Religious Enlightenment, 108
frogtown, 159
Frost, Gavin Dr. and Mrs. 314
Frum, David 307
Fuhr Mr., 193
Fulton, 91, 92
Fulton, Missouri, 92
fur trade, 13, 14, 16, 21, 24, 25, 27, 28, 40, 54, 61, 62, 63, 77

G

Gallaher Street, 132
Gamble, 92; Hamilton 85, 91
Gamble Governor, 91, 93
gambling 46, 50, 215, 238, 277, 281, 282, 283, 348, 356
G.A.R., 177
G.A.R. Hall, 167
Gardenhire, 84; James 84
Garfield, James 111
Garlichs, Adelheid 137; Hermann Reverend 141, 274
Gasconade County, 104, 141, 174
gaslights, 204
Gatzweiler, Friedrich 85
Gemini program, 328
Gemuetlichkeit, 146, 147, 162, 275, 307, 347
General Assembly, 32, 59, 94, 175, 239
General Motors, 330
General Motors Assembly Plant, 305, 355
General Quarter Sessions, 35
Gentry, William 104
geographical conditions, 116
Gerdemann, Heinrich Wilhelm 139
German Catholics, 107
German community, 100
German Day, 150
German Evangelical Synod, 142

German Evangelicals, 106, 141
German farmers, 116
German Home Guards, 85
German immigrants, 8, 13, 79, 82
German immigration, 43, 152
German Jews, 152, 155, 156
German *Kulture*, 134, 167, 274
German Language, 134
German Lutherans, 105
German Methodists, 106
German parishes, 153
German Republic in Arkansas, 134
German *Wehrmacht*, 263
German-Americans, 130, 163, 165, 236, 346
Germans, 13, 92
Gerteis, Louis Historian 81
Gervais, Joseph 24
Geyer, Henry C. 80, 81
Giddings, Salmon Reverend 48
Giessen Society, 134
Gilbert, M. 52
Gilmore, 330
Glasgow Missouri, 129
Glennon, John J. 287
Goebel, R. 152
Goellner, Glen 297; William 317
Goldwater, 303, 319; Barry 303
Goldwater-Wallace, 303
Governor Hearnes' Citizen Committee on Delinquency and Crime, 315
goyim, 156
Grabenhorst, Frederick Lieutenant 105
Grand Army of the Republic, 95
Grand River, 17
Granges, 126
Grant, 103; Ulysses S. General 99
Grant administration, 101, 103

Grantham, Taliaferro Captain 72

Gratiot Street prison, 87, 88, 89

Grau's cut, 248

Graves, Joseph 320

Great Britain, 5, 14

Great Depression, 78, 206, 208, 211, 239, 263, 273, 326

Great Society, 257, 317

Greeley, 103; Horace 103

Green, 174; James 34

Green Mules, 287

Green's Bottom, 126

Greens Bottom District, 247

Griewe, Arlie 301

Griffith, Daniel 71; Daniel A. 133; Daniel Judge 116; Daniel Judge of St. Charles Township 116; Samuel 34, 71, 133

Griffith family, 71

Groce, D. Oty 238

Gronefeld, Henry 116

Gross, Dowell 168

Gross-Algermissen Germany, 127

Grosvenor, William 101, 145

Grothe, Isidore 168; John 168

GROWTH INC, 310

Grundy County, 104

Guillet, 22; Bernard 22

gumbo, 128

Gumbo Flats, 241

Gut, Edward 151; E.F. 85

Guttermuth, 168

H

Haake, Joe 299

Hackman, John Captain 104

Hackmann, 117

Haenssler, R.C. 151, 196; R.C. Republican 178

Hafferkamp, Johann Wilhelm 117

Hahn, Darlene 224

Haiti, 27

Hamburg, 139, 162, 207, 211, 213, 254

Hammond, Samuel 41

Hampton Village, 273

Hancock, 104

Hancock Amendment, 350

Hancock District, 247

Hanneke, John C. 320

Hannibal, 122

Hannibal and St. Joseph Railroad Company, 120

Hannibal and St. Louis Railroad, 122, 127

Hannibal & Northwestern Railroad, 123

Hanover, 6, 114, 136, 139, 164, 347

Harbor Town, 334

Hardach, Henry 138

Hardin, 104; Charles Henry 103; T.L. Dr. 218

Harding, Edward Major 88; Warren 184

Hardwoods, 12

Harmon, Lloyd Reverend 225

Harmonie-Verein, 139

Harold, Leonard 139

Harrington, F.L. Dr. 298

Harris, Willie 154

Harrison, 37; William Henry governor of Indiana Territory 34, 37, 46

Harrison Frontier Land Act, 51

Harvester, 76, 105, 139, 142, 173, 207, 211, 227, 236

Havanna Cuba, 13, 177

Hawthorne Elementary School, 309

Hayes, Rutherford B. 106

Hazelwood, Missouri 268

Hearnes, Warren Governor 317, 323

Heidelbaugh, George 334

Heintzelmann, Ken 216

Helfert, George 251

Hempstead, Edward 35, 36, 38, 43, 77

Henderson, 95; John B.

Missouri Senator 100

Hennings, Thomas C. 299

Hepp, Joseph T. 286

Herald, Nathan Major of Dardenne Township 116

Herman Heinrich Sandfort, 116

Hermann, Missouri 11, 301

Hermann Dietrich Sanfort, 117

Hermann *Licht-Freund*, 108

Hess, Abe 214; Julius 156

Hesskamp, Hermann Arnold 117

Heuerleute, 114

Hickory Grove Christian Church, 49

High Tech Corridor, 330, 354

Highway 40, 7, 186

Historia Domus, 178

Historic District, 15

History of St. Charles County, 103, 193

hivernants, 24

hobos, 211

Hoch Deutsch, 136

Hoehn, J. Philipp Lieutenant 104

Hoffman, Henry S. 245

Holiday, Cleo 324

Hollenbeck, 279; C. Fred 279; Fred 218

Hollrah, Johann Dietrich 116; John Captain 105; John D. 85; Martin J. 245

Home Guard, 87, 90

Home Rule Charter, 324

Homestead Act, 118

homesteads, 32

Hoover, 189; G. 85; Herbert 187, 188; J. Edgar 225, 226, 227, 273

Hoover administration, 213

Hoovervilles, 211

Hopkins, Harry 244

Horst, 284

Hot Stove League, 285

House of Representatives, 36,

44, 219
Housman, J.E. Jr. 204
How, John 85
Howard, 36; Benjamin 35
Howard County, 59, 65
Howard General, 39
Howard Governor, 38
Howell, 20, 211, 254, 357;
    Frances of Dardenne
    Township 116; Francis 34;
    Francis Jr. 154; Thomas 75
Howell family, 70
Howell Prairie, 70
Howell's Ferry, 75
Howell's Ferry Road, 127
Hub Furniture, 156
HUD, 315
Hudson Bay Company, 63
Hughes, Charles Evans
    Republican 179; E.M. Judge
    161
Humphrey, Hubert 317
Humphreys, 89; James 88
Hungate, William
    Congressman 305, 322, 326
hunter-farmer, 69
hunting grounds, 37
Huntsville Missouri, 129
Hurley, Jay Secretary of War
    226; Patrick J. Secretary of
    War 213
Hurt, R. Douglas Historian 62
Husmann, George 118

I
I-370 corridor, 7
Ickes, Harold 243
Iffrig, Albert 178; Frank 300
Illinois Central Railroad, 124
Illinois country, 5, 14
Illinois River, 18
Immaculate Conception
    Parish, 143
Immaculate Heart of Mary,
    275
Immanuel Lutheran Church,
    105
Independent Workers

Organization, 250
Indian artifacts, 345
Indian attacks, 29, 37
Indian haters, 55
Indiana, 38
industrial parks, 329
industrial production, 190
Infant Hercules, 11
Intendant, 18, 63, 64
International Shoe Company,
    195, 213, 239, 252, 255, 268
interracial marriages, 346
Interstate 70, 7
Interstate Highway Act, 257,
    258, 271
Interstate Highway system, 6
Iowa, 23, 121
Iowa Indians, 23
Irish, 108, 347
Irish Catholics, 121
ironclad oath, 98, 101
Irving, Washington 21

J
Jackson, 43, 45, 174; Andrew
    40, 43, 83; Andrew General
    39, 44; Claiborne Fox 80, 85,
    86 Kenneth 320; Kenneth T.
    262, 265
Jackson Resolutions, 80
Jacksonians, 43, 44, 45
Jacobism, 130
Jacoby, Fred 150; Ludwig 143
Janning, Fred 242
Japanese aliens, 219
Jaycees Park, 213
Jayhawker, 92
jazz bands, 287
J.C. Penney Company, 214
Jefferson, 35, 174; Thomas
    President 35; Thomas
    President of the United States
    20, 34
Jefferson City, 6, 42, 49, 132
Jenkins, J.M. Dr. 214
Jensen, Richard 112
Jesuits, 82, 276
Jewel, Mary E. 183

Jewish congregation, 349
Jewish families, 156
John Birch Society, 303, 317
Johns, John Jay 106, 112, 149,
    157, 177; John Jay Elder 109
Johnson, 304; Andrew
    President 100; Charles
    Montgomery Captain 94;
    Charles Montgomery Dr. 86;
    Doris Abling 245; John 54;
    Paul 236
Joliet, Louis 14
Jolly, B.H. 253
Josephville, 112, 139, 143, 173,
    280
Jugendverein, 138
Jung, T. George 126
Jungermann Road, 117
Jung's Station, 126
Junior Baseball Association,
    285
Junto, 35, 41

K
K Line, 122
Kamper, Ken 74
Kamphoeffner, 137
Kamphoefner, Walter 99, 115,
    116, 131, 135, 136
Kampville, 279
Kansas City, 6
Kansas City Airport, 344
Kansas City Athletics, 283
Kansas Indians, 23
Kansteiner, Charles 234, 251
Kaplan, Abraham 156;
    Benjamin 156; Jacob 156;
    Julius 156; Samuel 156
Karrenbrock, Webster, Judge
    321
Kaskaskia, 14, 21
Katholicher Hausfreund, 146
Katy Railroad, 126, 354
Katy Trail, 7, 10, 354
Kaufmann, Aloys Mayor 269
Kearny, Stephen General 80
Keeble, 89; R.B. 89; Richard B.
    88

444

Keeble v. Humphreys, 89
keel-boat, 74
Keen, Eli 132, 160, 161
Kefauver Hearings, 282
Kem, James P. Republican 294, 296
Kemper, Henry 107
Kennedy, John F. Senator 302
Kennedy-Johnson, 303
Kenrick, Frances P. Bishop 99, 100, 130
Kentucky, 8
Keokuk, Chief 40
Keokuk hydroelectric project, 200
Keokuk Iowa, 122
Kern, L.A. 132
kerosene illumination, 200
Kessler, Rudolph G. 245
Khoury League, 285
Kibby, Timothy Colonel 7
Kiel Auditorium, 256
Kienker, Harry 234
King, Andrew Judge 89; Martin Luther Dr. 314; R.J. "Bus" 316, 318
King Charles VI, 15
Kingshighway, 138
Kinnamore, Charles Judge 318
Kirkendall, Richard Historian 295
Kirkpatrick, James 319
Kisker, 117
Kleeschulte Constable, 168
Kleppner, 175; Paul 106, 107; Paul Historian 103
Klondike Quarry, 355
KMOX, 201
Knights of America, 173
Knights of Columbus, 349
Knights of Labor, 186
Knippenburg, H.F. 151, 175
Knothole Gang, 217
Know-Nothing Party, 82, 97, 111
Koch, Edward Father 152
Koerner, Gustave 136

Kohl-Jeck, 284
Kohn, Louis 155
Kohn's Big Boot, 155
Korean conflict, 270, 296
Krainhardt, Theodore Father 143
Krekel, 80, 83, 86, 88, 89, 91, 92, 143; Arnold 83, 85, 87, 89, 91, 92, 95, 96, 98, 107, 108, 122, 131, 132, 138, 148, 170; Nicholas 122
Krekel's Dutch, 92
Ku Klux Klan, 169
Kultur, 163, 167
Kulturkampf, 107, 144, 145, 152, 163, 164, 316

L

La Mamelles, 7
La Mothe, 127
Labiche, Francois crewmember 34
Lackland, Joseph H. 233
Ladies' Guild of Trinity Episcopal Church, 212
LaFollette, 185; Robert 188, 235
Laissez faire, 303
Lake Michigan, 125
Lake St. Louis, 357
Lamarque, Mary 100
Lambert International Airport, 343, 344
Land Clearance for Redevelopment, 291, 337
Land Law of 1800, 51
Landmark Missionary Baptist, 275
Langenbacher, Robert County Extension Agent 168, 192, 210; 258
Latin farmers, 82, 135
Laurin Madame, 23
law and order, 314
Lawler, 357; Catherine 229, 231; Frank Alderman 295, 296; James 173, 270; J.W. 270

Le Dru Father, 23
Leavenworth, 6
Lecompte, Janet 21, 25
LePage, Antoine 24
Les Petite Cotes, 15, 21, 24, 26, 345
Lesseur, Francis 18
Lewis, 34; John L. 248; Meriwether 34, 35, 37, 62, 63; Russell B. Dr. 132; Russell B. Dr. of Flint Hill 152
Lewis and Clark, 62, 63, 346
Lewis and Clark Bridges, 219, 232, 240, 271
Lewis and Clark Vocational Technical School, 310
Liberal Republicans, 103
Liggett and Myers Tobacco Co., 124
Lincoln, 64, 91, 93, 94, 97; Abraham 80, 83, 84
Lincoln administration, 90
Lincoln County, 36, 37, 251
Lincoln County slickers, 46
Lincoln Institute, 132
Lincoln School, 154, 243
Linden Wood, 61
Lindenwood, 154, 215
Lindenwood College, 44, 61, 94, 134, 154, 168, 183, 189, 198, 215, 220, 264, 273, 275, 294, 302, 312, 336, 346
Lindenwood College Board of Directors, 154
Lindenwood University, 23, 43, 346
Linn, Elaine Goodrich 218
Linnemann, 293, 300; Kathryn 183, 203; Robert Senator, 295, 296, 300, 301
Lions Club, 354
Lisa, Manuel 39
Little Crow, 24, 55
Little Dixie, 13, 72, 158
Little Ice Age, 8
Little Rock, 300
Lloyd, William C. 19

local mean time, 129
loess, 7
Lohmar, Shirley 324
Louisiana, 5, 13, 14, 122
Louisiana Gazette, 38
Louisiana Missouri Unionists, 93
Louisiana Purchase, 33, 67
Lovejoy, Elijah 57
Lucas, John B. 35
Luetkenhaus, Leo 318, 319
lumber, 12
Lutheran, 142
Luzon, Charles Leander 19, 53
Lyon, Nathaniel 85, 86, 87

M

Machens, 122, 127, 203, 247, 248, 357; Henry 85, 105, 127
Machens-West Alton Telephone Company, 203
Mackay, James 20, 31, 34
Madison, President 24, 35, 55
Madison Street, 268
Madrid, 13
Maffett, 50
Mahon, Joseph T. 299
Main Street Mall, 325
Maine, 302
maize, 28
Major Governor, 231
Mallinckrodt, Anita 46, 59; Conrad 139; Emil 135, 157; Julius 107, 108, 135
Mallinckrodt Chemical Works, 270
Mamelle Hills, 335
Marais Croche and *Marais Temps Claire,* 8, 246
Marbury vs. Madison, 68
March of Dimes, 286
Marechal, Joseph 24
Marian piety, 276
Marion County, 37
Mark Twain, 335
Marquette, Father Jacques 14
Marriage 20, 22, 23, 27, 99. 137, 138, 144, 161, 173, 219,

263, 284, 311, 345
Marshall, John Justice 56
Marten, Frances 87, 104
Marthasville, 126, 142
Marthasville Road, 127
Martin, Douglas V. Mrs. 242
Mary Ridge, 266
Mason, A.S. 89; Thomas J. 124
Mason-Dixon Line, 104, 113
Masonic charter, 49
Massman Construction, 250, 251
mass-production, 201
Mastercard International, 355
Mathers, Thomas 76
Matson, 202, 207; Richard 126
May Company, 343
McCausland, David 80
McCloud, Robert 42
McCluer, Franc Dr. 294
McClurg Governor, 101, 102, 103, 107
McColloch, Andrew 283, 299, 301, 303, 319
McCormick, Cyrus 128
McCoy, William T. 324
McCulloch Captain, 204
McDaniel, 237; Lawrence 237
McDearmon, 104; James R. 44; John 101; John Democratic county clerk 98; John K. Colonel 104
McDermott, John Francis 19
McDonnell Aircraft, 255, 270, 271, 328, 329
McDowell, 253; Newton 253
McDowell Medical College, 87
McElhiney, William Dr. 44, 71, 87, 93, 117, 133, 159
McElvaine, 218
McGovern, George 319
McGurk, John Justice 68
McKiddy, Gary 88, 243
McKinley, 176; William Governor of Ohio 175
McKinley School, 154
McNair, Alexander 43;

Alexander Colonel 64; Governor 32, 42
McNair Park, 310
Mechlenburg, 114
Mehring, Henry 144
Meier, Red 275
Meigs, Return J. Jr. 35
Meining, D.W. 64, 73
Melvin Price lock and dam, 9, 11
Memorial Hall, 167, 263
Mercantile Library Association, 6
Mercantilist economic policies, 25
Mercer County, 104
Mercury spacecraft, 272
Merrill Major General, 88
Methodist, 48, 174, 275
Methodist Episcopal Church South, 134
Metrolink, 353
Mexico, 80
Mexico Road, 127
Meyer, Arlie 317, 319; Fred 319; Louis 107; Marvin 326
Meyer's grapes, 119
Miami University of Ohio, 104
middle ground, 22, 23, 24, 37, 45
Mid-rivers, 18
Mid-Rivers Mall, 336
military school, 153
Miller, Roy D. 238
Milligan, Jacob 229
Millington, Seth Dr. 34
Millville, 89, 124
Minor, Virginia 184
Mintert, Stanley 326
Mintrupp, Fred 234
Mispagel, Anton 189
missile gap, 302
mission school, 122
Mississippi River, 5, 6, 8, 14, 15
Mississippi River bluffs, 10
Mississippi Valley Association, 260

Mississippian culture, 7, 12
Missouri, 6, 12
Missouri Commission on Human Rights, 324
Missouri Conservation Commission, 269
Missouri *Demokrat*, 101
Missouri Department of Conservation, 8
Missouri Department of Natural Resources, 357
Missouri Department of Transportation, 356, 357
Missouri Gazette, 37
Missouri General Assembly, 65, 131, 153
Missouri National Guard, 349
Missouri Point, 127
Missouri Retail Association, 284
Missouri River, 6, 8, 14, 80
Missouri River Bridge, 127
Missouri River Bridges Committee, 332
Missouri State Guard, 86
Missouri State Labor Council, 284
Missouri State Militia, 91
Missouri Supreme Court, 68, 281
Missouri Synod Lutheran Church, 105, 130, 141, 142
Missouri Territory, 38
Missouri Valley Authority (MVA), 248
Missouri wine industry, 118
Missouri Women's Suffrage Association, 181
Missourian, 40, 42, 76
Missouri-Kansas pipeline, 239
Missouriton Grange, 126
mixed marriages, 284
MKT Railroad, 248
Moberly, 121
Mobile Homes, 298, 320
Moniteau County, 39
Monroe, James President 38, 42, 55, 65
Monroe County, 37
Monte Carlo night, 282
Montgomery, 64, 84
Montgomery County, 36, 37, 103
Montreal, 15
Morgan v. City of St. Louis, 66
Morgner, Albin 138
Morrill Act, 118
Mothers of the Sacred Heart, 131
Motley, Guy 168
Mount Zion Missionary Baptist, 159
Mowatt, Mary 133
Moynihan, Daniel Patrick 274
Mt. Zion Methodist Church in O'Fallon, 88
Mudd, James R. Dr. 152,198, 279
Muegge Road, 117
Mueller, Rudolph W. Republican 175
Mueller Road, 335
Muench, 80, 101, 135; Friedrich 82, 91, 103, 107, 108, 117, 127, 131, 134, 135
Muhm, Oscar Dr. 152
Mullanphy, John 51
Mullanphy Slough Levee District, 247
multicultural world, 22
Municipal Band of St. Charles, 307
Municipal League, 234, 235
Musick, 20
Musick Ferry, 77
Mutual Fire Insurance Company of St. Charles, 138
Myers, 124; George H. 124
Myrtle Street Prison, 87

N
Nagel, 42, 141; Paul 9, 11, 53; Professor 156; Rudolph 89
Nahm, Laura Dr. 281
Napoleonic Wars, 70
Nashville, Tennessee, 49
Natchez tribe, 56
Nathaniel, 25
National Academy of Sciences, 118
National Aeronautical and Space Administration, 272
National Bank of St. Charles, 120
National Currency Act, 119
National Defense Commission, 253
National Flood Insurance Act, 326, 351
National Flood Insurance Program, 345
National Foundation for Infantile Paralysis, 287
National Guard of Missouri, 153
National Industrial Recovery Act (NIRA), 241
National Recovery Administration (NRA), 232, 241
National Road, 44, 76
National Turnpike, 6
National Youth Administration, 243
Native Americans, 13, 22, 36, 45, 345
naturalized citizens, 165
Nazis, 220, 224
Negroe Advancement Association, 287
Negroes, 56, 92, 99, 101, 231, 287, 290
New Deal, 208, 232, 238, 239, 241, 257, 297, 351
New Federalism, 318
New Haven Phone Company, 203
New Madrid, 17, 35
New Melle, 97, 99, 103, 105, 136, 138, 143, 173, 202, 213, 227, 236, 280, 347

New Melle Band, 150
New Orleans, 13, 15, 19, 21
New York Children's Aid
  Society, 122
New York City, 298
Niccoli, Frank 324
Nichols, Grace 320
Nichols Country Club Plaza,
  273
Niedner, 171; Paul 261; Robert
  218, 295; Robert St. Charles
  County Prosecuting Attorne
  282
Nixon, 318; Richard 302, 305,
  315, 317, 323
Non-Partisan Court Plan,
  292, 349
Norfolk and Western
  Railroad, 331
North Central Association of
  Colleges, 154
North Missouri Railroad, 7,
  13, 114, 122, 125, 153, 241
North Missouri Railroad
  Bridge, 79
Northwest Ordinance, 27, 34
Norton's Virginia Seedling,
  119
Null, George M. 224
Nye, Gerald Senator 235

O

Obermark, Irv 275
O'Connor, Sandra Day 324
Octoberfest, 347
Odelia Sister, 152
Oetting, Alf 232, 301; Alf
  Representative 296
O'Fallon, 123, 132, 134, 139,
  158, 168, 173, 325; John 57,
  122
O'Fallon Cornet Band, 150
Office of Price
  Administration, 220
Ohlms, 357; Henry 189; Henry
  F. Republican 232
Old Monroe, 34, 122
Old Town St. Peters, 18

Oldenberg, 114, 136
O'Leary, Father, 186
Olive Street, 132
Olivet Presbyterian Church,
  48
Olson, Audrey 176; Edna
  McElhiney 17, 59, 93, 121,
  153; John Mayor 149, 200,
  204
Omaha, Nebraska, 6
O'Malley, Joseph C. Senator
  294
On the Origin of Species, 170
Orchard Farm, 105, 127, 129,
  139, 142, 173, 278, 353
Orchard Farm School
  District, 321
ordinaries de la nature, 23
O'Reilly, Alejandro 15, 56
Orf, Sample 84
Osage, Indians, 10, 12, 14, 17,
  37, 174, 345
Osage County, 104
Osnabruck District, 136
Osthoff, Hermann 116
Ostrom, Vincent 342
Our Lady of Fatima, 276
Our Lady of the Rivers, 277
Overall, Samuel Dr. 133
Ozark Dome, 6, 7

P

Pacific Railroad, 120
Page Avenue Bridge, 332, 349,
  353
Page Avenue extension, 7, 241
Panic of 1837, 120
Paris France, 6, 20
Park, Guy Democratic
  Governor 233
Park Board, 289
Park Ridge Apartments, 298,
  314
Parker, 107; Sherman 347;
  Thomas A. Superintendent of
  Schools 131, 132
parochial schools, 144, 146,
  147, 155. 167, 169, 173. 175,

265, 277, 279, 280, 281, 307,
  312, 348, 350
Parr, John C. 181
Patrons of Husbandry, 126
Paule, Ernie 301
Pearl Harbor, 219, 225, 255
Peck, Charles 32; H.H.
  Reverend 159; John Mason
  49
Peerless, 204
Pendergast, 237; "Boss" of
  Kansas City 229
Pendleton, Jim 288
Penrose, C.B. 52; J.H. 52
Pentecostals, 275
Perry, Street 174
Perry County, 104
Pershing's Crusaders, 180
Peruque Creek, 89, 123
Peruque Creek Bridge, 89
Peters, Delbert Mayor 325;
  Jacob 116
Pettus, William 42
Pezold, William Father 254,
  279, 280
Pfaff, John George 116
Phillips, Kevin 106, 318
Phoebe, 160
Pick, Lewis A. Colonel 248
Pieper, Henry F. Judge 105,
  151, 189
Pierce, Franklin 44
Piernas, Pedro 15
Pietistic Methodists, 106
Pike Street, 7
Pike County, 37, 93
Pilgrims, 149
pirogue, 27
Pitman, David K. 132; John
  Colonel of Dardenne
  Township 36, 76, 116
Plackemeier, Lester Sheriff
  168, 282, 295, 303; Mel 298
plank roads, 77
Planning and Zoning
  Commission, 299
Platte River, 80
Plaza Drive-In, 273

448

Plaza Shopping Center, 273
Point Prairie, 104, 139
Polski, Paul 155; Samuel 155
Poor Farm, 212
Pornography, 313
Portage de Sioux townships, 139
Portage des Sioux, 7, 10, 18, 24, 34, 38, 39, 40, 112, 136, 144, 162, 173, 213, 246, 255, 260, 276, 277, 326, 346
Portrait and Biographical Record, 107
post roads, 75
Post-Dispatch, 328, 330
postmaster of St. Louis, 35
potato famine, 121
potatoes, 28, 115
Powell, Ludwell Mayor of St. Charles 44, 49, 80, 133, 254
Powell Terrace, 254, 263
Praeger, Robert 166
Prairie du Chien, 17, 21
Prairie du Rocher, 21
Prairie Haute, 264
Pratt, Benjamin 153
Presbyterian Church, 134
Presbyterians, 48, 106, 174
Pretorius, Emil 103
Price, Sterling General, 89, 98
Primm, James Neal 45, 159; Wilson Judge 19
Probate Court, 35
Prohibition, 63, 96, 103, 106, 109, 164, 167, 168, 169, 170, 174, 176, 184, 187, 188, 189, 214, 215, 228
Promise of America, 314
prostitution, 17, 22
Protestant Americans, 13, 20, 141, 275
Protestant Bible, 111
Protestant Britain, 15
provost marshal, 87-91, 104
Prussia, 79, 114
Public Housing Administration, 264

public land, 29
public library, 183, 203
public mail delivery, 75
Public Service Commission, 331
public swimming pool, 287
Public Works Administration (PWA), 243
Pundmann, Ed 324
Pundmann Ford, 222
Putnam County, 104

Q
Quantrill's Raiders, 93
Quebec, 21, 24, 28
Quebec City, 14

R
race hatred, 224
Radical Republicans, 79, 90, 91, 99, 100, 130, 131, 145, 146, 287
Radical Union Party, 94, 99
Ralls County, 37
Ramsay family, 39
Randolph, Boswell 96
Randolph Street, 93
Raskob, 190
Rauch, 357; Celeste 167; Frank 242, 265; Lucy 324; Olive 167
Rayfield, Harold 316
RCA, 201
Reagan, Ronald 323, 324, 325
Rec-Plex, 356
Red Cross, 167, 212
Red Republicanism, 108
Reed, James Senator 182, 188
Reeves, Benjamin 76
Regional Sewer District, 337
register of marriages, 20
Regot, A.F. 169
Reineke, Henry 122
Reisdorff, Joseph Father 143, 146
religious freedom, 97
Reller, Francis X. Senator 283, 301, 302, 303
Reller "Landslide", 303

rendezvous, 39, 71
Renno, E. Lee 173
Rensmann, William J. 144
rent controls, 222
Republicaner, 146, 173
Republicans, 79, 81, 96, 102, 175
research park, 330
Reservoir Street, 89
Reveille, 42
Revolutionary War, 177
Reynal, Antoine 46; Antoine Dr. 28
Rice's Grove, 86
Ringe, Louis J. 226
Ringling, John 241
Rinsche, Mary Elizabeth 174
Riverboat Gambling, 347
roaring twenties, 171
Robert, Johnson and Rand Shoe Company 196
Roberts, Earl 324
Robinson, Jackie 288
Rock River, 38
Rock Road Bridge, 241
Rodgers, Latona 167
Roe v. Wade, 323
Roemer, John L. Dr. 154, 168
Rohlfing, Carl 299
Roosevelt, 294; Franklin D. 236-239, 241; Theodore 148, 177, 178, 179, 185
Roosevelt Coalition, 228, 230
Roosevelt Place, 159
Roosevelt's "fireside chats", 228
Rorabaugh, W.J. 70, 71
Rose Bowl, 219
Rosecrans, William S. 93, 94
Rosenblum, Samuel 155
Rotary Club, 263
Rothensteiner, 146
Roxy Theatre, 313
Royal Domain, 138
Rue Royal, 138
Rules for Rural Missouri Teachers, 145
Rules of Morales, 18

Ruluff, 32
Rum, Romanism, and Rebellion 111
Rummel's Military Band, 150
Rupp, Phil 242
Rural Electrification Authority (REA), 246
Rush, Fred 320
rush hour, 207
Russian Jews, 155, 156
Russians, 300
Rutgers, Aaron 35

S

Sabbath, 50, 106, 109, 134, 162, 163
Sable, Pointe du 40
Sabotage, 220
Sac, 17, 24, 37, 38, 39
Sac and Fox, 10, 17
Sacred Heart Order in St. Charles, 53, 54
Saeger, Louis 154
Salem District School, 132
salt licks, 76
Salt River, 76
Sammelmann, Raymond 251
San Carlos, 11, 17, 23, 24, 26, 31
Sandfort, 357; Heinrich Conrad 146; Hermann Dietrich 117; Hermann Heinrich 116; John H. Judge 169; Robert 174
Sanford, Alexander Colonel 57; John F.A. 58
Santa Fe trade, 74, 80
Santa Fe Trail, 10, 76
Saturday Evening Post, 266
Saucier, 18; Francis 18, 35
SBC Communications, 355
scalp lock, 12
Schaberg, Mary Jane 324
Schaffer, Roy Reverend 281
Scheffer, Wilbert 249
Schierding, George 117
Schluersburg, 97, 139, 202
Schmidt, W.A. Father 143

Schnare, Edward Mayor 234
Schnatmeier, Omar State Representative 232, 280, 295, 296, 297, 320, 323,
Schnippeled beans, 274
schnorrers, 156
Schoenich, Henry 151
Schofield, John Brigadier General 88, 93
school choice, 348
school for slaves, 131
School Sisters of Notre Dame, 153, 275
Schroeder, Joseph 144; Walter 173
Schulte, Franz family 152
Schultenhenrich, Ham 216
Schultz, Bob 92; David 86
Schurz, Carl 83, 100, 101, 103, 107, 111, 116, 138, 350
Schwendemann, Charles 320
Scopes Monkey Trial, 170, 171
Scott, Dred 57, 58; Felix 44, 58; John 40, 41, 43, 45
Second French Empire, 79
Second Industrial Revolution, 195
Second Reconstruction, 287
Second Vatican Council, 284
Second World War, 239
Selective Service Act, 181, 219
Sellers, 67; Charles 69
Seminoles, 40
Sevier, John 55
Sewers, 198, 330, 333, 335, 337, 338, 341
sex education, 313
sexual relations, 21, 22, 171, 307, 311, 313, 314
Shapiro, Charles 155
Shea, William 325
Shelby County, 37
Shelton, Pines H. 44
Sherman, William Tecumseh General 86
Shiloh Church, 87
shoe factory, 148, 193, 195,

207, 252, 268
Sibley, George 44, 50, 55, 76, 81, 82, 134; Mary Easton 48, 61, 183
Sibley Hall, 134
Sibley Street, 264
Sigmund, Judy 164
Silo Youth Center, 311
Simmons, Hezekiah 336
Simon, Joseph A. 258
Sioux, Indians, 10, 12, 28, 38
Sister Cities Program, 347
Sisters of St. Francis, 144
Sisters of St. Mary, 152, 198, 255, 331
Sisters of the Most Precious Blood, 144, 275, 279, 312, 350
sit down strikes, 232
Sixth Missouri Infantry, 152
Slater, Samuel captain 56
slave block, 47
slave pen, 87
slave revolt, 56
slave state, 57
Slaveholding, 45, 85, 116
slavery, 21, 42, 90, 130
slaves, 26, 91, 93, 157
slickers, 46
Sloan, W. Glenn 248
smallpox epidemic, 152
smallpox sisters, 152
Smartt, Joseph Gillespie 255
Smartt Field, 255
Smith, 184, 188, 189; Al 230, 302; Al a Catholic 187; George Commerce president 269; John Captain 149; Margaret Chase United States Senator 302
Smith, Adam, 61
Social Security Act, 229, 243
socialism, 130, 226
Soil Conservation and Domestic Allotment Act, 245
Sommershauser Pastor, 212
Soulard, Antoine 18

Soviet Union, 302, 307

Spain, 15

Spainhower, James 319

Spanish, 13, 14, 17, 20, 25, 239

Spanish administration, 15, 19, 20, 21, 33, 75

Spanish crown, 31

Spanish fort, 43, 355

Spanish Lake, 319

Spanish land grant, 34, 248

Spanish rule, 13, 20, 28

Spanish trade policies, 15

Spanish-American War, 152

Spellmann, Dennis President 346

Spencer, 20; Robert 34, 35, 36

split-shift, 308

spring planting, 28

Springfield, Missouri, 40

Sputnik, 307

SSM Healthcare, 355

St. Charles, Missouri, 6, 17, 42, 59, 64, 167, 174, 207, 216, 287, 302

St. Charles and Western Plank Road Corporation, 77

St. Charles Borromeo, 17, 20, 43, 53, 82, 121, 153, 178, 244, 277

St. Charles Bridge, 121

St. Charles Clarion, 67

St. Charles College, 43, 49, 60, 86, 88, 134, 153

St. Charles Cornet Band, 150 Broadhead, 86

St. Charles County, 5, 37, 103, 104, 141

St. Charles County Directory, 155

St. Charles County Portrait and Biographical Record, 113

St. Charles County v. Dardenne Realty Co., 351

St. Charles Fur Trading Post, 28

St. Charles High School, 154, 217, 218, 243

St. Charles Hills, 335

St. Charles Hotel, 161, 273

St. Charles Incandescent Light and Power, 200

St. Charles Journal, 110, 173, 190

St. Charles Lanes, 215

St. Charles Manufacturing, 191

St. Charles Military Band, 167

St. Charles News, 102, 110

St. Charles Post, 309

St. Charles Retail Merchants Association, 148

St. Charles Rock Road, 260

St. Charles Savings Bank, 151

St. Charles School District, 308

St. Charles West High School, 309

St. Cletus Parish, 312

St. Dominic High School, 277

St. Genevieve, 15

St. John Evangelical Church, 151

St. John United Church of Christ, 331

St. Johns A.M.E., 159

St. Joseph, 6

St. Joseph Hospital, 152, 214, 275, 276, 291

St. Joseph Parish, 254, 279

St. Joseph's Carmelite Nursing Home, 152

St. Louis, Missouri, 6, 13, 17, 21, 65, 141, 174, 196

St. Louis and Hannibal Railroad, 241

St. Louis Anti-Abolitionist Society, 57

St. Louis Area Rent Advisory Board, 263

St. Louis Building Trades Council, 250, 251

St. Louis Cardinal Football team, 283

St. Louis Cardinals, 217, 283

St. Louis fur businesses, 26

St. Louis Hawks basketball team, 283

St. Louis Kansas City and Northern Railroad, 6

St. Louis Metropolitan Region, 13

St. Louis University, 108

St. Louis World's Fair, 205

St. Mary's College in O'Fallon, 312

St. Mary's Institute, 144, 275

St. Mary's Machine Co., 196

St. Mary's Oil Engine Company, 196

St. Paul, 112, 139, 173

St. Paul M.E., 159

St. Peters, 17, 112, 122, 127, 139, 155, 173, 211, 216, 246, 357

St. Peter's Church, 150, 152, 153, 165, 167, 174

St. Peters District, 247

St. Robert Bellarmine, 312

St. Theodore, 213, 280

St. Vincent, 212

Stark, Lloyd Governor 237, 241

State Board of Education, 277, 292

State Bureau of Labor, 128

State Constitutional Convention, 96

State Highway Department, 241

State Militia, 90

State Republican Convention, 101

statehood, 33, 41

Ste. Genevieve, 17

steamboats, 12, 57, 73, 74

Steeple Chase, 267

Steiner, John 107

Stephen Douglas Democrats, 84

Stephenson, Thomas 324

Sterling Aluminum Corporation, 268, 298, 329
Stettinius, Edward R. Secretary of State 269
Stevenson, Adlai 295
Stewart, Herbert 317
Stimson, Henry L. 219
stock market, 239
Stoddard, 34; Amos 34
Stone, Ed 319
Strong, George Captain 87
Strother, French 94, 95
Stumberg, 357; Bernard Kurt Dr. 152, 154; Cordelia 215, 224; H.K. 218, 224, 282, 293, 295, 302, 321; Johann Heinrich 154; John Henry Dr. 105, 153, 154, 177, 194
Stumberg family, 154
Sublette, William 62
subsistence farmer, 69
Sunday-closing laws, 50, 106, 109, 162, 163, 277, 283, 284, 347
Sunflower Island, 88
Supreme Court, 67, 254, 316
Syllabus of Errors, 145
Symington, Stuart 296, 302

T

Taft, Robert Senator 294; William Howard 177
Taft-Hartley, 300
Taillon, Charles 17, 23; Commandant 20; Don Carlos 17
Tainter, George W. Dr. and Mrs 95, 222
Talley, John Dr. 152, 320
Tally, Darby 295
Talmadge, James Congressman 57
tavern license fee, 18
Taylor, Daniel G. 85; Zachary Lieutenant 39
Taxes 18, 19, 49, 55, 59, 60, 151, 155, 158, 182, 187, 189, 190, 191, 197, 203, 206, 213, 229, 232, 233, 234, 237, 238, 243, 245, 267-280, 302, 305, 307, 308, 309, 310, 314, 315, 317, 318, 321, 322, 325, 330, 333, 335, 338, 339, 341, 343, 350, 353, 354, 355, 356

Teasdale, Joseph 323
Tecumseh, 38
Tecumseh Street, 159
telephones 197, 201-203
temperance 50, 106, 109-111, 126, 137, 139, 163, 167, 174, 176
Temple Israel, 156
Tennessee, 8
Tennessee Valley Authority, 233, 248
Tenskatawa, 38
Territory of Missouri, 35
Texas, 80
Texas Junction, 127
The Alcoholic Republic, 70
The Bombers, 287
The Cross of Culture A Social Analysis of Midwestern Politics, 103
The Emerging Republican Majority, 318
The Observer, 57
The Western Star, 42
Thelen, David Historian 109
Thibault, Joseph 24
Thoele, Dietrich 116
Thompson, Ronald M. 165, 173; W.C. 50
Three Sisters, 7
Thro, Adolph Mayor 255, 357
Thro's Clothing, 172
Tiebolt, Charles 342
Tilden, Samuel 104, 106, 107
Title IX, 315
tobacco, 28, 69, 72, 115-117, 124
Toedtmann, C.W. 301
Tojo, Hideki Japanese General 224
Toonerville, 254
town lots, 27

Town of Boone's Trails, 357
Townsend, 21
T.R. Hughes Field, 356
Trail to the Village of the Missouris, 74
Trailer Camp, 298
Trans-Mississippi, 33
Travis, J. Edward "Brick" 214, 218, 242, 271, 286
Treatise on Religion and Christianity, Orthodoxy and Rationalism 108
Treaty of Ghent, 39, 40
Treaty of Paris, 5, 20
Treaty of San Il Defonso, 63
Trendley, Joseph 122
Trinity Episcopalian Church, 49
Trio Mobile Home Park, 320
Trolley League game, 216
Troy, Missouri 34, 89, 117, 295
Trudeau, Governor Zenon 12, 17, 18, 23
Truman, 292; Harry 239; Harry President 291; Harry S. 229, 231, 232, 238, 301; Harry S. President 264, 294
Tuhomehenga, 23
Turner, Gary 325; Gary Mayor 342; Ike and Tina 311; Nat 56
Turpin, William Judge 321
Tyler, Oliver W.H. Dr. 291
typhoid, 198

U

Unemployment, 208
Union, 41
Union Electric, 234
Union regulars, 89
Union Savings Bank, 151
United Nations Charter, 269
United Shoe Workers of America, 252
United States Air Force Academy, 269
University of Missouri, 118,

269, 330
University of Missouri Research Park, 354
Upper Louisiana, 13, 15, 20
U.S. Department of Justice, 165
U.S. Highway 40, 7

V

Van Burkleo, William 38
Vandalia, Illinois, 76
Vashon High School, 160
Vatican, 108, 146
Vatterott, 265
Verhaegen, Peter J. Father 108
Veterans Memorial (Page Avenue) Bridge, 270, 349
Veterans Service Committee, 284
Vicksburg, Mississippi, 87
Victorian social mores, 21
Victory Corps, 220
Vietnam War, 316, 326
Village of All Saints, 254
Vincennes, 21
Vine Hill Telephone Exchange, 202
Vineyards, 119
Virginia, 8, 117
Virginia and Kentucky, 34
Virginia Night Hawks, 287
Voelker, Frederick E. Historian 62
Vogt, Henry Mayor 291, 298, 309, 325; Richard 85
Von Bock, Johann Baron 134
voyageurs, 21, 26, 45, 345

W

WAAC's, 224
Wabash Railroad, 241, 243
Wabash region, 38
Wagner, David 92
Wagner Act, 248
Walbridge, Cyrus 177
Walker, Barbara 323
Wallace, Henry 294
Walnut Grove Grange, 126
Walsh, Robert of Baltimore 39

Walters Transit Co., 205
Walther, C.F. Dr. 130
Wappelhorst, Herbert 326; Norbert Park Superintendent 289, 329
War Bonds, 165
War Department, 249
War Industries Board, 180
War of 1812, 39, 40, 41
War on Poverty, 316, 317
Warren, 64, 84, 174; Earl 289; Robert 342
Warren County, 36, 37, 82, 103, 104, 131, 141
wartime measure, 184
Washboard Avenue, 271
Washington, Melvin 289, 290, 324
Washington D.C., 6
Washington, Missouri, 216
Washington School District, 278
Washington Temperance Group, 50
Watergate scandal, 305, 319, 322
Waterloo, Illinois, 343
Watson, Samuel S. Judge and Mrs. 134, 254
WAVE's, 224
Webb, Charles K. 324
Webster, Daniel Senator 11
Webster College, 287
Wegener, Walter 181
Weil, 156; Dave 214; Emil 155
Weinrich, 99, 209, 357; Anna 226; Conrad 85, 91, 99, 109; William 171, 209, 226
Welch, James 49
Weldon, Joseph and John 34
Weldon Spring, 139, 142, 207, 208, 220, 227, 236, 238, 254, 267, 325, 353, 357
Weldon Spring ordnance plant, 224, 225
Wells, Carty Judge 44
Wentker, Benedict 152; Joseph 250, 251

Wentz, Erasmus Livingston 124
Wentzville, 49, 89, 98, 124, 144, 150, 154, 158, 213, 236, 278, 325
Wentzville Business and Professional Women, 268
Wentzville High School, 310
Wentzville Hotel, 89
Wentzville Rotary Club, 354
Wentzville Union, 173
West Alton, 127, 132, 246, 248, 250, 279, 353
Westerfeld, Clarence 234
Wester-Kappeln, 139
Westliche Post, 100
Westminster College, 294
Weston, Jacob 131
wetland permits, 352
Wheeler-Rayburn Bill, 233
Whig Convention, 45
Whig Party, 33, 42, 44, 45
whipping post, 47
whiskey ring, 161
white, 287; David L. 324; Richard 22, 40
white devils, 38
Wildwood, Missouri, 357
Wilke, Herman 85, 94; John 202; John H. 83; John Mrs. 139; Otto 261
Wilkie, Wendell 235, 238
Wilkins, Robert John 317
Wilkinson, James Governor 35
Willbrand, J.C. 198
Williams, F. Arlene 324; Frank 290; R. Hal 106
Willmes, F.X. Father 152
Willner, Harry 156
Willner family, 155, 156
Willott, Road 117
Wilmer, Bernard 117
Wilson, 179; Andrew 43; Marcela 296; Woodrow 177, 179
Wilson President, 166, 178, 179, 180, 184
Windthorst, Ludwig 107

wine, 115, 119
Wisconsin Synod, 106
Wolf, Gene 298; Saul 214, 275
Wolfson, Joseph 155
Women's Christian
   Temperance Union, 163
Women's interscholastic
   sports, 315
Wood River Illinois, 34
woodchopper, 12
Woodland Indians, 12
Woods, Zadock 34
Woods' Fort, 39
Woodson, Charles F. 90; John
   Captain of Callaway

Township 116
Woolfolk Judge, 184, 251
World War II, 257, 266, 293
Worley, Kenneth Delegate 323
Wussler, Henry J. 324
Wyeth, John 25

Y

Yankee idea, 133
Yankee Merchants and the
   Making of the Urban West,
   77
Yankees, 77, 113, 137
yeomen farmers, 32, 69, 70, 78
YMCA, 310, 348
Young Men's Dramatic Club,

150
Youth in Need, 311

Z

Zeisler's orange soda, 218
Zeitgeist, 273
Zumbehl, 117; Johann Dietrich
   116
Zumbehl Road, 320, 333
Zumwalt, John 30, 34